CATIA V5 2024 GUIDE FOR BEGINNERS

MASTAFE CERLDAWELL

INTRODUCTION

Welcome to the "Catia V5 2024 Guide for Beginners," where your journey into the world of advanced computer-aided design (CAD) begins. Whether you aspire to become a proficient CAD designer, are seeking to enhance your engineering skills, or simply have a passion for precision and innovation, this guide is your doorway to mastering one of the most powerful design software suites in the industry.

In this guide, we will delve into the fundamentals of CATIA V5, a version that stands at the pinnacle of design sophistication, offering users an array of tools for product development and innovation. As you turn each page, you will discover that this book is more than just a manual; it is a pathway to unleashing your creative potential, streamlining design processes, and bringing your most complex ideas to life.

CATIA, or Computer-Aided Three-dimensional Interactive Application, is a multi-platform software suite for CAD, CAM, CAE, and PLM. It is developed by the French company Dassault Systèmes and has become an indispensable tool in numerous industries, including aerospace, automotive, and manufacturing. As the digital era progresses, the ability to create detailed models, assemblies, and drawings in CATIA is a sought-after skill in the engineering job market. With CATIA V5 2024, this skillset is taken to new heights with enhanced features and improved user experience.

As we embark on this educational adventure, you will learn that CATIA V5 is not just about the technicalities of software manipulation. It is about developing a mindset geared towards innovation, efficiency, and precision. Throughout this guide, you will gain not only the technical expertise needed to navigate and utilize CATIA V5 but also a conceptual framework that will enable you to think like a designer and an engineer.

We will start with the basics, gradually building a solid foundation before advancing to more complex concepts. Beginning with an overview of CATIA V5's environment, you'll become comfortable with the interface, learning how to start projects and set up your workspace. From there, we will guide you step-by-step through the modeling process, teaching you how to bring your ideas from rough sketches to three-dimensional reality.

Sketching is the language of design in CATIA V5, and you will learn to 'speak' it fluently. From simple lines and arcs to complex curves and geometry, you'll master the essential tools and techniques to translate your ideas onto the digital canvas. As your confidence grows, you'll explore advanced sketch features, enabling you to tackle more intricate designs with ease.

However, true mastery of CATIA V5 is not achieved until one can manipulate sketches into solid forms. You'll learn about sketch-based features such as pad, pocket, shaft, groove, and hole, which serve as the building blocks for your models. You'll understand how to use reference elements to guide your design process and ensure accuracy and precision in every project.

Beyond the individual parts, you'll learn to think in systems through our sections on assembly design. You'll understand both bottom-up and top-down assembly approaches, each providing unique advantages depending on your design needs. And, as no design is complete without proper documentation, you will learn to create detailed drawing views and enrich them with dimensions and annotations, enabling clear communication and facilitating the manufacturing process.

While this guide is tailored for beginners, it does not shy away from the complexities that will allow you to grow into an experienced user. You'll be introduced to advanced techniques, including multi-body modeling and the use of formulas to drive your designs. Each concept is presented with clarity and supported by practical examples, ensuring that even the most sophisticated techniques become approachable.

Our guide is more than a set of instructions; it is an invitation to explore and innovate. With each new skill acquired, you will find yourself envisioning possibilities that stretch beyond the scope of this book. CATIA V5 2024 empowers you to go beyond mere execution into the realm of creation.

As you navigate through the essentials of CATIA V5 with this guide, you will not only be preparing yourself for the demands of the modern design and engineering fields but also joining a community of forward-thinkers who share your passion for creation and innovation. Together, we will explore the depths of design potential and emerge ready to face the challenges of tomorrow's engineering landscape.

So, ready your mind and prepare your creative spirit. The path to mastery awaits, and the "Catia V5 2024 Guide for Beginners" is your faithful companion on this transformative journey.

Continuing from where we left off, let's delve deeper into the multifaceted world of CATIA V5 and set the stage for the transformative learning experience that awaits.

The story of CATIA begins in the 1970s, emerging from the aerospace industry's need for precise 3D design and manufacturing tools. Its evolution has mirrored the technological advancements of the past several decades, growing from a specialized software into a comprehensive suite that defines the cutting edge of CAD, CAM, and PLM systems. CATIA has been the birthplace of myriad innovations, from groundbreaking aerospace projects to revolutionary automotive designs. In this edition, CATIA V5 2024, the software continues to build on its legacy, offering users enhanced features, an optimized interface, and unparalleled design capabilities.

Understanding CATIA's rich history not only provides context but also helps new users appreciate the power and prestige of the software they are about to master. This guide is designed to be your mentor, breaking down complex ideas into digestible lessons that build upon each other seamlessly. Each section is meticulously crafted to ease the beginner into CATIA V5's environment without overwhelming them, gradually unfolding the software's capabilities as one's proficiency increases.

As we dive into the program's interface, you will learn about the workbenches—a term CATIA uses to describe its task-oriented environments—and how to navigate through them with ease. You'll find that CATIA V5 is a universe unto itself, with tools tailored for every aspect of the design process. This guide will help you orient yourself within this universe, providing you with the skills to move from one workbench to another, understanding the purpose and function of each tool at your disposal.

Moving forward, we'll delve into the heart of CATIA V5's power: modeling. Starting with basic geometrical forms, you will soon be piecing together complex shapes and surfaces. Each lesson is designed to build your confidence and understanding, ensuring that by the time you approach more challenging concepts, you are well-prepared and capable. We will tackle common obstacles that beginners face and provide practical tips to overcome them, smoothing your path to becoming a proficient modeler.

Your progression in sketching will be methodical and satisfying. Beginning with lines and shapes, you will advance to creating detailed sketches that serve as blueprints for 3D models. We will explore the subtleties of constraint-based sketching—how it can both guide and liberate your designs. By learning the language of CATIA's sketch tools, you will soon be speaking in arcs, splines, and constraints, articulating your ideas with precision and clarity.

When it comes to bringing sketches to life, CATIA V5 provides an extensive toolbox for creating solid features. In this guide, we dissect these tools, like the Pad and Pocket, and their real-world applications. You will not only learn how to use these features but also why and when to use them. This deeper understanding ensures that your knowledge is not just theoretical but practical and applicable to real-life design challenges.

Reference elements are the unsung heroes of precise modeling, and you will learn to harness their power effectively. This guide will introduce you to the strategic use of planes, axes, and points, which serve as the invisible framework upon which your models are constructed. As you progress, you will find these elements to be indispensable in maintaining accuracy and control over your designs.

Dress-Up features might sound like an aesthetic afterthought, but in CATIA, they are essential to refining and finalizing designs. Fillets, chamfers, and drafted faces are just a few of the enhancements we will cover, teaching you how to add both functional and aesthetic value to your creations.

As your designs grow in complexity, so will your need to manage their parameters. CATIA V5 shines in its ability to allow dynamic modifications through parametric modeling. This guide will reveal how to make your designs not only accurate but also adaptable, ready to evolve as requirements change.

Modeling with bodies introduces you to the concept of multi-body design, an advanced technique where separate bodies are modeled within the same part environment. This approach allows for complex assemblies and the exploration of interactions between different model components. Through hands-on exercises, you will learn to think and design in multiple dimensions, preparing you for the challenges of advanced engineering projects.

Copying objects and features is about more than just duplication; it's about understanding the relationships and dependencies within your model. This guide will teach you efficient methods to replicate features, ensuring consistency and saving valuable time in the design process.

We will then take a leap into the advanced realm with complex sketch-based features, pushing the envelope of what you thought possible within a sketch environment. This will pave the way to utilizing formulas—a feature that allows your models to be driven by mathematical relationships, empowering you to create intelligent and responsive designs.

The art of assembly design will take you from the macro to the micro, teaching you how to think both holistically and in detail. You will learn the strategies for creating robust assemblies, whether you're starting from the ground up (bottom-up) or conceptualizing the whole to guide the parts (top-down).

Finally, we close the circle by bringing designs to their necessary conclusion: the creation of detailed drawing views. In these sections, we discuss how to communicate your design intent through drawings, providing all the necessary specifications for manufacturing. This includes the intricacies of dimensioning, annotating, and presenting exploded views, ensuring that what you have designed can be accurately and efficiently brought to life.

In the pages that follow, you'll not only learn the "how" but also the "why" behind each step in the design process, enabling you to make informed decisions and foster innovation. By the end of this guide, you will not only be familiar with CATIA V5 2024, but you will also have developed a foundation of design principles that will serve you in any CAD environment.

This is just the beginning. The real journey unfolds with each project you undertake, each challenge you overcome, and each design you bring forth into the world. Welcome to the community of CATIA V5 designers. Welcome to a world of endless possibilities. Welcome to "Catia V5 2024 Guide for Beginners."

CONTENTS

introduction

Contents

CHAPTER 1: INTRODUCING CATIA V5

WELCOME TO CATIA V5

CATIA V5 is a powerful CAD (Computer-Aided Design) software that has become an essential tool in numerous industries for the creation, modification, analysis, and optimization of complex designs and systems. With its advanced features and capabilities, CATIA V5 enables professionals and beginners alike to transform their innovative ideas into reality, while ensuring high efficiency and accuracy.

What to Expect from This Guide

This guide is meticulously crafted to usher you into the world of CATIA V5 2024, providing step-by-step tutorials, practical examples, and tips to maximize your learning experience. Expect to gain a foundational understanding that will not only equip you to navigate through the software with ease but also to leverage its functionalities to fulfill your design aspirations. Each section is designed to build upon the previous one, ensuring a smooth learning curve.

How to Use This Book

To get the most out of this book, it is recommended that you follow the chapters in sequence, especially if you are a newcomer to CATIA V5. Practical exercises are provided to reinforce the concepts discussed. It's advisable to have CATIA V5 2024 installed on your computer so you can practice as you read. Feel free to revisit topics for clarity, and utilize the resources provided at the end of each chapter to expand your understanding.

WHAT IS CATIA?

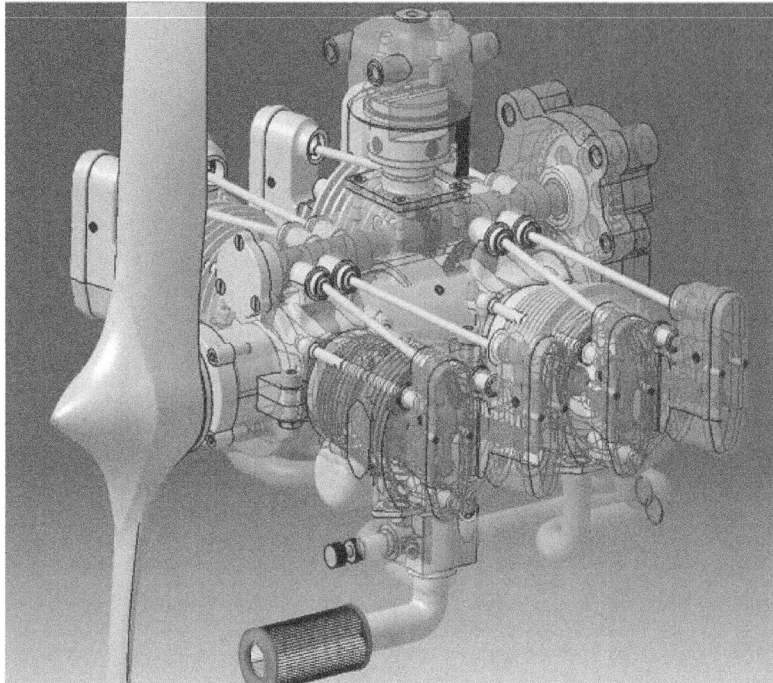

Definition of CATIA

CATIA, which stands for Computer Aided Three-dimensional Interactive Application, is a leading CAD software suite developed by Dassault Systèmes. It is renowned for its sophisticated 3D design capabilities, computer-aided manufacturing (CAM), and computer-aided engineering (CAE) functionalities. CATIA is not just a design tool; it's a comprehensive platform for product lifecycle management (PLM), allowing for collaboration and innovation across the entire process of product development.

The Role of CATIA in Design and Manufacturing

In design and manufacturing, CATIA is the cornerstone that enables designers and engineers to create high-precision models and simulations. The software's advanced features allow for the development of everything from simple sketches to intricate assemblies. CATIA's integral role extends to validating the designs and simulating how they would behave in real-world conditions, thus bridging the gap between concept and production.

Industries and Disciplines That Use CATIA

CATIA is the backbone of many industry giants in various sectors, including aerospace, automotive, industrial machinery, electronics, and consumer goods. For instance, automotive companies use CATIA to design cars with high precision and performance. Aerospace companies rely on its powerful tools for creating airframes and systems that meet strict aviation standards. The versatility of CATIA makes it a universal language among disciplines such as mechanical engineering, systems engineering, and industrial design.

THE EVOLUTION OF CATIA

A Brief History of CATIA

CATIA's journey began in the late 1970s when it was developed as an in-house application by the French aircraft manufacturer, Dassault Aviation. Originally created to develop Dassault's Mirage fighter jet, the software rapidly evolved into a commercial product that transformed the design and manufacturing processes across industries.

Key Milestones in CATIA Development

Throughout its evolution, CATIA has seen numerous upgrades, with each version bringing significant improvements in usability, functionality, and integration. The shift from mainframe computers to PC-based systems in the 1990s marked one of the significant transitions that made CATIA accessible to a wider audience.

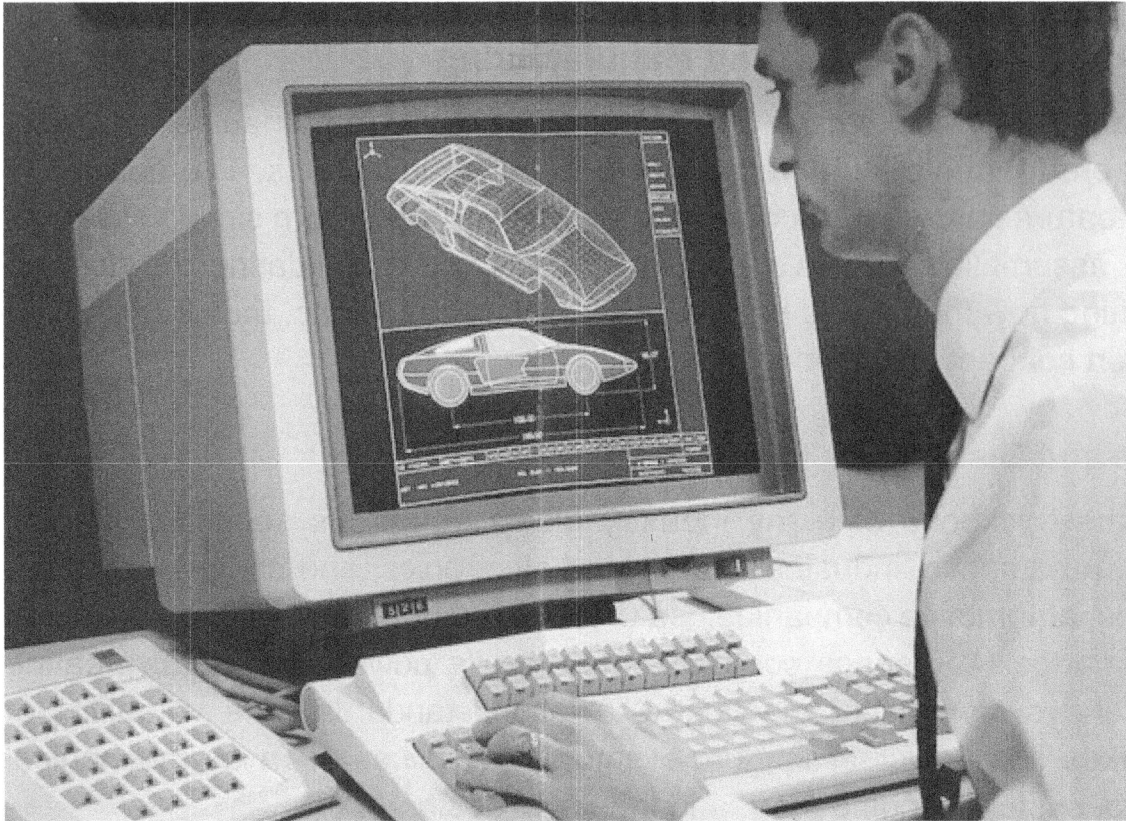

CATIA V5's Place in the Evolution Timeline

CATIA V5 was a game-changer upon its release, offering enhanced 3D capabilities and user-friendly interface. It introduced parametric and associative modeling techniques that allowed for quicker and more flexible design changes. As a milestone in CATIA's timeline, V5 solidified Dassault Systèmes' presence in the PLM market.

What's New in CATIA V5 2024

With the 2024 version, CATIA V5 introduces new features and enhancements that cater to the ever-evolving challenges of product design. Key updates include improved user experience with more intuitive interfaces, enhanced collaboration tools for better team integration, and advanced analytics for optimizing design performance. The latest version also focuses on interoperability, ensuring seamless integration with other Dassault Systèmes products and third-party applications.

GETTING CATIA V5

Securing your access to CATIA V5 is the first step in exploring the possibilities of this innovative CAD software. Dassault Systèmes has tailored a variety of subscription options and licensing arrangements to cater to different user needs, from independent professionals to large enterprises.

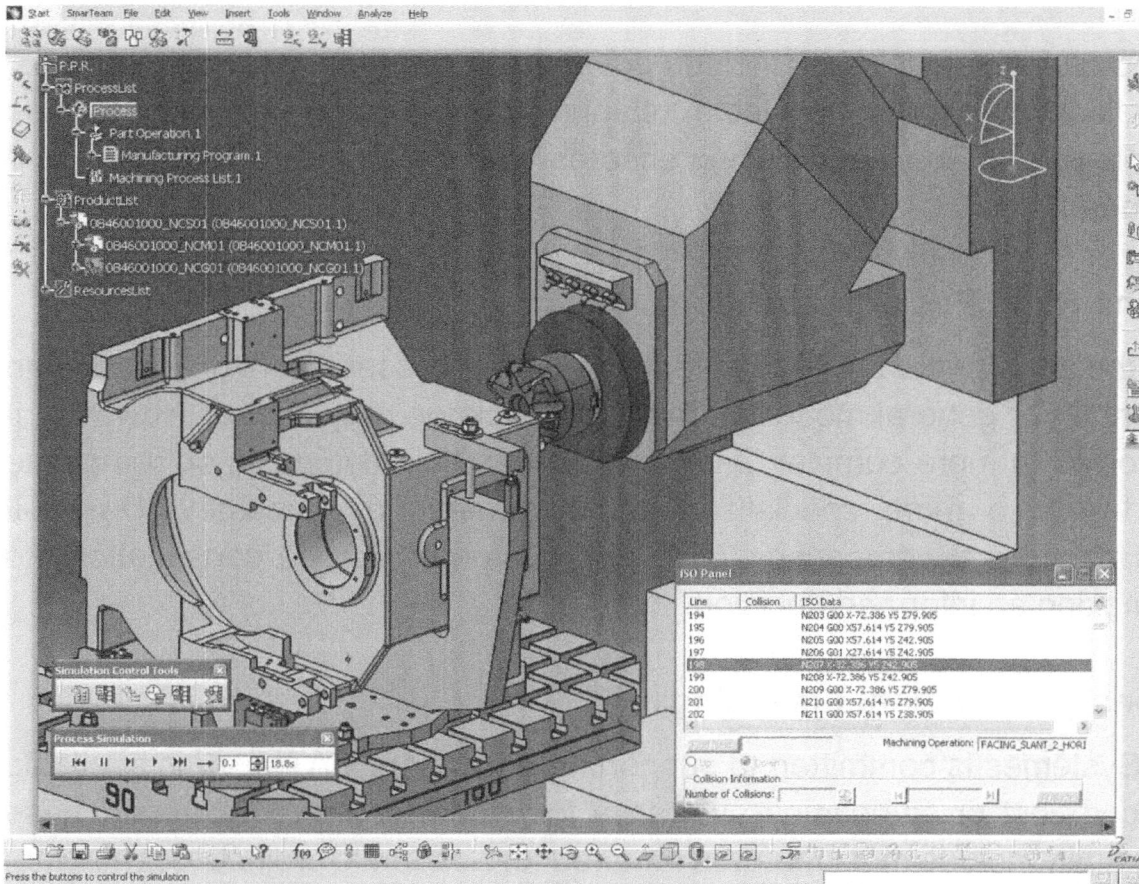

Subscription Options

Dassault Systèmes offers CATIA V5 primarily through a subscription-based model. Subscriptions can be monthly or annual, providing flexibility depending on your project timeline and budget. The subscription service grants you access to the latest software updates, technical support, and cloud-based services, ensuring your software remains current and competitive.

Price Structures and Licensing

The pricing structure of CATIA V5 is tiered, reflecting the diverse range of functionalities available. Basic packages cater to general 3D design needs, while more comprehensive packages include advanced simulation and analysis tools. Corporate licenses are also available, offering scalable solutions for companies with multiple users. This tiered pricing ensures you only pay for the features and tools you need.

Finding the Right Package for Your Needs

Selecting the appropriate CATIA package requires an assessment of your design requirements. For general modeling, the base package may suffice. However, if you're involved in more complex projects, such as fluid dynamics or composite material design, a more specialized package may be necessary. Dassault Systèmes provides a comparison chart and customer service consultations to assist in making an informed decision.

Educational and Student Licensing

Dassault Systèmes is committed to supporting education. CATIA V5 is available at a reduced cost or sometimes even free for students and educators. These licenses usually include most features required for academic projects but may not be used for commercial purposes. This commitment ensures that the next generation of designers and engineers have access to professional tools during their formative learning years.

INSTALLING CATIA V5

With the right subscription and license in hand, the next step is to properly install CATIA V5 on your system. Ensuring that your computer meets the necessary specifications will facilitate a smooth installation process and optimal software performance.

System Requirements

Before installation, verify your system adheres to the recommended requirements, which include a multi-core processor, ample RAM (typically 16 GB or more), and a dedicated graphics card. Additionally, ample storage space and a compatible operating system, such as Windows 10 or newer, are essential.

Step-by-Step Installation Guide

Installation is typically initiated through the Dassault Systèmes' download manager, which manages the download and installation of the software components. A detailed guide accompanies the software package, guiding you through the process, from account setup and software download to installation and initial launch.

Troubleshooting Common Installation Issues

Common issues during installation include compatibility problems, insufficient user permissions, and disrupted internet connections. The troubleshooting guide addresses these common pitfalls, and Dassault Systèmes' support can assist with more complex issues.

Setting Up Your Workspace

Once installed, configuring CATIA to your personal workflow preferences is a critical next step. This may involve setting up toolbars, importing custom settings, or establishing templates that align with your project requirements.

THE DESIGN PHILOSOPHY OF CATIA

Understanding the design philosophy of CATIA is crucial for leveraging the software's full potential. CATIA is built on the principles of precision, collaboration, and innovation.

The Core Principles of CATIA Design

CATIA's core principles revolve around creating a seamless and intuitive design experience. It promotes precision in modeling, ensuring designs are accurate and robust, capable of being used throughout the product lifecycle, from conceptualization to manufacturing.

How CATIA Supports the Design Process

CATIA supports the design process by facilitating a multidisciplinary approach. It allows for simultaneous work on mechanical, electrical, and fluidic systems within a single unified environment, ensuring all components of a design work in harmony.

Understanding the User Interface

CATIA's user interface is designed to be both powerful and accessible. Familiarizing yourself with its layout, toolbars, and menus is essential. The interface can be customized to better suit your workflow, enabling you to access frequently used tools more quickly.

Customization for Efficiency

Efficiency in CATIA is heightened through customization. This includes creating macros for repetitive tasks, custom commands, and personalized shortcuts. The software allows you to adapt the workspace to suit individual preferences, leading to a more efficient design process.

DEVELOPING THE CATIA MINDSET

Adopting a CATIA mindset is about more than just learning to use the software; it's about embracing a design philosophy that enhances creativity, precision, and efficiency. CATIA V5 2024, with its rich set of tools and functionalities, requires a mindset that balances technical skill with innovative thinking.

Thinking Like a Designer

To think like a designer in CATIA means to see the software not just as a collection of tools but as a canvas for innovation. It involves understanding the needs and constraints of the project, envisioning the end product, and planning the design process. A designer's mindset is inquisitive, constantly questioning how each element of the design can be improved or how different aspects of the model will interact.

Problem-Solving with CATIA

CATIA is a problem-solving ally. Whether you're dealing with space constraints, material selection, or design functionality, CATIA's suite offers simulation and analysis tools that help identify and rectify issues early in the design process. Adopting a problem-solving approach means actively using these tools to preempt challenges and test solutions.

Best Practices for Beginners

For beginners, it is essential to start with best practices that will serve as the foundation for all future CATIA projects. This includes:

- Familiarizing yourself with the user interface before starting your first project.

- Learning to organize your work with layers and groups.

- Starting with simple models and gradually increasing complexity.

- Regularly using the help function and tutorials provided within CATIA.

- Saving work frequently and creating backups.

Embracing Complexity Gradually

One of the key strategies for learning CATIA is to build your skills progressively. Begin with simple parts and assemblies, and as you become more comfortable, introduce more complex features like surfacing and kinematics. This gradual approach allows you to become confident with the basics before tackling the advanced functionalities that CATIA offers.

THE FUTURE AND BEYOND WITH CATIA

As technology evolves, so does the landscape of CAD/CAM/CAE. Being future-ready with CATIA means staying informed about emerging trends and preparing to integrate new features into your workflow.

Upcoming Trends in CAD/CAM/CAE

Innovations like artificial intelligence, cloud computing, and virtual reality are changing the way designers and engineers use CATIA. Future versions of CATIA will likely incorporate more of these technologies, providing tools that predict user actions, enable real-time collaboration across the globe, and allow for immersive design experiences.

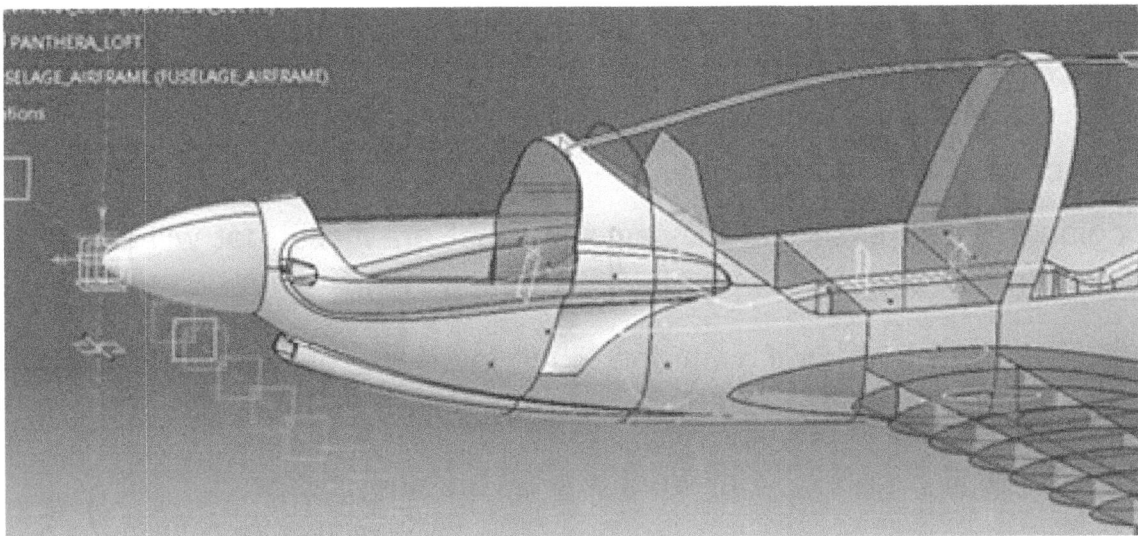

Preparing for Advanced CATIA Modules

As you look to the future, preparing for advanced modules involves deepening your understanding of the software's current capabilities and where it's heading. Engaging with the CATIA community and staying abreast of Dassault Systèmes' updates can help you anticipate and learn new modules quickly.

The Role of CATIA in Future Design Innovations

CATIA is poised to play a crucial role in future design innovations, especially in areas like sustainable design, advanced materials, and smart manufacturing. By using CATIA, you can contribute to these innovations, creating designs that are not only technologically advanced but also environmentally responsible and economically viable.

1.8.4 Continuing Your CATIA Education

To continue your education in CATIA, consider online courses, certification programs, and workshops. Additionally, engaging with user forums, attending webinars, and reading industry publications will help you stay connected with the CATIA ecosystem and lifelong learning.

CHAPTER SUMMARY

Key Takeaways

Developing a CATIA mindset involves thinking creatively and embracing the role of a designer.

Gradual complexity adoption and problem-solving are critical to mastering CATIA.

The future of CATIA includes embracing trends in technology that influence CAD/CAM/CAE.

Review Questions and Exercises

At the end of this chapter, review questions and exercises will be provided to reinforce the concepts covered. This might include creating simple sketches, using basic features, or exploring the software's help functions.

Additional Resources for Further Learning

For further learning, this section will guide you to additional resources such as tutorials, user community forums, Dassault Systèmes support pages, and educational literature.

By understanding the CATIA mindset, you set the stage for becoming not just proficient in using the software, but also for being a part of the next generation of designers who will shape the future of innovation. The journey through CATIA V5 2024 is one of continuous learning, problem-solving, and creative exploration, and this chapter is your launchpad.

CHAPTER 2: INITIATING YOUR JOURNEY WITH CATIA V5

2.1 INTRODUCTION TO CATIA V5

CATIA is a three-dimensional CAD/CAM/CAE software which was developed and sold by Dassault Systèmes, France in the late I 970 s. The software was first used for designing the Mirage fighter plane. The application has since expanded in to the automotive, aerospace and shipbuilding industries. CATIA is competing in the market with other three-dimensional CAD/CAM /CAE software such as Pro/Engineer, Siemens X, Autodesk Inventor, SolidWorks and Solid Edge.

Up until CATIA V4, non-manifold solid engines were adopted to create individual surfaces which were then connected to construct the final model. However, in CATIA V5, you can construct a solid model in a similar manner to other three-dimensional CAD/CAM/ CAE systems because it adopts a NURBS based parametric solid and surface modeling technique.

A feature is the very basic unit of modeling. The models created in CATIA V5 are combi- nations of features, and those features may be associated with each other directly or indirectly. Therefore, if you create a model by taking into account the relationships between the features, you can easily modify the specification of one feature, and all subsequent features dependent on the modified feature are updated as a res ult. The downstream associativity of the features increases the flexibility of the modeling process.

In parametric modeling, parameters are used to define the standard shape and size of the geometry. The parameters arc specified in the feature definition dialog boxes and the features are recorded in the specification tree in CATIA V5. You can therefore modify the parameters of a feature at any time during the modeling process, which allows you to make the model with ease. The holes in Fig 1-1(a) are created in a Circular Pattern feature which allocates 6 as the number of holes. Here, the number of holes represents the parameter and the Circular Pattern is the feature. If you modify the parameter, i.e. number of hole s to 8, the model can be updated simply as shown in Fig 1-1(b).

<Reference: Wikipedia>

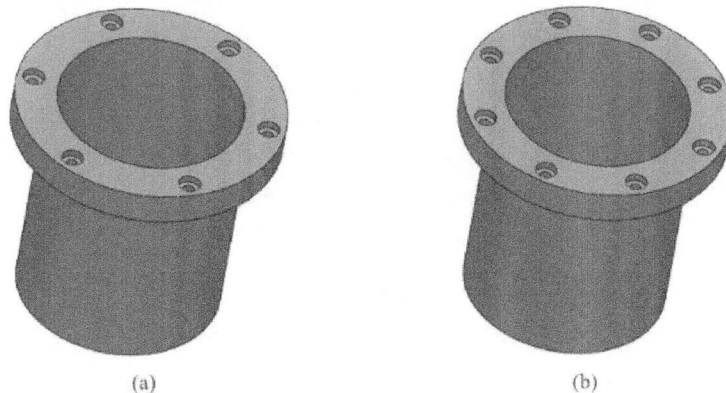

(a)   (b)

Fig 1-1 Modification of the Model

13

2.2 WORKBENCHES IN CATIA V5

There are many workbenches in the category of mechanical design in CATIA V5. A workbench is a modeling environment which contains functions to complete the desired work. The mechanical design workbenches in CATIA V5 include Part Design, Wire- frame and Surface Design, Assembly Drafting, Generative Sheetmetal Design and others. Th is book explains the basics of using workbench es such as Part Design, Assembly and Drafting through specially arranged exercises.

2.3 EXECUTING CATIA V5

To execute CATIA V5 you can choose Start > All Programs> CATIA P3 > CATIA P3 V5-6 R2014. You may either double click the icon in the background of Windows or click the fast-executing facility.

The startup screen shown in Fig 1-3 is of the Product Structure workbench. The startup screen can change according to the modeling condition. You can use one of two methods to create a new part file when creating a model.

Fig 1-2 Executing CATIA V5

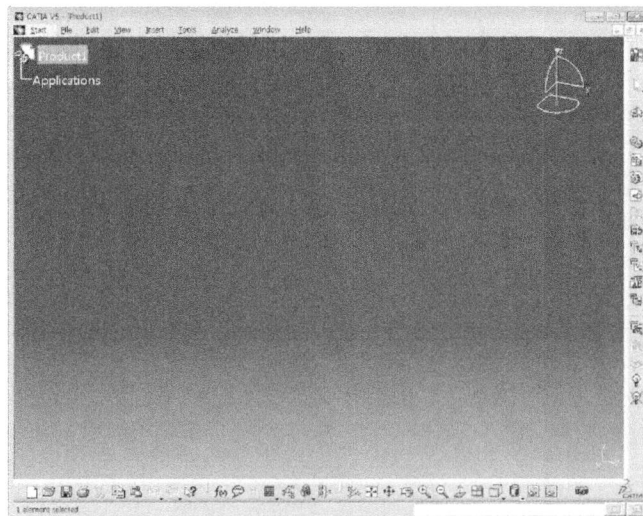

Fig 1-3 Screen Shot of CATIA V5

2.3.1 Choosing File > New in the Menu Bar

Select File > New in the me nu bar and the dialog box shown in Fig 1-4 appears. Choose the type of new file and press OK in the dialog box. The corresponding workbench is invoked.

We will choose Part in the List of Types option area to invoke the Part Design workbench. You may type Part in the Selection input box. After specifying the type of new file press OK in the dialog box. The Part Design workbench as shown in Fig 1-5 is invoked.

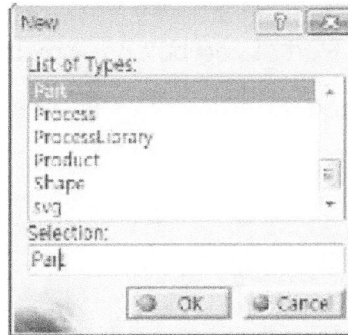

Fig 1-4 New Dialog Box

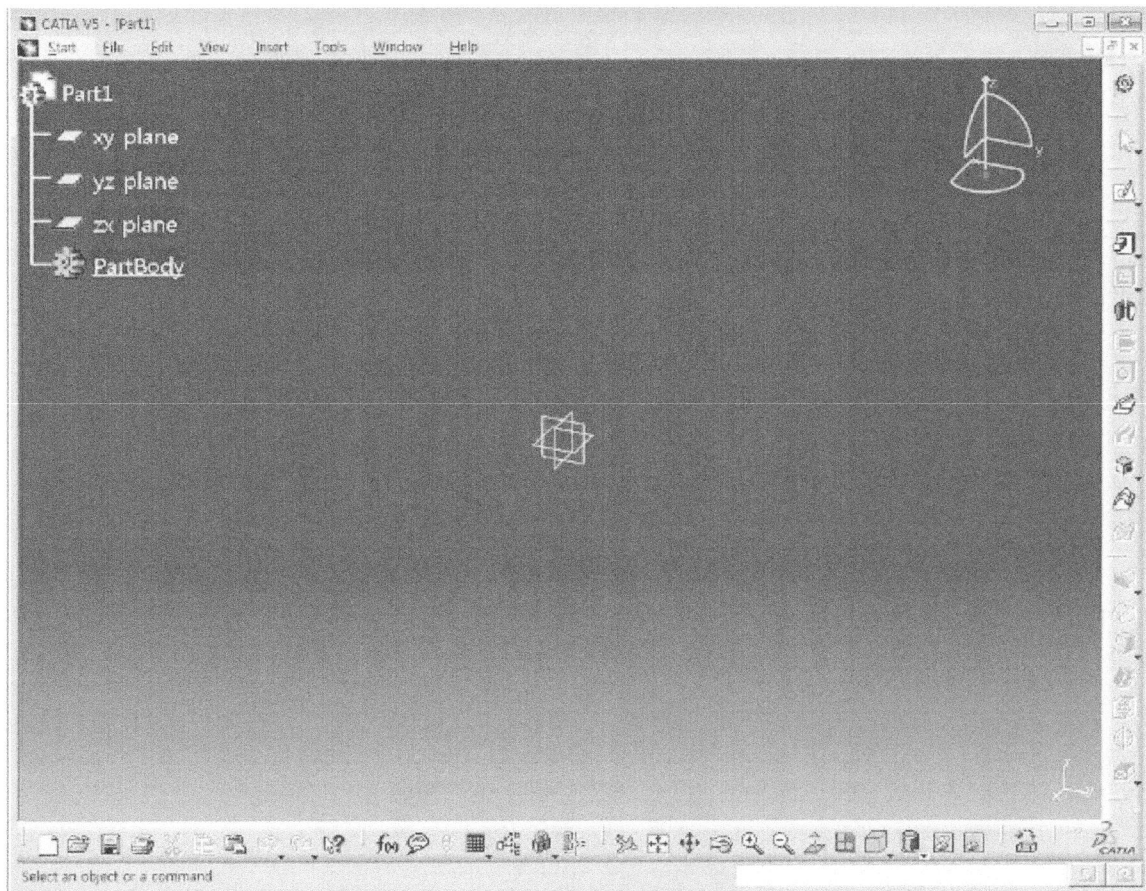

Fig 1-5 Part Design Workbench

2.3.2 Selecting Workbench in the Start Menu

You can start a new part file by closing the default product file and choosing the Part Design workbench in the Start button of CATIA V5. Keep the following process to start a new part file in this method.

1. Choose File > Close in the me n u bar to close the default product file without saving it.
2. Click the Start button of CATIA V5 and choose Mechanical Design > Part Design in the Start menu as shown in Fig 1- 6.
3. Enter a part name in the New Part dialog box as shown in Fig 1-7.

The Part Design workbench is invoked as shown in Fig 1- 8. Note that the name of the pat1 is specified in the Spec Tree.

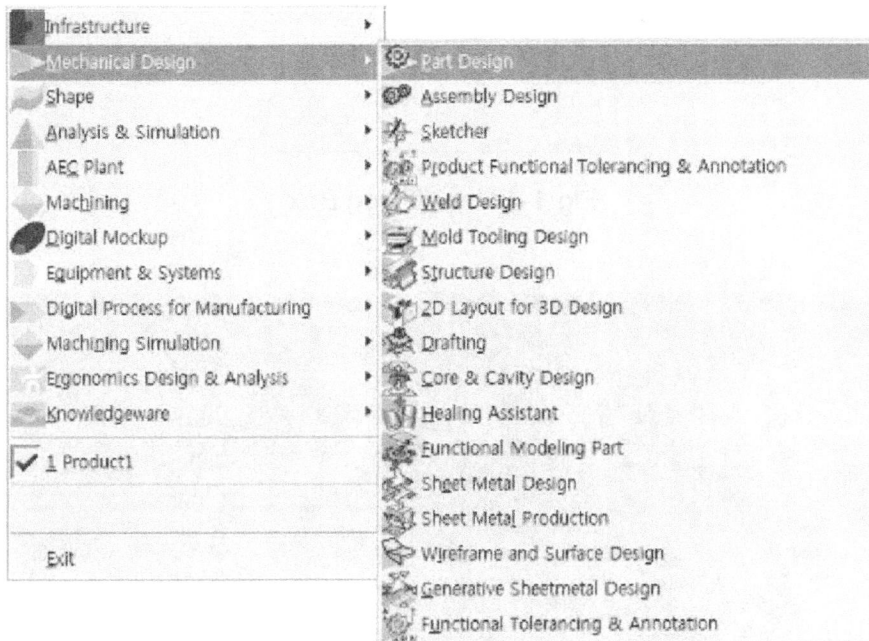

Fig 1-6 Invoking the Part Design Workbench

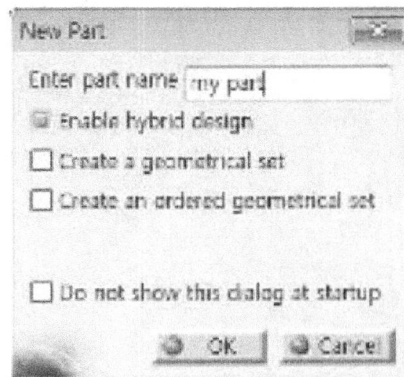

Fi g 1-7 New Part Dialog Box

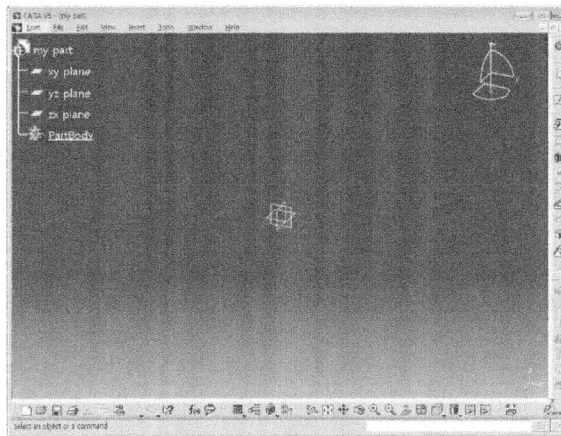

Fig 1-8 Part Design Workbench

2.4 LAYOUT OF THE CATIA V5 SCREEN

Fig 1-9 shows the layout of CATIA V5 in the Part Design workbench. Users can customize the layout of the screen with the help of the customization tool.

2.4.1 Specification Tree

The specification tree shows the mode ling history of a part. You can modify the shape of a model by accessing the specification of a feature. The specification tree can be hidden by choosing View > Specification Tree from the me nu bar.

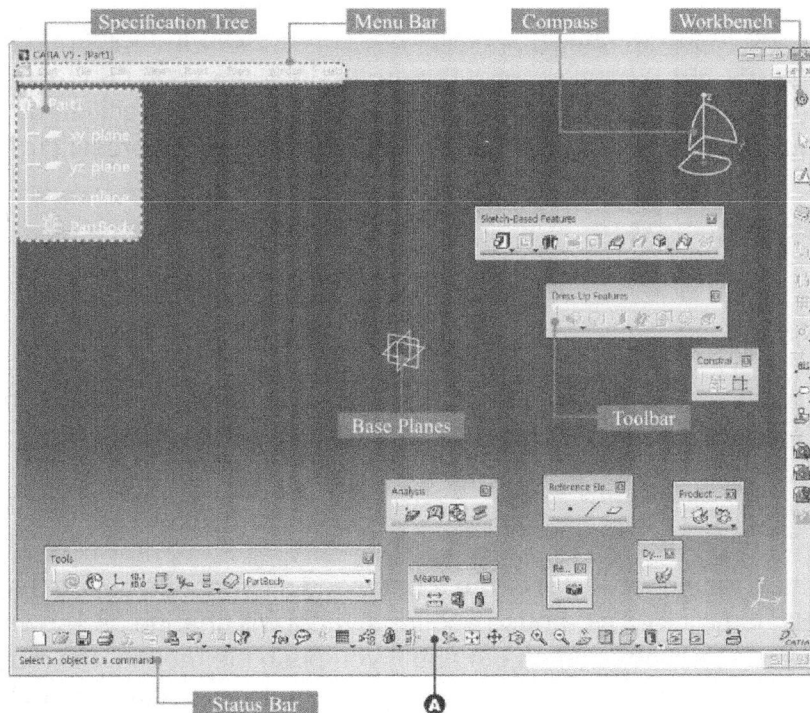

Fig 1-9 Layout of CAT IA V5 Screen

2.4.2 Menu Bar

You can execute a number of functions to create a model or set preferences.

2.4.3 Compass

Compass is used to translate or rotate a screen. You can also translate or rotate a model or component.

2.4.4 Workbench

This icon informs the workbench that you are currently in. Clicking in this area, the Wel- come to CATIA V5 dialog box appears.

2.4.5 Status Bar

The status bar notifies the user what to do to complete the current function.

2.4.6 Base Planes

Base planes are three planes that are created automatically. You cannot delete base planes.

2.4.7 Toolbar

Functions that are used in the modeling process are categorized in toolbars. Commands that are available in the menu bar are presented as icons in the toolbars. You can take the toolbars out in the graphics window by dragging the beginning point of a toolbar as specified by (A) in Fig 1-9 from the toolbar area. You can drop the toolbar horizontally or vertically by pressi.t1g the Shift key.

2.5 VIEW OPERATIONS

2.5.1 Pan

To pan the screen, press mouse button 2 and drag. A mouse pointer as shown in Fig 1-10 appears and the screen will pan while maintaining the view angle.

2.5.2 Zoom In/Out

Press the middle button (or wheel: MB2) of the mouse and dick mouse button 3 (MB3: right click) or mouse button 1 (MB1: left click). The mouse pointer symbol will change as shown in Fig 1-11. If you pull the mouse, the mode I will be zoomed out and if you push the mouse, the model will be zoomed in. You can hold the Ctrl key while pressing MB2 (middle button) to attain zoom in/out mode.

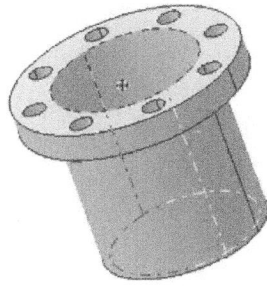

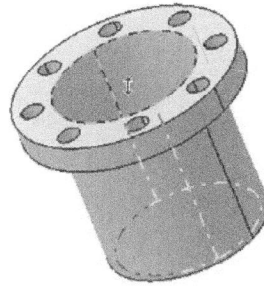

Fig 1-10 Pan   Fig 1- 11 Zoom In/Out

2.5.3 Rotate

To rotate the model, press MB2 (middle button) and either MB1 (left button) or MB3 (right button) at tbc same time. A dashed circle appears on the screen as shown in Fig 1-12, and if you move the mouse, the screen, i.e., the view ang le, will be rotated. You can press the middle button and the Ctrl key at the same time and drag the mouse to rotate the model.

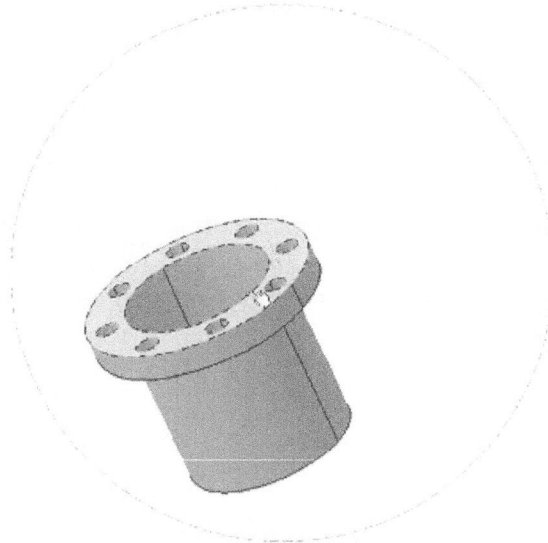

Fig 1-12 Rotate

2.5.4 Quick Pan

Place the mouse pointer at a specific location and click MB2 (middle button). The model will quickly pan so that the location is positioned at the center of the scree n.

2.6 VIEW TOOLBAR

Fig 1-13 shows the View toolbar. You can perform view operations which were explained earlier with the icons in the View toolbar.

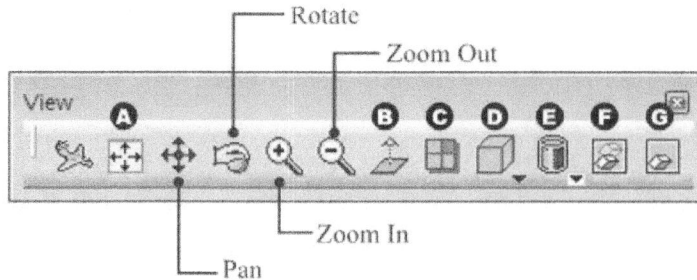

Fig 1-13 View Toolbar

2.6.1 Pan, Rotate, Zoom In, Zoom Out

To pan, rotate and zoom in/ out, press each icon in the View toolbar and drag the mouse while pressing the 1B] (left button) of the mouse.

2.6.2 Fit All In ((A) in Fig 1-13)

To fit the model so that it occupies the full screen, select the Fit All In icon in the View toolbar. Press this button when you have lost sight of the mode l and you cannot see anything on the screen.

2.6.3. Normal View ((B) in Fig 1-13)

If you press the Normal View icon in the View toolbar, the status bar message informs you to select a plane. On selecting a plane, the model view changes to normal for the selected plane. Fig 1-14 (a) shows a general three-dimensional view and Fig 1- 14 (b) shows the model view after aligning norma l to the top plane of the model.

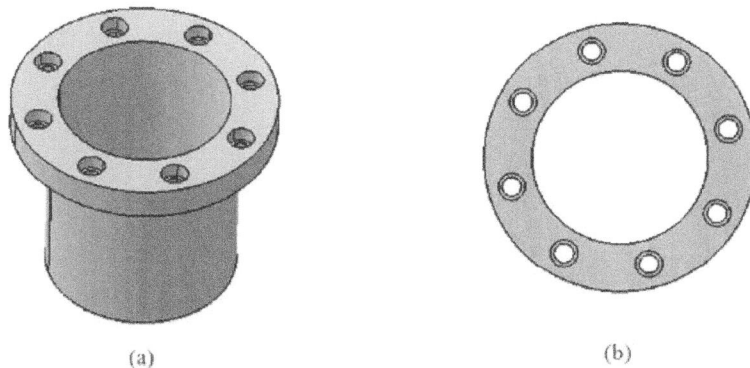

(a)   (b)

Fig 1-14 Aligning Normal View

2.6.4 Create Multi-View ((C) in Fig 1-13)

If you press this icon. The screen is split into four. You can specify a different view direction for each screen.

20

2.6.5 Quick View

Pressing the small downward symbol specified by (D) in Fig 1- 13 allows you to drag out the Quick View toolbar as shown in Fig 1-15. If you press the Shift key while you are dragging the toolbar, you can place the toolbar horizontally.

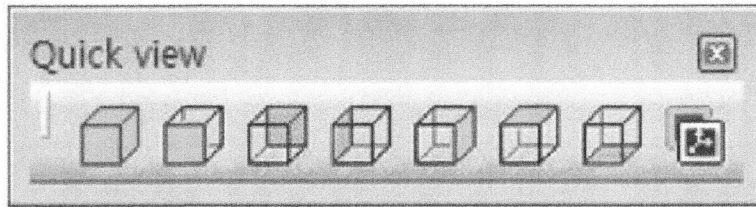

Fig 11-15 Quick View Toolbar

Using tools in the Quick View toolbar, you can quickly align the view direct ion to one of the standard views as shown in Fig 1-18.

Pressing the Named View icon in the Quick View toolbar, the Named View dialog box as shown in Fig 1-16 appears. You can save the current view angle by specifying its name in the dialog box.

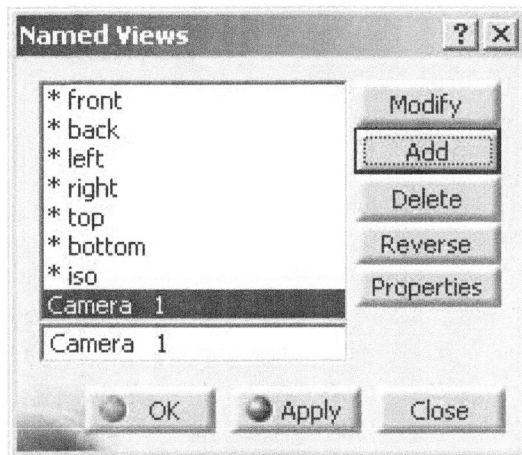

Fig 1-16 Named Views Dialog Box

2.6.6 View Mode

You can drag out the View Mode toolbar from (E) in Fig 1-1 3. You can set the view mode of the model by using too ls in this toolbar. Fig 1-19 shows the view modes available in CATIA V5.

Fig 1-17 View Mode Toolbar

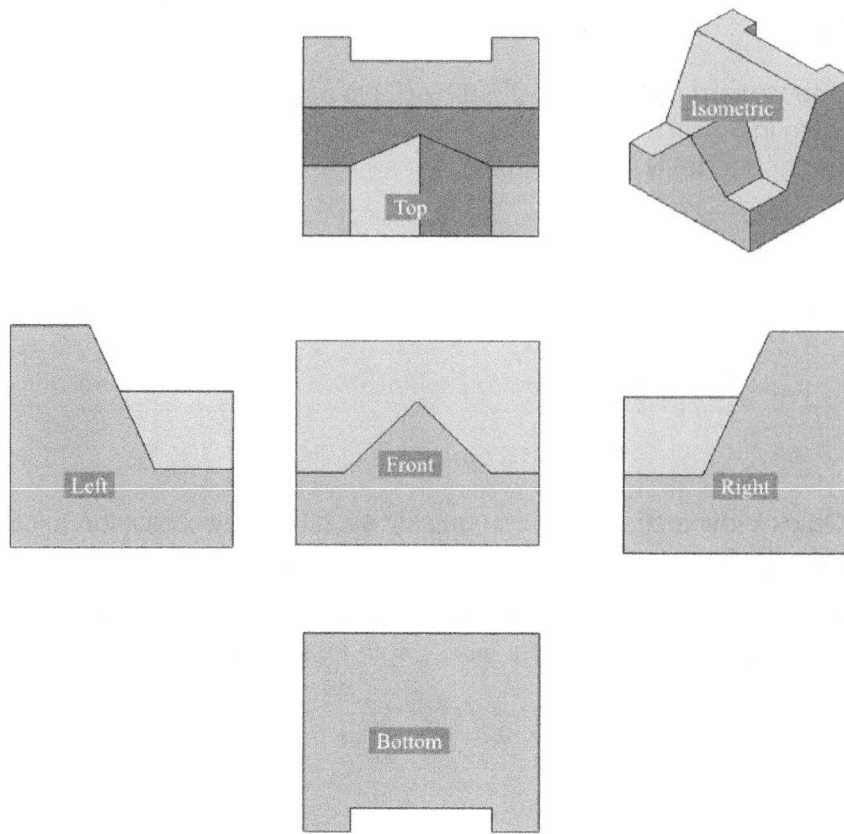

Fig 1-18 Standard Views

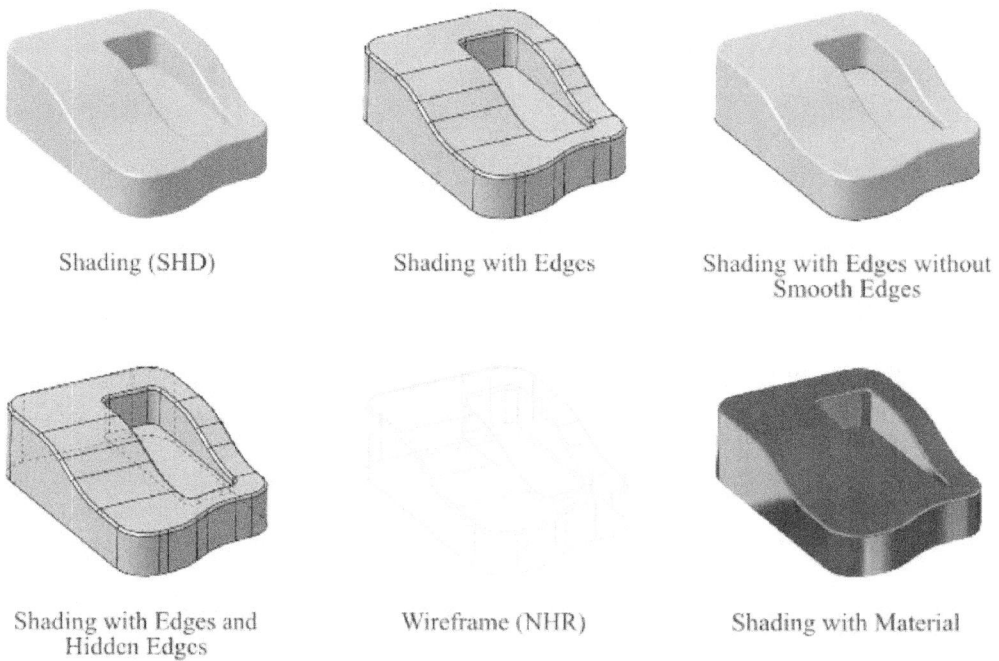

Shading (SHD)

Shading with Edges

Shading with Edges without Smooth Edges

Shading with Edges and Hidden Edges

Wireframe (NHR)

Shading with Material

Fig 1-19 View Modes

To apply the Shading with Material view mode, you have to first apply the mate rial ac- cording to the following procedure.

1. Press the Apply Material button ⬛ from the lower part of the CATIA V5 screen.
2. Select Part Body in the Specification Tree or in the graphic window.
3. Choose material in the Material Library dialog box as shown in Fig 1-20.
4. Press the Shading with Material button in the View Mode tool bar.

2.6.7 Hide/Show ((F) in Fig 1-13)

You can hide or show modeling objects by using the Hide/Show button in the View tool - bar. Press this button then select the object(s) to hide. There are two graphic spaces in CATIA V5: a modeling space and a non-modeling space. If you hide an object, the object moves from the modeling space to the non-modeling space, and the object will not be visible.

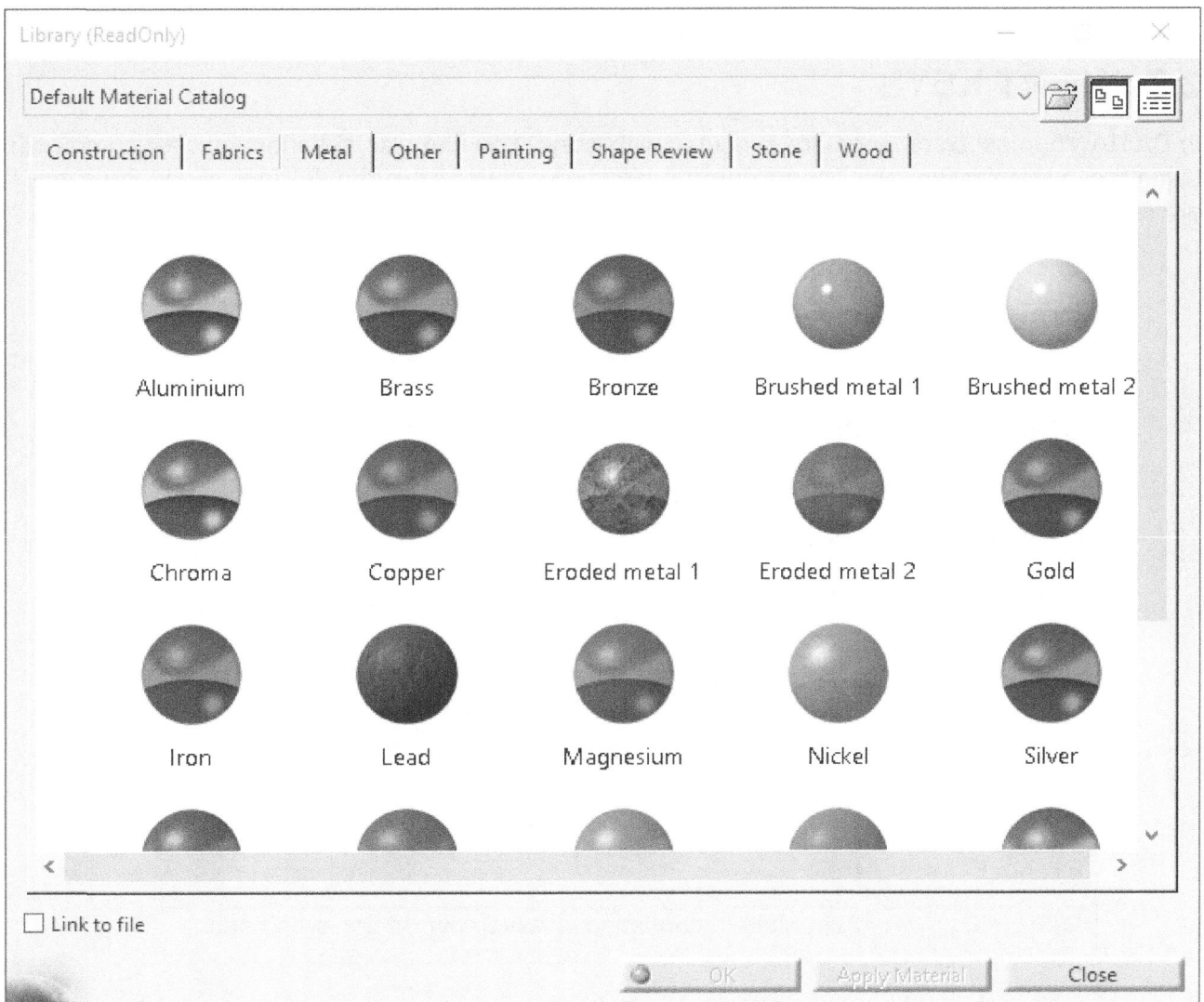

Fig 1-20 Material Library Dialog Box

2.6.8 Swap visible space (G in Fig 1-11)

Pressing this button, the visibility of the two spaces is switched, i.e., you can see objects in the non-modeling space. If you switch the visible space, the background color changes to indicate that you are in the non - modeling space. You can continue the modeling process in the non -mode ling space, but the result will be created in the modeling pace and cannot be seen. Jr you use the Hide/Show button in the non-modeling space, the object moves to the modeling space.

Restoring the position of toolbars

You can restore the position of toolbars according to the following steps.

1. Select **Tools** > **Customize** from the menu bar.
2. Select the **Toolbars** tab in the **Customize** dialog box.
3. Press the **Restore Position** button.

2.7 SHORT KEYS

In CATIA V5, most commands are executed with icons. You can also set short keys for commands using the customization tool. The following table shows several system de- fault sho11 keys which are commonly used.

Short Keys	Commands
CTRL + Z	Undo
CTRL + Y	Repeat
CTRL + S	Save
ALT + ENTER	Properties
CTRL + F	Search
CTRL + U	Update
SHIFT + F2	Specification Overview
F3	Hide or show the Specification Tree
SHIFT + F3	Activate or deactivate the Specification Tree
SHIFT + F1	What's This?
F1	Help
CTRL + D	Fast Multi-Instantiation in Assembly Design workbench

2.8 SYSTEM OPTIONS

Selecting Tools > Options from the menu bar, the Options dialog box as shown in Fig 1-21 appears. In the left side of the dialog box specified by (A) in Fig 1-21, the options are categorized. The option s related to display can be set by pressing General > Display on the left. Pressing the Visualization tab on the right of the dialog box lets you set the method of how to display the model on the screen.

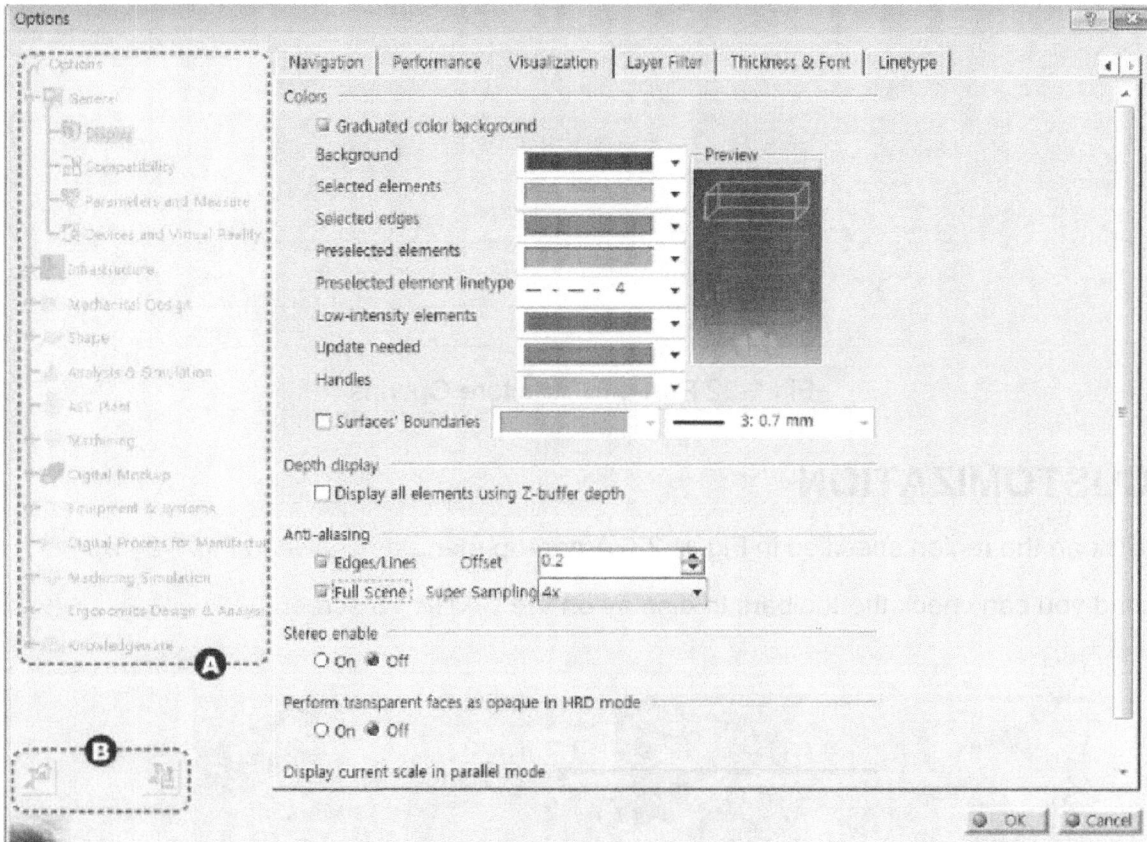

Fig 1- 21 Display Options

Expand Infrastructure in the category specified by (A). An option category Part Infra- structure appears and if you select it, the corresponding options are shown on the right of the dialog box as shown in Fig 1-22. With the Keep link with selected object option in the General tab checked, you can create features that are linked with other features.

Expand the category of Mechanical Design on the left of the dialog box. You can set the options related to Assembly Design, Sketcher and Drafting, etc. If you check the automatic update option in the General tab of the Assembly Design category, the location and orientation of the com ponent is updated automatically while you are const raining in the Assembly Design workbench. In the Sketcher category, you can set options regarding the grid, sketch plane, constraints, etc. Note that we will not change any option located in the Sketcher category throughout this textbook unless otherwise stated.

The two buttons specified by (B) in Fig 1-21 are used to reset the options to default or to dump the parameters set in the Options dialog box.

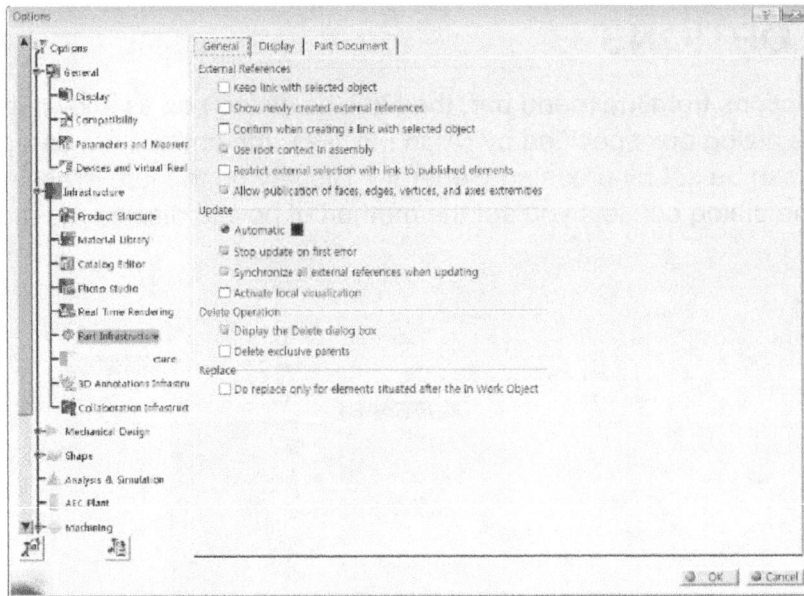

Fig 1-22 Part Infrastructure Options

2.9 CUSTOMIZATION

Right click on the region specified in Fig 1- 23. A pop-up menu as shown in Fig 1-24 appears and you can check the toolbars to display on the CATIA V5 screen.

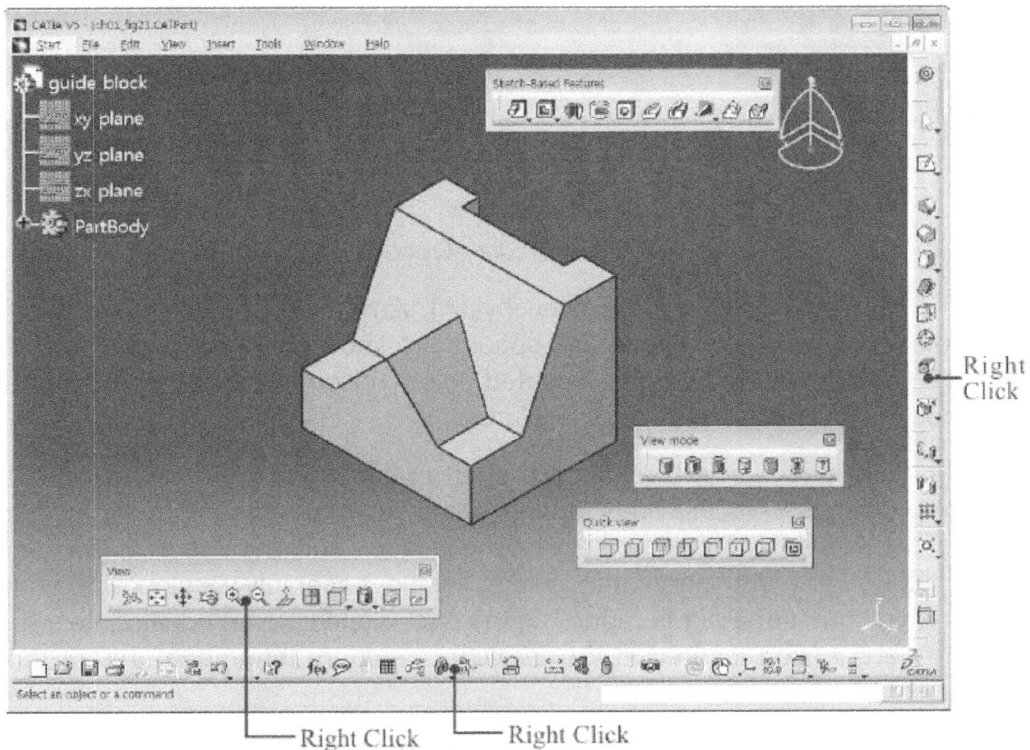

Fig 1- 23 Area to Invoke Pop-up Menu

26

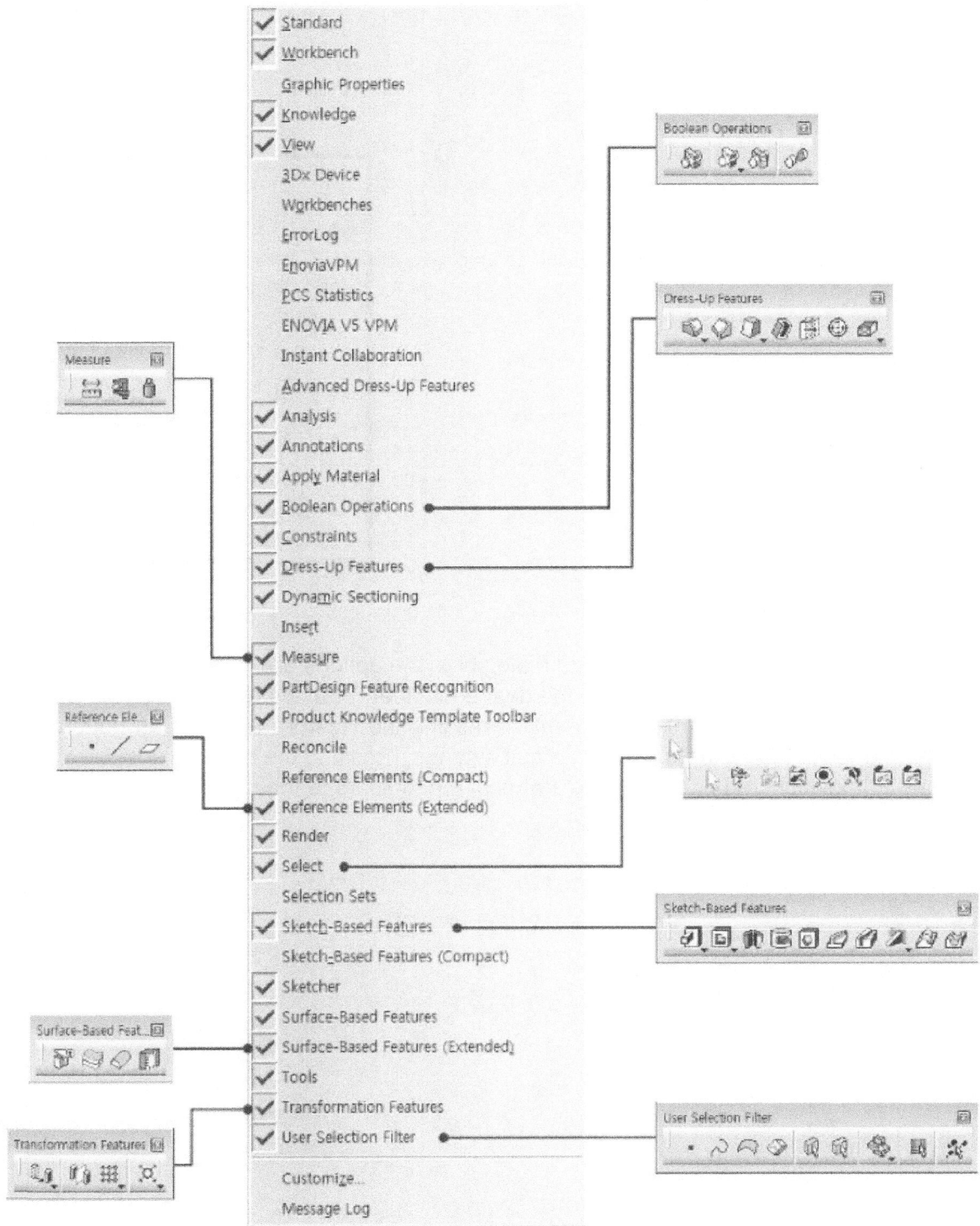

Fig 1- 24 Various Toolbars

Select Tools > Customize from the menu bar or select Customize in the pop-up menu shown in Fig 1-24. The Customize dialog box a shown in Fig 1- 25 appears and you can set the start menu in the Start Menu tab.

Select a workbench in the Favorite workbench list and you can also set a hot key in the Accelerator option to switch to the workbench quickly.

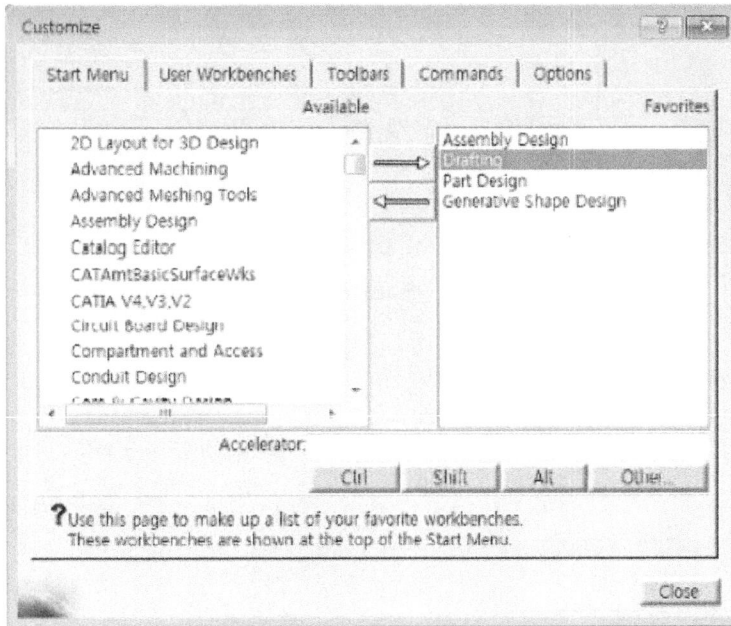

Fig 1-25 Start Menu Tab

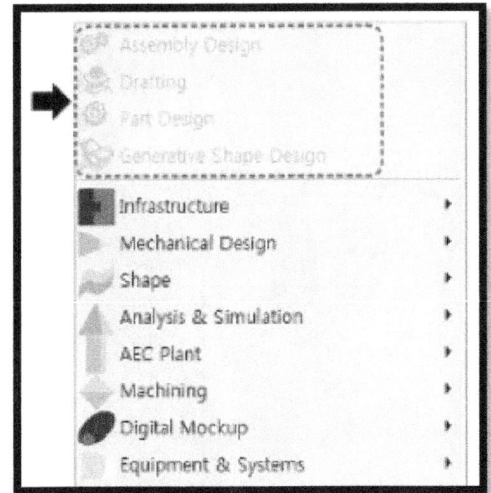

Fig 1-26 Start Menu

Pressing the Toolbars tab in the Customize dialog box, the options are changed as shown in Fig 1-27. You can add or remove commands in the desired toolbar. You can also create your own toolbar to contain commands that you use frequently. Pressing the Restore all contents button, you can restore commands in the toolbars to their default settings. Pressing the Restore position button, you can restore the position and/or display the status of the toolbars to their default settings.

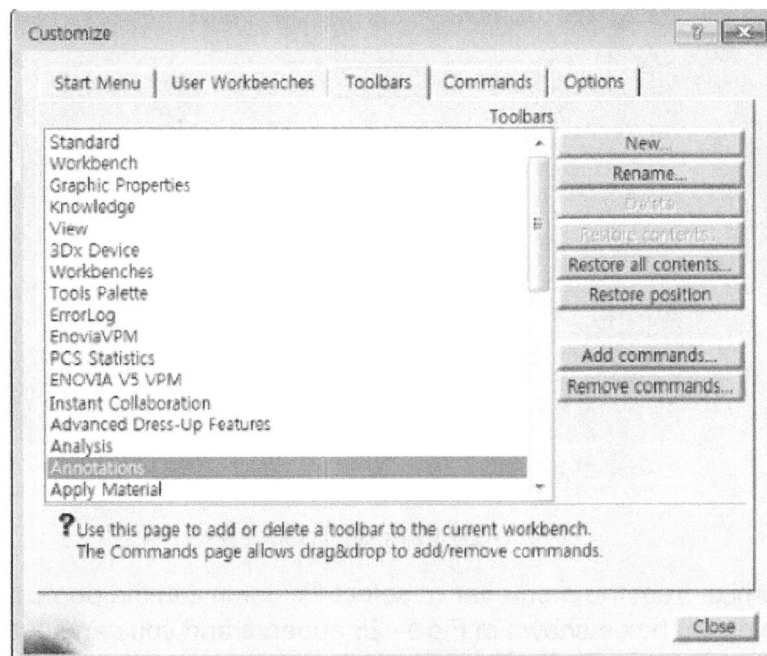

Fig 1-27 Toolbars Standard

Fig 1- 28 shows options in tbc Commands tab. You can drag a command from the Commands list in the dialog box and drop it onto the desired toolbar. You can also set short keys for each command by pressing the Show Properties button. n1e command proper- ties option is available a shown in Fig 1-29 where you can set a short key in the Accelerator input box.

I n the Options tab, you can set the size of the icons. If you check the Tooltips option, a brief explanation on the command will be displayed when you hover the mouse pointer over an icon. In the User Interface Language dropdown list, you can choose your own language as the inter face if it is available. Note that you have to ex it and run CATT A VS again after changing the user interface language. You can also lock the position of toolbars with the option in th e Options tab.

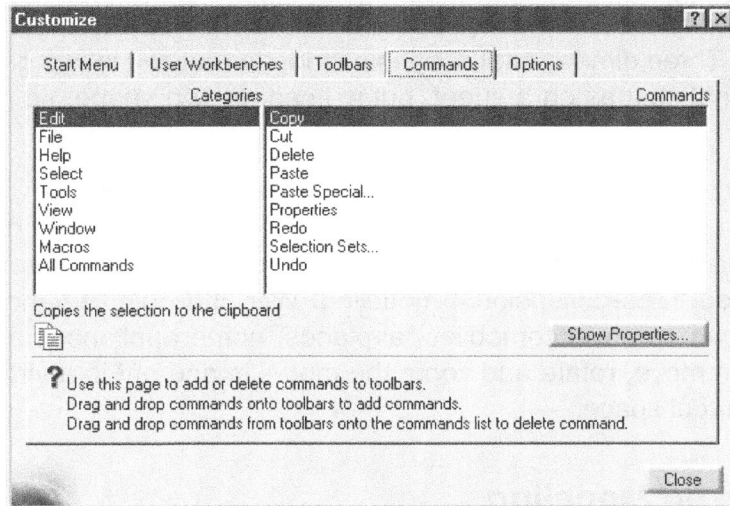

Fig 1- 28 Commands Tab

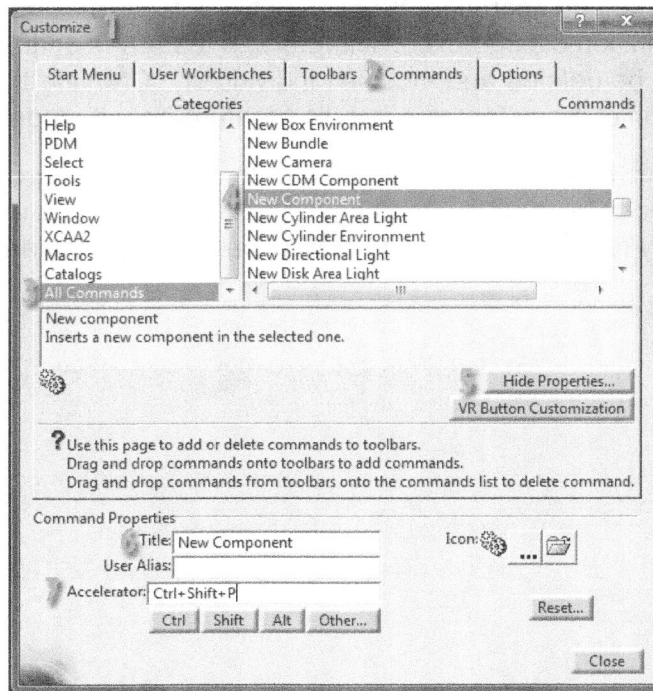

Fig 1- 29 Commands Tab (Show Parameters)

CHAPTER 3: THE A TO Z OF MODELING BASICS IN CATIA V5

3.1 TERMS AND CONCEPTS

3.1.1 Three-Dimensional Modeling

All objects in the real world are three dimensional. However thin an object may be, it has thickness and therefore volume. Three dimensional shapes cannot be realized in two dimensions. We cannot create three dimensional shapes on a sheet, but we can draw a shape, so it appears to be three dimensional.

With the development of computers and graphic processors, we can now establish three dimensional shapes in a virtual space on Olu- computer system. We can define a surface from, wireframes and we can define the volume with closed surfaces . Creating three dimensional shapes on a computer is called three-dimensional modeling. With the help of various three-dimensional design software, we can create automobiles, airplanes, home appliances and other objects in a graphic space. We can move, rotate and zoom the model in and out in a virtual three-dimensional space just as we do in real space.

3.1.2 Feature Based Modeling

Three dimensional models can be created by combining many basic features. A feature defines a basic shape through a command operation. You can define a feature using a command and several options in the feature definition dialog boxes. Therefore, a feature is understood to be the smallest unit of modeling that can be defined and modified individually. Creating three dimensional models based on the accumulation of many features is called feature-based modeling.

Fig 2- 1 shows some basic features which can be create d by extruding or revolving wire- frames. (A) and (B) can be created by extruding a rectangular or circular wireframe along one direction. (C) and (D) can be created by revolving a rectangular or circular wire frame around an axis.

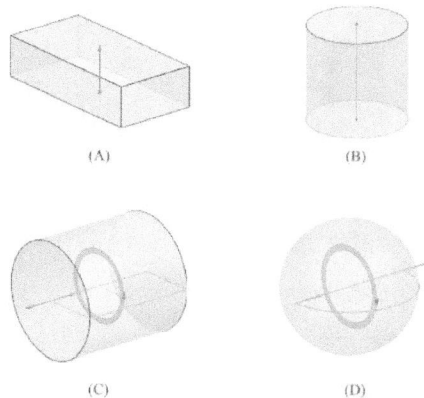

(A)

(B)

(C)

(D)

Fig 2-1 Some Basic Features

3.1.3 Sketch Based Feature

Some features cannot be defined without sketches. These features are called sketch based features. The hexahedron in Fig 2-1 (A) can be create.cl by extruding a rectangular sketch along a specific direction. In CATIA V5, you can create the extruded shape by using the Pad command. Therefore, a pad feature is a sketch based feature. The shapes (C) and (D) in Fig 2- 1 are created by revolving sketches around a respective axis. In CATIA V5, a revolved shape can be created using the Shaft command. Therefore, a shaft feature is a sketch based feature. The commands to create sketch based features are grouped in the Sketch-Based Features toolbar.

In CATIA V5, there are features called dress-up features. Dress-up features do not need sketches but need a three-dimensional geometry. Therefore, you cannot define dress-up features as the first feature because there is no geometry at the beginning of a new model file. Fig 2-2 shows the Sketch-Based Features and Dress-Up Features toolbars that appear in the Part Design workbench.

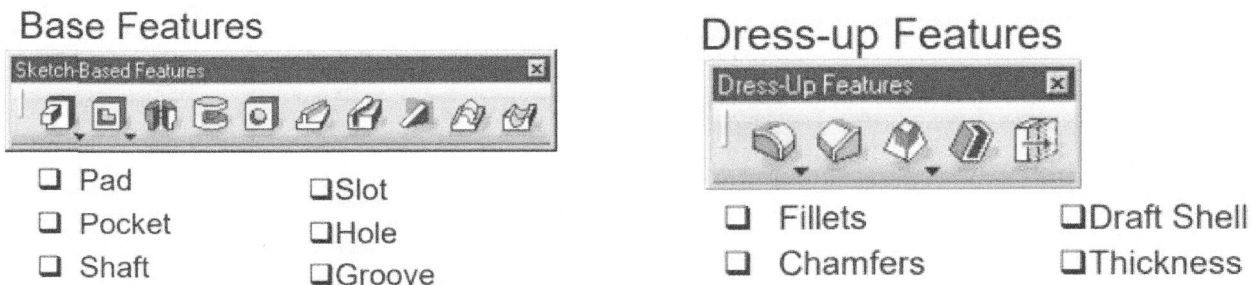

Base Features

Sketch-Based Features

☐ Pad   ☐ Slot
☐ Pocket   ☐ Hole
☐ Shaft   ☐ Groove

Dress-up Features

Dress-Up Features

☐ Fillets   ☐ Draft Shell
☐ Chamfers   ☐ Thickness

Fig 2-2 Sketch-Based Features and Dress-Up Features Toolbars

3.1.4 History Based Modeling

Features created in CATIA V5 are grouped in the specification tree in order. Looking at the specification tree, you can understand the modeling history of a pa t1. You can also modify the feature definition options by accessing the feature definition dialog box. This is called history-based modeling. Fig 2-3 shows each modeling step of a part with the specification tree. The following explains each step.

1. Create a sketch on the xy plane.
2. Extrude the sketch along the Z direction with the Pad command.
3. Create a second sketch on the top planar face of the geometry.
4. Extrude the sketch with the Pad command and add to the existing body.
5. Apply fillet to the edges.
6. Hollow out the body with the Shell command.
7. Create a third sketch on a side wall.
8. Extrude the sketch with the Pocket command and remove the body.

The order of feature creation is very crucial in creating the desired model. If you apply the Shell command (step 6 in Fig 2-3) before applying the Fillet (step 5 in Fig 2-3), you will not be able to create the proper thickness for the filleted surface.

31

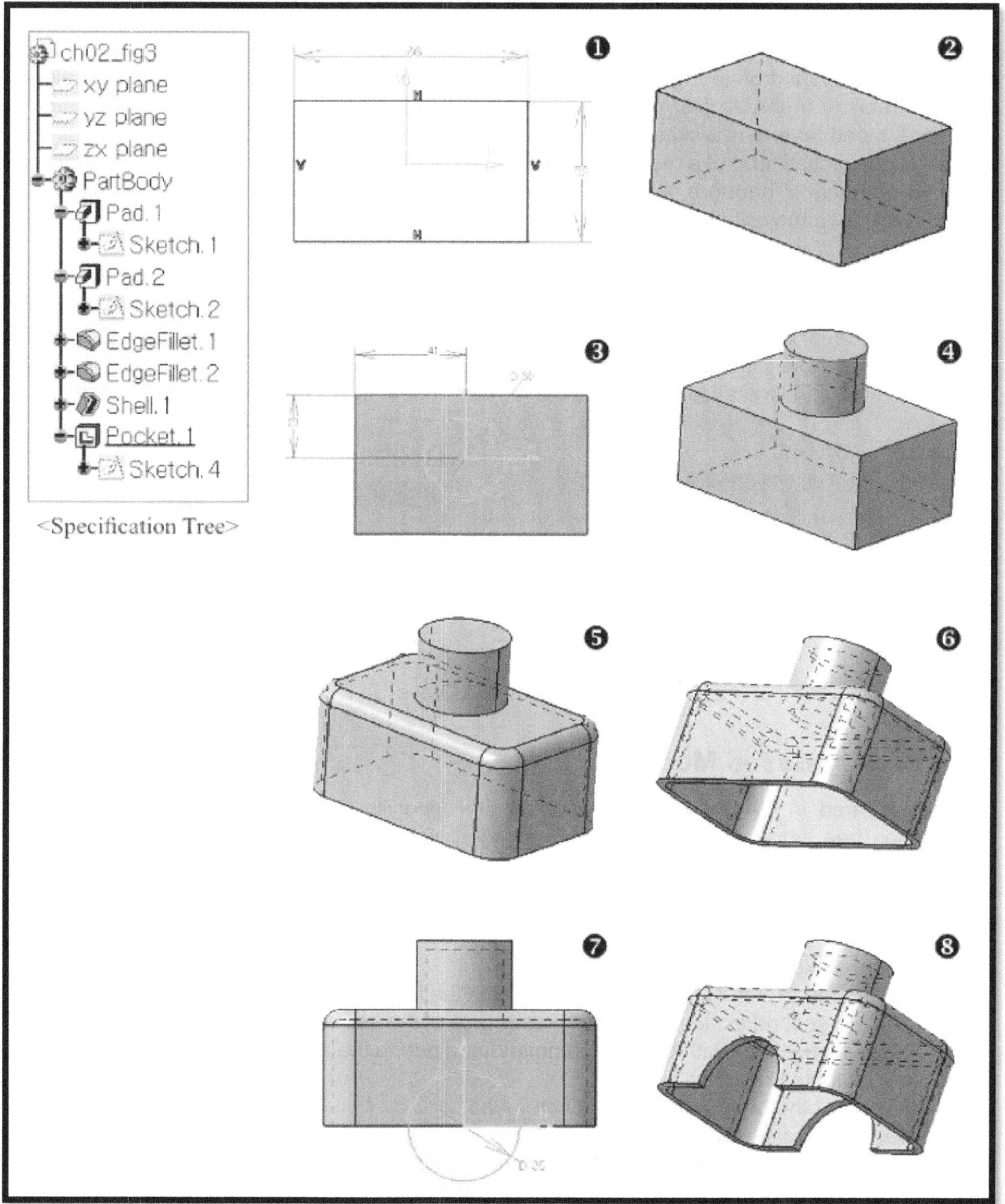

Specification Tree

```
ch02_fig3
├── xy plane
├── yz plane
├── zx plane
└── PartBody
    ├── Pad. 1
    │   └── Sketch. 1
    ├── Pad. 2
    │   └── Sketch. 2
    ├── EdgeFillet. 1
    ├── EdgeFillet. 2
    ├── Shell. 1
    └── Pocket. 1
        └── Sketch. 4
```

<Specification Tree>

Fig 2-3 Modeling History

3.2 INTRODUCTION TO CATIA V5 MODELING PROCESS

In this section, we will learn the general process of modeling with CATJA V5 by following the steps illustrated in Fig 2-3.

3.2.1 Creating a Part File

When you are executing CATIA V5 for the first time, the scree n will appear as shown in Fig 2-4. This is the Product Structure workbeJ1ch. In this textbook, we will set the type of file while we are creating a new file, and you will start the new file in the designated workbench. Therefore, close the file that automatic a11y s tarts in the Product Structure workbench by choosing File> Close in the menu bar. If you have set the favorite work- benches as shown in Fig 1-25, the Welcome to CATIA V5 dialog box with be invoked. Check the Do not show this dialog at startup opt ion and close the dialog box. The dialog box will not appear when you execute CATIA V5 in the future. You can invoke the Welcome to CATIA V5 dialog box by clicking the Workbench icon as designated by the arrow in Fig 2-4.

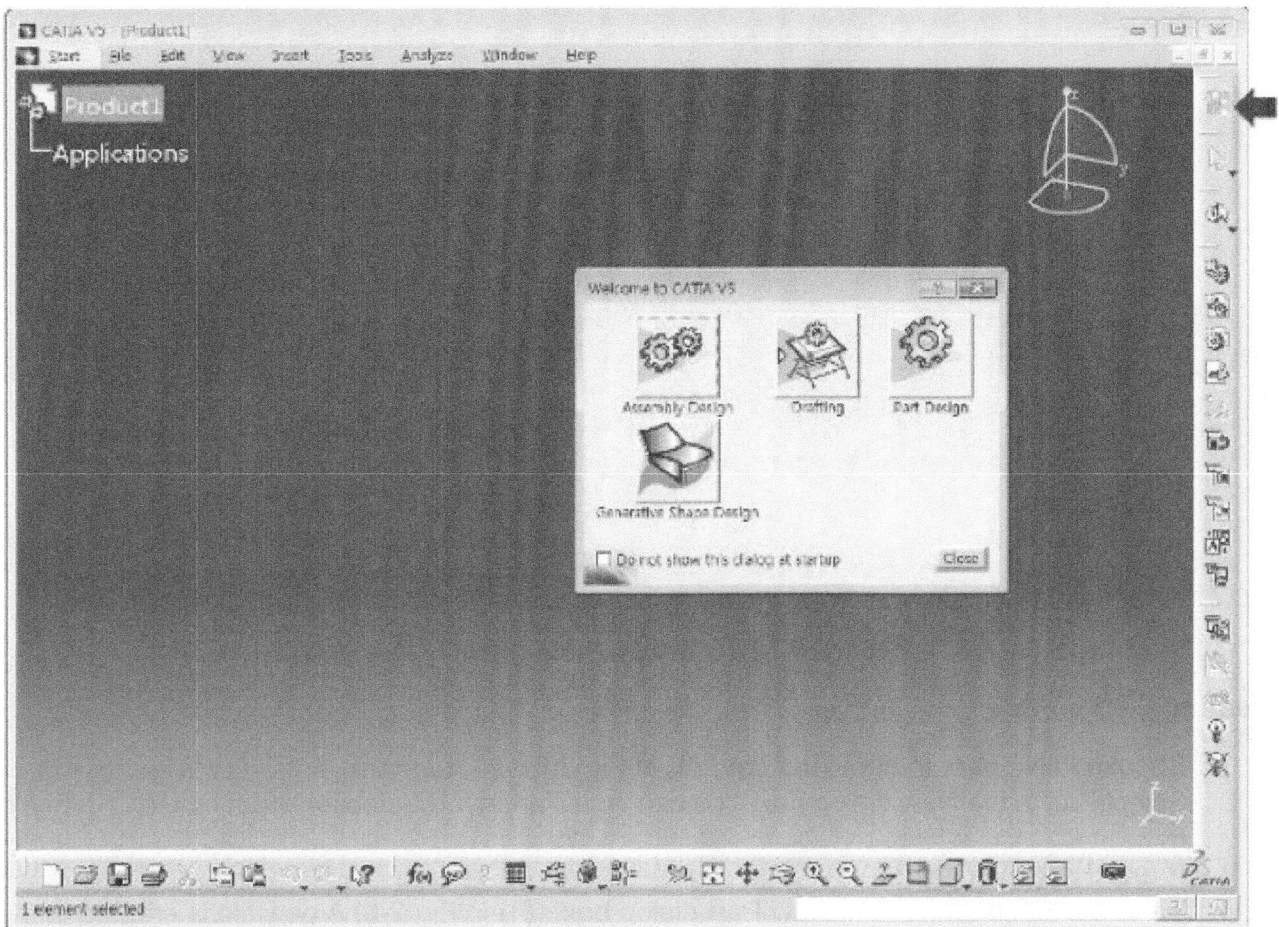

Fig 2-4 CATJA V5 Screen on Execution

Exercise 1: Creating a New Part File

The CATIA V5 screen after closing the Assembly Design workbench will appear as shown in Fig 2-5. Now, let's create a new part file.

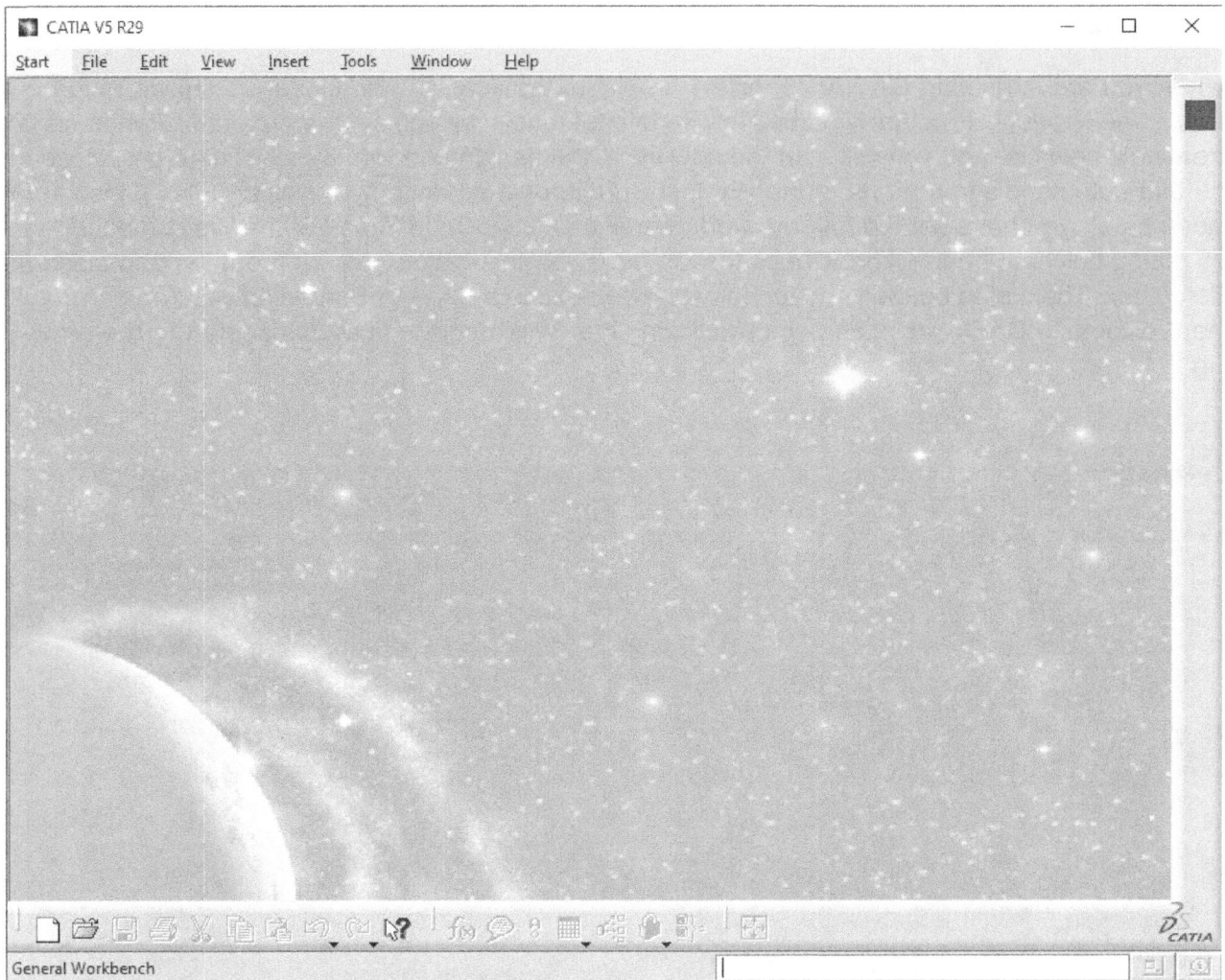

Fig 2-5 CATIA V5 Screen after Closing the Assembly Design Workbench

Creating the Part File

1. Choose File > New in the menu bar. ((1) in Fig 2-6)
2. Select Part in the New dialog box. You can type Part in the Selection input box. ((2) in Fig 2-6)
3. Press OK. ((3) in Fig 2-6)
4. Press the OK button in the New Part dialog box. ((4) in Fig 2-6) A new file is created in the Part Design workbench.

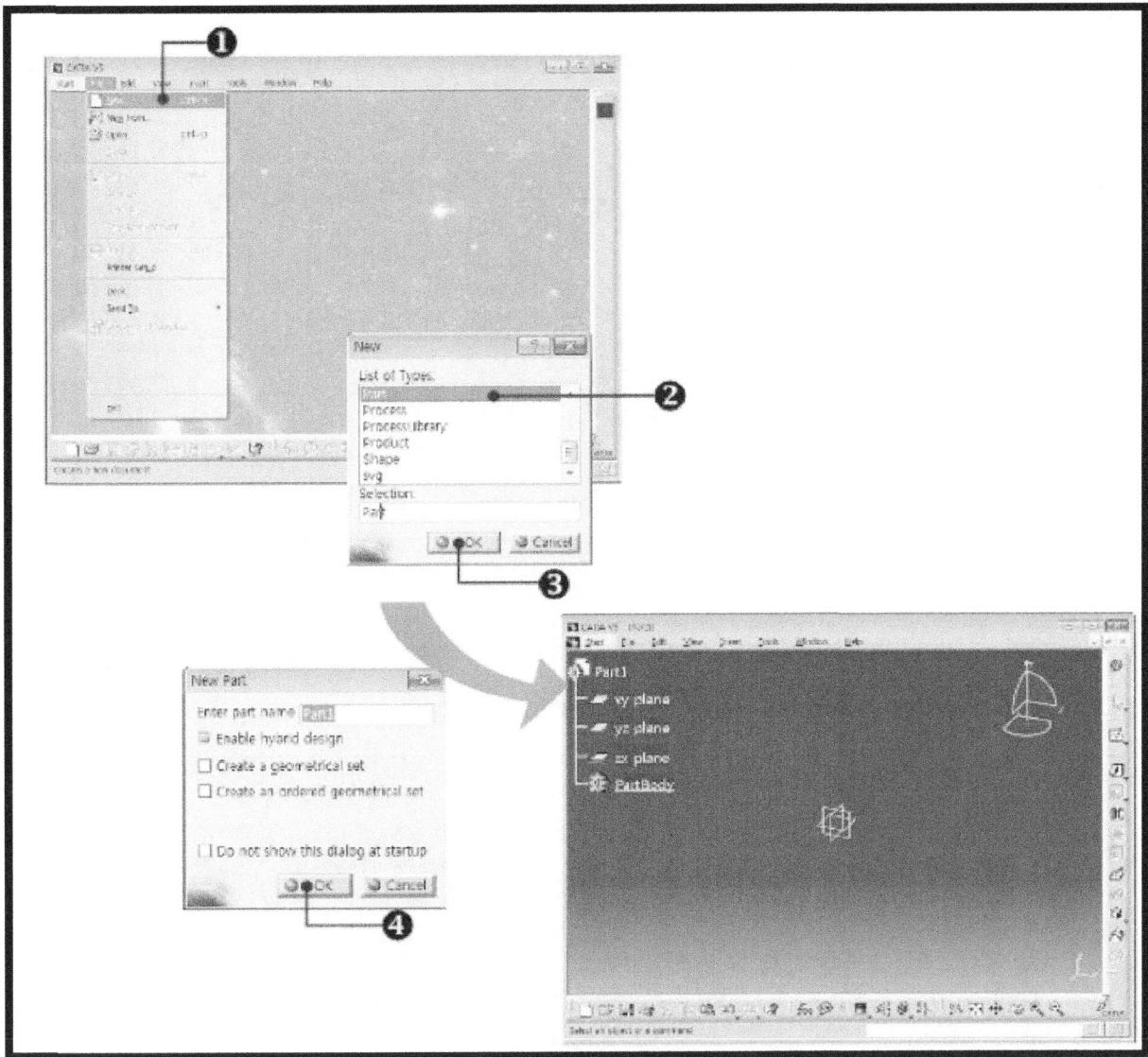

Fig 2- 6 Creating a New Part File

Product Naming (Part Number)

1. Place the mouse pointer on "Part 1" (1) in Fig 2-7) and press MB3 (mouse button 3). Choose Properties from the pop-up menu.
2. Press the Product tab in the Properties dialog box and type "ch02_my part" in the Part Number input box. Then press OK.
3. Note that the topmost name in the specification tree has been changed to "cb02_my part".
4. Choose File > Save from the menu bar.
5. Select a folder and name the file to "ch02_my part".

Fig 2-8 shows the CATIA V5 screen after completing the steps to create a new part file.

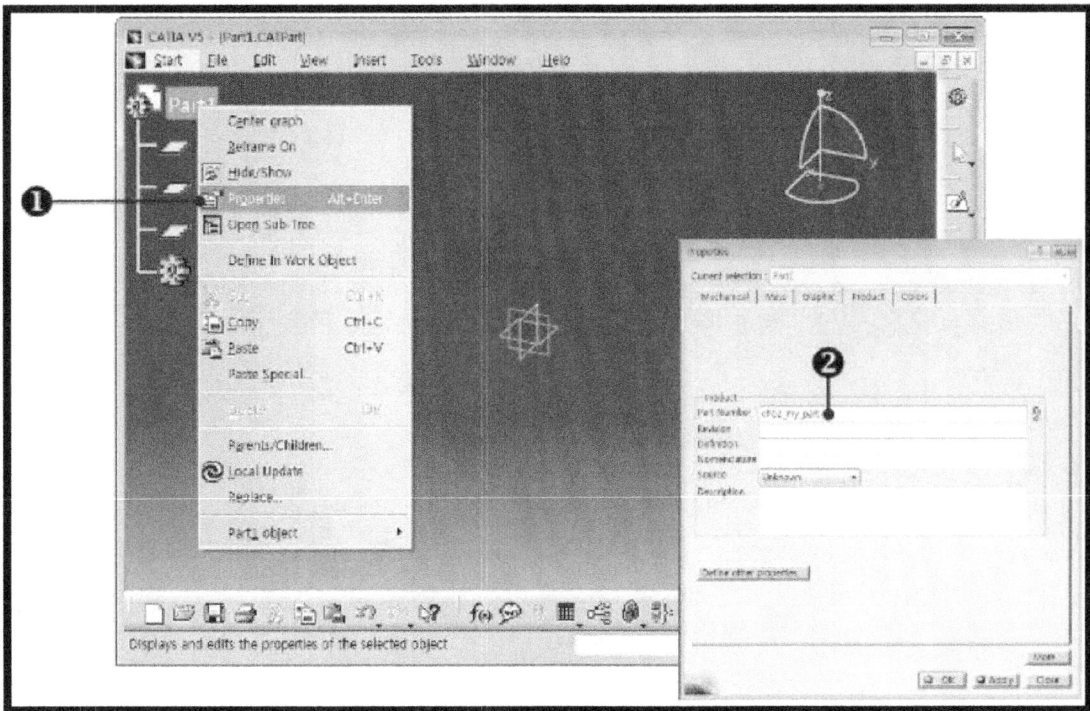

Fig 2-7 Product Naming

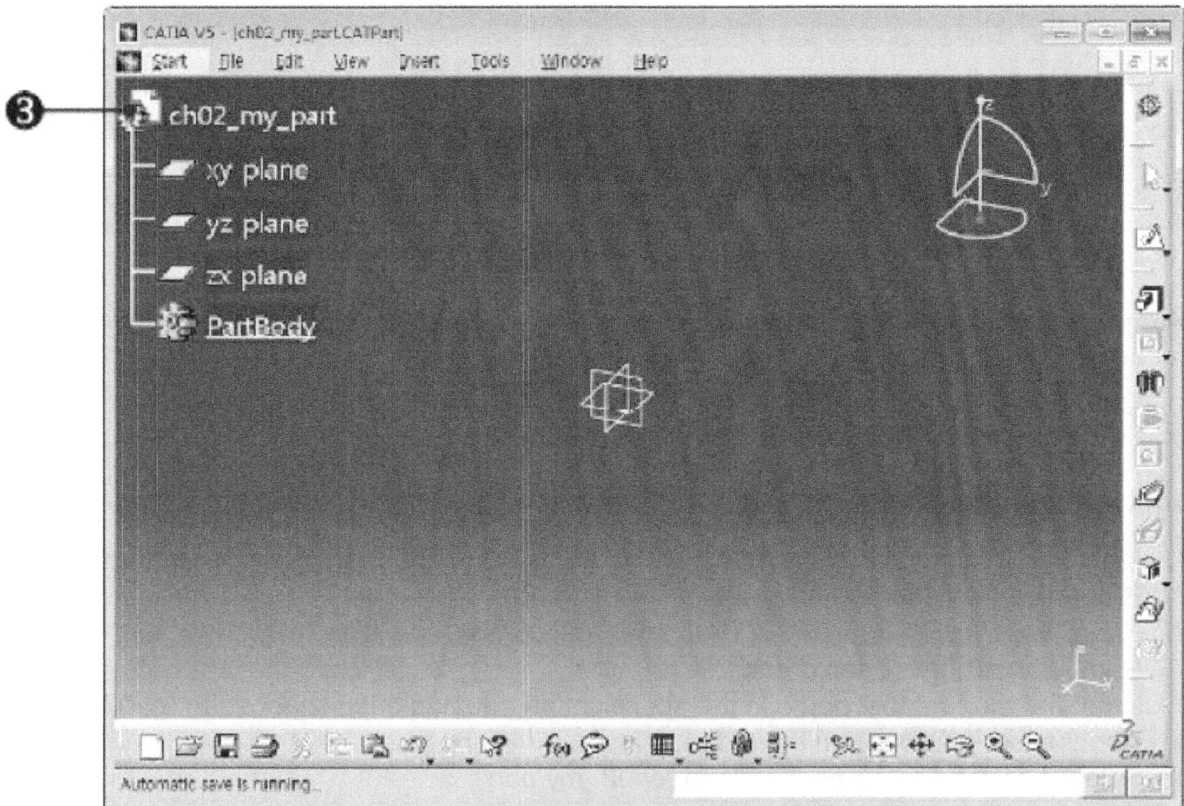

Fig 2-8 CATIA V5 Screen

3.2.2 Creating the first Sketch

Creating a sketch is the first step in three dimension al modeling. After creating the sketch, we create 3D geometry using the Pad or Shaft command and then proceed with the next step to complete the modeling process.

Exercise 2: Creating the First Sketch

Let's create a sketch on the xy plane.

Starting Sketch

1. Press the Sketch button.
2. Read the message in the status bar. You have to select a plane to create the sketch on.
3. Select the xy plane in the specification tree. You can select the xy plane in the graphic area.

Fig 2-10 shows the screen of the Sketcher workbench. Several toolbars are invoked.

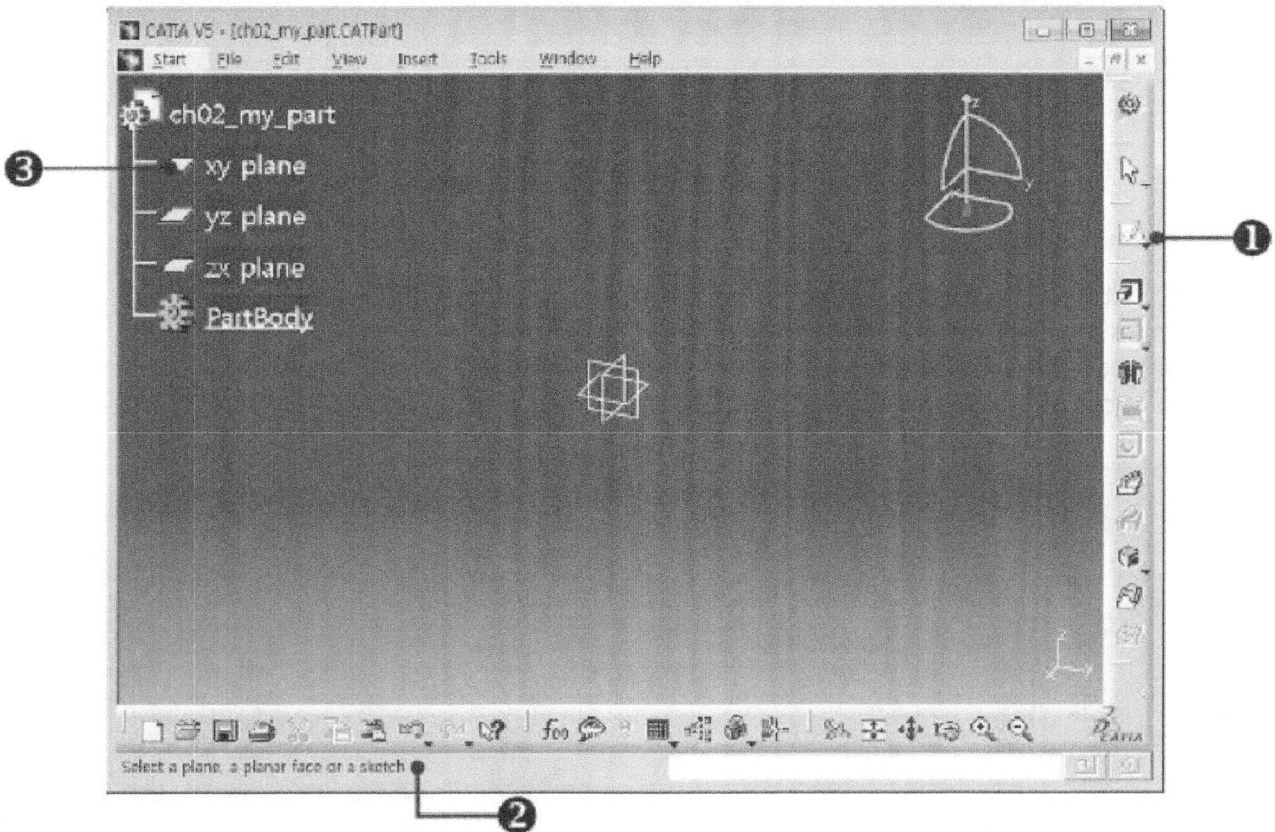

Fig 2-9 Invoking the Sketcher Workbench

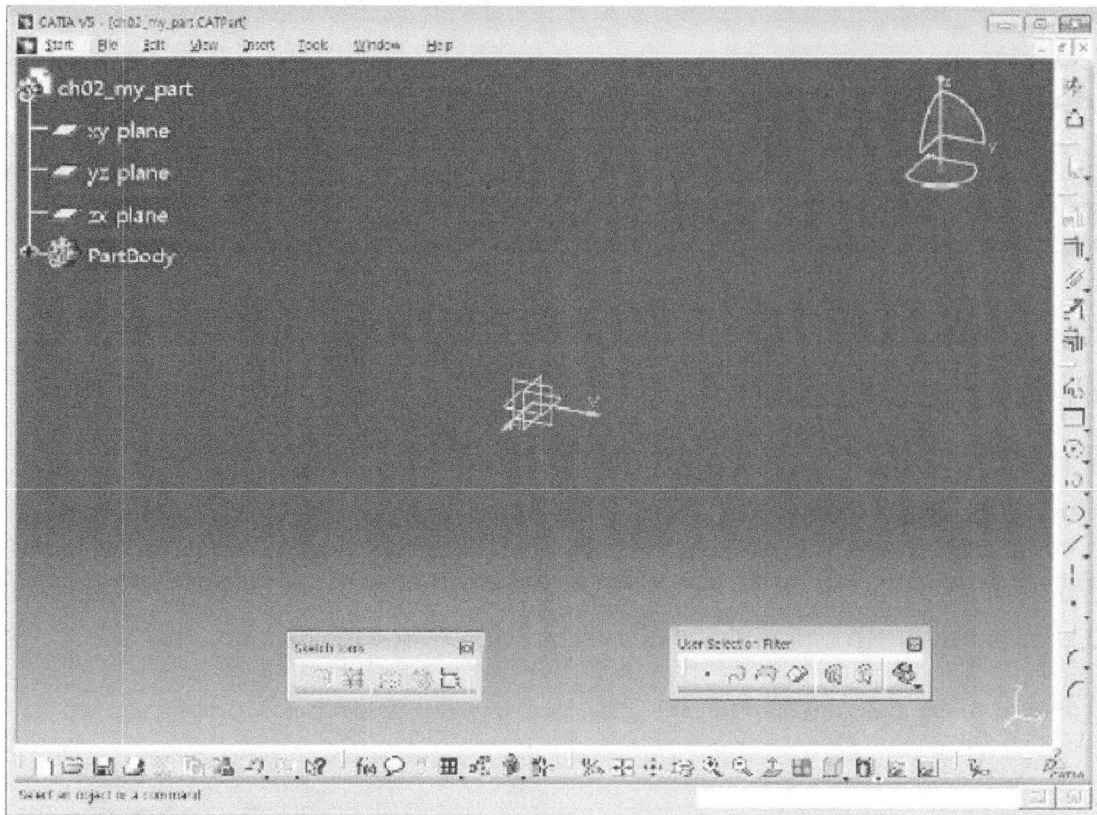

Fig 2-10 Screen of the Sketcher Workbench

Taking out a Toolbar

1. Select the Profile toolbar with the left click and drag it into the graphic area.
2. Press the Shift key. The toolbar is laid horizontally.
3. Release the mouse button on the desired location in the graphic area.
4. Take out the Profile, View, Sketch tools and Constraints toolbars as shown in Fig 2-11.

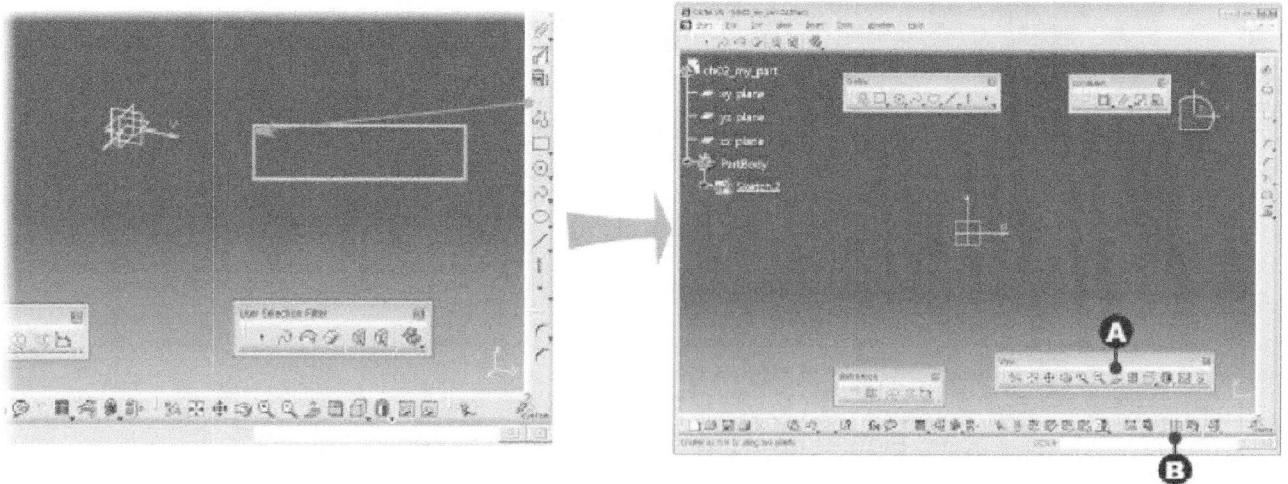

Fig 2-11 Dragging a Toolbar

Create Sketch Curves

1. Click the Normal View ((A) in Fig 2-11) icon in the View toolbar. The sketch plane is aligned to the screen.
2. Click the Grid ((B) in Fig 2-11) icon in the Visualization toolbar. Sketch grid is displayed.
3. Click the Rectangle icon in the Profile toolbar. ((3) in Fig 2-12)
4. Click MB1 (left button) of the mouse at a point (4) in Fig 2-12.
5. Move the mouse pointer around point (5) in Fig 2-12 and click MB1 (left button). A rectangle is created. Note that the curves in the rectangle are selected in orange.
6. Click MB1 (left button) at an arbitrary point ((6) in Fig 2-12) in the graphic area. The curves are deselected in white.

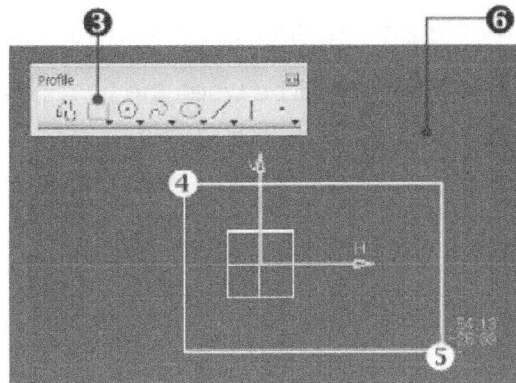

Fig 2-12 Creating a Rectangle

Dimensioning

1. Choose the Constraint button ((1) in Fig 2-13) in the Constraint toolbar.
2. Select the two curves (A) and (B) in order and pick the area (C) as the location.
3. Double click the dimension 0 in Fig 2-13 and type 52 in the Value input area in the dialog box as shown in Fig 2-14. Then press OK.

(Note) Defining a Sketch

In this chapter, we will not fully define the sketch. Therefore, your sketch may be different to the images in this textbook. We will learn about constraining sketches in detail in chapters 3 and 4.

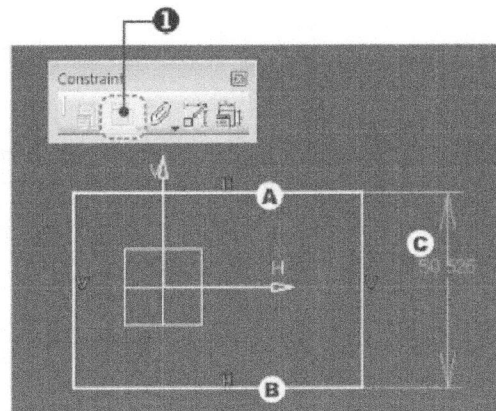

Fig 2-13 Creating a Dimension

39

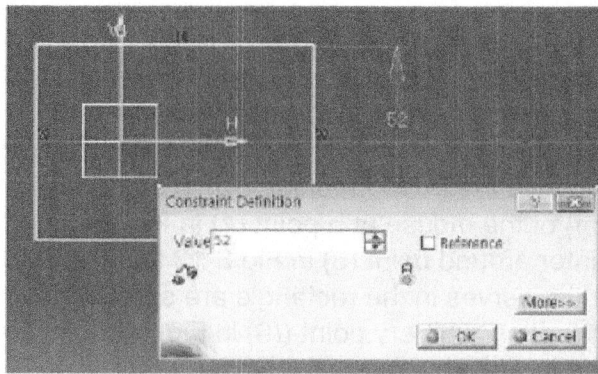

Fig 2-14 Modifying a Dimension Value

4. Create the dimension (4) in Fig 2-15 between the two lines (A) and (B).
5. Double click the dimension and change its value to 86.

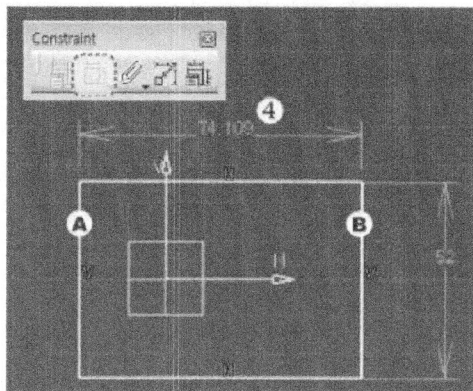

Fig 2-15 Creating the Second Dimension

6. Click the Exit workbench button designated by the arrow in Fig 2-16.
7. Click the empty area in the screen with MB1 (left button) to deselect the sketch.
8. Click the Isometric View icon in the View toolbar. Fig 2- 17 shows the Part Design workbench after exiting the Sketcher workbench.

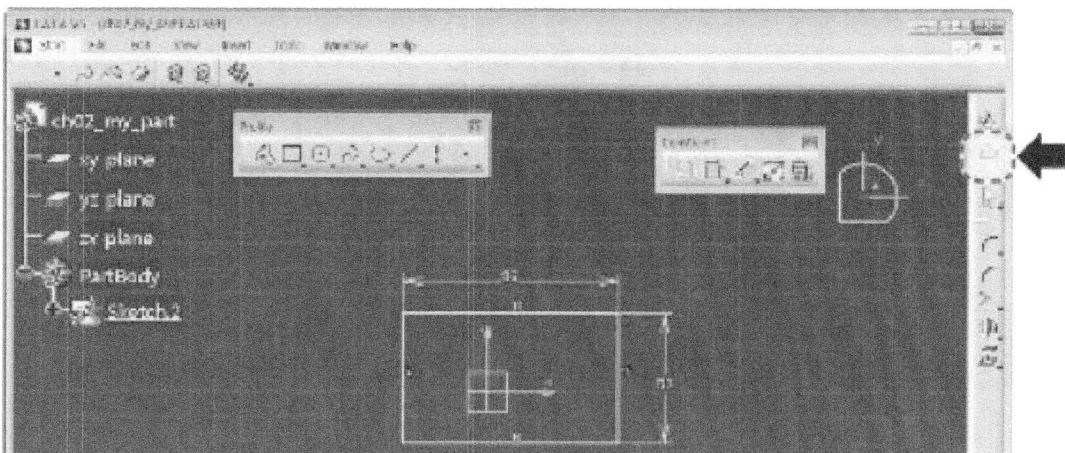

Fig 2- 16 Exiting the Sketcher Workbench

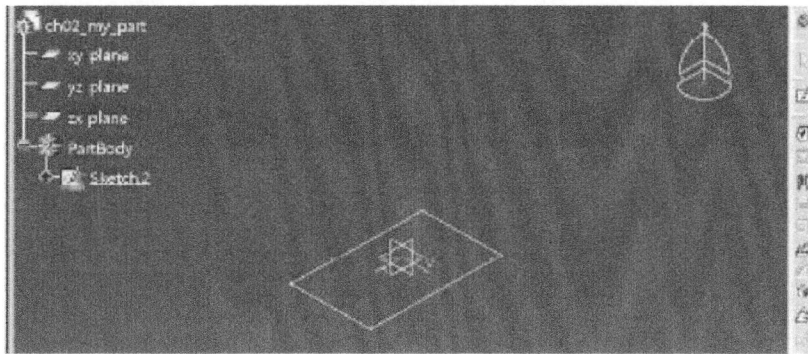

Fig 2-17 Part Design Workbench

3.2.3 Extruding the Sketch

Using the Pad command in the Sketch-Based Features toolbar, we can extrude the sketch to create a 3D geometry.

Exercise 3: Creating a Pad Feature

In this exercise, we will create a 30 feature with the Pad command.

1. Take out the Sketch-Based Features toolbar as shown in Fig 2-18 and click the Pad icon in the toolbar. The Pad Definition dialog box appears as shown in Fig 2-18.
2. Select the rectangular sketch created earlier. A preview of the 3D feature is shown in the graphic area.
3. Enter 20 in the Length input area of the dialog box and press OK. Fig 2-19 shows the Pad feature created. The features are selected in orange.
4. Click an empty area of the screen with MB1 (left click) to deselect it.

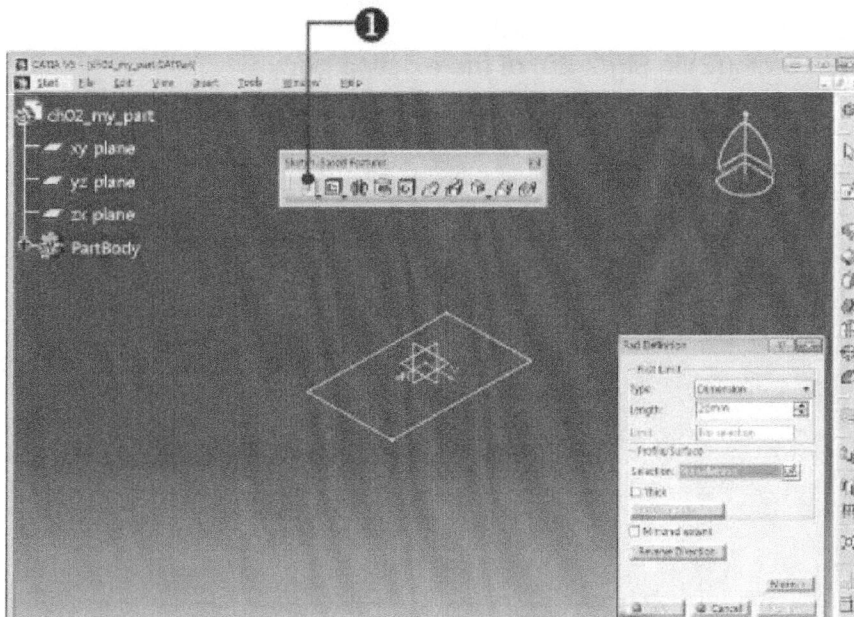

Fig 2-18 Executing the Pad Command

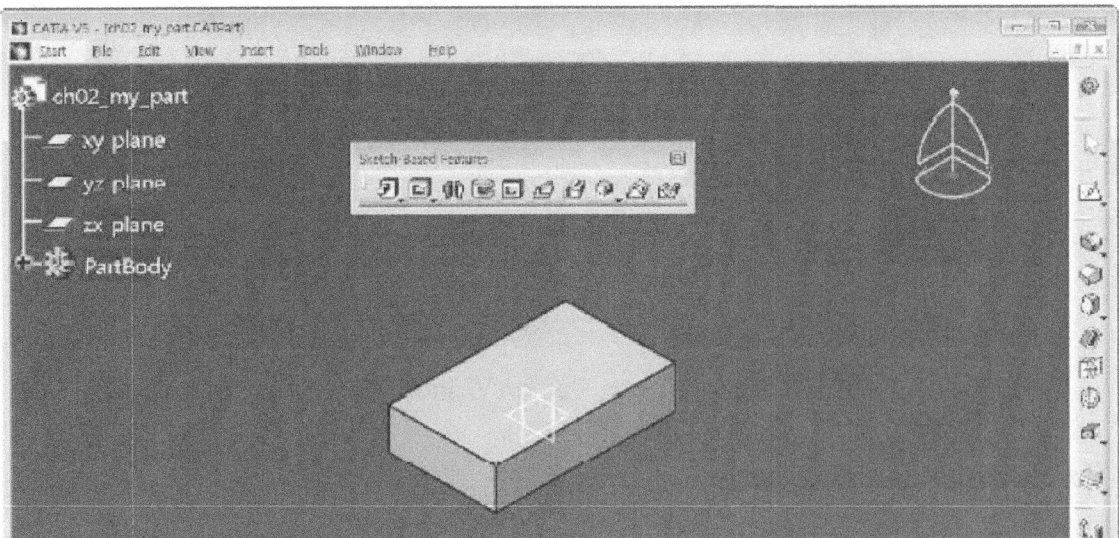

Fig 2- 19 Pad Feature Created

3.2.4 Creating the Second Feature

We have created just one Pad feature. However, most 3D models cannot be completed with just one Pad operation. We have to create additional features by repeatedly creating sketches on the plane of the 3D geometry.

Exercise 4: Creating the Second Feature

Let's create the second sketch on the top plane of the 3D feature and create the second Pad feature.

Create the Second Sketch

1. Press the Sketch icon. ((1) in Fig 2-20)
2. Select the top face ((2) in Fig 2-20) of the existing body.

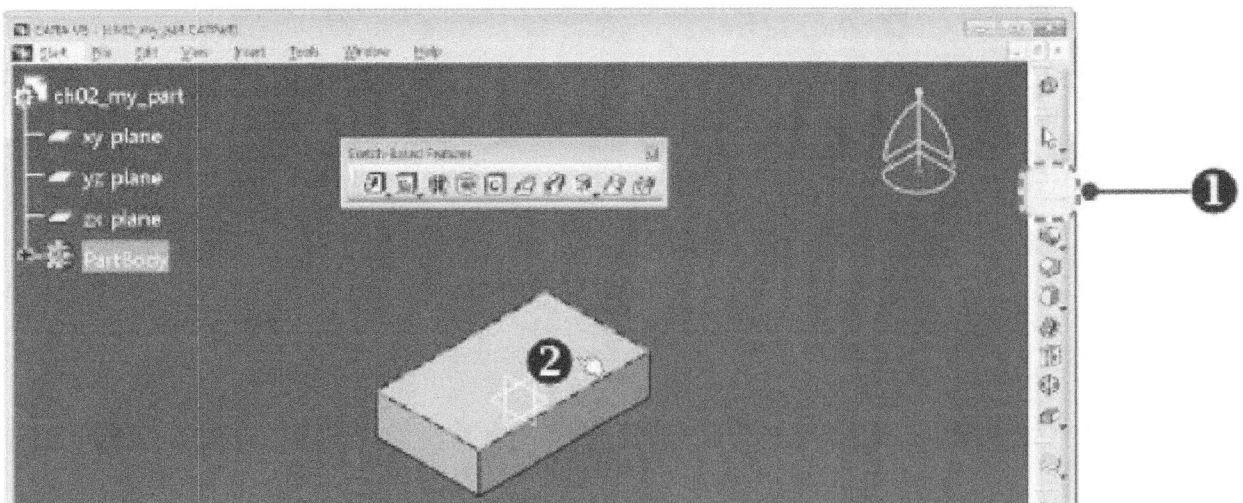

Fig 2-20 Creating a Sketch

3. Click the Normal View icon ((3) in Fig 2-21) in the View toolbar.
4. Click the Snap to Point icon ((4) in Fig 2-21) in the Sketch tools toolbar to deactivate it.
5. Click the Circle icon ((5) in Fig 2-2 1) in the Profile toolbar.
6. Press the Shift key and create a circle as shown in Fig 2-21.
7. Deselect the circle by clicking on an empty space in the graphic area.

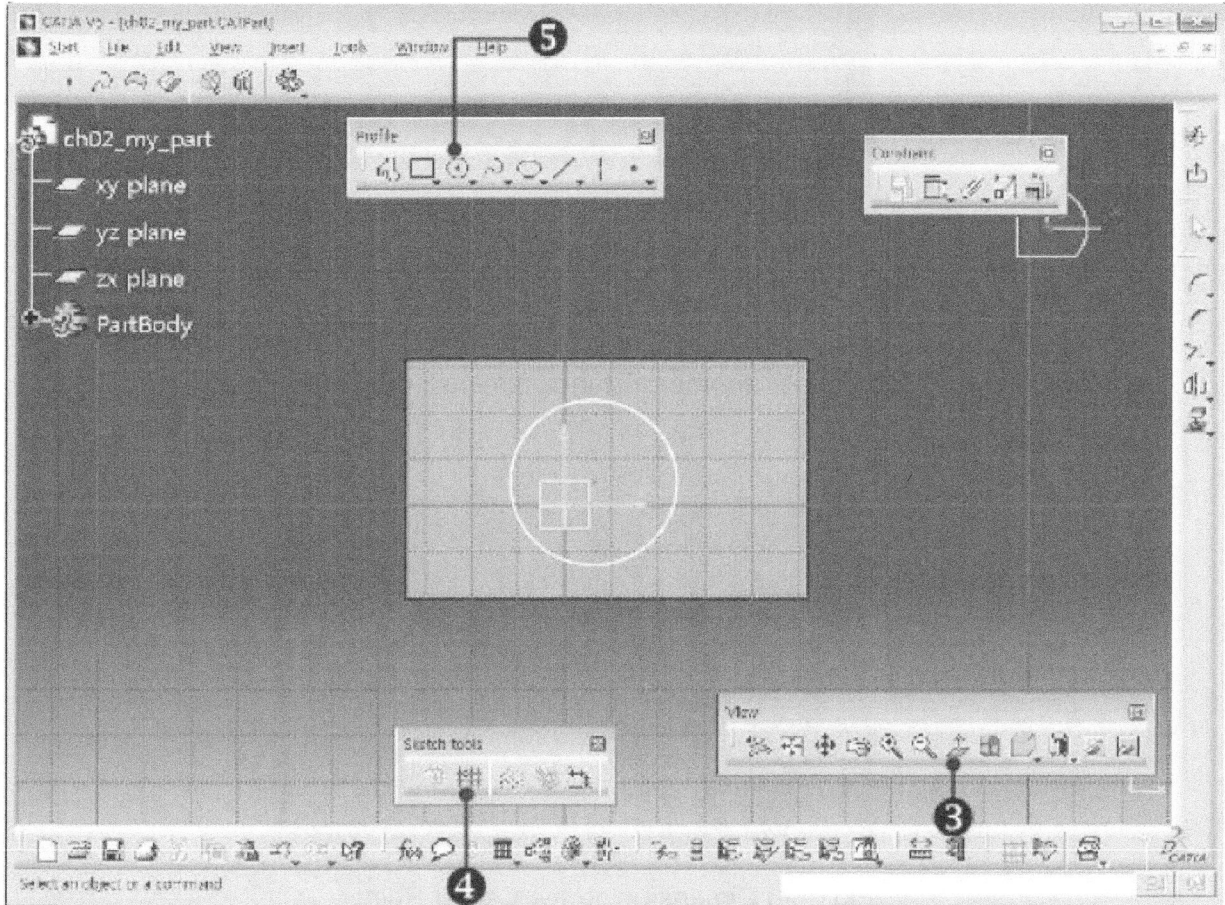

Fig 2-21 Creating a Circle

(Note) Deselecting Elements and Shift Key

1. After creating a sketch curve, it is selected. Deselecting the sketch is good practice to prevent confusion when constraining the sketch curves.
2. Pressing the Shiff key while creating the sketch curves disables snapping to other sketch elements.

Dimensioning

1. Click the Constraint icon in the Constraint toolbar.
2. Select the circle and create a diametral dimension as shown in Fig 2-22.

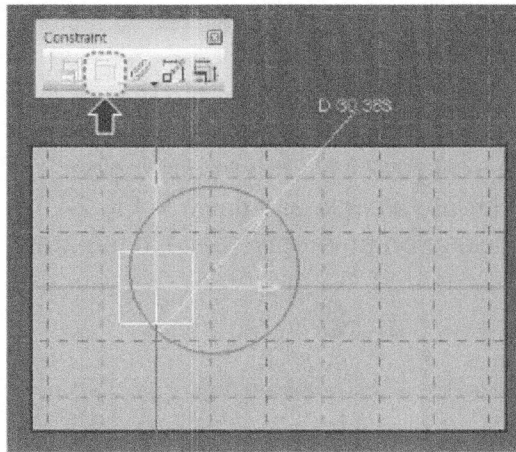

Fig 2-22 Creating a Diametral Dimension to a Circle

3. Click the Constraints button again and select the edge (A) and center point of the circle (B) as shown in Fig 2-23 to create the distance dimension (3).
4. Click the Constraints button again and select the edge (C) and center point of the circle (D) as shown in Fig 2-24 to create another distance dimension (4).

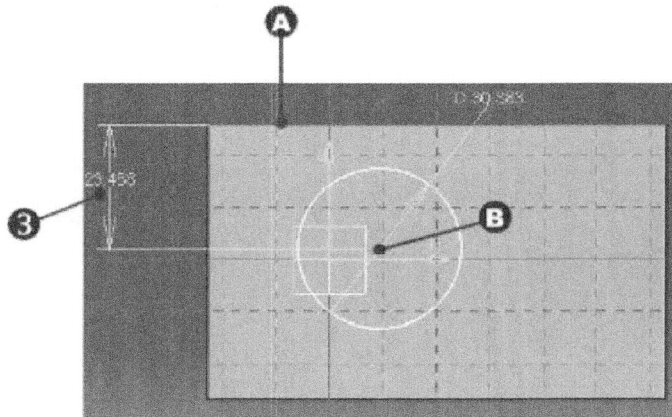

Fig 2-23 Dimensioning the Center Point

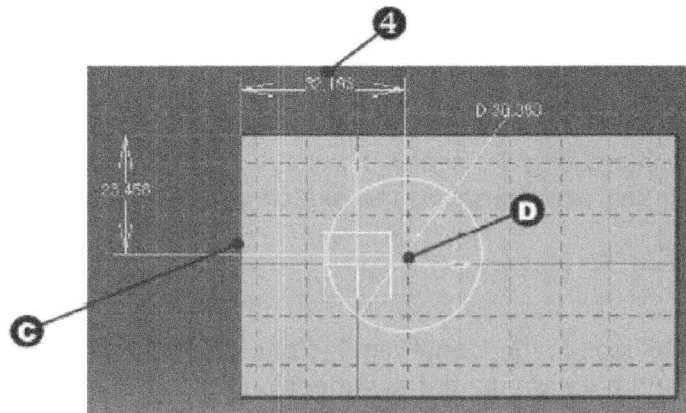

Fig 2-24 Dimensioning the Center Point

44

5. Double click each dimension and modify it as shown in Fig 2-25. Note that the color of the circle has changed to green.
6. Exit the Sketcher workbench.
7. Deselect the ketch and click the Isometric View icon in the View toolbar.

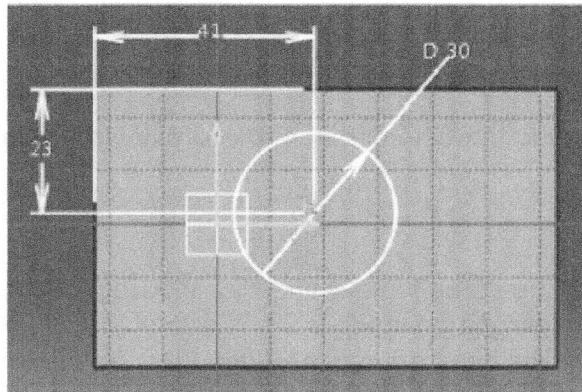

Fig 2-25 Modified Dimension Values

Create a Pad Feature

1. Click Shading with Edges with Hidden Edges in the View Mode toolbar.
2. Click the Pad icon in the Sketch Based Features toolbar and select the circle in the sketch.
3. Press the OK in the Pad Definition dialog box. (Length = 20mm)
4. Deselect the feature by clicking on an empty space in the graphic area with MB1 (left click).

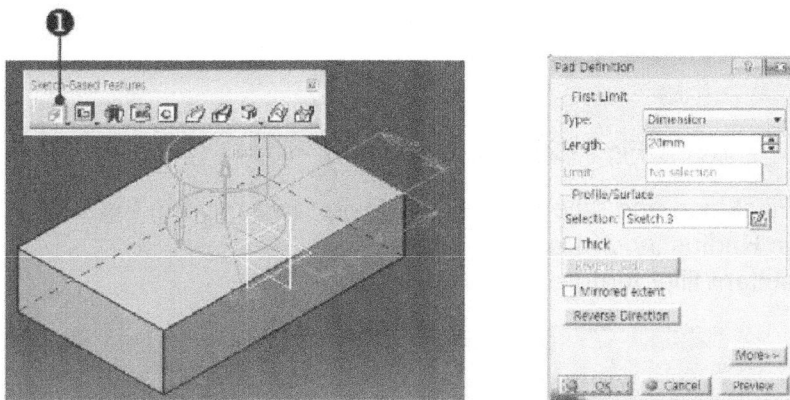

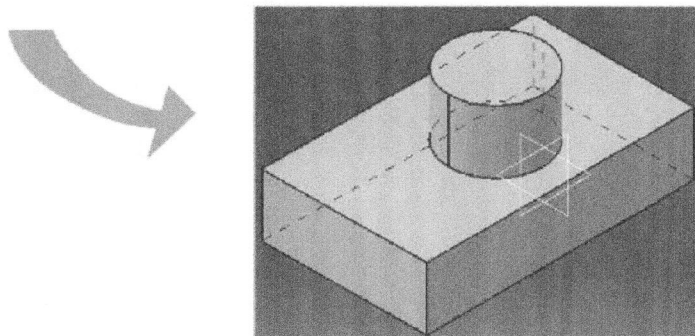

Fig 2- 26 The Second Pad Feature

3.2.5 Additional Modeling

After creating basic features using commands in the Sketch-Based Features toolbar, we create additional features to modify the 30 geometries. Commands in the Dress-Up Features toolbar is used in this step.

Exercise 5: Additional Modeling

Let's modify the 3D shape using the commands in the Dress-Up Feature s toolbar. We will apply fillet and shell commands.

Apply Fillet

1. Take out the Dress-Up Features toolbar and click the Edge Fillet icon.
2. Select the four edges designated in Fig 2-27.
3. Enter 10mm in the Radius input area in the Edge Fillet Definition dialog box and press OK.
4. Deselect the fillet feature by clicking an empty space of the graphic area.

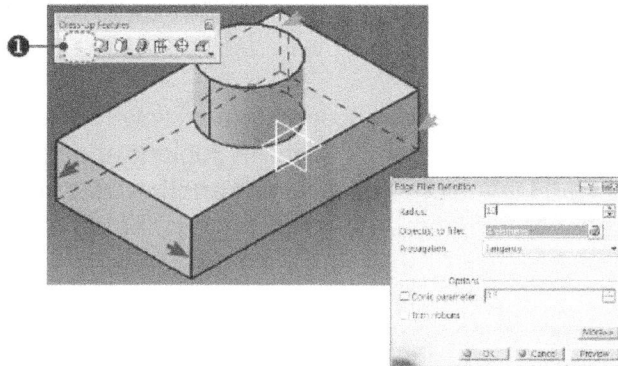

Fig 2- 27 Edges to Apply Fillet

5. Click the Edge Fillet icon and select the edge designated by O in Fig 2-28.
6. Enter 5mm in the Radius input area and press OK.
7. Deselect the resultant fillet feature.

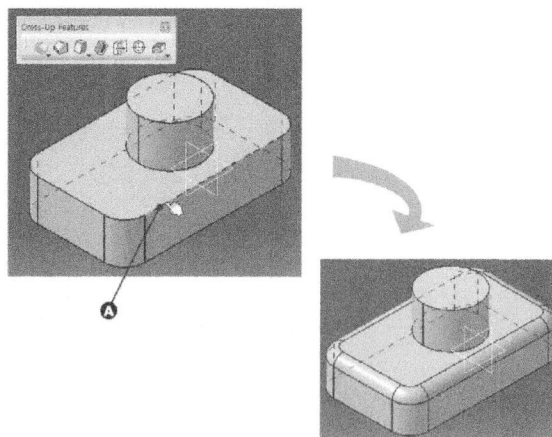

Fig 2 - 28 Applying the Second Fillet

46

Apply Shell

1. Click the Shell icon in the Dress-Up Features toolbar.
2. The Shell Definition dialog box appears and the status bar message reads "Select a face to be removed."

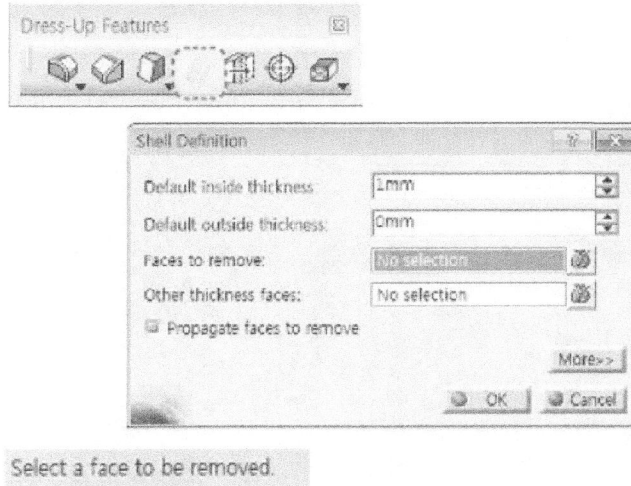

Fig 2-29 Executing Shell Command

3. Rotate the mode] as shown in Fig 2-30 and select the face (A).
4. Note that the face appears in the Faces to remove selection area.
5. Enter 3mm in the Default inside thickness input area and press OK.

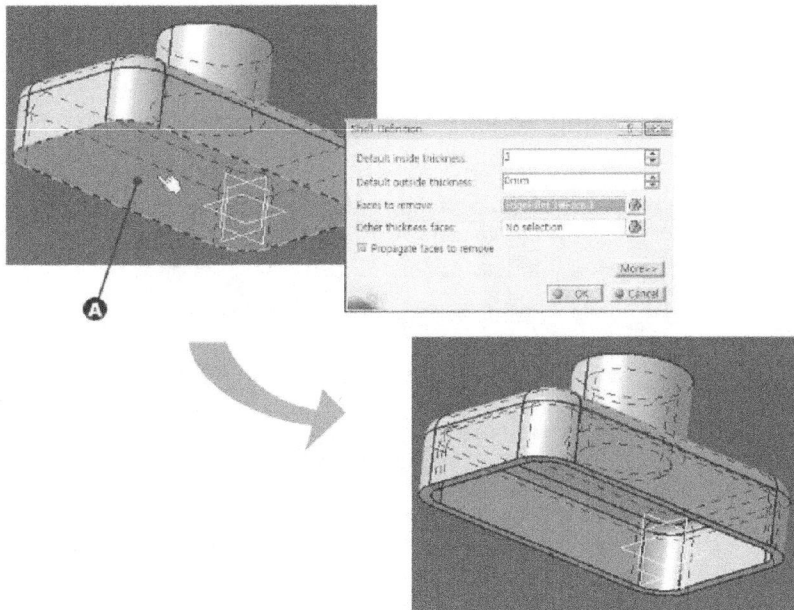

Fig 2-30 Hollowing out the Body

3.2.6 Removing the Body

Using the Pocket command in the Sketch-Based Features toolbar, you can remove the body by extruding a sketch.

Exercise 6: Removing the Body

Let's remove the side wall with a circular sketch by using the Pocket command.

Create a Sketch

1. Press the Sketch icon and select the face designated by (A) in fig 2-31.

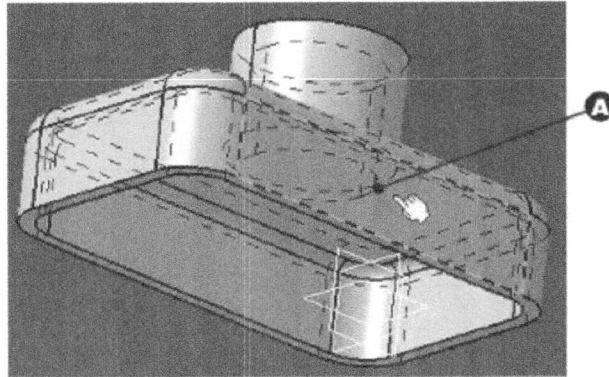

Fig 2-31 Sketch Plane

2. Click the Normal View icon in the View toolbar.
3. Click the Circle icon in the Profile toolbar.
4. Create a circle as shown in Fig 2-32. The center of the circle is located at the center of the lower edge.
5. Apply a 25mm diameter to the circle.
6. Exit the Sketcher.
7. Deselect the sketch by clicking an empty space of the graphic area.
8. Restore the isometric view.

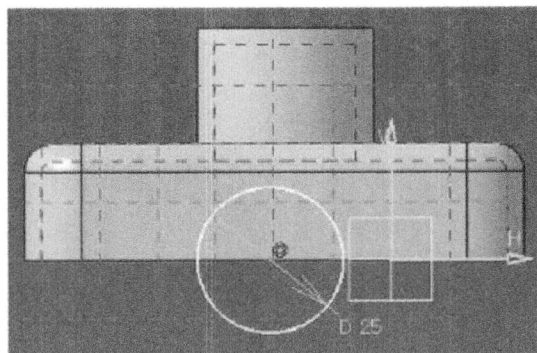

Fig 2-32 Creating a Circle

Create a Pocket Feature

1. Click the Pocket icon in the Sketch -Based Features toolbar.

2. Select the circle created earlier.

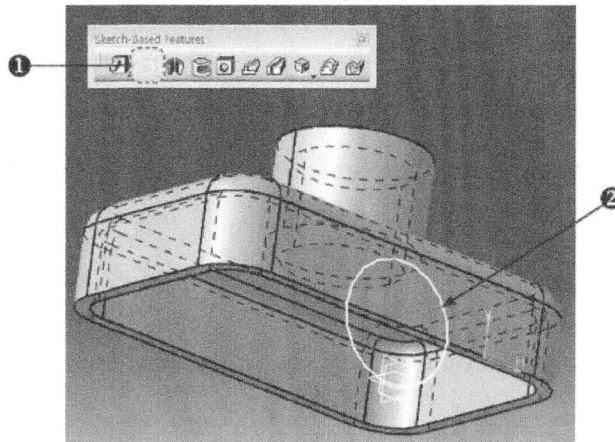

Fig 2-33 Circle to Select

3. Set the Pocket Definition dialog box as shown in Fig 2-34. Note tha t the Type of Fi r st Limit is Up to last.
4. Press OK and deselect the feature.

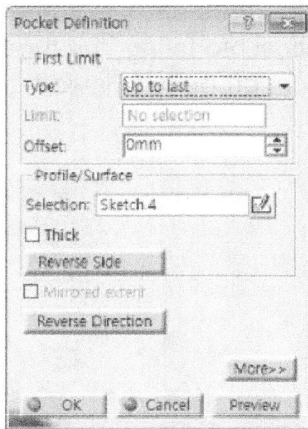

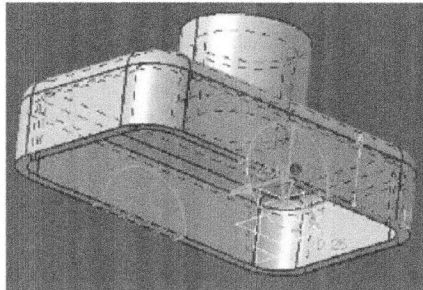

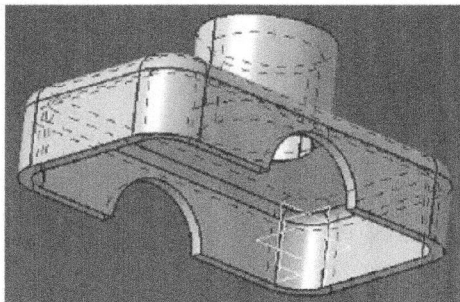

Fig 2-34 Final Model

End of Modeling

1. Save the file. We will use the file in the next Exercise.
2. Choose File > Close in the men u bar to close the part file.

3.3 Summary of the Modeling Process

If a 3D model consists of many pads, pockets and other features, keep in mind the following guidelines to create models while avoiding mistakes.

Step 1: Create a sketch.

- Define the sketch plane.
- Create the sketch curves and define their shape with constraints.

Step 2: Create 3D geometry.

- Create features that are added to the body: Pad, Shaft, Rib, etc.
- Create features that remove the body: Pocket, Groove, Hole, Slot, etc.

Step 3: Finish the modeling by creating dress-up features.

In step 2, it is recommended to create all features that add material to the body and then create features tl1at remove material from the body. Additional features are recommended to be created at the final step. However, this is just a guideline. Tn practical modeling, the three steps are applied repeatedly as required. Note that if the modeling order is not properly followed, the result may differ from your desired outcome.

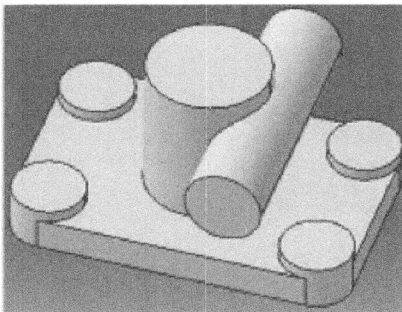

| (a) Add Material | (b) Remove Material | (c) Detail Modeling |

Fig 2-35 General Modeling Process

3.4 USING THE SPECIFIC AT ION TREE

You will be usi11g the specification tree frequently when you create and modify models. Therefore, you have to be accustomed to using the specification tree. Click the + symbol designated by (A) in Fig 2-36 to expand the branch. Click the - symbol to collapse it.

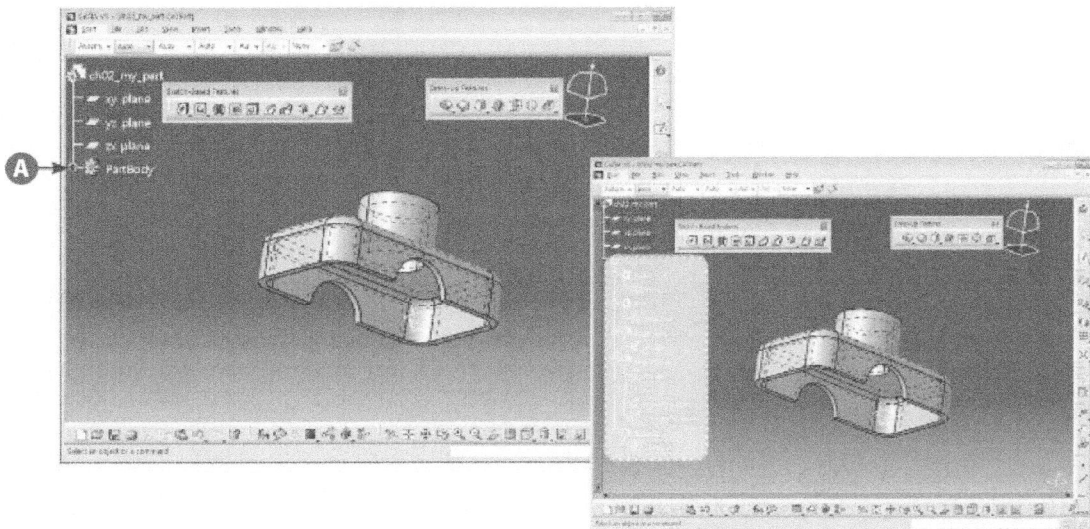

Fig 2-36 Expanding the Branch

Click the branch line designated by (B) in Fig 2-37 with MB1 (left click). The model is dimmed out and you are in specification tree manipulation mode. In this mode, you cannot pan, rotate or zoom the model in/out with the mouse.

Press MB2 (middle button) in this mode and move the mouse. The specification tree can be moved as shown in Fig 2-38. If you press MB1 (left button) and MB2 (middle button) at the same time and move the mouse, you can zoom in or out on the specification tree.

To exit from specification tree mode, you can click the branch line once again or you can click the coordinate system designated by (C) in Fig 2-38.

If you click the branch line and move the mouse, you can move the specification tree to the desired location. If you rotate the wheel on the mouse, the specification tree moves up and down. If you press the Ctrl key and rotate the wheel, the specification tree is zoomed in or out.

Fig 2- 37 Entering Specification Tree Mode

51

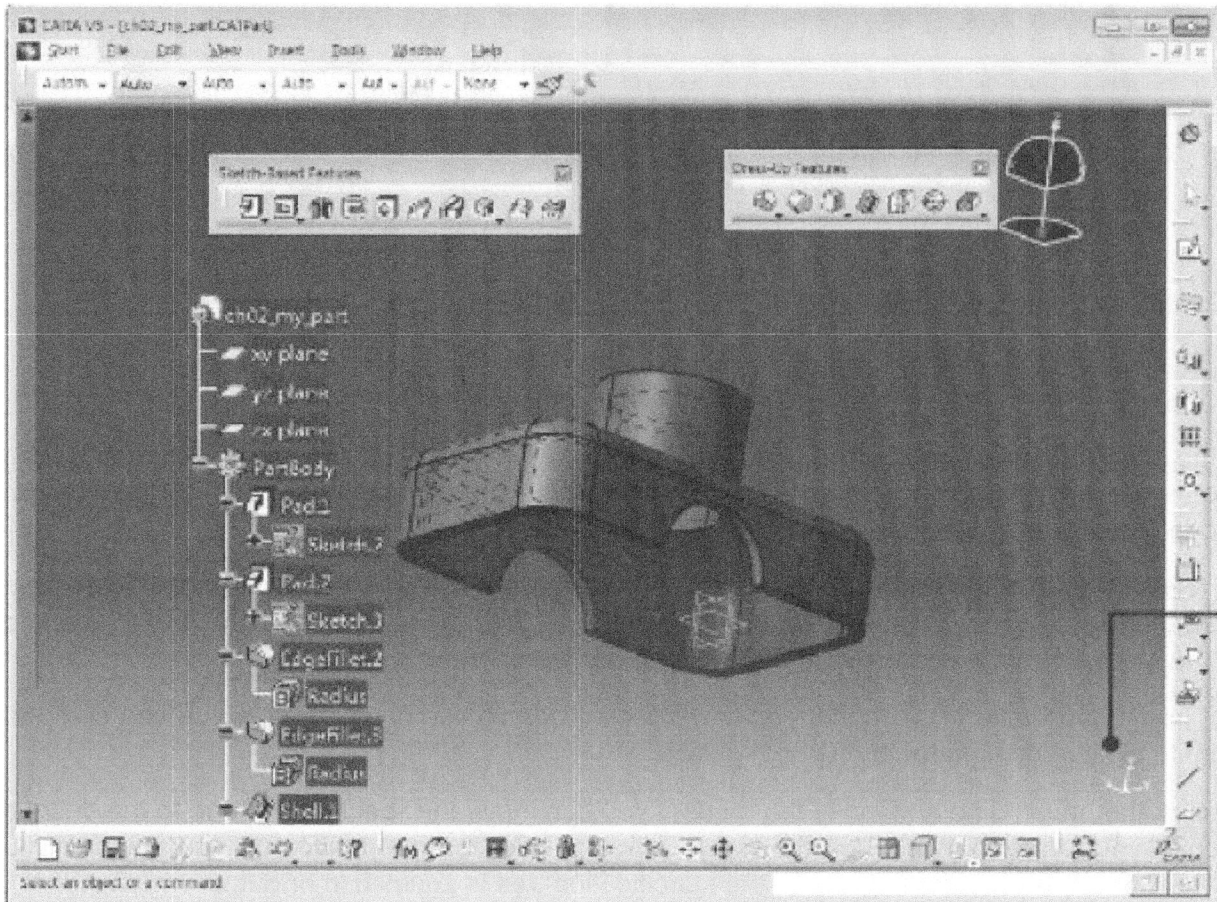

Fig 2-38 Moving Specification Tree

(Note) Using F3 Key

- Pressing the F3 key can hide or show the specification tree.
- Pressing Shift+ F3 key allows you to enter or exit from specification tree manipula-tion mode.

Right click on an item in the specification tree brings up a pop-up menu as shown in Fig 2-39. If you select Center graph in the pop-up menu, the item in the specification tree is shown at the vertical center of the screen. Fig 2-40 shows the result of the Center graph option at the top item. If you select Reframe On on an item in the pop-up menu the item will be zoomed in or out to fit the screen and the center of rotation is reset. You can reset the specification tree by choosing Reframe graph by right clicking in the specification tree manipulation mode.

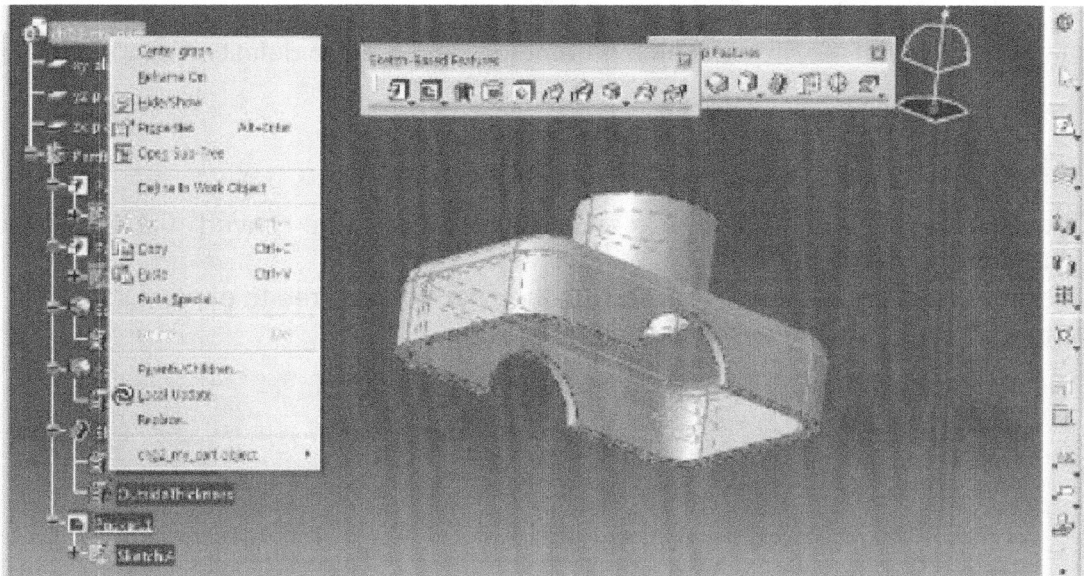
Fig 2-39 Pop-up menu

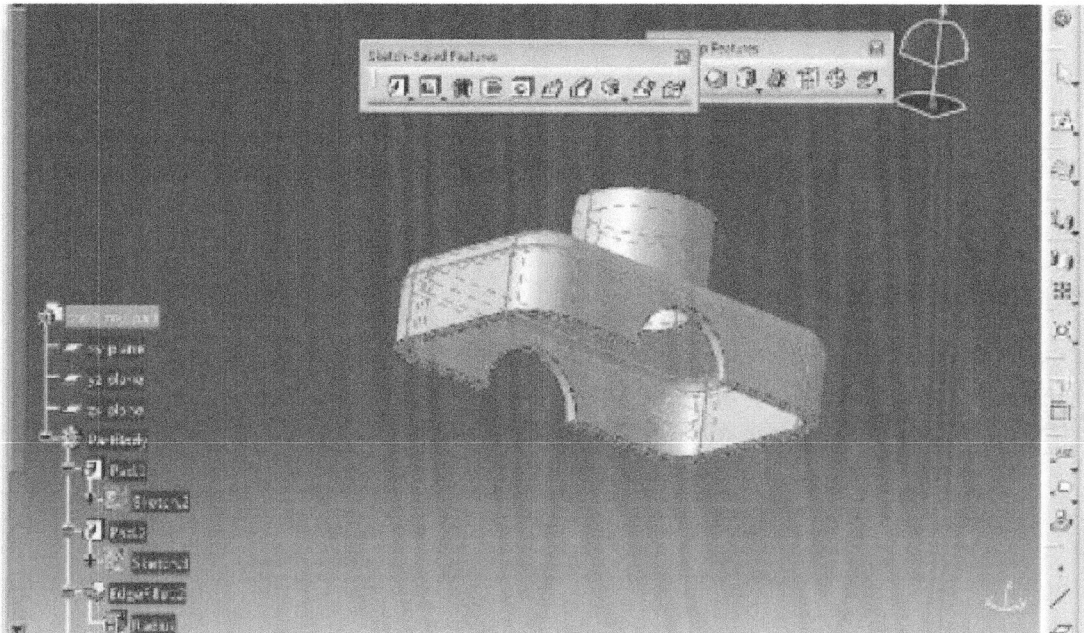
Fig 2-40 Result of Center Graph

3.5 MODIFICATION OF THE MODEL

To take advantage of parametric modeling, we have to know how to modify a model. There are two approaches to modifying a model.

1. Modifying the feature definition option
2. Modifying the sketch

Exercise 7: Modification of the Model

Let's get the basic idea of modifying sketch parameters and feature definition options by opening the model saved in Exercise 06.

Open the File

1. Choose File > Open in the menu bar to open the saved file in Exercise 06 (ch02_mypart.CATPart).
2. Click the + symbol in front of PartBody in the specification tree to expand it.
3. Change the view mode to Shading with Edges.

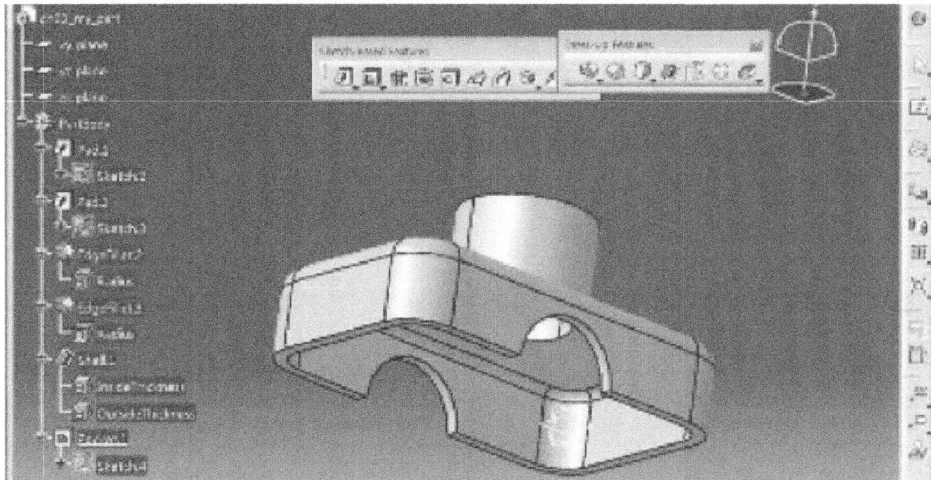

Fig 2-41 Expanded Tree

Modify the Feature Option (Pad.1)

1. Double click on Pad.1 feature in the specification tree shown in Fig 2-41.
2. Modify the Length value in the Pad Definition dialog box to 35.
3. Press OK in the dialog box and deselect the feature.

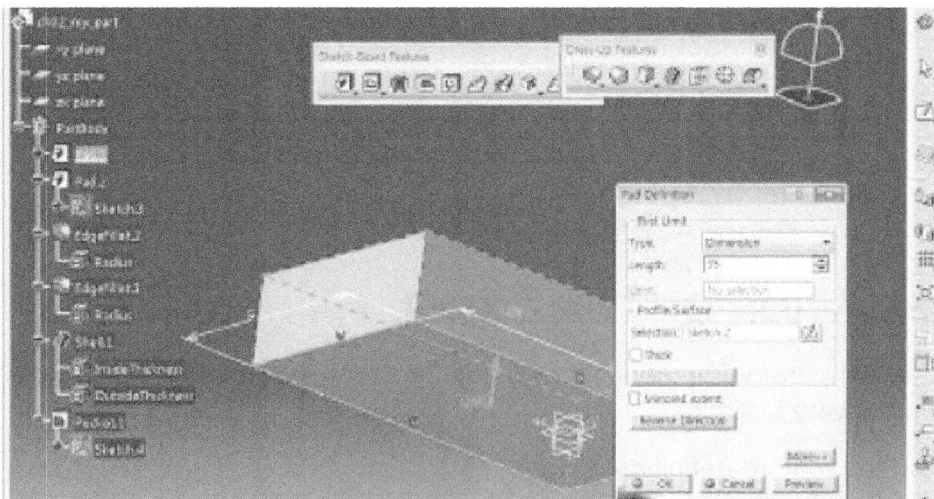

Fig 2-42 Modifying Pad Option

Modify the Sketch Dimension (Sketch.4)

1. Double click Sketch.4 by expanding the Pocket. I feature in the specification tree. The Sketcher workbench is invoked as shown in Fig 2-43. Click the Normal View icon once or twice in the View toolbar to align the sketch plane like the figure.
2. Double click on the dimension D25 specified by (2) in fig 2-43.
3. Modify the diameter to 35mm and press OK.
4. Press the Exit workbench button ((4) in Fig 2-43).

On exiting the Sketcher workbench, the geometry is updated automatically. This is be- cause the Update option in Fig 1-22 is set to Automatic.

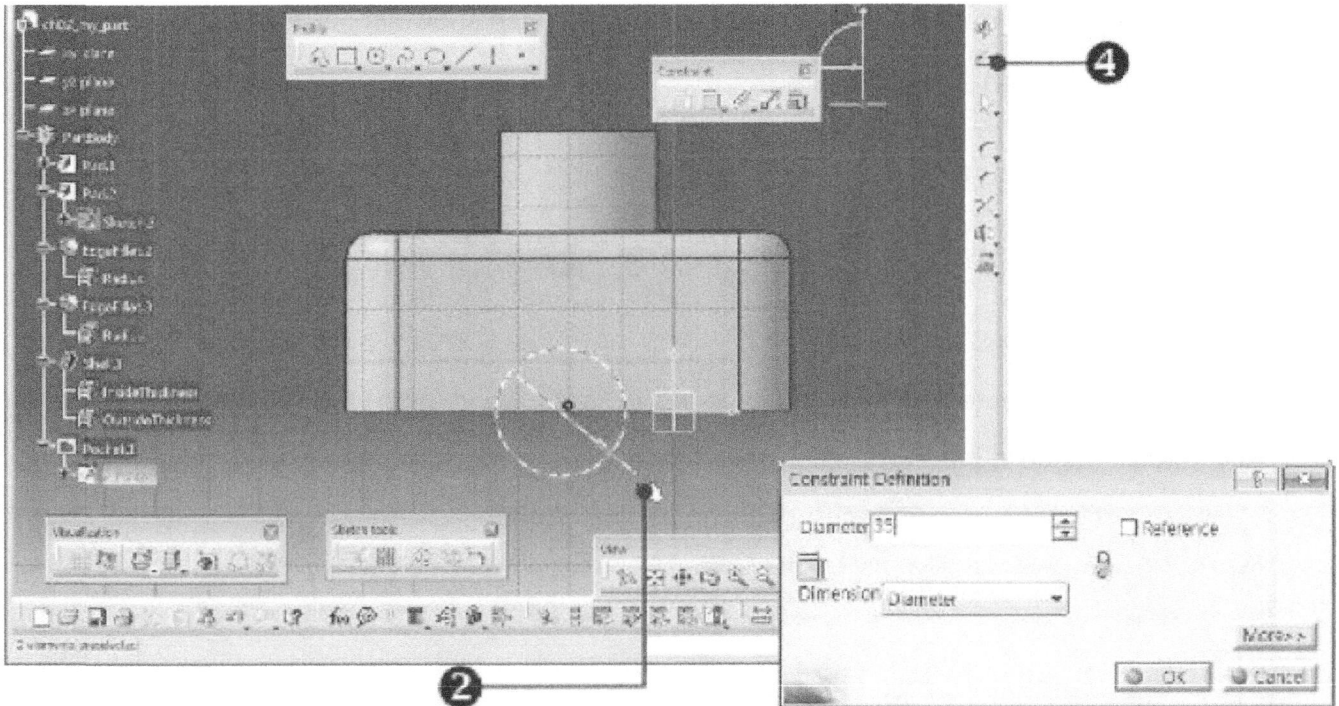

Fig 2-43 Modifying the Sketch Dimension

(Note) Identifying the Loaded Files

- Select Windows in the menu bar to identify the files that are currently loaded. The checked file is the active part.

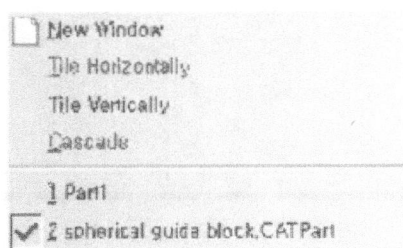

Fig 2-44 Identifying the Loaded Files

55

CHAPTER 4: MASTERING THE ART OF SKETCHING

4.1 SKETCHER WORKBENCH

4.1.1 Introduction

A sketch is required when creating features using commands in the Sketch-Based Features toolbar. The Pad feature shown in Fig 3-2 is created using the sketch shown in Fig 3-1.

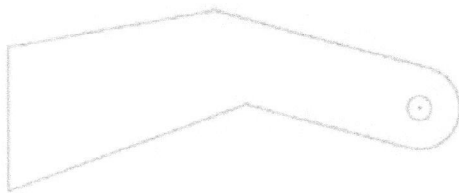

Fig 3-1 A Sketch   Fig 3-2 A Pad Feature

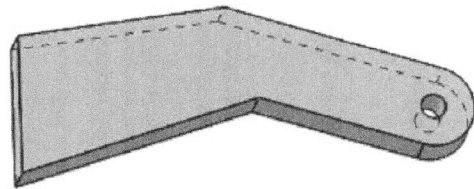

If you are going to create a sketch, you have to switch the workbench to the Sketcher.

Press Sketch button in the Part Design workbench to invoke the Sketcher workbench.

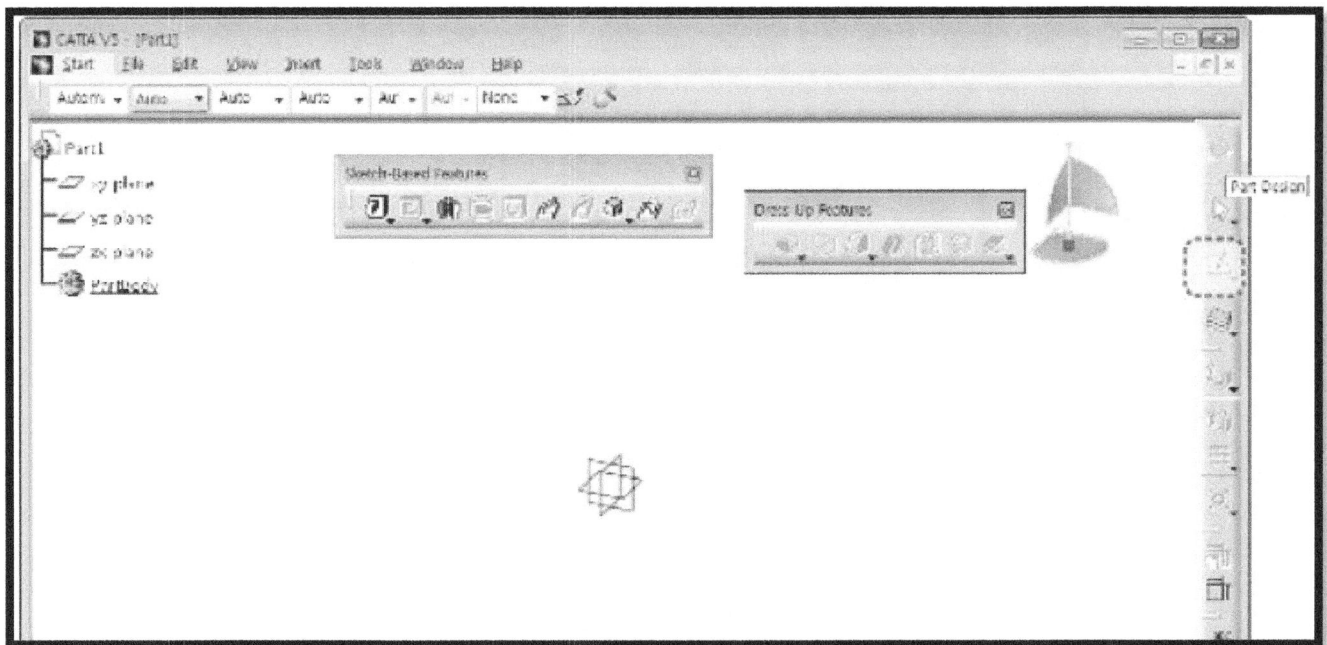

Fig 3-3 Part Design Workbench

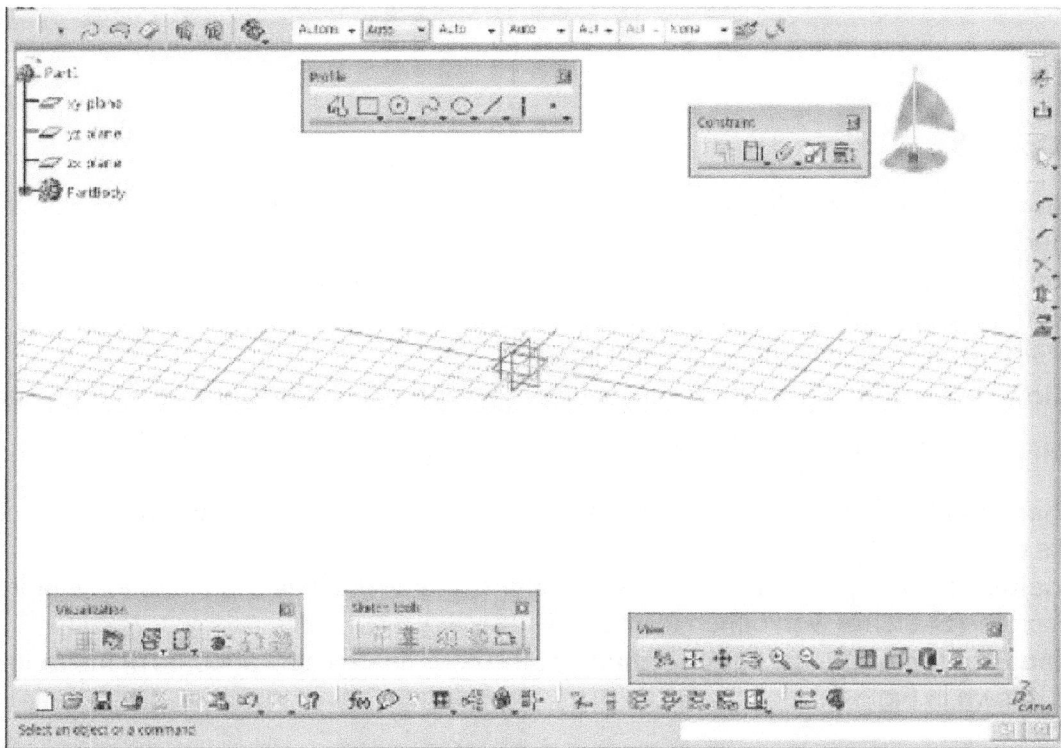

Fig 3 - 4 Sketcher Workbench

4.6.7 Options for Sketcher Workbench

If you choose Tools > Options in the menu bar, an Options dialog box as shown in Fig 3-5 appears. Expand the item Mechanical Design on the left and select Sketcher. The options for the Sketcher workbench appear on the right.

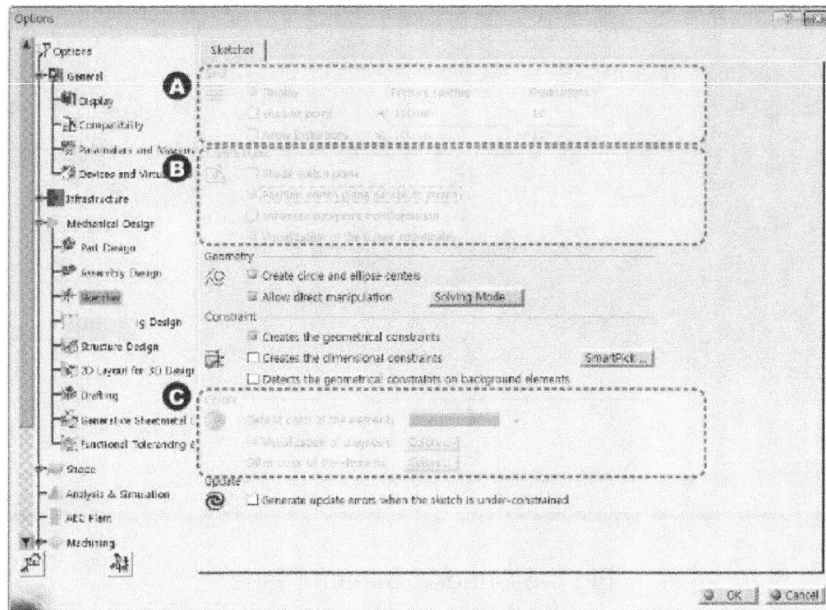

Fig 3- 5 Sketcher Options

57

(A) Grid Options

- **Display:** dis plays grid lines on the sketch plane. Fig 3-4 shows the grid lines with this option checked.
- **Snap to point:** snaps to the grid line when you are creating curves.
- **Primary spacing:** spacing of grid lines
- **Graduations:** spacing of dotted grid lines
- **Allow Distortion:** allows different spacing between horizontal and vertical grid lines.

(B) Sketch Plane Options

- **Shade sketch plane:** displays the sketch plane in gray. Fig 3-6 shows the sketch plane with this option checked.
- **Position sketch plane parallel to screen:** the sketch plane is aligned to the monitor screen when the Sketcher workbench is invoked.
- **Visualization of the cursor coordinates:** the coordinate value appears at the mouse cursor as shown in Fig 3-7.

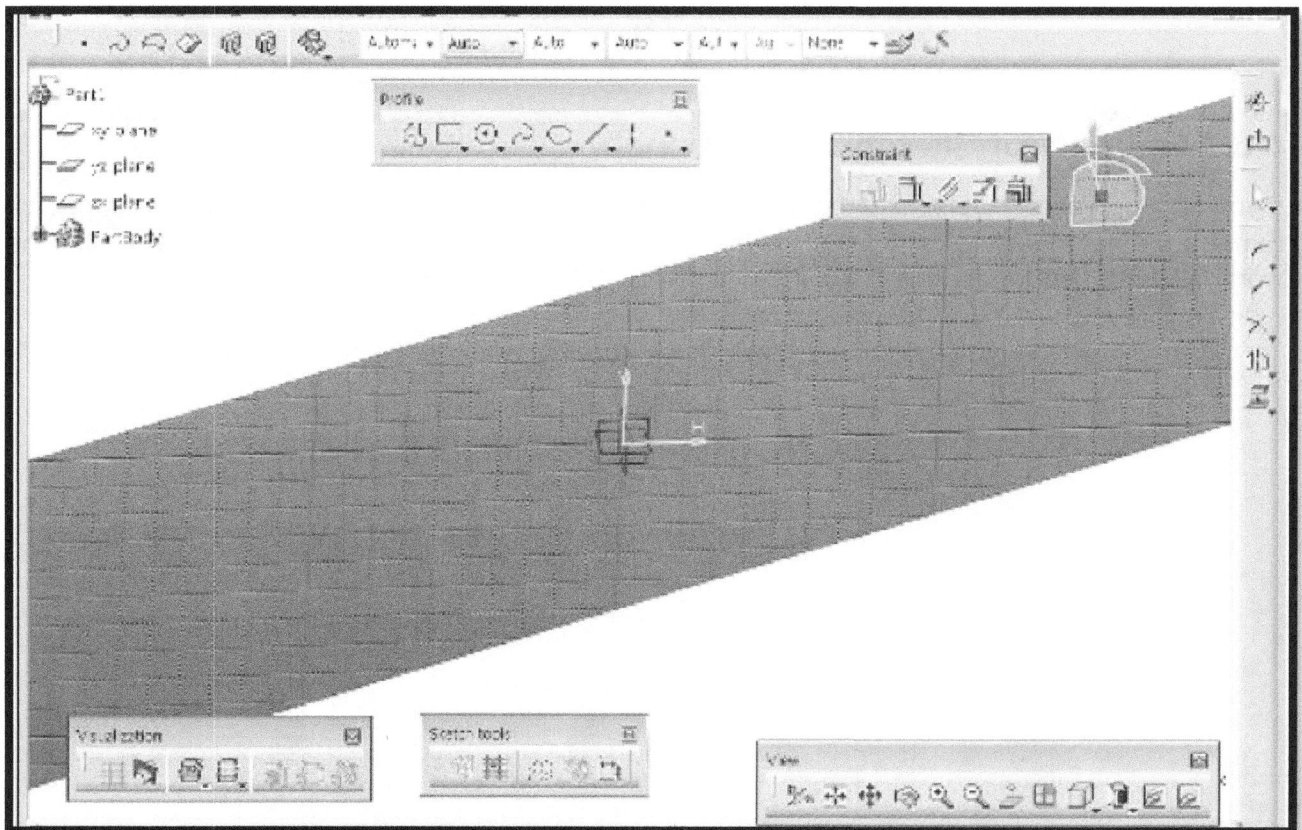

Fig 3-6 Shaded Sketch Plane

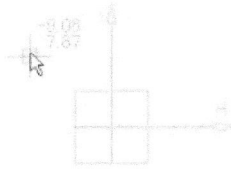

Fig 3- 7 Coordinate Value

(C) Colors Option

- **Default color of the elements:** sets the color of sketch elements such as curves, lines, points, etc. Tue default color for sketch elements is white. But in this textbook, we will use black on a white background to improve visibility.

Other sketch options will be referred to when required.

4.6.8 Units

Expand the General item on the left of the Options dialog box and select Parameters and Measure. If you select the Unit ta b on the right, the options shown in Fig 3-8 will appear. You can set units for length angle, time etc. The option designated by (A) shows 3 for the decimal places for read/write numbers.

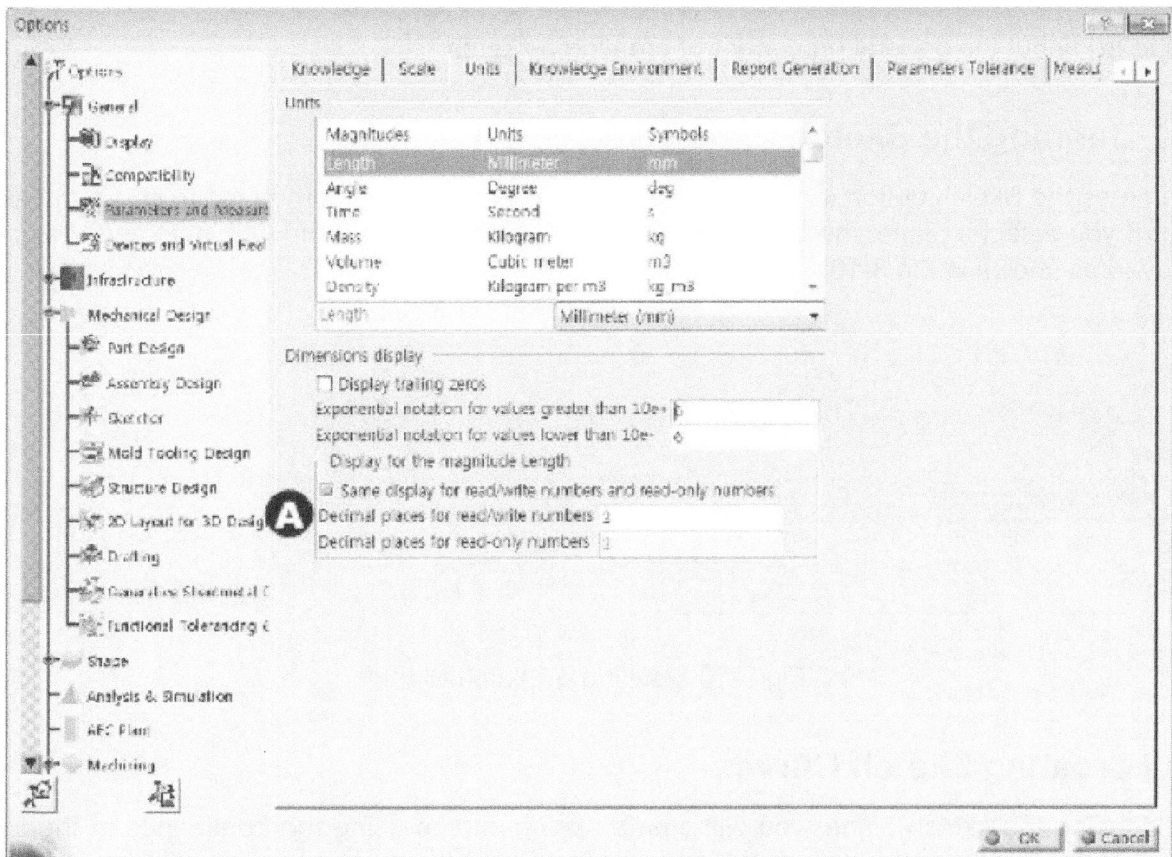

Fig 3-8 Units Options

59

4.2 SKETCH ELEMENTS

Expand the Spec Tree in the Sketcher workbench to view the base elements of the sketch as shown in Fig 3-9. There is one origin at the location (0, 0) and the HDirection and VDirection a1Tows are displayed in yellow. The base elements are the reference for defining the shape of the sketch curves.

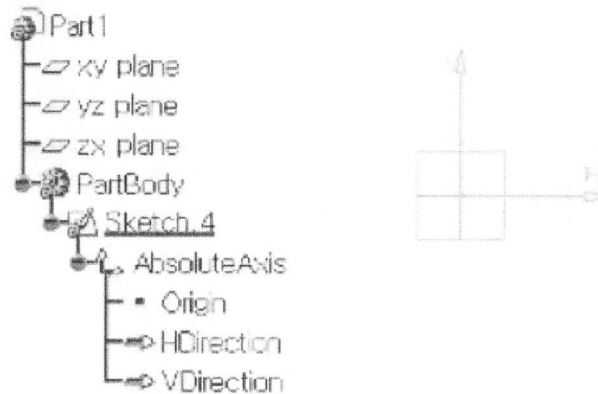

Fig 3-9 Sketch Elements

4.3 SKETCH PROCEDURE

Let' s learn about the general procedure of creating a sketch.

4.3.1 Defining the Sketch Plane

If you press the Sketch button in the Part Design workbench, you arc prompted to select the sketch plane. If you select a plane, the Sketcher workbench is invoked and the Origin, H and V axes are displayed as shown in Fig 3-10.

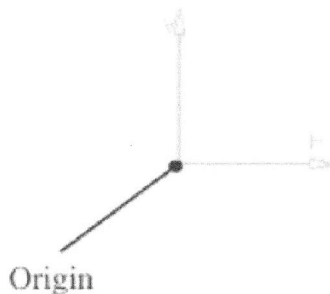

Fig 3-10 Defining a Sketch Plane

4.3.2 Creating Sketch Curves

After defining the sketch plane, you will create sketch curves using the commands in the Profile toolbar. At this stage, you can create the curves roughly, but the size and shape of the sketch should be as similar as possible to the desired outcome.

60

4.3.3 Constraint

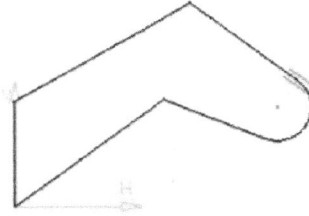

Fig 3-11 Roughly Created Sketch

Define the sketch curves exactly as you want using constraints. Fig 3-12 shows a sketch that is defined fully.

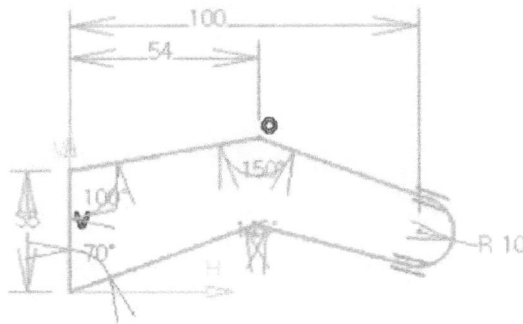

Fig 3-12 Fully Defined Sketch

4.3.4 Exit the Sketch

Press the Exit workbench button after completing the sketch.

4.4 CREATING A SKETCH

Using the icons in the Profile toolbar shown in Fig 3-13, you can create sketch curves in various ways.

Fig 3-13 Profile Toolbar

- **Profile:** creates lines and arc continuously.
- **Predefined Profile:** creates various predefined shapes.
- **Circle:** creates circ les or arcs.
- **Spline:** creates splines or connects curves with a spline.

- **Conic:** creates conic curves such an ellipse, hyperbola, etc.
- **Line:** creates lines.
- **Axis:** creates Jines that are to be used as axes.
- **Point:** creates points.

4.4.1 Line

Using the Line command, you can create a line by selecting two points. When you click the Line icon in the Profile toolbar, the Sketch Tools toolbar is changed as shown in Fig 3-14.

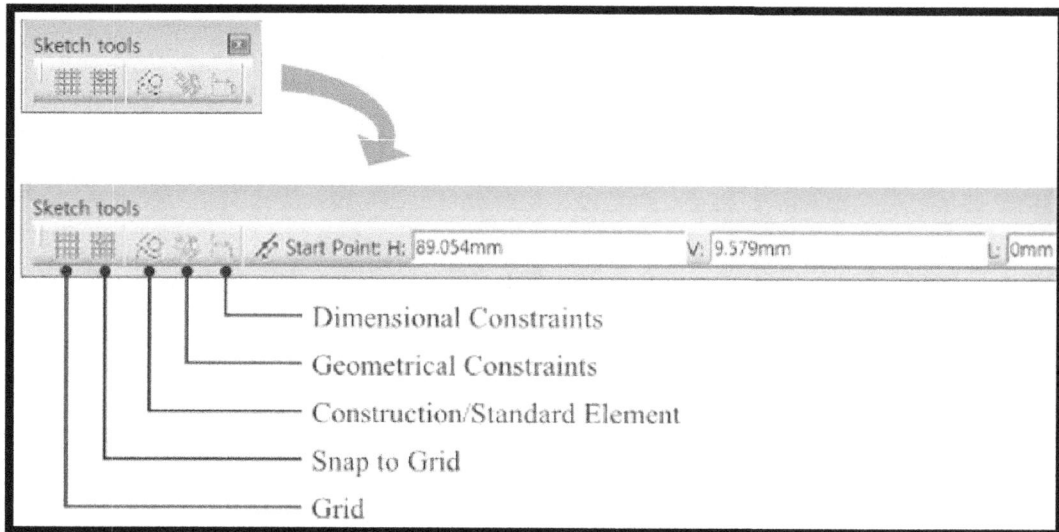

Fig 3-14 Sketch Tools Toolbar

- **Grid and Snap to Grid:** are the same as checking the Display option (A) in Fig 3-5.
- **Construction/Standard Element:** converts the attribute of the curve.
- **Geometrical Constraints:** adds geometrical constraints v,1hen you are creating curves.
- **Dimensional Constraints:** adds dimensional constraints when you are creating curves with input values.

Note that the Geometrical Constraints and the Dimensional Constraints buttons have to be turned on throughout this textbook.

Exercise 8: Creating Lines with snap

1. Create a new part file and click the Sketch icon.
2. Select the xy plane in the Spec tree.
3. Click the Line icon in the Profile toolbar.
4. Locate the mouse cursor at the origin and click MB I when the mouse pointer is changed as shown in Fig 3-1 5. The shut point of the line coincides with the origin point.
5. Move the cursor as shown in Fig 3-1 6 and click MB1. The line is created and selected. Click an arbitrary po int on the screen to deselect the line.

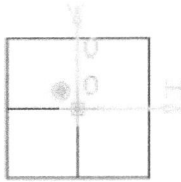

Fig 3-15 Selecting Origin Point

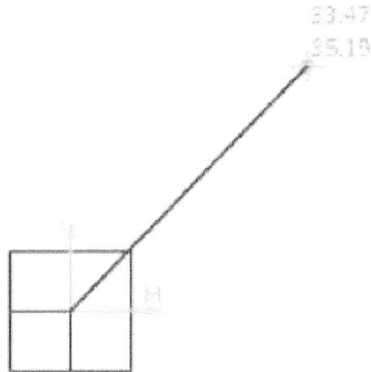

Fig 3-16 Creating a Line

6. Click the Line icon and select the end point of the existing line when the mou e cursor is changed as shown in Fig 3- 17. The symbol means that the start point of a new line is coincident with the end point of the existing line.
7. Move the cursor as shown in Fig 3-18 and click MB1 when the perpendicular symbol appears at the corner. It means that the two lines arc ensured to be perpendicular each other.
8. Deselect the line.
9. Move the mouse cursor on the second line as specified by the an-ow in Fig 3-19, select the line by pressing MB1 and drag it downwards as shown in fig 3-19. Note that the coincidence of the end points and the perpendicularity are maintained.
10. Exit the sketcher workbench by pressing the Exit Workbench icon.

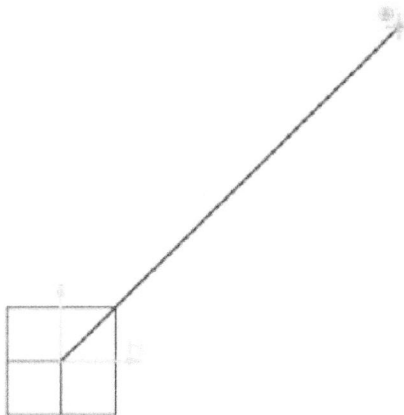

Fig 3-17 Selecting the End Point

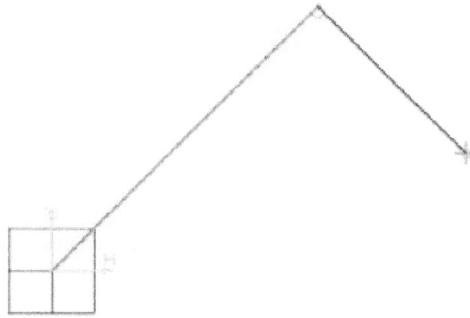

Fig 3 - 18 Perpendicular Line

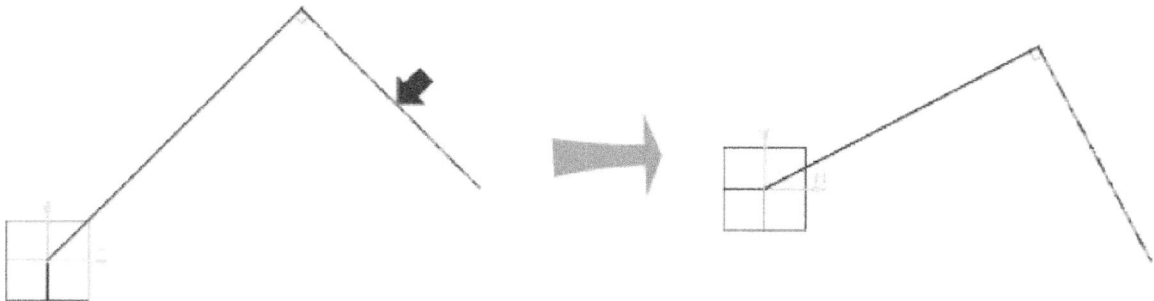

Fig 3-19 Dragging a Line

4.4.2 Profile

Using the Profile icon in the Profile toolbar, you can create lines and arcs continuously.

The Profile command can be terminated in the following way.

1. Press the ESC key two times. Curves that have been created up to that point will be selected. If you press the ESC key one more time, the curves will be deselected.
2. Double click MB1 (mouse button 1) at the final point. The Profile command is terminated, and the curves are selected.
3. Press the Select icon.

Fig 3- 20 Select Icon

When you are creating curves using the Profile command, the Sketch Tools toolbar is changed as shown in Fig 3-21.

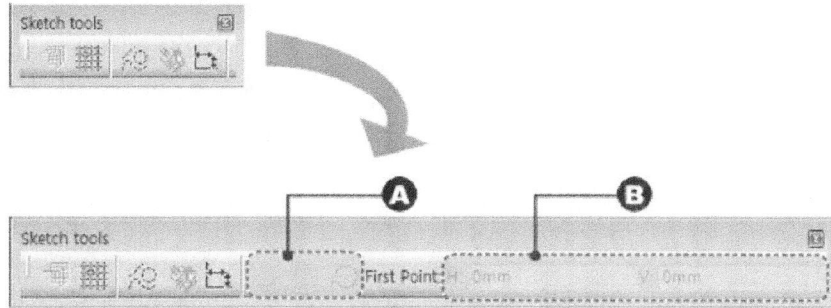

Fig 3-21 Sketch Tools Toolbar

(A) in Fig 3-21

- These buttons appear only when you arc using the Profile comm and.
- You can create lines, tangent arcs and three point arcs continuously by pressing the corresponding button.

(B) in Fig 3-21

- Shows the location of the m use cursor.
- You can specify the location of the. po in t by typing values in the H and V input box.
- Press the Tab key to activate the input box.

Exercise 9: Using Profile Command

1. Click the Profile icon in the Profile toolbar.
2. Locate the mouse cursor over the extended line of the H axis as shown in Fig 3-22 and click the MBI.
3. Click the other points in order as shown in Fig 3-23. For the last point (6) click the location of the first point (1). The curves are closed, and the Profile command is terminated automatically.

The curves are still selected. If you click on an empty area of the graphic area, the curves are deselected.

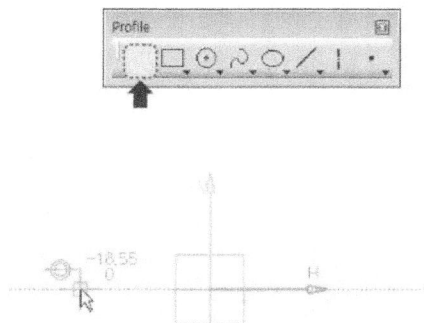

Fig 3-22 First Point

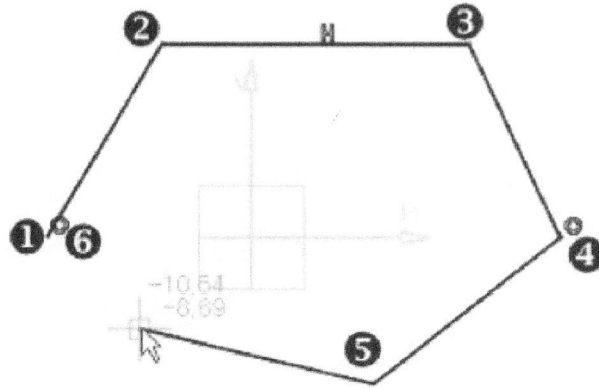

Fig 3 - 23 Selecting Points Consecutively

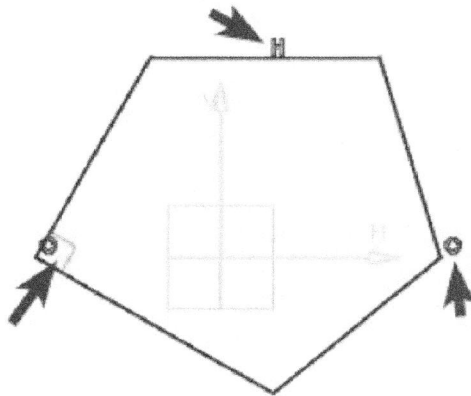

Fig 3-24 Closed Sketch Curves

(Note) Geometrical Constraints

The symbols designated by the arrows in Fig 3-17 imply that geometrical constraints have been applied.

4.4.3 Predefined Profile

The second icon group in the Profile toolbar can be dragged out. Using commands in the

Predefined Profile toolbar, you can create various predefined shapes easily.

Exercise 10: Creating Predefined Profile

Let's practice creating various predefined shapes as illustrated below.

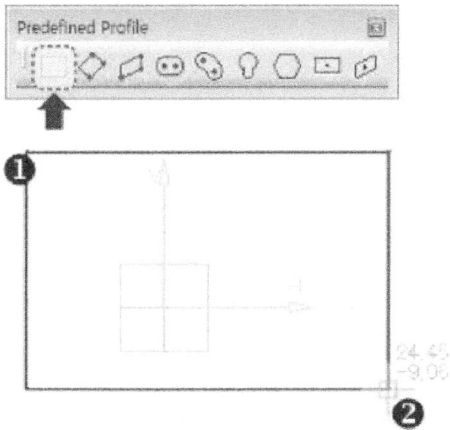

Fig 3-25 Rectangle

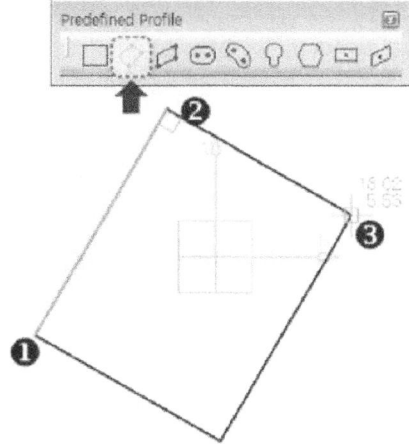

Fig 3-26 Oriented Rectangle

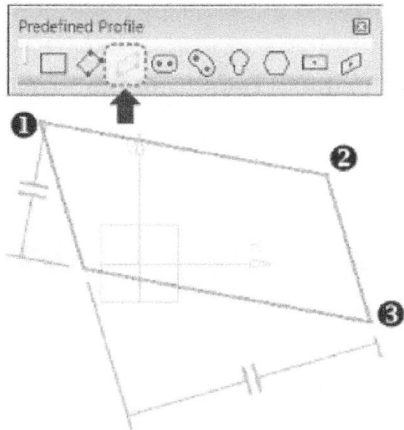

Fig 3-27 Parallelogram

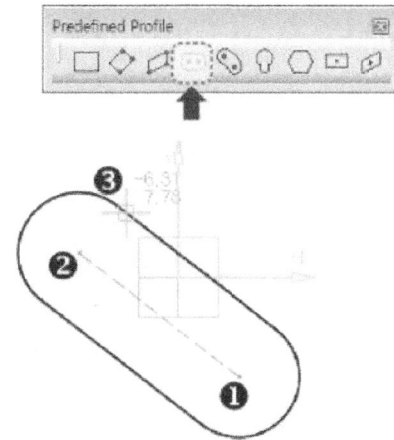

Fig 3-28 Elongated Hole

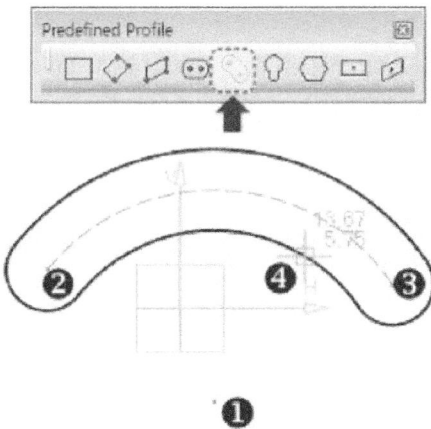

Fig 3- 29 Cylindrical Elongated Hole

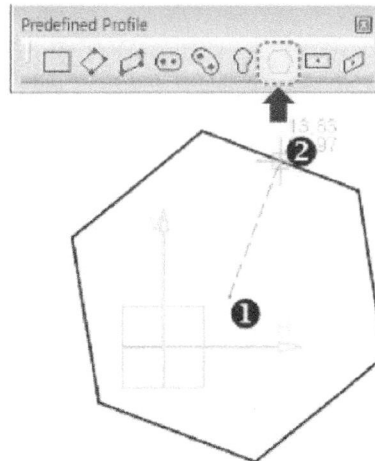

Fig 3-30 Hexagon

67

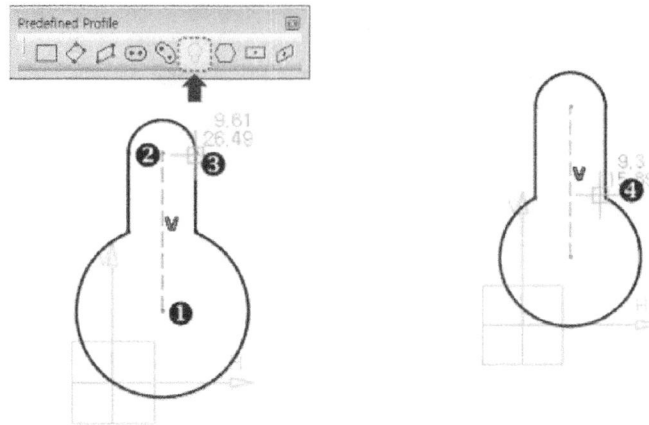

Fig 3-31 Keyhole Profile

4.4.4 Other Sketch Commands

You can drag out the Circle, Spline, Conic, Line and Point tool bars from the Profile toolbar. Fig 3-32 shows the respective tool bars.

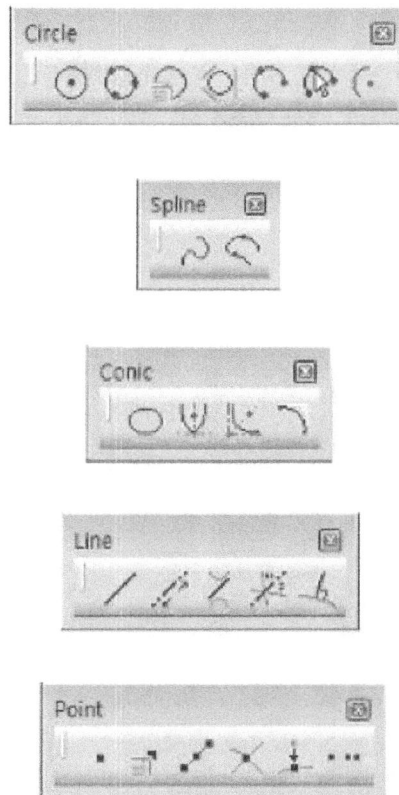

Fig 3-32 Other Sketch Toolbars

Exercise 10: Creating Circles

Let's practice creating circles and arcs in various ways.

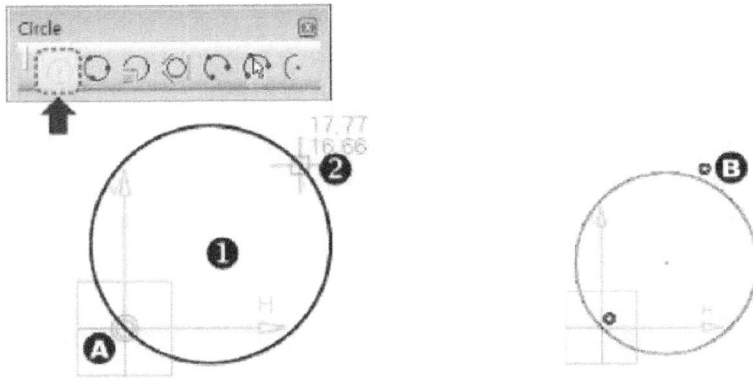

Fig 3-33 Circle

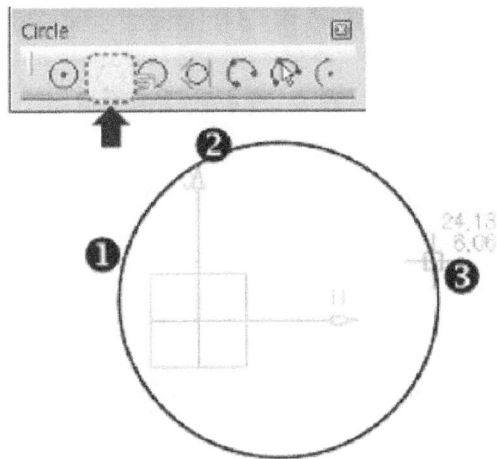

Fig 3-34 Three Point Circle

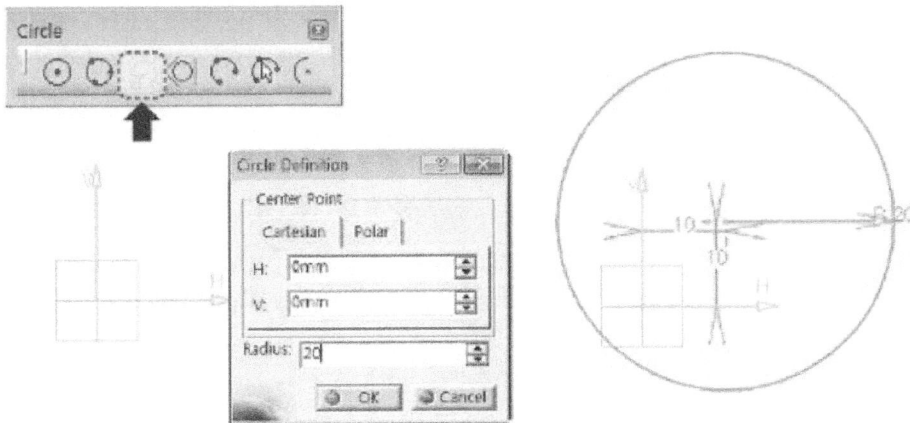

Fig 3- 35 Circle Using Coordinates

(Note) Point at the Center of a Circle

- When you are creating a circle or arc, a point is created at the center. This is because the Create circle and ellipse centers option in Fig 3-5 has been checked.

(Note) Shift Key and Sketch tools Option

1. If you do not want to recognize the constraint (A) in Fig 3-33, press the Shift key.
2. If you do not want to create the constraint (B) in Fig 3-33, turn off the Geometric Constraints button in the Sketch tools toolbar. Do not forget to turn this button ON throughout this textbook.

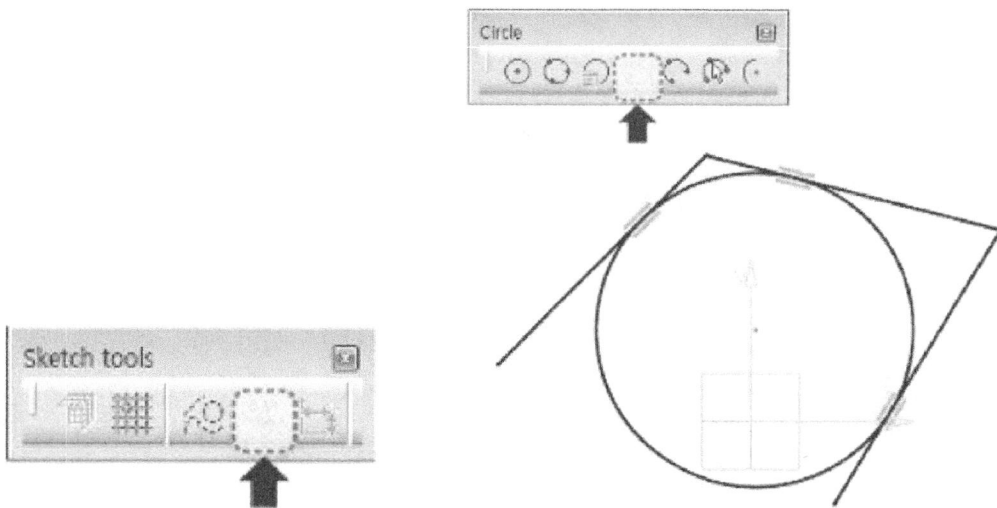

Fig 3-36 Tri-Tangent Circle

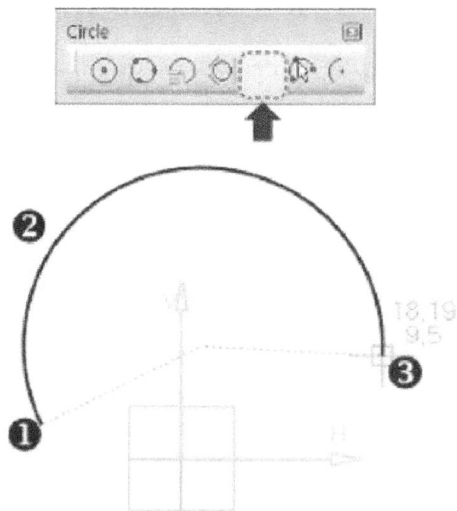

Fig 3-37 Three Point Arc

Tangent?

The lines and the circle in Fig 3-36 are said to be tangent to each other.

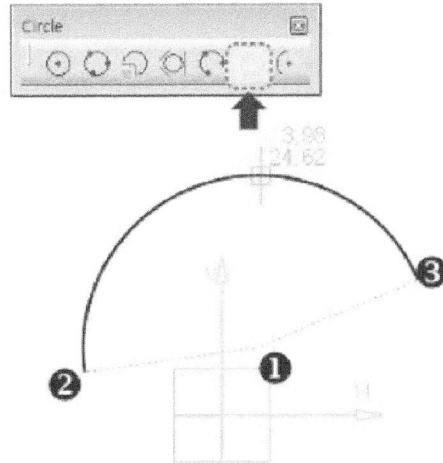

Fig 3- 38 Three Point Arc Starting with Lim its

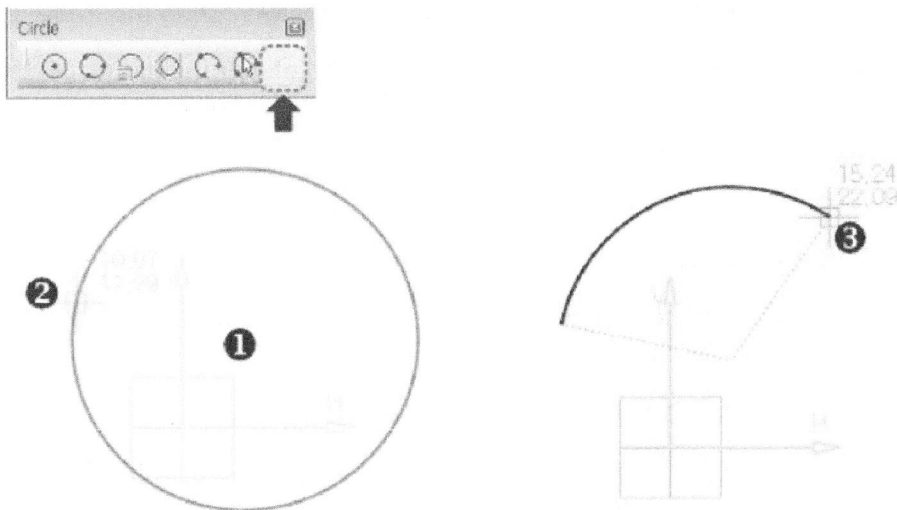

Fig 3-39 Arc

4.5 DELETING SKETCH ELEMENTS

If you are not executing any commands in CATIA V5, you are in fact executing a Select command. Therefore, you can select an object by clicking MB1 (mouse button I). Selecting curves, dimensions and the symbols of geometrical constraint and pressing the Delete key will delete them.

4.5.1 Select Toolbar

Drag out the Select too I bar as shown in Fig 3-40 and you can use many selection options.

The default selection option is Rectangle Selection Trap.

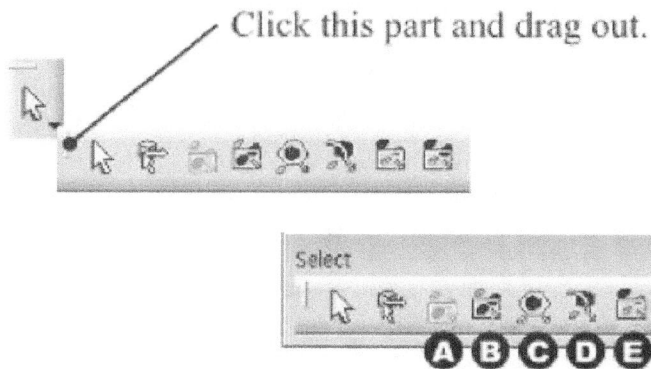

Fig 3-40 Select Toolbar

(A) Click MB1 and drag. The elements that are completely rectangular! Tap are selected.

(B) The elements that intersect the rectangular trap boundary are selected.

(C) Define polygon trap by clicking MB 1. Double click MB 1 for the last point. The Clements that are completely in the polygon trap are selected.

(D) Drag the mouse with MB1 clicked. The elements intersecting the trace arc selected.

(E) Click MB1 and drag. The elements that are completely outside the rectangular trap are selected.

(F) Select the elements outside of the rectangular trap including the elements that intersect the trap boundary.

(Note) Deleting Base Elements

- You cannot delete the base sketch elements, H and V axes or the origin.

4.6 CONSTRAINING SKETCH CURVES

Until now, you might have created sketch curves arbitrarily. However, a sketch that is not defined exactly as required or desired has no meaning in mechanical design. We have to define the size and shape of sketch curves exactly as we want them and then use them to extrude or revolve to create the 3D features.

In parametric modeling software such as CATIA V5, you can precisely define the sketch by using two types of constraints.

    (1) Geometrical Constraint

    (2) Dimensional Constraint

With geometrical constraints, you will define the shape of the curves by defining their relationship with other sketch elements. With dimensional constraints, you will use numerical values to define the distance, length, radius, diameter, angle, etc. The two types of constraints are combined to fully define the shape and size of the sketch elements. You can delete or modify constraints after applying them.

72

For example, if you want to fully define a po int, you need two distance dimensions as shown in Fig 3-41. If you want to fully define a circle, you have to define the location of the center point and the diameter of the circle as shown in Fig 3-42 (a). You can apply a tangent constraint as shown in Fig 3-42 (b) instead of the. vertical distance, provided that the distance is the same as the radius of the circle.

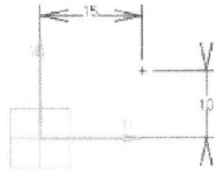

Fig 3-41 Constraining a Point

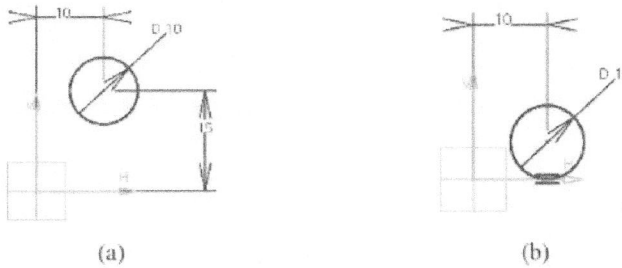

(a)   (b)

Fig 3- 42 Constraining a Circle

4.6.1 Dimensional Constraint

You can apply a dimensional constraint by clicking the Constraint icon in the Constraint toolbar as shown in Fig 3-43. Dimension types are determined automatically acc ordin g to the combination of selected elements.

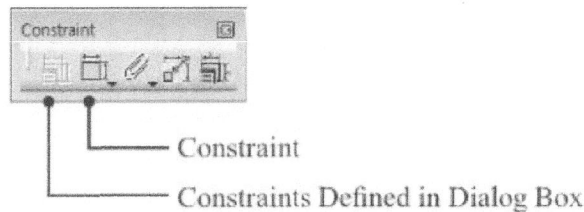

Fig 3-43 Constraint Toolbar

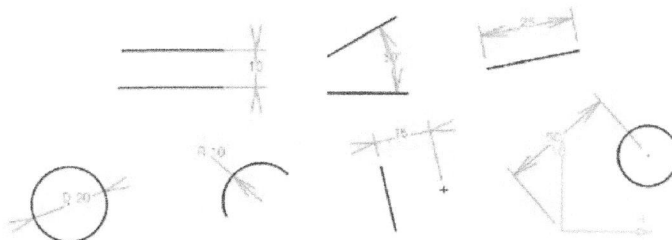

Fig 3-44 Various Types of Dimensions

73

(Note) It's amazing!!!

- By double clicking the dimension value and modifying it, you can modify the size or shape of the sketch element. This is the standard method for modifying sketches in a parametric modeler. You can delete the sketch element and create a new one only when parametric modification cannot be applied to obtain the desired shape.

4.6.2 Geometrical Constraint

There are two met hods in applying geometrical constraints.

(1) sing the Constraints Defined in Dialog Box icon.

(2) sing the Constraint icon.

If you select the sketch elements first, the Constraints Defined in Dialog Box button will be activated. You can apply geometrical constraint according to the following procedure.

(1) Select the sketch elements to apply the constraint to. You can select one or more elements with the Ctrl key.

(2) Click the Constraints Defined in Dialog box icon.

(3) Select the type of constraint in the dialog box.

(4) Press OK.

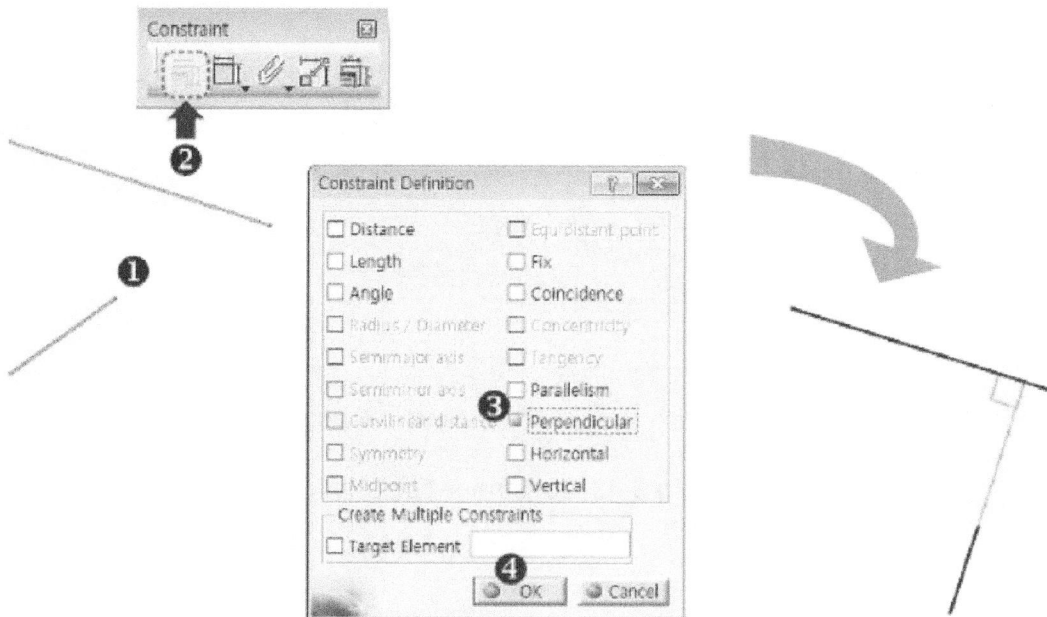

Fig 3-45 Applying Geometrical Constraint

(Note) It's amazing!!!

After applying a geometrical constraint, the sketch elements are adapted to the constraint. This is a key characteristic of parametric modeling.

You can apply a geometrical constraint with the Constraint icon according to the following procedure.

(1) Click the Constraint icon.

(2), (3) Select the objects ((2) and (3)) in Fig 3-46). The dimensional value appears.

(4) Press MB3 (right click).

(5) Select the type of constraint from the pop-up menu.

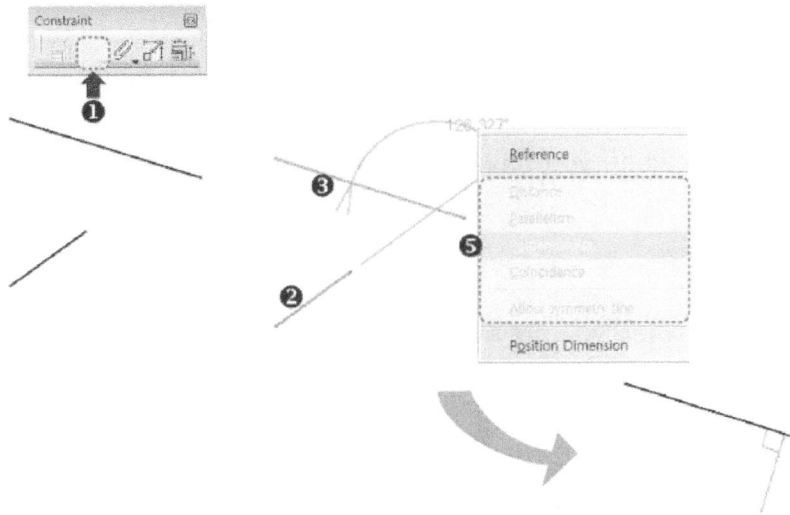

Fig 3-46 Applying Geometrical Constraint

(Note) Types of Constraints

Look at the dialog box shown in Fig 3-45. Some types of constraints are not activated. This means that you cannot apply constraints between the selected element(s). Only the types of constraints applicable to the selected sketch element(s) appear in the pop- up menu as shown in Fig 3-46.

4.6.3 Types of Constraints

The following types of constraints are applicable in the Constraint Definition dialog box shown in Fig 3-45.

Distance

This constraint is activated when you have selected two points, one point and a line and two parallel lines. You can define the distance between the two sketch elements.

Length

This constraint is activated when you have selected a line. You can define the length of the line.

Angle

This constraint is activated when you have selected two lines that are not parallel to each other. You can define the angle between the two lines.

Radius/Diameter

This constraint is activated when you have selected a circle or arc. You can define the radius or diameter of the circle or arc.

Semi-major axis

This constraint is activated when you have selected an ellipse. You can define the length of the semi-major axis.

Semi-minor axis

This constraint is activated when you have selected an ellipse. You can define the length of the semi-minor axis.

Symmetry

This constraint is activated when you have selected two sketch elements and an axis of symmetry. The two sketch elements are constrained to be symmetrical against the axis of symmetry.

Midpoint

This constraint is activated when you have selected a point and a line. The point is constrained at the middle of the line.

Equidistant point

This constraint is activated when you have selected three points. The distance of the first two points to the third point is constrained to be the same.

Fix

This constraint is always activated. The selected elements are constrained to be fixed. This constraint is used when you need to fix the location of the imported curves.

Coincidence

Point vs. Point: The location of the two points is constrained to be the same.

Line vs. Line: The two lines are aligned.

Point vs. Curve: The point is constrained on the curve.

Circle vs. Circle: The location and diameter of two circles are constrained to be the same.

Concentricity

This constraint is activated when you have selected two circles or arcs. The center of the two elements is constrained to be the same. You can constrain a point and a circle with this constraint.

Tangency

This constraint is activated when you have selected two curves or one line and a curve. The two elements are constrained to be tangent to each other.

(Note) Meaning of Point

Points in the CATIA V5 Sketcher include the center point of a circle or ellipse, the end point of a curve or line, the control point of a spline and the physical point, which are created with commands in the Point toolbar.

Parallelism

This constraint is activated when you have selected two lines. The two lines are constrained to be parallel to each other.

Perpendicular

This constraint is activated when you have selected two Lines. The two lines arc con- strained to be perpendicular to each other.

Horizontal

This constraint is activated when you have selected a line. The line is constrained to be parallel to the H axis.

Vertical

This constraint is activated when you have selected a line. The line is constrained to be parallel to the V axis.

Exercise 11: Creating a Rectangle Symmetric to H and V Axes

1. Click the Rectangle icon from the Profile toolbar.
2. Create an arbitrary rec tangle as shown in Fig 3-47. The Horizontal and Vertical constraints are created automatically.
3. Deselect the curves by clicking on an empty area.
4. Press Ctrl key and select the curves (A) and (B) as shown in Fig 3-48.
5. Click the Constraint Defined in Dialog Box icon.

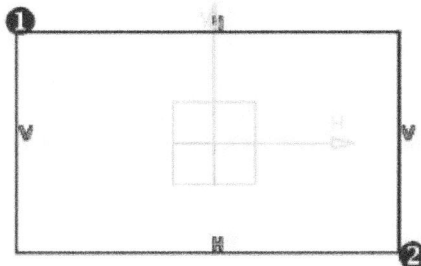

Fig 3-47 Creating a Rectangle

77

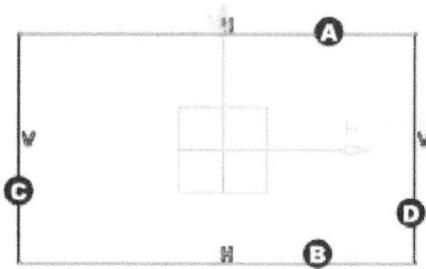

Fig 3-48 Applying a Distance Constraint

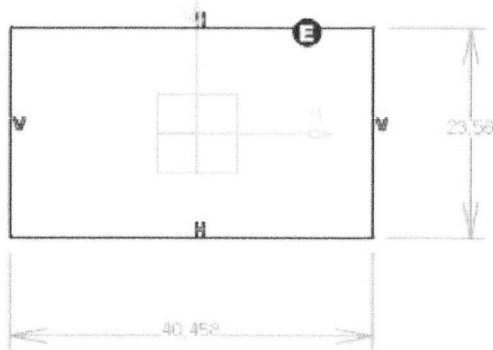

Fig 3-49 Dragging Line

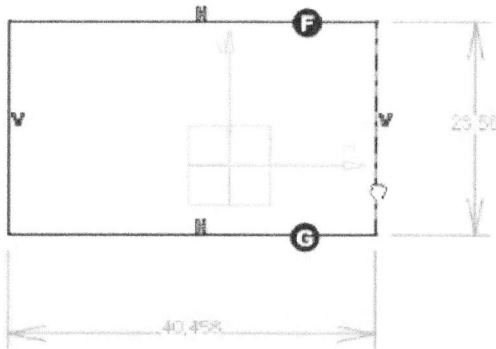

Fig 3-50 Applying Symmetry constraint

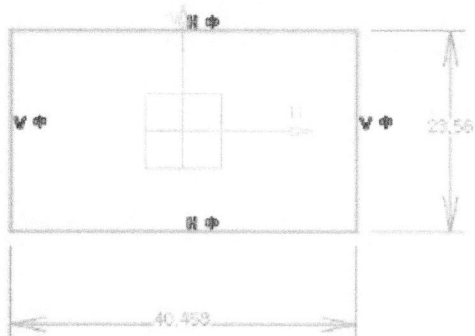

Fig 3- 51 Iso-constrained Sketch

6. Check the Distance option in the dialog box and pre s OK.
7. Create a distance constraint between the line (C) and (D) shown in Fig 3-48 in the same way.
8. Drag the line (E) shown in Fig-49 so the origin is one sided.
9. Select the lines (F) and (G) shown in Fig 3-50 and the H axis as the third element.
10. Click the Constraint Defined in Dialog Box icon and select the Symmetry option.

(Note) Iso-constrained

The color of the curve turns green.

11. Select the lines (C) and (D) in Fig 3-48 and the V axis as the third element.
12. Apply the Symmetry constraint. The result of constraining is shown in Fig 3-51.

(Note) Iso-constrained

The iso-constrained curves cannot be dragged.

4.6.4 Status of Constraint

The shape and size of the sketch curves are defined by using constraints. Lines shown in Fig 3-51 have their size and location defined exactly. The lines cannot be dragged freely. This status of constrain t is called iso -const rained.

If the sketch is constrained partially as shown in Fig 3-50, it is called under-constrained. The color of the sketch in this status is white by default. You can drag the under-con- strain ed sketch along the free direct ion.

Let's add a half dimension (A) as shown in Fig 3-52. The color of the line turns to magenta. The reason we apply dimensions is to define its size. We can modify the value by double clicking on it. The distance 40.458 between the two lines is defined and the two lines are constrained to be symmetrical. Therefore, the half dimension is of course 20.229 and you cannot modify this value by itself. Even if you double click the dimension and type in another value, the half distance will not be adapted. This status of constraint is called over-constrained. If you exit the sketcher with the sketch is over-constrained, an update diagnosis is invoked.

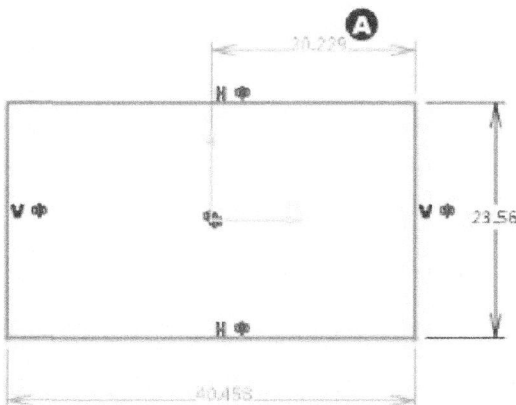

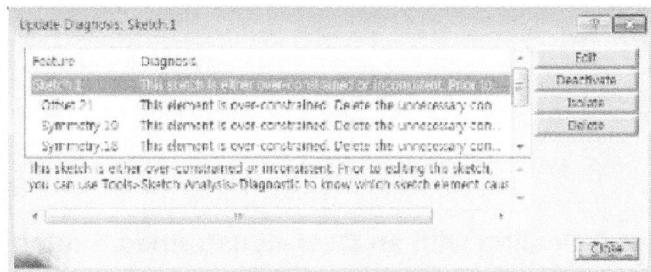

Fig 3-52 Over-constrained Sketch and Update Diagnosis

(Note) Which status is preferable?

79

- Of course, the iso-constrained sketch is the goal of constraining. Although you can create 3D features with an under-constrained sketch, it is not recommended. You must avoid creating an over-constrained sketch.

4.6.5 Verifying the Status of Constraint

There are several ways to verify the status of constraint.

Color

You can verify the status of constraint by the color of the sketch curves.

- **Under-constrained:** White
- **Iso-constrained:** Green
- **Conflicting constraint:** Red
- **Over-constrained:** Magenta

Symbol

Double click on the dimension. The Constraint Definition dialog box as shown in Fig 3-53 appears. You can modify the dimension value and verify if the dimension is normal or not If you double click the green dimension , the symbol in the dialog box is shown as in Fig 3-53 (a). If you double click the over constrained dimension ((A) in Fig 3-52) the symbol is shown as in Fig 3-53 (b). You can also verify the status of the geometrical constraint by double clicking on it. The symbol in Fig 3-53 (c) depicts the geometrical constraint.

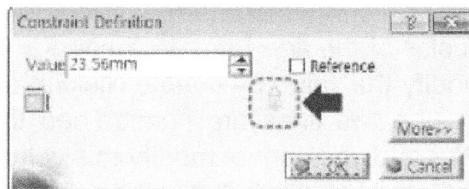

(a) Normal Dimension   (b) Over-constrained Dimension

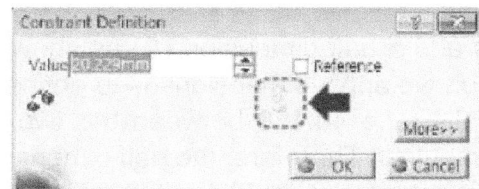

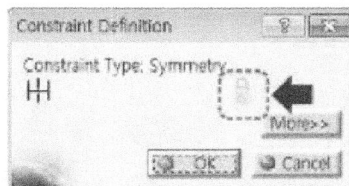

(c) Normal Geometrical Constraint

Fig 3-53 Symbols Representing the Status of Constraint

(Note) Dealing with an Over-constrained Sketch

- **Dimension:** You can delete or convert to a reference dimension. If you check the Reference option in the dialog box shown in Fig 3-53, the dimension is not considered as a constraint. The reference dimension cannot be modified.
- **Geometrical Constraint:** Delete it.

If you want to resolve the over-cons trained status shown in Fig 3-52, you may delete one of the three constraints: 20.229, 40.458 or the symmetric constraint. When you decide to delete a geometrical constraint, it is recommended that you deactivate it first and examine the impact. If the deactivation does not have any impact on the sketch, you can delete it.

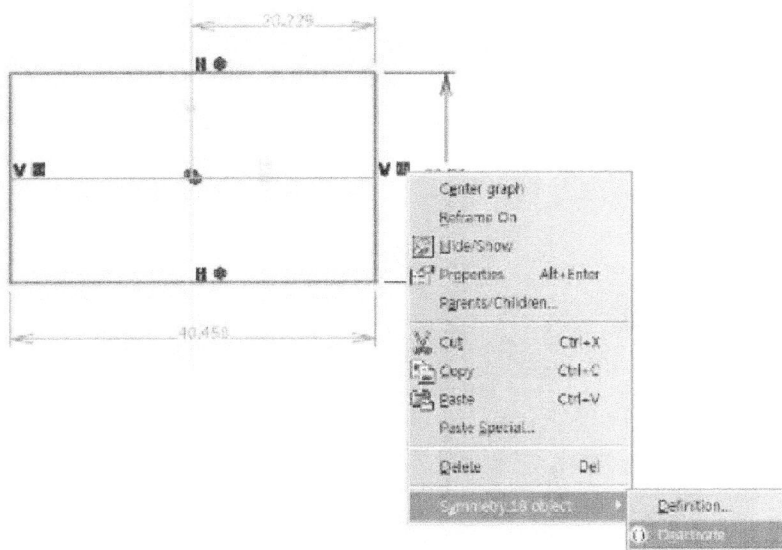

Fig 3-54 Deactivation of Geometrical Constraint

Drag

Partially constrained sketch elements can be dragged. Pick the curve or point (control

point, end point, center point of a circle, etc.) with MB1 and drag it.

Using the Analysis Tool

Using the commands in the 20 Analys is toolbar shown in Fig 3-55, you can analyze the status of the sketch constraint.

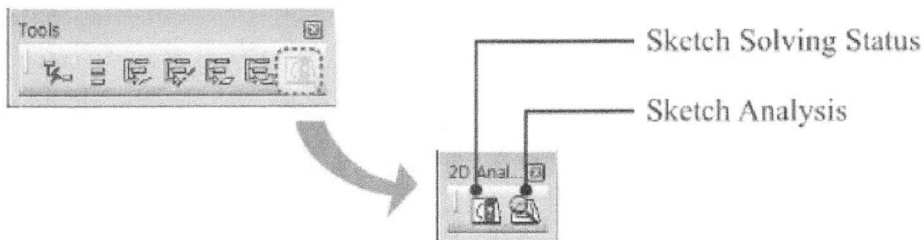

Fig 3-55 Analys is Tools

Click the Sketch Solving Status icon in the 2D Analysis toolbar. A dialog box as shown in fig 3-56 appears and the result of the evaluation is displayed.

If you press the Sketch Analysis button in the Sketch Solving Status dialog box, another dialog box as shown in Fig 3-57 (a) appears and tells the status of each sketch element. Over-constrained sketch elements arc highlighted. You can delete the over-constrained sketch curves or constraints.

81

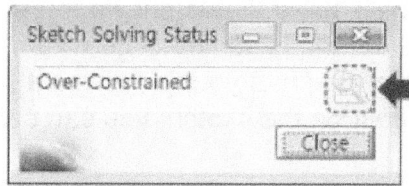

Fig 3- 56 Sketch Solving Status Dialog Box

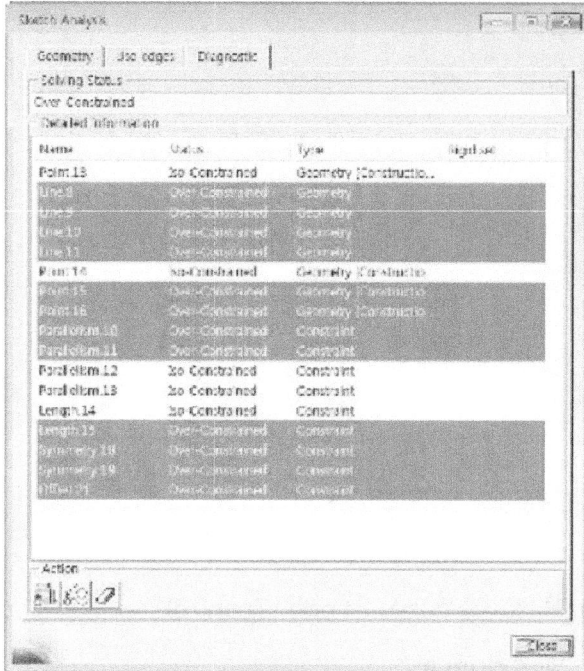

(a)

(b)

Fig 3- 57 Sketch Analysis Dialog Box

1. Create a new part file and invoke the Sketcher workbench by selecting the xy plane as the ketch plane.

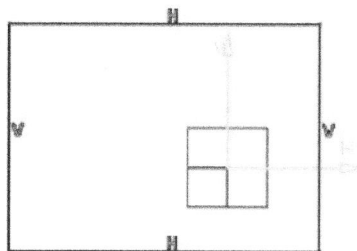

Fig 3-58 Rectangle

2. Create a rectangle so that the origin is one-sided as shown in Fig 3-58.
3. Deselect the sketch curves by clicking an empty space in the graphic area.
4. Click the Constraint icon in the Constraint toolbar.
5. Create a distance dimension between the two lines ((1) and (2) in Fig 3-59).

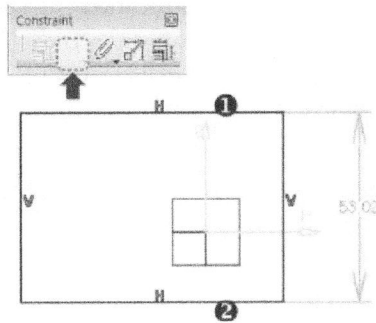

Fig 3-59 Dimensioning

(Note) Icon is turned off.

- After creating a dimension, the Constraint icon is turned off automatically. If you want to create constraints consecutively, double click the Constraint icon.

6. Double click the Constraint icon and create a horizontal distance constraint between the two lines ((3) and (4) in Fig 3-60). Note that the Constraint icon is not turned off.

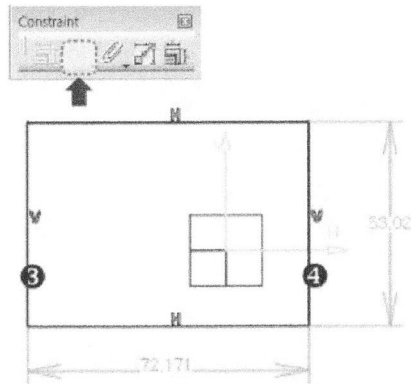

Fig 3-60 Dimensioning

7. While the Constraint icon is on, select the line (1) and (2).
8. Press MB3 (right click) and choose the Allow symmetry line option ((3) in Fig 3-61) in the pop-up menu.

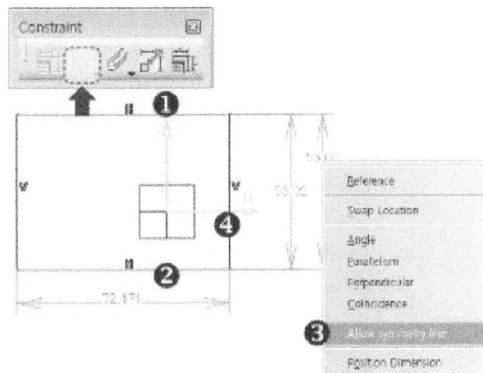

Fig 3-61 Applying Symmetry Constraint

83

9. Select the H axis ((4) in Fig 3-61). The two lines (1) and (2) become symmetric and the symmetry symbols appear on the lines.
10. Apply symmetric constraint between the line (3), and (4) in Fig 3 - 60 in the same way. Select the V axis as the symmetric axis.

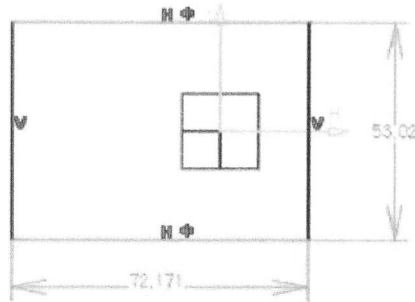

Fig 3-62 Result of Symmetry Constraint

11. Check that the sketch is iso-constrained.
12. Click the Select icon to release the constraint icon.

(Note) Which method is better?

- The method in Exercise 4 is considered to be more convenient than that of Exercise 3.

Exercise 12: Constraining an Arc

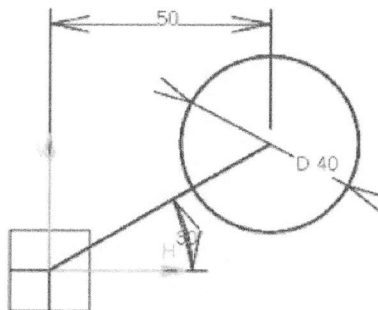

Fig 3-63 An Arc

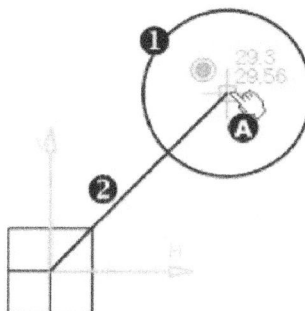

Fig 3-64 Line and Arc

84

1. Create an arc on the first quadrant.
2. Create a line between the origin and the center of the circle. Note that the Coincidence constraint has to be created.
3. Double click on the Constraint button.
4. Select the circle (A) in Fig 3-65 to create a diametral dimension.

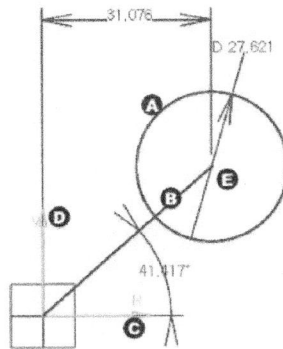

Fig 3-65 Dimensioning

5. Create an angular dimension by selecting the line (B) and the H axis (C) in Fig 3-65.
6. Create a distance dimension between the V axis (D) and the center of the arc (E).
7. Press the ESC key twice to turn off the Constraint icon.

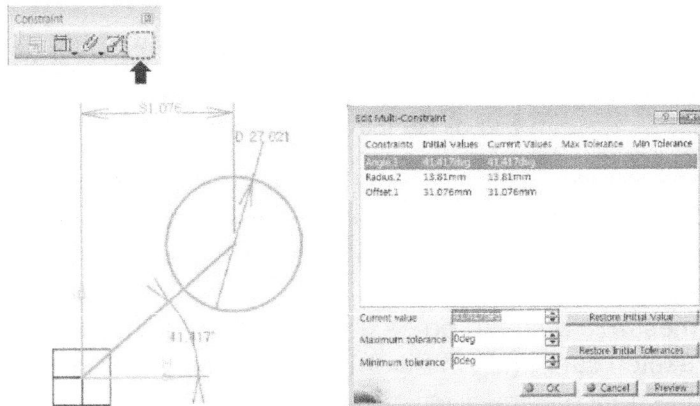

Fig 3-66 Modifying Several Dimensions

8. Click the Edit Multi-constraint icon in the Constraint toolbar.

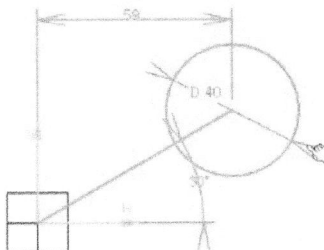

Fig 3-67 Repositioning the Dimension

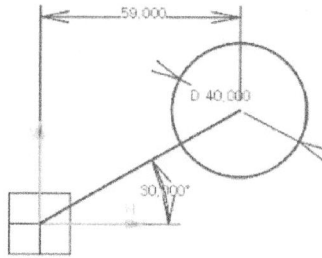

Fig 3-68 Repositioning the Dimension

9. Highlight each dimension value as shown in Fig 3-66 and modify it. Note that the radius is displayed for the diametral dimension.
10. Drag each dimension to move it to a proper location as shown in Fig 3-67.

(Note) Dragging Dimension

- You can drag the dimension value or the dimension arrow.
11. Exit the Sketcher workbench.

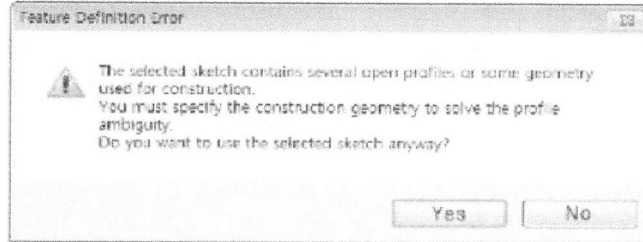

Fig 3- 69 Error Message

12. While the sketch is selected, click the Pad icon in the Sketch Based Features toolbar.
13. An error message as shown in Fig 3-69 appears. Note that the profile curve must not intersect. We have to convert the line into a construction element so that the line does not contribute to defining a profile.
14. Press No in the message box and press Cancel in the Pad Definition dialog box.
15. Double click the sketch curve ((A) in Fig 3-70) or Sketch.1 ((A) in Fig 3-70) in the Spec Tree. The Sketcher work- bench is invoked.

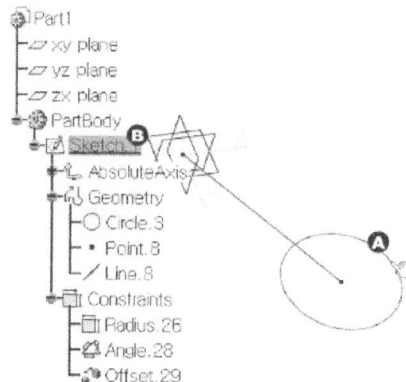

Fig 3-70 Modifying the Sketch

86

16. Select the line (1) in Fig 3-71 and click the Construction/Standard Element icon ((2) in Fig 3-71) in the Sketch tools toolbar.

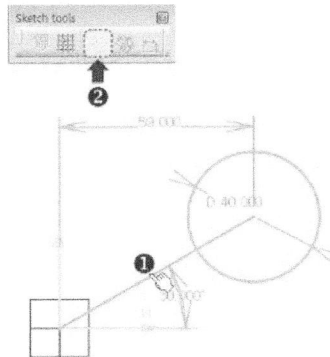

Fig 3-71 Changing the Attribute of a Curve

17. Confirm that the line has been con-verted to a dashed line.
18. Click the Construction/Standard Element icon to turn it off.
19. Exit the Sketcher workbench.
20. Confirm that the line is not visible.

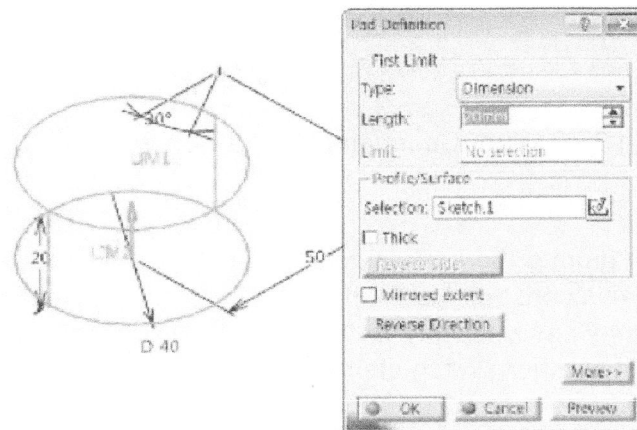

Fig 3-72 Extruding with Pad Icon

21. Click the Pad icon in the Sketch- Based Features toolbar to extrude the profile by 20mm.

(Note) Construction Element / Standard Element

- **Construction Element:** The construction element does not contribute to defining a profile but can be used as a reference in constraining the sketch elements.
- **Standard Element:** The standard element contributes to defining a profile. You can convert the attribute of the sketch curves by using the Construction/Standard Element button in the Sketch tools toolbar.

4.6.6 Other Sketch Constraints and Commands

Contact Constraint ((A)in Fig 3-73)

Constrains two elements to be in contact with each other. You can apply either a Concentricity, Coincidence or Tangency constraint.

Fix Together ((B) in Fig 3-73)

This constraint fixes the selected sketch elements together. The fixed elements can be thought of as one object.

Auto Constraint ((C) in Fig 3-73)

With this command you can constrain the sketch elements automatically.

Animate Constraint ((D) in Fig 3-73)

With this command you can animate a dimension.

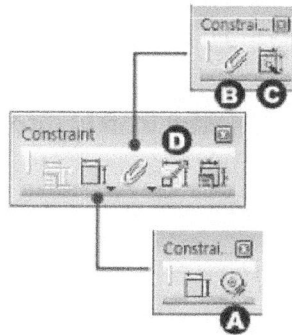

Fig 3-73 Other Commands in the Constraint Toolbar

(Note) Do not apply Fix constraint.

- The Fix constraint among the geometrical constraints are not used to define the shape of the sketch curve. This constraint is used to fix sketch objects that are imported from another CAD system. Sometimes you may fix some sketch elements temporarily to evaluate the status of constraint of other sketch elements. You have to delete the Fix constraint after its temporary use.

Exercise 13: Creating a Sketch and Padding

Create an equilateral triangle as shown in fig 3-74 so that the center of the side is on the origin. iso-constrain the sketch and pad it by 200mm.

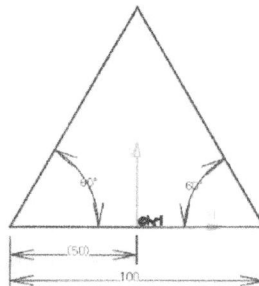

Fig 3-74 Equilateral Triangle

1. Press the Shift key and create an arbitrary triangle with the Profile command just similar to the given size and shape.
2. Apply the Coincidence constraint between the lower side and the H axis.
3. Apply the Midpoint constraint between the lower side and the origin.
4. Create a 100mm dimension.
5. Create a (50mm) dimension as a reference.
6. Create an angular dimension.

Exercise 14: Creating a Sketch and Padding

Create a sketch as shown in Fig 3-75 and pad it by 20mm.

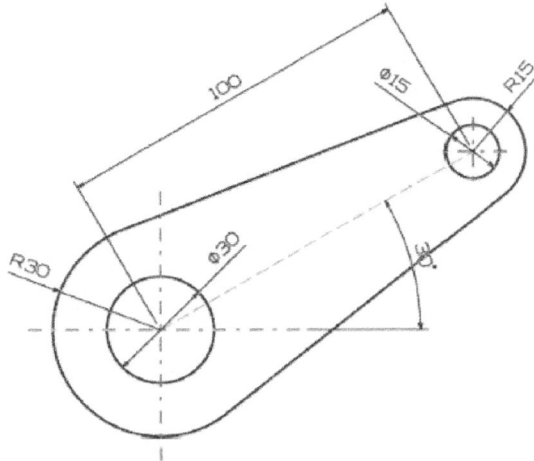

Fig 3-75 Link Part

(Note) Hint

- The iso-constrained sketch is shown in Fig 3-76.

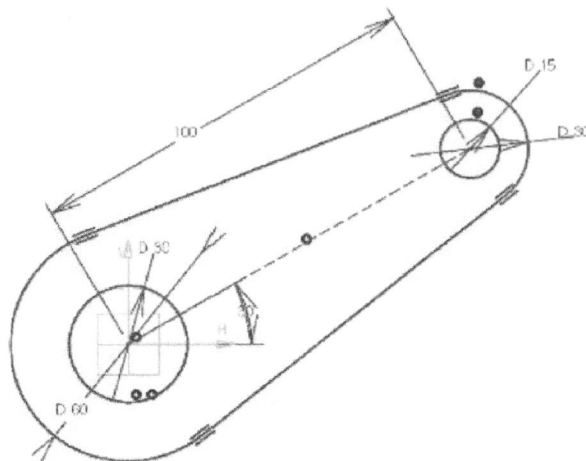

Fig 3-76 Iso-constrained Sketch

CHAPTER 5: ELEVATING YOUR SKETCHING SKILLS

5.1 MODIFYING SKETCH CURVES

You can modify sketch curves using commands in the Operations tool bar.

5.1.1 Fillet

A fillet connects two curves with an arc.

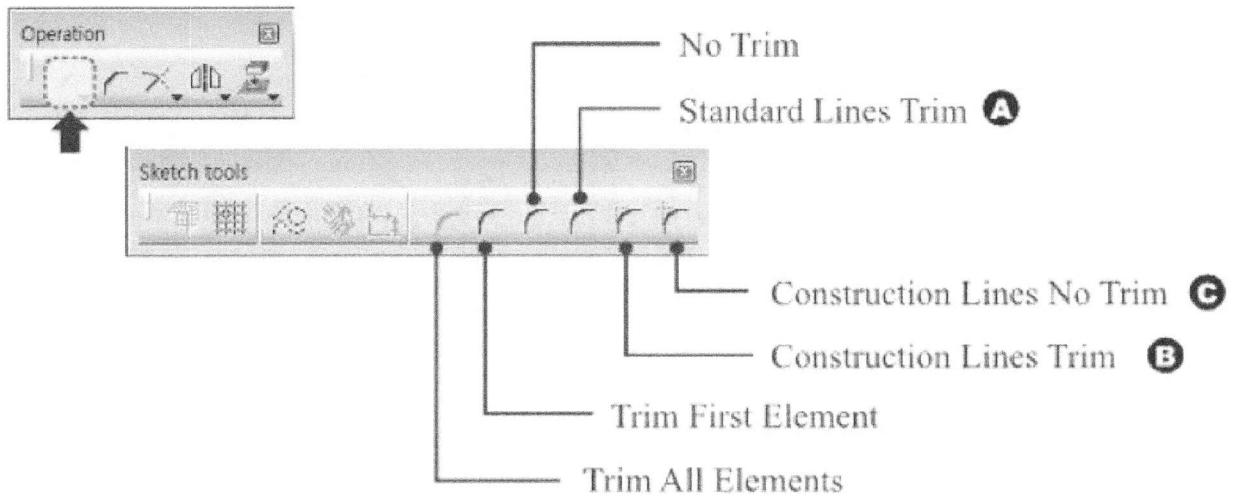

Fig 4 - 1 Trim Option of Fillet

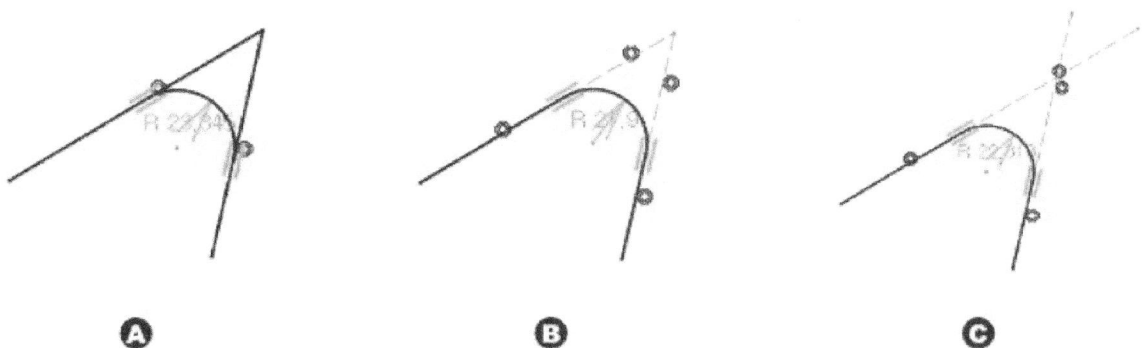

Fig 4 - 2 Results of Each Trim Option

5.1.2 Chamfer

A chamfer connects two curves with an inclined line.

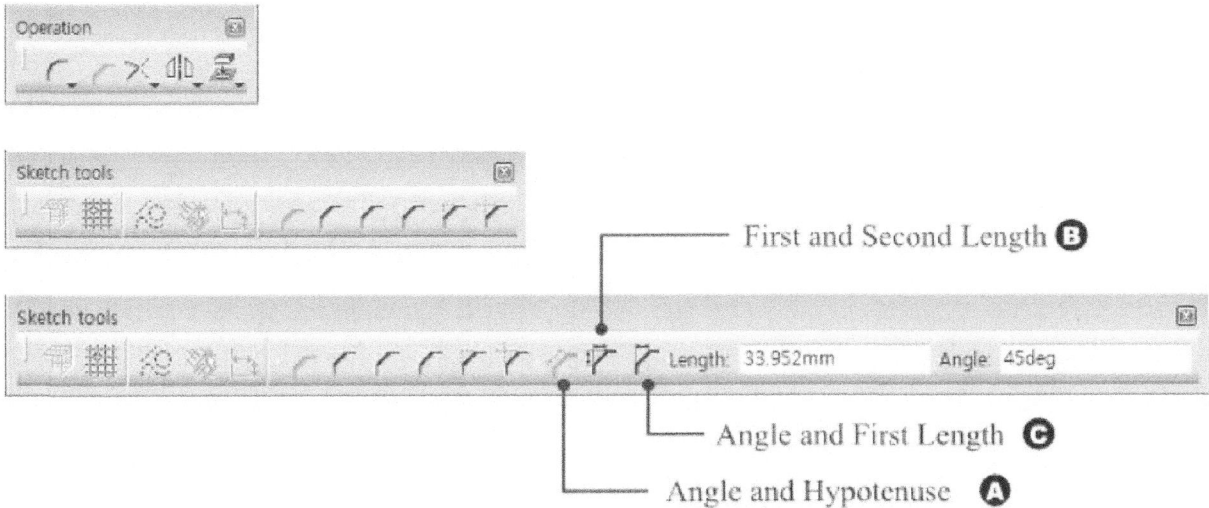

First and Second Length **B**

Length: 33.952mm   Angle: 45deg

Angle and First Length **C**

Angle and Hypotenuse **A**

Fig 4- 3 Types of Chamfer

Procedure

(1) Click the Chamfer icon in the Operations toolbar. The Sketch tools toolbar is expanded to show trim options.

(2) Select a trim option.

(3) Select two curves to apply the chamfer to. The Sketch tools toolbar is expanded to show types of chamfer and corresponding input boxes.

(4) Select the type of chamfer.

(5) Enter values in the Angle and Length. (Press the Tab key to activate the input box.)

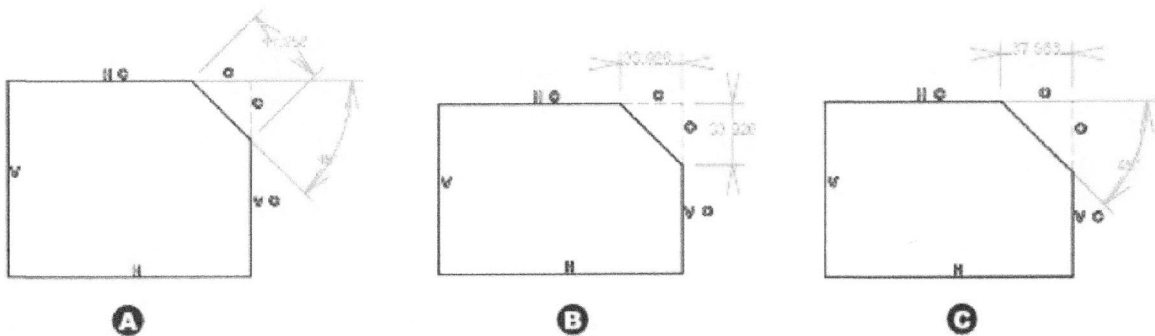

A   **B**   **C**

Fig 4-4 Types of Chamfer

5.1.3 Relimitation

Re-define the end point of the curve.

91

Trim

Trim out the selected curves. You can trim all of the selected curves or only the first curve.

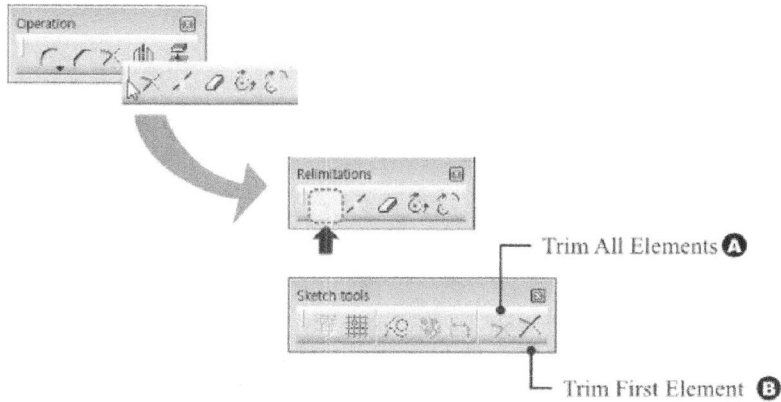

Fig 4- 5 Trim Options

Quick Trim

You can trim out the selected part of a curve with regard to the boundary curve(s).

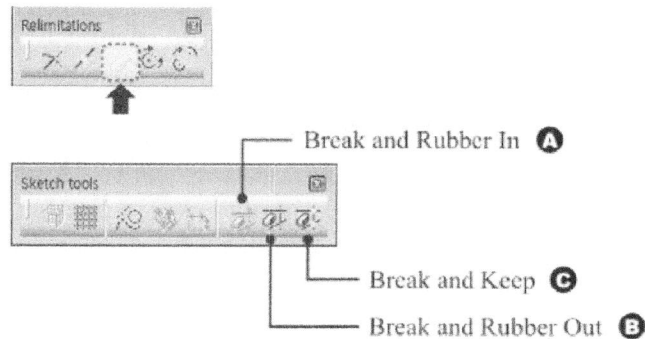

Fig 4- 6 Quick Trim Options

5.2 TRANSFORMATION

5.2.1 Mirror

Mirror the sketch elements against an axis. The symmetry constraints are created automatically.

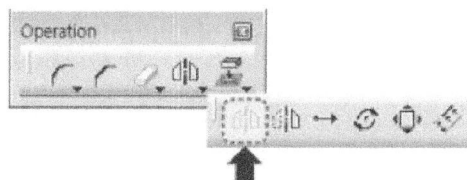

Fig 4-7 Mirror Icon

Exercise 15: Mirror

1. Create an axis ((A) in Fig 4-8) with the Axis icon in the Profile toolbar.
2. Create lines as s how n in Fig 4-8 with the Profile icon in the Profile toolbar.
3. Click the Select icon to deselect the curves.
4. Click the Mirror icon in the Opera-tions toolbar.

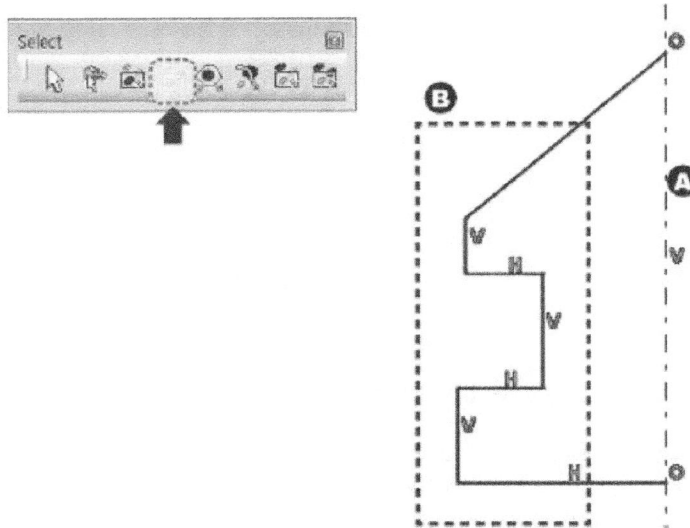

Fig 4-8 Half Sketch and Axis

1. Change the selection trap to Intersecting Rectangle Selection Trap and drag the selection window, as designated by (B) in fig 4-8.
2. Read the status bar message and select the axis (A). The lines are mirrored as shown in Fig 4-9.
3. Drag the line (A) in Fig 4-9. The symmetry constraint is maintained and you can achieve the result as shown in Fig 4-10.

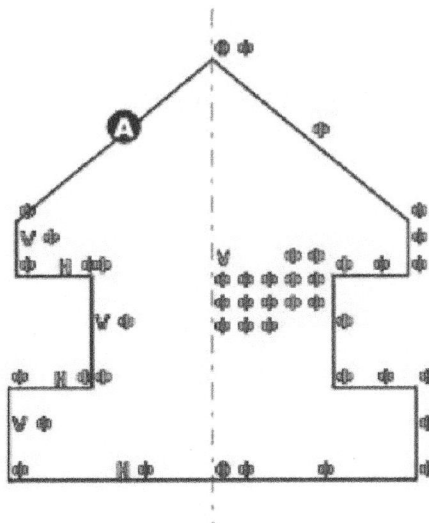

Fig 4-9 Result of Mirror

93

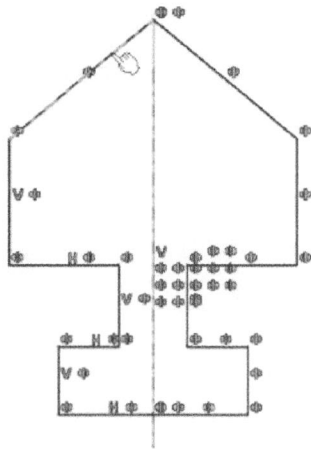

Fig 4-10 Dragging

(Note) Symmetry Axis

The following elements can be used as the symmetry axis.

1. Base axis of the sketch (The H and V axis).
2. An axis line that is created with the Axis command.
3. A line created as a construction element.

5.2.2 Symmetry

Mirror the sketch curves and delete the original curves.

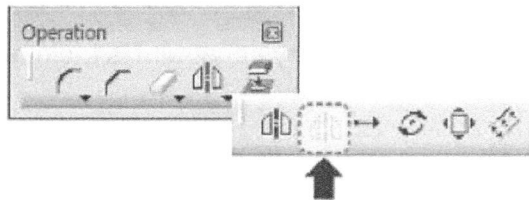

Fig 4-11 Symmetry Icon

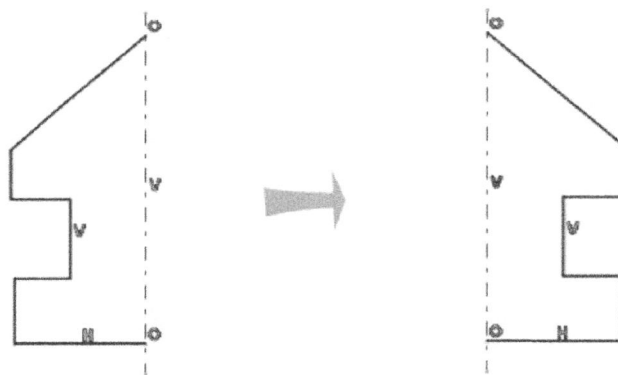

Fig 4-12 Curves Mirrored with Symmetry Command

5.2.3 Translate

Use the Translate command in the Transformation tool bar to move or copy the sketch elements.

Procedure

(1) Select the sketch elements to move or copy.

(2) Click the Translate icon in the Trans formation toolbar.

(3) Specify the start point.

(4) Set the options in the dialog box.

(5) Specify the end point.

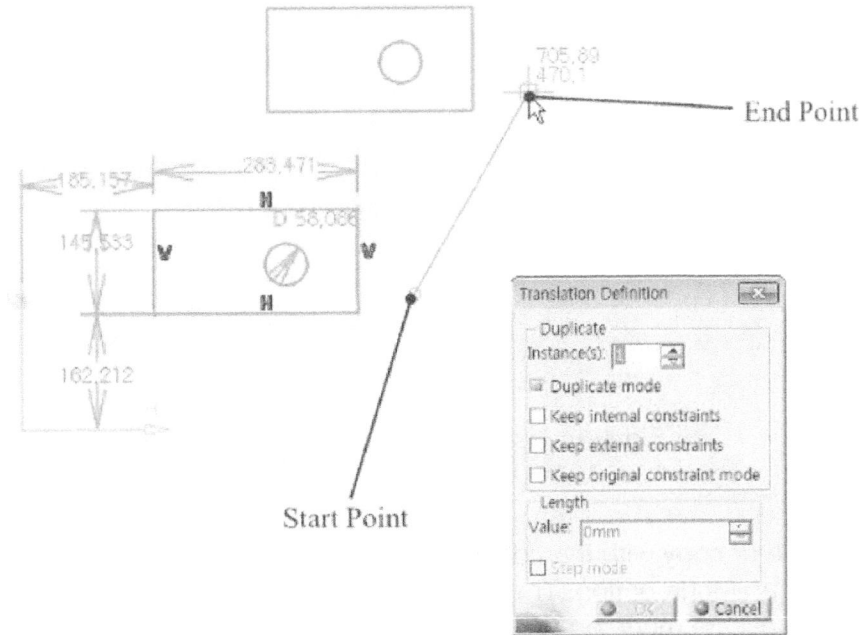

Fig 4-13 Using the Translate Command

(Note) Selecting Elements

- It is recommended to select the elements before clicking the Translate icon. You can use the Ctrl key to select several elements at once. If you press the Translate icon first, you cannot use the Ctrl key to select elements one by one but use the selection window.

5.2.4 Rotate

Use the Rotate command in the Transformation toolbar to rotate or copy the sketch elements.

Procedure

(1) Select the sketch elements to rotate or copy.

(2) Click the Rotate icon in the Transformation toolbar.

(3) Set the options in the dialog box.

(4) Specify the center of rotation.

(5) Specify the start point of the rotation angle.

(6) Specify the end point of the rotation angle.

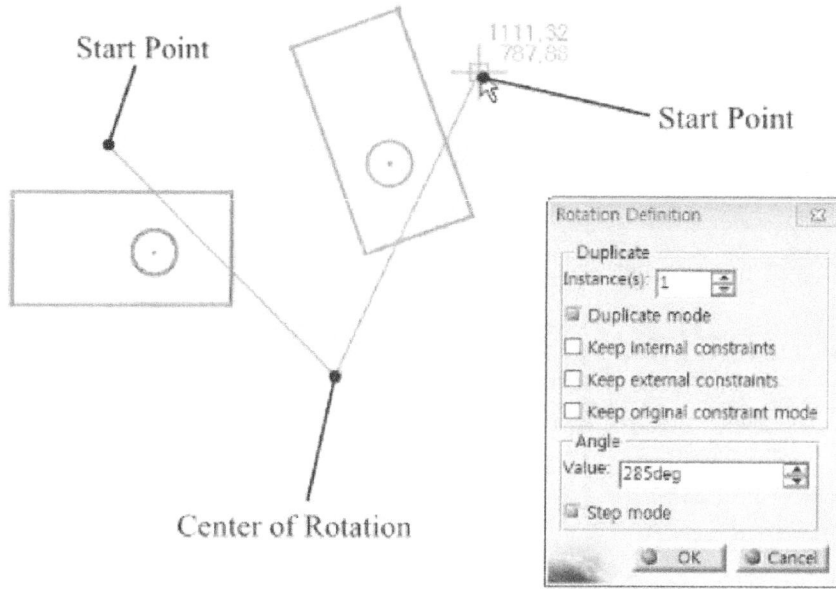

Fig 4-14 Using the Rotate Command

(Note) Option

1. You can rot.at e or copy with the constraints maintained.
2. Turn on the Snap Mode option. The rotation angle is snapped at 5° intervals.
3. Turn on the Duplicate mode option. You can specify the number of instances to be copied.

5.2.5 Scale

Using the Scale command in the Transformation toolbar, you can magnify or reduce the size of the sketch elements.

Procedure

(1) Select the sketch elements to magnify or reduce.

(2) Click the Scale icon in the Transformation toolbar.

(3) Set the options in the dialog box.

(4) Specify the base point.

(5) Specify the end point or input the scale value.

96

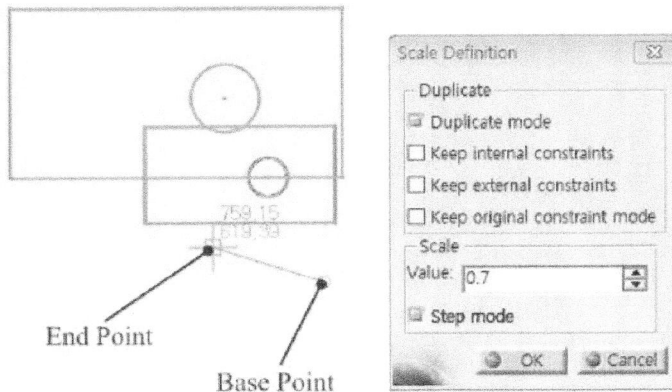

Fig 4-15 using the Scale Command

5.2.6 Offset

Using the Offset command in the Transformation toolbar, you can offset sketch curves along one direct ion or both directions.

Procedure

(1) Click the Offset icon in the Transformation toolbar.

(2) Choose a Propagation option in the Sketch tools toolbar.

(3) Select the sketch curves.

(4) Set the direction of offset.

(5) input the amount of offset. (You can press the Tab key to move to the input box or you can specify a point on the screen.)

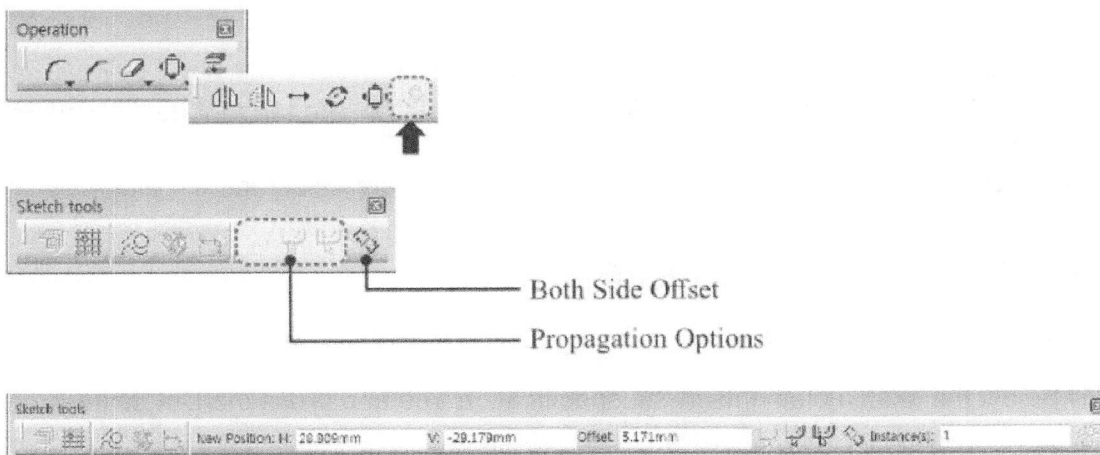

Fig 4-16 Offset icon and Options

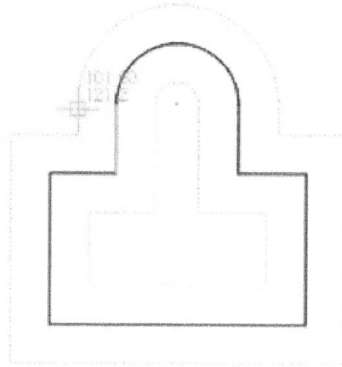

Fig 4-17 Both Side Offset

(Note) Propagation Options

The Propagation option defines the se lection method in the case where curves are connected. Fig 4-18 shows the result of each option when you select the connected sketch at the location specified by (A) with the respective propagation option.

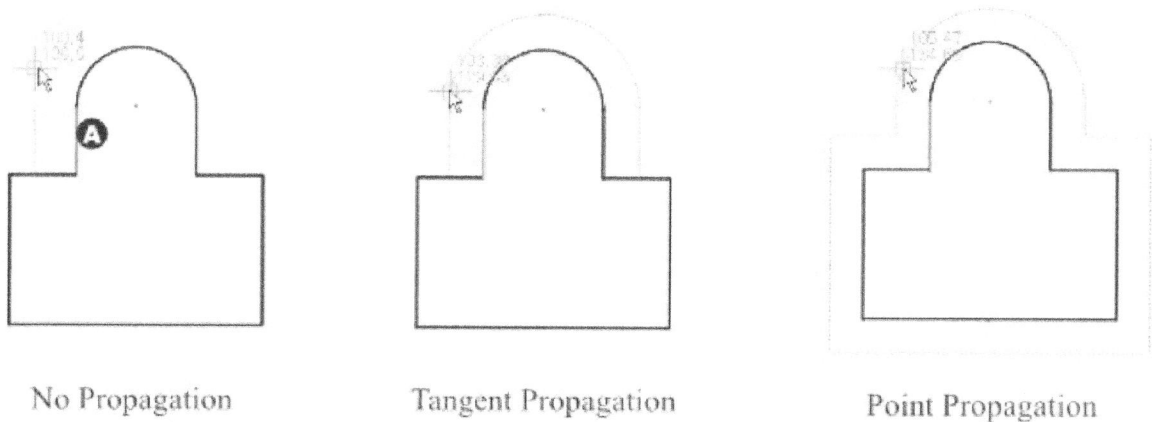

No Propagation   Tangent Propagation   Point Propagation

Fig 4-18 Propagation Options

- **No Propagation:** Only the curve (A) is selected.
- **Tangent Propagation:** The curve (A) and the curves that are tangent continuous to (A) arc selected.
- **Point Propagation:** All the curves connected with (A) are selected.

5.3 DELETING 1 SKETCH ELEMENTS

You can delete sketch elements such as curves, points, constraints, etc.

(1) Select the sketch elements in the specification tree and press the Delete key.

(2) Select the sketch elements in the specification tree and press MB3 > Delete.

(Note) How to identify the related sketch elements

(1) Move the mouse cursor to a specific constraint. The related sketch elements are highlighted as shown in Fig 4-19 (a).

(2) Pres MB3 (right click) on a specific constraint in the Spec Tree or on a symbol in the graphic area and choose the Parent/Children option in the pop-up men u. You can identify the related sketch elements in the Parent and Children dialog box as shown in Fig 4-19 (b). If you select the elements in the dialog box, they are highlighted in the graphic area.

The identification method is effective only in the Sketcher workbench.

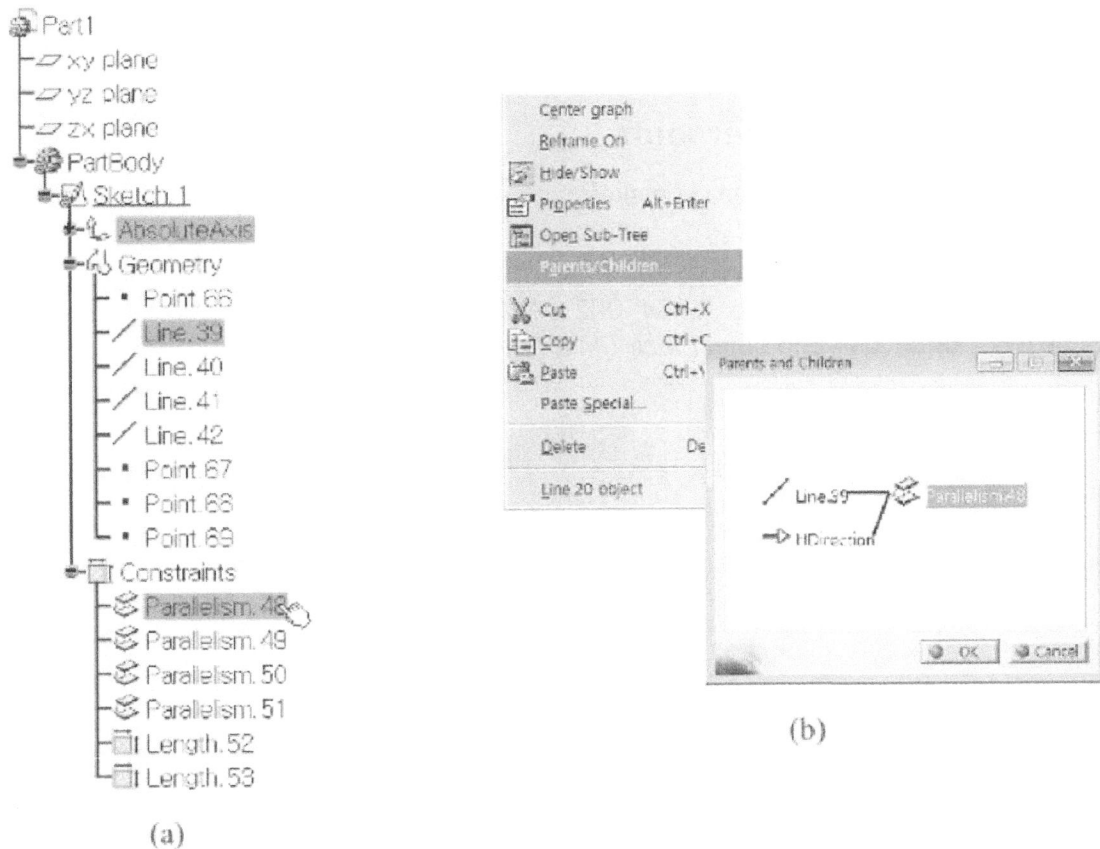

Fig 4-19 Identifying the Related Elements

5.4 CREATING SKETCH ELEMENTS FROM 3D GEOMETRY

You can create points or curves on a sketch plane from existing 30 geometries such as vertex, edge or face.

(1) Project 30 Element: Projects edges or vertices on a sketch plane.

(2) Intersect 30 Elements: Creates sketch elements by intersecting the current sketch plane and the 3 D geometry. If the plane is intersected with a face, a line is generated. If the plane is intersected with an edge, a point is generated.

(3) Project 3D Silhouette Edges: Projects the silhouette edges of the 3D geometry on the sketch plane.

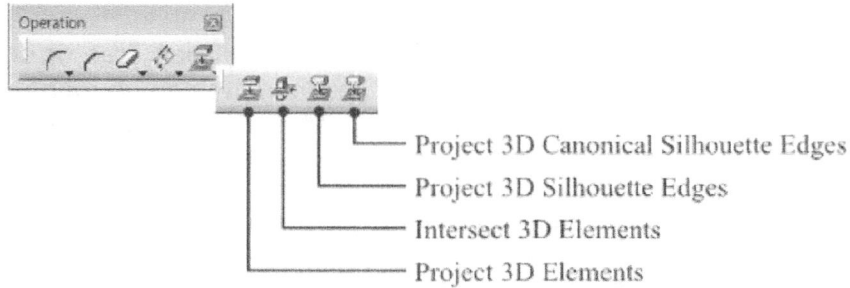

Project 3D Canonical Silhouette Edges
Project 3D Silhouette Edges
Intersect 3D Elements
Project 3D Elements

Fig 4-20 3D Geometry Tools

Exercise 15: Project 3D Elements

In this exercise, we will project edges on a sketch plane to create a 3D geometry.

Project and Pad

1. Open the file for the exercise. (ch04_002.CATPart)
2. Click the Sketch icon and select face (A) as the sketch plane.

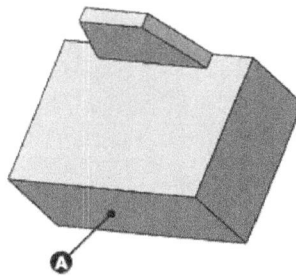

Fig 4-21 Sketch Plane

3. Rotate the model view as shown in Fig 4-22.
4. Click the Project 30 Elements icon in the Operation toolbar.

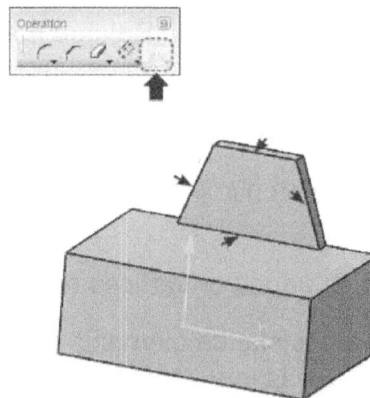

Fig 4-22 Edges to Project

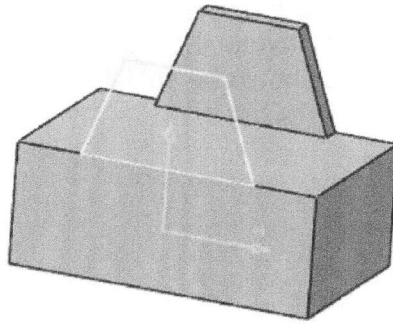

Fig 4-23 Projected Curves

5. Select the four edges specified in Fig 4-22. The curves are projected on the sketch plane in yellow.
6. Exit the Sketcher workbench.

(Note) Yellow Curve?

The yellow-colored curves mean that they were created from a 3D geometry with a link. If you modify the source geometry parametrically, the curves also change.

(Note) Aligning to Sketch Plane

- You may rotate the 3D model while you are sketching. You can return to the sketch view by pressing the Normal View button in the View toolbar. If you press this button one more time, the sketch plane is revered.

- Click the Pad icon.
- Enter 10mm as the length of the First Limit and press OK.

Modifying the Source

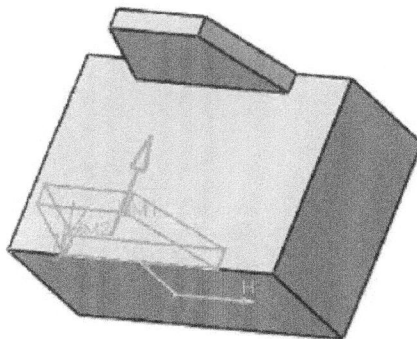

Fig 4-24 Pad

101

1. Expand the Spec Tree as shown in Fig 4-25.
2. Double click the second sketch to invoke the Sketcher workbench.
3. Modify the sketch dimensions as shown in Fig 4-26.

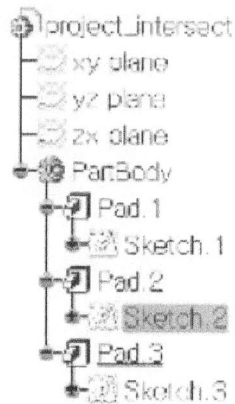

Fig 4-25 Sketch to modify

4. Exit the Sketcher workbench. The projected sketch changes as shown in Fig 4-27.

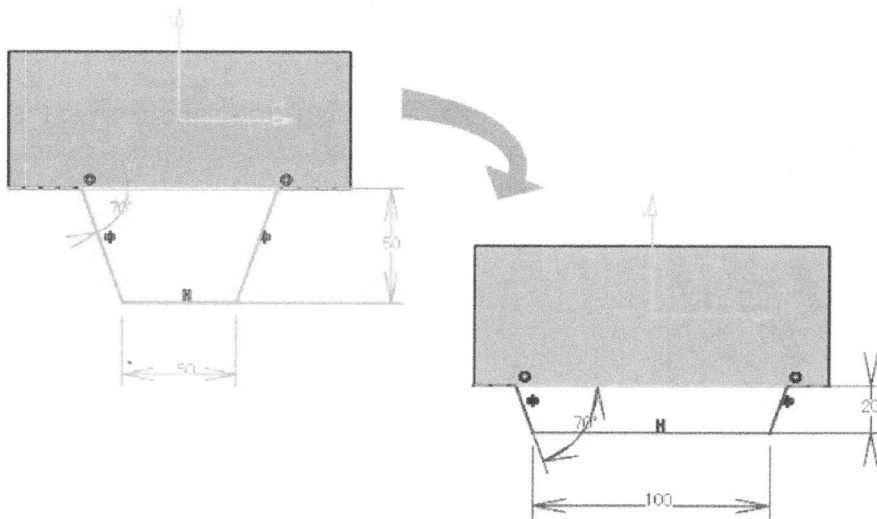

Fig 4- 26 Modifying the Source Sketch

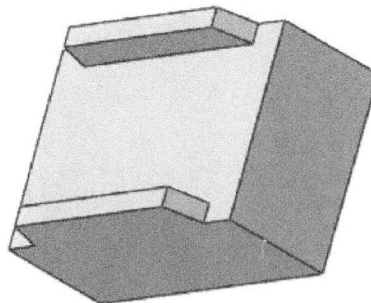

Fig 4-27 Updated model

(Note) projected Element

The elements created by the link with the 3D geometry are registered in the Spec Tree as shown below.

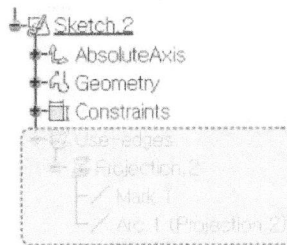

Exercise 16: Intersect 3D Elements

In this exercise, we will intersect a face with the sketch plane and Pad the sketch to create a rib.

1. Open the given part file. (ch04_003.CATPart)
2. Place the mouse curser in the yz plane in the Spec Tree and press MB3 > Hide/Show.

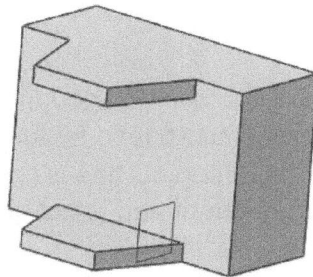

Fig 4-28 Given Part

3. Select the yz plane.
4. Click the Sketch icon.
5. Rotate the model as shown in Fig 4-29.
6. Click the Intersect3D Elements icon in the Operation toolbar.
7. Select the two faces ((A) and (B)) consecutively as shown in Fig 4-29. Two yellow curves are generated.

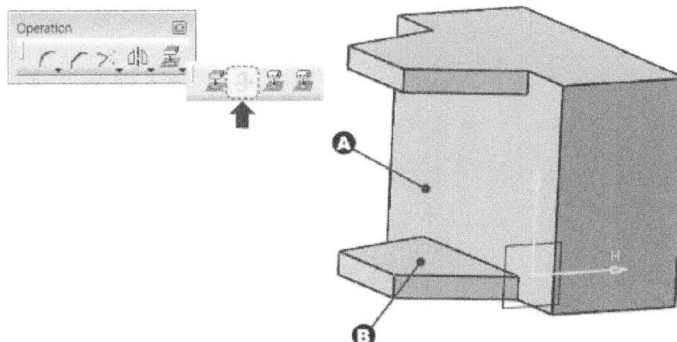

Fig 4-29 Intersect

103

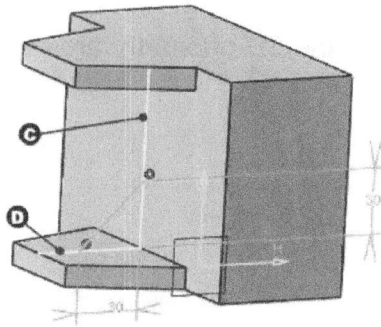

Fig 4-30 Sketch

8. Create an additional line as shown in Fig 4-30 and is o-constrain it.

Trim

Now, let's trim out the unnecessary portion of the intersect line.

1. Click the Quick Trim icon in the Operation toolbar.
2. Select the portion (C) and (D) as shown in Fig 4-31.

(Note) Trim of Linked Curve

- The trimmed-out portion of the curve is converted into a construction element which is not used in defining the profile of the sketch-based features.
- Note that the selected portion of the intersect line is converted lo a da shed li ne. The dashed line is considered a construction element and is not seen outside of the Sketch workbench.
3. Exit the Sketcher workbench.

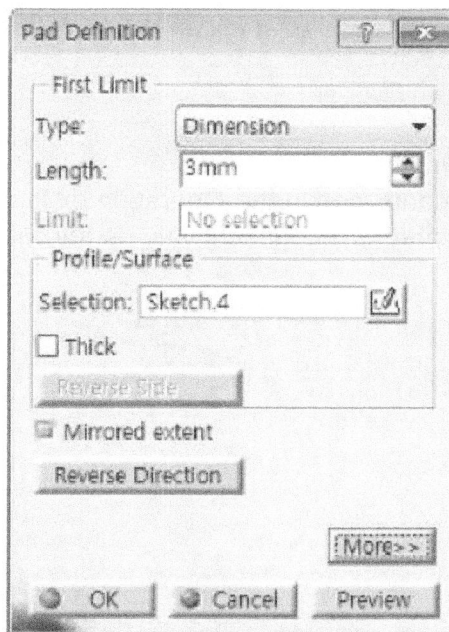

Fig 4- 31 Pad Definition Dialog Box

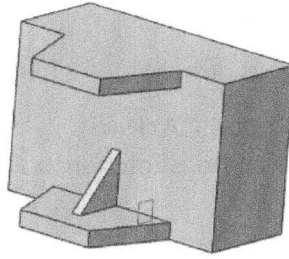

Fig 4-32 Final Model

Pad

While the sketch is selected, click the Pad icon in the Sketch-Based Features toolbar.

Set the options of Pad as shown in Fig 4-31. Enter 3mm as the length of the First Limit and check the Mirrored extent option.

Press OK in the dialog box. A rib feature is created as shown in Fig 4-32.

5.5 POSITIONED SKETCH

Using the Positioned Sketch command, you can specify the H, V direction and the Origin of the sketch plane. Fig 4-33 shows the Sketch Positioning dialog box.

- **Type:** Choose Positioned in the Type dropdown list and select a sketch plane as the Reference. The Origin and Orientation opt ions are activated. Choosing Sliding is the same as pressing the Sketch button in the Part Design workbench.
- **Reference:** Select a planar face as the sketch plane.
- **Origin:** Specify the Origin of the sketch plane. The default type is Implicit which means that the origin is determined by the software according to the shape of the sketch plane.
- **Orientation:** Define the direction of the base sketch axis, i.e., the H and V axes.
- **Reverse H:** Reverse the direction of the H axis.
- **Reverse V:** Rever c the direction of the V axis.
- **Swap:** Swap the H and the V axes.

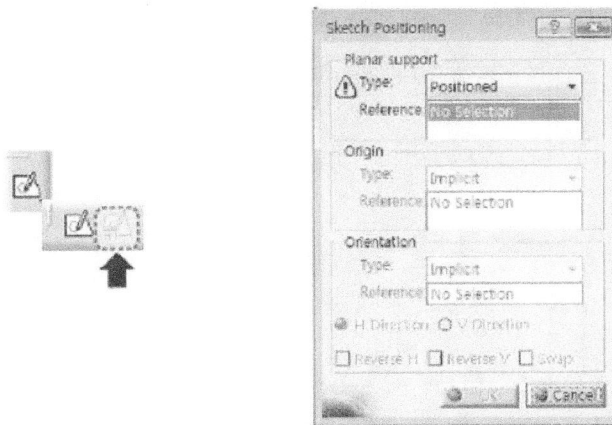

Fig 4-33 Positioned Sketch Icon and Dialog Box

Exercise 17: Positioned Sketch

Let' s learn how to re-define the origin and direction of a sketch plane.

1. Open the given part file. (ch104 _004.CATPart)
2. Click the Positioned Sketch icon in the Sketcher toolbar.
3. Select the face (1) shown in Fig 4-34.

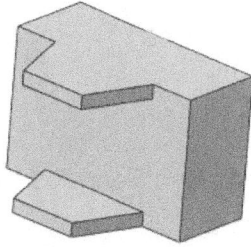

Fig 4-35 Sketch Axis and Origin

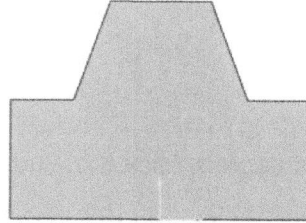

Fig 4-36 Aligned Sketch Plane

4. Select the Middle point in the Origin dropdown list in the Sketch Positioning dialog box.
5. Select the edge (2) in Fig 4-34.
6. Check the Reverse H and Reverse V option so that the direction appears as shown in Fig 4-35.
7. Press the OK button in the dialog box. The sketch view is aligned as shown in Fig 4-36.

(Note) Reverse the Sketch View

- Click the Normal View icon in the View toolbar. The sketch normal view is reversed.

5.6 LINKING SKETCH DIMENSIONS

A sketch dimension can be linked with other sketch dimensions using a formula.

Looking at the sketch in Fig 4-37, the dimension named Offset.6 is linked to Offsct.8. Therefore, if you modify the value of Offset.8, the value of Offset.6 is also changed. The symbol f(x) marked behind Offset.6 means that the dimension is linked with another dimension.

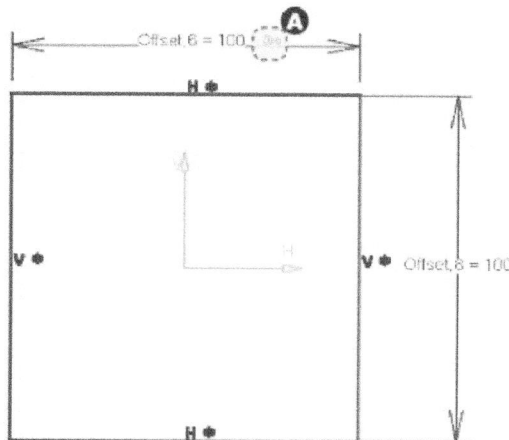

Fig 4-37 Linking Dimensions

(Note) Displaying the Name of the Dimension

Press MB3 (right click) on the sketch dimension and select the Name/Value Display option from the pop-up menu specified by (B) in Fig 4-38.

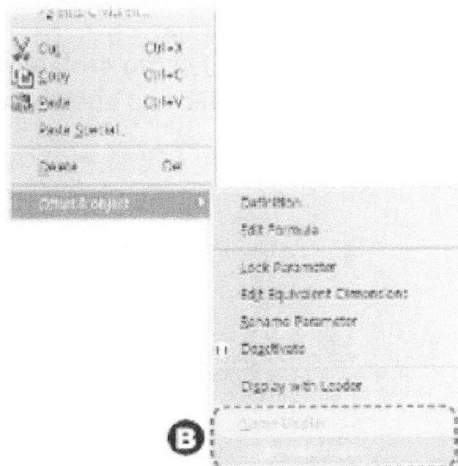

Fig 4-38 Dimension Display Option

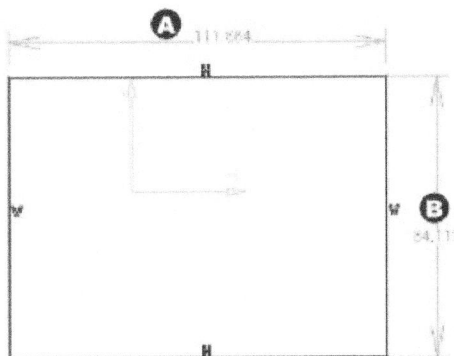

Fig 4-39 Rectangle

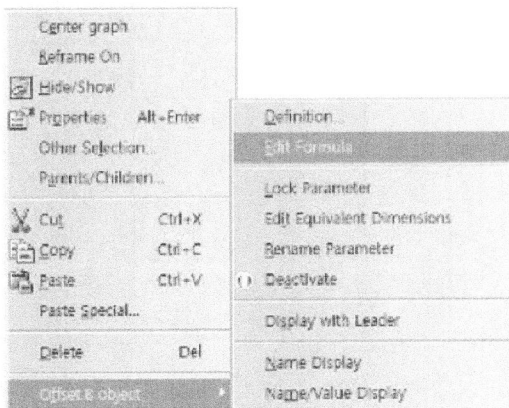

Fig 4-40 Pop-up Menu

1. Create a new part file and define a sketch on the xy plane.
2. Create a rectangle as shown in Fig 4-39 and apply dimensions. Note that the symmetric constraint should not be applied.
3. If you have double clicked the Constraint button, release it. The Select button should be activated.
4. Press MB3 (right click) on the dimension (A) in Fig 4-39 and select Edit Formula in the pop-up menu shown in Fig 4-40. He Formula Editor as shown in Fig 4-41 appears.

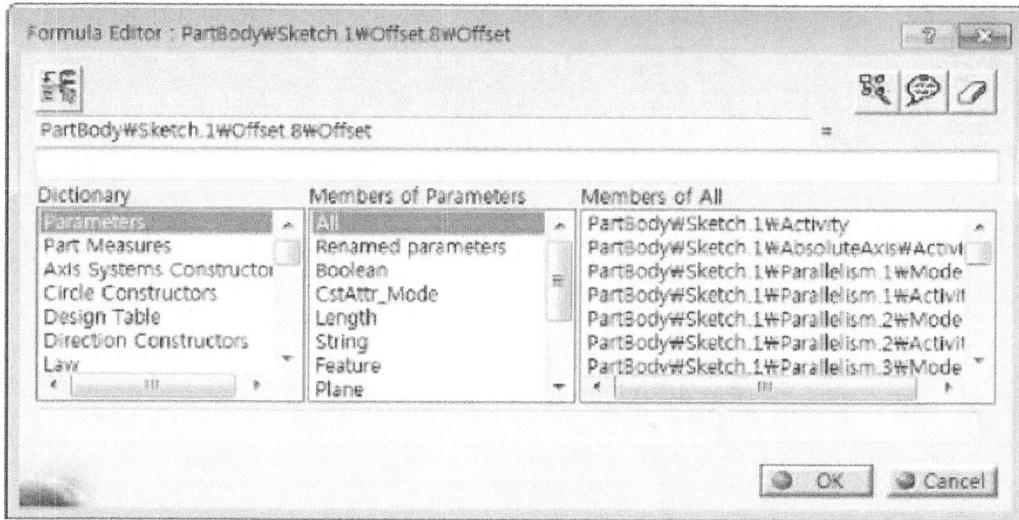

Fig 4-40 The Formula Editor

5. Select the dimension (B) shown in Fig 4-39.
6. Press OK in the dialog box. The two dimensions are linked together. If you modify the value of dimension (B) in Fig 4-42 as 100, dimension (A) is also changed. The sketch is not yet iso- constrained because we did not apply a symmetry constraint. We will attain symmetry by applying a half dimension.

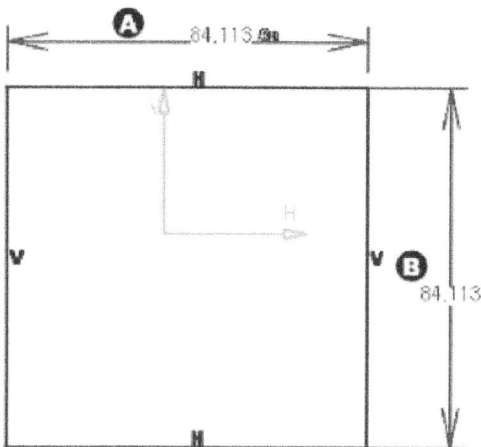

Fig 4-42 Linking Dimensions   Fig 4-43 Linking a Half Dimension

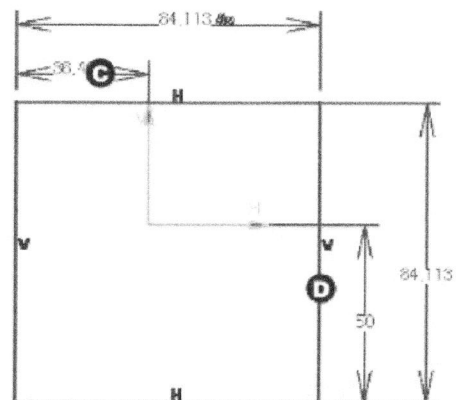

7. Apply dimensions0 and8 between the side and base axes. The location of the rectangle has been defined and the sketch is now iso-constrained.
8. Activate the Select button and press MB3 on dimension0 and select Length.* object > Edit Formula from the pop-up menu . The Formula Editor shown in Fig 4-44 appears.
9. Select dimension O in Fig 4-42 and type /2 behind the name of the variable appearing in the (E) input area. Dimension (C) is linked to a half of dimension (A).

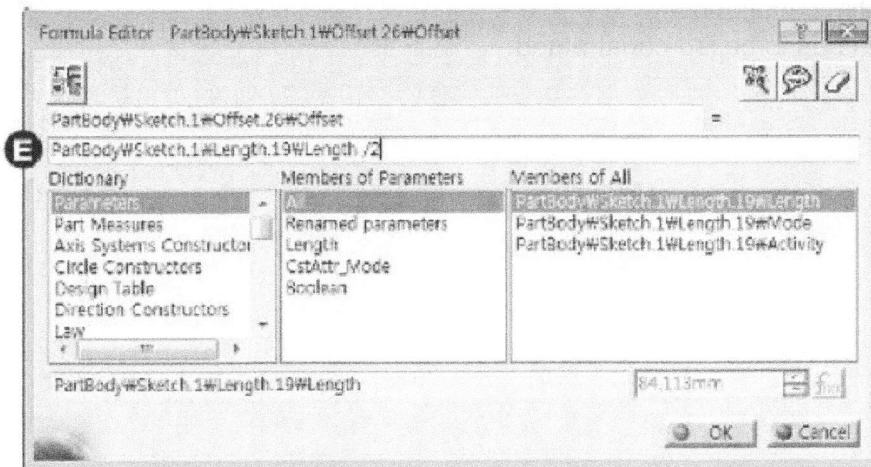

Fig 4-44 Formula Editor

Link dimension (D) to one half of dimension (B). The final sketch is as shown in Fig 4-45. If you modify the dimension of (B) to 200, all Jinked dimensions are changed, and the origin of the sketch is still located at the center of the square.

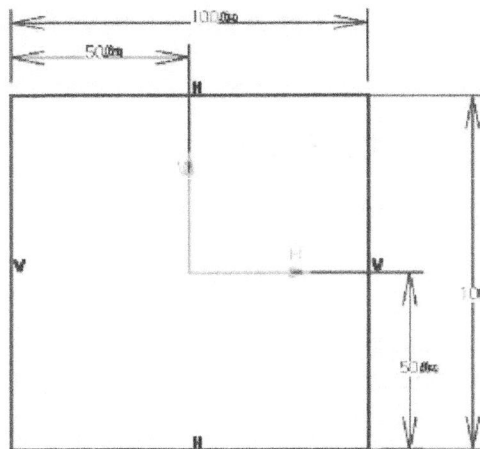

Fig 4-45 Final Sketch

(Note) Modifying the Name of a Dimension

- Place the mouse cursor on the dimension, right click and choose Properties. You can modify the Feature and Name in the Feature Properties tab. Or you can modify   the name of a din1ension by double clicking the dimension and pressing the More button in the Constraint Definition dialog box.

Exercise: Four Hole Plate (ch04_006.CAT Part)

Create a sketch as shown in Fig 4-46 and pad it by 20mm.

Requirements

1. Locate the sketch origin as specified.
2. Apply a Fillet command.
3. The sketch has to be iso-constrained.

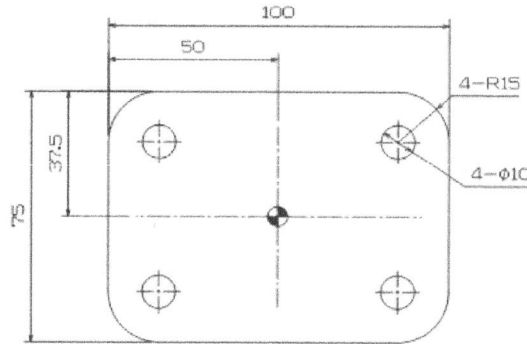

Fig 4- 46 Four Hole Plate

(Note) Do not apply Fix constraint.

- The Fix constraint among the geometric al constraints are not used to define the shape of the sketch curves. This constraint is used to fix sketch objects that are imported from another CAD system. Sometimes you may fix some sketch elements temporarily to evaluate the status of constraint of other sketch elements. You have to delete the Fix constraint after its temporary use.

Exercise 18: Arm (ch04_007.CATPart)

Create a sketch as shown in Fig 4-47 and pad it by 20mm.

Requirements

1. Locate the sketch origin as specified.
2. The sketch has to be iso-constrained.

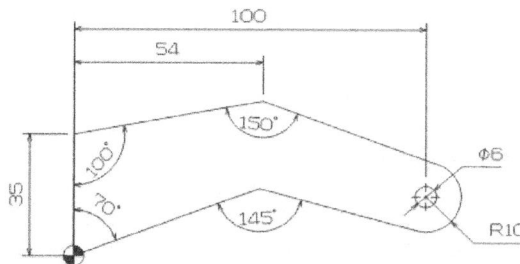

Fig 4-47 Arm

(Note) Applying Constraints in Combination

- Two types of constraints are combined to fully define the shape and size of sketch elements. If the geometry changes abruptly by applying a constraint, you will have to undo the constraint and try another constraint. You can drag the sketch curves or points near to the desired location.

Exercise 19: Sketch with Fillet (ch0 4_008.CATPart)

Create a sketch as shown in Fig 4-48 and pad it by 20mm.

Requirements

1. Locate the sketch origin at the bottom center.
2. The sketch has to be iso-constrained.

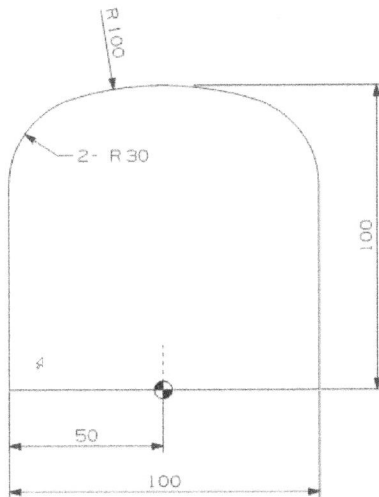

Fig 4-48 A Sketch with Fillet

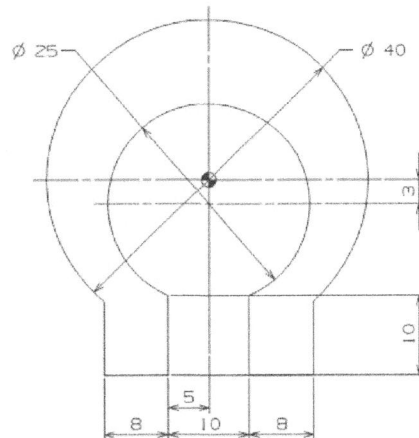

Fig 4-49 Flat Pin

Create the sketch sho.vn in Fig 4-49 and pad it by 20mm.

Requirements

1. Locate the sketch origin as specified.
2. The sketch has to be iso -constrained.

Exercise 20: Creating Symmetric Sketch – 2 (ch04_010.CATPart)

Create the sketch shown in Fig 4-50 and pad it by 20mm.

Requirements

1. Locate the sketch origin as specified.
2. The sketch has to be iso-constrained .

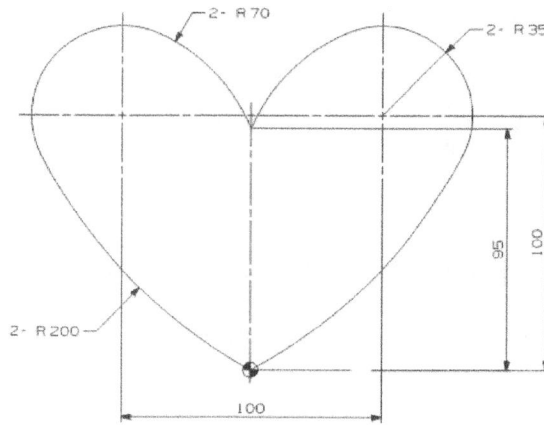

Fig 4-50 Symmetric Sketch

Exercise 21: Link – 1 (ch04 _011.CATPart)

Create a sketch as shown in Fig 4-51 and pad it by 20mm.

Requirements

1. Locate the sketch origin as specified.
2. The sketch has to be iso-constrained.

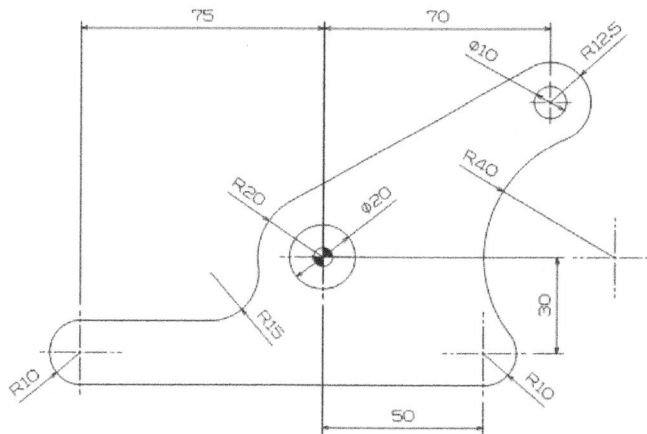

Fig 4-51 Link 1

Exercise 22: Flange Cover (ch04_012.CATPart)

Create a sketch as shown in Fig 4-52 and pad it by 20mm.

Requirements

1. Locate the sketch origin as specified.
2. The ketch has to be iso -constrained.

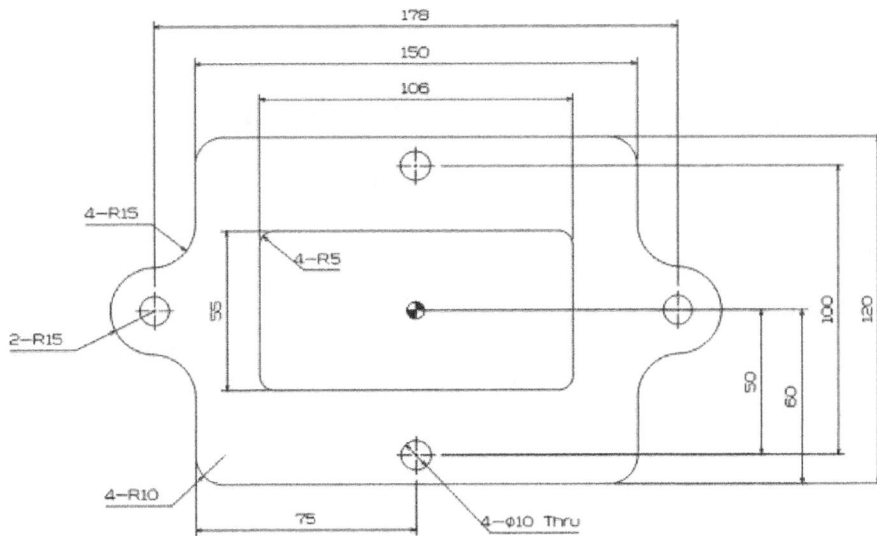

Fig 4 - 52 Flange Cover

Exercise 23: Link – 2 (ch04_013.CATPart)

Create a sketch as shown in Fig 4-53 and pad it by 20mm.

Requirements

1. Locate the sketch origin as specified.
2. The sketch has to be iso -constrained.

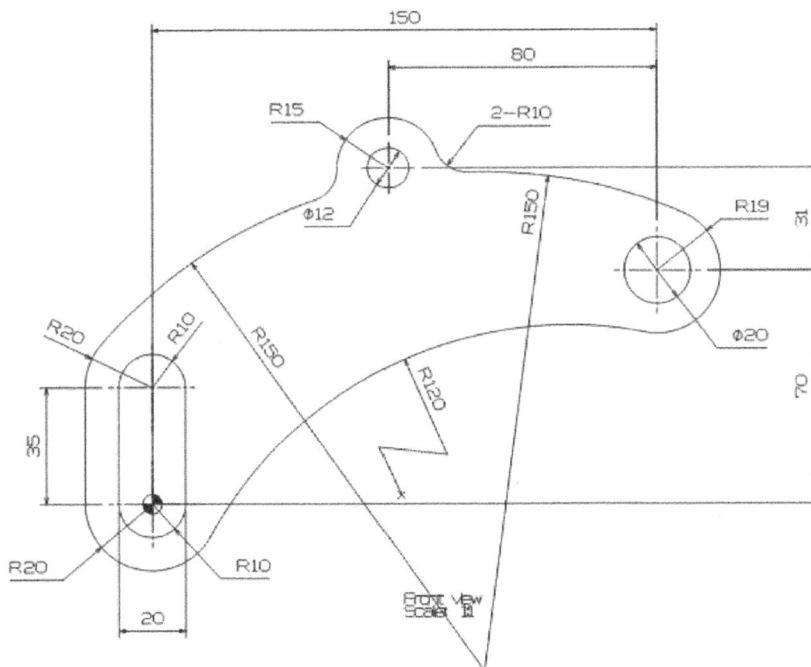

Fig 4-53 Link 2

Exercise 24: Spanner Head (ch0 4_O1 4.CAT Part)

Create a sketch as shown in fig 4-54 and pad it by 20mm.

Requirements

1. Locate the sketch origin as specified.
2. Link the two dimensions designated by O with a formula so that they are always the same.
3. The end points of R28 arc and R45 arc meet at the point specified by 0.
4. The sketch has to be iso-constrained.

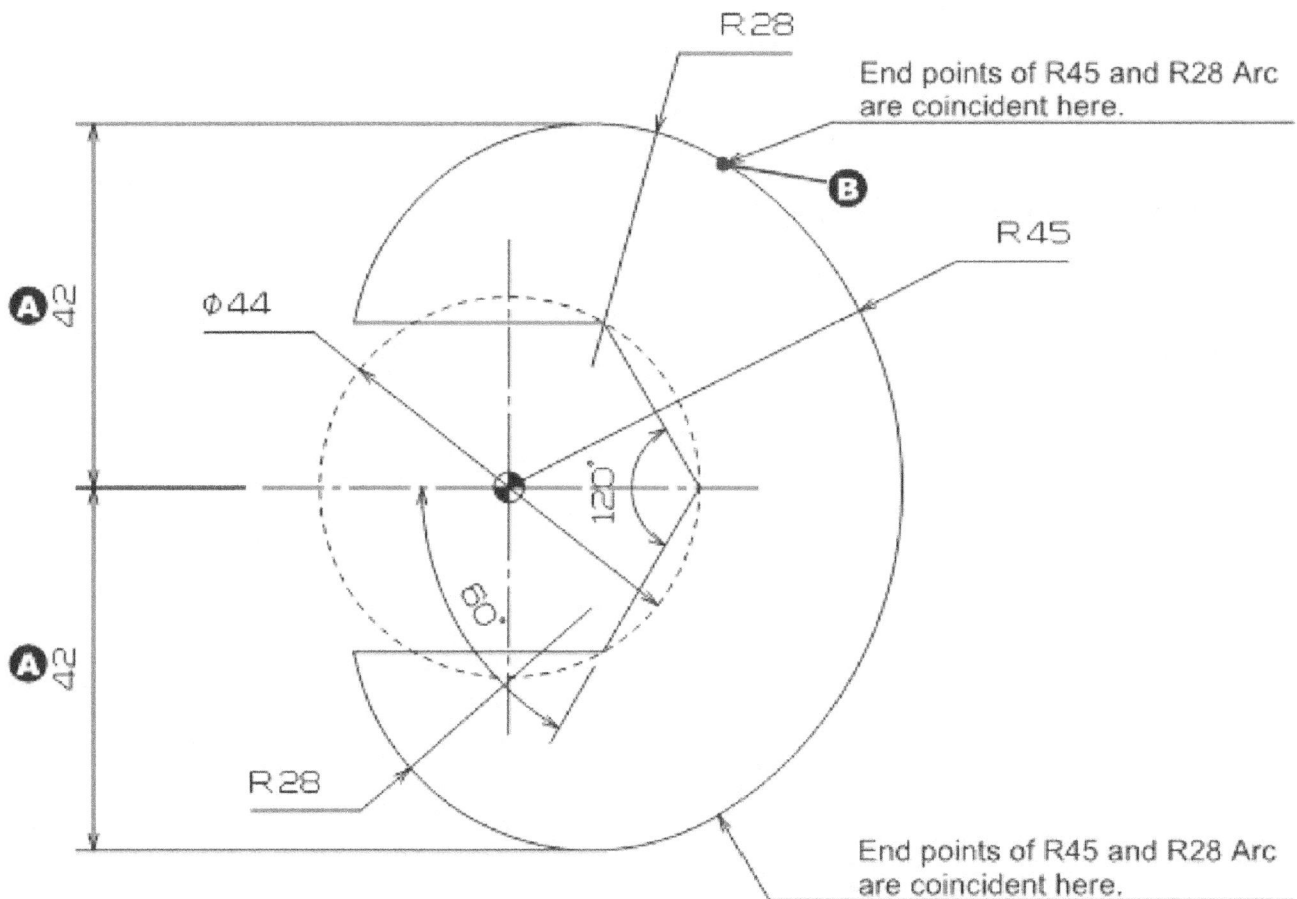

Fig 4-54 Spanner Head

Fig 4-54 Spanner Head

CHAPTER 6: CRAFTING SOLIDS: PAD, POCKET, SHAFT, GROOVE AND HOLD

5.1 PAD

Using the Pad command in the Sketch -Based Features toolbar, you can extrude a profile or surface to create a 3D geometry. the 3D geometry created with the Pad command is added to the existing geometry.

Procedure

1. Click the Pad icon in the Sketch-Based Features toolbar.
2. Select the profile or surface. If you select a face or surface, you have to specify the direction.
3. Define the First Limit option.
4. Set other options in the Pad Definition dialog box and press OK.

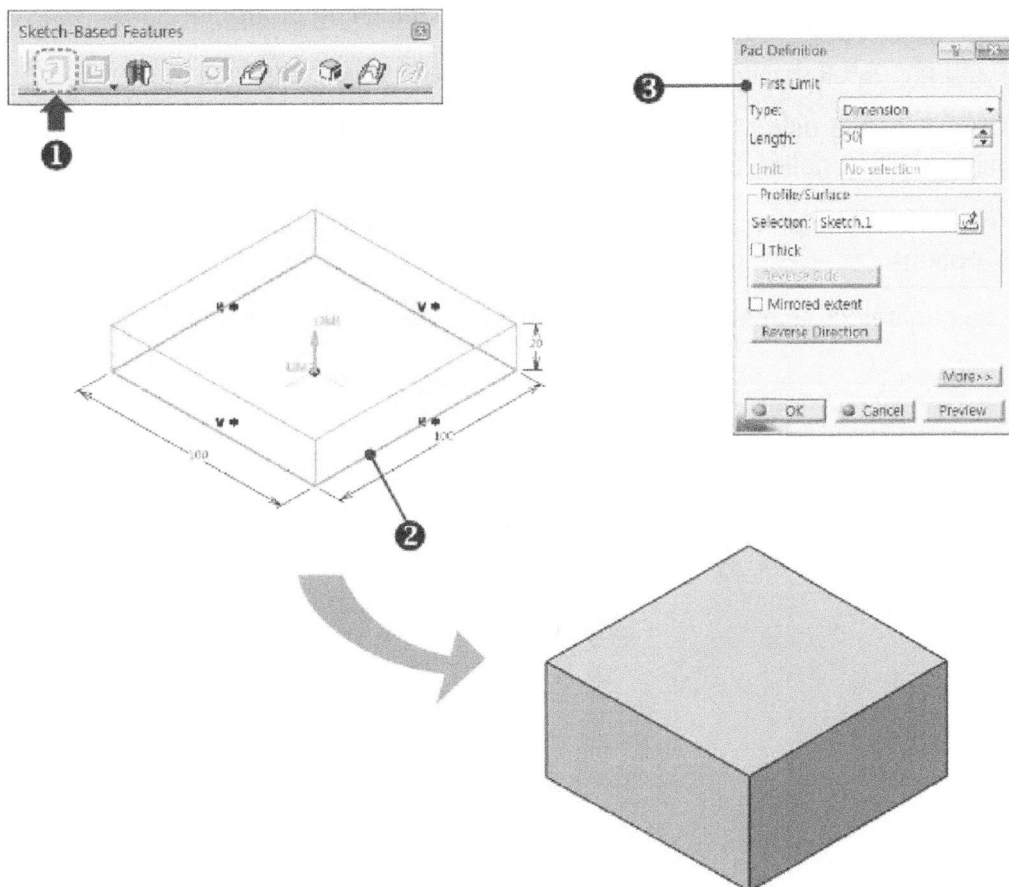

Fig 5-1 Pad Definition Dialog Box

115

5.2 PROFILE

Among the sketch curves created in a single sketch feature as shown in Fig 5-2, you can create a Pad feature as shown in Fig 5-3 by extruding the rectangle. The rectangle con- tributes to constructing the Pad feature and is called a profile.

You can use either a portion of the sketch or all of the sketch curves as the profile provided that the curves meet the requirements.

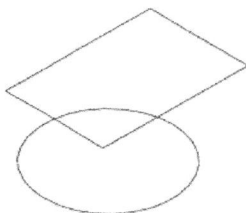

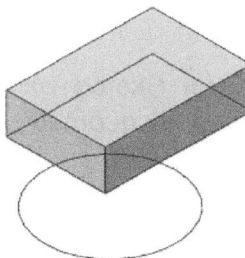

Fig 5-2 Sketch   Fig 5-3 Pad Feature

5.2.1 Characteristics of a Profile

When you define a profile, you have to bear in mind the following characteristics.

(1) If you choose a closed profile, you can create a solid body.

(2) When you are using an open profile as the profile of the first Pad feature, you have to choose the Thick option to create a. solid body.

(3) You cannot use an intersecting profile for a single Pad feature unless you are using the Thick option.

(4) You can select as many profile as you want unless they are intersecting.

Fig 5- 4 Open Profile

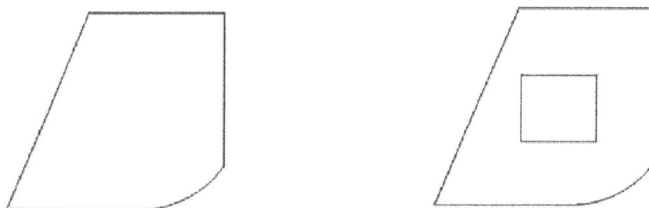

Fig 5-5 Closed Profile

116

Fig 5-6 Intersecting Profile

(Note) What is a Solid Body?

- There are two types of bodies in CATIA V5. A solid body is a geometry that has volume. If a geometry is closed by sur faces, you can define the material inside the surface provided that the geometry is a so lid body. Note that geometry close d by surfaces cannot always constitute a so lid body.
- The other type of body is a sheet body which does not have volume. A geometry closed by surfaces but not filled with material is called a sheet body. Modeling with a sheet body is outside of the scope of this textbook.

Exercise 25: Selecting a Portion of a Sketch as the Profile (ch05_001.prt)

1. Create a sketch as shown io Fig 5-7. You may skip iso-constraining.
2. Exit the Sketcher.

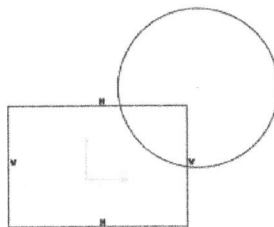

Fig 5-7 Sketch

3. Deselect the sketch and display the isometric view.
4. Click the Pad icon in the Sketch• Based Features toolbar.
5. Press MB3 (right click) on the Selection field ((A) in Fig 5-8) in the Pad Definition dialog box.

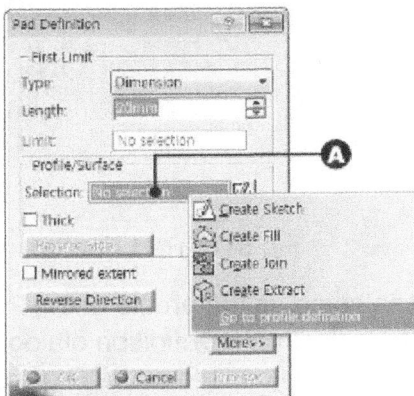

Fig 5-8 Defining Profile

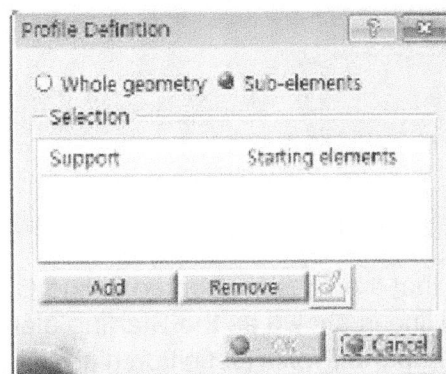

Fig 5-9 Profile Definition Dialog Box

117

6. Choose Go to profile definition in the pop-up menu. The Profile Definition dialog box as shown in fig 5-9 appears.
7. Select the Sub-elements option.

(Note) Deselecting

- You can deselect features by clicking in an empty part of the graphic area with MB1 (left click) or by pressing the ESC key twice.

8. Select the line (B) as shown in Fig 5-10.

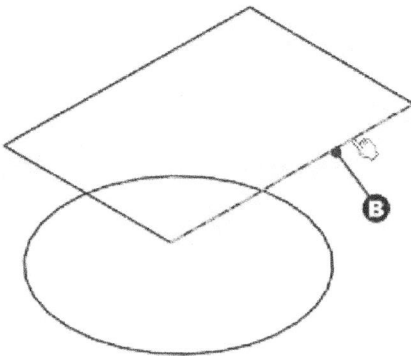

Fig 5- 10 Selecting the Starting Element

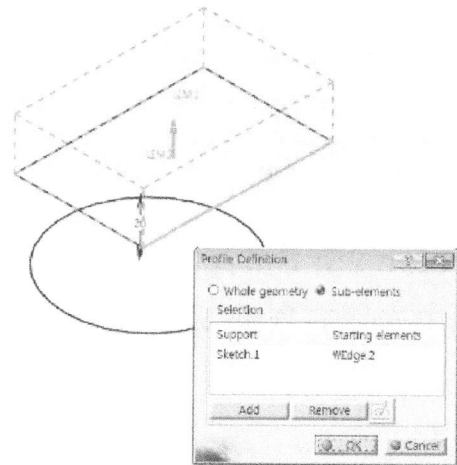

Fig 5-11 Preview

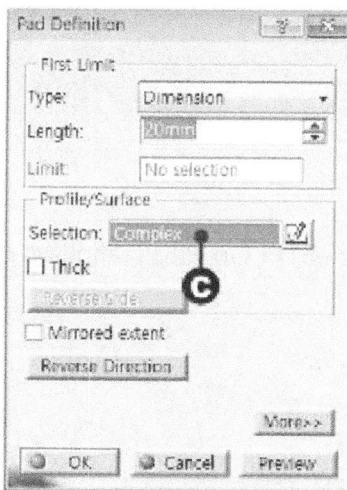

Fig 5- 12 Profile Defined

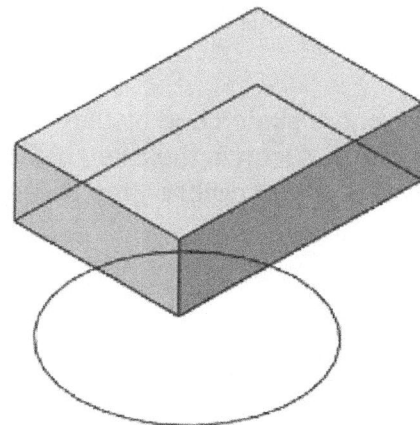

Fig 5-13 Pad Feature

9. Confirm that the lines connected to line O are selected as the profile of the Pad feature. The selected line is shown as the Starting element in the Profile Definition dialog box.
10. Press OK in the Profile Definition dialog box. The Selection field of the Profile/Surface option changes as designated by8 in Fig 5-12.
11. Press OK in the Pad Definition dialog box. Fig 5-13 shows the resultant Pad feature.

5.2.2 Understanding Multiple Loops

You can create a pad feature by choosing several closed loops that do not intersect each other. If there is a clos e d loop within another closed loop, the internal area is created as an empty volume as shown in Fig 5-14. If the closed sections are separated from each other, each loop is created as multiple solid bodies as shown in Fig 5-15.

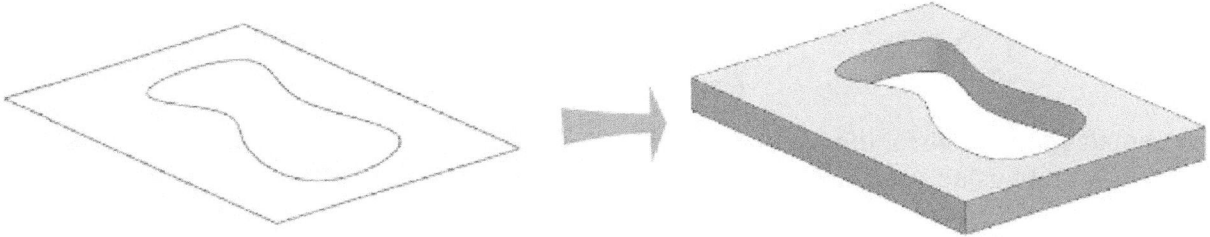

Fig 5-14 internal Loop

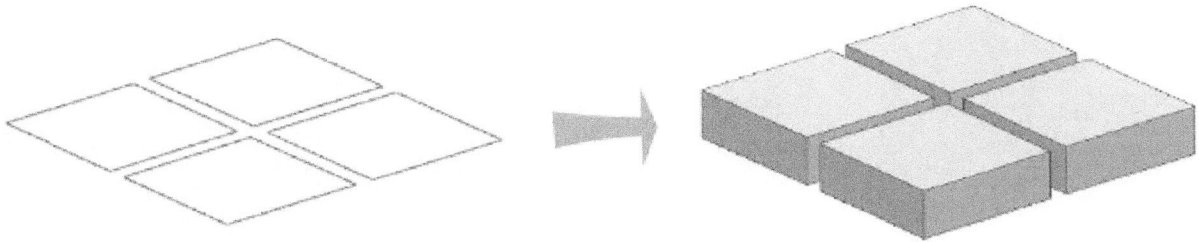

Fig 5-15 Separated Loops

5.2.3 Using an Open Profile as the First Pad Feature

If you select an open profile while you are creating the first Pad feature, an error message as shown in Fig 5-16 appears.

Press the Yes button in the message box. If you check the Thick option in the Pad Definition dialog box, the Thin Pad option is available on the right of the dialog box by pressing the More button and you can create the first solid feature using an open profile.

You can also use the Thick option to create a thin walled Pad feature with a closed profile.

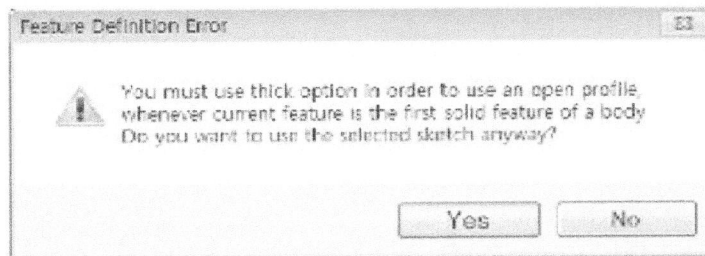

Fig 5-16 Error Message

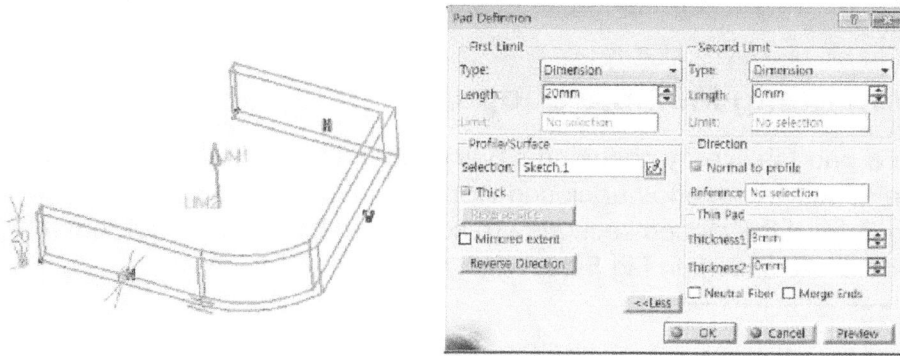

Fig 5-17 Thick Option

If you use an open profile for the second and later Pad features, you can add material to the existing solid body without using the Thick option. Note that you have to specify the side and direction.

Exercise 26: Pad with an Open Profile (ch05_002.CATPart)

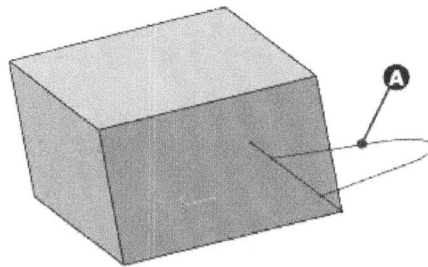

Fig 5-18 Given Pan

1. Open the given part file. (ch05 _002.CATPart)
2. Click the Pad icon in the Sketch- Based Features toolbar.
3. Invoke the Profile Definition dialog box as shown in Fig 5-19 and select the curve (A) specified in Fig 5-18.

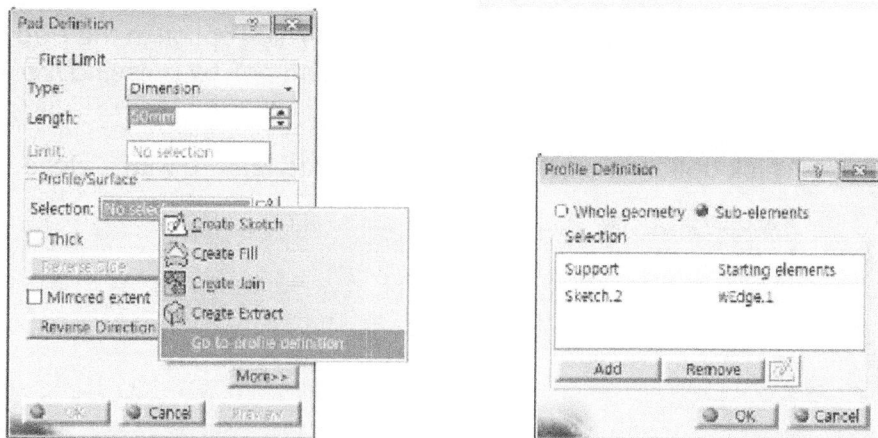

Fig 5-19 Profile Definition

120

4. A preview is shown as in Fig 5-20. The preview shows that an open profile has been selected.
5. Click the head of the arrow specified by (A) to reverse it.

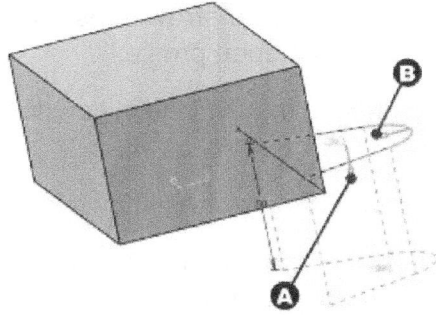

Fig 5- 20 Preview

6. Press the OK button in the Profile Definition dialog box.
7. Input the Length of the First Limit as 20 and press OK. The resultant model is shown in Fig 5-22.

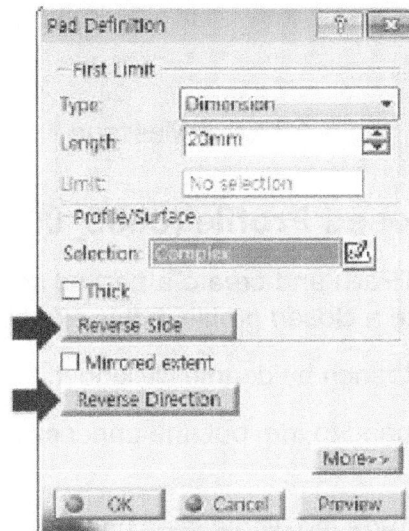

Fig 5- 21 Pad Definition Dialog Box

Fig 5-22 Pad Feature Created

121

5.2.4 Side and Direction Arrows

If you press the Reverse Side button in the Pad Definition dialog box, the direction of the arrow (B) in Fig 5-20 is reversed. If the direction of the side arrow does not point to the existing mate rial, you cannot create and add a pad feature with an open profile.

If you press the Reverse Direction button in the Pad Definition dialog box, the direction of the arrow (A) in Fig 5-20 is reversed.

In the following cases, you may encounter an error as shown in Fig 5-23.

1. The length of the first limit is higher than the exist in g geometry.
2. The side arrow ((B) in Fig 5-20) points outward.
3. The direction arrow ((A) in Fig 5-20) points downward.

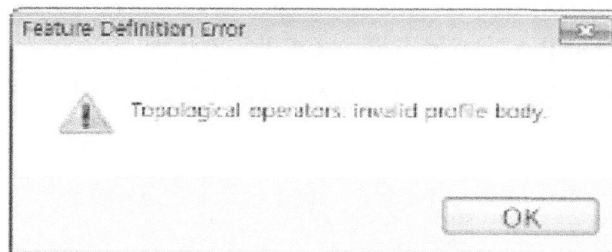

Fig 5- 23 Error Message

Exercise 27: Pad with a Closed Profile (ch05_003.CATPart)

Open the give n file (ch05_003.CATPart) and create a part as shown in Fig 5-22 according to the following procedure. You have to use a closed profile in this exercise.

(1) Invoke the Sketcher workbench by double clicking the second sketch.

(2) Use the Quick Trim command to trim out the unnecessary portions ((A) and (B) in Fig 5-24) of the projected curve.

(3) Exit the Sketcher and extrude the whole sketch with the Pad command.

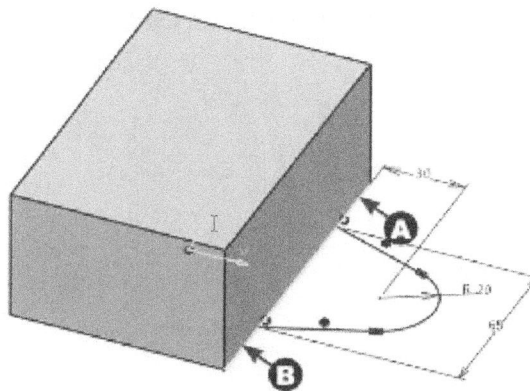

Fig 5-24 Curve to be Trimmed Out

122

5.2.5 Mirrored Extent

Using the Mirrored extent option in the Pad Definition dialog box, you can create a Pad feature along both sides.

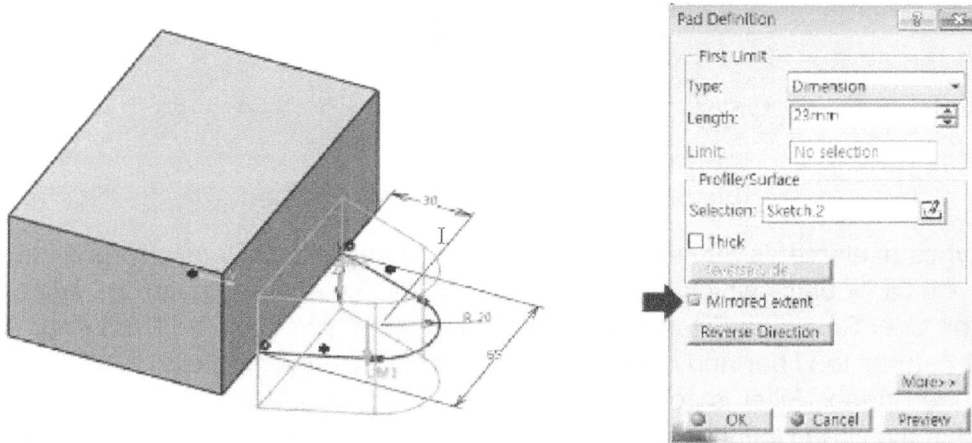

Fig 5- 25 1inored Extent Option

5.3 HIDE AND SHOW

The sketch feature may still be shown in the graphics window after creating a pad feature. You can hide the sketch feature by right clicking on the feature in the Spec Tree and choosing Hide/Show in the pop-up menu as shown in Fig 5-26. Hidden features can be shown by right clicking on the feature and choosing Hide/Show in the pop-up menu.

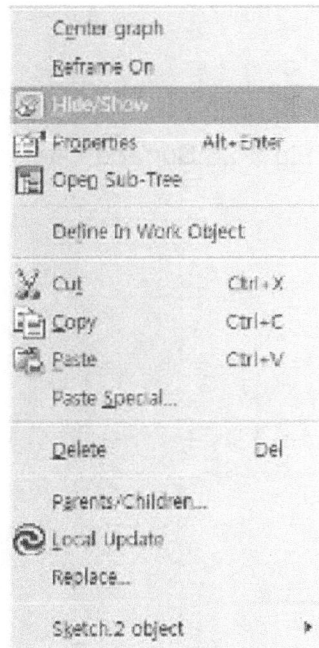

Fig 5 - 26 Hide/Show Option

5.4 USER SELECTION FILTER

When you select elements, you can filter types of elements in the User Selection Filter toolbar as shown in Fig 5-27.

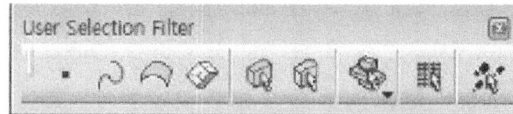

Fig 5-27 User Selection Filter Toolbar

Note that types of elements for select ion are confined automatically for a select ion step. This means that you can identify which type of objects you can select for the current selection step by looking at the User Selection Filter tool bar. For example, if you click the Draft Angle icon in the Dress-Up Features too l bar and cli ck the Face{s} to draft selection field in the Draft Definition dialog box, the Surface Filter is activated as shown in Fig 5-28. If you click the Pulling Direction selection field in the Draft Definition dialog box, the Curve Filter and Surface Filter are activated as shown in Fig 5-29.

Fig 5-28 Surface Filter

Fig 5-29 Curve Filter and Surface Filter

Exercise 28: Cre a ting a Solid Body

Create the solid model shown in Fig 5-30.

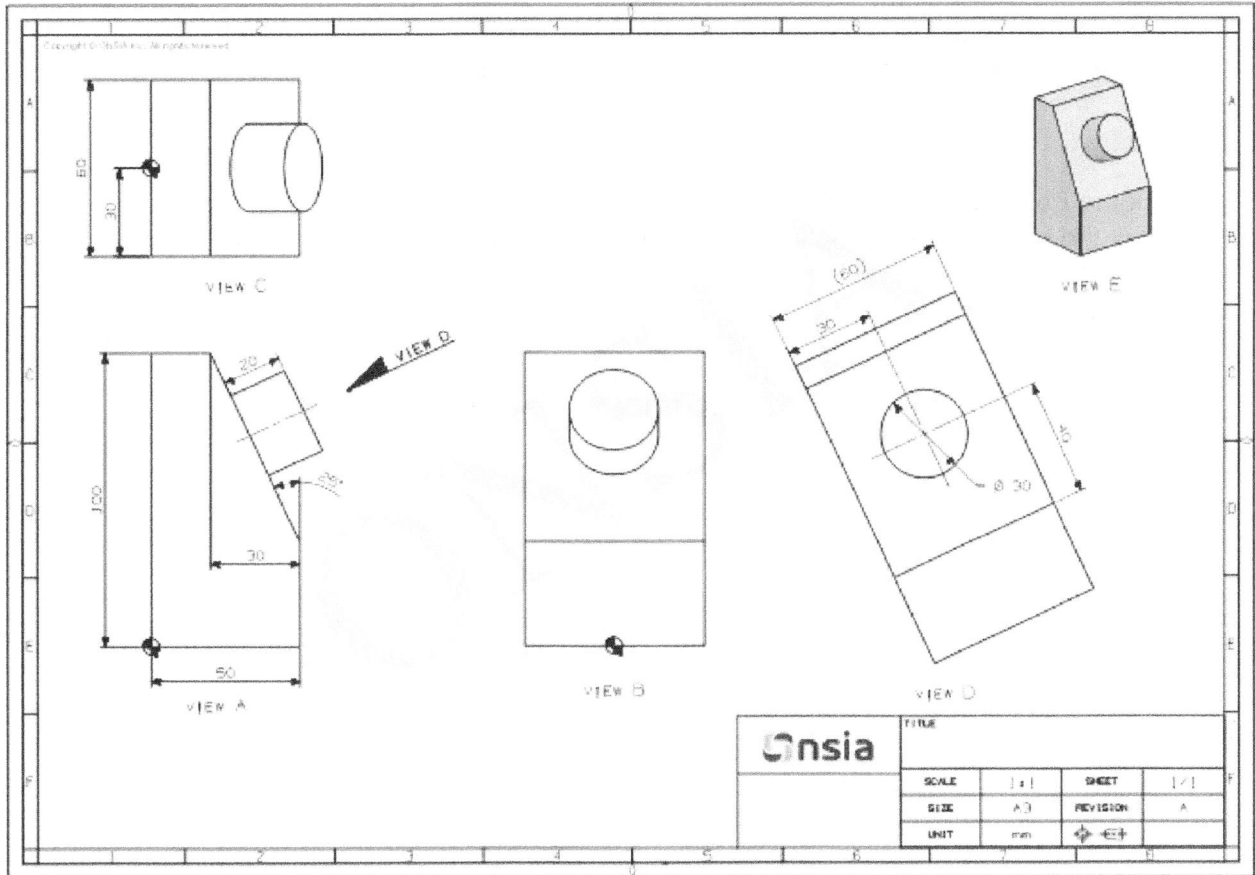

Fig 5-30 Drawing for Exercise 04

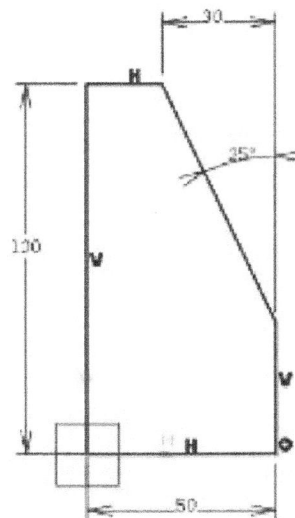

Fig 5-31 First Sketch

Creating a File and a Sketch

1. Create a part file with the name of ch05_ex04.CATPart.
2. Select the yz plane in the Spec Tree and click the Sketch icon.
3. Create a sketch and iso -constrain it as shown in Fig 5-31.
4. Exit the sketcher. Note that the sketch feature is selected.

First Pad

1. Click the Pad icon in the Sketch-Based Features toolbar.
2. Select the Mirrored extent option in the Pad Definition dialog box.
3. Enter 30mm in the Length input box.
4. Click OK in the dialog box.

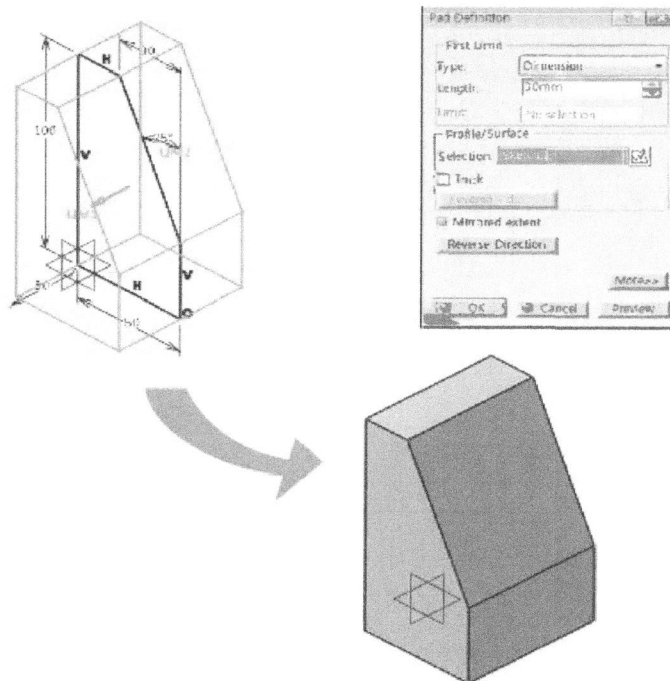

Fig 5-32 First Pad Feature

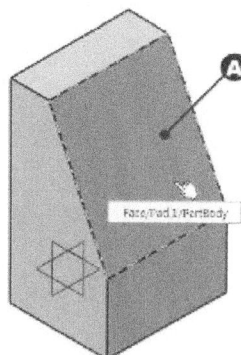

Fig 5-33 Sketch Plane

Second Sketch

1. Click the Sketch icon.
2. Select the plane designated by (A) in Fig 5-33.
3. Create the second sketch as shown in Fig 5-34.

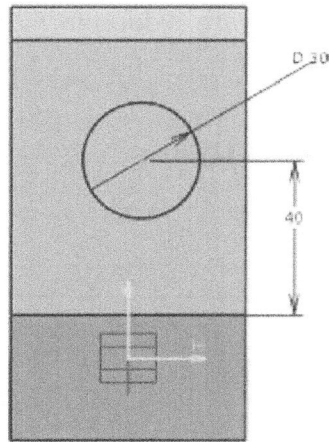

Fig 5-34 Second Sketch

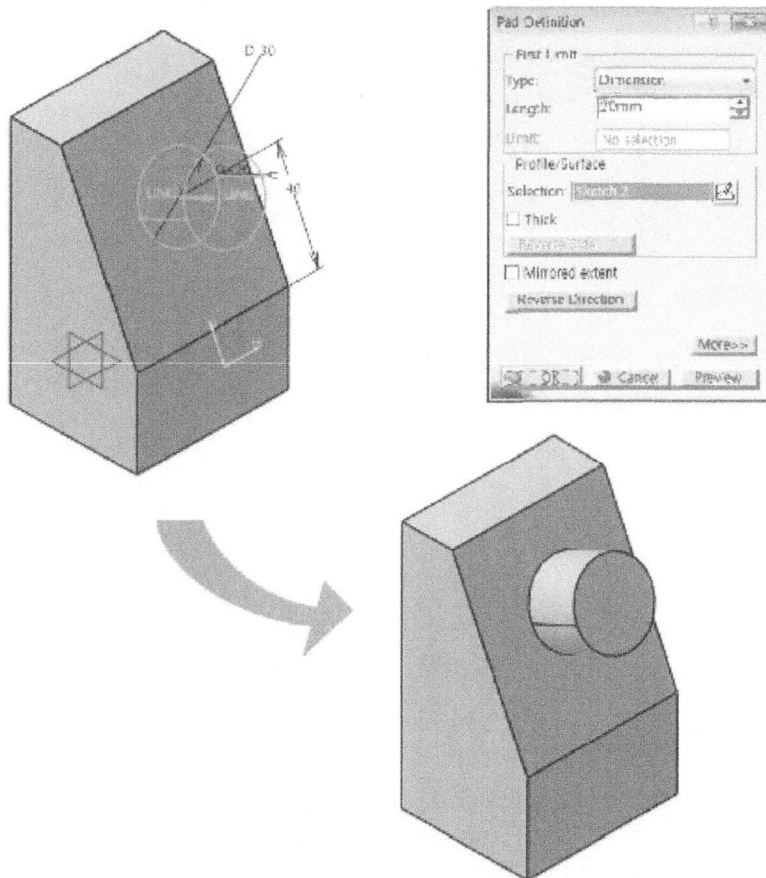

Fig 5-35 Second Pad

4. Exit the sketcher and make sure that the sketch feature is selected.

Second Pad

1. Click the Pad icon in the Sketch Based Features toolbar.
2. Enter 20mm in the Length input box.
3. Click OK in the dialog box. Planes are hidden in Fig 5-35. Note that sketch features arc hidden automatically.

Exercise 29: Creating a Solid Body

Create the solid model shown in Fig 5-30.

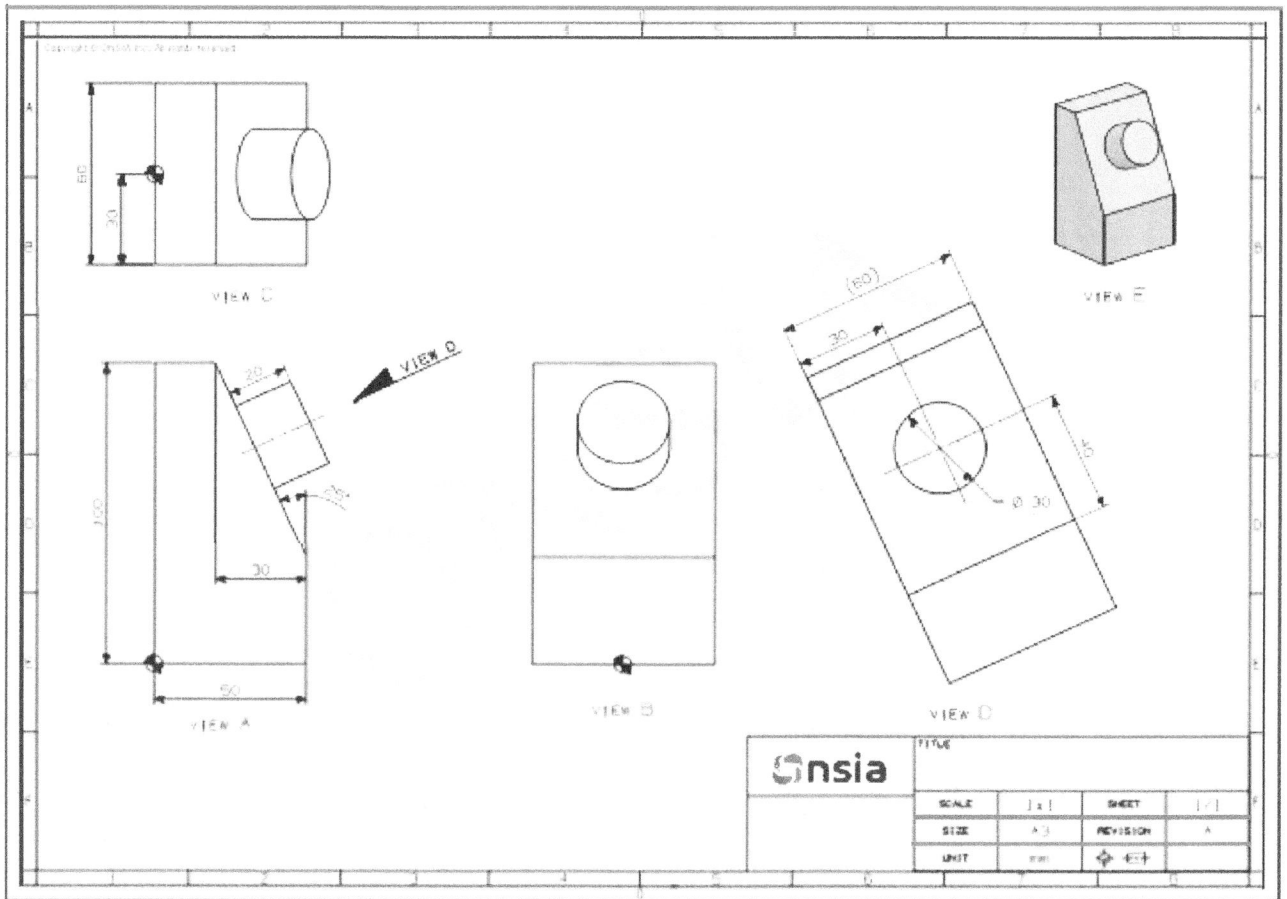

Fig 5-30 Drawing for Exercise 04

Creating a File and a Sketch

1. Create a part file with the name of ch05_ex04.CATPart.
2. Select the yz plane in the Spec Tree and click the Sketch icon.
3. Create a sketch and iso-constrain it as shown in Fig 5-31.
4. Exit the sketcher. Note that the sketch feature is selected.

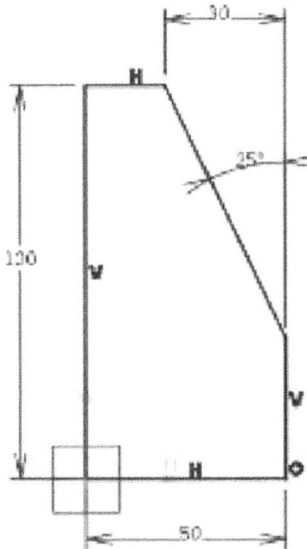

Fig 5-31 First Sketch

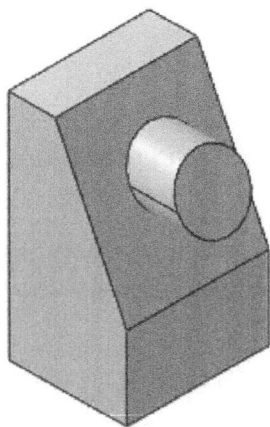

<Isometric View>   <Front View>

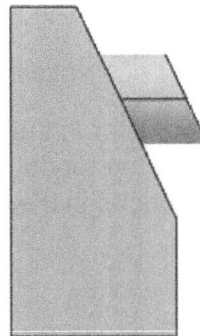

Fig 5-37 Modified Pad Direction

Save

1. Click the Isometric View icon in the View toolbar.
2. Save the part file.
3. Choose File> Close in the menu bar.

(Note) Deleting a Sketch-Based Feature

- You can delete the last feature created in Exercise 04. Place the mouse cursor on the last Pad feature in the Spec Tree and press MB3 > Delete. The Delete dialog box shown in Fig 5-38 appears. Be aware that if you check option (A), the sketch will also be deleted. You may delete the sketch if it is not being used for other features.

129

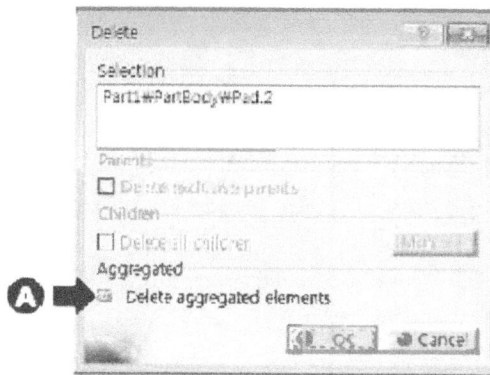

Fig 5-38 Delete Dialog Box

5.5 GRAPHIC PROPERTIES

Using the tools in the Graphic Properties toolbar, you can modify graphic properties of elements.

Fig 5-39 Graphic Properties Toolbar

You can modify the color of a solid body according to the following procedure.

1. Click the Volume Filter in the User Selection Filter toolbar.
2. Select volumes in the model. You can choose several volume by pressing the Ctr! key.
3. Select graphic options in the Graphic Properties tool bar. Fig 5-40 shows modified color with 75% opacity.

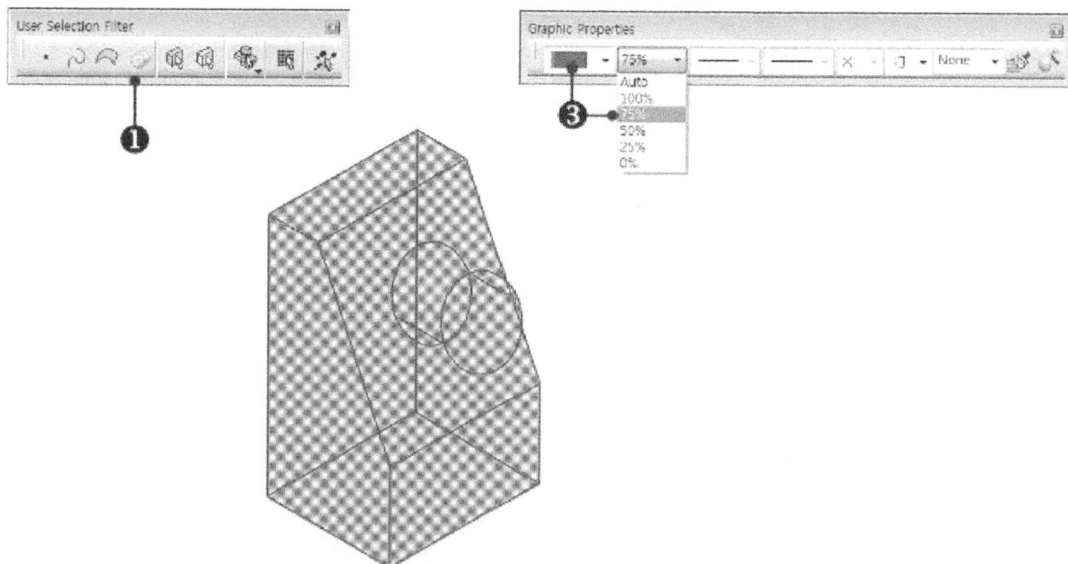

Fig 5-40 Modifying Graphic Properties

130

5.6 LIMIT OF PAD

The following limit options are available in the Type dropdown list of the First Limit option of Pad.

1. Dimension
2. Up to next
3. Up to last
4. Up to plane
5. Up to surface

If you choose Dimension as the type, you can enter the Length of the pad. The value is always retained even though the model will be changed. You can modify the input value by dragging the LIM1 or LIM2 text in the graphics window.

Other types define the limit by giving relations with the existing geometry. If you modify the geometry, the related limit is updated.

If you press the More button in the Pad Definition dialog box, the Second Limit option is available. You can see that the same types of limit can be applied for the second limit.

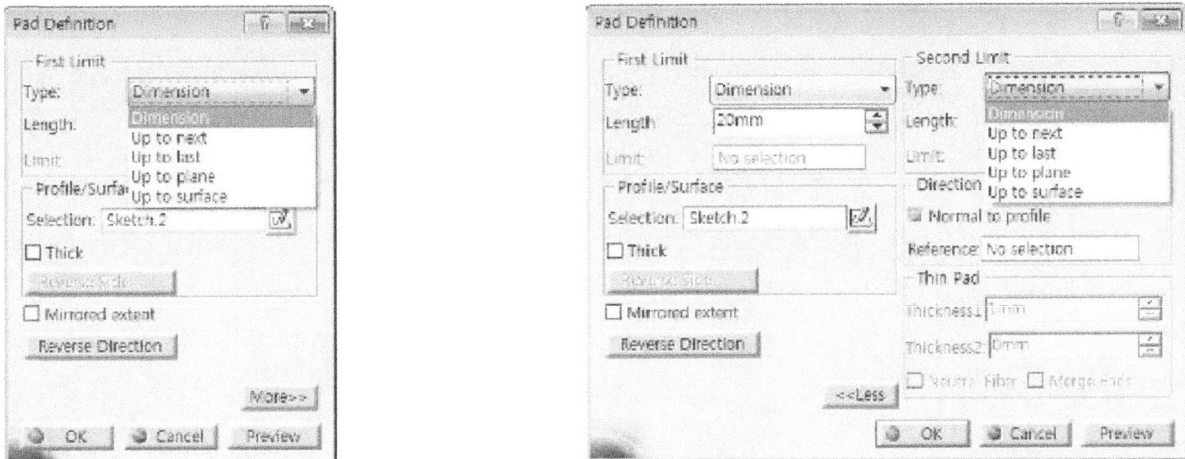

Fig 5- 41 Types of Limit

5.6.1 Up to Next

Limit is defined by the geometry which is met first along the extrusion direct ion. The limit of the feature has to be fully enclosed by the first geometry it meets.

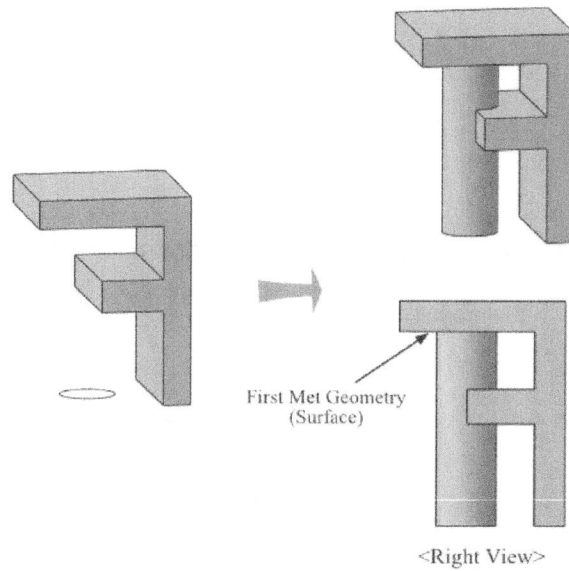

Fig 5-42 Limit: Up to Next

5.6.2 Up to Plane

The limit is defined by selecting a planar surface in the 3D geometry. The surface is ex- tended when the limit of extrusion is not fully enclosed by the surface.

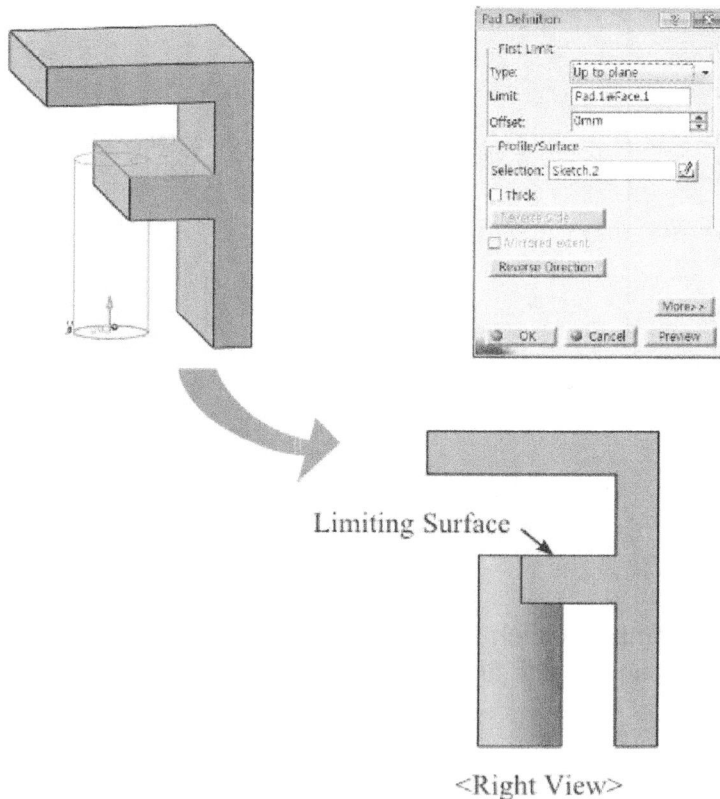

Fig 5-43 Limit: Up to Plane

(Note) Usage of the Up to Plane Option

You can pad a profile up to the selected plane.

- You cannot select the curved surface as the limit.
- You can pad a profile up to the reference plane. Reference planes will be explained in Chapter 8.

5.6.3 Up to Surface

The limit is defined by selecting a surface in the 30 geometries. When the limit element is modified after extrusion, the extrude limit will be updated. Note that the limit has to be fully enclosed by the selected surface. You can select a reference plane as the limit.

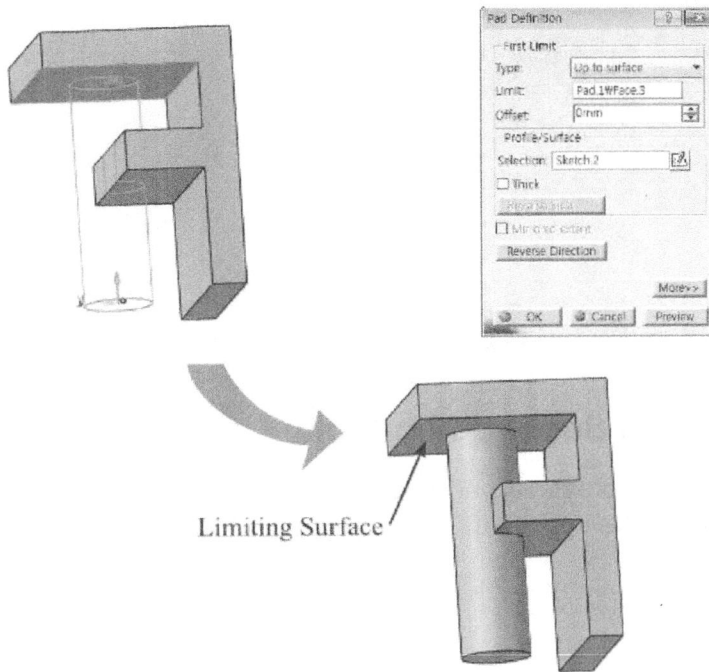

Fig 5-44 Limit: Up to Surface

If the start and/or end limit of a pad feature is defined by using the Up to Surface option, the limit has to be fully enclosed by the limiting surface, otherwise an alert message is invoked as shown in Fig 5-45. With the Up to Plane limit option, the limiting surface will be extended such that the limit can be defined for the pad feature.

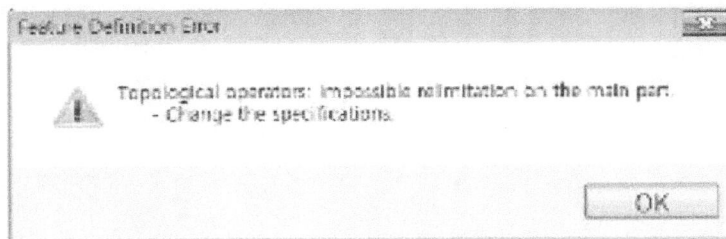

Fig 5-45 Error Message

133

5.6.4 Up to Last

The profile is extruded until the end of the geometry. Fig 5-46 shows the result of removing material from the existing body by using the Pocket command with the Up to Last limit option. The Pocket command will be explained later in this chapter.

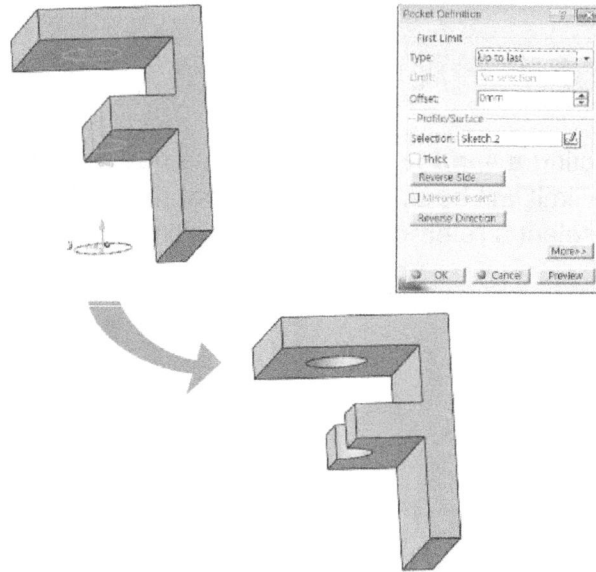

Fig 5-46 Limit: Up to Last

Exercise 30: First and Second Limit (ch05_005.CATPart)

Open the given part file and create a pad feature as shown in Fig 5-47 by selecting two limiting surfaces. Note that you have to specify the first and second limits as shown in Fig 5-48.

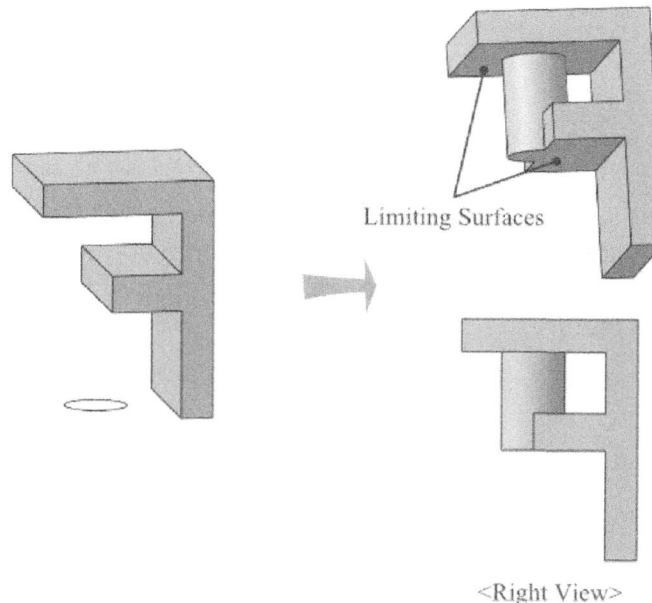

Fig 5-47 Model with Two Limits

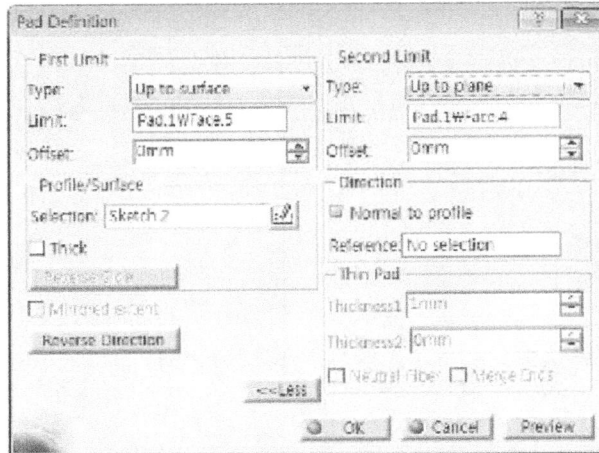

Fig 5-48 Pad Definition Dialog Box

5.6.5 Offset of Limit Plane or Surface

Offsetting a surface or plane means moving it constantly along a specified direction by a specified distance.

If you specify Up to next, Up to last, Up to plane or Up to surface as the type of limit, the Offset option is activated as shown in Fig 5-49. Using this option, you can offset the limit plane or surface normal to the selected plane or surface by a specified distance.

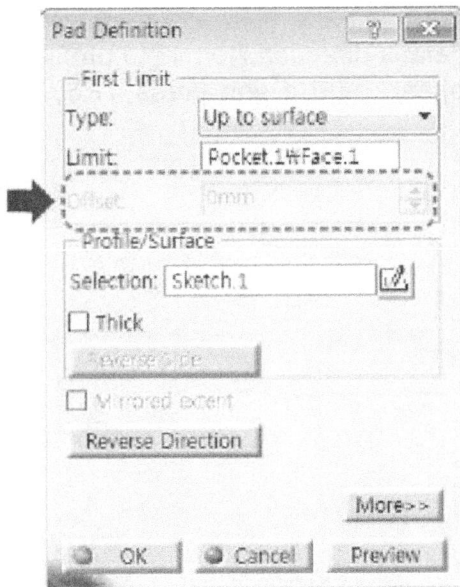

Fig 5-49 Offset Option

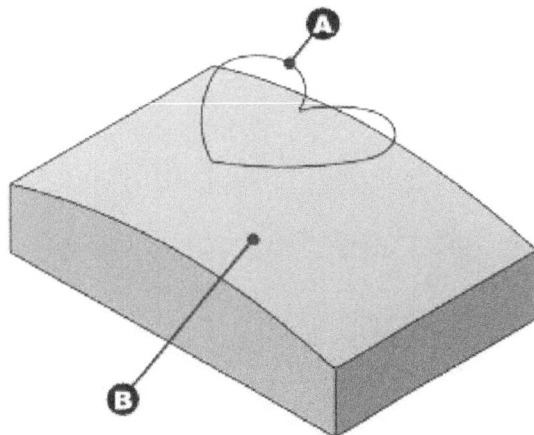

Fig 5- 50 Pad with Offset Option

To practice offsetting the limit surface, open the file for exercise ch05_fig50.CATPart. Click the Pad icon in the Sketch-Based Features toolbar, select the sketch specified by (A) in Fig 5-50. Expand the Pad Definition dialog box, press the Reverse Direction button in the dialog box, choose Up to last as the type of the first limit. Choose Up to surface as the type of the second limit, select surface

(B) as the limit surface. Enter 10mm in the Offset input box. Press the Preview button in the dialog box and click OK.

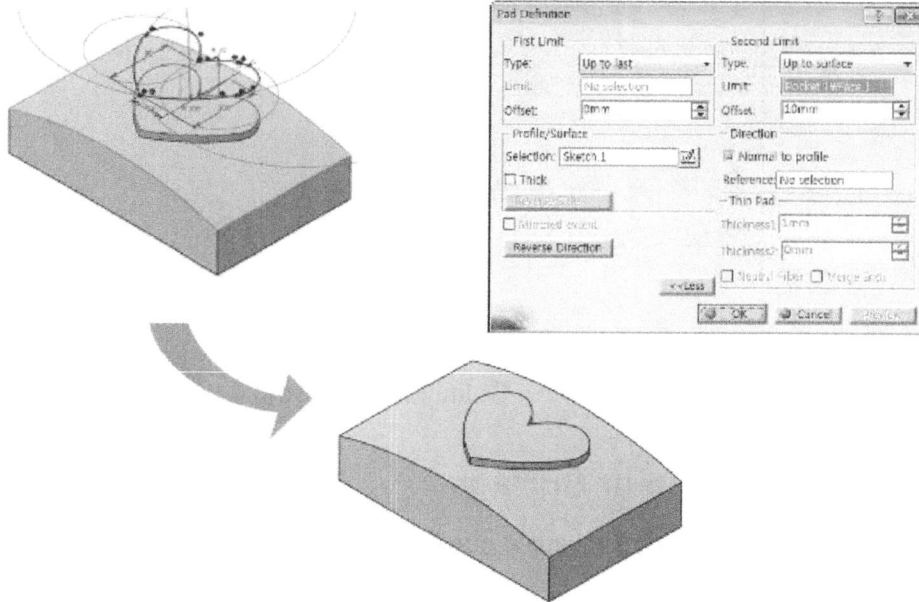

Fig 5-51 Pad with Offset Option

5.7 PAD OF SURFACE

You can pad a plana r or curved surface. In this case, the default direction Normal to profile cannot be applied. The warning message shown in Fig 5-52 appears and if you press YES, you are prompted to select a direction.

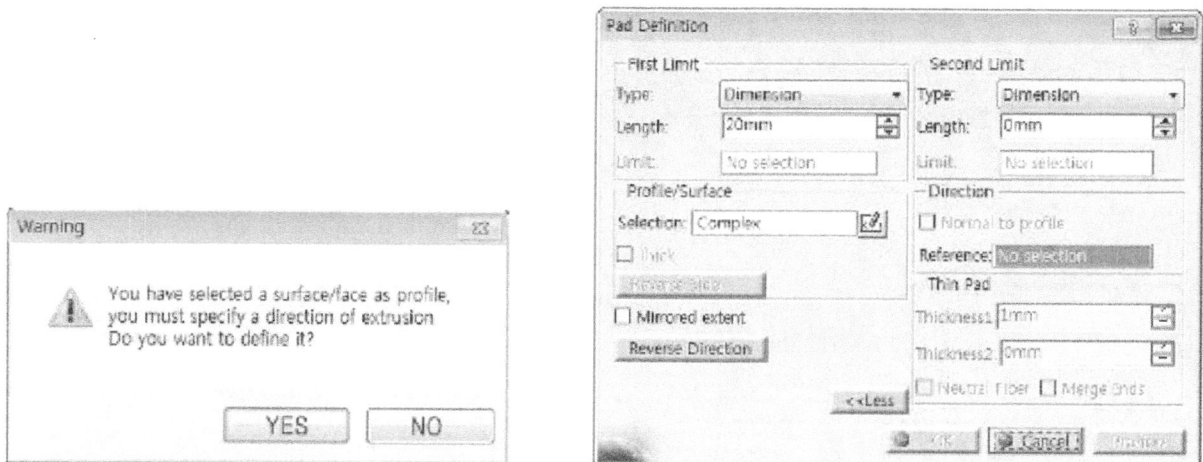

Fig 5-52 Warning Message

Fig 5-53 shows specifying the pad direction by selecting edge (A). Note that you can specify the normal direction by selecting a plane or the axis direction by selecting a cylindrical surface.

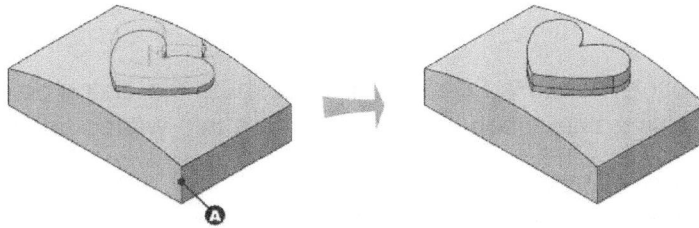

Fig 5-53 Pad Direction by Edge

(Note) Dragging Lim1 and Lim2

- You can drag the LIM1 and LIM2 symbol shown in the preview. If you place the mouse cursor near the text, the pointer changes to a hand symbol and you can drag the limit by pressing MB 1 (left click).

(Note) Shortcut Key

If you press MB3 (right click) on a feature in the S pec Tree, a pop-up menu as shown in Fig 5-55 appears. You can see that among the options in the pop-up men u, some of the letters are underlined. This means that you can execute the option command by simply pressing MB3 on the feature and typing the corresponding underlined character.

For example, if you want to delete a feature, press MB3 on the desired feature and type "d" on the keyboard. If you want to show or hide a feature, you can press MB3 on the feature and type "h" on the keyboard.

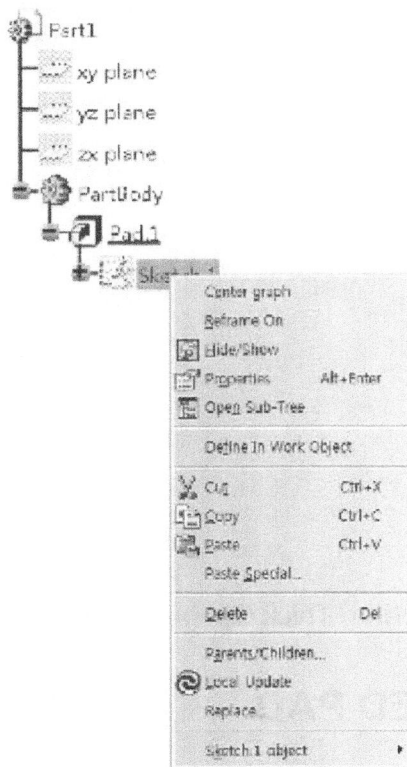

Fig 5-55 Pop-up Menu

137

5.8 THIN PAD

If you check the Thick option in the Pad Definition dialog box, the dialog box expands and the Thin Pad option is available. Using this option, you can create a thin-walled pad feature.

- **Thickness 1:** Offset of profile along one side.
- **Thickness 2:** Offset of profile along the other side.
- **Neutral Fiber:** Offset Thickness I along both sides.
- **Merge Ends:** Extend the end of the profile up to the existing surface.

Fig 5-56 shows a Pad feature with the Merge Ends option turned on. The short ends of the profile curve are extended until they reach the next available surface or plane.

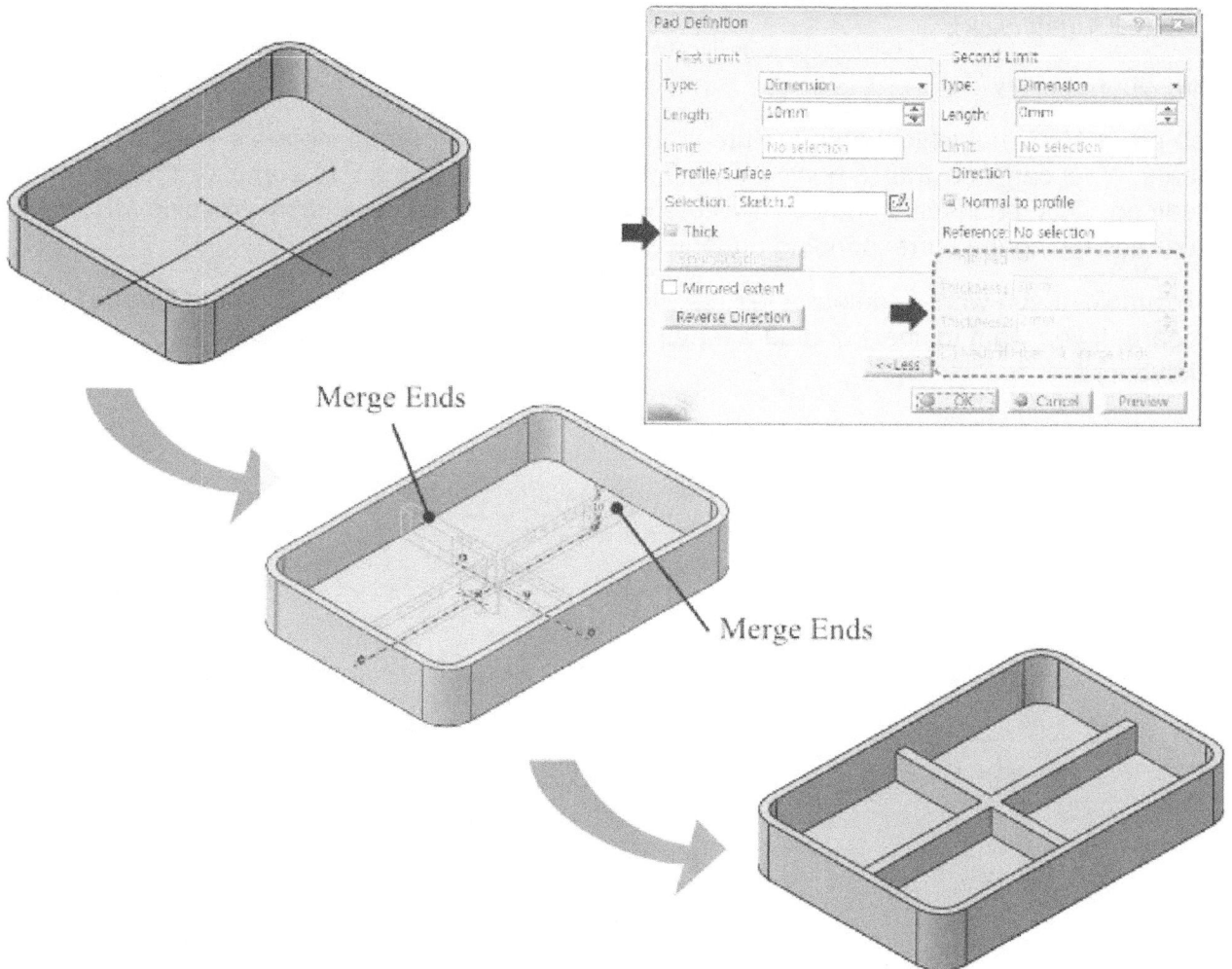

Fig 5-56 Applying Thick Option with Merge Ends Option

5.9 DRAFTED FILLETED PAD

Using the Drafted Filleted Pad command, you can apply a fillet and draft while you are creating a Pad feature. We will learn about fillet and draft in Chapter 9.

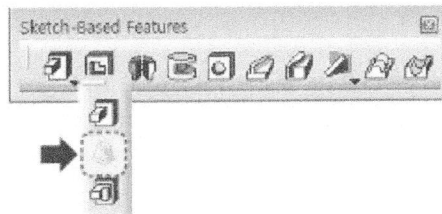

Fig 5-57 Drafted Filleted Pad Icon

Exercise 31: Drafted Filleted Pad (ch05_006.CATPart)

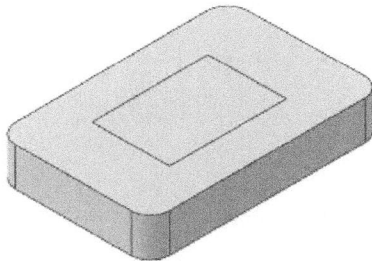

Fig 5-58 Given Part

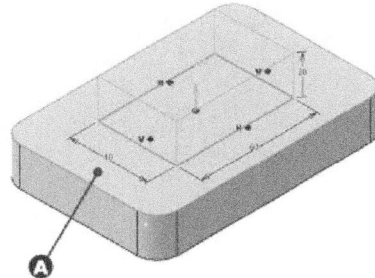

Fig 5-59 Second Limit

1. Open the given part file. (ch05_006.CATPart)
2. Click the Drafted Filleted Pad icon in the Pads toolbar.
3. Select the sketch as the profile.
4. Type 20mm in the First Limit input box. The status bar message prompts you to elect the second limit.
5. Select the face O in Fig 5-59 as the second limit.
6. Type I 0deg in the Angle input box and select the Second limit as the Neutral element.
7. Set the Fillets option as shown in the dialog box in Fig 5-60 and press OK.

Fig 5-61 shows the result part and the meaning of fillet options.

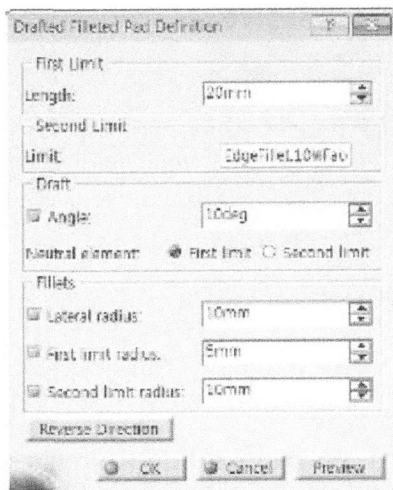

Fig 5-60 Fillet Options

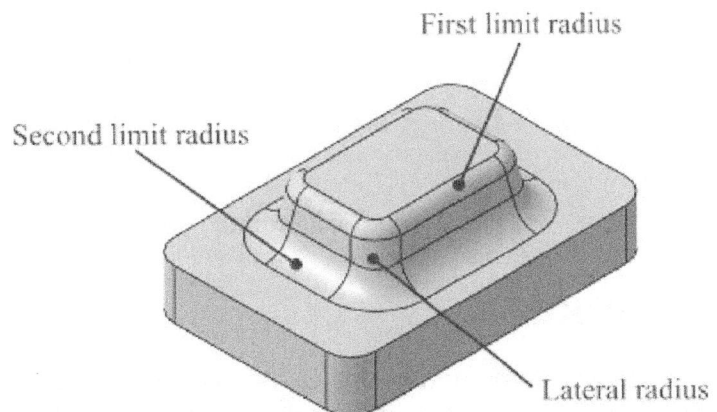

Fig 5-61 Result

5.10 MULTI-PAD

With the Multi-Pad command you can create a Pad feature using a sketch that is divided into several closed domains. You can apply different thickness es for each domain. Moreover, you can apply zero thickness for the domain if required.

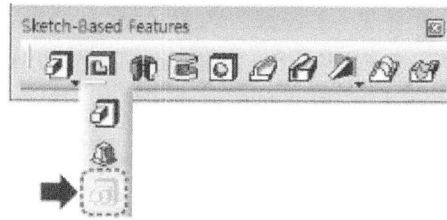

Fig 5-62 Multi-Pad Icon

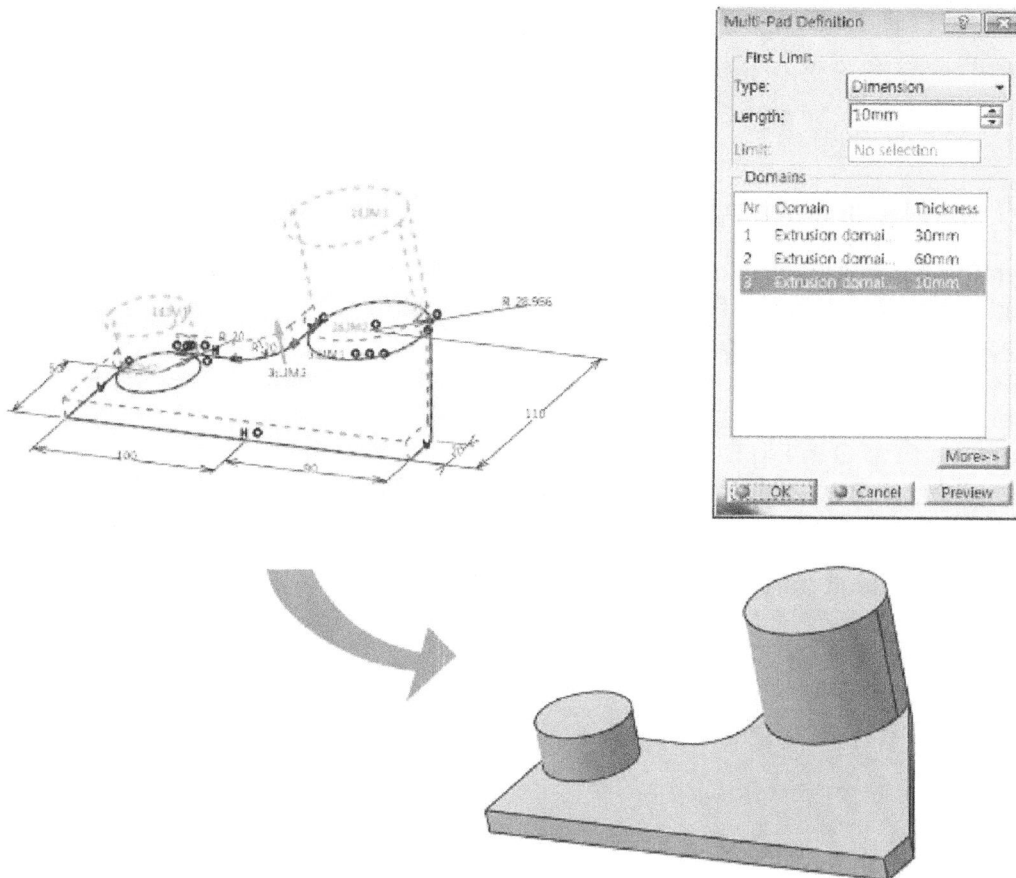

Fig 5-63 Modeling with Multi-Pad Command

5.11 POCKET

With the Pocket command in the Sketch-Based Features toolbar, you can extrude a profile and remove material from the existing solid body. The Pocket icon is activated only when at least one solid body exists. Therefore, you cannot create a Pocket feature as the first feature.

Fig 5-64 shows creating a pocket feature using a closed profile.

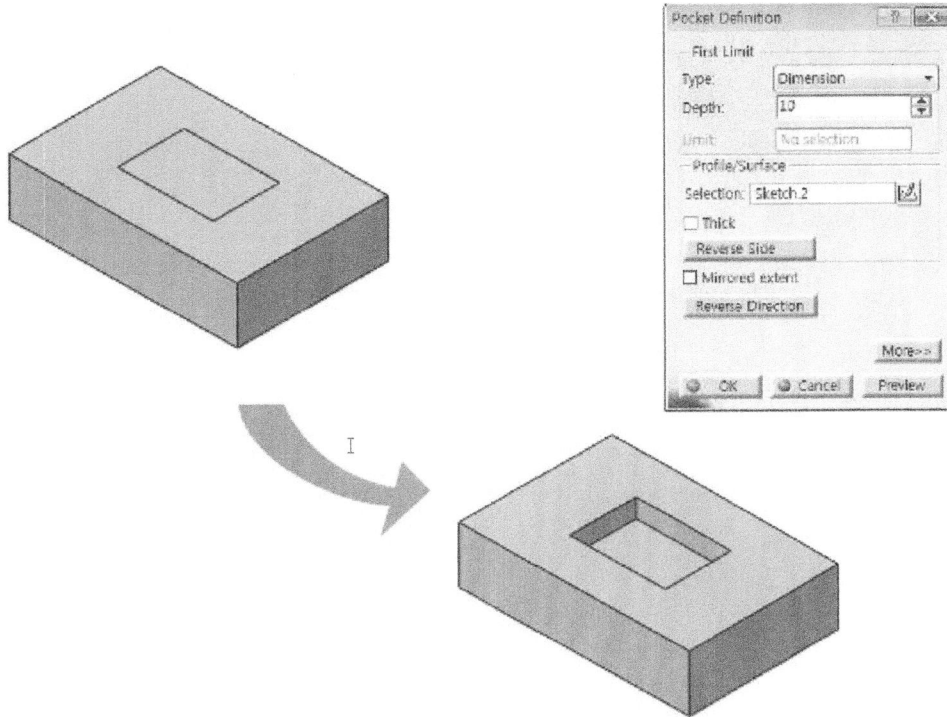

Fig 5-64 Pocket with Closed Profile

If you use the Thick option for the closed profile, you can obtain the pocket result as shown in Fig 5-65.

Fig 5-66 shows creating a pocket feature with an open profile. .otc that the side and dir- ection arrow should be aligned such that it can remove mate rial from the existing solid body as shown in the figure.

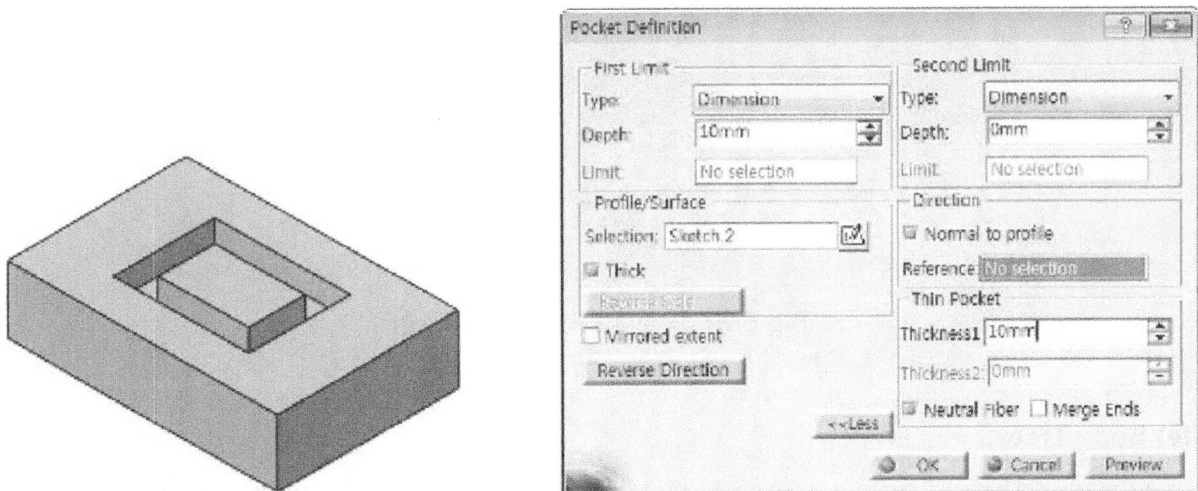

Fig 5-65 Closed Profile with Thick Option

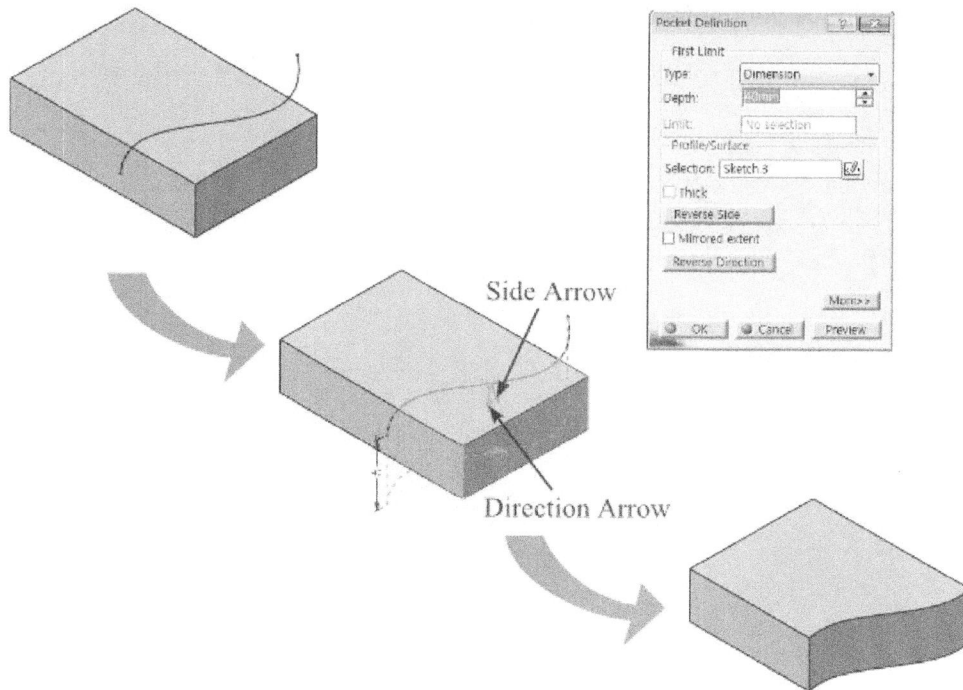

Fig 5-66 Open Profile

5.12 DRAFTED FILLETED POCKET

This command is the same as the Drafted Filleted Pad except that it removes material from the existing part.

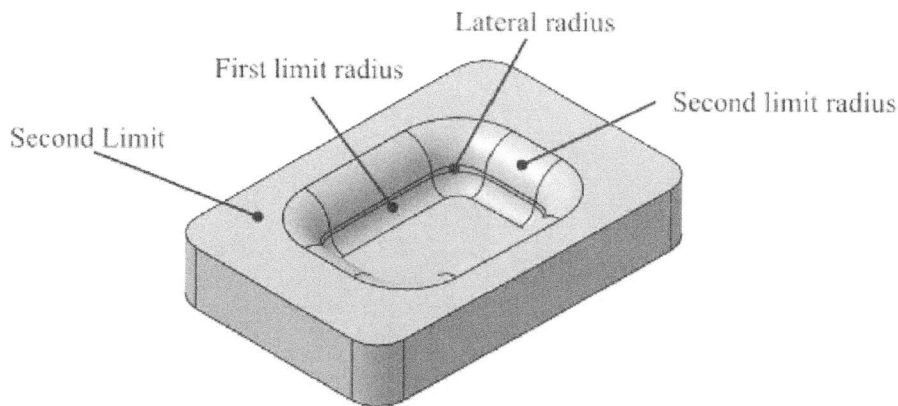

Fig 5-67 Drafted Filleted Pocket

(Note) Spec Tree

Drafted Filleted Pad and Pocket are recorded in the Spec Tree a individual Pad or Pocket, Fillet and Draft as shown in Fig 5-68, and not as a single feature. Therefore, if you want to modify the draft angle or fillet radius, just double click the feature and modify the value in the respective dialog box.

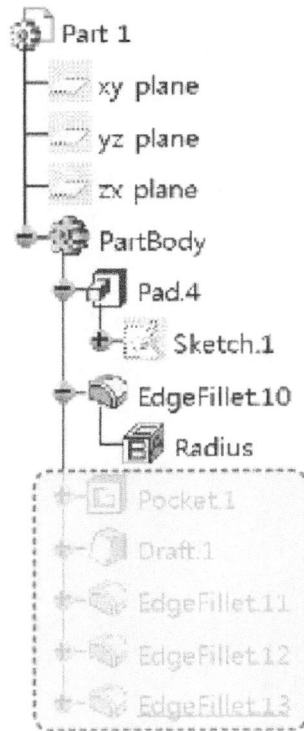

Fig 5-68 Spec Tree after Drafted Filleted Pocket

5.13 MULTI-POCKET

This command is the same as the Multi-Pad except that it removes material from the existing part.

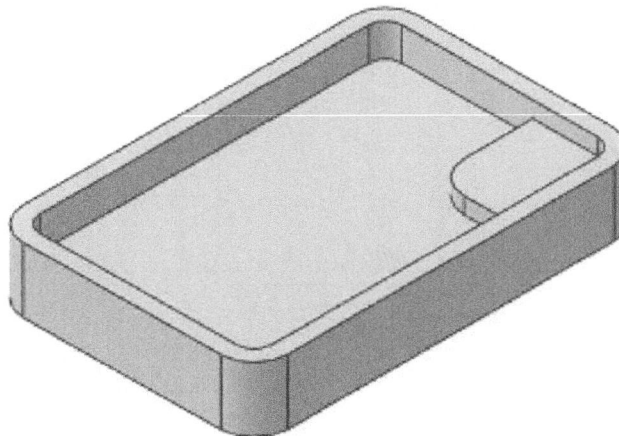

Fig 5-69 Multi-Pocket

(Note) Multi Domain

- Each domain in Multi-Pad or Multi -Pocket has to be closed, and the curves at the intersection have to be divided. You can divide a line or curve by using the Break or Quick Trim command in the Sketcher work bench.

Exercise 32: Guide Block Modeling (ch05_007.CATPart)

Requirements

1. The end of the feature (A) must always terminate at the face (B). (Use a proper limit option.)
2. The feature (C) always removes the part body up to the last.

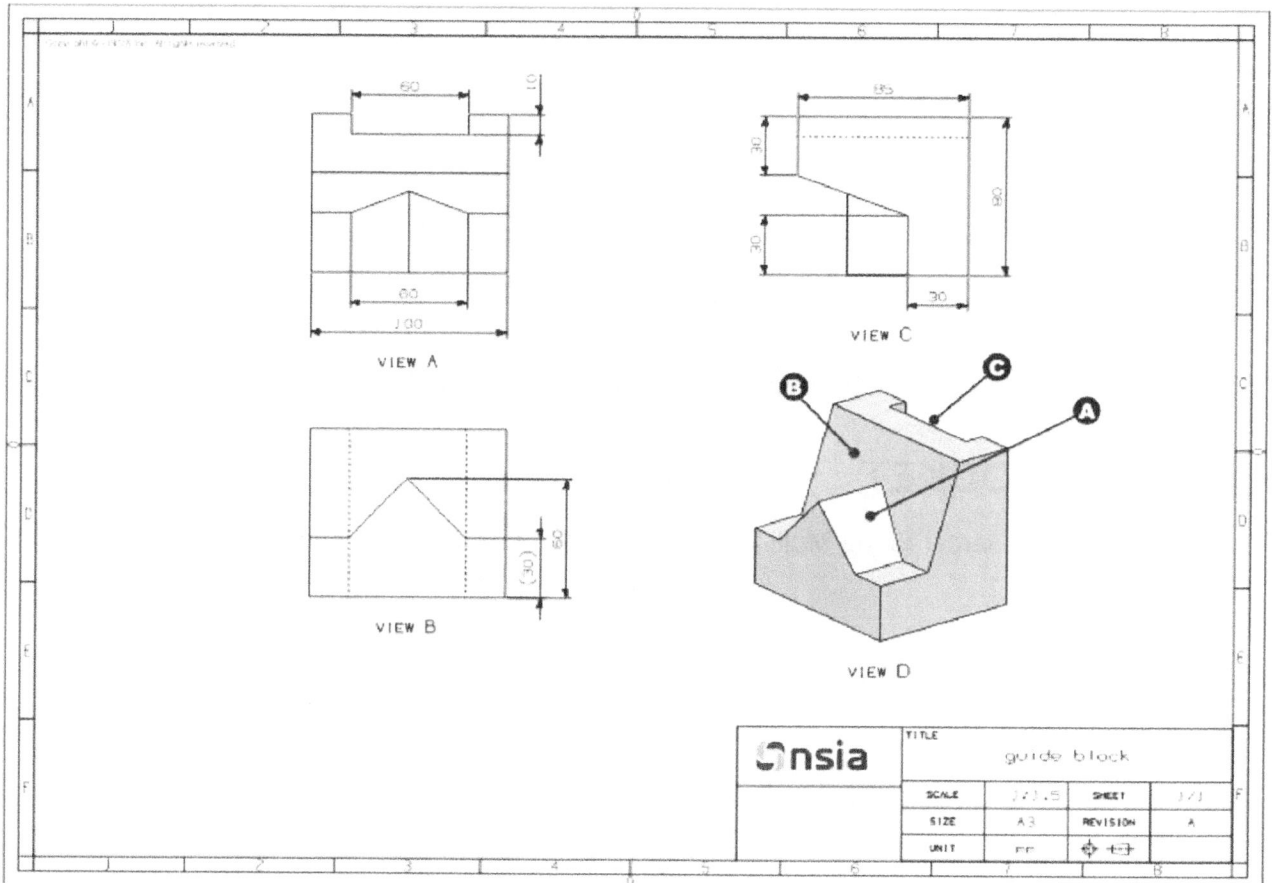

Fig 5-70 Guide Block

First Sketch

1. Create a sketch on the zx plane as shown in Fig 5-71.
2. Exit the Sketcher.

144

First Pad

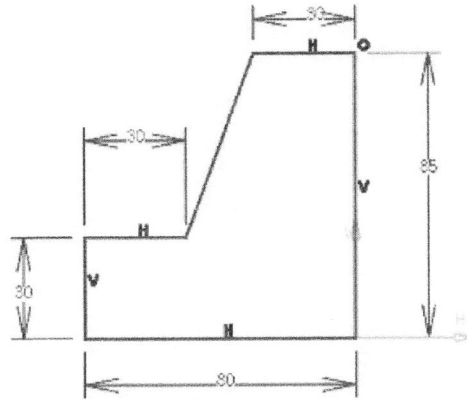

Fig 5-71 First Sketch

1. Click the Pad icon.
2. Select the sketch created in the first sketch.
3. Check Mirrored extent in the dialog box and enter 50 mm as the Length.
4. Press OK.

Second Sketch

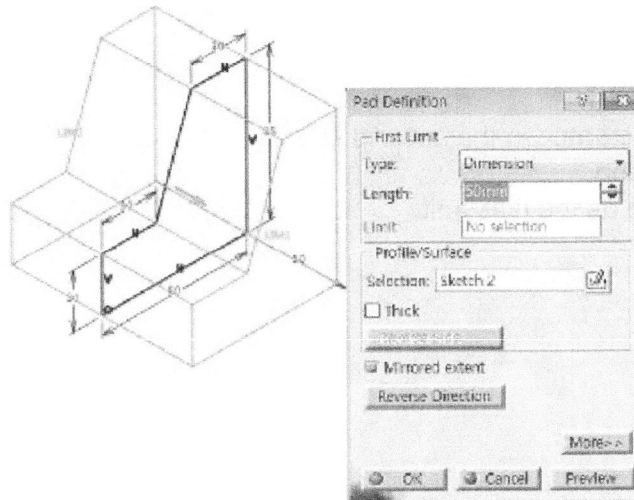

Fig 5-72 First Pad

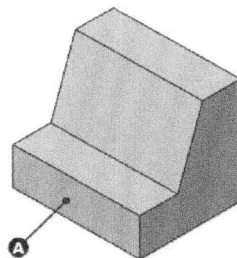

Fig 5-73 Second Sketch Plane

1. Invoke the Sketcher workbench by selecting the face (A) in Fig 5-73 as the sketch plane.

(Note) Mirrored extent

- The Mirrored extent option is recommended when the geometry is symmetric to the sketch plane because the origin will then be located at the center of the feature. The location of the origin can make your modeling process simpler or more difficult.

2. Create a sketch as shown in fig 5-74. Note that you have to create a triangle to form a closed profile and apply coincidence and symmetric constraints as shown in figure.
3. Exit the Sketcher.

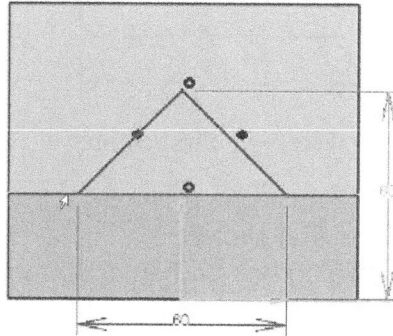

Fig 5-74 Second Sketch

Second Pad

1. Click the Pad icon.
2. Select the sketch created in the second sketch as the profile.
3. Confirm the direction.
4. Select Up to plane as the first limit.

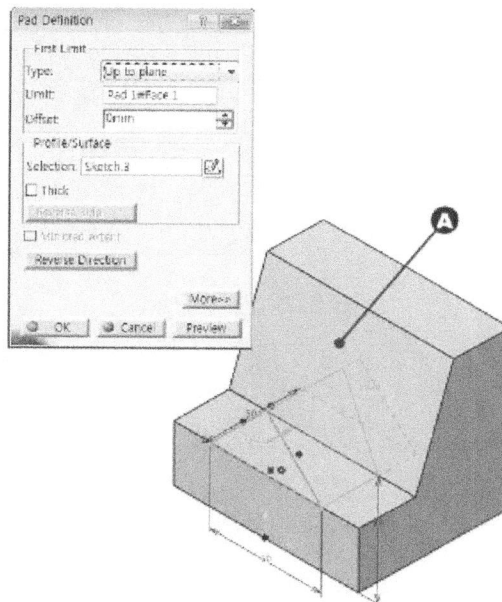

Fig 5-75 Second Pad

5. Select the face (A) as shown in Fig 5-75 and press OK.

(Note) Design Intent

- The intention of a designer can be reflected in the modeling process and options. According to the requirement of this exercise, the second pad has to be extruded up to the face (A) shown in Fig 5-75. This means that the Pad feature must always terminate at the face (A) regardless of any future modification of the dimension in the first sketch.

Third Sketch

Fig 5-76 Third Sketch Plane

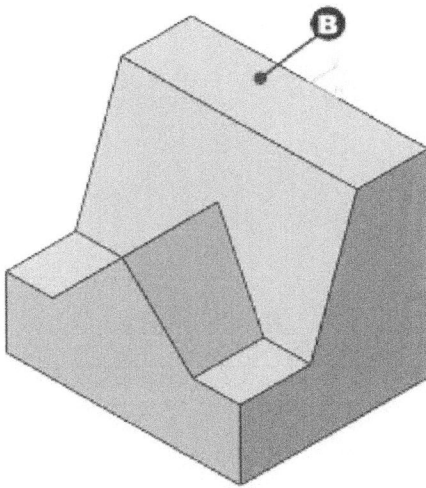

Fig 5-77 Third Sketch

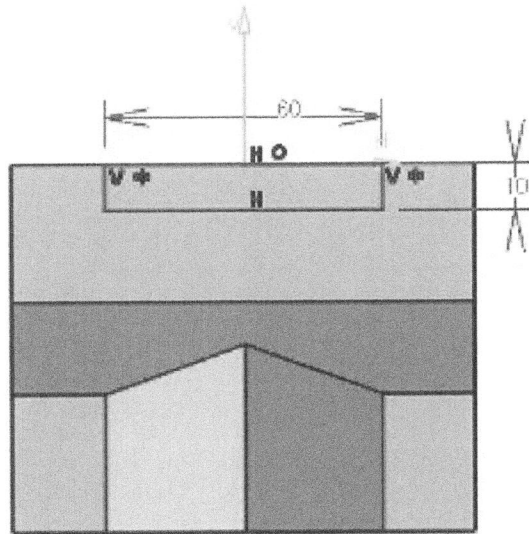

Fig 5-78 Completed Model

1. Click the Positioned Sketch icon and select the face (B) as shown in Fig 5-76.
2. Turn on the Reverse H option and the Swap option in the Sketch Positioning dialog box so that the sketch axes appear as in Fig 5-76.
3. Press the OK button in the dialog box.

(Note) Positioned Sketch

- If you align the sketch axis properly, creating a sketch referring to the drawing becomes easier.
4. Create a rectangle as the third sketch as shown in Fig 5-77 and iso-constrain it.
5. Exit the Sketcher.

Third Pad

1. Click the Pocket icon.
2. Choose Up to last as the first limit and press OK. Fig 5-78 shows the completed part.

Exercise 33: Flange Part (ch05_008.CATPart)

Create the flange part referring to the given drawing.

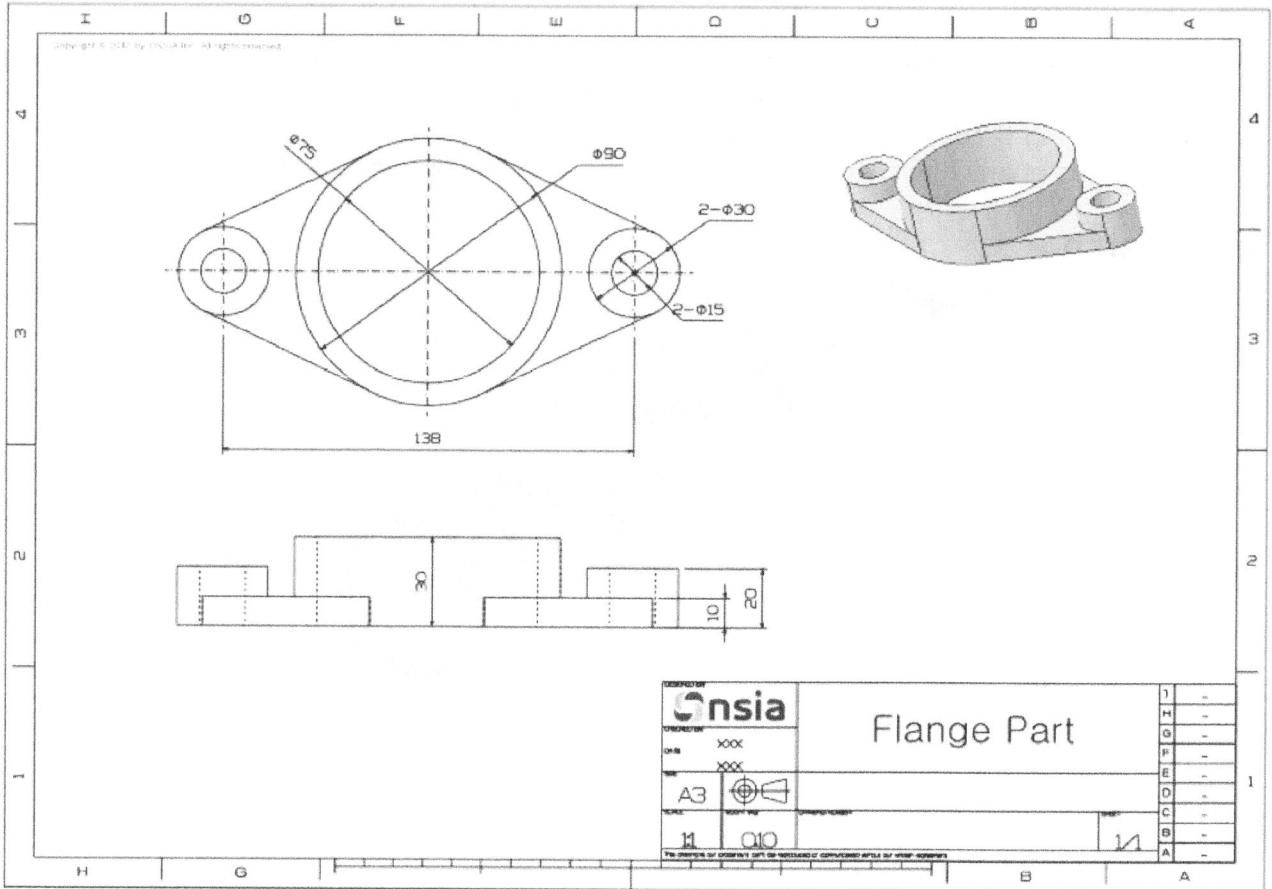

Fig 5-79 Flange Part

Step 1: First Sketch

1. Create a sketch on the xy plane as shown in Fig 5-70 and apply the major dimensions.

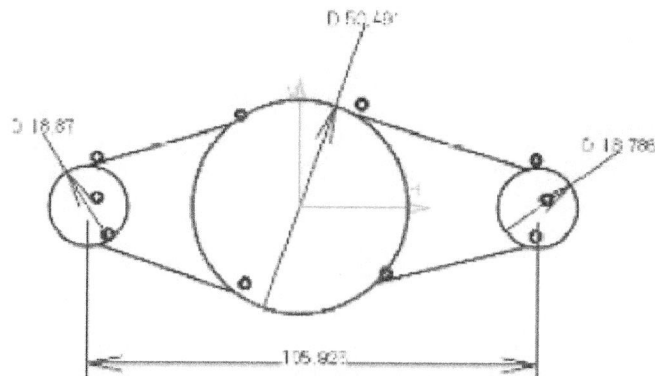

Fig 5 - 80 Rough Sketch

148

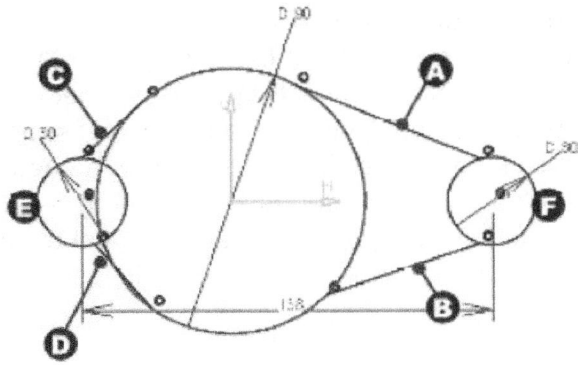

Fig 5-81 Modifying Dimension

2. Modify the dimension values by using the Edit Multi-Constraint command in the Constraint toolbar. The sketch should appear as in Fig 5-81.

(Note) Creatin g a Sketch Roughly

- When you create a sketch roughly, it is recommended that you draw it as close to the given dimensions as possible, referring to the coordinate value appearing at the mouse cursor or in the Sketch Tools toolbar. If it is too different from the given dimension or shape, you may have to re-draw it.

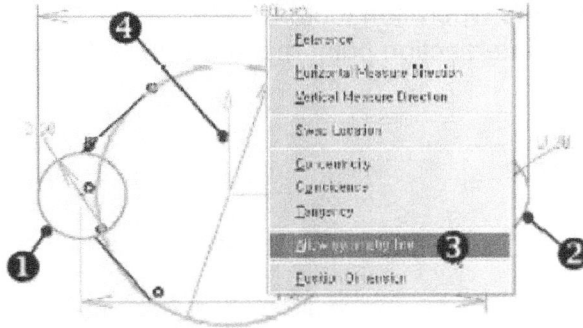

Fig 5-82 Symmetry Constraint

3. Apply the Symmetry constraints. Lines (A) and (B) in Fig 5-81 are symmetric to lines (C) and (D), respectively, with respect to the V axis. Circle (E) is symmetric to circle (F) with respect to the V axis. After applying the Symmetry between the two circles with the diametral dimensions are both ap plie d, the sketch changes to over-constrained.

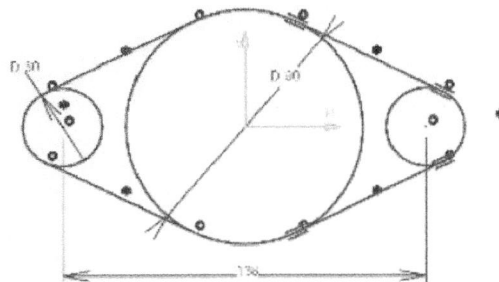

Fig 5-83 Iso-constrained Sketch

149

4. Delete the diametral dimension of circle (F).
5. Apply a Tangency constraint so that lines (A) and (B) are tangent to the circles. Lines (C) and (D) also become tangent because they are symmetric to lines (A) and (B). If the geometry changes abruptly by applying the Tangency constraint, you will have to undo the constraint and drag the sketch curves or points near to the desired location before applying the constraint. The sketch up to this step is shown in Fig 5-83. We will create a Multi-Pad with different thicknesses for each profile domain. We first have to break the sketch curves at the intersection.

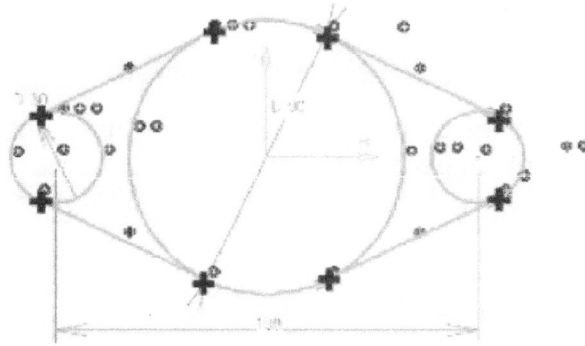

Fig 5-84 Break Points

6. Click the Break icon in the Operation toolbar.
7. Break the circles at the intersection point marked by + in Fig 5-84.
8. Exit the Sketcher.

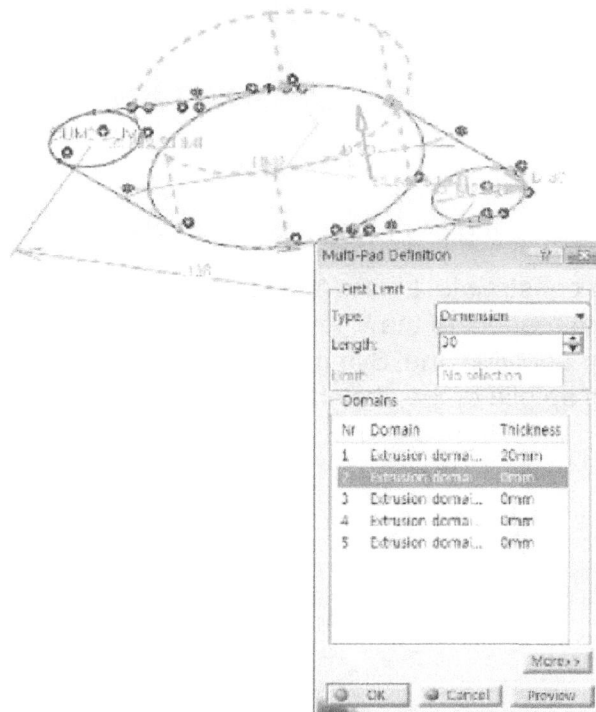

Fig 5-85 Applying Multi-Pad

Step 2: Multi-Pad

1. Click the Multi-Pad icon in the Sketch-Based Features toolbar.
2. Enter the thickness for each domain in the Length input box of the Multi-Pad Definition dialog box as shown in Fig 5-85.

Step 3: Second Sketch

1. Create a sketch on the bottom plane as shown in Fig 5-86.
2. Exit the Sketcher.

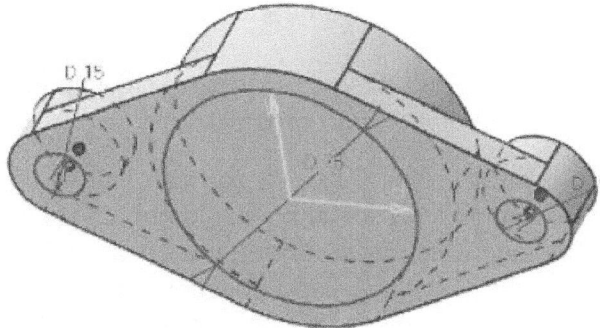

Fig 5-86 Second Sketch

Step 4: Pocket

1. Press the Pocket icon and select the sketch created in Step 3.

Fig 5-87 Completed Model

2. Choose Up to last as the first limit in the Pocket Definition dialog box and press OK. Fig 5-87 shows the completed model.

(Note) 0 mm Thickness

• Step 3 and Step 4 can be created in Step 2 as a single Multi-Pad operation. To do this, you have to create the circle for the holes in the first sketch and input zero thickness for the corresponding profile domain.

SKETCH BASED FEATURE (SHAFT, GROOVE, HOLE)

6.1 SHAFT

Using the Shaft command in the Sketch-Based Features toolbar, you can revolve a pro- file or surface to create a 3D geometry. The 3D geometry created with the Shaft command is added to the Part Body.

Procedure

1. Create a sketch.
2. Click the Shaft icon in the Sketch-Based Features toolbar.
3. Select the profile or surface.
4. Select an axis of revolution if you have not created an axis in the profile sketch.
5. Input the limit angle of the revolution and press OK.

If you press the button designated by (A) in Fig 6-1, you can invoke the Sketcher workbench and modify the sketch that you selected as the profile. If you did not create a sketch in advance, you can create a new sketch while running sketch base d features such as Pocket, Pad and Shaft etc. by pressing the Sketcher button in the dialog box and specifying the sketch plane. After creating the sketch, you can ex it the Sketcher as usual and the sketch is selected as the profile.

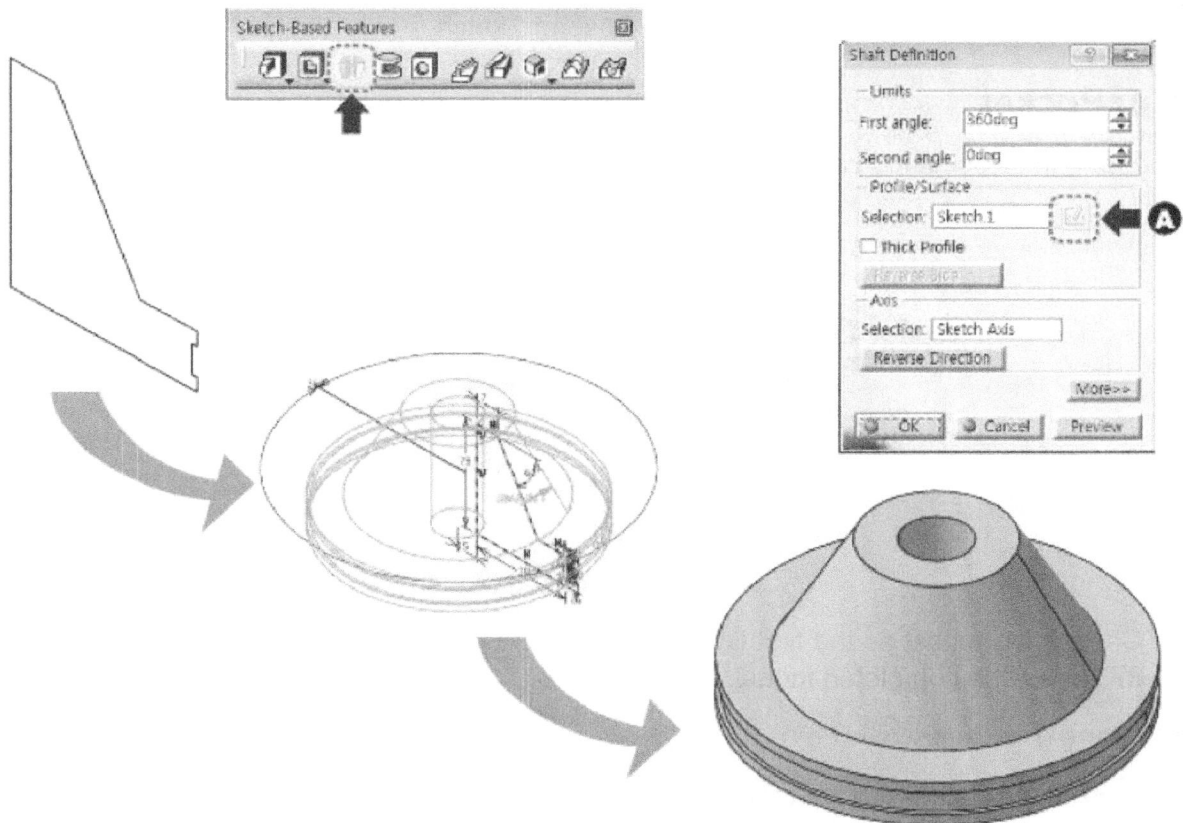

Fig 6- 1 Creating a Shaft Feature

Exercise 34: Creating a Shaft Feature (ch06_001.CATPart)

Creating a Sketch

1. Create a new part tile.
2. Create a sketch on the yz plan e as shown in Fig 6-2. Create an axis line as specified by (A) using the Axis command in the Profile toolbar.
3. Exit the sketcher.

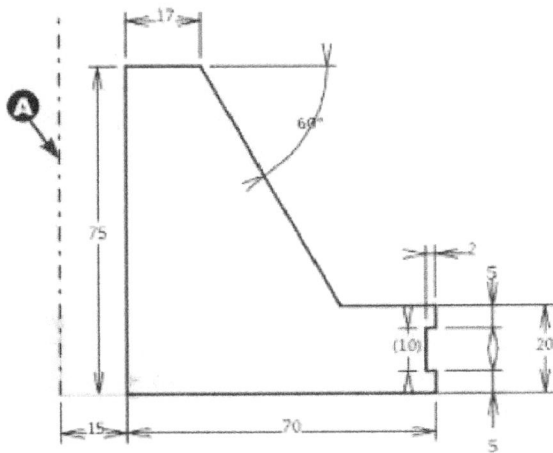

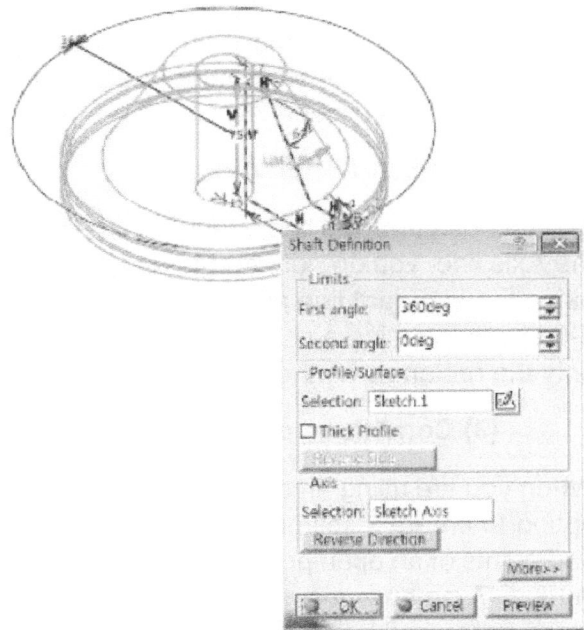

Fig 6-2 Sketch   Fig 6-3 Preview of Shaft

Creating a Shaft Feature

1. Click the Shaft icon in the Sketch- Based Features toolbar while the sketch is selected. The shaft feature is previewed as shown in Fig 6-3. Note that the Sketch Axis is selected as the Axis in the Shaft Definition dialog box. 1f you have not created an axis line in the sketch, you have to define the shaft axis explicitly.
2. Click OK in the dialog box. Fig 6-4 shows the shaft feature created.

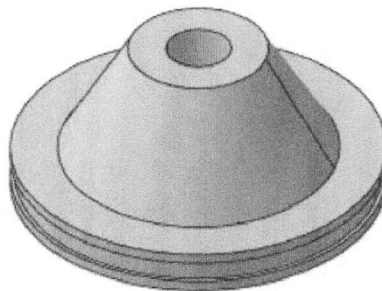

Fig 6- 4 Shaft Feature Created

6.1.1 Characteristics of Profile and Axis of Shaft

When you define the profile and axis for a Shaft feature, you have to bear in mind the following characteristics.

(1) General Rule for Profile and Angle

You can create a solid body by revolving a closed profile. You can select as many profiles as you want unless they are intersecting, provided that they are all closed. You cannot use an intersecting profile for a single Shaft feature under any circumstances. Va lues in the First angle and Second angle should not exceed 360°.

(2) Type of Shaft Axis

You can use the Axis line, standard line or linear edge as an ax.is of the Shaft. When you are using the Axis line, you do not need to select it in the Axis selection field in the dialog box. When you are using the standard line as the shaft axis, you have to select the axis in the Axis selection field. Fig 6-5 shows creating a shaft feature using the standard line as an axis. Note that you have to select only the rectangle as the profile.

(3) Conditions of Profile and Axis

When you are using an open profile as the profile of the first Shaft feature, you have to use the Thick option to create a solid body. However you can create a solid body with an open profile when the end points of an open profile are on the axis as shown in Fig 6-6. If you define a shaft ax.is as shown in Fig 6-7, an error message is dis played as shown in Fig 6-8.

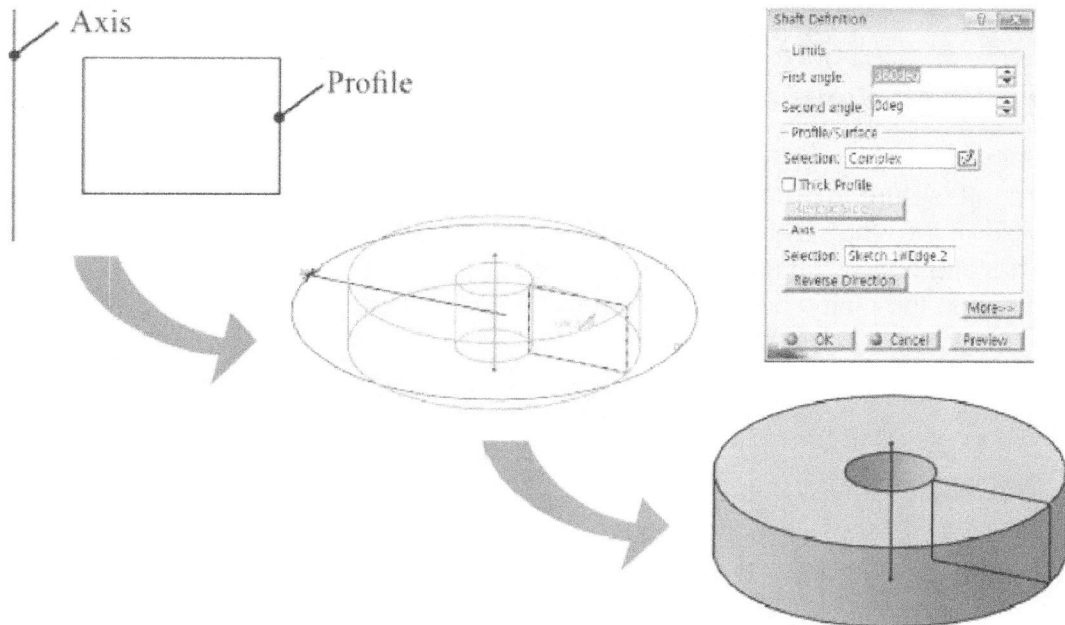

Fig 6-5 Using Standard Line as an Axis

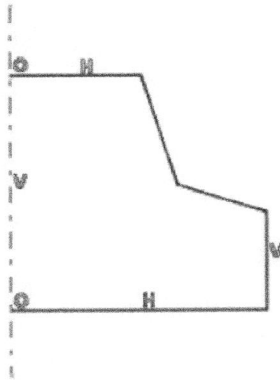

Fig 6-6 Open Profile

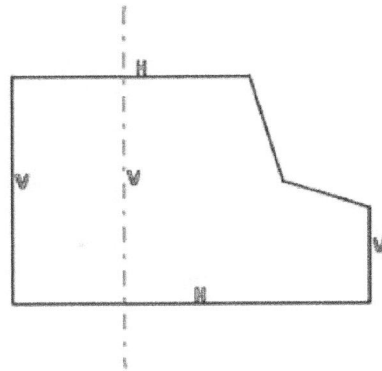

Fig 6-7 Axis Intersecting the Profile

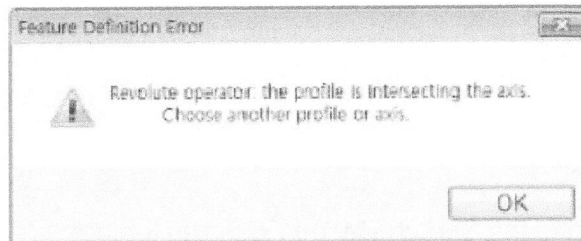

Fig 6-8 Error message

6.2 GROOVE

Using the Groove command in the Sketch-Based Features toolbar, you can revolve a profile and remove mate ria l from the existing soli d body. The Groove icon is activated only when at least one solid body exists. Therefore, you cannot create a Groove as the first feature.

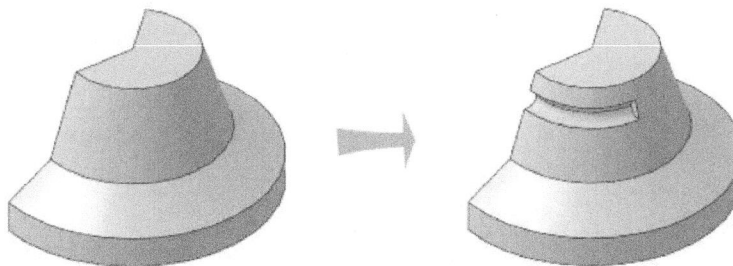

Fig 6-9 Groove Feature

Exercise 35: Creating a Groove Feature (ch06_002.CATPart)

Let's create a groove feature after creating a sketch.

Step 1: Sketch

Open the given part file. (ch06 _002.CATPart)

155

Invoke the Sketcher workbench by specifying the plane O in Fig 6-10 as the sketch plm1e.

Create a circle as shown in Fig 6-11 and iso-co11s train it.

Exit the Sketcher.

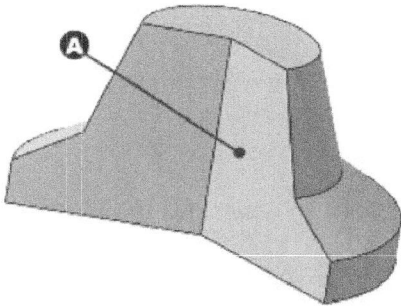

Fig 6-10 Sketch Plane

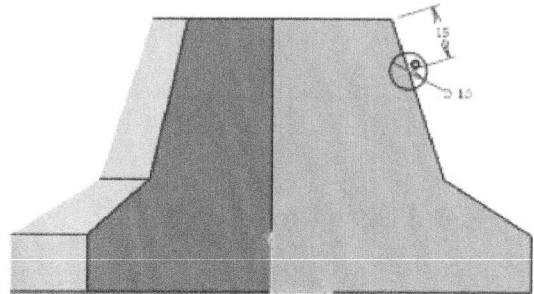

Fig 6-11 Sketch

Step 2: Groove

1. Click the Groove icon in the Sketch-Based Features toolbar.
2. Select the sketch created in Step 1.
3. Select the axis of revolution ((B) in Fig 6-12).
4. Press the Reverse Direction button in the dialog box if required such that the direct ion of the arrow appears as shown in Fig 6-12 (C).

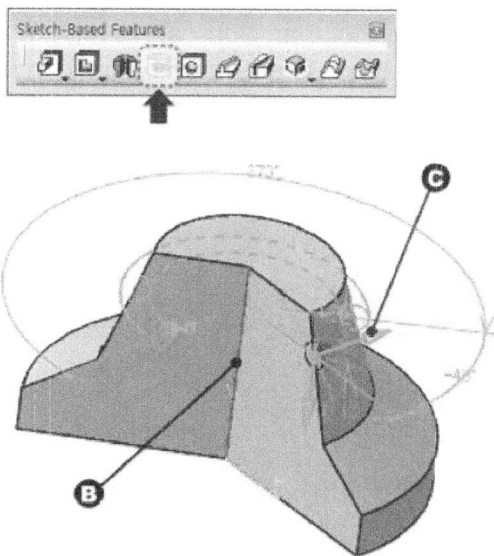

Fig 6-12 Selecting Sketch and Axis

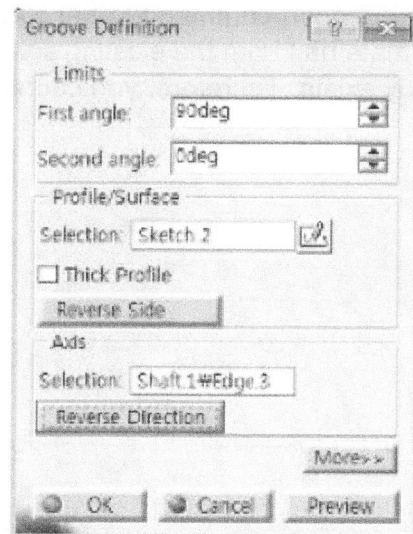

Fig 6-13 Limit Values

5. Enter the limit values as shown in Fig 6-13. The preview is updated.
6. Press the OK button. Fig 6-15 shows the groove feature created.

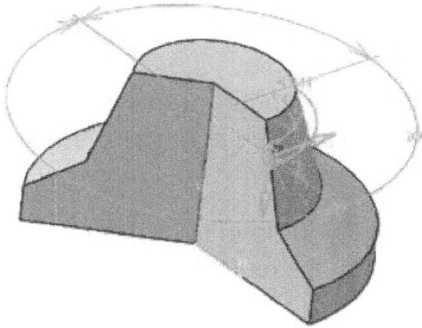

Fig 6-14 Preview

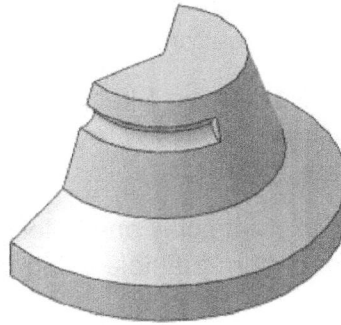

Fig 6-15 Groove Feature

6.3 HOLE COMMAND

Using the Hole command in the Sketch-Based Features tool bar, you can easily create standard holes that are frequently used in mechanical parts.

You can create five types of standard holes in CATIA V5.

1. Simple Hole
2. Tapered Hole
3. Counterbored Bole
4. Countersunk Hole
5. Counter drilled Hole

Fig 6-16 shows the section of each standard hole.

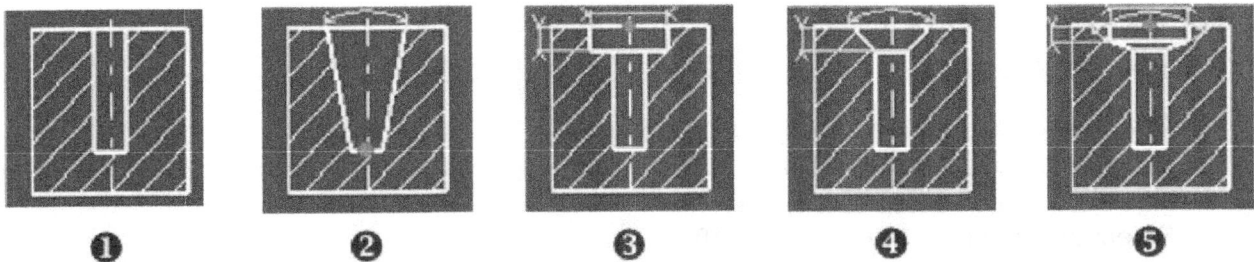

Fig 6-16 Section of Standard Holes

Remember that you can create holes by using the Pocket or Groove commands if you do not know how to use the Hole command.

6.3.1 Creating a General Hole

You can create a general hole according to the following procedure.

1. Click the Hole icon in the Sketch-Based Features toolbar.
2. Select a plane onto which to create a hole.
3. Set the Extension, Type and Thread Definition in the Hole Definition dialog box.

4. Invoke the Sketcher by pressing the Positioning Sketch button and define the location of the hole center. Then exit the Sketcher workbench.
5. Press the OK button.

If you press the Positioning Sketch button, you can define the location of the hole center by using the sketch constraint. You may modify the location of the hole later by accessing the sketch feature in the Spec Tree.

Note that you can create only one hole in a single operation. If you have to create a hole recursively, you can copy or pattern the hole using the command. in the Patterns toolbar.

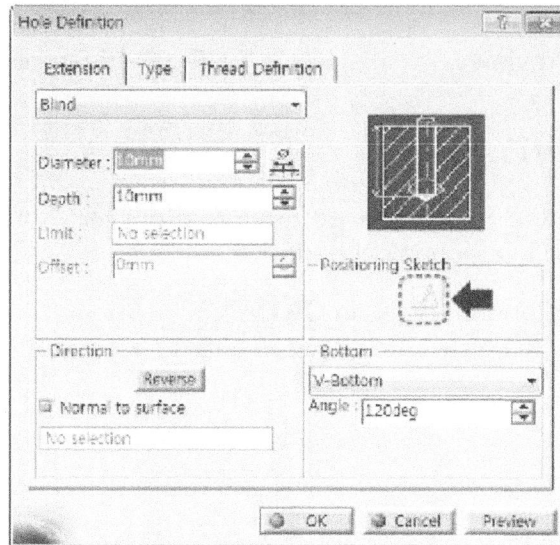

Fig 6-17 Hole Definition Dialog Box

Exercise 36: Ceating a General Hole (ch06_003.CATPart)

1. Open the given part file. (ch06_003.CATPart)
2. Click the Hole icon in the Sketch- Based Features toolbar. Read the message in the status bar.
3. Select the face (A) shown in Fig 6-18.

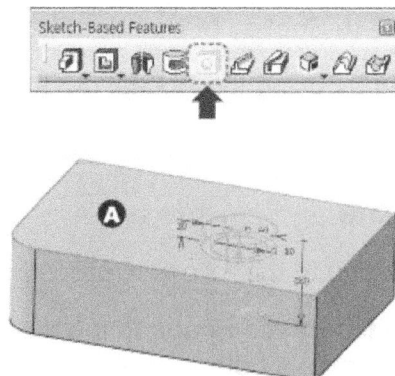

Fig 6-18 Plane for Hole

4. Set the options in the Extension and Type tab in the Hole Definition dialog box as shown in Fig 6-19 and press OK. A counter bored hole is created at an arbitrary location as shown in Fig 6-20.

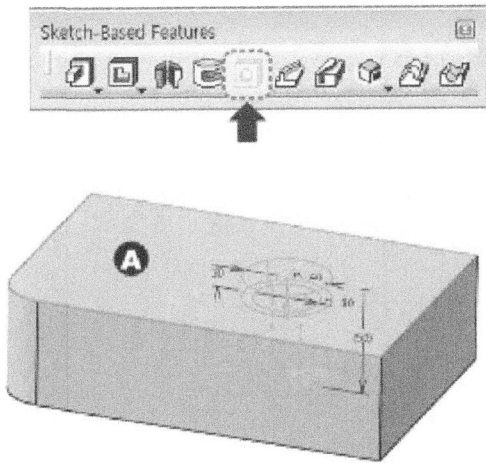

Fig 6-19 Options

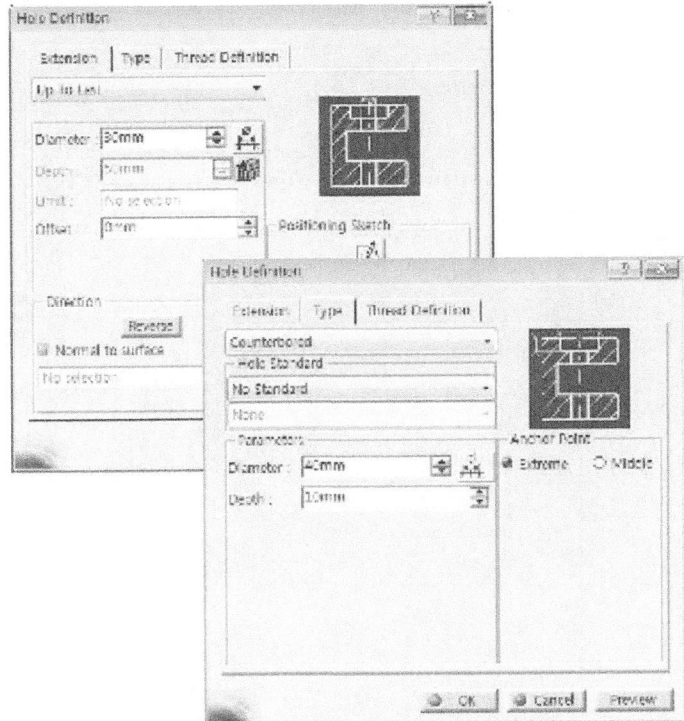

Fig 6-20 Counterbored Hole Created

5. Double click the Sketch feature un- der the Hole feature in the Spec Tree. The Sketcher workbench is invoked.

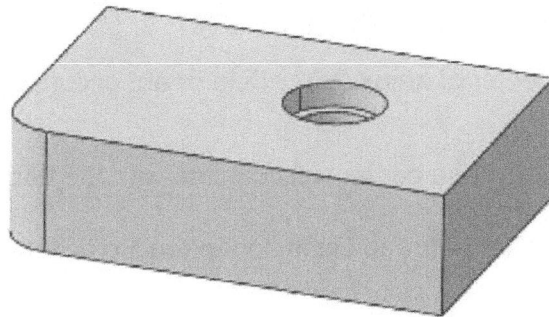

Fig 6- 21 Define the Location

6. Press the Constraint icon and define the location of the point as shown in Fig 6-21.
7. Exit the Sketcher. The location of the hole is updated.

(Note) Anchor Point

- The Anchor Point option in the Type tab of Hole Definition dialog box defines the location of the base point in the hole section.

159

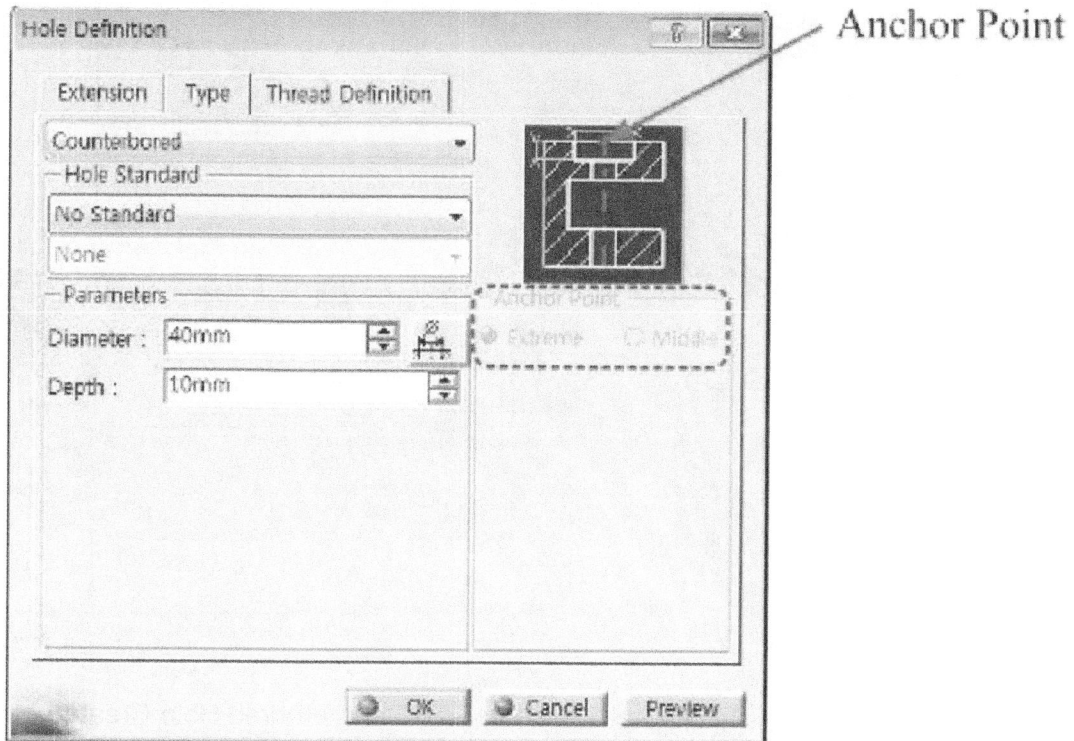

Fig 6-22 Anchor Point Option

6.3.2 Creating a Hole at an Existing Center

You can create a hole at the center of an existing circle or arc according to the following procedure.

1. Click the Hole icon.
2. Select a circle or an arc whose center will coincide with the center of the hole.
3. Select a plane.
4. Set the Extension, Type and Thread Definition in the Hole Definition dialog box.
5. Press the OK button.

Exercise 37: Creating a Hole at an Existing Center (ch06_004.CATPart)

Open the part file ch06_004.CATPart and create a simple hole whose center is co incident with the center of an existing arc. The number in Fig 6-23 corresponds to the procedure explained above.

160

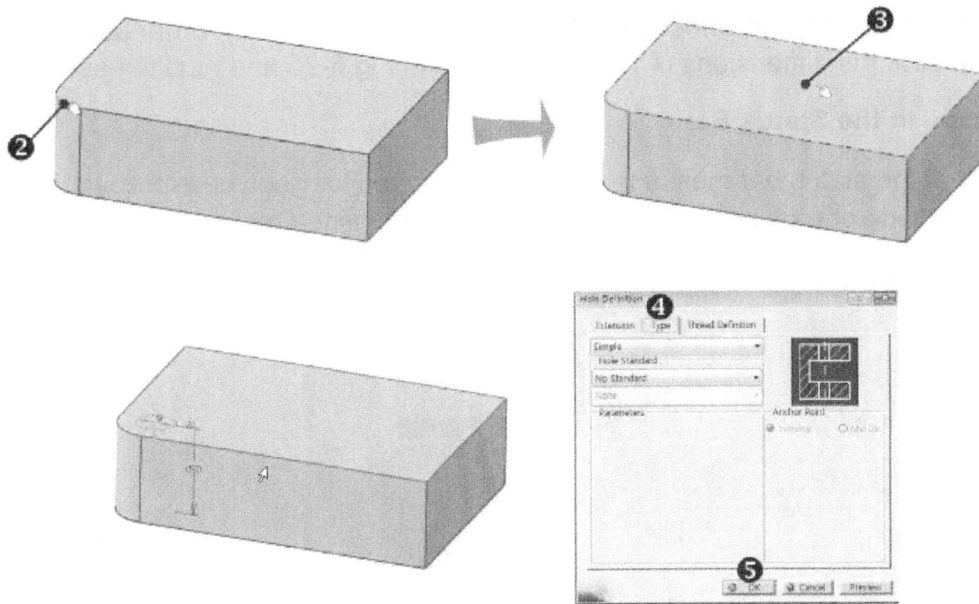

Fig 6-23 Creating a Simple Bole

6.3.3 Creating a Hole at a Distance from Existing Edges

You can create a hole at a distance from the existing linear edge(s) according to the following procedure.

1. Click the Hole icon.
2. Select one or two linear edge(s).
3. Select a plane.
4. Set the Extension, Type and Thread Definition in the Hole Definition dialog box.
5. Press the OK button.

Open the part file ch06_005.CATPart and create a countersunk hole at a location measured from the existing edges.

Exercise 38: Creating a Hole at a Distance from Existing Edges (ch06_005.CATPart)

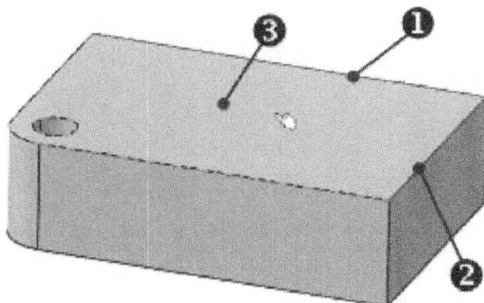

Fig 6-24 Selecting Edges and Plane

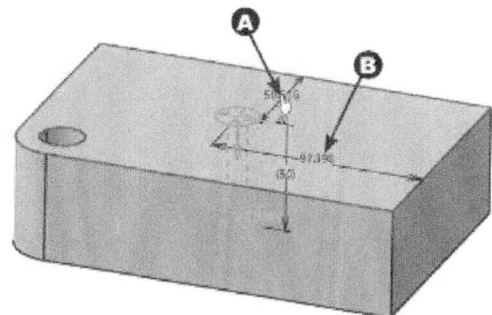

Fig 6-25 Modifying the Dimensions

1. Click the Hole icon and select the edges (1), (2) and plane (3) in order as shown in Fig 6-24.
2. Double click the dimensions (A) and (B) shown in Fig 6-25 and modify each value to 40mm.

(Note) Message in the Status Bar

- Note that the status bar message after pressing the Hole icon is as follows.
- "Select a face or a plane. Optionally select a point or line first to posit io n the sketch."

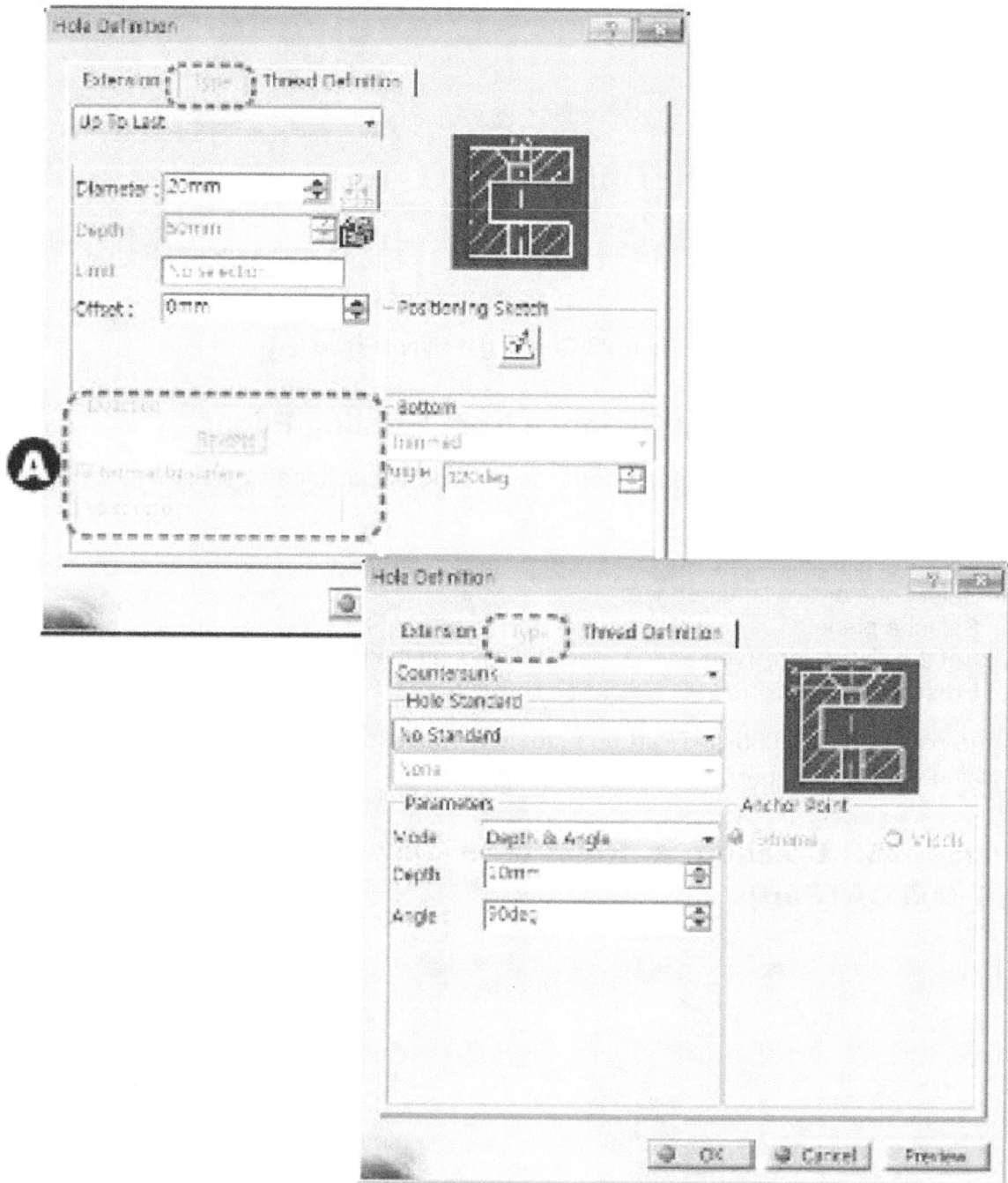

Fig 6-26 Type and Extension Option

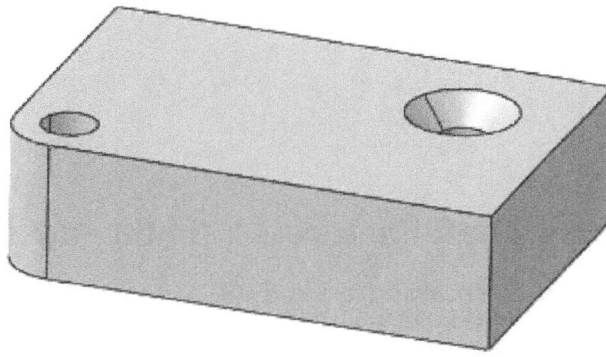

Fig 6-27 Countersunk Hole Created

Exercise 39: Creating a Shaft Feature – I (ch06_006.CATPart)

Create a solid model referring to the drawing in Fig 6-28.

1. All sketches have to be iso-constrained.
2. You should not use the Fix constraint.
3. Use the Shaft command just once.

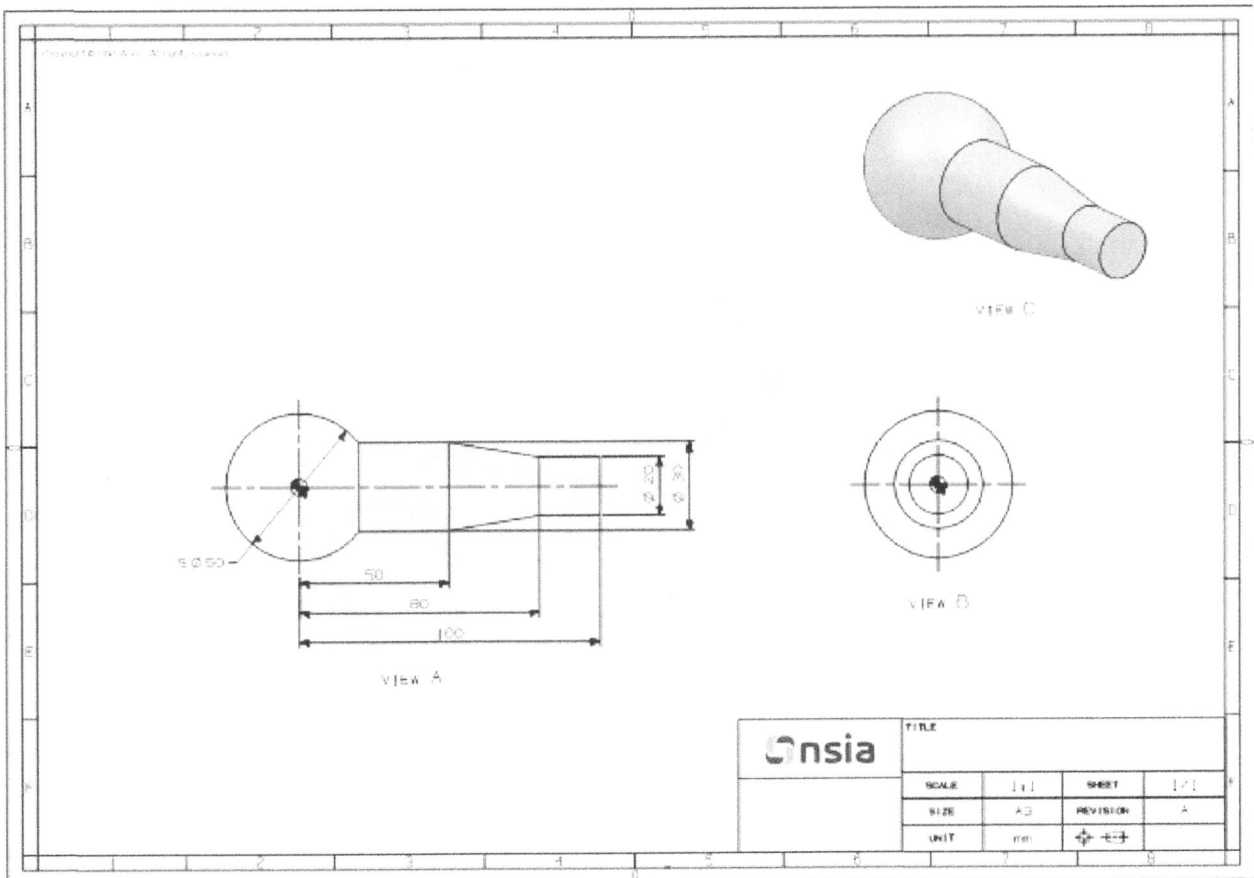

Fig 6-28 Drawing for Exercise 06

163

Exercise 40: Creating a Shaft Feature – II (ch06_007.CATPart)

Create a solid model referring to the drawing in Fig 6-29.

1. All sketches have to be iso-constrained.
2. You should not use the Fix constraint.

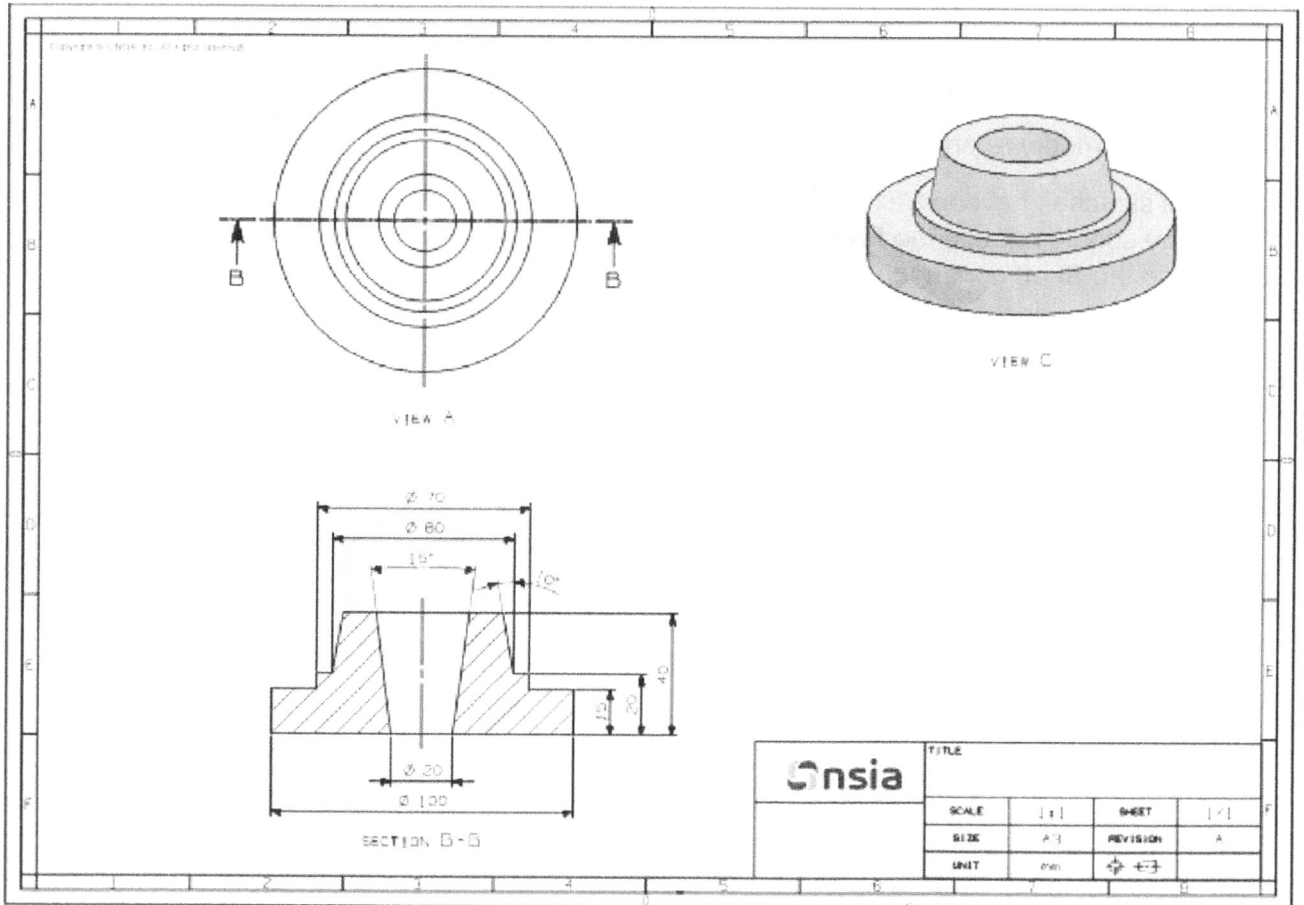

Fig 6-29 Drawing for Exercise 07

Exercise 41: Creating Holes (ch06_008.CATPart)

Create a solid model referring to the drawing in Fig 6-30.

1. All sketches have to be iso-con trained.
2. You should not use the Fix constraint.
3. Use the Hole co mm and to create holes.

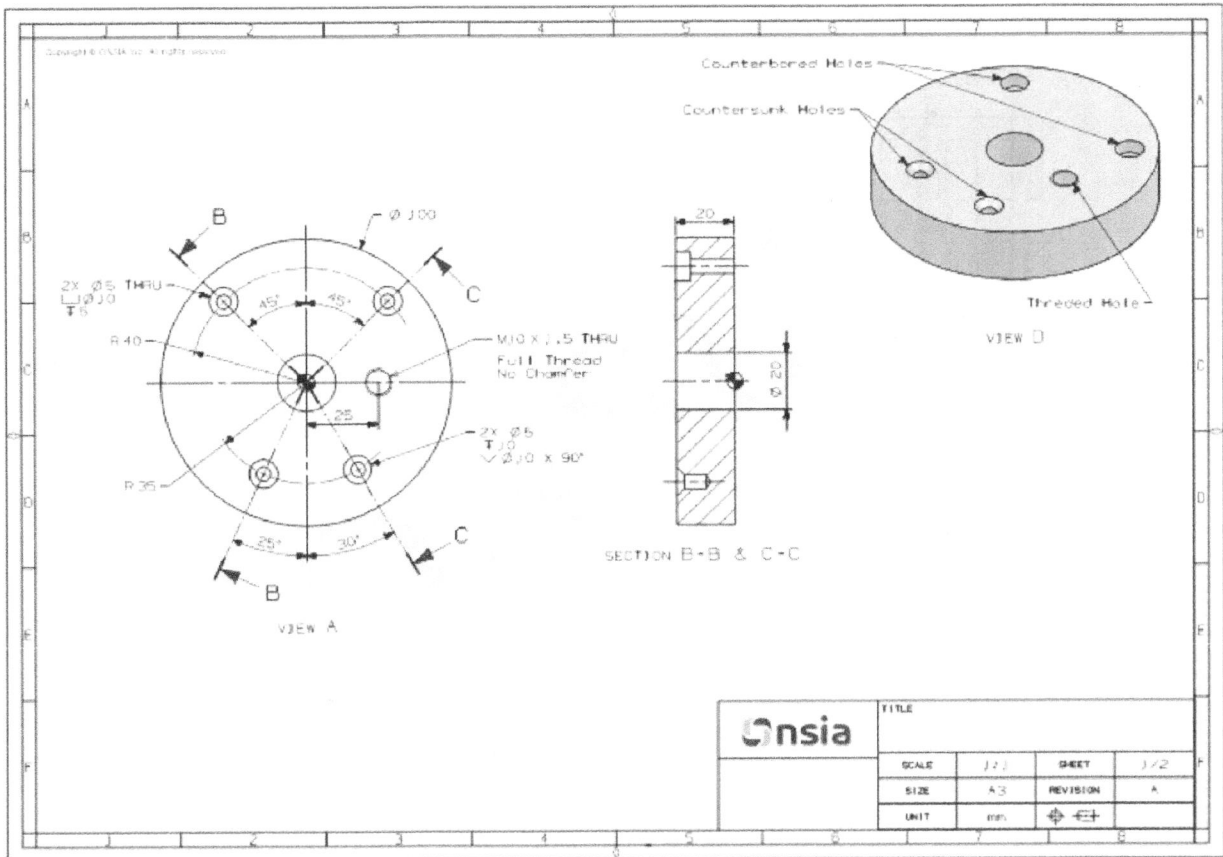

Fig 6-30 Drawing for Exercise 41

Exercise 42: Creating a Part (ch06_009.CATPart)

Create a solid model referring to the drawing in Fig 6-31.

1. Use the Hole command to create holes.

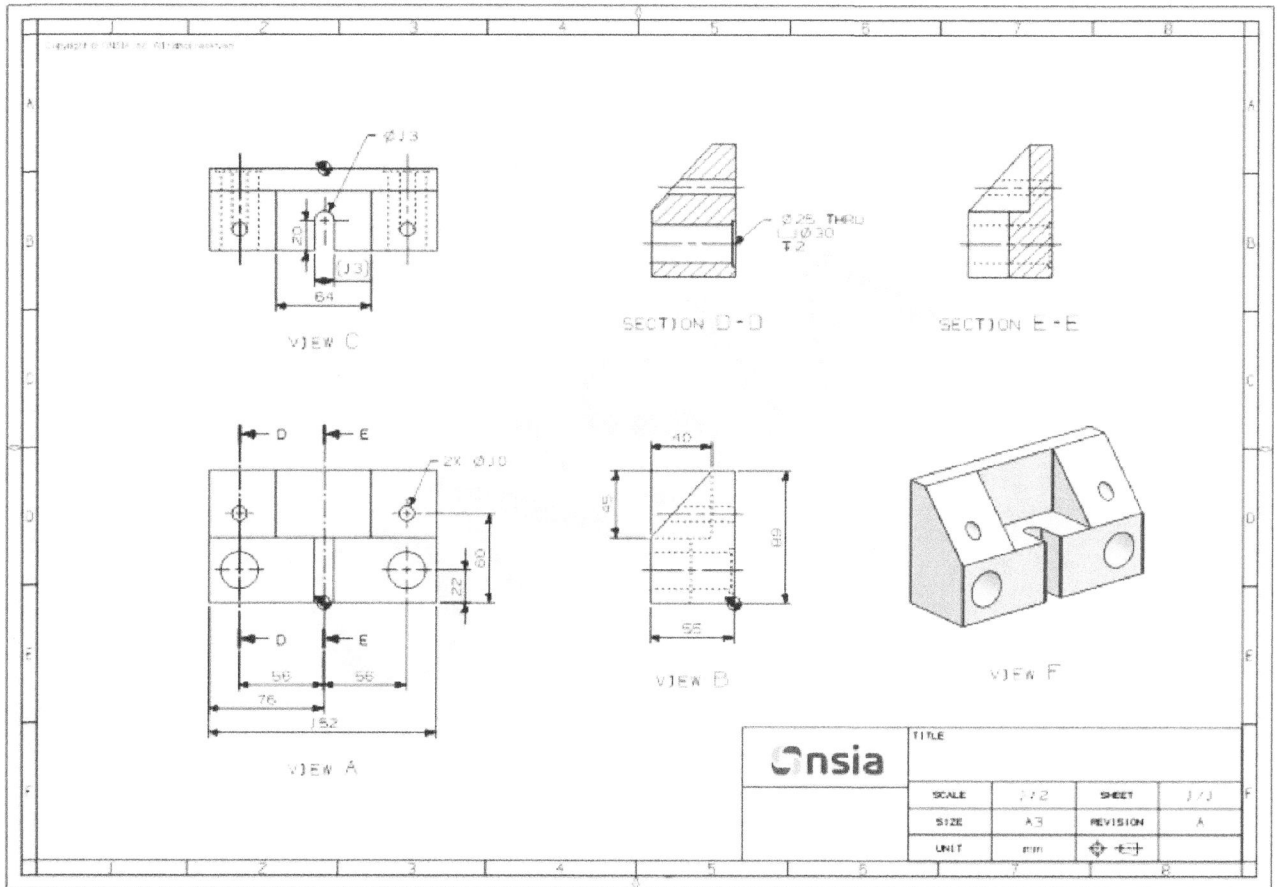

Fig 6-31 Drawing for Exercise 42

Exercise 43: Creating a Part (ch06_010.CATPart)

Create a spherical guide block referring to the drawing in Fig 6-32.

Requirements

1. The diameter of the four holes specified by (A) are linked such that if you modify one, all other holes are updated.
2. The Pocket feature designated by (B) in Fig 6 - 32 has to remove the sphere completely regardless of the radius of the sphere.
3. The Pad feature designated by (C) has to end on the spherical surface.

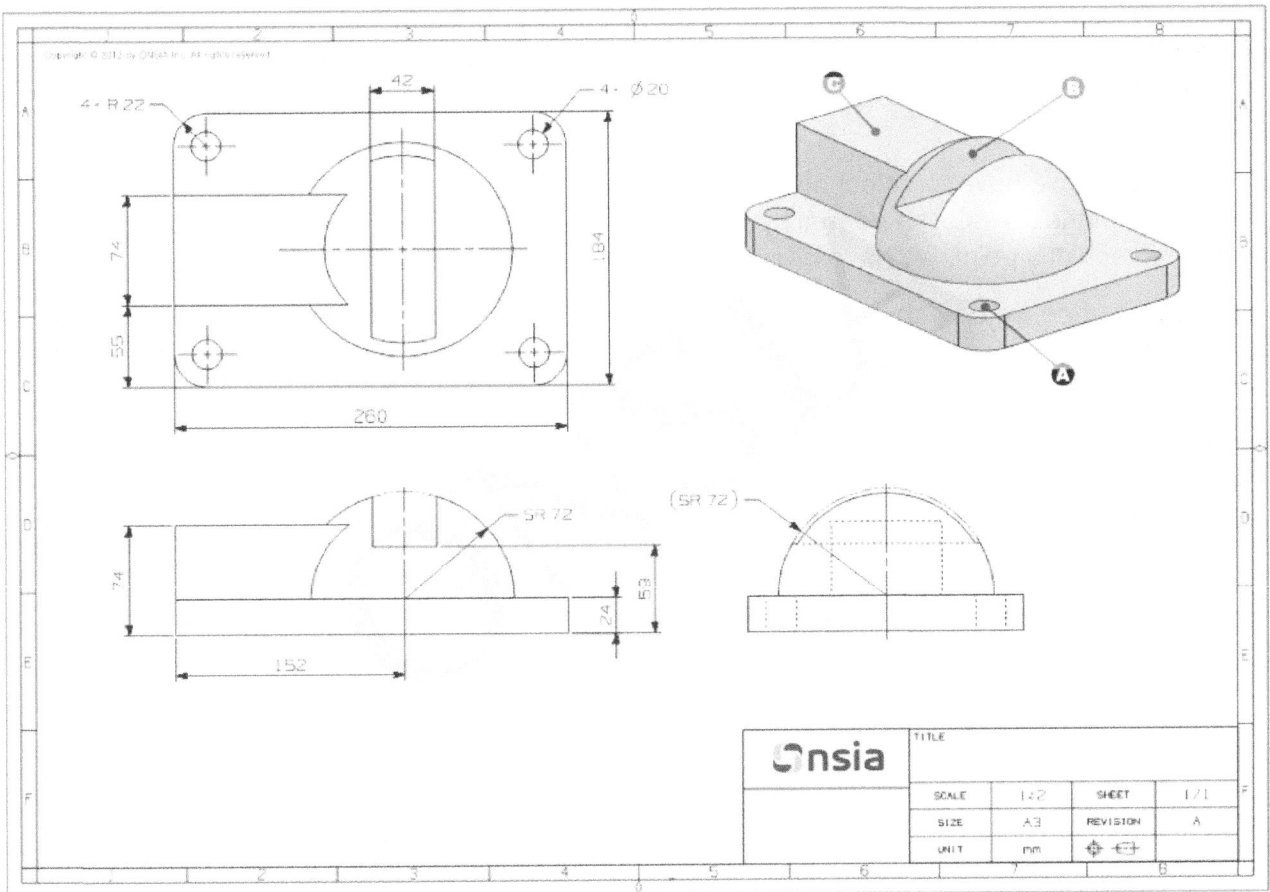

Fig 6-32 Spherical Guide Block

CHAPTER 7: UTILIZING REFERENCE ELEMENTS FOR PRECISION

7.1 REFERENCE ELEMENTS

In chapters 1 through 6, we used planes, lines and points for the following purposes.

- **Planes:** for defining sketch planes and for limiting planes using the Pad and Pocket commands
- **Lines:** for defining direction using the Pad, Pocket and Translate commands
- **Points:** for defining the location of a hole, start and end points using the Rotate and Translate commands.

That is to say, we selected planes, linear edges or points in cases where the modeling process required us to select those elements to define a feature. We have been able to select a planar plane onto which to create a sketch. We have been able to select a plane to define the limit of Pad or Pocket features.

In cases where we have to select an object to define the direction, we have been able to select a linear edge, plane (to select a normal direction) or cylindrical surface (to select an axial direction). If we need to select a point, we have been able to select a vertex, or a point created in Sketcher.

However, what do we do if there is no exact object for what we have to select? In such cases, we have to create the required plane, point or line with reference to the existing geometry. The geometry elements that are created for this purpose are called Reference Elements.

For reference element we cannot define mass or volume and they are not considered as part geometry.

Reference elements are always defined with reference to existing geometries and maintain associativity with them. Therefore, if the parent geometries are changed parametrically, the reference elements will be updated. The associativity can be broken using the Isolate command.

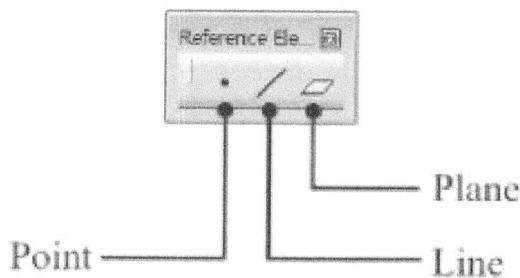

Fig 7-1 Reference Elements Toolbar

Fig 7-1 Reference Elements Toolbar

7.2 REFERENCE PLANE

Reference planes have the following characteristics.

- A reference plane does not have area and thickness.
- A reference plane does not have a boundary. ft is an infinite plane. The rectangular plane shown in the part geometry is just a symbol to show the existence of the reference plane.

If you click the Plane icon in the Reference Elements toolbar, the Plane Definition dialog box as shown in Fig 7-2 appears. There are many methods for defining the reference plane in the Plane type dropdown list. Other options in the dialog box are changed according to the selected definition method.

The following types of planes are widely used.

1. Offset from plane
2. Angle/ Normal to plane
3. Tangent to surface
4. Through three points
5. Nonnal to curve

While you are defining the reference elements, it is strongly recommended that you carefully read the prompts in the status bar.

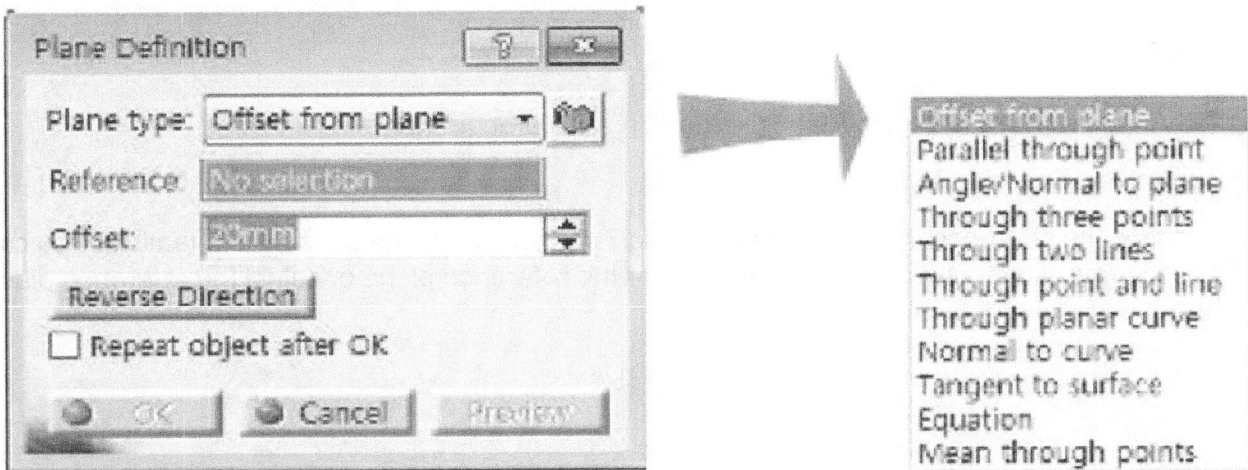

Fig 7-2 Plane Definition Dialog Box

7.2.1 Usages of a Reference Plane

The following are three typical usages of reference planes.

(1) Sketch Plane

The feature designated by the arrow in Fig 7-3 is created by padding a sketch defined on a reference plane slanted 45 degrees from the yz plane.

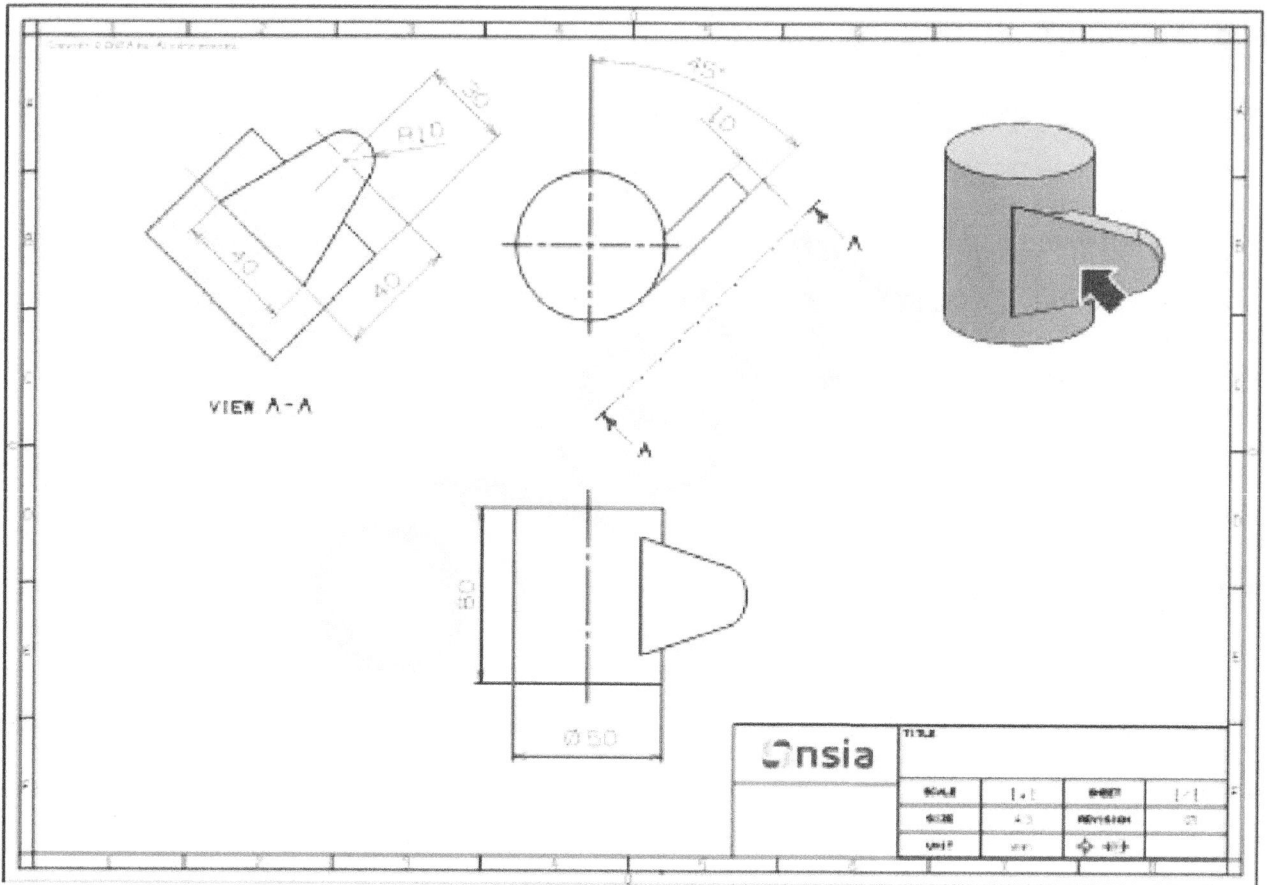

Fig 7-3 An Example of a Sketch Plane Defined on a Reference Plane

(2) Control the Size of a Feature

If you define the reference planes as shown in Fig 7-4, you can define the size of a feature. You can either constrain sketch elements with reference to the reference plane or select the reference plane as the limiting element to define a Pad feature.

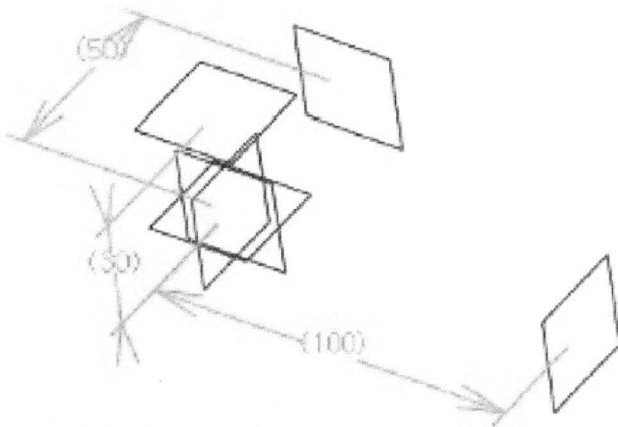

Fig 7-4 Three Reference Planes Defined at a Distance

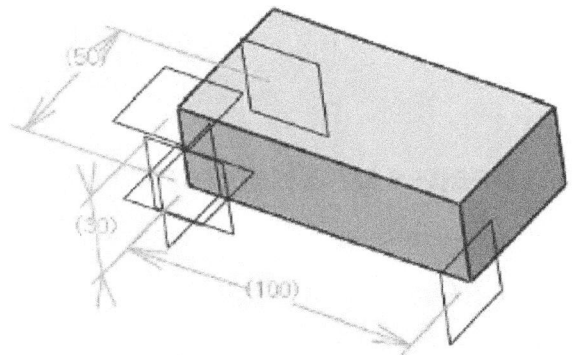

Fig 7-5 A Pad Feature

170

(3) Tool Object of the Split Command

The cut plane designated by the arrow in Fig 7-6 is created with the Split command. You can select a reference plane as the Splitting Element.

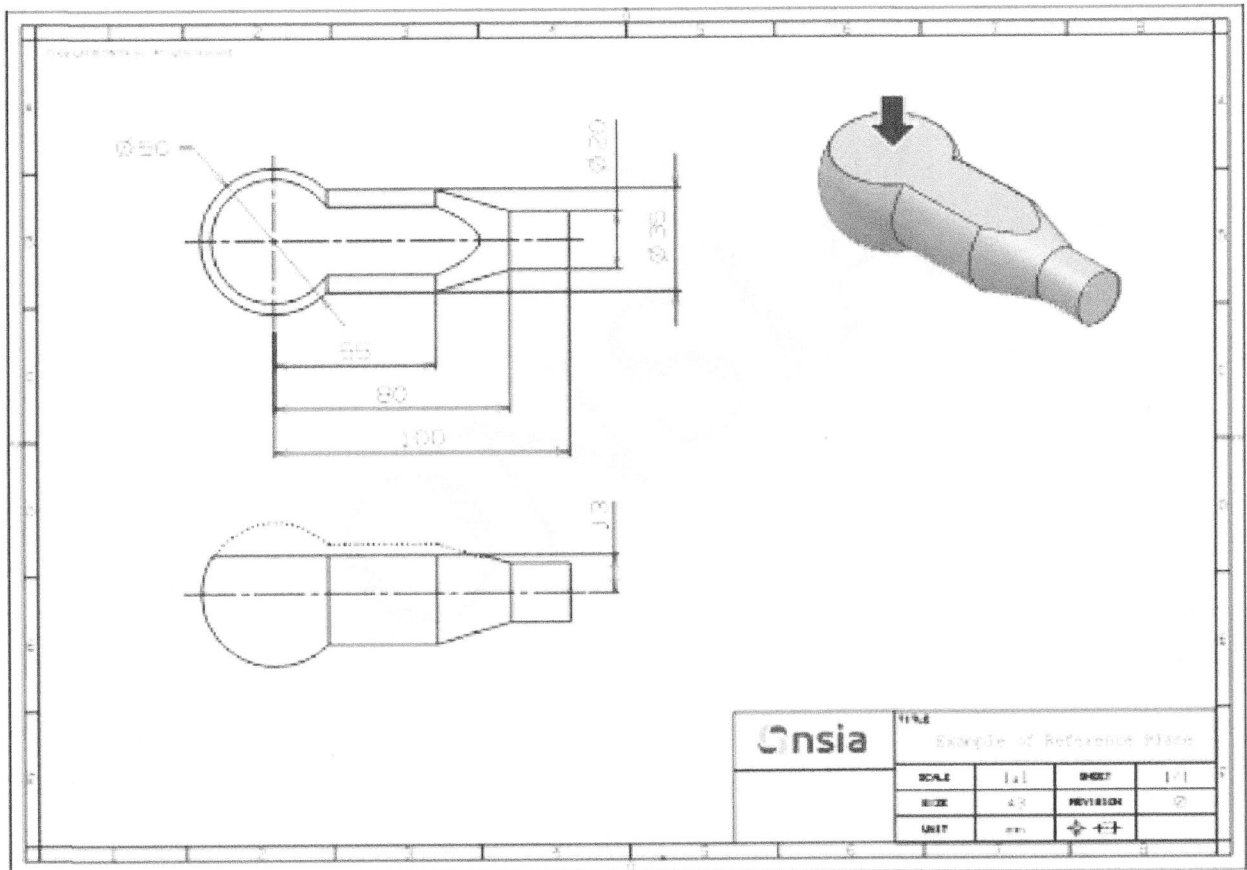

Fig 7-6 Splitting a Solid Body with a Reference Plane Reference Plane

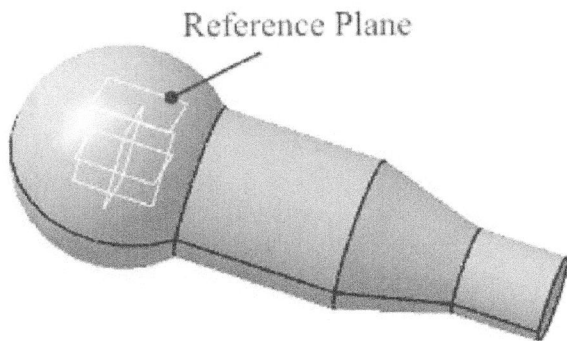

Fig 7-7 Before Splitting

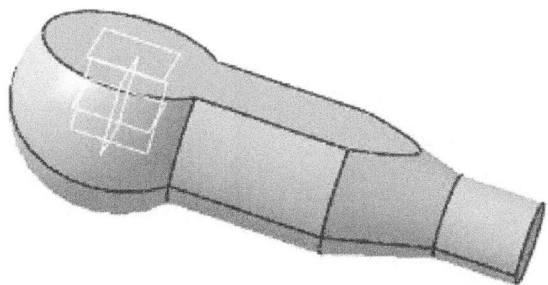

Fig 7- 6 After Splitting

7.2.2 Types of Reference Plane

You can identify various types of reference planes in the Plane Definition dialog box. If you select a type in the dropdown list, other options in the dialog box will change accordingly. You can define a reference plane by carefully reading the status bar messages for the corresponding options.

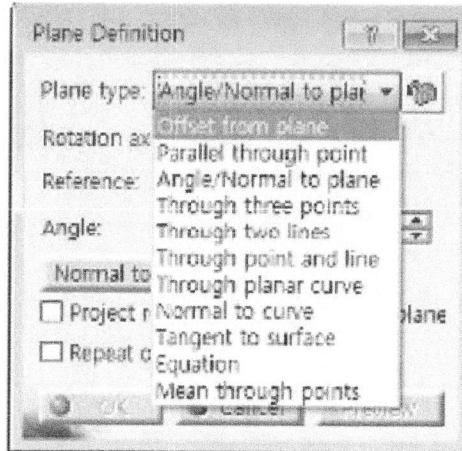

Fig 7-9 Types of Reference Plane

Exercise 44: Offset from Plane (ch07_001.CATPart)

With the Offset from plane type, you can create a reference plane at a distance from an existing planar face or another reference plane. Let's learn how to create the Offset from plane type reference plane.

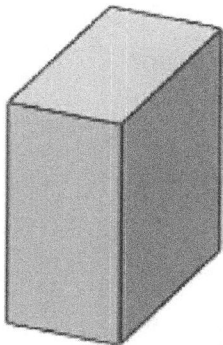

Fig 7-10 Reference Plane (Offset from plane type)

Fig 7-11 A Block

Fig 7-12 Face to Select

Opening the Given Part

1. Open the given part ch07_001.CATPart.
2. Hide the xy, yz and zx planes as shown in Fig 7-11.

Creating a Reference Plane

1. Click the Plane icon in the Reference Elements toolbar.
2. Select Offset from plane in the Type dropdown list.
3. Select the plane designated by the arrow in Fig 7-12 as the reference.
4. Enter 50 in the Offset input box.
5. Select the Repeat object after OK option in the dialog box. A preview is shown like in Fig 7-14.

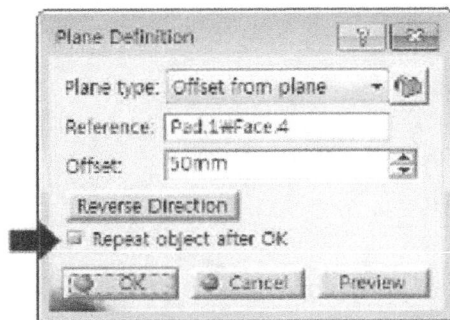

Fig 7-13 Plane Definition Dialog Box

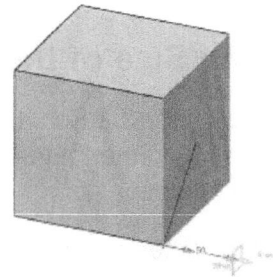

Fig 7-14 Preview

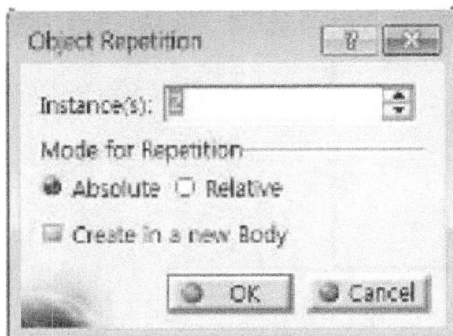

Fig 7-15 Object Repetition Dialog Box

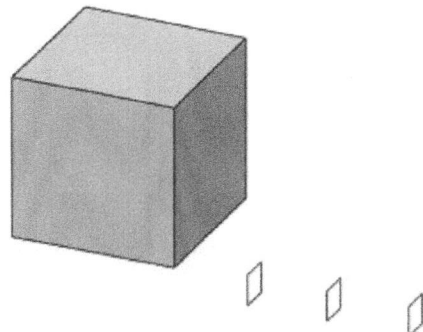

Fig 7-16 Reference Plane Created

173

6. Press the OK button in the dialog box. The Object Repetition dialog box is invoked as shown in Fig 7-15.

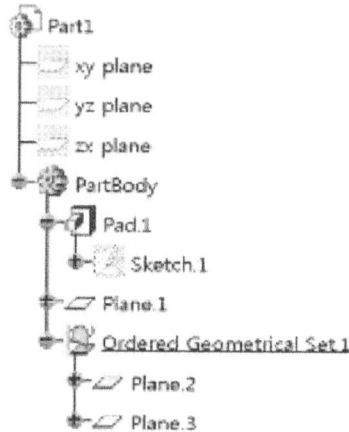

Fig 7-17 Spec Tree

7. Set the options as shown in the figure and click OK. Fig 7-16 shows three reference planes that have been created. Note that two more planes are created after clicking OK in the Plane Definition dialog box according to the setting in the Object Repetition dialog box. Fig 7-17 shows the specification tree after creating the reference planes. Now, let's modify the size of the block.

Modifying the Size of the Block

1. Double click the Sketch. I feature under the Pad. I feature.
2. Modify the dy dimension from 100 to 50.
3. Exit the sketcher.

Confirm that the distance between the side plane of the block and the first reference plane is maintained to 50 mm.

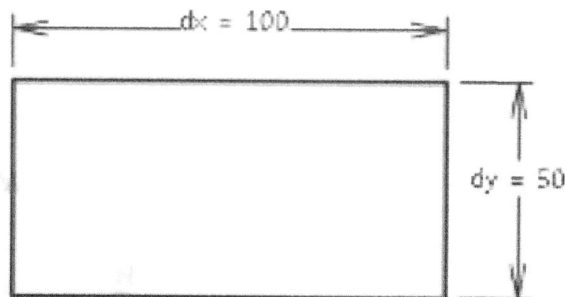

Fig 7 - 19 Modified Dimension

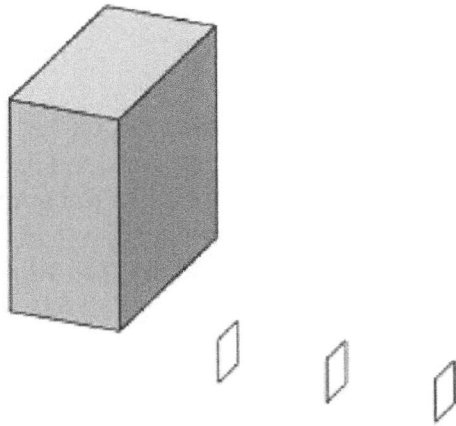

Fig 7-18 Modified Pad Feature

Exercise 45: Angle/Normal to Plane – 1 (ch07_002.CATPart)

Let's create a model by defining an angled reference plane. We will create an Angle/Normal to plane type reference plane using the automatic type change function.

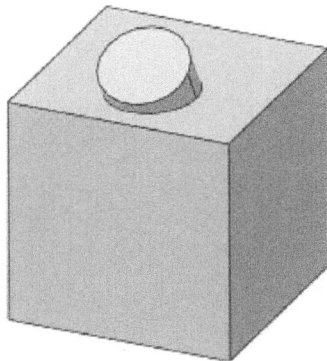

Fig 7-20 Model to Create

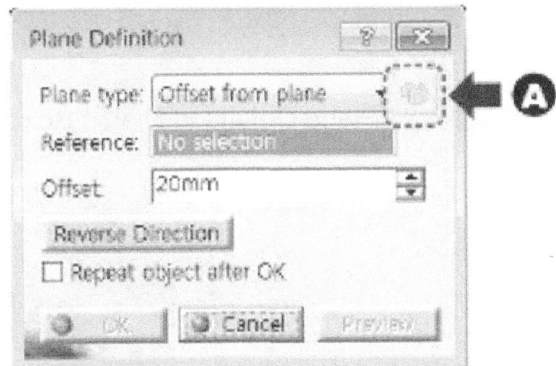

Fig 7-21 Plane Definition Dialog Box

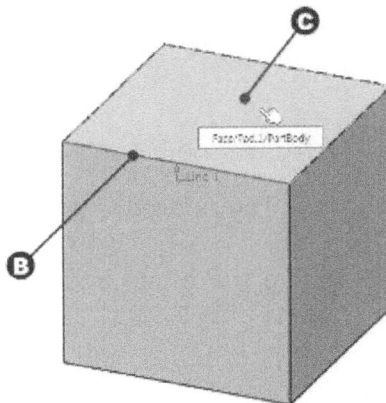

Fig 7-22 Selecting an Edge and Plane

Creating a Reference Plane

1. Open the given part ch07_002.CATPart.
2. Hide the xy, yz and zx planes.
3. Click the Plane icon in the Reference Elements tool bar.
4. Set the options as shown in Fig 7-21. Note that the plane type is set to Offset from plane and that the button specified by (A) is unlocked. It means that the plane type will change automatically according to the selection of geometry.
5. Select the edge and plane as specified by Q and0 in Fig 7-22. Note that the Plane type option changes as shown in Fig 7-23.

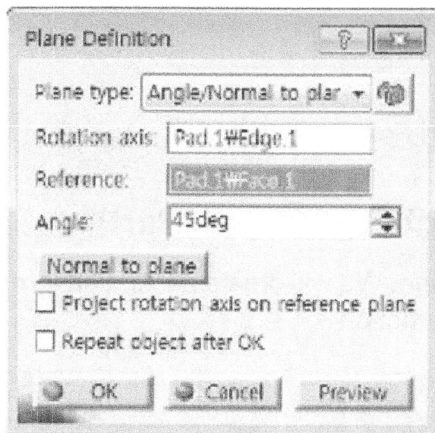

Fig 7-23 Plane Definition Dialog Box

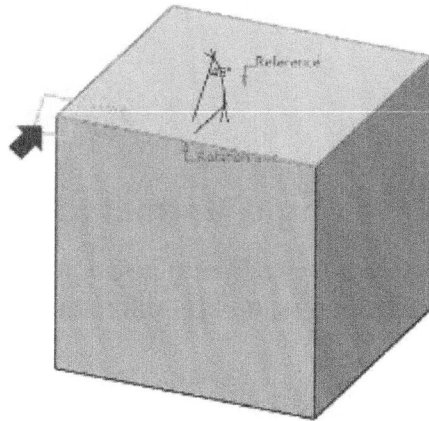

Fig 7-24 Preview

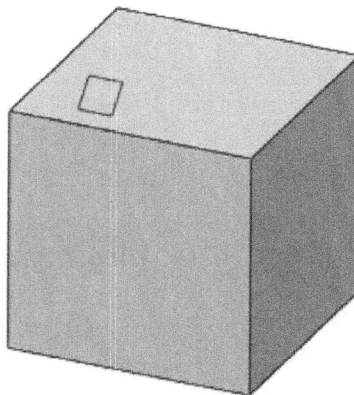

Fig 7-25 Reference Plane Created

6. Enter 45 deg in the Angle input box. The reference plane is previewed as designated by the arrow in Fig 7-24.
7. Move the plane symbol by dragging the Move text and click OK in the dialog box. The reference plane is created as shown in Fig 7-25.

Modeling with Reference Plane

1. Define a positioned sketch as shown in Fig 7-26. Note that the origin of the sketch axis is at the middle point of the edge.

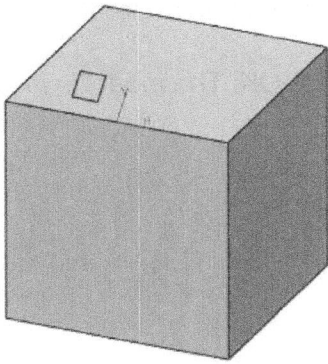

Fig 7-26 Sketch Plane

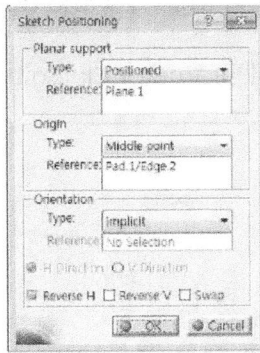

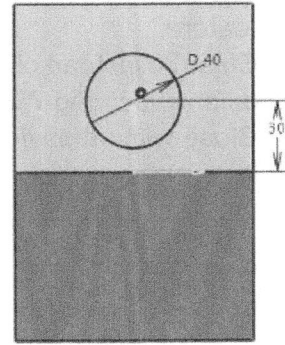

Fig 7-27 Sketch

2. Create a circle and iso-cons train it as shown in Fig 7-27.
3. Create a pad feature as shown in Fig 7-28. The reference plane is hidden for graphic simplicity.

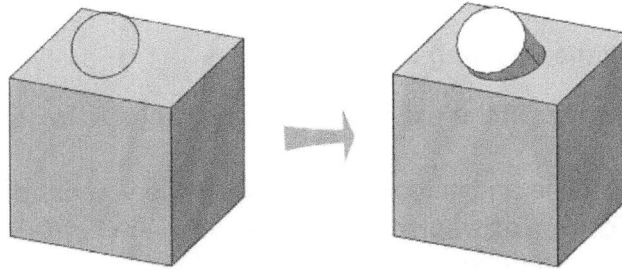

Fig 7-28 Pad Feature Created

Modifying the Model

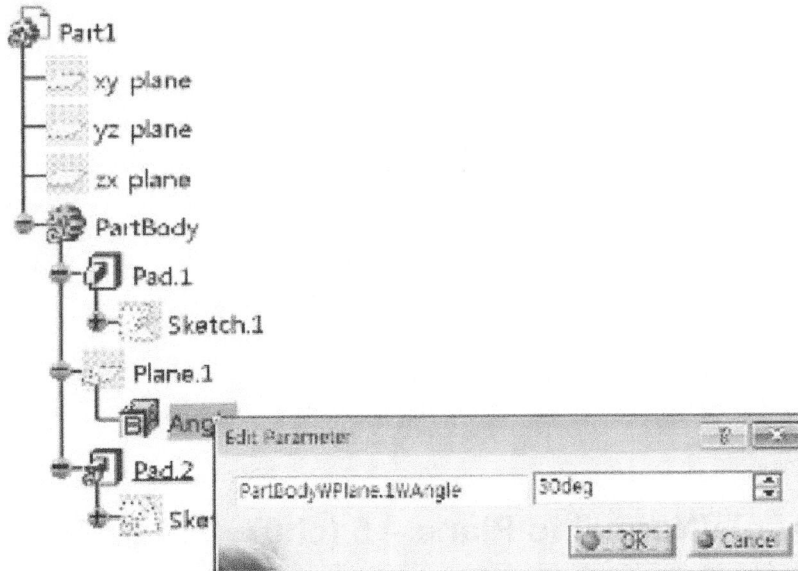

Fig 7-29 Modifying Angle

177

1. Expand the Spec Tree as shown in Fig 7-29 and double clic k the Angle under the Plane. 1 feature.
2. Enter 30 instead of 45 in the Edit Parameter dialog box and press OK. The model is modified as shown in Fig 7-30.
3. Close without saving the file.

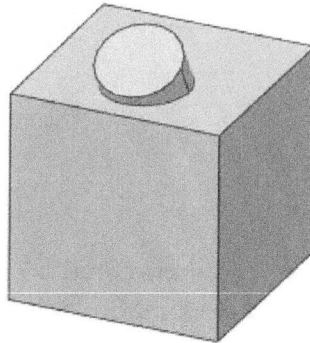

Fig 7-30 Result of Modification

(Note) Creating an Axis while Defining a Plane

- If there is no linear object in the existing geometry, we have to create one before defining a plane.
- You can also create a line and select it as an axis while you are defining a reference plane.
- Right click on the Rotation axis selection area as shown in Fig 7-31. A pop-up menu appears and you can create the required line with the Create Line me nu. When we are defining an object while running a command, a Running Command window appears and shows you the current step of the definition.

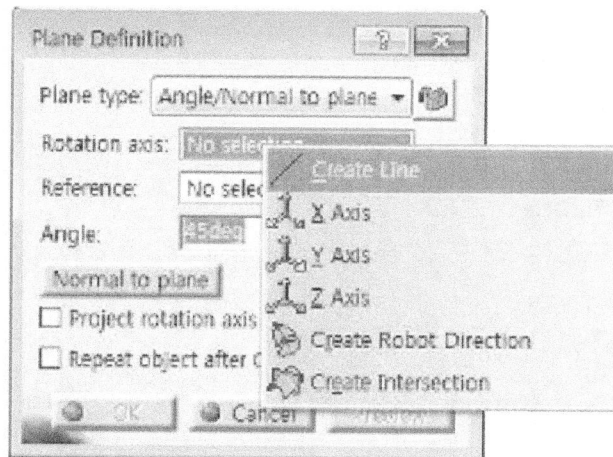

Fig 7-31 Pop-Up Menu

Exercise 46: Angle/Normal to Plane – 5 (ch07_003.CATPart)

Let's create a 45° angled reference plane with respect to the yz plane. Refer to the dashed rectangle shown in Fig 7-32 to identify the location and angle of the reference plane to create.

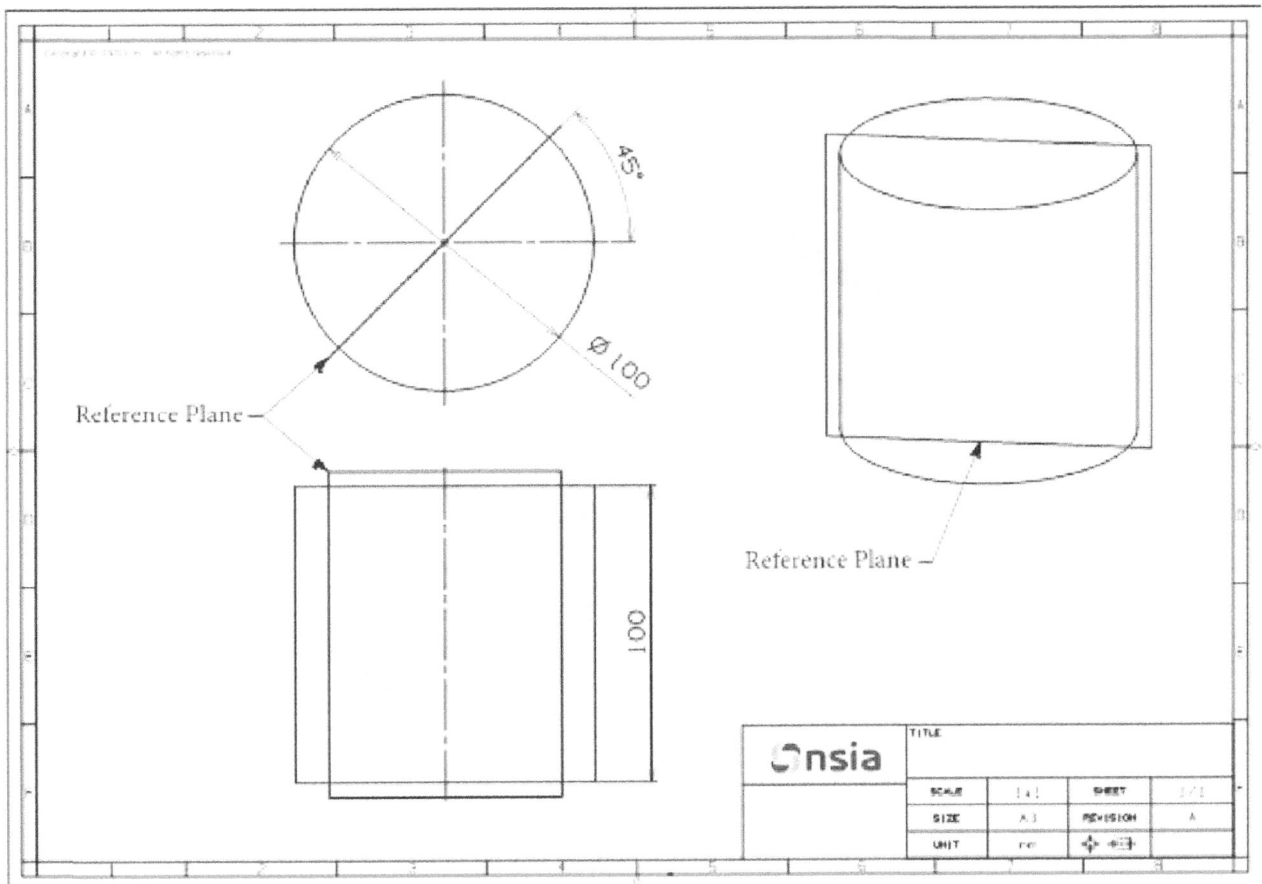

Fig 7-32 Drawing for Reference Plane

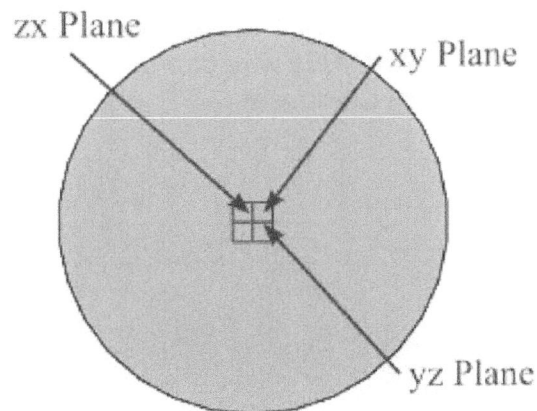

Fig 7-33 Top View

Opening the Given Part

1. Open the given part ch07_003.CATPart.
2. Display the top view as shown in Fig 7-33. Identify each base plane as shown in the figure.

179

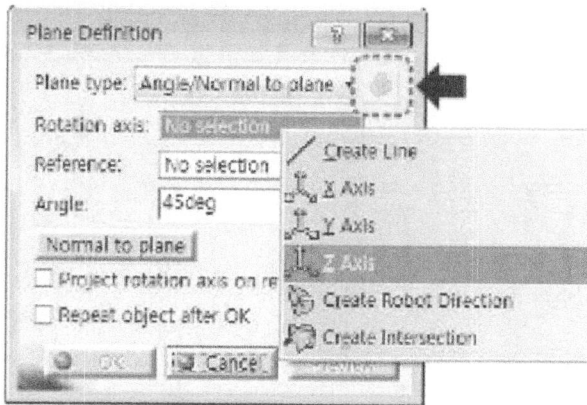

Fig 7-34 Plane Definition Dialog Box

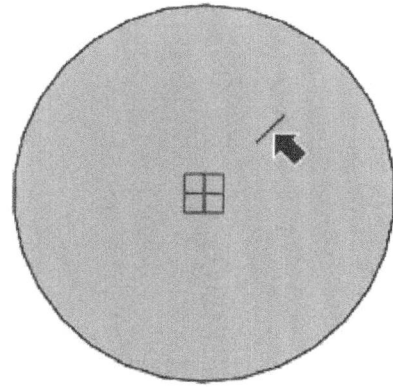

Fig 7-35 Reference Plane Created

Creating the Reference Plane

1. Click the Plane icon in the Reference Elements tool bar.
2. Choose Angle/Normal to plane in the Plane type dropdown list.
3. Lock the automatic type change button.
4. Right click on the Rotation axis selection field and choose Z Axis in the pop-up menu. You are prompted to select the reference plane in the status bar.
5. Select the yz plane.
6. Enter 45 deg in the Angle input box.
7. Move the plane symbol as shown in Fig 7-35 and click OK in the Plane Definition dialog box.
8. Close without saving the file.

(Note) Creating Points while Defining a Plane

Right click on the Point select ion area. A pop- up menu as shown in Fig 7-36 appears and you can create the required point with the Create Point menu. You can also create a point using other methods that appear in the pop-up menu. This way of creating the required object to select while running a command is called a Stacking Command.

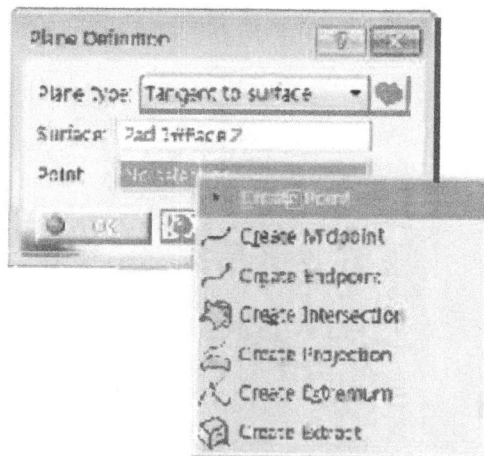

Fig 7-36 Point Pop-up Menu

180

Exercise 47: Tangent to Surface (ch07_004.CATPart)

Let's create a reference plane which is tangent to a cylindrical face and passes through a specific point.

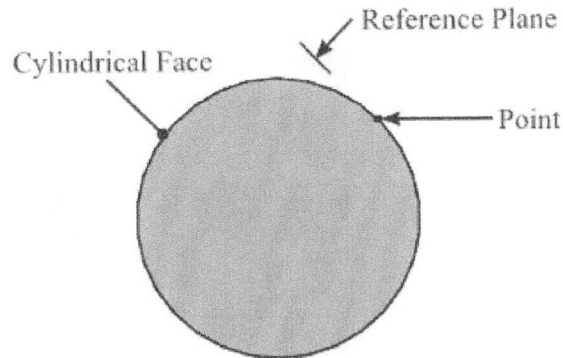

Fig 7-37 Reference Plane to Create

Opening the Given Part

Fig 7-38 Top View
Fig 7-39 Selecting an Edge

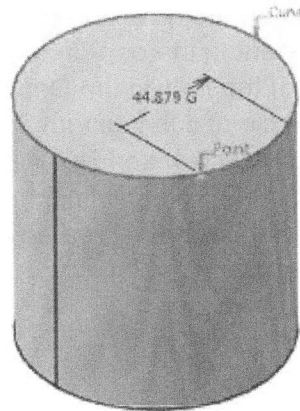

Opening the Given Part

1. Open the given part ch07_004.CATPart.
2. Hide the xy, yz and zx planes.
3. Display the top view as shown in Fig 7-38. Note that the horizontal direction of the model coincides with the y direction.
4. Display the iso metric view.

Creating a Point

1. Click the Point icon in the Reference Elements tool bar.
2. Choose On curve in the Point type dropdown list.
3. Select the upper circular edge of the cylinder as shown in Fig 7-39. The point is previewed.

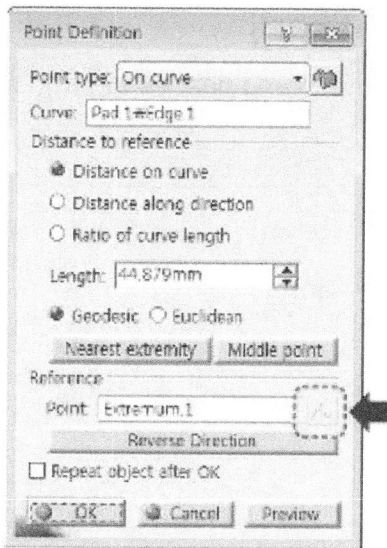

Fig 7-40 Point Definition Dialog Box

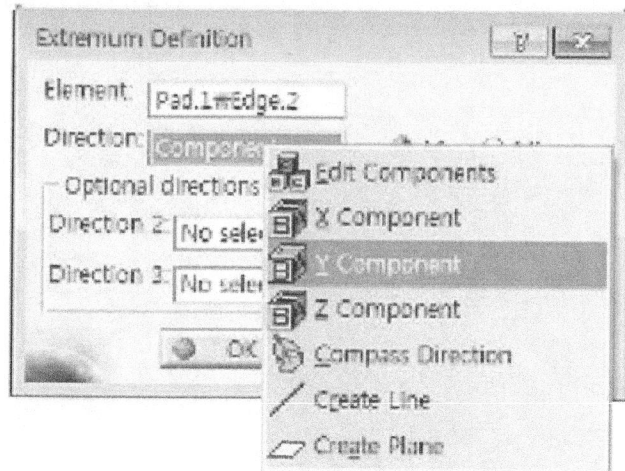

Fig 7-41 Extremum Definition Dialog Box

4. Click the Extremum icon in the Point Definition dialog box as specified by the arrow in Fig 7-40. The Extremum Definition dialog box is invoked as shown in Fig 7-41.
5. Right click on the Direction selection field in the Extremum Definition dialog box and choose Y Component in the pop-up me nu.
6. Click OK in the Extremum Definition dialog box.
7. Choose Ratio of curve length in the Distance to reference option and enter 0.125 in the Ratio in put box as shown in Fig 7-42.
8. Click OK in the Point Definition dialog box. The point is created as shown in Fig 7-43. Note that the point has been created at the location of 12.5% of the full circular edge with reference to the Y maximum point.

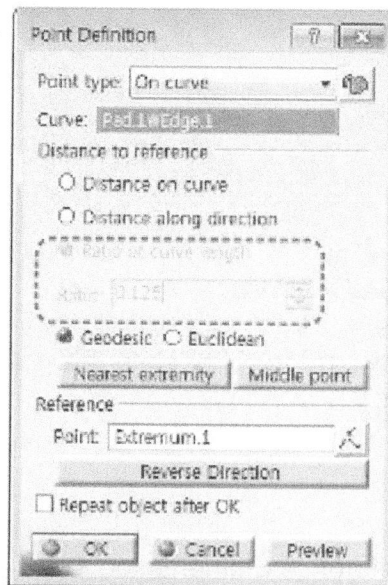

Fig 7-42 Point Definition Dialog Box

182

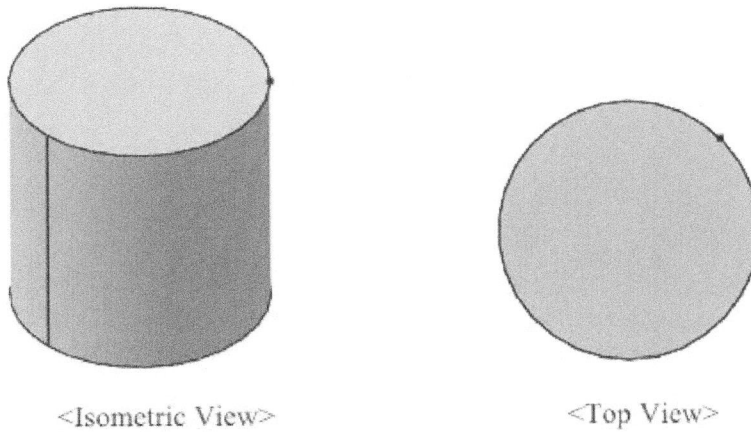

<Isometric View>   <Top View>

Fig 7-43 Point Created

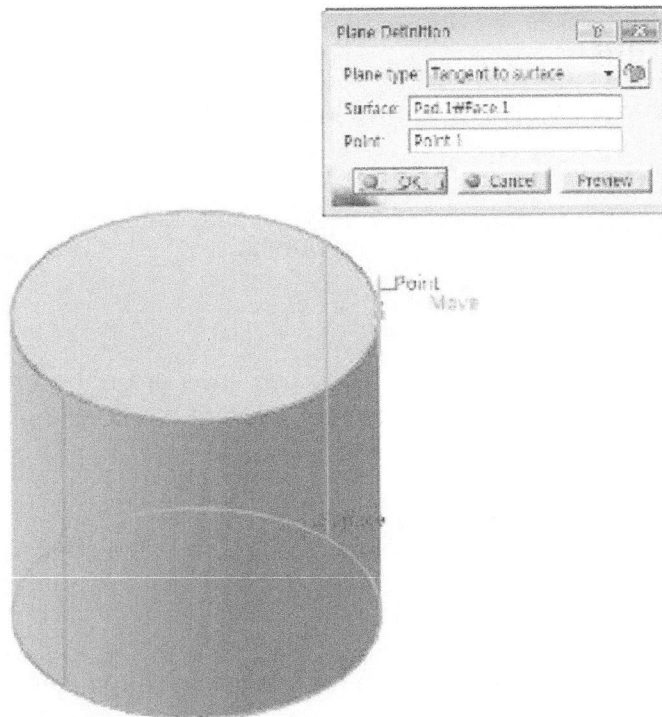

Fig 7-44 Selecting Surface and Point

Creating the Reference Plane

1. Restore the isometric view.
2. Click the Plane icon in the Reference Elements toolbar.
3. Choose Tangent to surface in the Plane type dropdown list.
4. Select the cylindrical surface and point for the respective selection field as shown in Fig 7-44.
5. Click OK in the Plane Definition dialog box.
6. Display the top view and move the plane symbol as shown in Fig 7-45.
7. Close without saving the file.

183

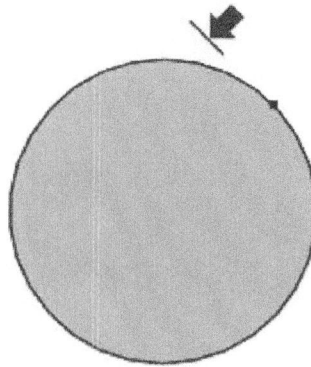

Fig 7-45 Reference Plane Created

7.2.3 Other Types of Reference Plane

Parallel through point

You can create a plane that is parallel to an existing plane and passes through a specific point.

Through three points

You can create a plane that passes through three points.

Through two lines

You can create a plane defined by two lines. If the two lines are not on the same plane, the start point of the second line (Line 2) is moved to the start point of the first li ne (Line 1).

Through point and line

You can create a plane defined by two end points of a line and one specific point.

Through planar curve

If a curve is defined on a plane, you can create a reference plane just by selecting the plana r curve.

Tangent to surface

You can create a plane that is tangent to an existing surface and passes through a specific point.

Normal to curve

You can create a plane that is normal to a curve at a specific point.

Equation

You can create a plane by defining constant values for a general equation of a plane.

$Ax + By + Cz = D$

You can create a plane by specifying the constants A, B, C and D. You can select a point instead of specifying the constant D.

Mean through points

You can create a mean plane with three or more points.

7.3 REFERENCE POINT

If the modeling process requires you to select a specific point and there is no such point in the existing geometry, you can create the point with the Point command in the Reference Elements toolbar.

The following types of points can be created.

1. Coordinates
2. On curve
3. On plane
4. On surface
5. Circle / Sphere / Ellipse Center
6. Tangent on curve
7. Between

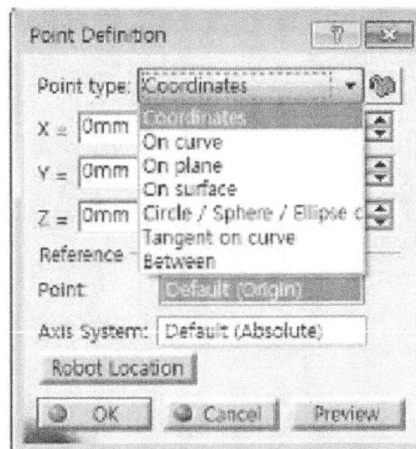

Fig 7-46 Point Definition Dialog Box

7.3.1 Coordinates Type

You can create a point by entering coordinate values with respect to a specific axis system. To practice creating this type of point, open the file ch07_fig47.CATPart, click the Named views icon in the Quick view toolbar and apply the pre-defined view named "my view" to the model as shown in Fig 7-48.

Producedure

1. Click the Point icon in the Reference Elements toolbar.

2. Set the point type to Coordinates.
3. Select the reference point. Otherwise, the absolute origin is selected as reference.
4. Select the reference axis system. Otherwise, the absolute axis system is selected as reference.
5. Enter the coordinate values in the respective input area and press OK.

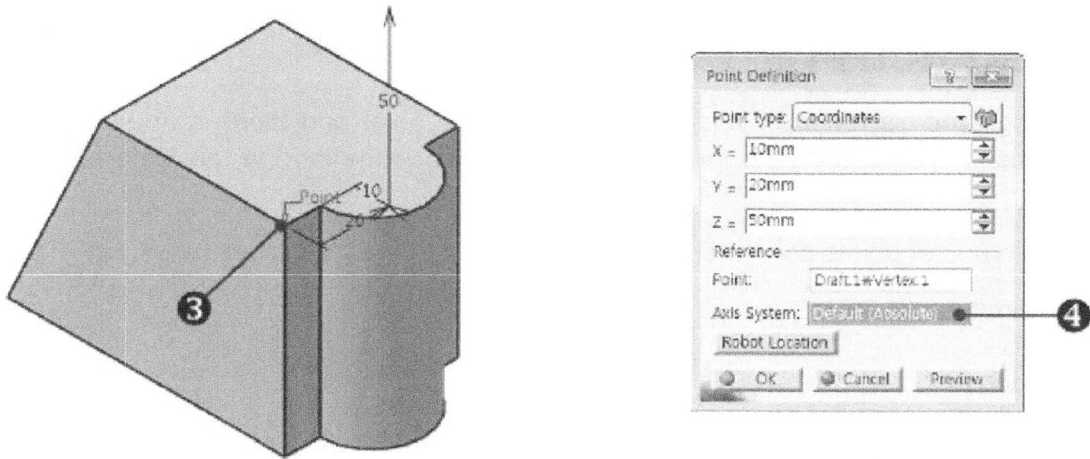

Fig 7-47 Creating a Point with the Coordinates Option

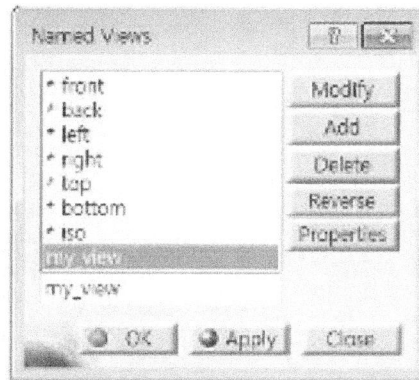

Fig 7-48 Applying Named View

(Note) Axis System

If you right cli ck on the Axis System select ion area in the Point Definition dialog box, the Create Axis System option is available in the pop-up menu. You can create a new axis system among the following three types.

- **Standard type:** You can define an axis system by specifying the origin and selecting the X, Y and Z direction.
- **Axis Rotation Type:** You can define an axis system by rotating an axis system that is defined according to the same method as the standard type.
- **Euler Angles Type:** You can define an axis system by defining Euler angles.

You can create the axis system in advance by using the Axis System icon in the Tools tool bar or by choosing Insert > Axis System in the menu bar.

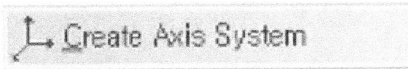

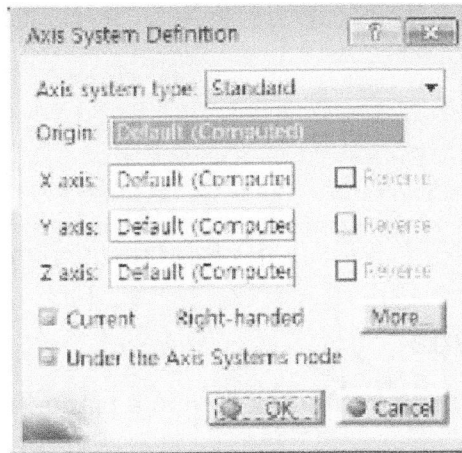

Fig 7-49 Axis System Definition Dialog Box

7.3.2 On curve Type

You can create a point at a specific location on a curve.

Procedure

1. Click the Point icon in the Reference Elements toolbar.
2. Set the Point type to curve.
3. Select a curve on which to create a point.
4. Select a point for reference. Oth er wise, an end point is selected as a reference.
5. Specify the location with a proper option.
6. Press the OK button.

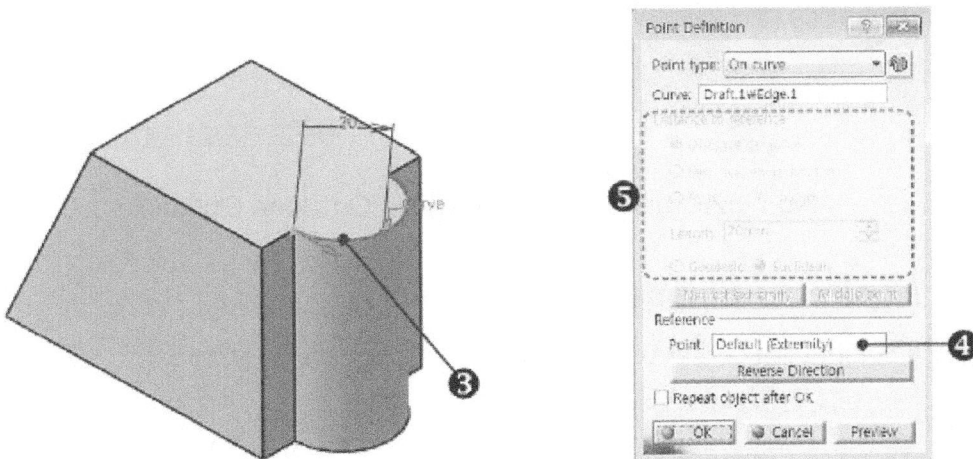

Fig 7-50 Creating a Point with the on curve Option

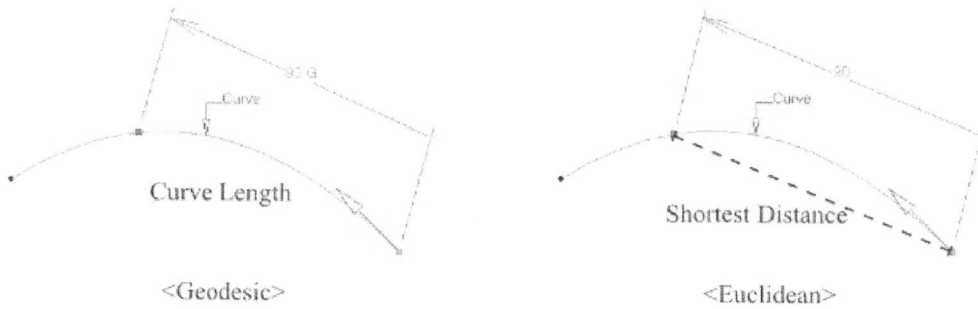

Fig 7-51 Measuring method

7.3.3 On plane Type

You can create a point at a specific location on a plane.

Procedure

1. Click the Point icon in the Reference Elements toolbar.
2. Set the Point type to On plane.
3. Select a plane on which to create a point.
4. Select a point for reference.
5. Enter the H and V values. You can press the Tab key to update the preview.
6. Press the OK button.

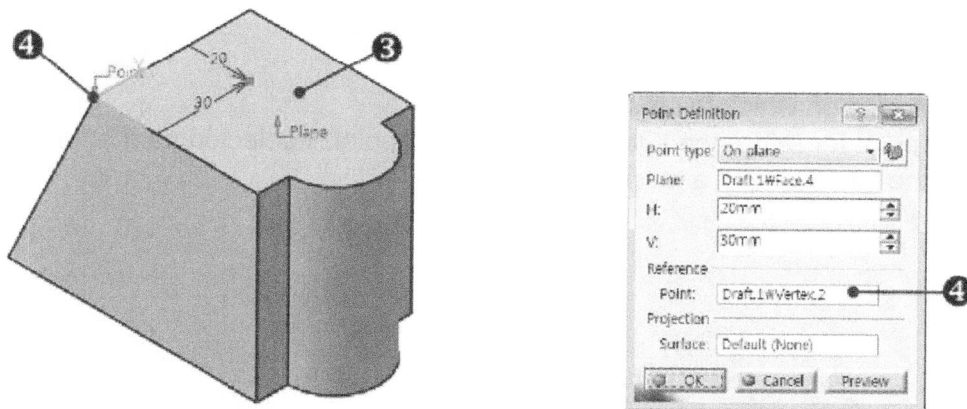

Fig 7-52 Creating a Point with the On plane Option

7.3.4 Circle / Sphere / Ellipse center Type

You can create a point at the center of an existing circle, sphere or ellipse.

Procedure

1. Click the Point icon in the Reference Elements toolbar.
2. Set the Point type to Circle/Sphere/Ellipse center.

188

3. Select the circle, sphere or ellipse on which to create a point at the center.
4. Press the OK button.

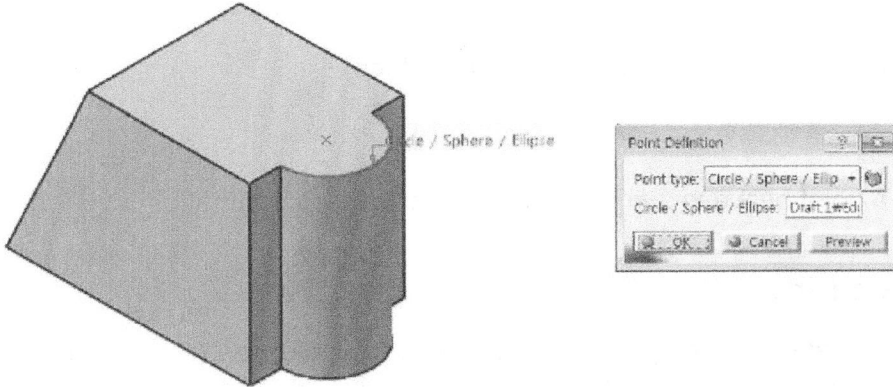

Fig 7-53 Creating a Point with the Circle / Sphere / Ellipse center Option

(Note) Caution

- You have to select the proper object for the reference. The Point type option 1s changed automatically according to your selection. For example, if you select a plane, the type is changed to On plane. If you select a surface, the type is changed to On surface.
- You can lock the type by pressing the type lock button.

7.3.5 Tangent on curve Type

You can create a point on a curve and tangent to a specified direct ion.

Procedure

1. Click the Point icon in the Reference Elements toolbar.
2. Set the Point type to Tangent on curve.
3. Select a curve to be tangent with.
4. Specify the direction.
5. Press the OK button.

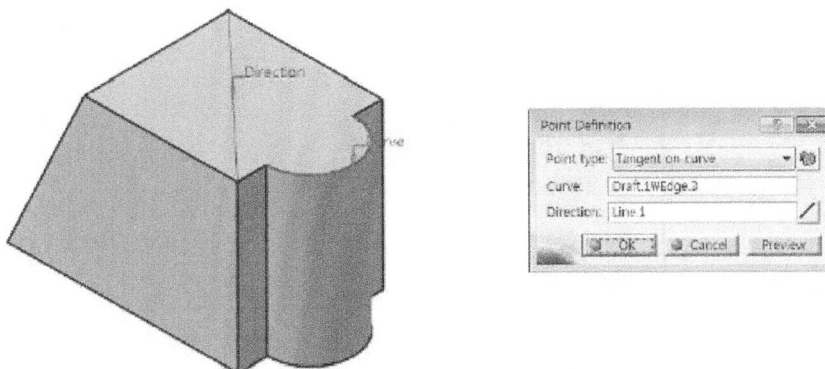

Fig 7- 54 Creating a Point with the Tangent on curve Option

7.3.6 Other Types of Reference Points

On surface

You can create a point at a specific location on a surface.

Between

You can create a point between two points at a specific location of ratio.

7.4 Reference Line

If the modeling process requires you to select a line or vector and there is no such object in the existing geometry, you can create the line with the Line command in the Reference Elements toolbar.

The following types of lines can be created.

1. Point -Point
2. Point-Direction
3. Angle/Normal to curve
4. Tangen t to curve
5. Normal to surface
6. Bisecting

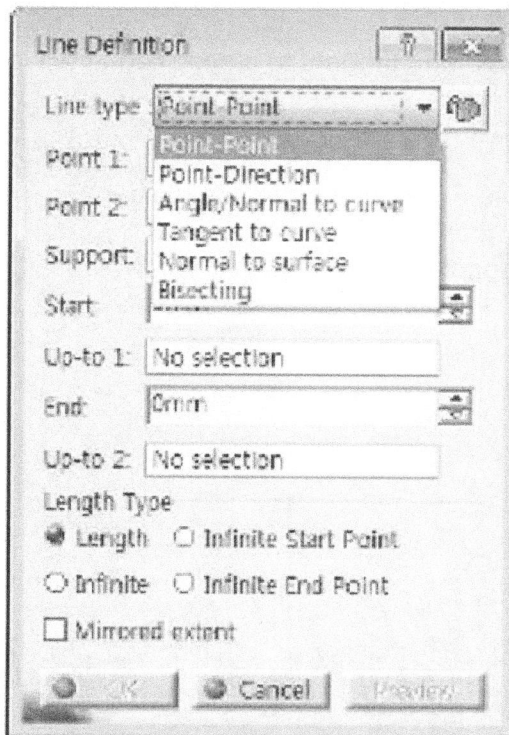

Fig 7-55 Line Definition Dialog Box

7.4.1 Usage of Reference Line

The following are two typical usages of reference lines.

1. Axis of Shaft or Groove Command

Fig 7-56 shows a Shaft feature created by selecting the reference line as the axis.

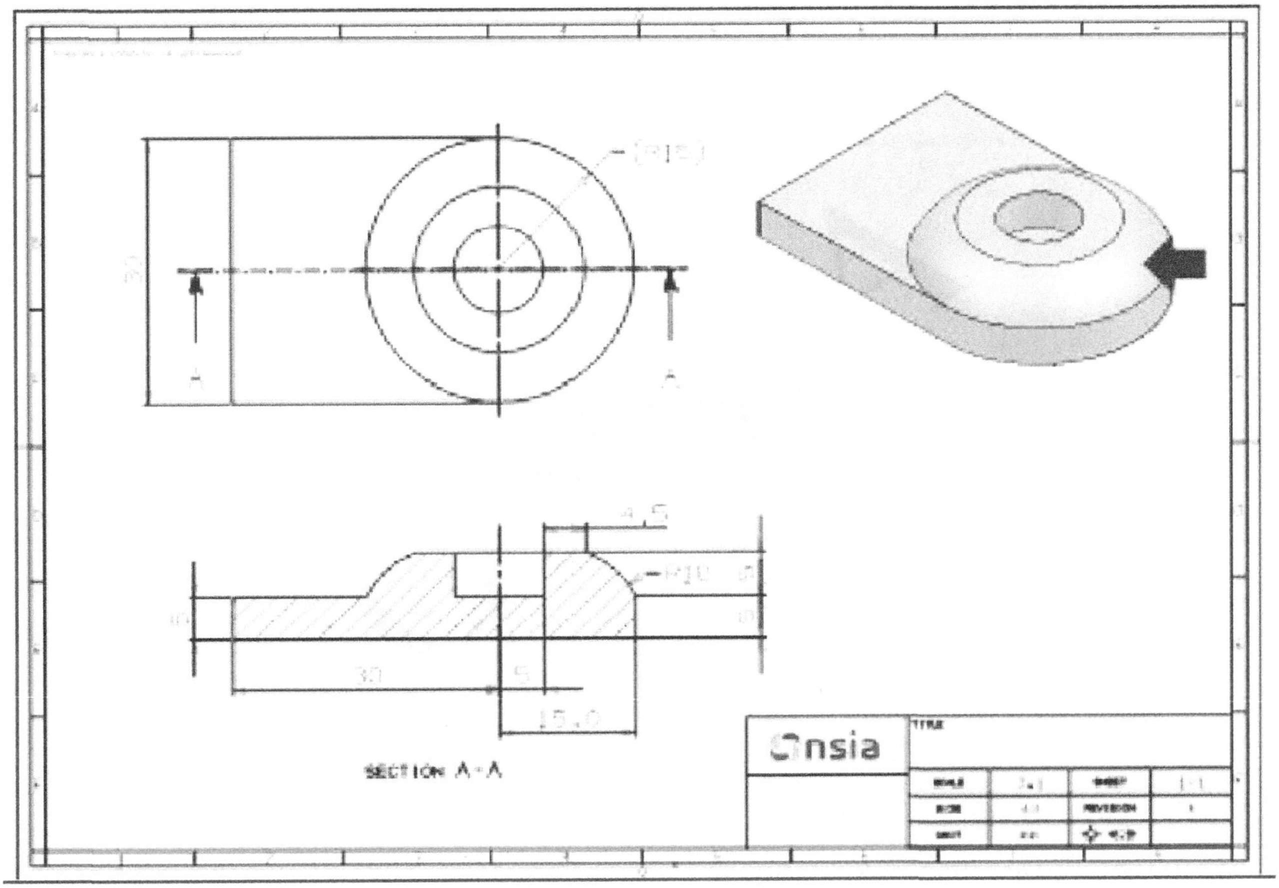

Fig 7-56 Shaft Feature

2. Reference Direction of Circular Pattern Command

Fig 7-57 shows a Circular Pattern feature created by se lectin g the reference line as the Reference Direction.

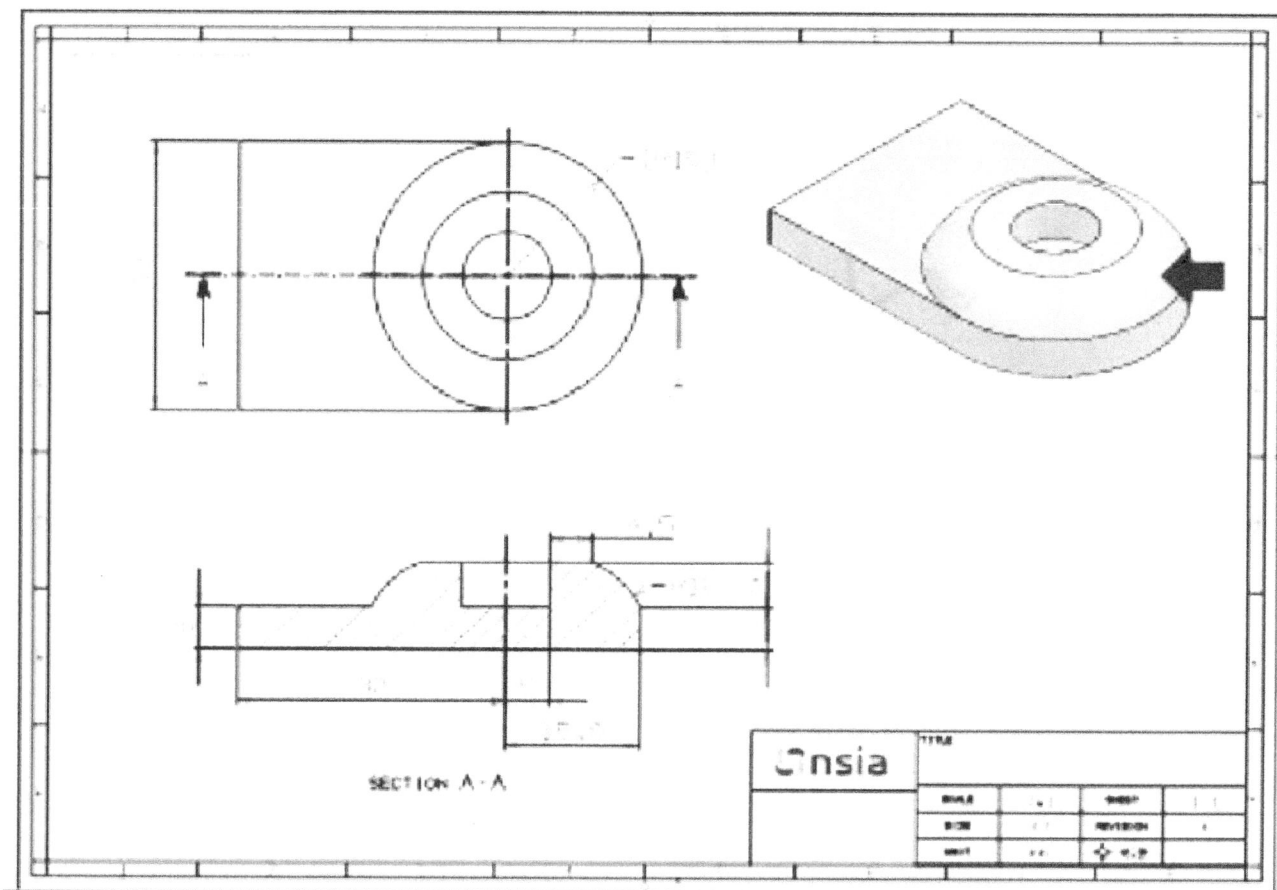

Fig 7- 57 Circular Pattern Feature

3. Reference Direction of Rectangular Pattern Command

Fig 7-58 shows the Rectangular Pattern feature created by selecting the reference line as the direction of array.

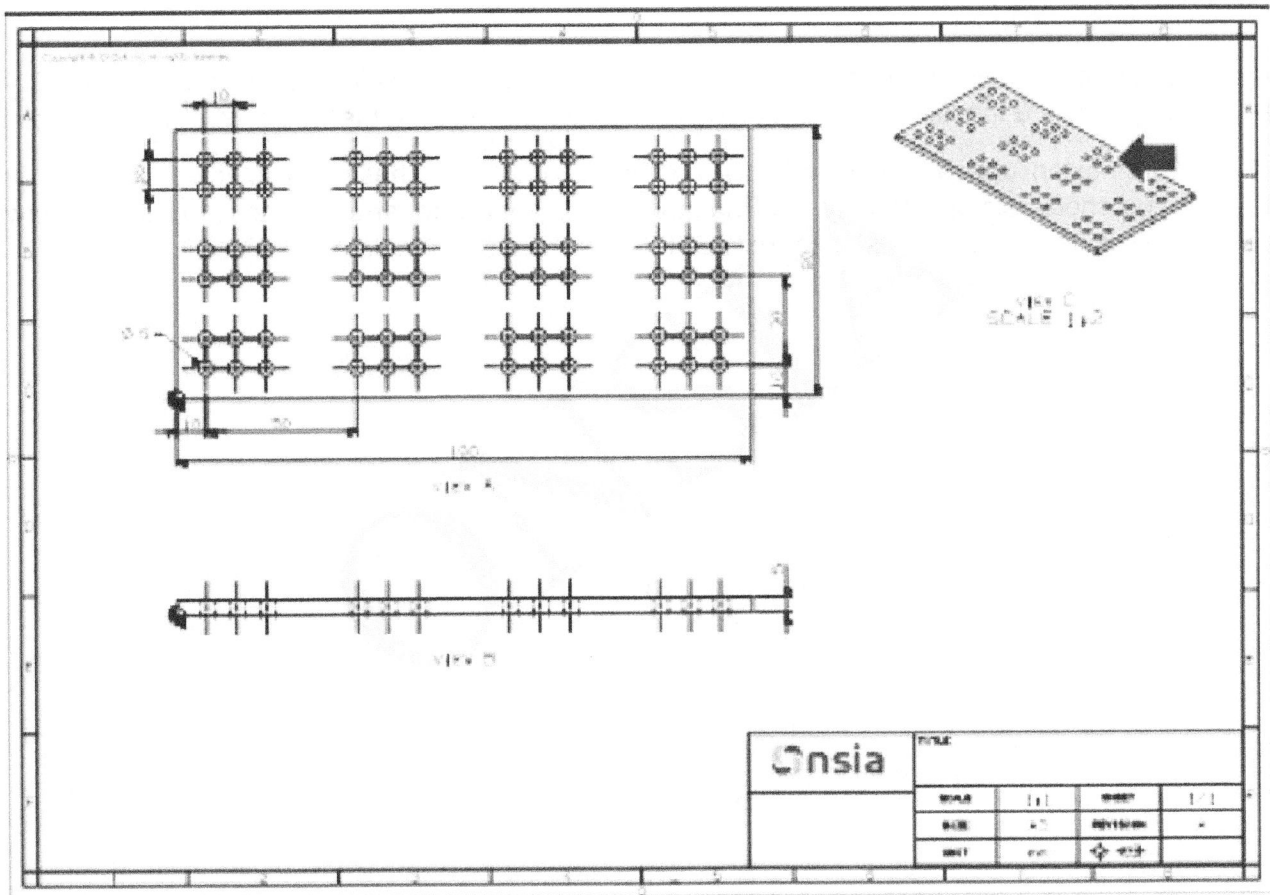

Fig 7- 58 Rectangular Pattern feature

7.4.2 Point-Point Type

You can create a line by connecting two points. You can select reference points or vertices.

To practice creating this type of line, open the file ch07_fig59.CATPart, click the Named views icon in the Quick view tool bar and apply the predefined "my_view" to the model.

You can create a line starting from a point and ending to another point.

Procedure

1. Click the Line icon in the Reference Elements toolbar.
2. Choose Point-Point in the Line type dropdown list.
3. Select Point 1 and Point 2.
4. Set the length options and press OK.

If you select Length in the Length Type option ((C) in Fig 7-59), you can extend the start and/or the end point of the line by dragging the respective symbols designated by (A) and (B) in Fig 7-59. Also, you can select the object by clicking the Up to 1 and Up to 2 selection field in the Line Definition dialog box.

If you select Infinite in the Length Type option, you can create an infinite line. In this case, the Start and End options are inactive. You can also create a line infinite at either the start or the end point.

The Mirrored extent option is activated only when the Length option has been selected as the Length Type. If you check this option, only the End input field is available, and the line connecting the two points is extended the same distance from both the sta1t and end points.

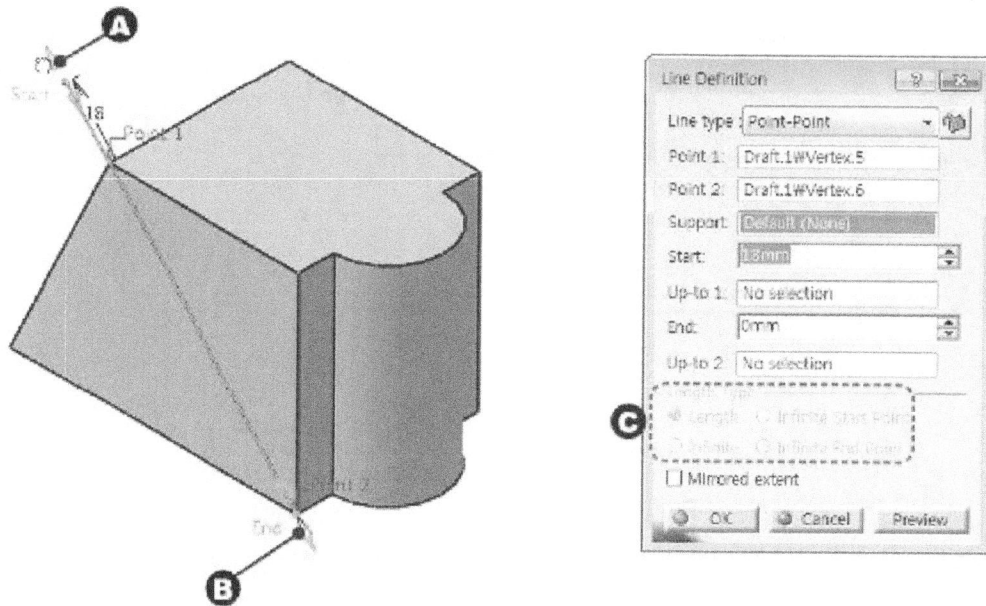

Fig 7-59 Creating a Line with the Point-Point Option

(Note) Applying Values in the Preview

- When you are entering numeric values in the input boxes, you can apply the value in the preview by pressing the Tab key. The value is updated in the preview and the cursor moves to the next available input box or button.

7.4.3 Point-Direction Type

You can create a line starting from a point along a specified direction.

Procedure

1. Click the Line icon in the Reference Elements toolbar and choose the line type.
2. Select a point.
3. Select an object to define the direction. You can define the direction by right clicking on the Direction selection field and choosing Create Line in the pop-up menu.
4. Set the length options and press OK.

If you specify a Support, the line is projected on the selected support plane or surface.

194

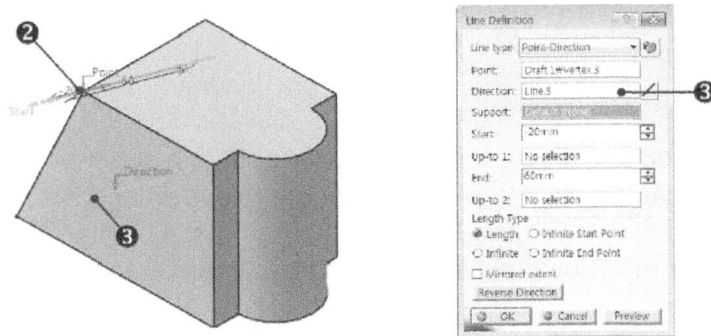

Fig 7-60 Creating a Line with the Point-Direction Option

(Note) Deselecting or Re-selecting an Object

When you have selected an object in the Support, Direction, Up-to 1 or Up-to 2 select ion area, the Other Selection or Clear Selection option s are available in the pop-up menu by right clicking on the selection area . You can deselect an object with the Clear Selection option and you can select a new object with the Other Selection option. Only the Other Selection option is available for required options such as the Point and Direction options.

7.4.4 Angle-Normal to curve Type

You can create a line starting from point (A) in Fig 7-61 and inclined about the tangent line (B) at point (A).

Procedure

1. Click the Line icon in the Reference Elements toolbar and choose the line type.
2. Select a curve ((2) in Fig 7-61)
3. Click the Support select ion field and select plane (C).
4. Click the Point selection field, right click and create a point on curve (2).
5. Enter the angle. Or you can press the Normal to Curve button.
6. Set the length options and press OK.

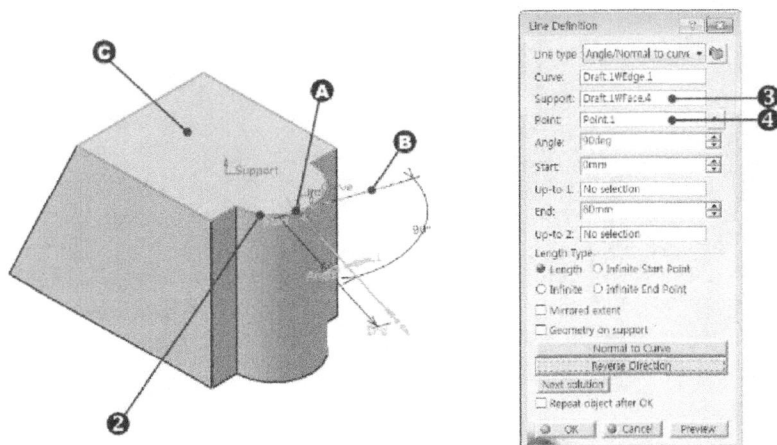

Fig 7- 61 Creating a Line with the Angle-Normal lo curve Option

195

7.4.5 Other Types of Reference Lines

Tangent to curve

- **Mono-Tangent:** You can create a line that is tangent to a curve or edge at a specified point.
- **Bi-Tangent:** You can create a line that is tangent to two selected curves. Note that the Next solution button is activated in the dialog box when two or more result s are available. You can select another result by pressing the Next solution button.

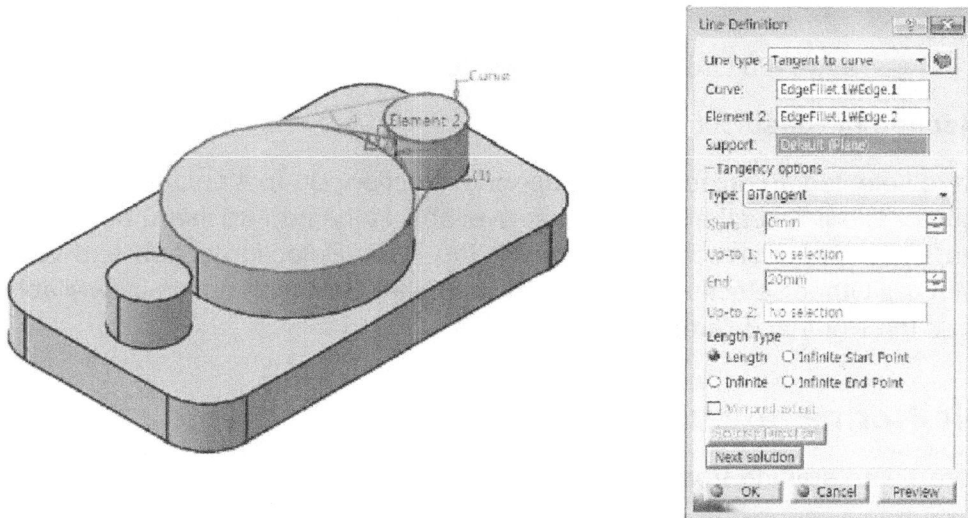

Fig 7-62 Tangent to curve Type (Bi-Tangent)

Normal to surface

You can create a line that starts from a po int and i s normal to the selected surface.

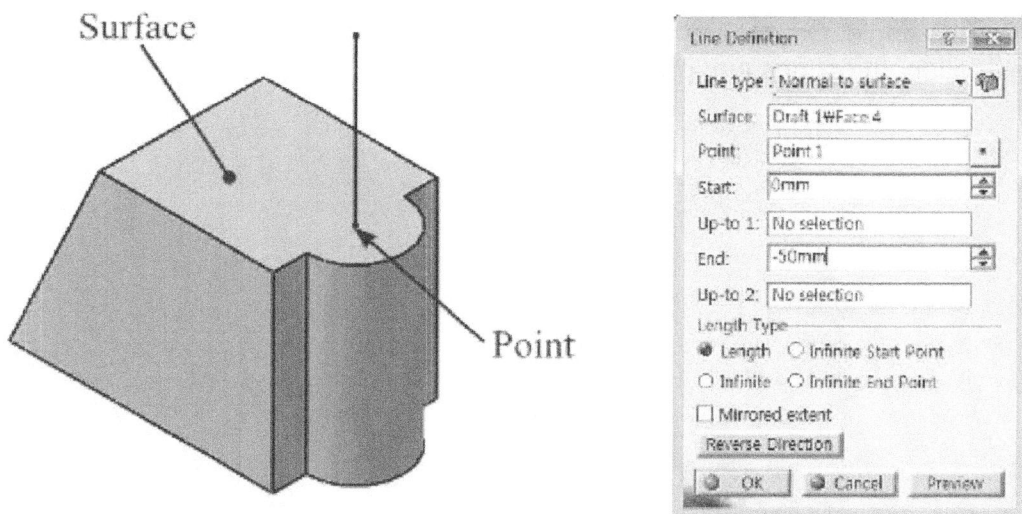

Fig 7-63 Normal to surface Type

Bisecting

You can create a line by bisecting two lines. The direction is calculated by adding the two vectors, and the length can be defined in the dialog box.

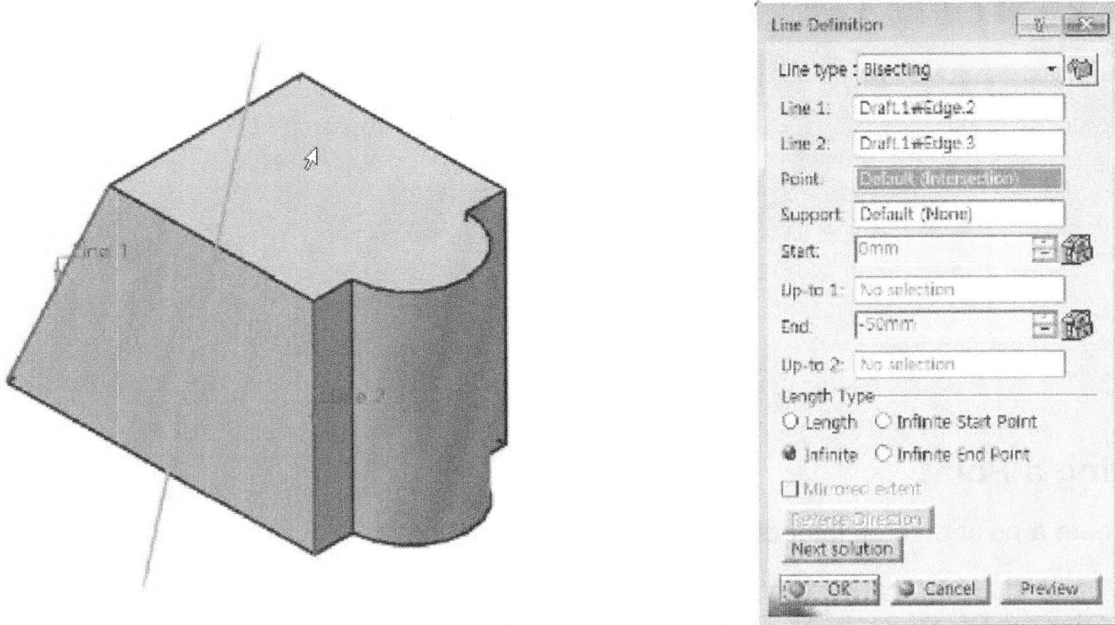

Fig 7-64 Bisecting Type

Exercise 48: Point-Direction Type Line (ch07_005.CATPart)

Create a reference line that passes through a point and copy a feature using the Circular Pattern command.

Fig 7 - 65 Model to Create

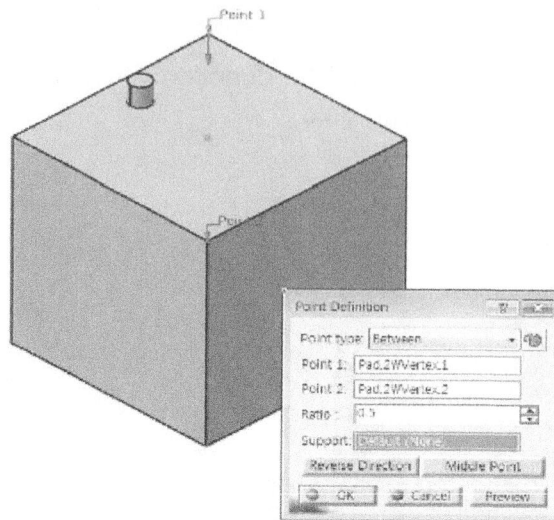

Fig 7-66 Creating a Point

Creating a Point

Let's create a point at the center of the upper plane.

1. Open the given part file ch07_005.CATPart.
2. Click the Point icon in the Reference Elements toolbar.
3. Choose Between in the Point type dropdown list.
4. Create a point by selecting two diagonal vertices as how n in Fig 7-66.

Creating a Line

Let's create a line normal to the upper plane that passes through the point created previously.

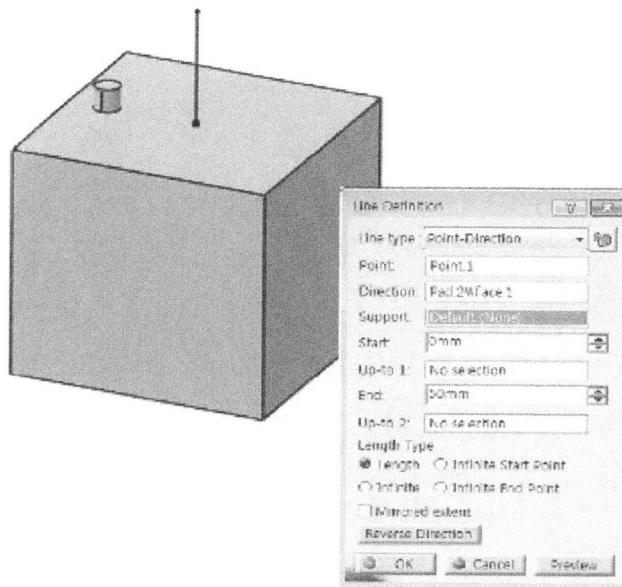

Fig 7-67 Creating a Line

1. Click the Line icon in the Reference Elements toolbar.
2. Choose Point-Direction in the Line type dropdown list.
3. Select the point and the upper plane for the respective selection field. Note that the normal direction is chosen if you select a planar surface.
4. Enter the end length to 50mm and click the Reverse Direction button if required.
5. Press OK.

Creating Circular Pattern

We will create a circular pattern of the cylindrical pad. Note that you have to select the feature first.

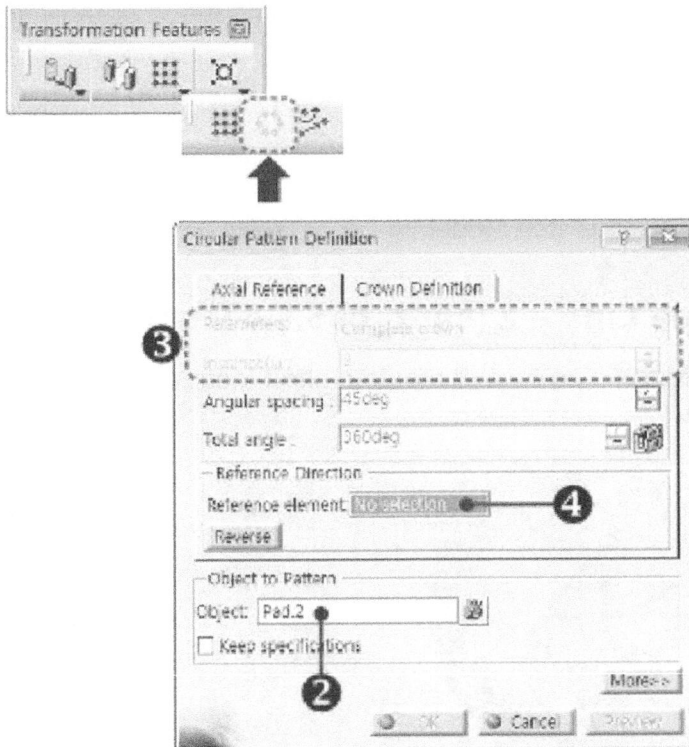

Fig 7-68 Defining Circular Pattern

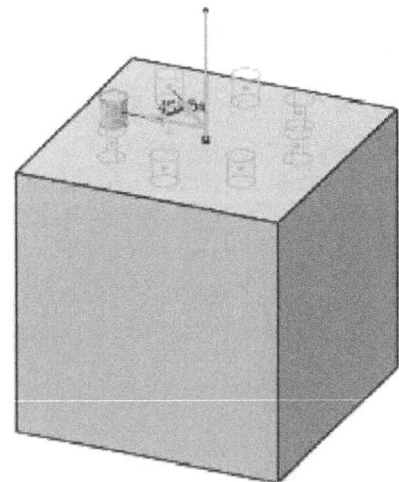

Fig 7-69 Preview

1. Select the cylindrical pad feature in the Spec Tree or in the model.
2. Click the Circular Pattern icon in the Transformation Features toolbar. Note that the selected feature is chosen in the Object selection field as designated by (2) in Fig 7-68.
3. Choose Complete crown in the Parameters dropdown list and enter 8 in the instance(s) input box.
4. Click the Reference element select ion field.
5. Select the line. A preview of the pattern is displayed as shown in Fig 7-69.
6. Click OK in the Circular Pattern Definition dialog box. Fig 7-70 shows the completed model.
7. Close without saving the file.

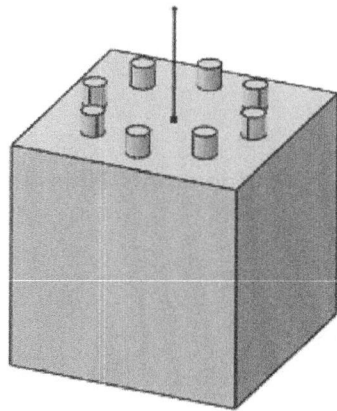

Fig 7-70 Completed Model

Exercise 49: Point-Direction Type Line – 2 (ch07_006.CATPart)

Let's create a reference line that passes through a po int and create a shaft feature.

Fig 7-71 model to Create

Creating a Chamfer

1. Open the given part file ch07_006.CATPart.
2. Click the Chamfer icon in the Dress Up Features toolbar.

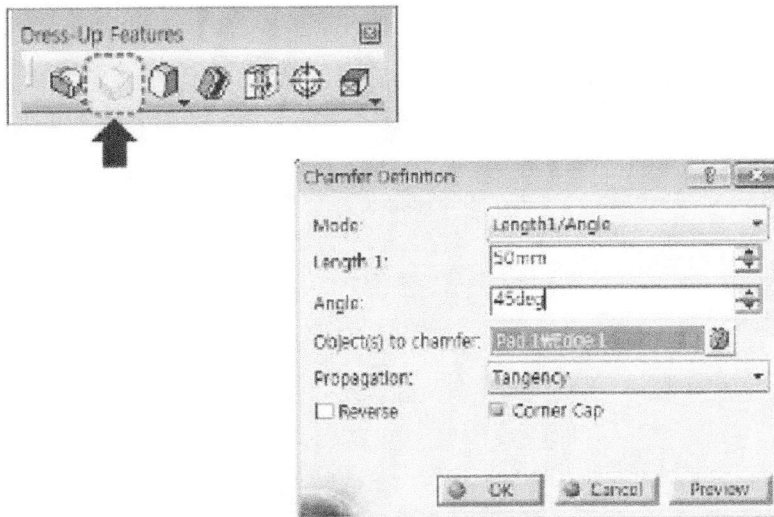

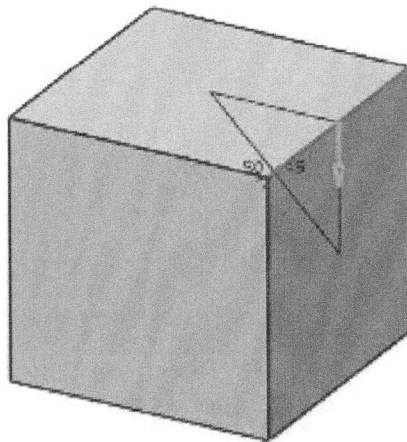

Fig 7-72 Defining Chamfer

3. Select the edge as shown in Fig 7-72.
4. Enter 50m m in the Length 1 input box in the Chamfer Definition dialog box and press the Tab key.
5. Click OK in the dialog box.

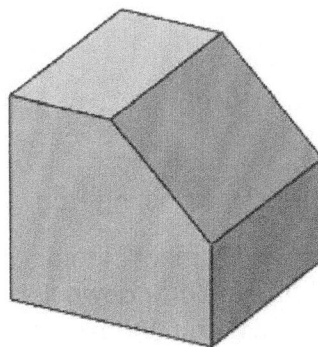

Fig 7-73 Chamfer Created

Creating a Line

Let' s create a line by defining an intersection point.

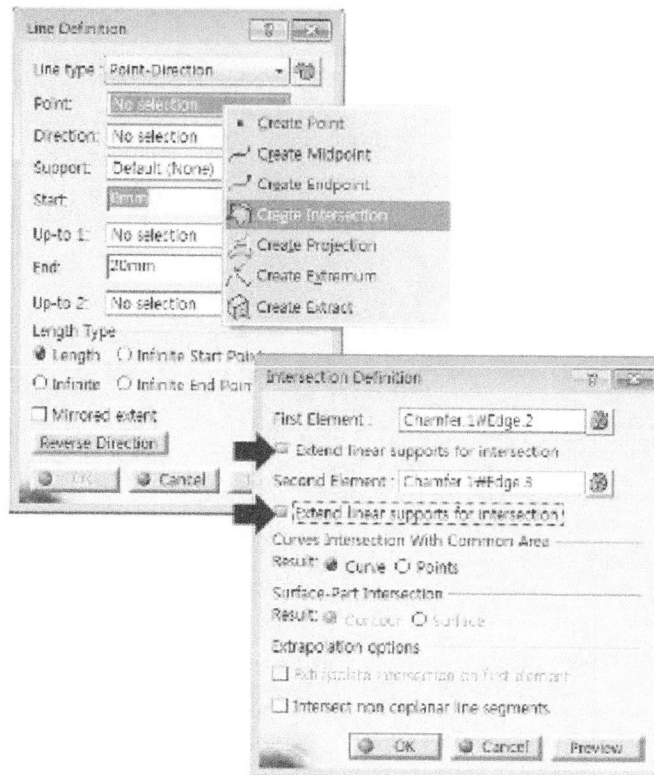

Fig 7-74 Defining an Intersection Point

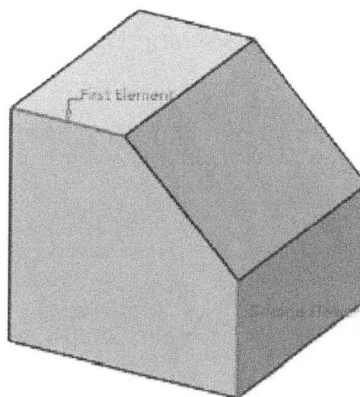

Fig 7-75 Selecting Edges

1. Click the Line icon m the Reference Elements toolbar.
2. Choose Point-Direction m the Line type dropdown list.
3. Right click on the Point selection field and choose Create Intersection in the pop-up menu.
4. Select the two edges as shown in Fig 7-75 and check the extend options as specified by the arrow in Fig 7-74.

5. Click OK in the Intersection Definition dialog box. Note that the Direction select io n field is highlighted in the Line Definition dialog box.
6. Select the edge specified by (6) in Fig 7-76. Line is previewed.
7. Enter 30mm in the End input box and click OK. Fig 7-77 shows the line created.

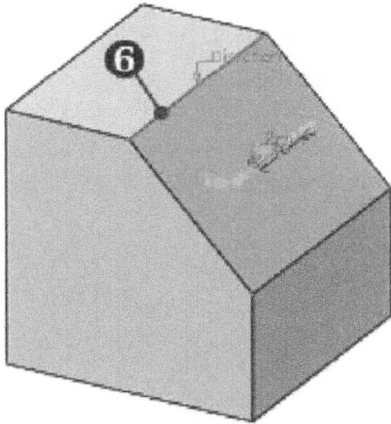

Fig 7-76 Sketching Direction Edge   Fig 7-77 Line Created

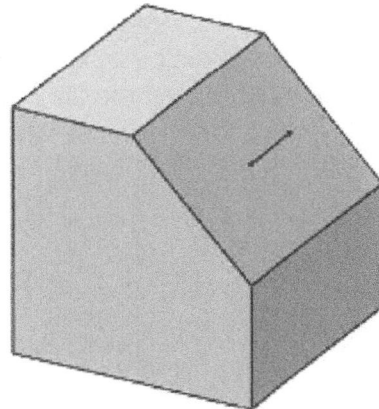

Creating the Sketch and Shaft Features

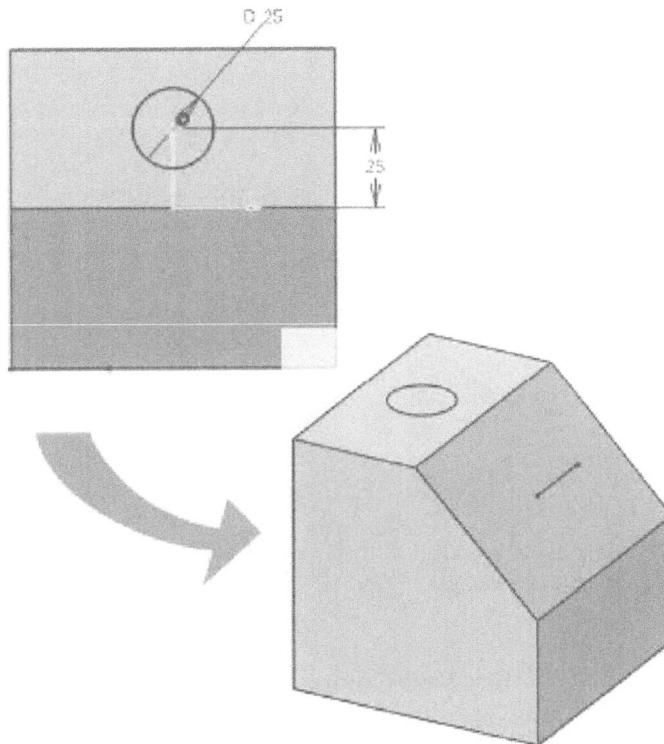

Fig 7-78 Sketch

1. Define a sketch plane on the upper face using the Positioned sketch command and create a circle at the center of the face as shown in Fig 7-78.

203

2. Exit the sketcher.
3. Click the Shaft icon in the Sketch- Based Features toolbar.
4. Select the sketch as the profile.
5. Select the line created in Fig 7-77 as the axis.
6. Enter 270deg in the First angle input box and press the Tab key. Click the Re- verse Direction button if required. The shaft feature is previewed as shown in Fig 7-79.
7. Click OK in the dialog box. Fig 7-80 shows the completed model.
8. Close without saving the file.

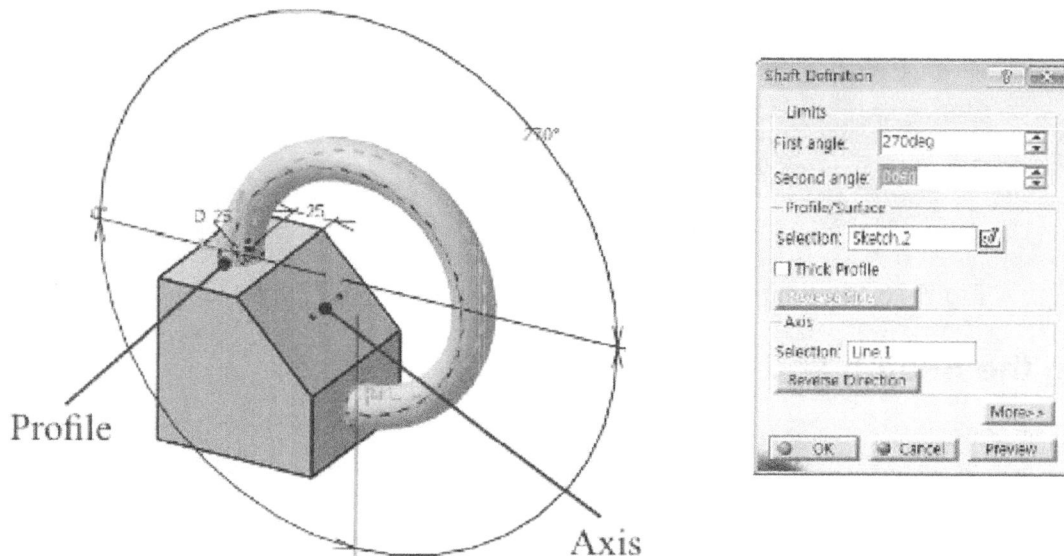

Fig 7-79 Creating the Shaft Feature

Fig 7-80 Completed Model

(Note) Positioning the Sketch Plane

- The sketch plane is positioned such that the H direction is aligned to right of the screen and the V direction is aligned to up. This option is set in the Sketch Plane option as shown in Fig 3-5 on page 61.

- If you uncheck the "Position sketch plane parallel to screen" option, the sketch plane is not aligned to screen when you are entering the Sketcher workbench. In this case, you can align the sketch plane in the Sketcher workbench by clicking the Normal View icon in the View toolbar. If you click the Normal View icon once again, sketch view is reversed.

Exercise 50: Reference Plane – Tangent to Surface

Create a solid model referring to the drawing in Fig 7-81.

Requirements

1. All sketch objects have to be iso-const rained.
2. Do not use the Fix constraint.

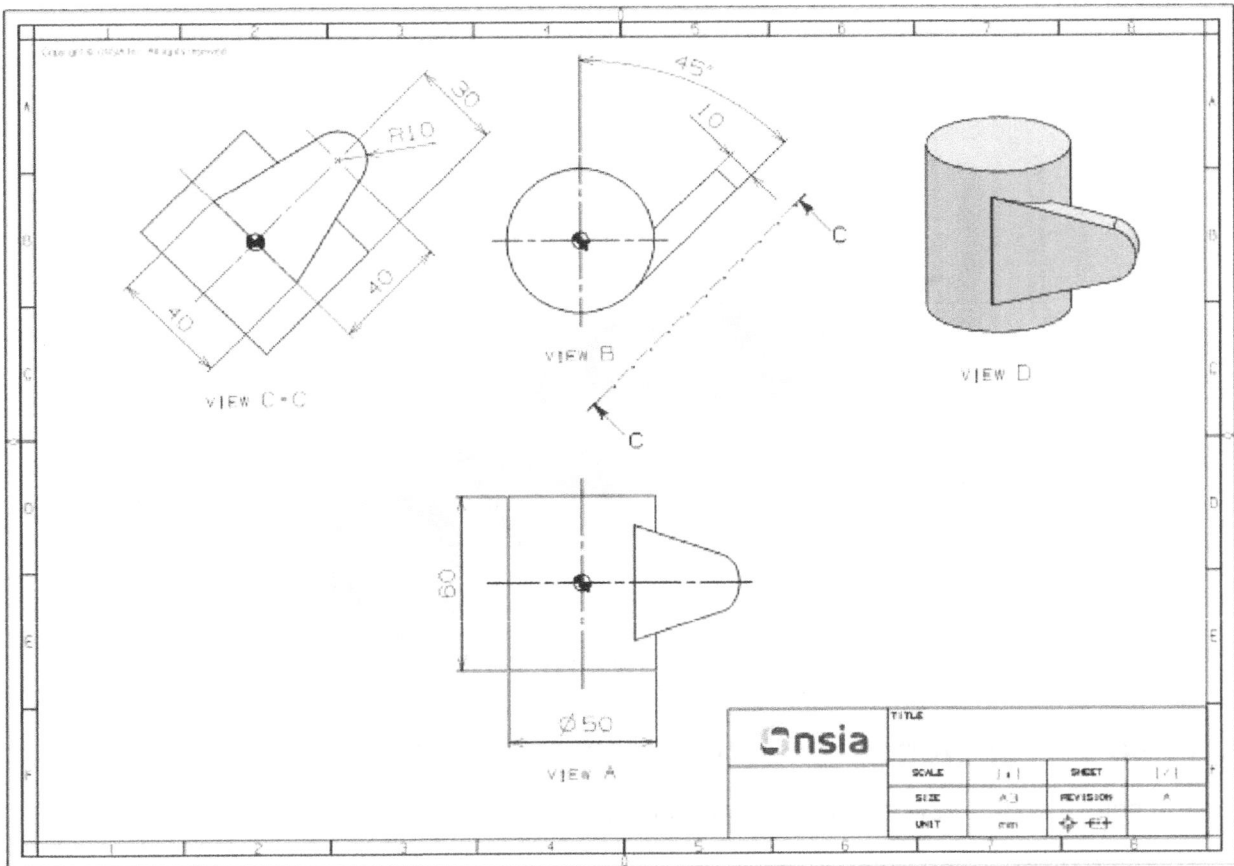

Fig 7-81 Drawing for Exercise 50

Exercise 51: Reference Plane – Offset from Plane (ch07_008.CATPart)

Create a solid model referring to the drawing in Fig 7-82.

1. All sketch objects have to be iso-constrained.
2. Do not use the fix constraint.

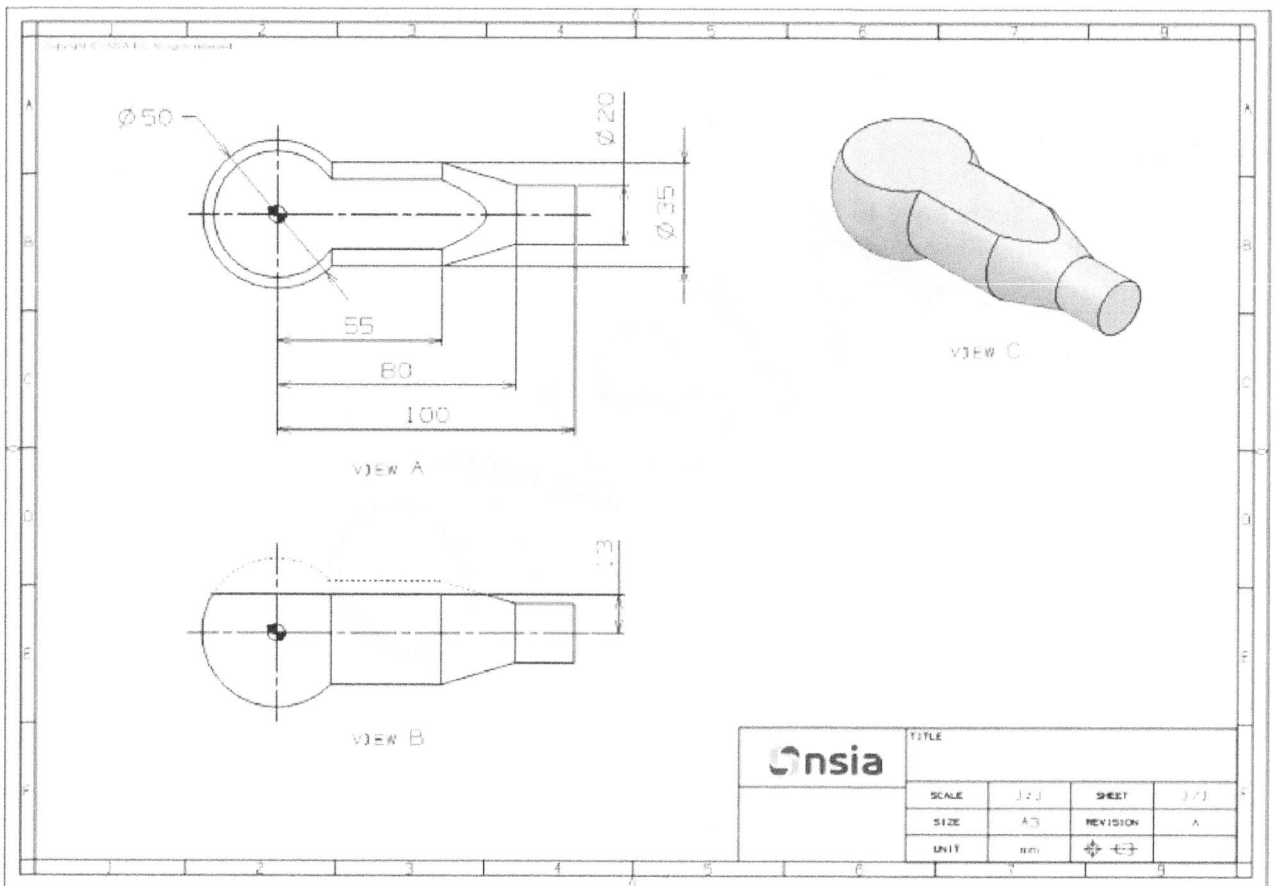

Fig 7-82 Drawing for Exercise 51

Exercise 52: Reference Line (ch07_009.CATPart)

Create a solid model referring to the drawing in Fig 7- 83.

ch07_009.CATPart

1. All sketch objects have to be iso -constrained.
2. Do not use the Fix constraint.

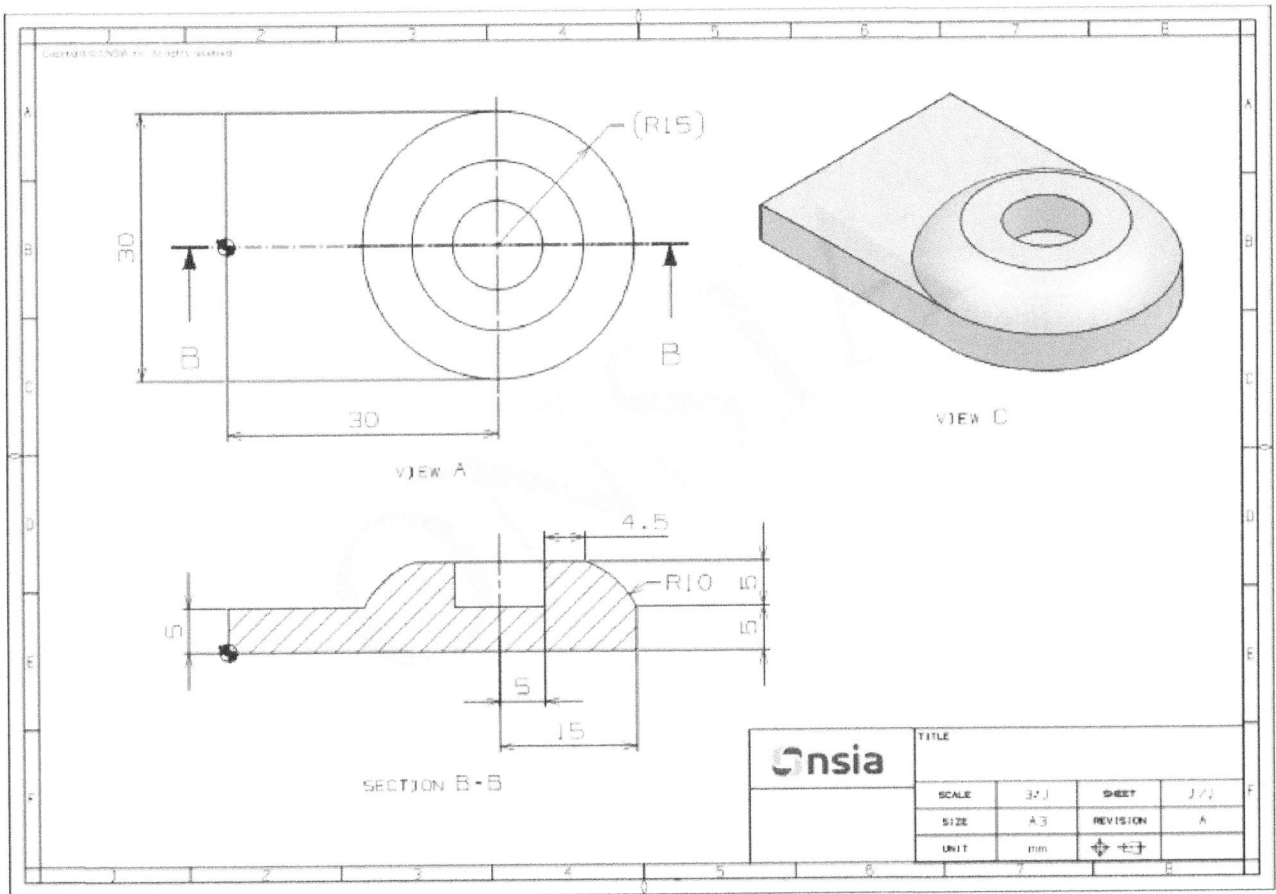

Fig 7.83 Drawing for Exercise 52

Exercise 53: Reference Plane – Angle/Normal to Plane (ch07_010.CATPart)

Create a solid model referring to the drawing in Fig 7-84.

1. The final result has to be a single solid body.
2. Use the Hole command to create holes.

Exercise 53: Reference Plane – Angle/Normal to Plane (ch07_011.CATPart)

Create a solid model referring to the drawing in Fig 7-85.

1. The final result has to be a single solid body.
2. Use the Hole command to create holes.

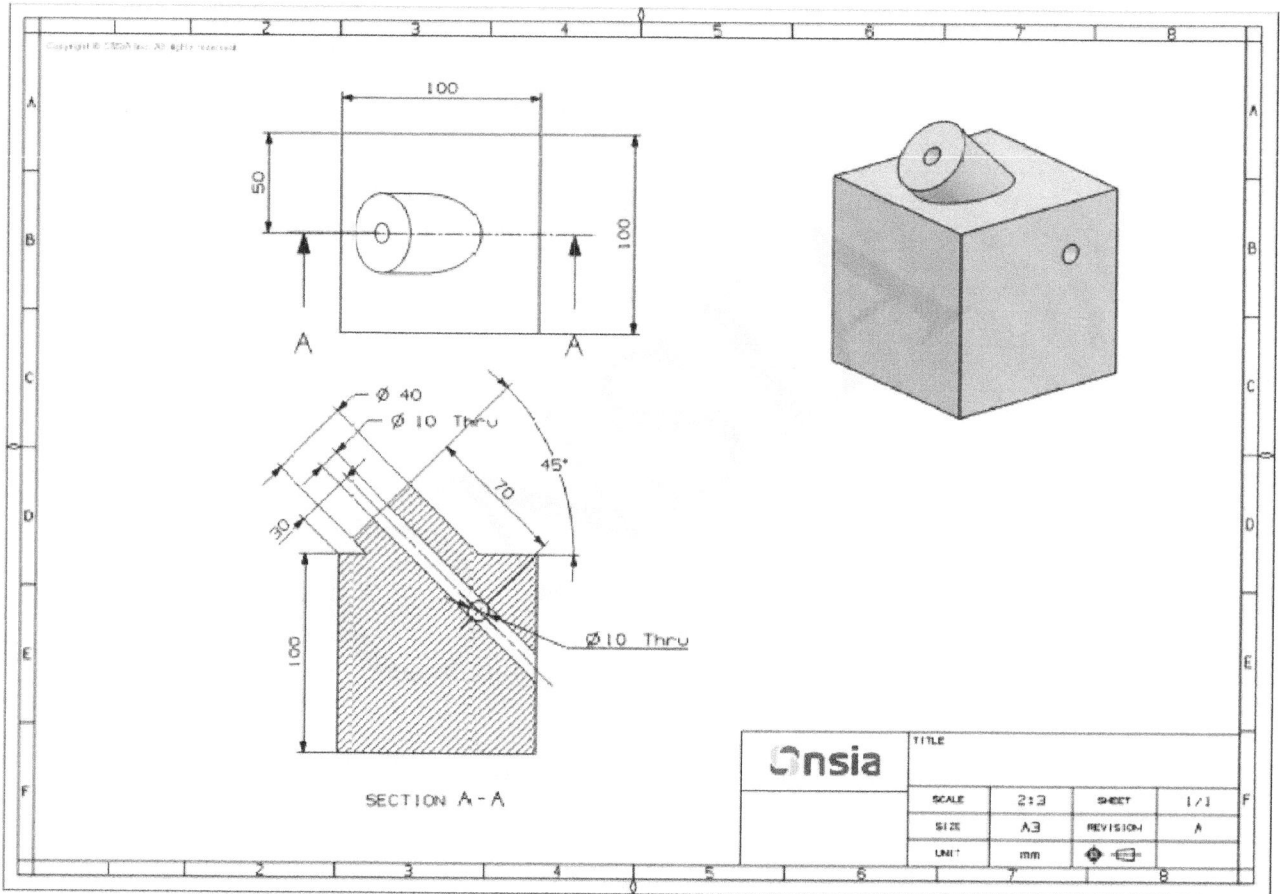

100

50

100

100

A   A

Ø 40

Ø 10 Thru

45°

70

30

100

Ø10 Thru

SECTION A-A

Onsia

TITLE			
SCALE	2:3	SHEET	1/1
SIZE	A3	REVISION	A
UNIT	mm		

Fig 7-85 Drawing for Exercise 53

208

CHAPTER 8: ADDING FLAIR WITH DRESS-UP FEATURES

8.1 DRESS UP FEATURES

Refer to the guidelines outlined in 2.3 on page 5l to avoid mistakes when creating your model.

1. Create a sketch.
2. Create 3D geometry.
   - Create features that arc added to the body: Pad, Shaft, Rib, etc.
   - Create features that remove from the body: Pocket, Groove Hole, Slot, etc.
3. Finish the mode ling by creating dress- up features.

After creating 3D features using the commands in the Sketch-Based Features toolbar, apply the commands in the Dress-Up Features toolbar to finalize the modeling process. However, bear in mind that this is just a guideline. In practical modeling the three steps arc applied repeatedly as required. Note that if the modeling order is not chosen properly, the result may differ from what you had intended. Dress-up features can be applied to existing edges, faces or vertices and do not require a sketch. The following four types of dress-up features will be explained in this chapter.

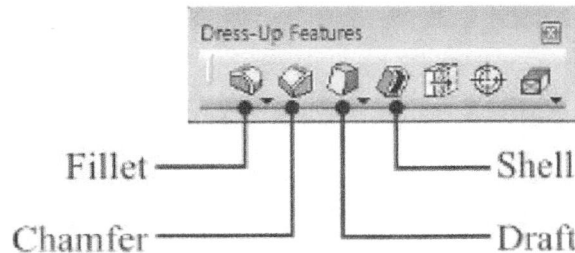

Fig 8-1 Dress-Up Features Toolbar

8.2 FILLET

We can apply fillets either on edges or between faces. the former is called an Edge Fillet and the latter is called a Face Fillet.

8.2.1 Edge Fillet

Edge fillets are applied to smoothen sharp edges. There are two types of sharp edges. Fig 8-2 (A) shows concave edges and (B) convex edges.

When a part has been manufactured, convex edges can damage the parts themselves, resulting in deterioration of product quality. They can even injure people who deliver or deal with the parts.

When a load is applied to a part, the stress will concentrate at the concave edges and a fracture may initiate from these edges. Using the Edge Fillet command, you can create fillets on the concave or convex edges in the 3D model. Some types of fillets arc created inevitably during the manufacturing process and some are required to improve the mechanical performance of the part.

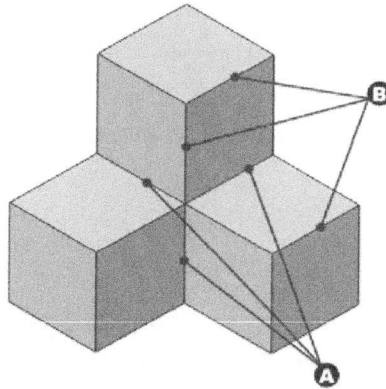

Fig 8-2 Types of Edges

8.2.2 Types of Edge Fillet

In CATIA V5, there arc four types of edge fillets available as shown in Fig 8-3.

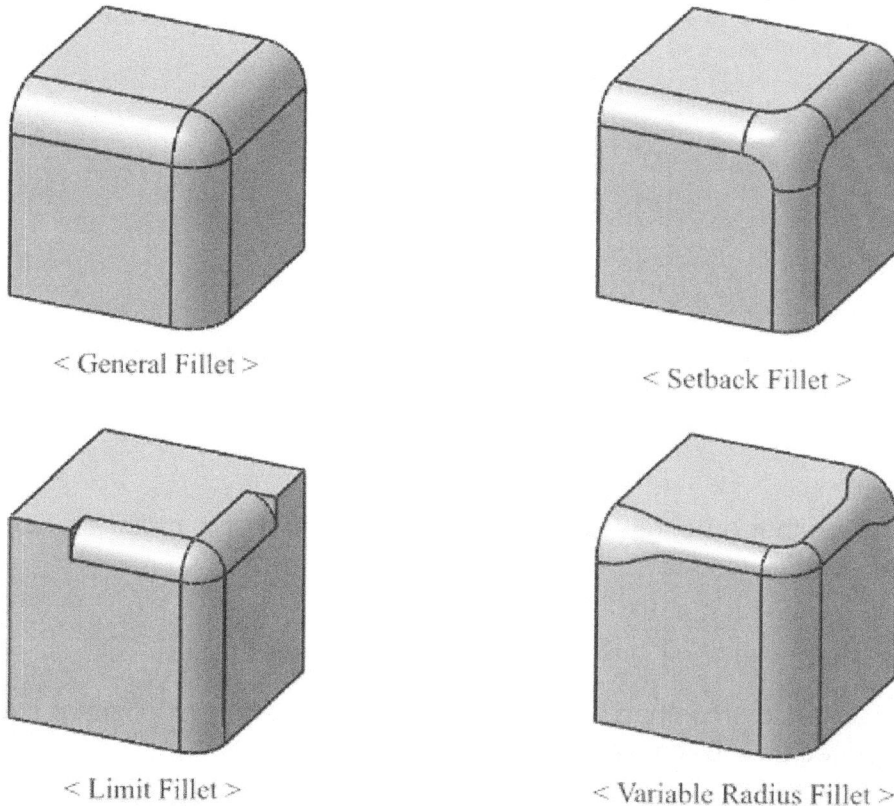

< General Fillet >

< Setback Fillet >

< Limit Fillet >

< Variable Radius Fillet >

Fig 8- 3 Types of Edge Fillet

A setback fillet can be applied on vertices where three or more edges meet. You can create a smoother fillet on vertices.

A limit fillet is applied on edges where you cannot create a complete fillet on the edge due to the complexity of the geometry. An edge fillet is limited to a portion of the edge by defining limiting elements such as points or planes.

You can also apply fillets on an edge with various radiuses at the specified points.

Setback fillets and limit fillets can be applied with the Edge Fillet command using the proper options. On the other hand, a variable radius fillet can be applied with the Variable Radius Fillet command in the Dress Up Features toolbar.

8.2.3 Procedure for Edge Fillets

The recommended procedure for edge fillets is as follows. Each step number corresponds to that in Fig 8-4.

1. Click the Edge Fillet icon in the Dress-Up Features tool bar.
2. Enter the fillet radius and press the Tab key.
3. Select the edges on which to apply the fillets.
4. Click OK.

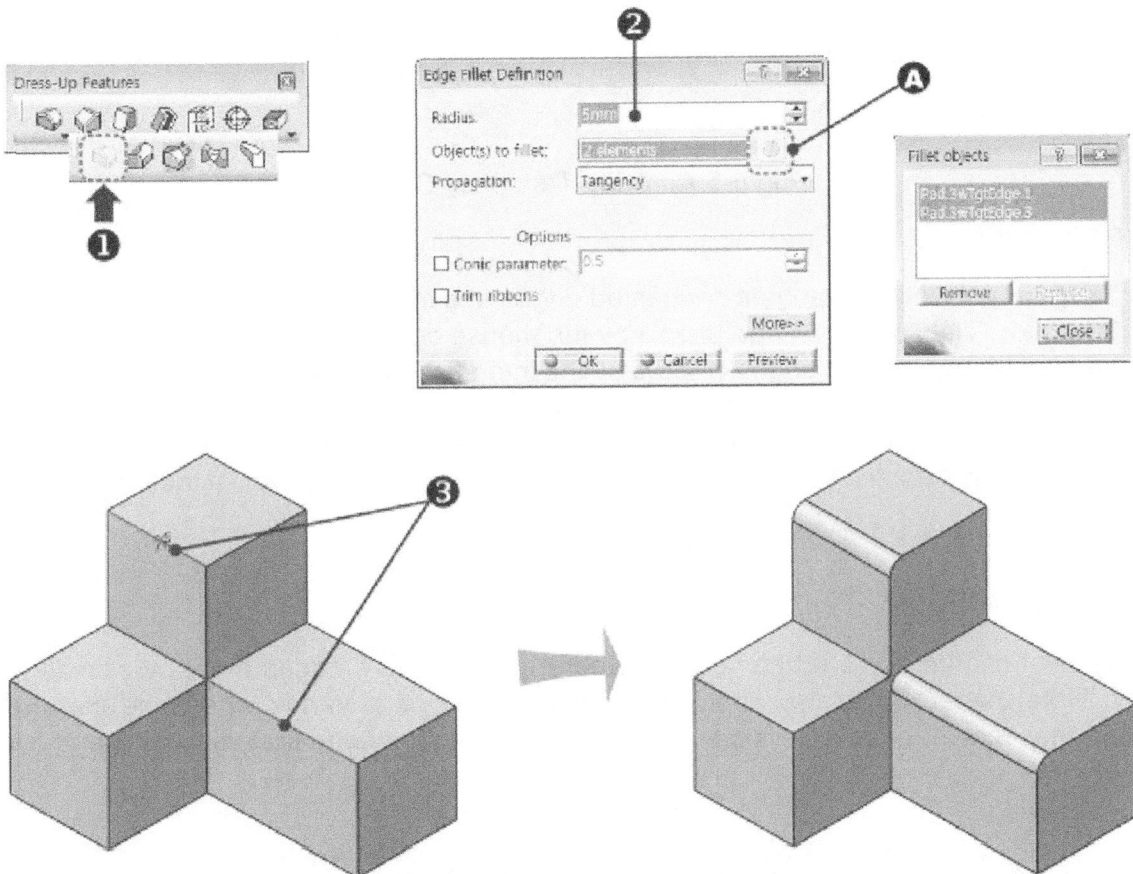

Fig 8-4 Applying Edge Fillet

211

- **Method 1:** Press the Ctrl or the Shift key and select the edges to deselect.
- **Method 2:** Press the multi selection button designated by (A) in Fig 8-4 in the Edge Fillet Definition dialog box. Select the edges to deselect in the Fillet objects dialog box and press the Remove button.

Exercise 54: Understand Propagation Option (ch08_001.CATPart)

1. Open the given file ch08_001.CATPart.
2. Apply RS fillet on the edges specified by (A) in Fig 8-5.
3. Click the Edge Fillet icon once again.
4. Set the Propagation option in the dialog box to Tangency.
5. Select the edge specified by (B) in Fig 8-5.
6. Enter a radius of 5mm and press OK.

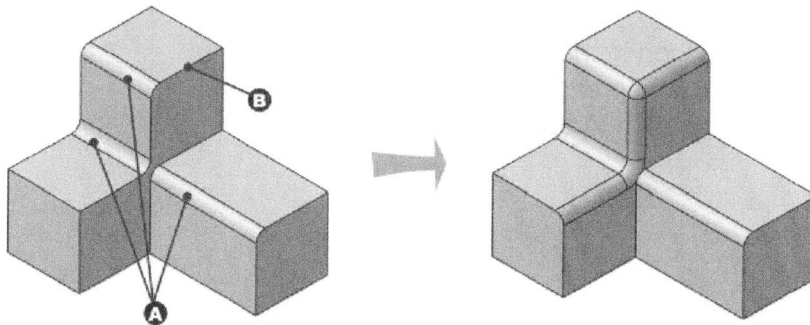

Fig 8-5 Applying Tangency Option

(Note) Propagation

1. **Tangency:** Fillets the tangent connected edges at a ingle pick.
2. **Minimal:** Fillets only the edge picked by the mouse pointer.
3. **Intersection:** Fillets all edges created by the intersection of the faces of the selected objects and the rest of the faces of the current body.
4. **Intersection with selected features:** Selecting the geometric features in the Object(s) to fillet and the Selected features fields automatically selects the edges at their intersection and fille to them.

8.2.4 Setback Fillet

A setback fillet can be app li ed on vertices where three or more edges meet by selectin g them together. Note that you can also apply the setback blend on a vertex where the con- vex and concave edges meet. Setback fillets can be applied by using the edge fillet with the Blend corner(s) option.

Exercise 55: Creating Setback Fillet (ch08_002.CATPart)

Let 's learn how to create a setback fillet through an exercise.

1. Open the given file ch08_002.CATPart.
2. Click the Edge Fillet icon.
3. Enter 5mm in the Radius input box in the dialog box and press the Tab key.
4. Select the three edges together as designated by (A) in Fig 8-6.

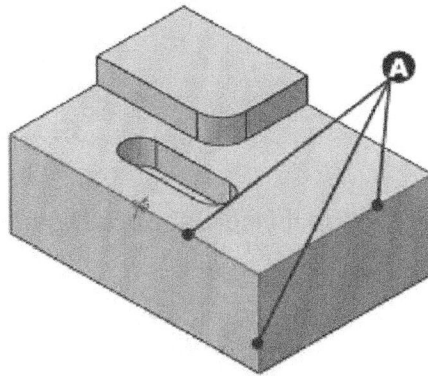

Fig 8-6 Edges to Fillet

5. Expand the dialog box, click the Edge corner(s) field and right click on the selection field.
6. Select the Create by vertex option in the pop-up menu.

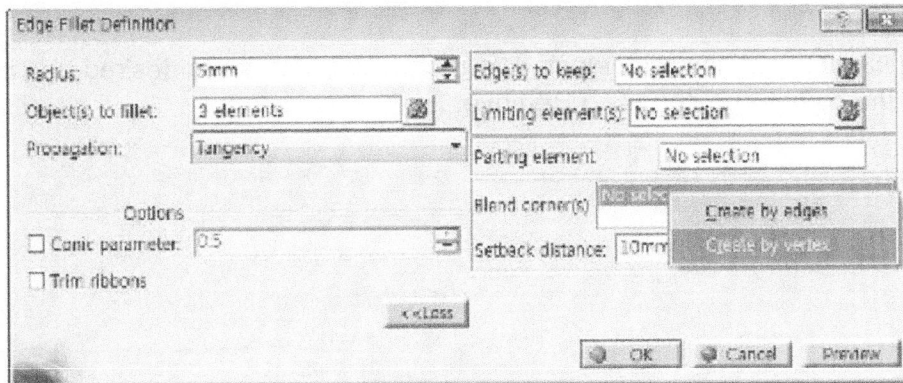

Fig 8-7 Blend corner(s) Option

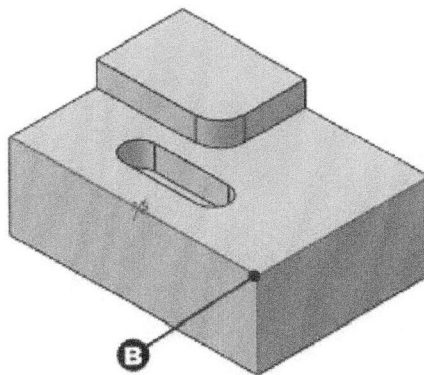

Fig 8-8 Selecting Vertex

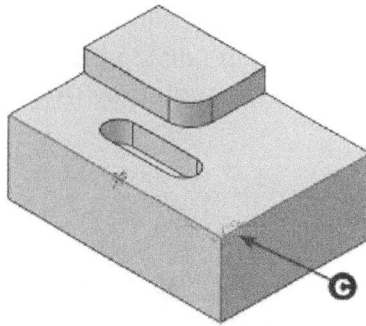

Fig 8-9 Mod if ying Set back Distance

7. Select the vertex specified by (B) in Fig 8-8.
8. Double click the dimension (C) shown an Fig 8-9 and enter the Setback distances. You can also enter the setback distance by choosing the Edit option in the pop- up menu of the Blend corner(s) option as shown in Fig 8-10.
9. Press the OK button in the Edge Fil- let Definition dialog box.

(Note) Selecting Comer

If you select the Create by edges option in the pop-up menu shown in Fig 8-7, the corner is selected automatically.

In cases where several vertices are selected, you can deselect the undesired one by right clicking on the name of the comer and choosing Remove.

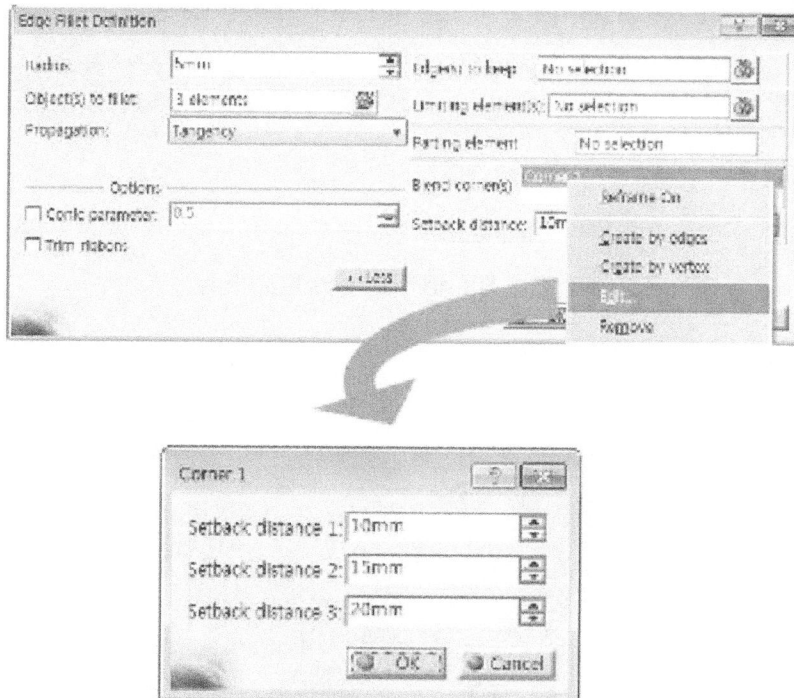

Fig 8-10 Modifying cutback Distance

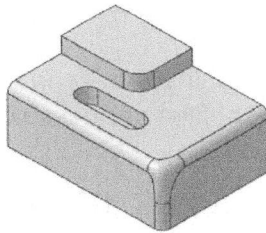

Fig 8-11 Result

8.2.5 Limit Fillet

By defining the limiting elements, you can create a fillet on a portion of an edge. Points and planes can be used as the limiting elements.

Create a limit -fillet according to the following procedure. The starting limit is located 20mm from the vertex as shown in Fig 8-12. The fillet goes up to the end of the edge.

Click the Edge Fillet icon, enter radius 5mm and press Tab.

Select the edge (A) shown in Fig 8-12.

Expand the dialog box by pressing the More button.

Right click on the Limiting element(s) se lection field and choose Create Point in the pop-up menu.

Define a point 20mm apart. from the vertex as shown in Fig 8-12.

Confirm the direction of the fillet by the arrow and press OK.

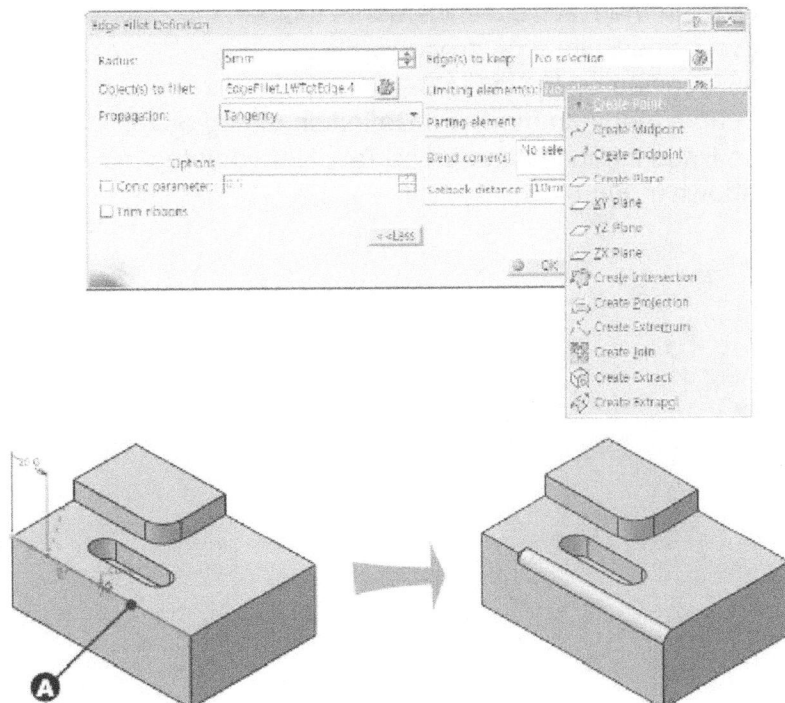

Fig 8-12 Creating a Limit Fillet

215

8.2.6 Variable Radius Fillet

A variable radius fillet can be created by using the Variable Radius Fillet but ton in the Dress-Up Features tool bar. You can specify different fillet radiuses on the desired location of an edge.

Exercise 56: Creating Variable (ch08_004.CATPart)

Let's create a variable radius fillet on an edge as shown in Fig 8-13.

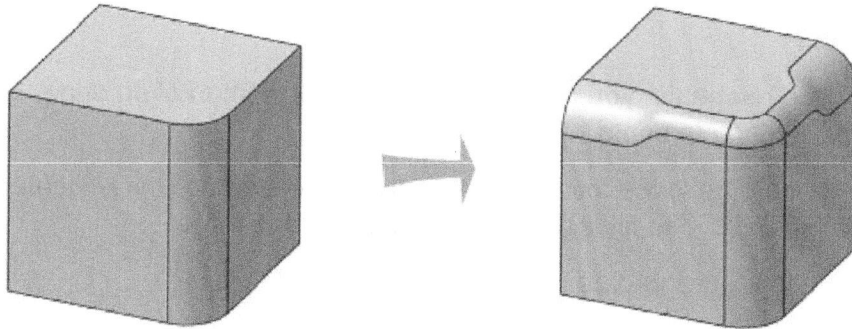

Fig 8-13 Variable Radius Fillet

Creating Points

Fig 8-14 Point Definition Dialog Box

1. Open the given file ch08_ 004.CATPart
2. Click the Point icon in the Reference Elements toolbar.
3. Choose On curve in the Point type dropdown list.
4. Select the edge specified by (A) in Fig 8-15.
5. Select Ratio of curve length in the Point Definition dialog box.
6. Enter 0.35 in the Ratio input box and press Tab. Note that the location ratio should start from the vertex (B) shown in Fig 8-15.

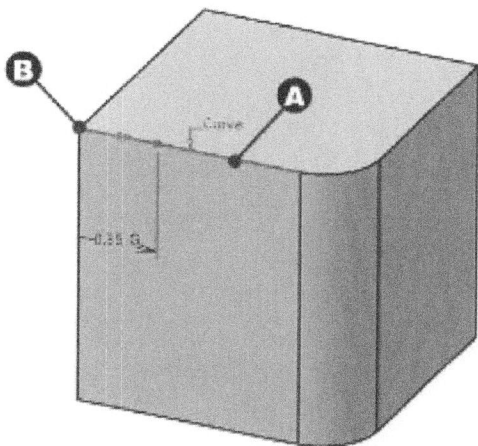

Fig 8-15 Point at 0.35

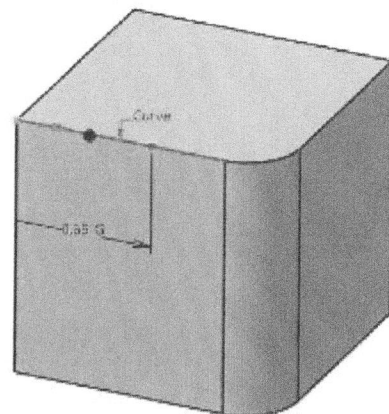

Fig 8-16 Point at 0.65

7. Create another point at the location of ratio 0.65 as shown in Fig 8-16.
8. Create two points on another edge specified by (C) in Fig 8-17 in the same way. Fig 8-18 shows the four points created on edges.

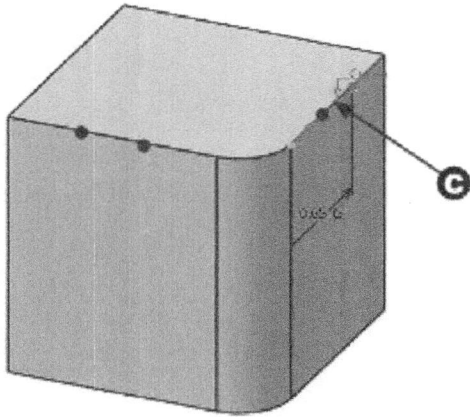

Fig 8-17 Point at another Edge

Fig 8-18 Points Created

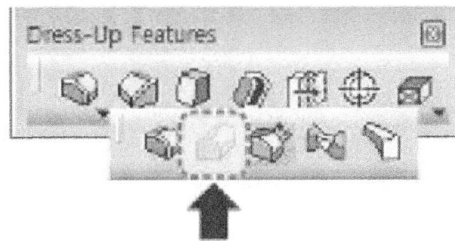

Fig 8-19 Variable Radius Fillet Icon

Applying Variable Radius Fillet

1. Click the Variable Radius Fillet icon in the Fillets (or Dress-Up Features) toolbar.

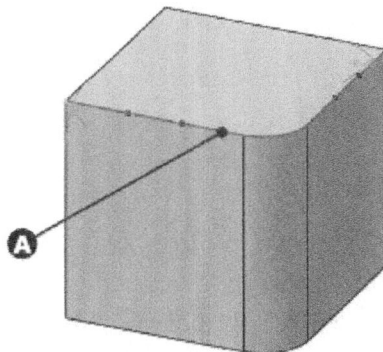

Fig 8-20 Edges to Select

2. Select the edges specified by (A) in Fig 8-20 with the Tangency propagation option.
3. Enter 20mm in the Radius input box and press Tab.

217

4. Click the Point multi selection field specified by (B) in Fig 8 - 21.
5. Select the four points created in Fig 8-18. Fig 8-22 shows the preview of variable radius fillet.

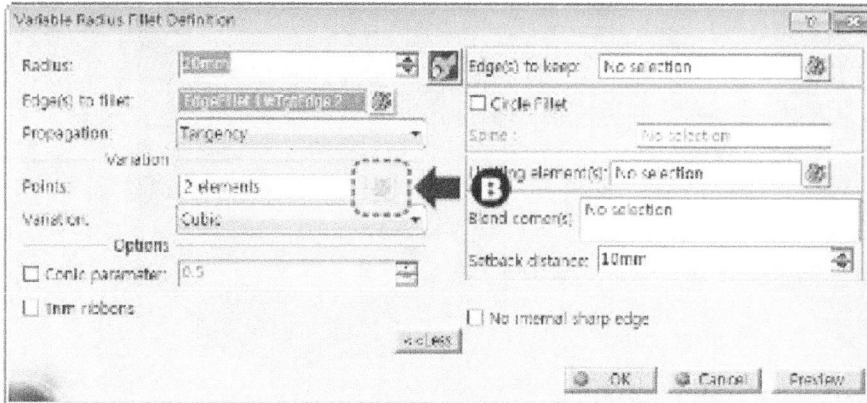

Fig 8-21 Selecting Variable Radius Points

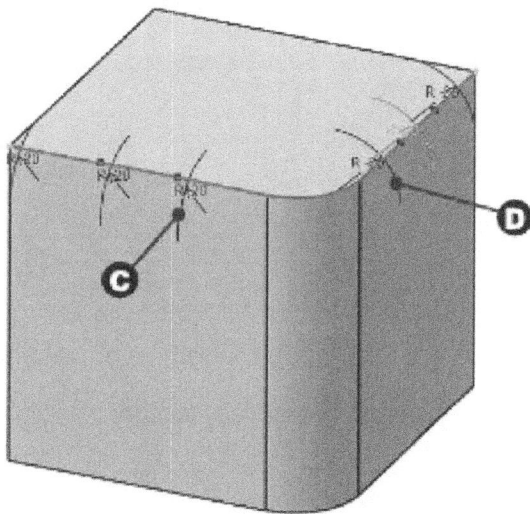

Fig 8-22 Variable Radius Points Specified

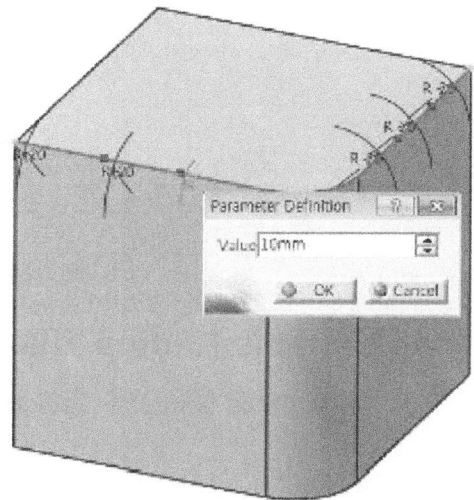

Fig 8-23 Modifying the Variable Radius

Modifying the Radius Value

1. Double click the dimension (C) shown in Fig 8-22.
2. Modify the value to 10mm and press OK.
3. Double click the dime ns ion 0 shown in Fig 8-22, modify the value to 10mm and press OK.
4. Press the OK button in the Variable Radius Fillet Definition dialog box. Fig 8-24 shows the result of variable radius fillet.

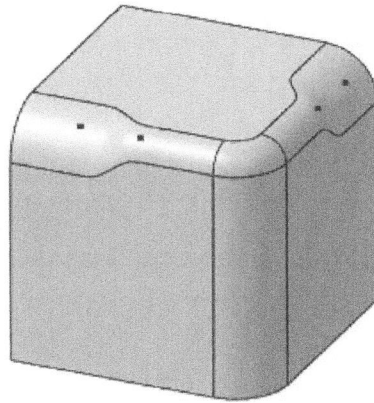

Fig 8-24 Result of Va1iable Radius Fillet

8.2.7 Edge to Keep Option

When the resultant surface of a fillet invades another edge, the edge line can be varied. If you want to prevent the edge from being varied, you can set the edge to be kept using this option.

Exercise 57: Creating Variable (ch08_005.CATPart)

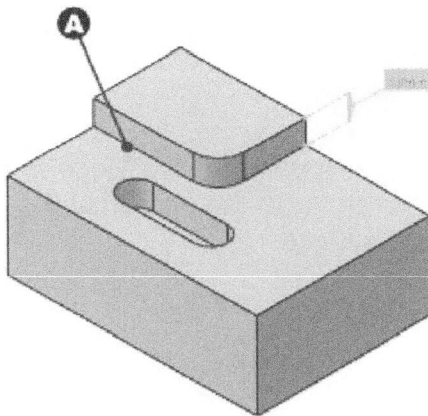

Fig 8-25 Edge to Fillet

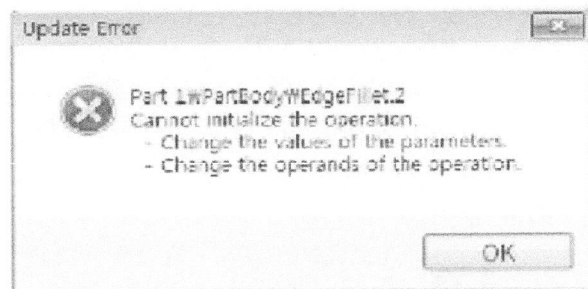

Fig 8-26 Error Message

1. Open the given file ch08_005.CATPart.
2. Click the Edge Fillet icon and select the edge (A) designated in Fig 8-25. Note that the Propagation option is Tangency.
3. Enter the radius 20mm and press the Tab key.
4. Click OK in the Fillet Definition dialog box. An error message appears as shown in Fig 8-26. You cannot apply an R20 fillet on the selected edge.
5. Press the OK in the Update Error message box. An error message as shown in Fig 8-27 appears.

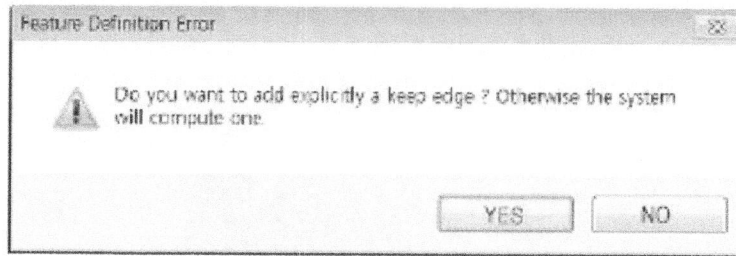

Fig 8-27 Keep edge Message

6. Press the OK in the error message box.

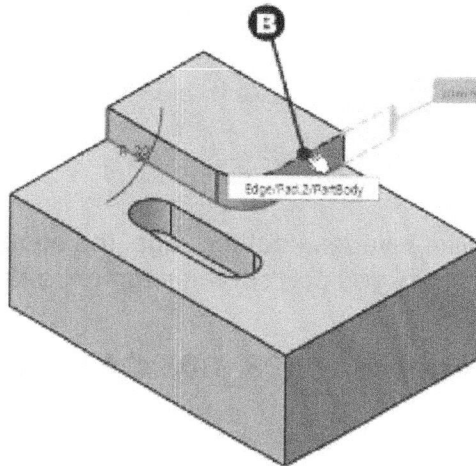

Fig 8-28 Selecting Edge to Keep

7. Select the edge (B) designated in Fig 8-28. The edge appears in the Edge(s) to keep selection field ((C) in Fig 8-29) in the dialog box.
8. Press the OK button. Fig 8-30 shows the resultant fillet surface.

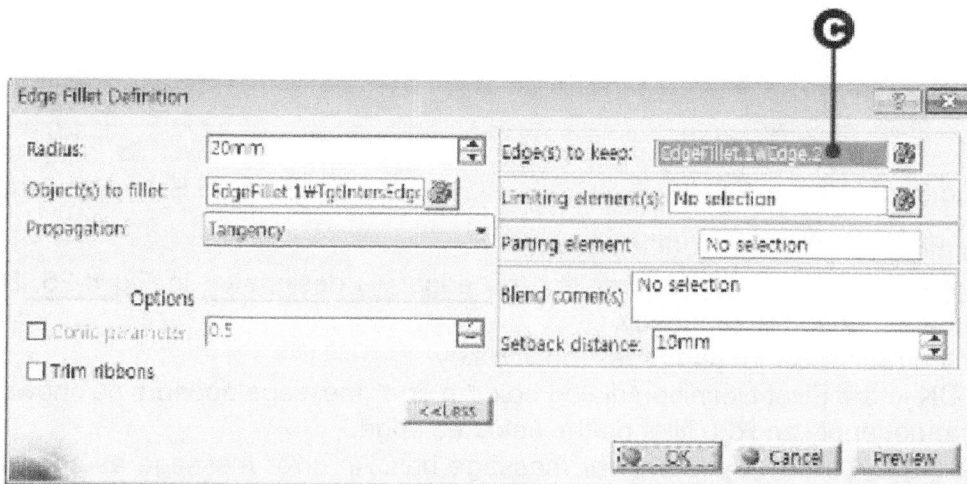

Fig 8-29 Edge Fillet Definition Dialog Box

(Note) Size of Fillet R

In general, the size of the fillet radius has to be larger or equal to the dimension (D) designated in Fig 8-30.

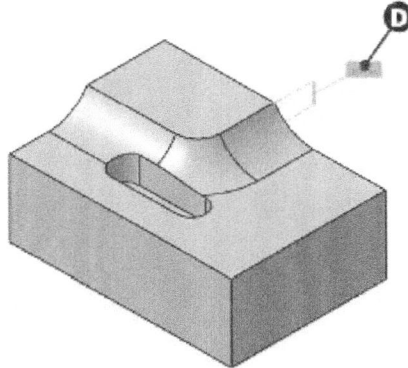

Fig 8-30 Result

(Note) Giving up of Other Edge

If you want to keep edge (A) in Fig 8-31, you have to concede that edge (B) will not be kept.

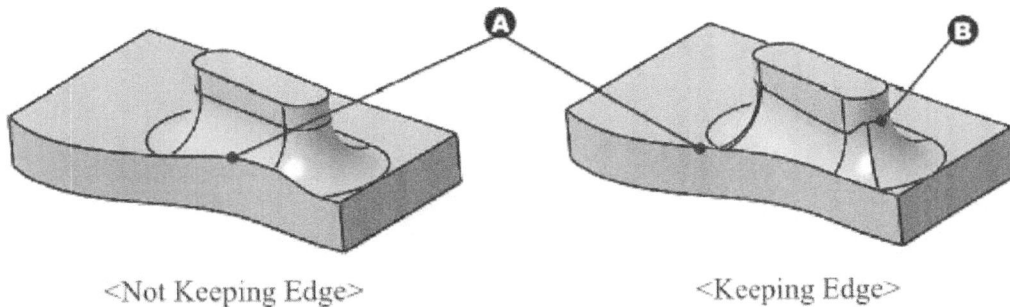

<Not Keeping Edge>   <Keeping Edge>

Fig 8-31 Comparison of Keeping Edge

(Note) Displaying the Result of measurement.

- If you want to display the result after measuring the distance, angle, etc. between the objects, follow the procedure below (the numbers con-es pond to the numbers in Fig 8-32).

  (1) Click the Measure icon in the Measure toolbar.

  (2) Press the Measure button in the Measure Between dialog boxes.

  (3), (4) Select the two objects between which to measure entities.

  (5) Check the Keep Measure option and press OK.

The result of measurement is recorded in the Spec Tree, and you can modify the definition of the measurement by double clicking it in the Spec Tree or on the screen.

If you place the mouse point on the dimension text (A) or on the dimension line (B) while the Measure Definition dialog box is invoked, you can drag them to another location.

If you do not check the Keep Measure option, the result disappears on the screen after pressing the OK button.

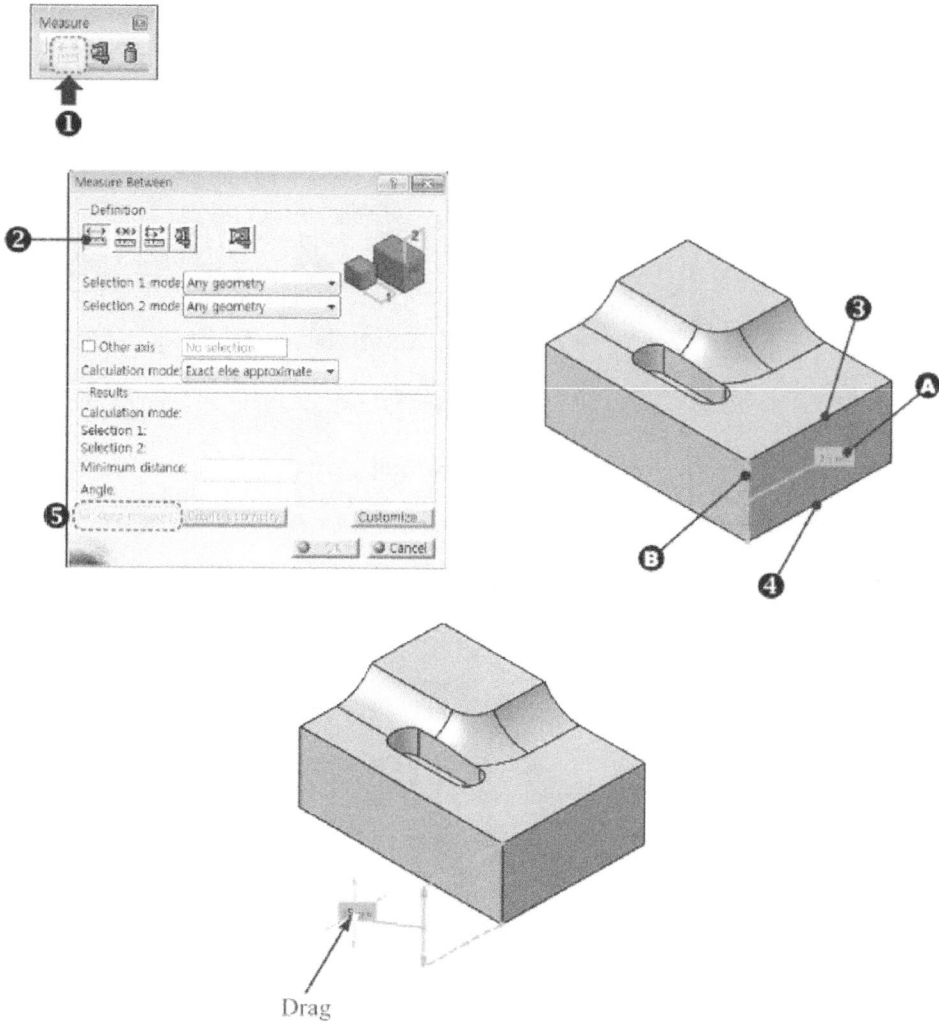

Fig 8- 32 Measuring Distance

(Note) Other Commands in the Measure Toolbar

- **Measure Item:** Measures the length of an edge, area of a surface, volume of a fea-ture or solid body by selecting the line, surface, feature or solid body, respectively.
- **Measure Inertia:** Measures the physical prope1ties of a surface or a solid body.

8.2.8 Face-Face Fillet

With the Face-Face Fillet in the Fillets toolbar, you can create a smooth connecting ur- face between two surfaces.

Procedure

1. Click the Face-Face Fillet icon in the Dress-Up Features toolbar.

2. Select the two surfaces between which to apply the fillet.
3. Enter the fillet radius and press OK.

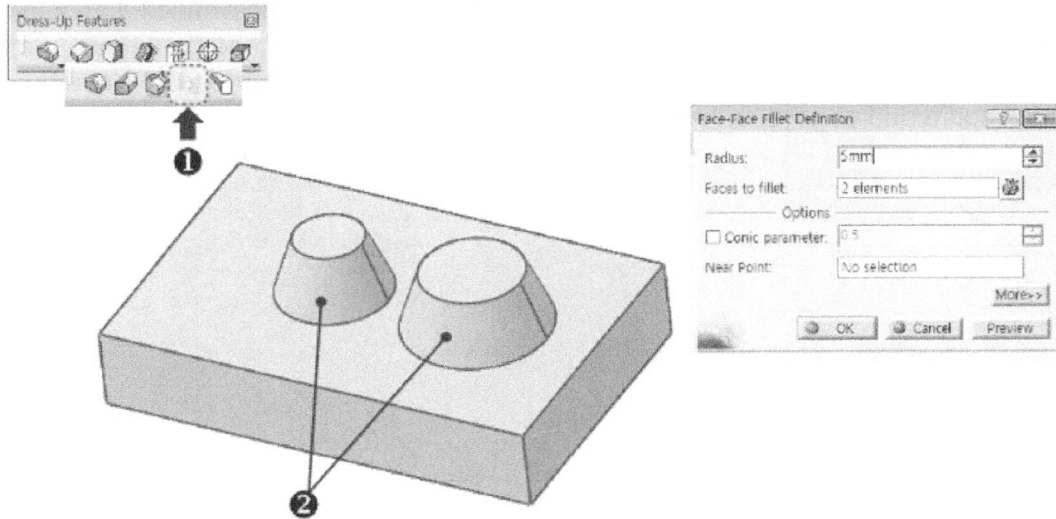

Fig 8-33 Procedure of Face-Face Fillet

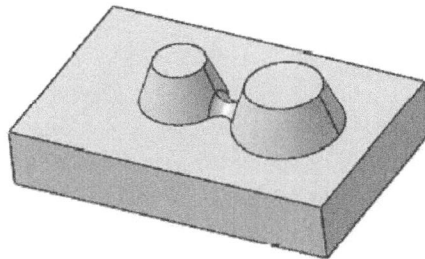

Fig 8-34 Result of Face-Face Fillet

(Note) Case of Face-Face Fillet

- You can connect two separate bodies into one single body by the fillet surface.

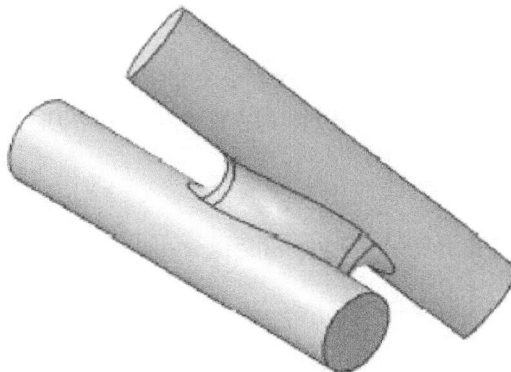

Fig 8-35 Applying Fillet between Two Bodies

Fig 8-36 shows the application of a fillet between two surfaces0 and O with the Hold Curve, Spine and Edge(s) to keep option. When you are creating a fillet using the Face-Face Fillet command, the shape of the fillet edge can be pre-defined as the Hold Curve. In this case, you have to specify the Spine at the same time. Note that the Radius input box is not available because the radius varies to keep the hold curve and edge(s) to keep.

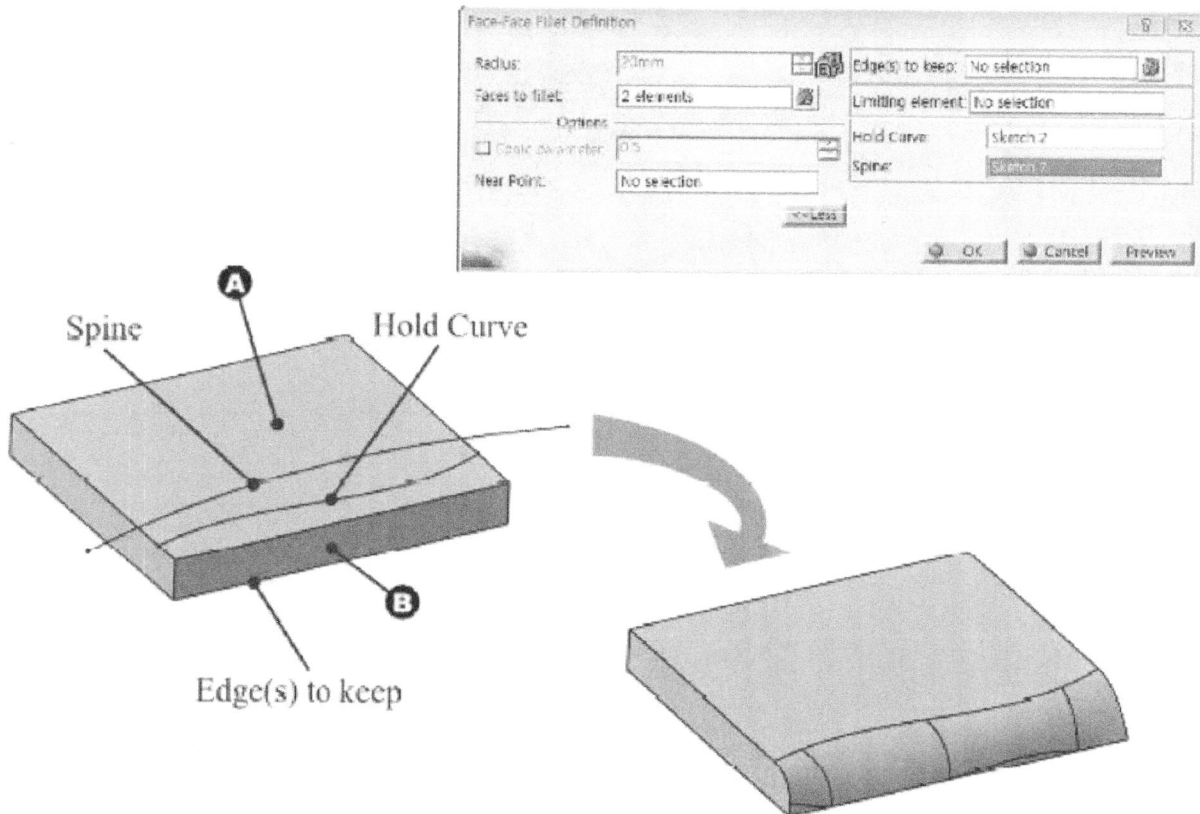

Fig 8-36 Using Hold Curve Option

8.2.9 Tri tangent Fillet

Using the Tri tangent Fillet command, you can create a fillet surface that is tangent to three surfaces as shown in Fig 8-38. This command is useful when you are filleting the sharp end of a thin feature.

Procedure

(1) Click the Tri tangent Fillet icon in the Fillets toolbar.

(2), (3) Select the two opposite faces.

(4) Select the face to remove (the third tangent surface) and press OK.

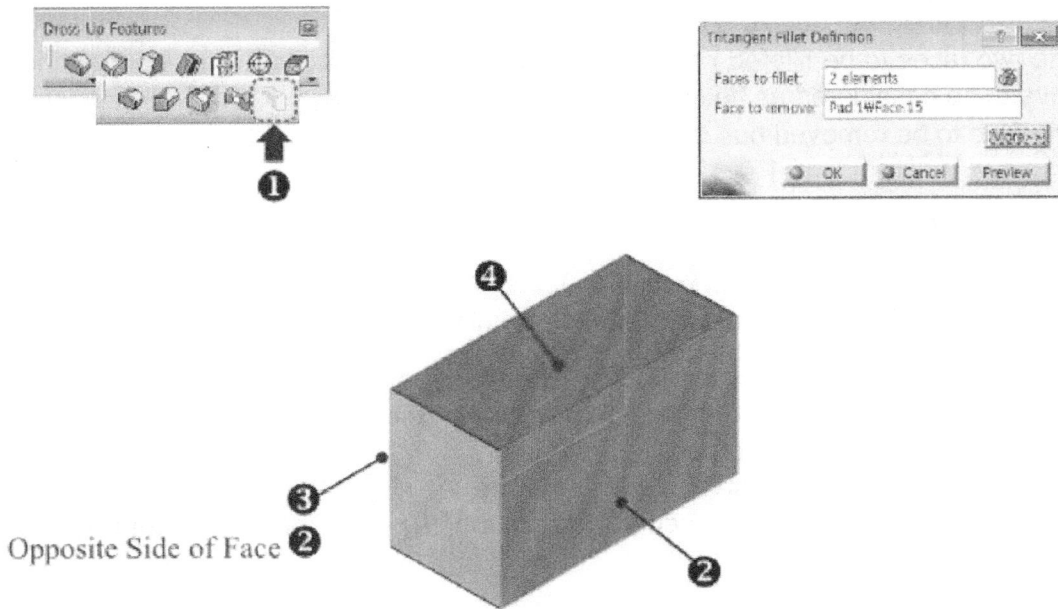

Fig 8-37 Procedure of Tri tangent Fillet

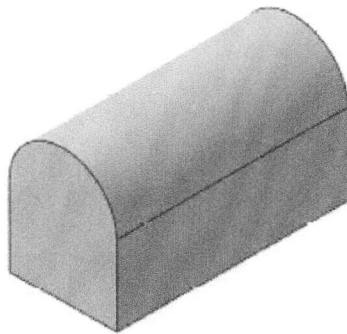

Fig 8-38 Result of Tri tangent Fillet

Exercise 58: Tri tangent Fillet (ch08_006.CATPart)

Open the given file ch08_006.CATPart and apply Tri tangent fillet as shown in Fig 8-39.

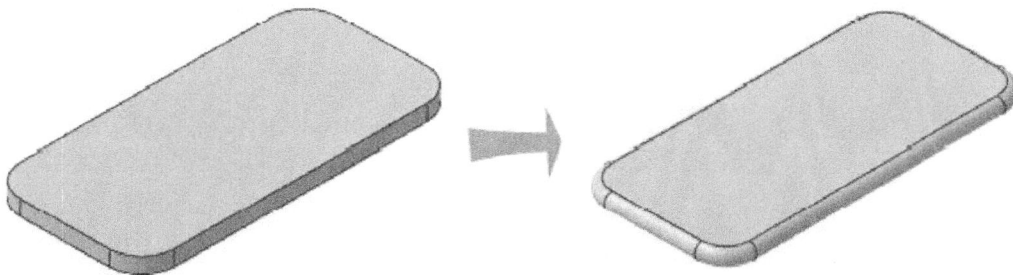

Fig 8-39 Applying Tri tangent Fillet

- The two faces to be filleted have to be separated. If the faces are tangent connected, they have to be considered as being selected at the same time.
- The face to be removed bas to co1U1ect the faces to fillet.

8.2.10 Guideline for Applying Fillet

Quite often you will not be able to create a satisfactory fillet for complex geometry. The following guidelines outline the steps to create a fillet successfully.

1. Apply the fillet for the larger radius first, and then proceed to the smaller ones.
2. Apply the fillet for the concentrated edges first by selecting the edges at the same time. You can apply setback for this case.
3. Apply fillets one by one, not as a single feature.
4. Apply the fillet for the separate edges first so that the edges to be selected later are tangent connected.

Exercise 59: Applying Fillet in Sequence (ch08_007.CATPart)

Apply fillet for the given part ch08_007.CATPart according to the suggested order.

Case 1: Different radiuses for each edge

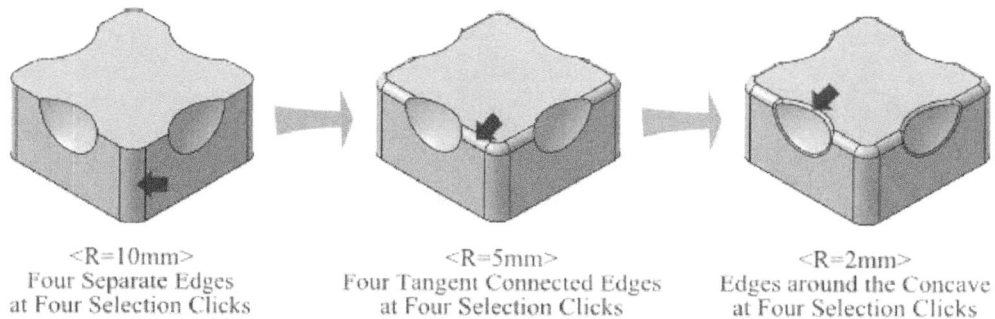

<R=10mm>	<R=5mm>	<R=2mm>
Four Separate Edges	Four Tangent Connected Edges	Edges around the Concave
at Four Selection Clicks	at Four Selection Clicks	at Four Selection Clicks

Fig 8-40 Applying Diffe rent Radiuses

Case 2: Same radius for each edge

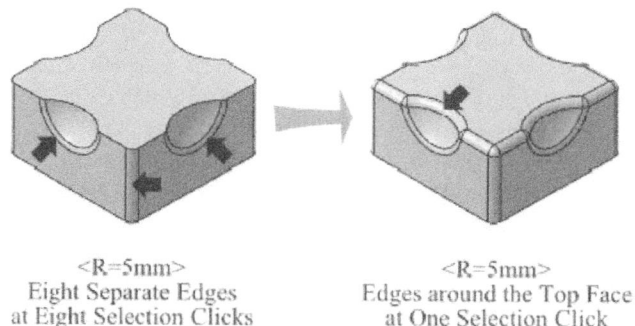

<R=5mm>	<R=5mm>
Eight Separate Edges	Edges around the Top Face
at Eight Selection Clicks	at One Selection Click

Fig 8-41 Applying Same Radius

Exercise 60: Applying Fillet in Sequence (ch08_008.CATPart)

Open the file ch08_008.CATPart and apply fillets as shown in Fig 8-42. The fillet radius is 3 mm for all edges except the bottom. Apply 10 mm setback distances.

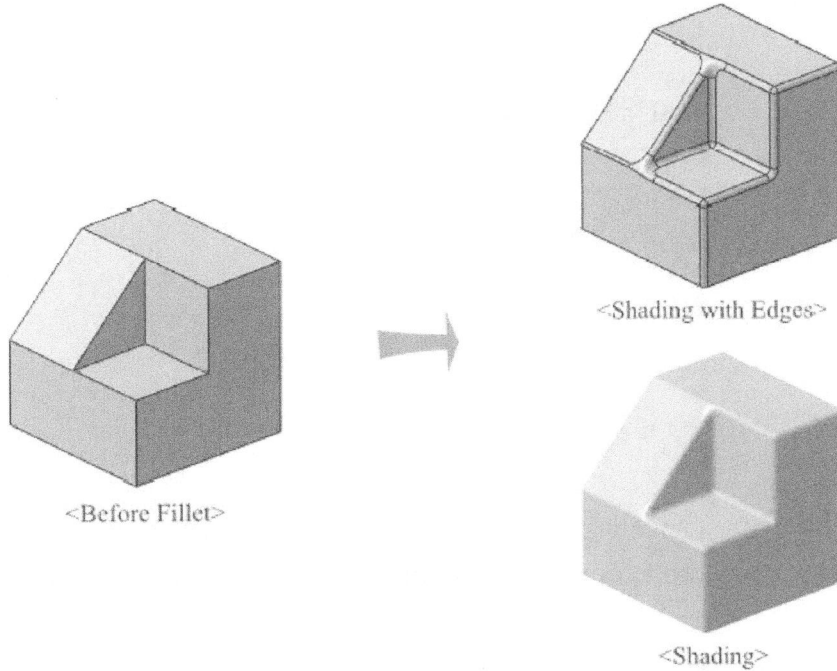

Fig 8- 42 Applying Fillet with Blend Corner(s) Option

(Note) Hint!

- Apply fillet three times as shown in Fig 8-43.

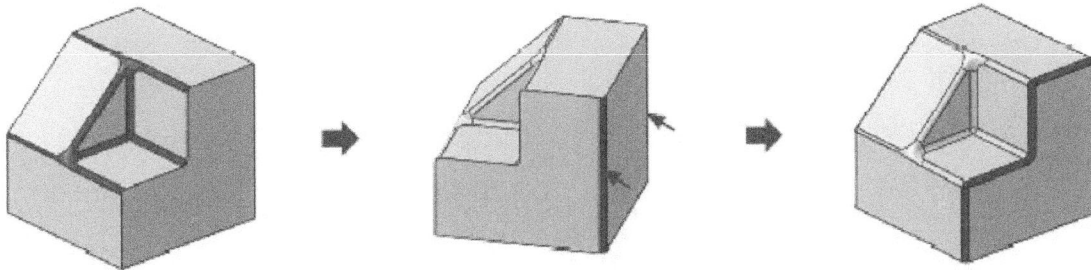

Fig 8-43 Applying Three Fillets in Sequence

8.3 CHAMFER

Sharp edges can be chamfered at a specified angle or by entering a distance from the sharp edge. Mate ria l can be removed or added to eliminate the sharp edge of a part. Fig 8-44 shows the case of removing material and Fig 8-45 shows the case of filling material. In manufacturing processes, a chamfer is frequently applied to the part itself. On the other hand. a fillet is applied to the mold and reflected on the part.

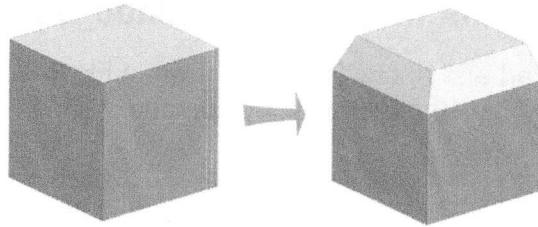

Fig 8-44 Removing Material by Chamfer

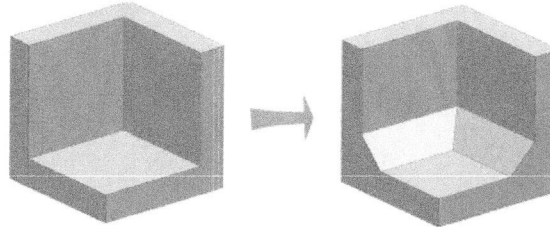

Fig 8-45 Adding Material by Chamfer

8.3.1 Procedure

Keep to the following procedure to apply chamfer on an edge. The step numbers correspond to the steps in Fig 6-69.

1. Click the Chamfer icon in the Dress-Up Features toolbar.
2. Select the Mode option.
3. Select the edges to apply chamfer. If you select a face, all the edges of the face are selected.
4. Enter parameters and press OK.

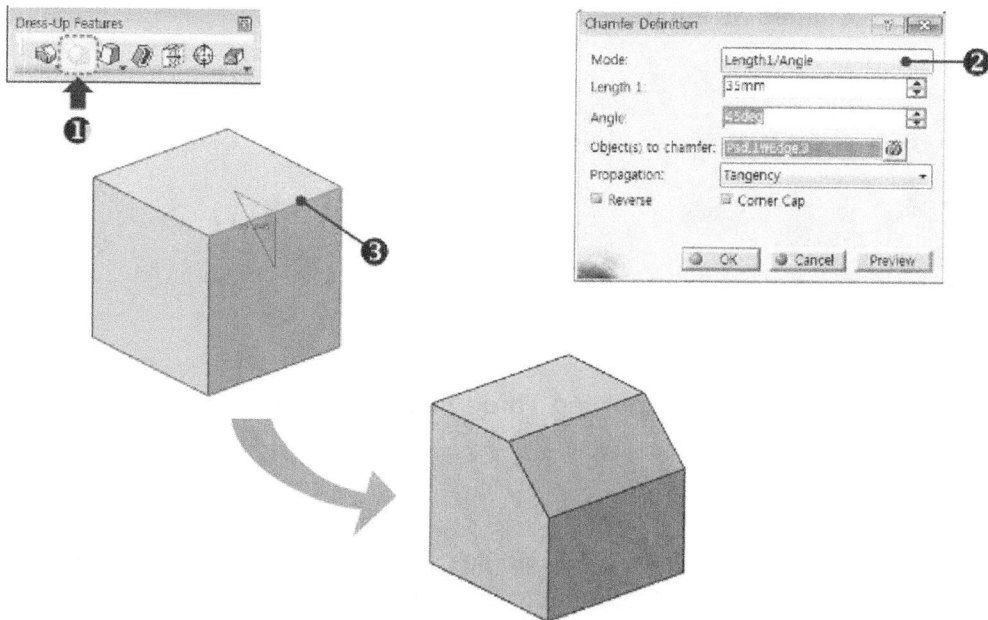

Fig 8-46 Applying Chamfer

8.3.2 Mode Option

- **Length1/Angle:** Enter the distance from the edge on a surface along the direction specified by the arrow and the angle from the surface.

Fig 8-47 Length1/Angle Mode

- **Length1/ Length2:** Enter two distances on the surfaces sharing the edge that is being chamfered.

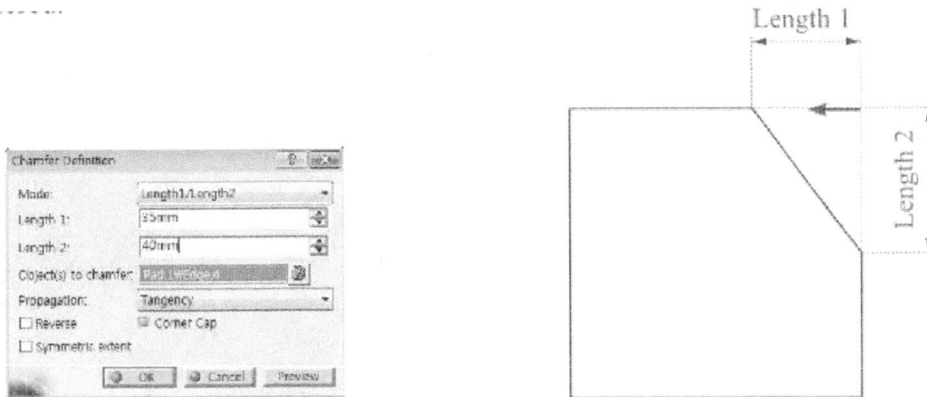

Fig 8-48 Length 1/ Length 2 Mode

- **Chordal length / Angle:** Enter the chordal length of chamfer and the angle from the surface specified by the arrow.

Fig 8-49 Chordal length/Angle Mode

229

- **Height/Angle:** Enter the height from the edge to be chamfered to the chamfer surface and the angle from the surface specified by the arrow.

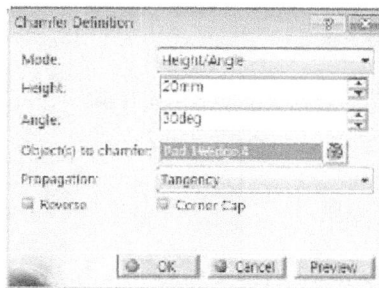

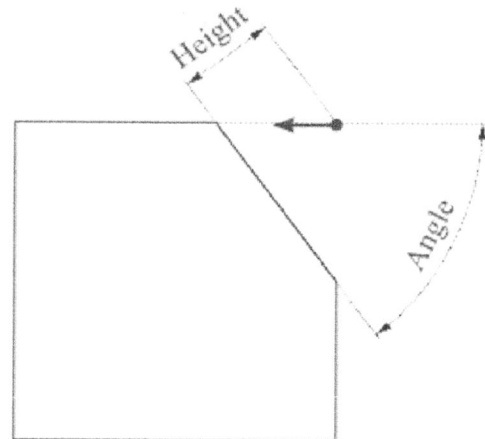

Fig 8-50 Height/Angle Mode

8.4 DRAFT

You can apply draft on a face with reference to the pulling direction of the upper mold. If the side face is not guaranteed a proper draft angle, the part cannot be separated from the mold. Fig 8-51 shows the side face before and after draft, where the pulling direction is upward.

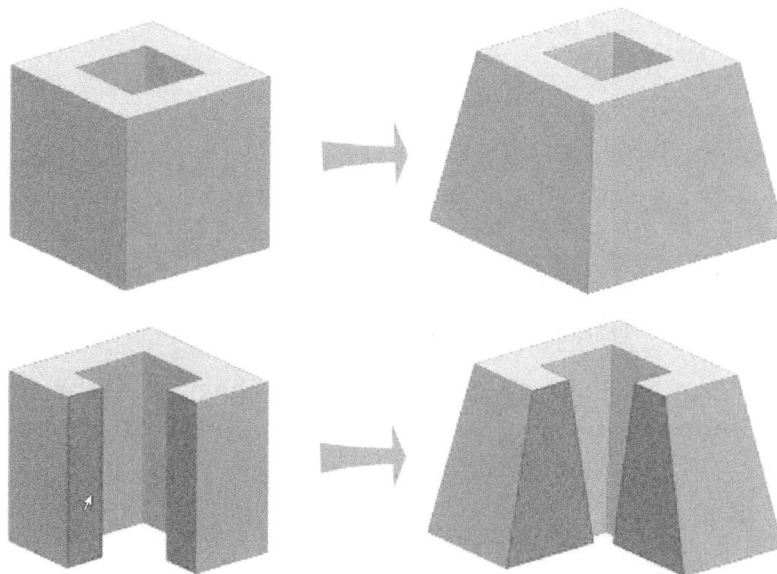

Fig 8-51 Before and After the Draft

Why does the side face of a part have to be slanted? This is a question that arises when you manufacture a part through a mold.

Fig 8-52 shows a part that will be manufactured out of plastic. You will design the upper mold (cavity) and the lower mold (core) as shown in Fig 8-53 and Fig 8-54, respectively.

The two molds are assembled as shown in Fig 8-55 where plastic resin will be injected into the vacant area as designated by @ in Fig 8-55. Temperature is applied to the mold for a while and the resin will become cured as designated by the black area in Fig 8-56. When the pa1t is cured sufficiently, the mold will be opened by pulling the upper mold upward to separate the part from the mold.

However, if the side face of the part or the corresponding face of the mold is parallel to the pulling direction, the side face will be damaged in the area designated by the arrows in Fig 8-57 because of the slip between the faces.

<Top>   <Bottom>

Fig 8-52 Sample Part

Fig 8-53 Upper Mold (Cavity)   Fig 8-54 Lower Mold (Core)

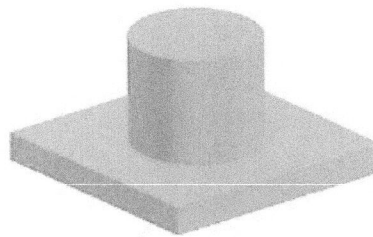

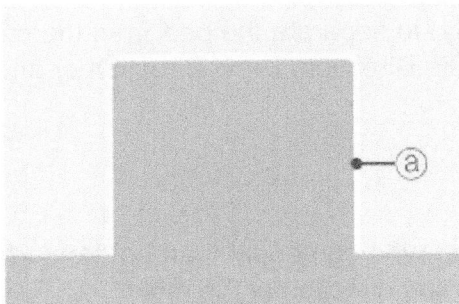

Fig 8-55 Assembled Mold   Fig 8-56 Cured Product (Black)

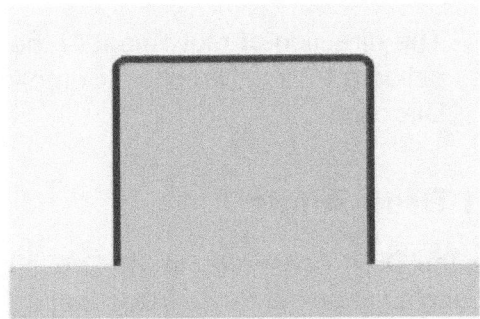

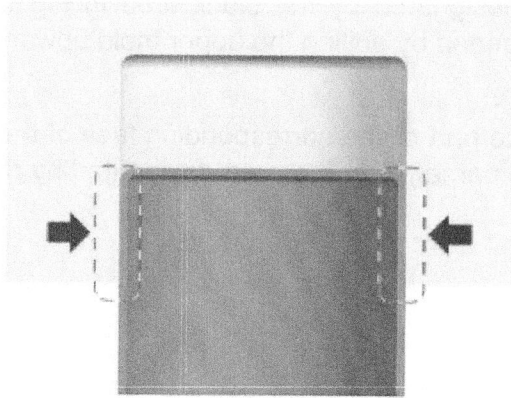

Fig 8-57 Side Face Where Slip Occurs

Damage to the side faces that occurs while the part is separated from the mold can be avoided by applying draft as shown in Fig 8-58. Positive angle draft means that the angle is applied so that the part can be separated easily as shown in Fig 8-59. If you apply a reverse angle draft, you cannot separate the part, or the part will be broken.

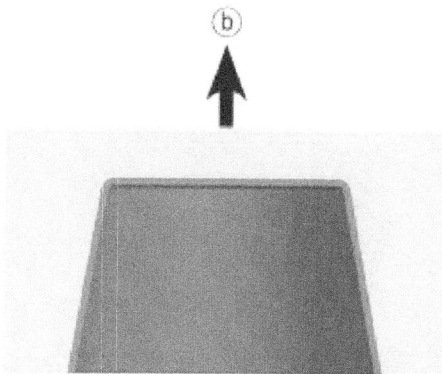

Fig 8-58 Part Applied with Draft Angle

Fig 8-59 Parting

(Note) Pulling Direction((b) in Fig 8-59)

- The direction of movement of the upper mold (cavity) to separate the part from the mold is called a Pulling Direction. Sometimes it is called a Die Direction, Draw Direction or an Eject Direction.

8.4.1 Draft Angle

Using the Draft Angle icon in the Dress-Up Features toolbar, you can apply draft on the surfaces. Draft angle is applied to the faces that are parallel to the pulling direction of the mold.

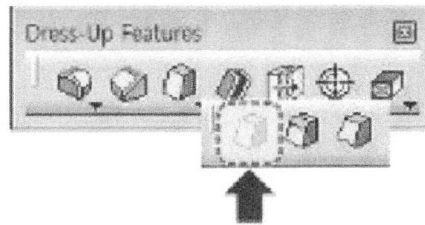

Fig 8-60 Draft Angle Icon

8.4.2 Neutral Face and Parting Face

- **Neutra Face:** The basis of the draft. The cut section by the neutral face does not change.
- **Parring Face:** The upper and lower molds meet at the par ting face. In view of the part, the parting face forms the parting edge on the surface. The parting edge is the boundary which divides the regions formed by the upper and lower molds.

The neutral face and the parting face can either be the same or not.

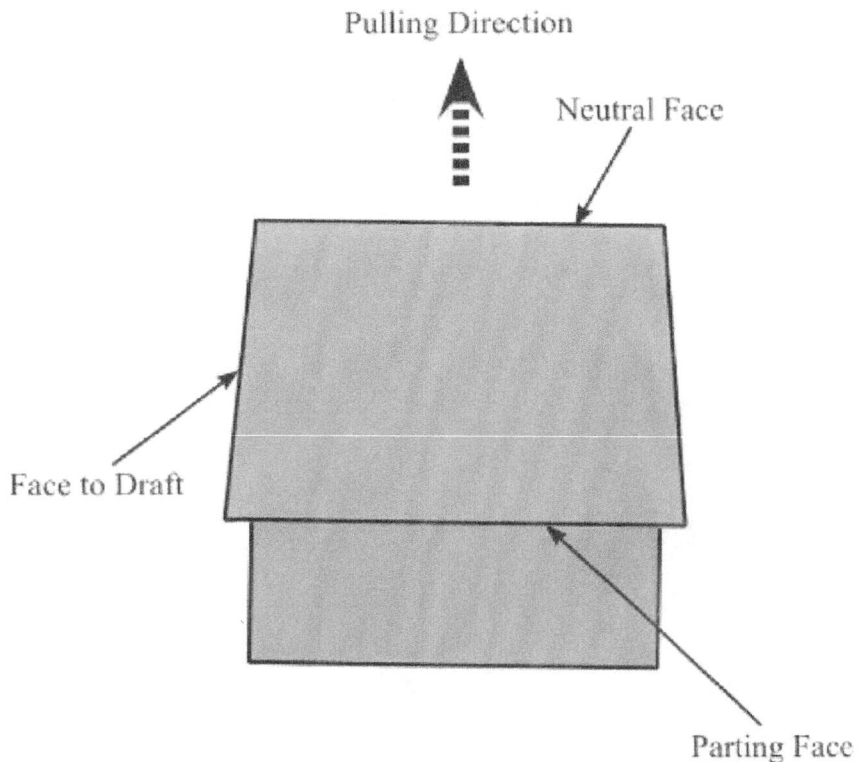

Fig 8- 61 Terms or Mold

Exercise 61: Draft Angle (ch08_009.CATPart)

Let's apply draft angle to the surfaces of given part supposing that the pulling direction and neutral face are as shown in Fig 8-62.

233

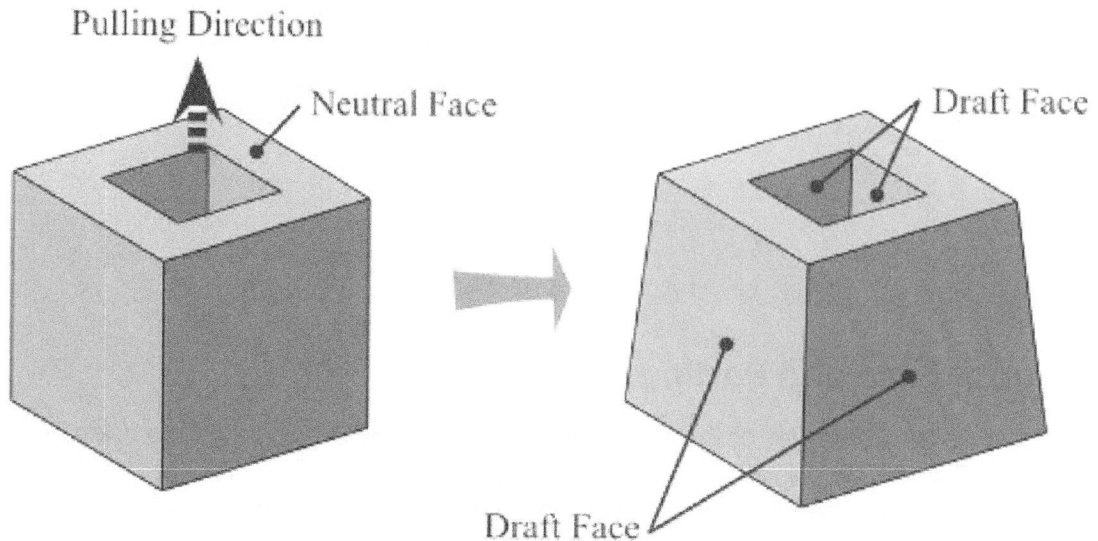

Fig 8-62 Applying Draft Angle

1. Open the given file ch08_009.CA · Part.
2. Click the Draft Angle icon in the Dress-Up Features toolbar.
3. Enter 5 deg in the Angle input box and press the Tab key. Note that the Face(s) to draft selection field is highlighted and you are prompted to select the faces to draft.
4. Select the eight faces to draft as shown in Fig 8-63.

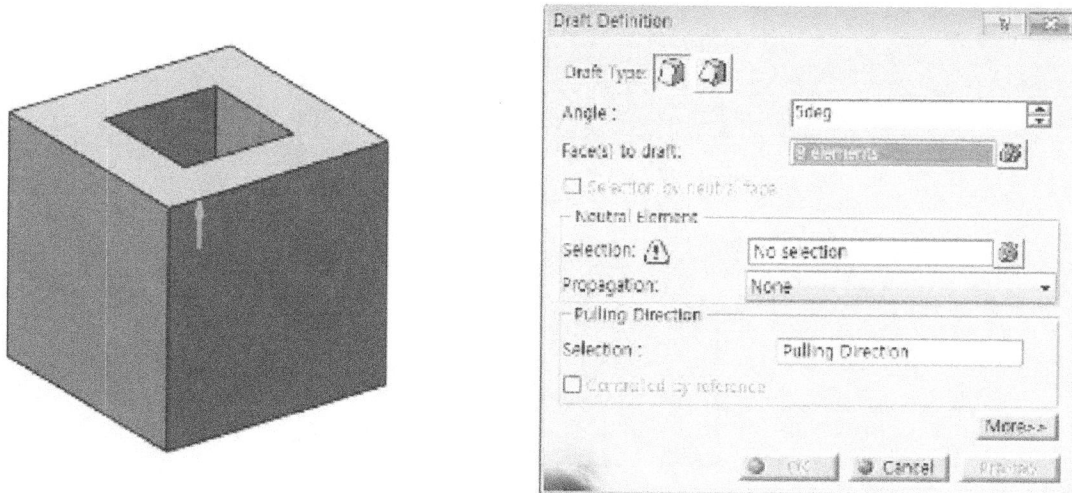

Fig 8-63 Face to Draft

5. Click the Selection field in the Neutral Element option.
6. Select the neutral face specified by the arrow in Fig 8-64. Note that the pulling direction is set normal to the neutral face. You can reverse the pulling direction by clicking the arrowhead.
7. Click OK in the Draft Definition dialog box. Fig 8-65 shows the result of the draft.

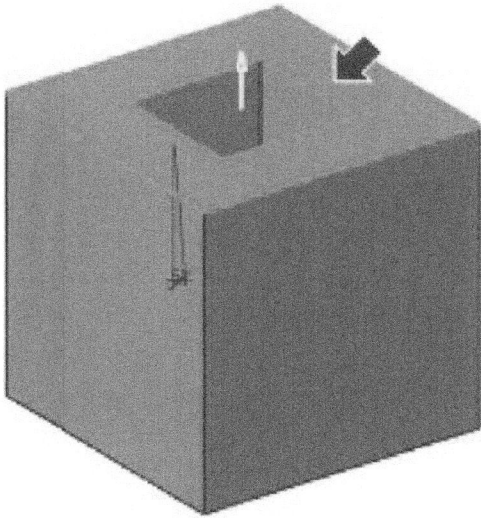

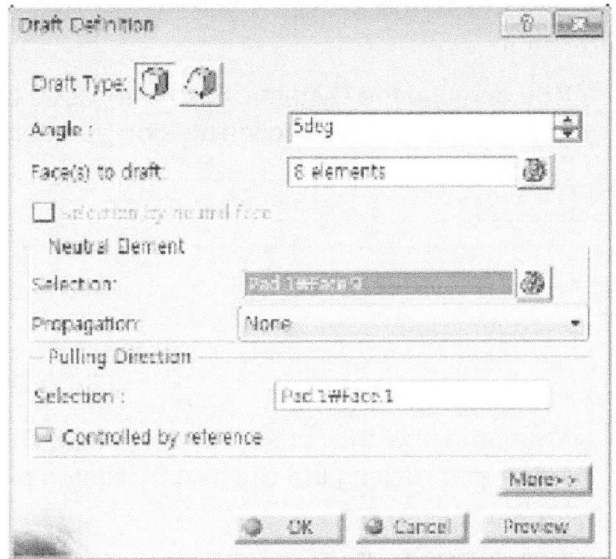

Fig 8- 64 Neutral Face

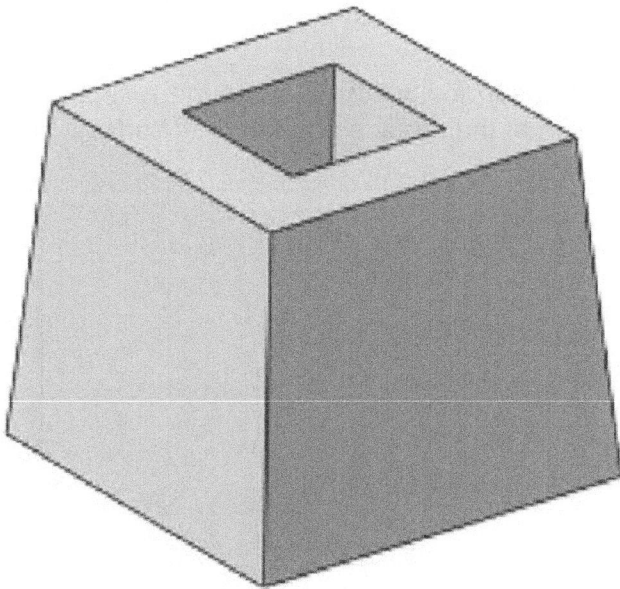

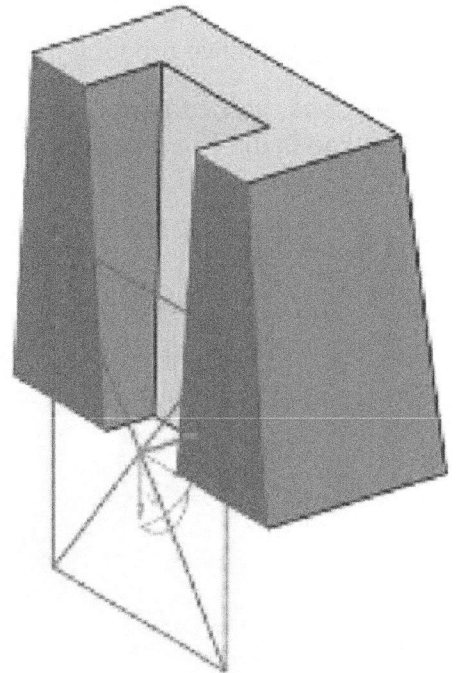

Fig 8-65 Completed Model

(Note) Controlled by reference

- If you select a neutral face, the pulling direction is defined normal to the neutral face. When the Controlled by reference option is turned on, if the neutral face is slanted, the pulling direction is updated.

(Note) Dynamic Sectioning

You can use the Dynamic Sectioning icon to show the section cut of a mode I as shown in Fig 8-65. C lick the Dynamic Sectioning icon and select a plane, e.g., the yz or zx plane.

Fig 8-66 Dynamic Sectioning Icon

You can show the cut section in the sketcher workbench by defining the sketch plane on a desired plane and clicking the Cut part by sketch plane icon in the Visualization toolbar.

8.4.3 Draft Reflect Line

The area marked by ⌇ in Fig 8-67 cannot be pulled out because the surfaces do not ensure the required draft angle. Even though the part is pulled out, the surface will be scratched, which will produce a defective product.

In this case, you can apply draft by creating tan gent surface with respect to the reflect line. The reflect line is the line that is formed by the intersection of the surface and the draft surface.

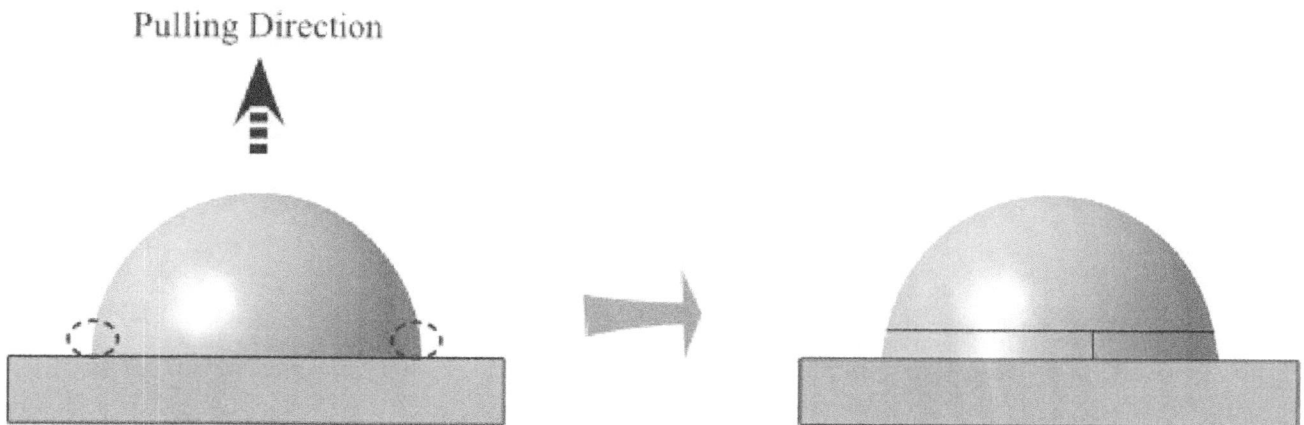

Fig 8-67 Pulling Direction and Tangent Face

Exercise 62: Applying Draft (ch08 _010.CATPart)

Apply draft angle of 5 degrees for the given part according to the specified pulling direction. Smooth edges are not displayed in figures.

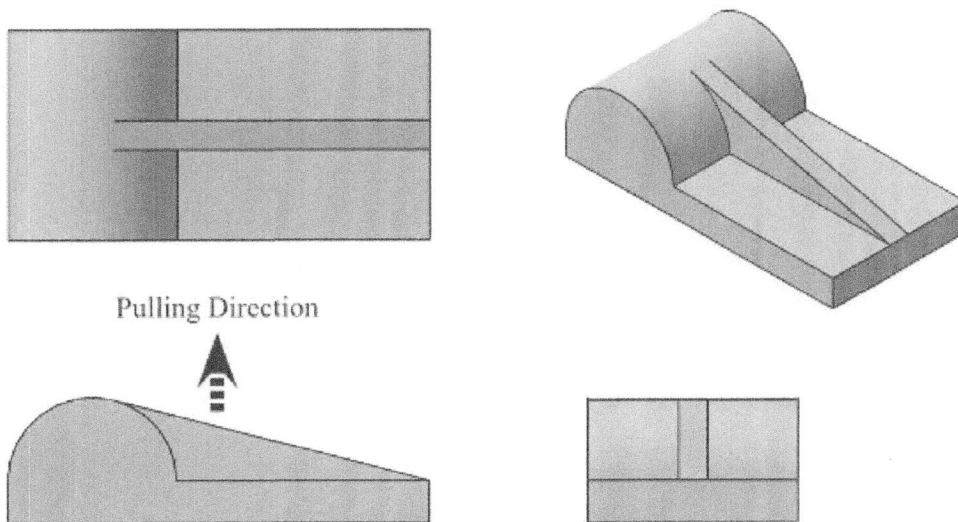

Fig 8-68 Before Applying Draft

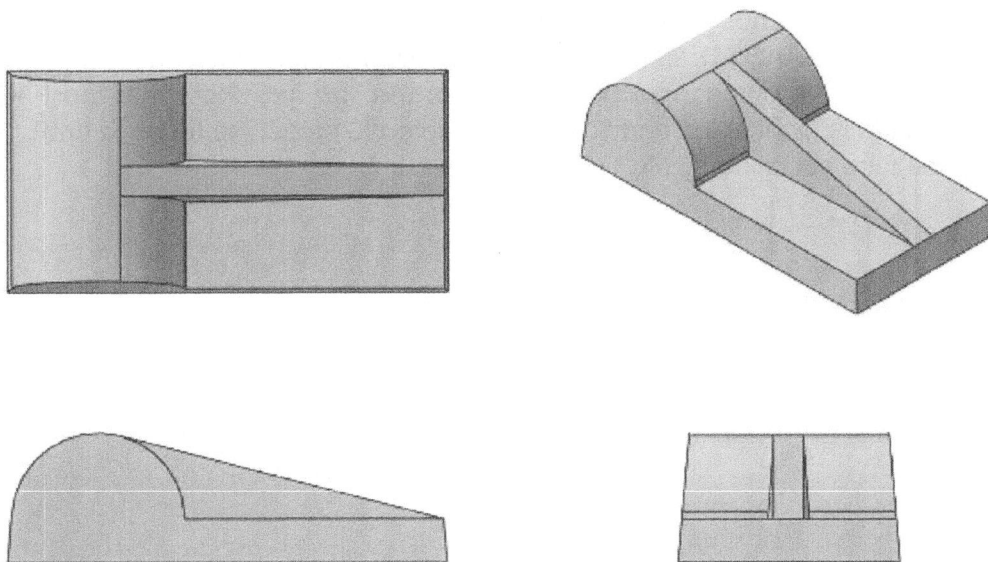

Fig 8-69 After Applying Draft

8.4.4 Variable Angle Draft

If you set the draft type as Variable, you can apply variable angle draft on a face at a specified po
int. You can also use the Variable Angle Draft icon in the Drafts toolbar. Vertex points can be chosen
as the variable ang le point. You can also create a point at a desired location by right clicking on the
Points selection field in the Draft Definition dialog box. Note that the draft face will be distorted on
account of the different draft angle at the specified points.

Exercise 63: Variable Angle Draft (ch08_011.CATPart)

Let's learn how to apply variable angle draft as shown in Fig 8-70.

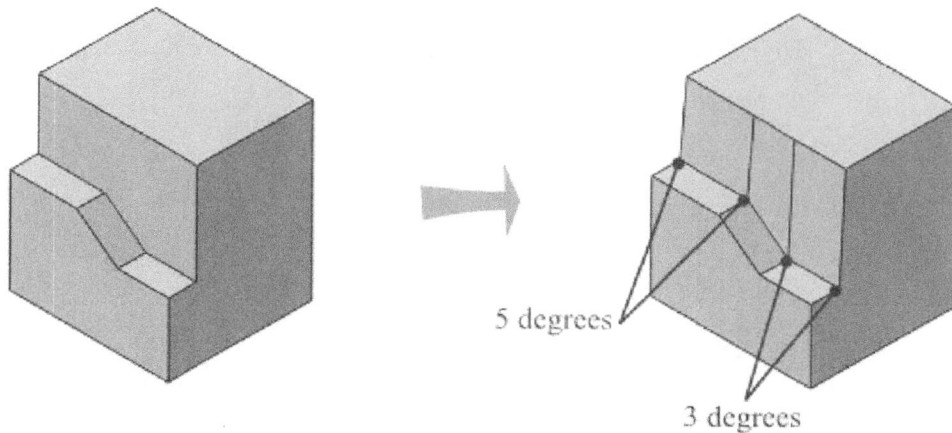

Fig 8-70 Variable Angle Draft

Selecting Faces to Daft

1. Open the given file ch08_011.CATPart.
2. Click the Variable Angle Draft icon in the Dress-Up Features toolbar.
3. Enter 5 deg in the Angle input box and press the Tab key. Note that the Face(s) to draft selection field is highlighted and you are prompted to select the faces to draft.
4. Select the face specified by (A) in Fig 8-71.

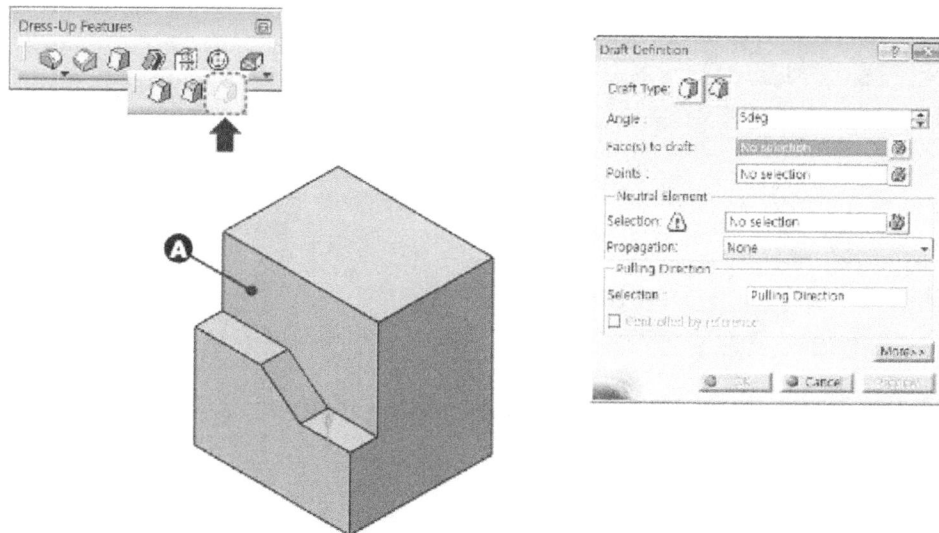

Fig 8-71 Face to Draft

Neutral Element. Variable Draft Points and Pulling Direction

1. Click the Neutral Element selection field.
2. Select the three faces specified by (B) in Fig 8-72. Note that two points are selected in the Points selection field. The location of the selected point may be different according to the selection order of the neutral faces.

3. Click the Points selection field and select a vertex other than the selected points. An en or message is displayed as shown in Fig 8-73.
4. Click OK in the message box.

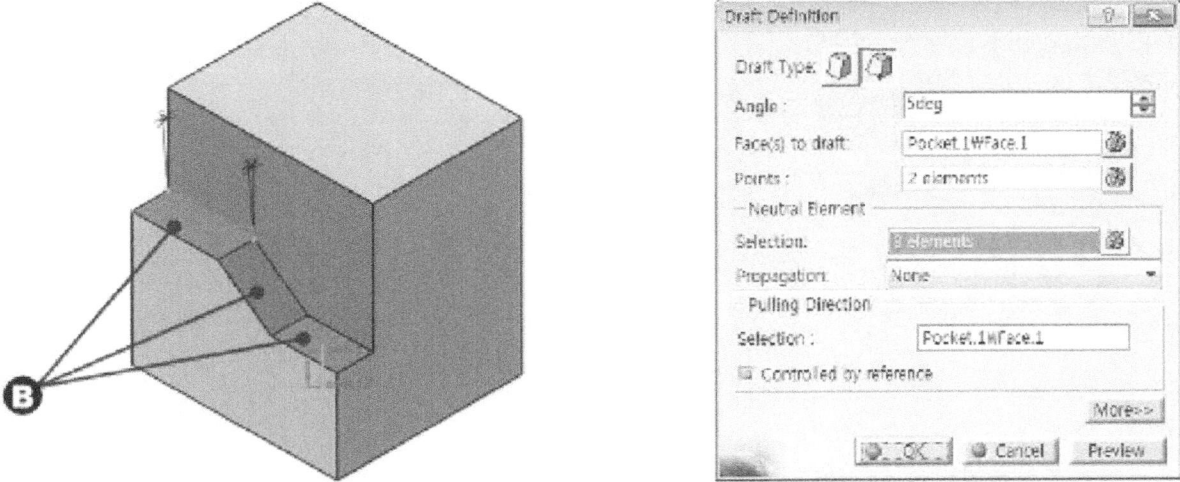

Fig 8-72 Neutral Element

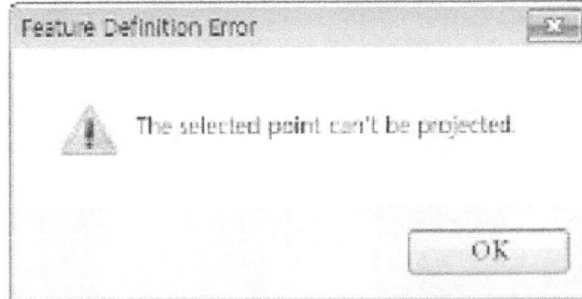

Fig 8-73 Error Message

Note that the pulling direction is specified automatically normal to the first neutral face. We have to modify the pulling direction.

5. Right click on the Pulling Direction selection field in the Draft Definition dialog box.
6. Choose Z Axis in the pop-up menu.
7. Click the Points selection field again and select the vertices other than the points selected automatically. Fig 8-75 shows the preview and dialog box after electing two more variable draft angle points.

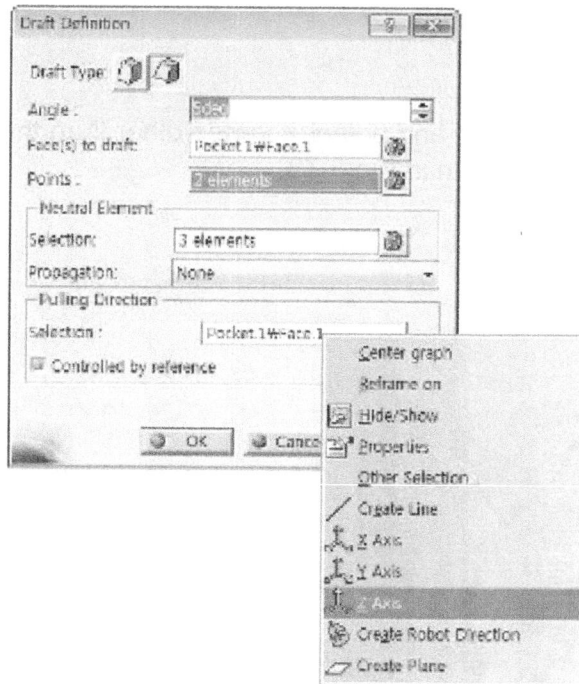

Fig 8-74 Pulling Direction

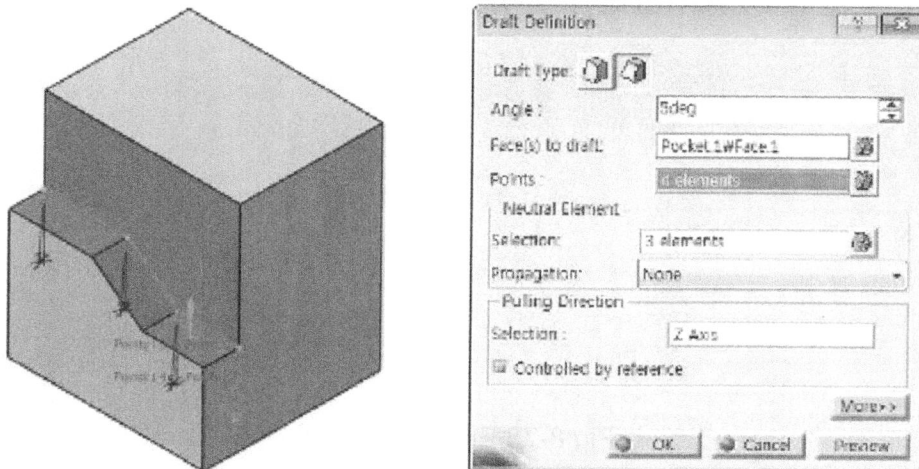

Fig 8-75 Variable Draft Angle Points

Applying Variable Angle

1. Double click the angular dimension in the model, enter 3 deg in the input box and press the Tab key.
2. Press OK in the Parameter Definition dialog box.
3. Double click another angle, modify the value to 3 deg as shown in Fig 8-77 and click OK.
4. Click OK m the Draft Definition dialog box. Fig 8-77 shows the result of draft with variable angle at the specified points.

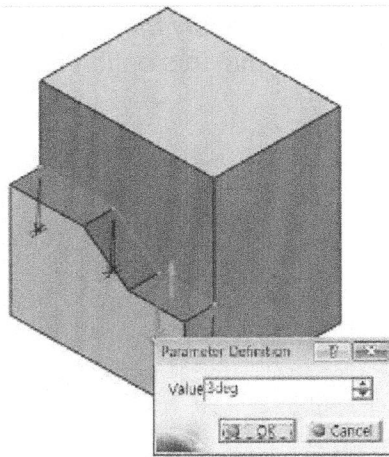

Fig 8-76 Modifying Angle

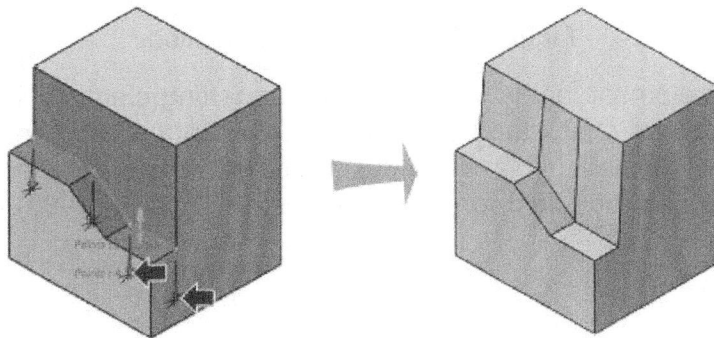

Fig 8-77 Completed model

8.4.5 Other Options in Draft

If you use a reference plane in the middle of the model as the parting element and neutral clement, the faces to draft are divided with respect to the parting clement Note that you have to expand the Draft Definition dialog box and check the Parting = Neutral option.

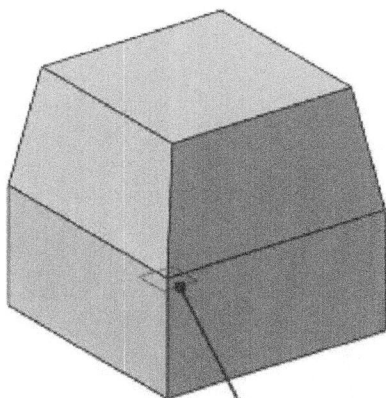

Neutral Element

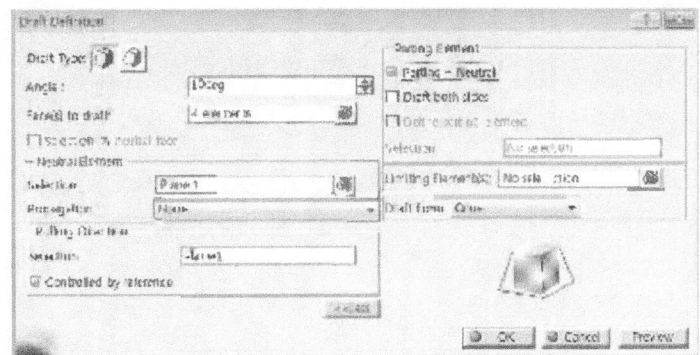

Fig 8-78 Parting = Neutral Option

If you use the Draft both sides option, you can apply the same draft angle for both sides of the faces to draft with respect to parting clement. Note that this option is available only when you have chosen the Parting = Neutral option.

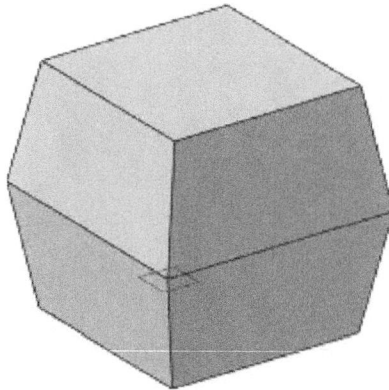

Fig 8-79 Draft Both Sides Option

You may use a neutral element that is different from the parting element. To do this, uncheck the Parting = Neutral option and check the Define parting element option in the dialog box. Click the selection field for parting element ((A) in Fig 8-80) and select the parting element in the model, e.g. Plane.1. Then click the selection field for neutral element ((B) in Fig 8-80) and select the neutral element, e.g. Face.5.

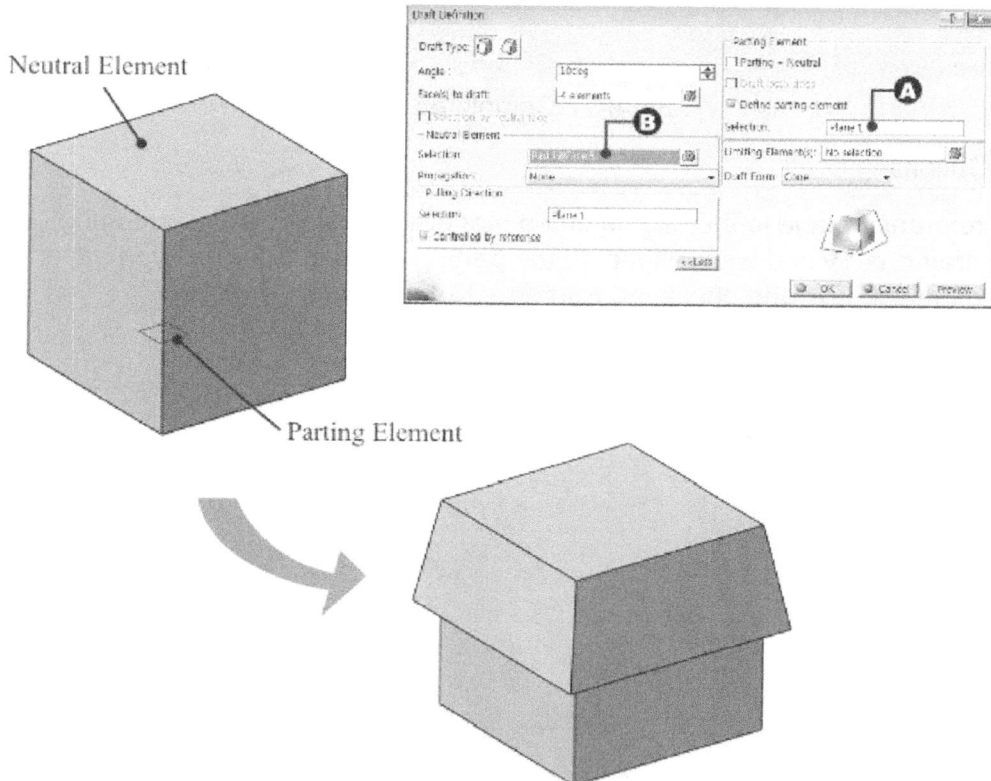

Fig 8-80 Neutral Element # Parting Element

8.5 SHELL

This command hollows out a solid body to create a thin wall.

Procedure

1. Click the Shell icon in the Dress-Up Features toolbar.
2. Enter default inside thickness and press the Tab key. Note that you are prompted to select. a face to remove.
3. Select the face to be removed. You can remove several faces.
4. Press the OK button.

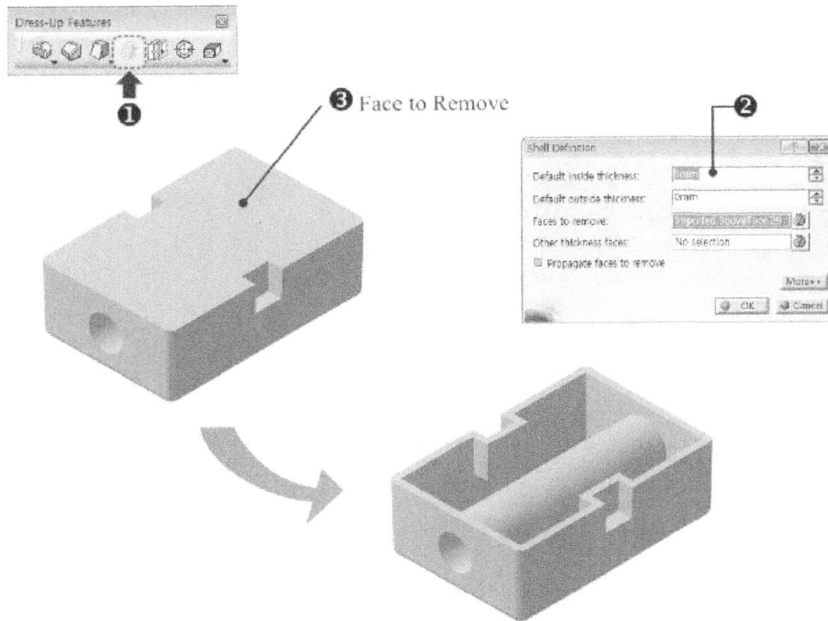

Fig 8-81 Procedure of Shell

You can select as many faces to remove as required. Fig 8-82 shows an example of specifying several faces to be removed.

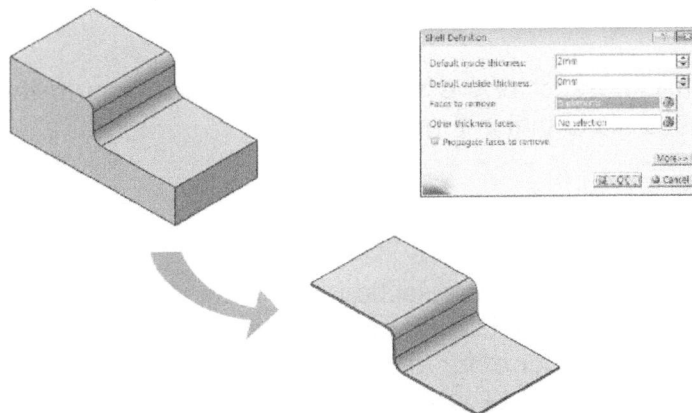

Fig 8-82 Specifying Several Faces to Remove

8.5.1 Outside Thickness

Thickness of shell command can be applied inside, outside or both sides. Fig 8-83 shows the volume of liquid that will be filled in the bottle. If you want to create a bottle that has the inner volume maintained, you have to apply the Shell command by ap plying the outside thickness.

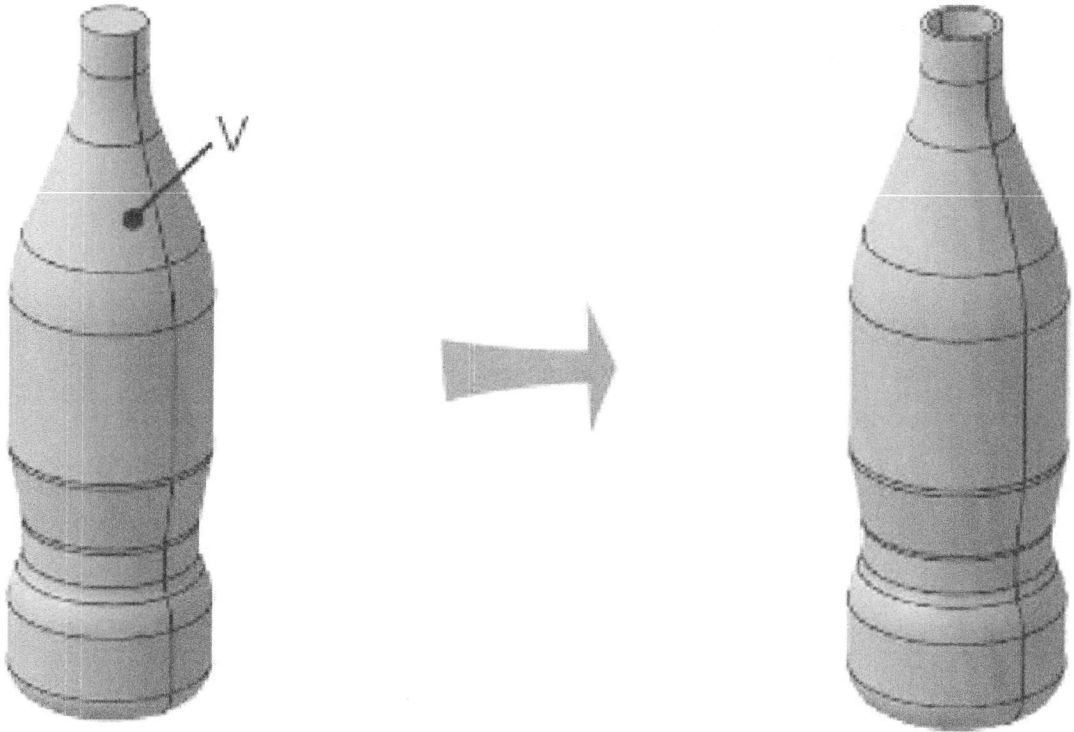

Fig 8-83 Applying Outside Thickness

8.5.2 Other Thickness Faces

You can apply various thicknesses for the specified faces according to the following procedure. Each step number corresponds to that in Fig 8-84.

1. Click the Shell icon.
2. Enter default thickness and press the Tab key.
3. Select faces to remove.
4. Click the Other thickness surfaces selection field.
5. Select surface to apply other thickness than the default thickness.
6. Double click the dimension for other thickness in the model.
7. Enter the thickness value in the Parameter Definition dialog box and click OK.
8. Click OK in the Shell Definition dialog box.

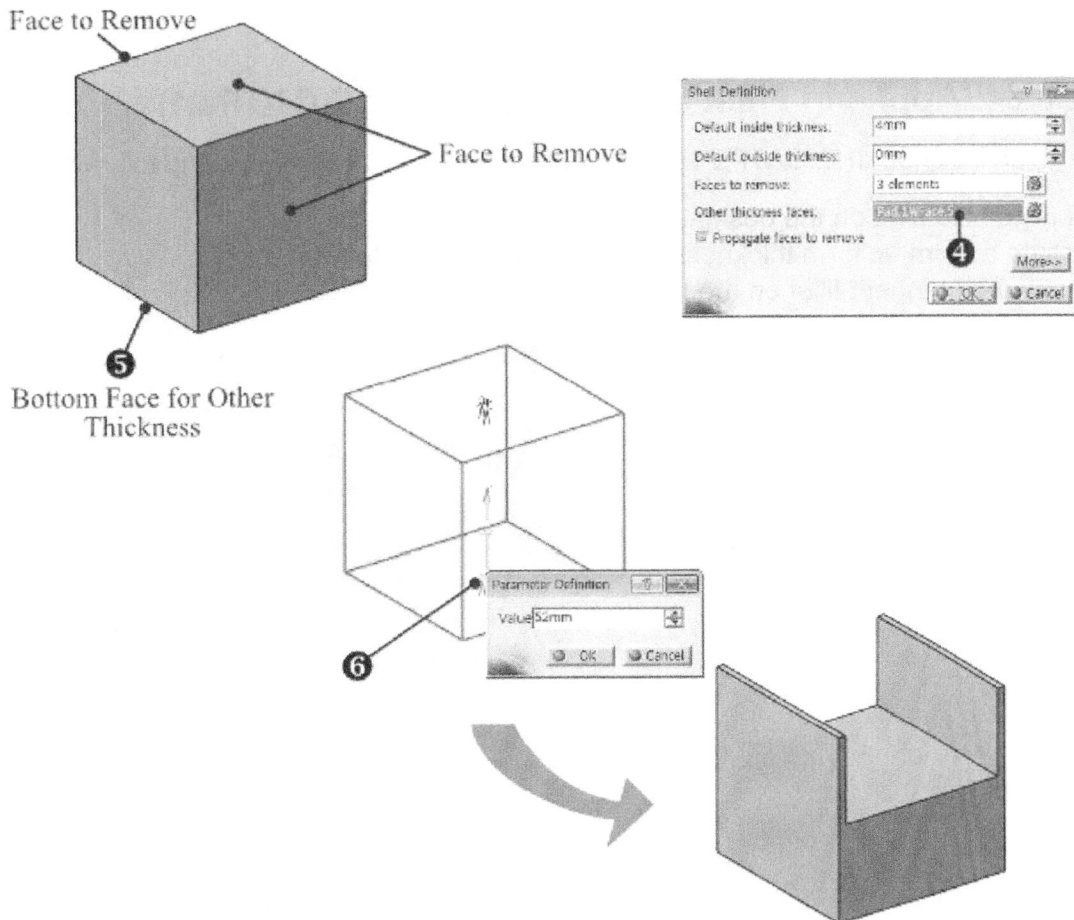

Fig 8-84 Procedure of Applying Other Thickness

Note that you can apply the Shell command for the solid body even though it has already been applied by the Shell command. You can create the model shown in Fig 8-85 by ap- plying additional Shell command to the resultant solid body shown in Fig 8-84.

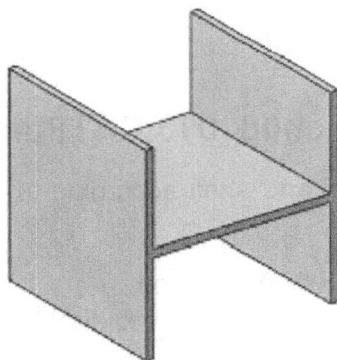

Fig 8-85 Applying Shell Twice

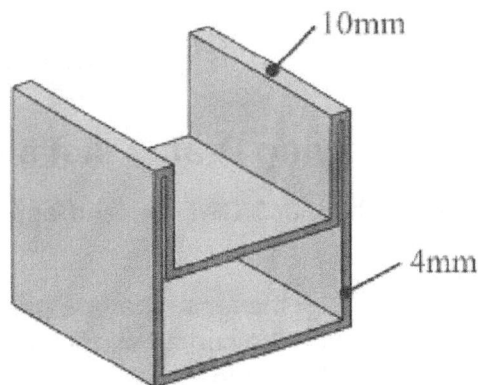

Fig 8-86 Applying Thickness

If the shell thickness is small enough with regard to the existing body, you can apply the Shell command to create the model as shown in Fig 8-86.

Exercise 64: Applying Fillet and Shell (ch08_012.CATPart)

Open the given file ch08_012.CATPart and apply fillet and shell according to the following directions.

1. Apply an R5 fillet on the designated edges.
2. Create a 3mm uniform thickness wall removing the bottom face.
3. Apply a Tri tangent fillet on the bottom edges.

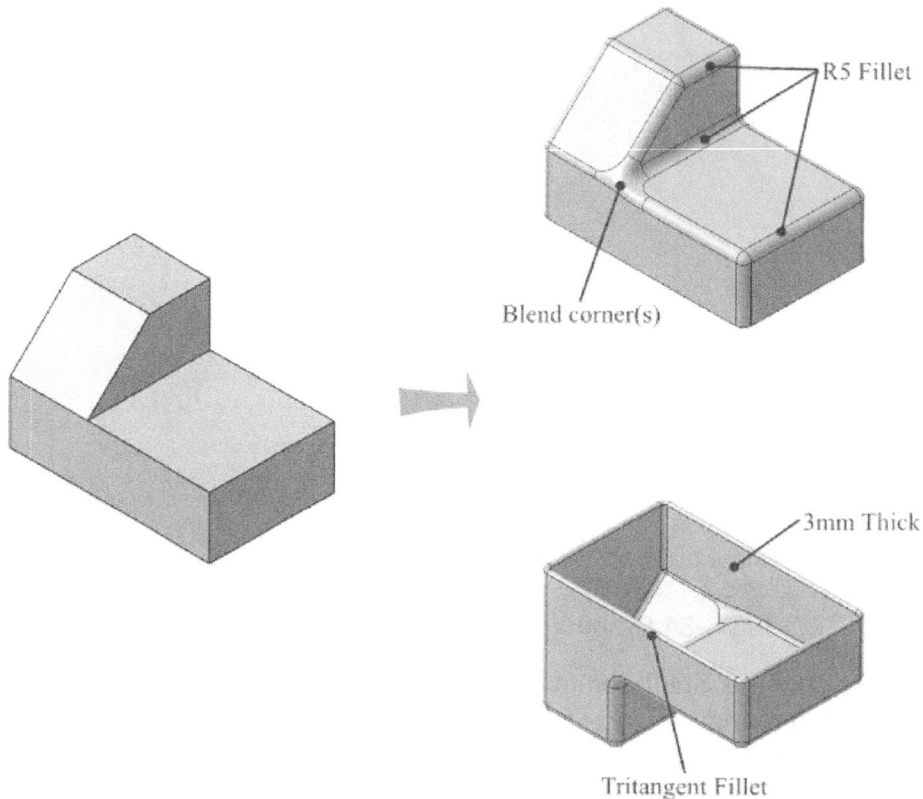

Fig 8-87 Applying Shell and Fillet

Exercise 65: Applying Draft, Fillet and Shell (ch08_013.CATPart)

Open the given file ch08_013.CATPart and apply draft, fillet and shell according to the following directions.

1. Apply 3dcg draft on the faces that are parallel to the pulling direction.
2. Apply 3deg draft on the curved surfaces that are tangent to the pulling direction. (se
3. the Draft Reflect Line icon.)
4. Apply an R3 fillet on all edges except for the bottom edges.
5. Create a 2mm thick uniform wall removing the bottom face.

The cut model on the right of Fig 8-88 is to show you the status of the cut section. You do not need to cut the model as illustrated.

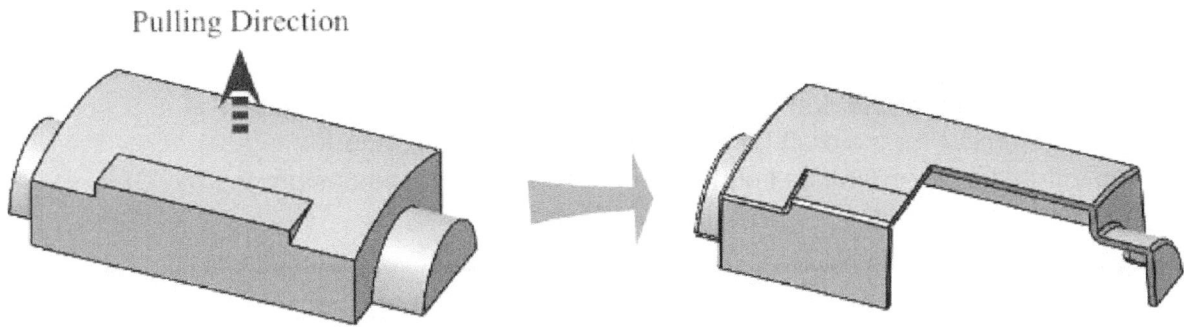

Fig 8-88 Applying Draft, Fillet and Shell

Exercise 66: Mounting Bracket (ch08_014.CATPart)

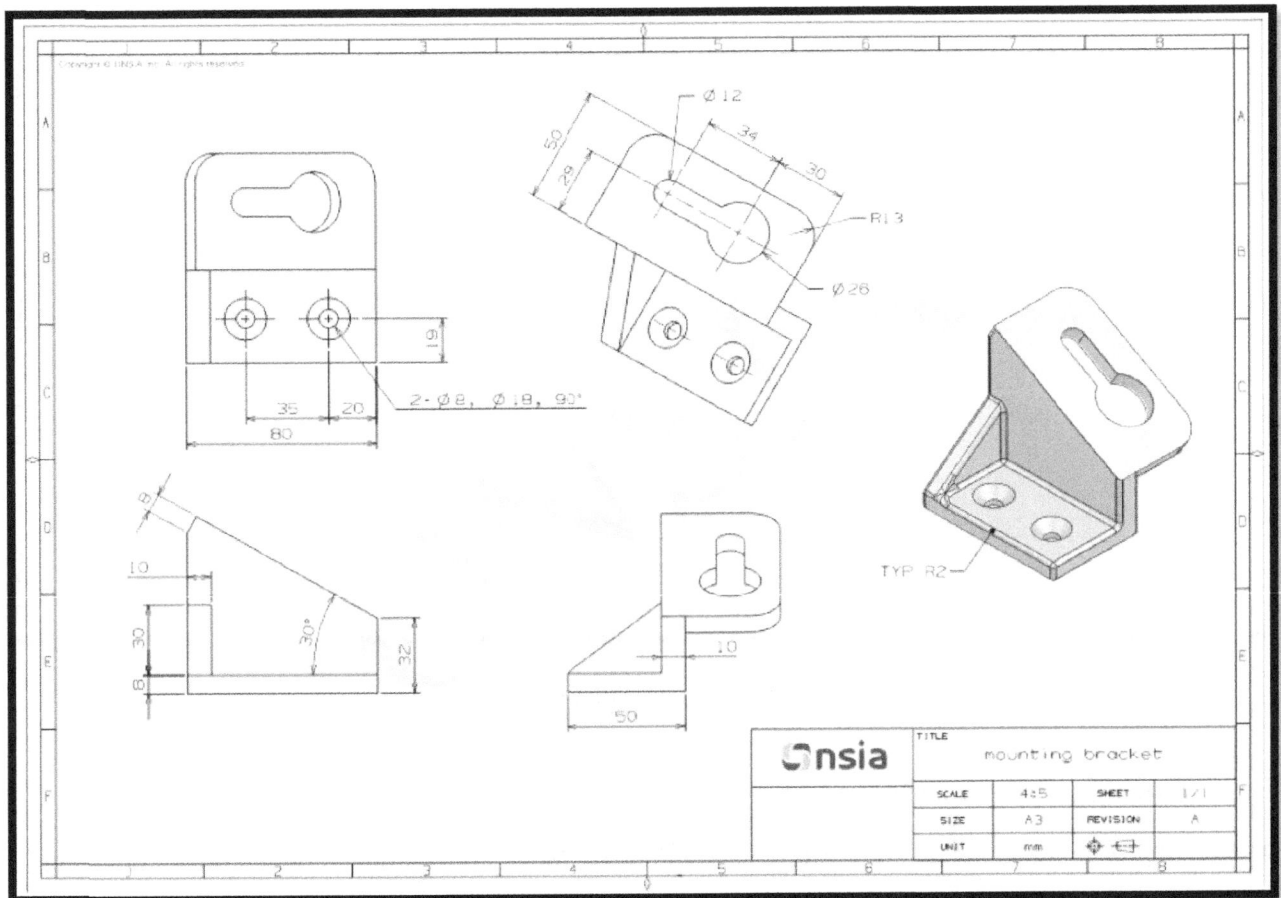

Fig 8-89 Mounting Bracket

Exercise 67: Plastic Cover (ch08_O1 5.CAT Part)

Create a plastic cover model as shown in Fig 8-90 according to the following directions.

1. Apply R3 fillet on all edges except for the bottom edges.

2. Neutral element for the draft faces specified by (A) is the bottom face (F).
3. Neutral element for the draft faces specified by (B) is the face (G).
4. Apply draft for the cylindrica l surfaces near the parting face designated by (C).
5. Wall thickness is 2mm.

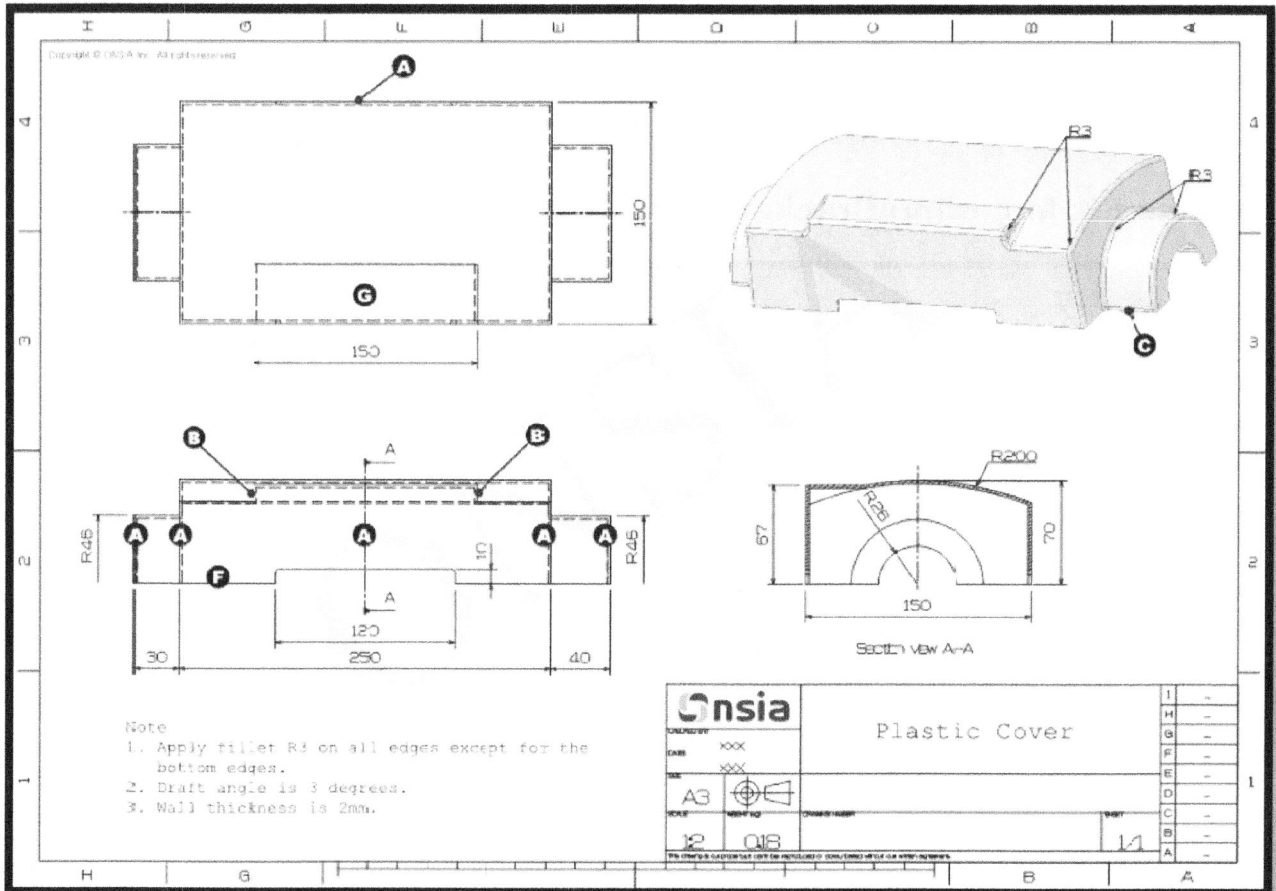

Fig 8-90 Plastic Cover

Exercise 68: Plastic Cover (ch08_O1 5.CAT Part)

Create the solid model referring to the drawing in Fig 8-91.

Refer to the following guides for the general modeling procedure.

1. Create all features that add material.
2. Create features that remove material.
3. Apply fillet last.

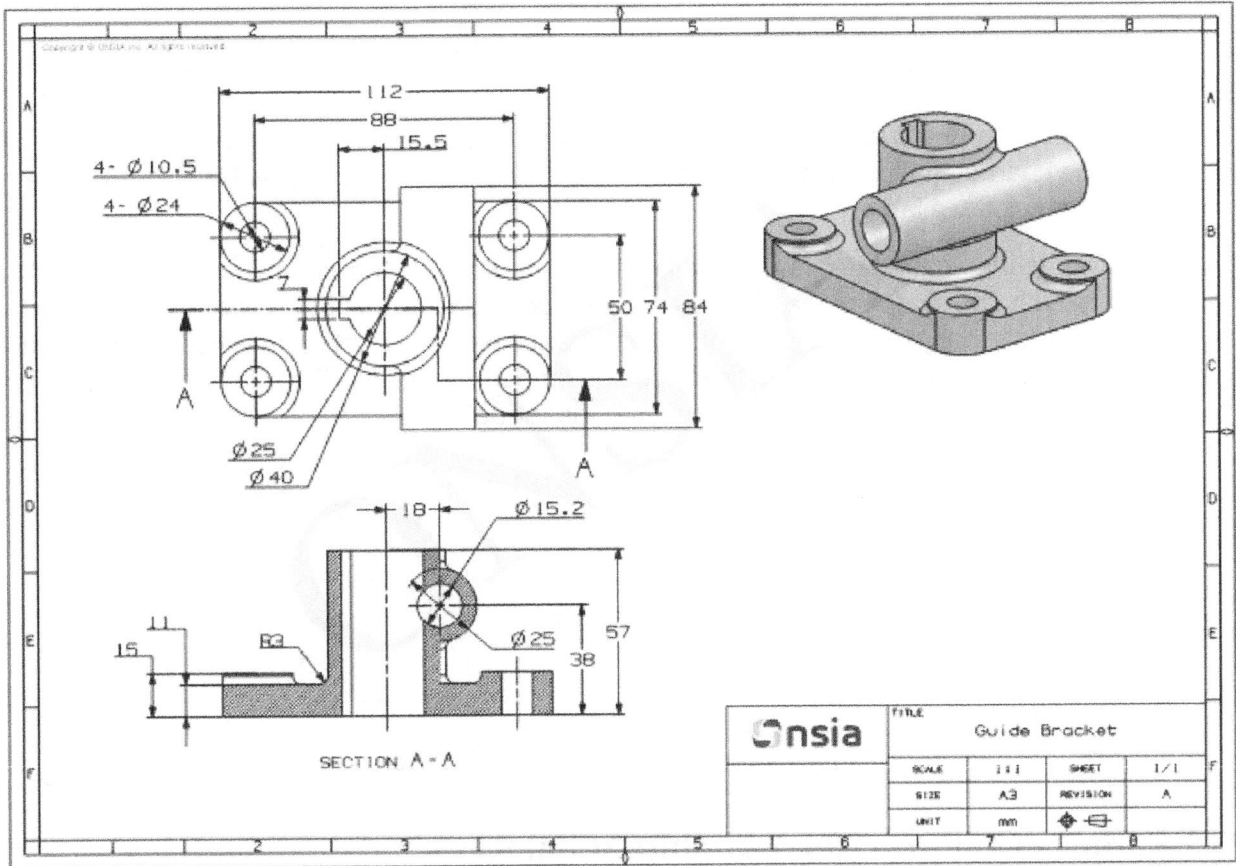

Fig 8-91 Guide Bracket

CHAPTER 9: THE DYNAMICS OF PARAMETRIC MODIFICATIONS

9.1 UNDERSTANDING PARAMETRIC MODIFICATION

If you discover that a feature of a part has been created incorrectly during or after the modeling process, you can take one of the following two approaches to correct this.

1. Delete the feature m1d create it correctly.
2. Modify the feature definition or profile.

In parametric modeling software such as CATIA V5, the second app roach is recommended as it best utilizes the characteristics of the software. The first approach should only be chosen when the second method is not available.

Fig 9- 1 shows the impact of parametric modification. If you modify the slant angle of feature (A) by modifying its sketch, the sketch plane of feature (B) will be updated due to the linkage. In this chapter we will learn how to modify features and consider the anticipated impact on the model. Note that we will encounter update errors because of linkages between the features. Therefore, we have to learn how to cope with errors generated when modifying the model.

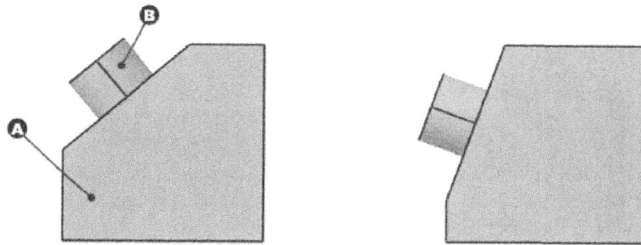

Fig 9-1 Impact of Feature Modification

9.1.1 Parent - Children Relationship of Features

If you have used an existing geometry to define a feature a link age is established between the features by default. Therefore, if you modify the existing geometry before defining a certain feature, the latter frame will be affected. The fom1er feature is called a parent feature and the latter feature is called a children feature.

The linkage between features must be considered when you are modifying a feature be- cause errors can be encountered on account of the loss of link information. You can break the Linkage, if required, to remove the errors.

In CATIA V5, you can examine the linkage between features using the Parents/Children pop-up me nu of the Spec Tree as shown in Fig 9-2. Parent features of Pad.2 in Fig 9-3 (a) are Sketch.1 and Pad,1. If you double click on Pad.1, the Parents and Children window will change as shown in fig 9-3 (b) to show the link information of the Pad.1 feature.

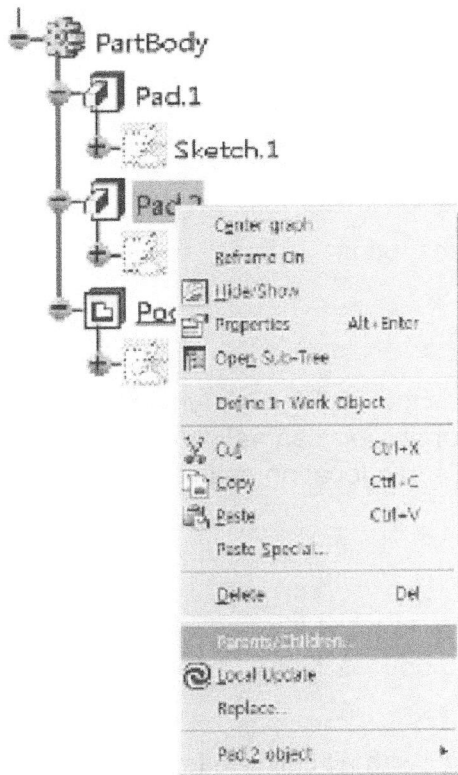

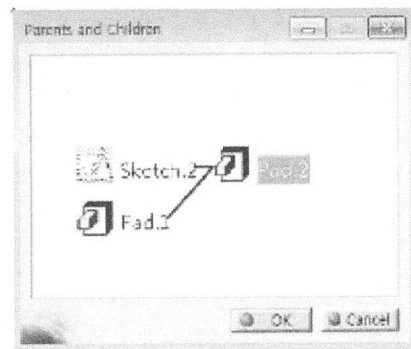

(a)

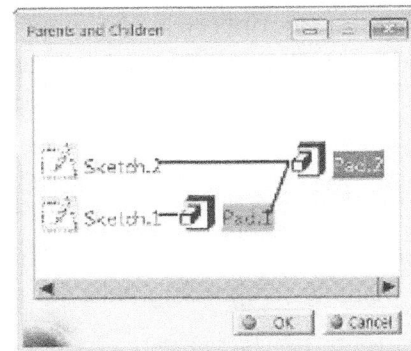

(b)

Fig 9-2 Pop-up Menu of Spec Tree   Fig 9-3 Parents and Children Window

9.1.2 Breaking Links (Isolate)

You can break links between features if required. If you break a link between certain features, the child feature is not affected by the modification of the parent feature.

If you want to break a link between features, select Isolate from the pop-up menu of the object of which to break a l ink as shown in Fig 9-4. Examples of breaking links are as below.

- Breaking a link of a sketch plane.
- Breaking a link of a reference element with 3D geometry or another reference element.
- Breaking a link of a sketch curve generated by the Project or Intersect Curve command.

251

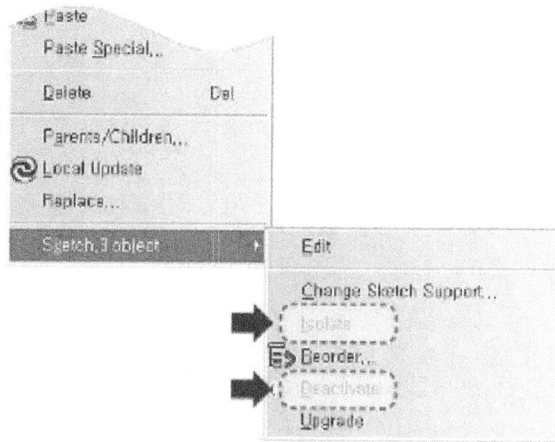

Fig 9-4 Isolate Option

9.1.3 Deactivate

Using the Deactivate option in the pop-up menu show in Fig 9-4, you can invalidate features temporarily. Because this does not delete the features, you can validate the features at any time using the Activate option which can be found at the same location as the Deactivate option.

9.2 DELETING A FEATURE

When you delete a certain feature, you have to bear in mind that the children features may have problems in building. Regarding links, there are two options that you can choose when deleting a feature.

- Delete all children: Delete the feature together with all children features.
- Delete aggregated element: Delete only the selected feature leaving the children features intact.

Fig 9- 5 Delete Dialog Box

If you delete only the parent features when there arc also children features, an update error as shown in Fig 9-6 appears and you have to resolve the problem.

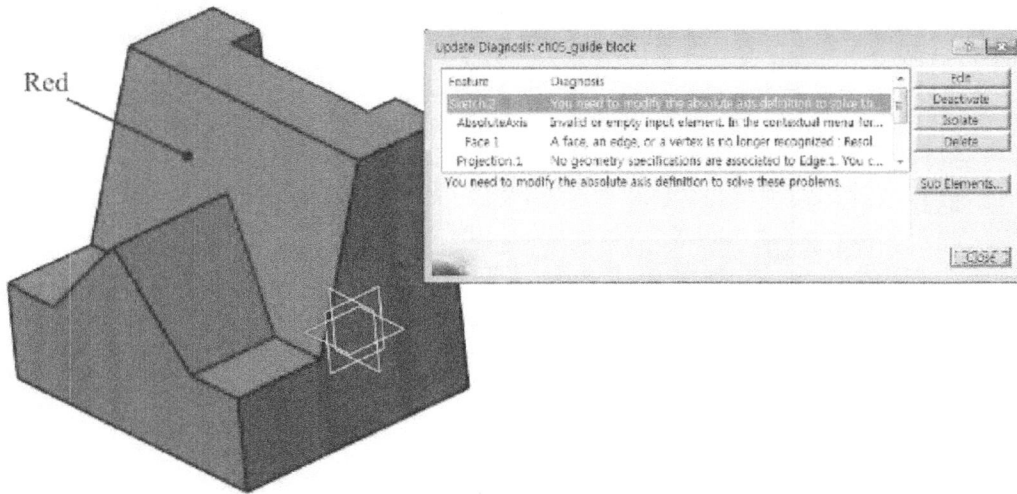

Fig 9-6 Update Error

9.3 MODIFYING A SKETCH

If you double click a sketch feature in the Spec Tree or double click on the sketch in the graphic window, the Sketch workbench is invoked. You can also press the Sketch button and select the sketch to modify to enter sketch modification mode.

Approaches to Modify a Sketch

1. Leave the sketch curves intact and modify the sketch dimensions or constraints. You can delete the constraints and re-define new ones.
2. Delete ketch curves or create new curves and iso-constraint the curves.
3. Change the sketch support and/or sketch axis.

You will take the first approach in most cases. The second approach may be taken when the first approach is not sufficient to obtain the desired sketch. The third approach is taken when you have to move the sketch plane to another plane or when you have to change the orientation and/or origin of the sketch plane.

9.3.1 Elements Constituting Sketches

Sketches have three types of elements as shown in Fig 9-7. The sketch axis is the reference of the sketch constraint and you cannot delete it. Sketch elements, which consist of points and curves, can be deleted, isolated or deactivated individually. Constraints can also be deleted and deactivated.

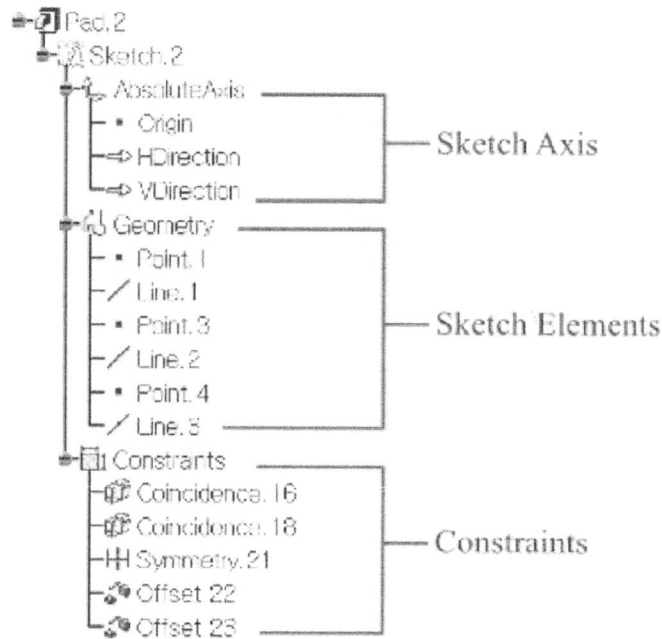

Fig 9-7 Elements Constituting a Sketch

Open the given file and modify the sketch dimensions to check that the children feature is updated.

1. Open the given file ch09_001.CATPart.
2. Place the mouse pointer on Sketch.1 under the Pad.1 feature in the Spec Tree right click and choose Hide/Show in the pop-up menu. The sketch will be shown.

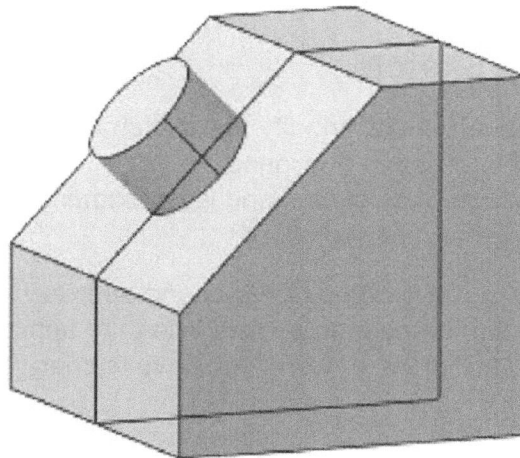

Fig 9- 8 Showing the Sketch

3. Double click Sketch.1 to enter the Sketcher workbench.
4. Delete the dimension (A) shown in Fig 9-9 and create the dimension (D) shown in Fig 9-10.
5. Double click the dimension (B) which is shown in Fig 9-9 and modify it to 60. Link the dimension (C) to the dimension 85 with a formula. The modified sketch is as shown in Fig 9-10.

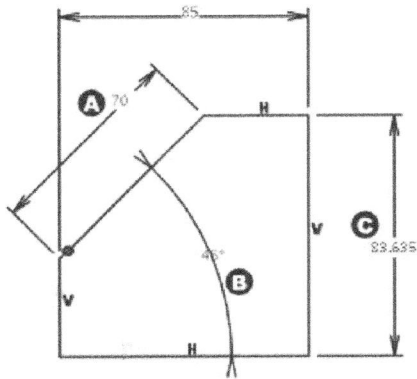

Fig 9-9 Given Sketch

(Note) Hide/Show

1. Hide features or show the hidden features.
2. You can hide or show the same types of features by choo sing Tools > Show or Tools > Hide in the menu bar.
3. You can hide or show a feature by right clicking and pressing the H key on the desired feature.

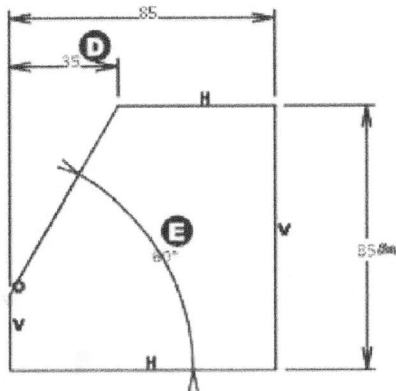

Fig 9-10 Modified Sketch

Press the Exit workbench butt on in the sketch. Fig 9-11 shows the modified model. Note that the sketch support of the cylindrical feature is 11pdated. It is recommended to continue with the next exercise.

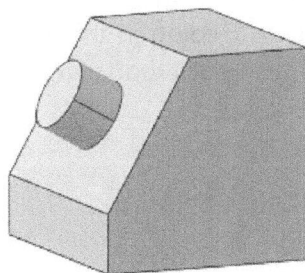

Fig 9-11 updated Model

255

(Note) Update Option

- If the Manual Update mode button in the Tools toolbar i s turned on, the co lor of the model turns red after modification. In this case, you have to update the model manually by pressing the Update button.
- You can choose Edit > Update in the menu bar. The shortcut key is Ctr! + U.
- For the remainder of this textbook, it is assumed that the Manual Update mode is turned off, which means that the model will be updated automatically after modification.

9.3.2 Changing Sketch Support

You can change the sketch plane by right clicking on the sketch feature and choosing Change Sketch Support in the pop-up menu. The warning message is displayed as shown in Fig 9-13. When you are changing the sketch plane, bear in mind that the objects selected to constrain the sketch curves are held. That is to say, if you have applied a dimensional or geometrical constraint with regard to an edge or vertex, you have to redefine the constraint if an incorrect result is generated. You may need to modify the horizontal or vertical reference.

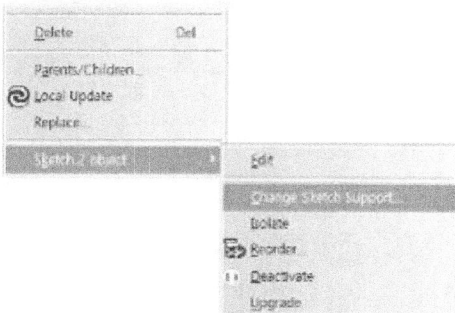

Fig 9-12 Change Sketch Support Menu

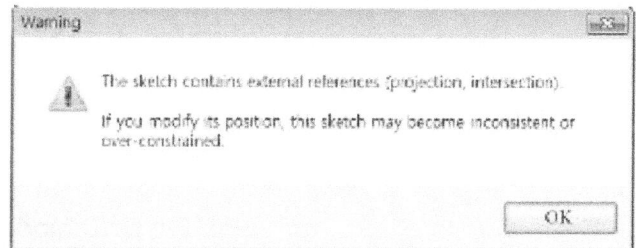

Fig 9-13 Warning Message

If you click OK in the warning message box, the Sketch Positioning dialog box, which is the same as what you have seen when you define a positioned sketch, is invoked as shown in Fig 9-14. You can reselect the sketch plane by choosing Sliding in the Type dropdown list in the Planar support option area, redefine the sketch origin and orientation.

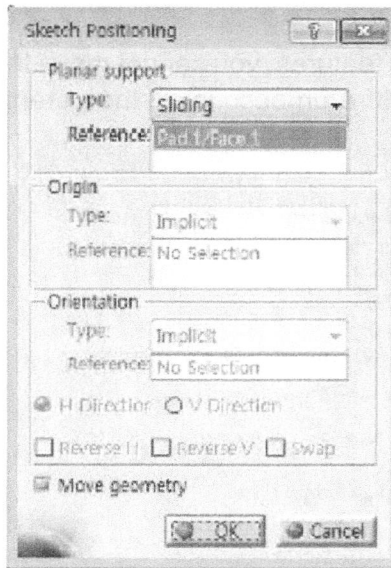

Fig 9-14 Sketch Positioning Dialog Box

9.4 REORDERING FEATURES

The modeling order has great effect in constructing a model. When the modeling order is not taken properly, you may have to repeat unnecessary modeling processes or you may not even be able to create the desired model.

When the modeling order is not correct, you can reorder the feature in the Spec Tree. If you right click on a feature, the Reorder option becomes available as shown in fig 9-15. This option allows moving the location of the feature before. or after the target feature.

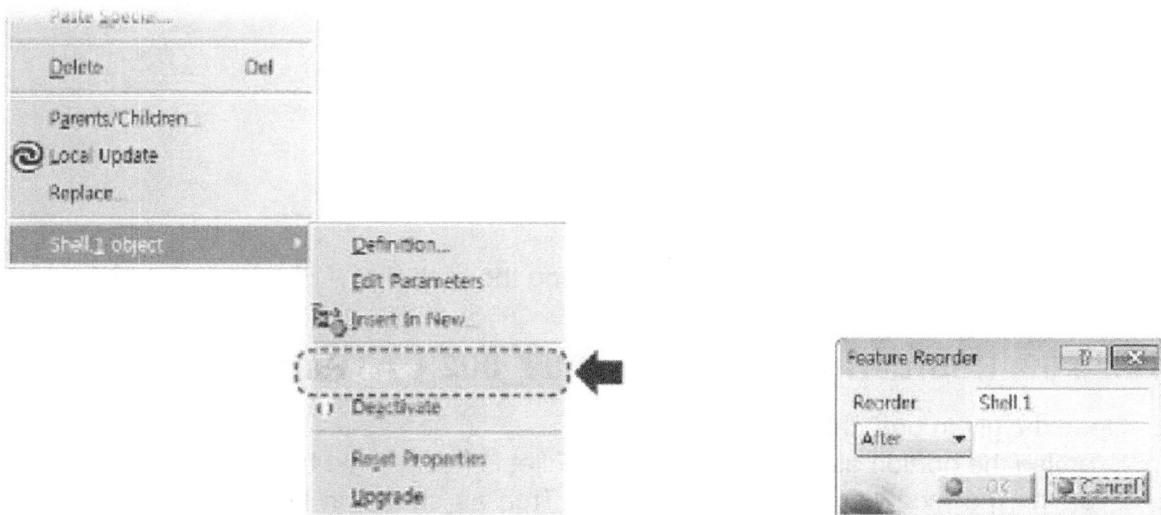

Fig 9-15 Reorder Option

You can reorder features using the drag and drop function. Fig 9-16 shows dragging the Shell feature and dropping after EdgeFillet.2.

Bear in mind that, when you reorder features, you cannot move the features earlier before the parent feature and later after the child feature on account of the parent/children relationship between the features.

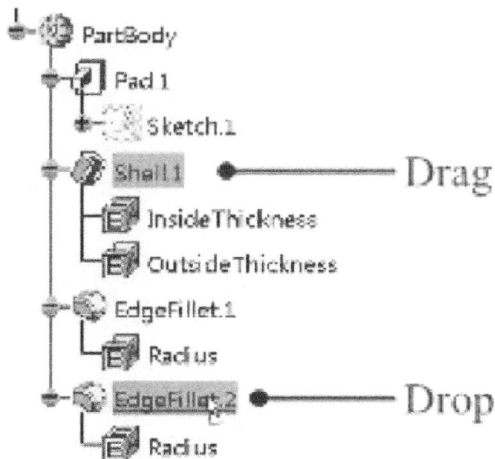

Fig 9-16 Drag and Drop of a Feature

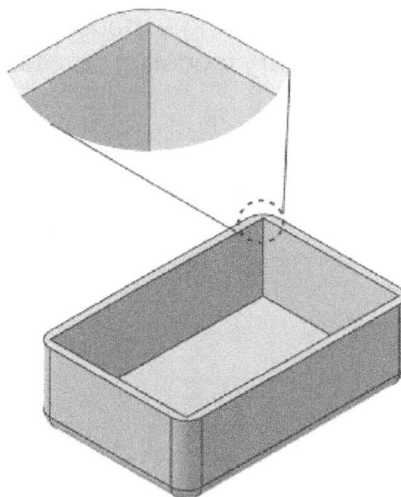

Fig 9-17 Examining the Model

Exercise 69: Reordering Features (ch09_002.CATPart)

1. Open the given part ch09_002.CATPart.
2. Examine the portion as shown in Fig 9-17. Fillet is not applied by the Shell feature.
3. Examine the modeling history in the Spec Tree as shown in Fig 9-18. Note that the fillet features are created after the shell feature.
4. Right click on the Shell. 1 feature and choose Shell.1 object > Reorder. You are promoted to specify a new location in the specification tree.

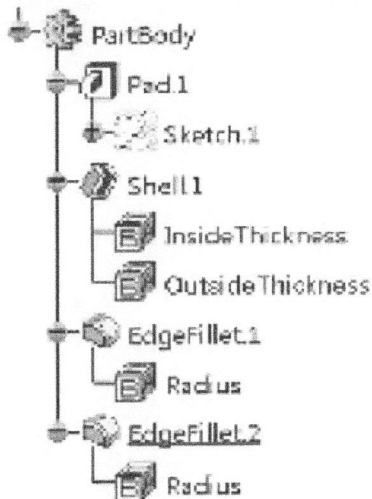

Fig 9-18 Modeling History

Make sure that After is selected in the reorder dropdown list and select the Edge- Fillet.2 feature in the Spec Tree. The model is shown like in Fig 9-20. You can see that the Pad. 1 feature is underlined in the Spec Tree as shown in Fig 9-21. This means that the feature is in work object.

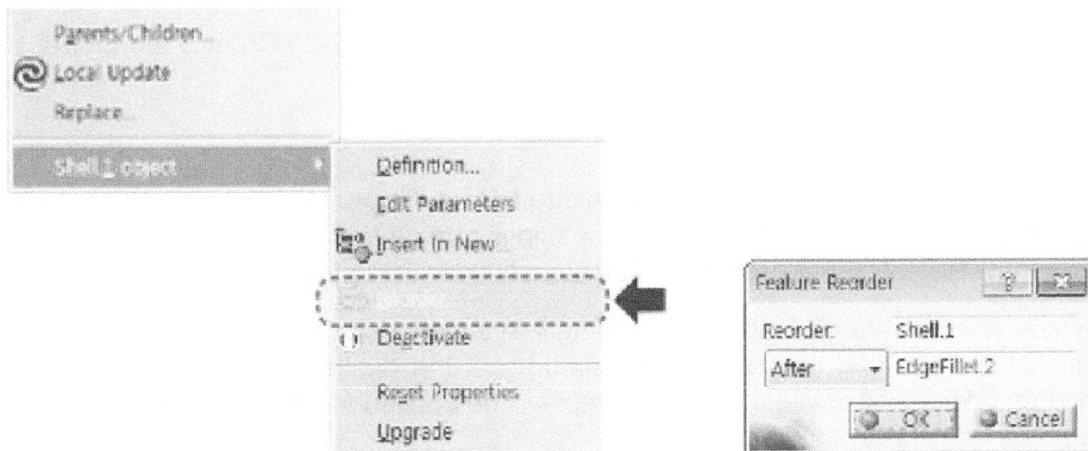

Fig 9-19 Reordering

Fig 9-20 Model after Reordering

5. Right click on the Shell.1 feature in the Spec Tree and choose Define in Work Object in the pop-up menu. The part is updated as shown in Fig 9-23.

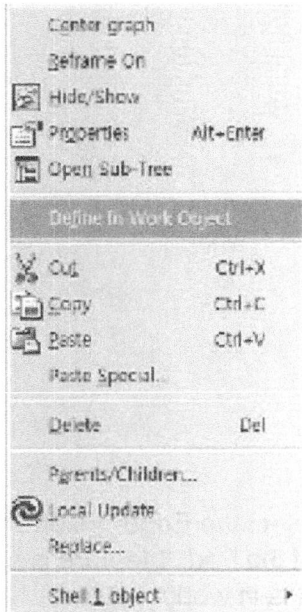

Fig 9-22 Define in Work Object Menu

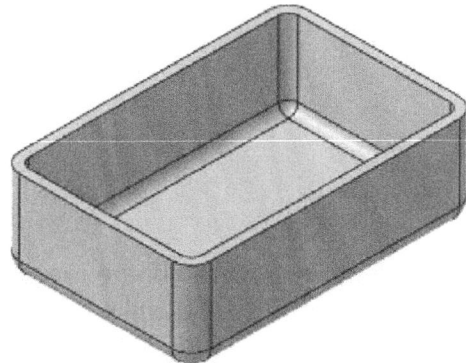

Fig 9-23 Comple ted Model

9.5 INSERTING A FEATURE

If you are changing the timeline location of a feature before the parent feature, you can- not use the reorder option unless the parent/children relationship is removed by using the Isolate option. Or you can create a new feature at the desired timeline location by using the Define in work object option.

You can insert features after a feature by defining it in a work object. The advantage of rolling back the modeling history is that you can create features at the desired location without establishing parent/children relationships with the features that will be applied afterwards. Note that the following features can be affected by inserting features.

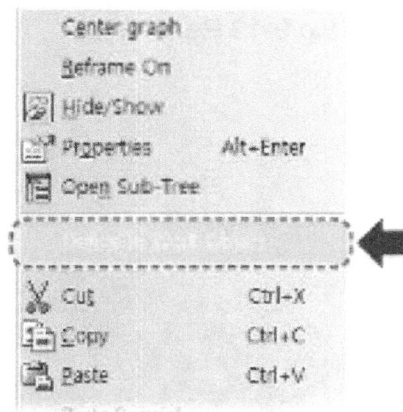

Fig 9-24 Define in Work Object Option

260

Exercise 70: Inserting a Feature (ch09_003.CATPart)

Let's create a hole such that the shell feature is applied to the hole feature as shown in Fig 9-25.

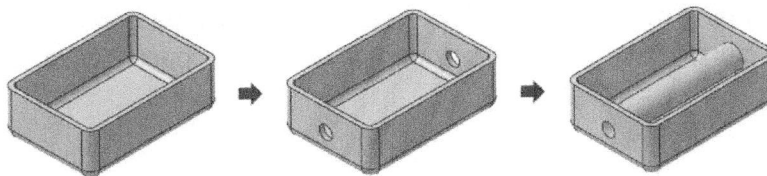

Fig 9-25 Adding a Feature

Creating a Hole

1. Open the given part file ch09_003.CATPart.
2. Click the Hole icon in the Sketch- Based Features tool bar.
3. Select the two edges (A), (B) and plane (C) consecutively as shown in Fig 9-26. Note that the edge (A) is created by the shell feature and the edge (B) is created by the fillet feature.

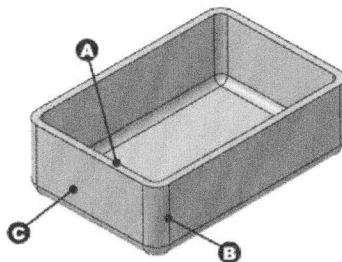

Fig 9-26 Selecting Edges and Plane for Hole

4. Modify the positional dimensions of the ho le feature, set the hole parameters as shown in Fig 9-27 and click OK in the Hole Definition dialog box.

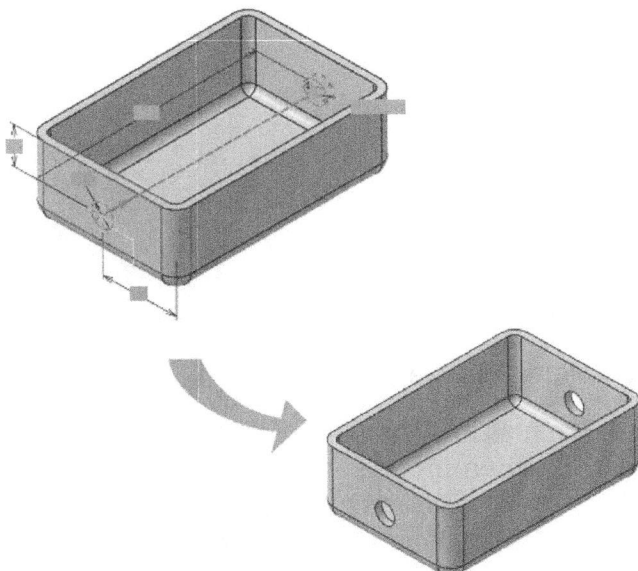

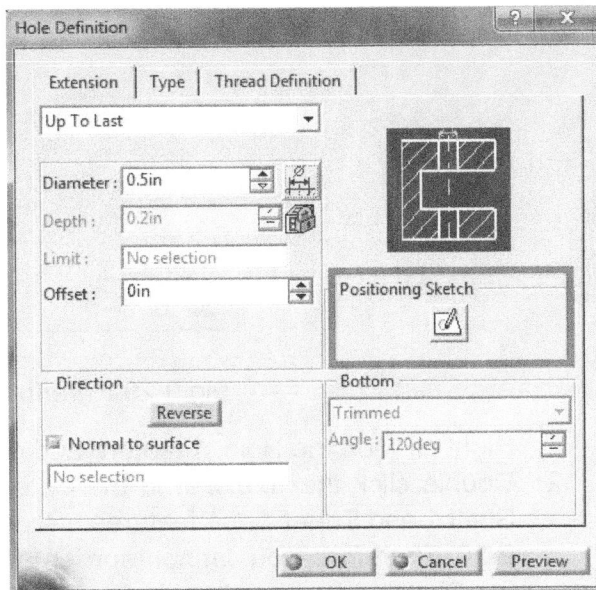

Fig 9-27 Creating a Hole

Reordering the Hole Feature

1. Drag the Hole. I feature in the Spec Tree and drop on the EdgeFillet.2 feature as shown in Fig 9-28. A warning message is displayed on the lower right corner of the graphics window. Note that you cannot reorder a feature earlier before the parent feature.

Fig 9-28 Drag and Drop

Let's identify the parents/children relationship of features.

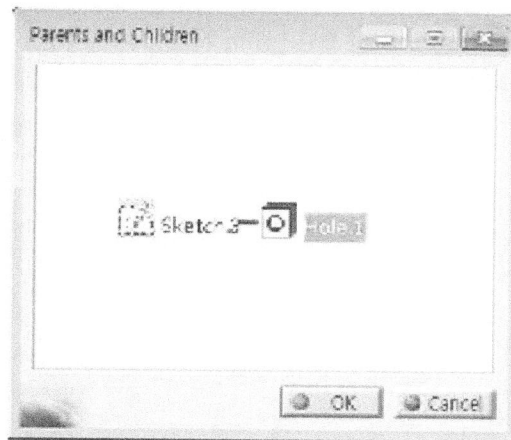

Fig 9-29 Parents and Children of Hole.1

1. Right click on the Hole. 1 feature and choo e Parents/Children in the pop-up menu.
2. Double click the Sketch.3 in the Parents and Children browser. You can see that Pad.1, Shell.1 and EdgeFillet.1 features are parent feature of the Sketch.3 feature as shown in Fig 9-30. Therefore, you cannot reorder the Hole. I feature before the Shell.1 feature. Note that the Sketch.3 feature should be reordered together with the Hole. 1 feature.

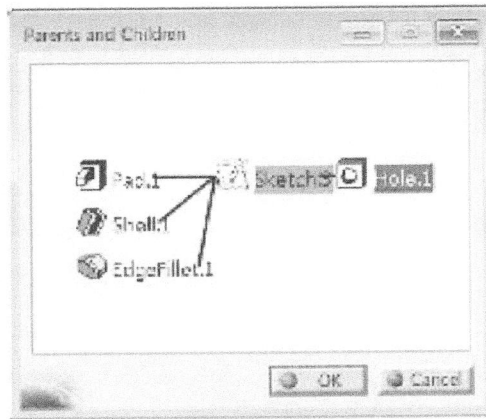

Fig 9-30 Parents and Children of Sketch.3

Creating the Hole Feature before the Shell Feature

1. Delete the Hole.1 and Sketch.3 feature.

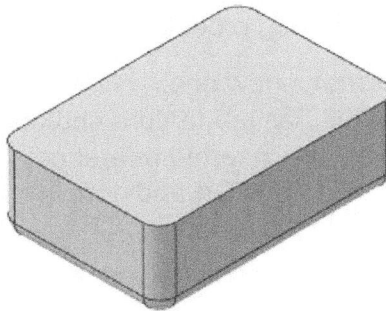

Fig 9-31 Rolled Back History

2. Right click on the EdgeFillet.2 in the Spec Tree and choose Define in Work Object in the pop-up menu. The modeling history is rolled back before the Shell.1 feature as shown ii1 Fig 9-31.
3. Create a hole feature as shown in Fig 9-32. Note that the parents/children relationship between the Hole feature and SheU. I feature is impossible intrinsically.

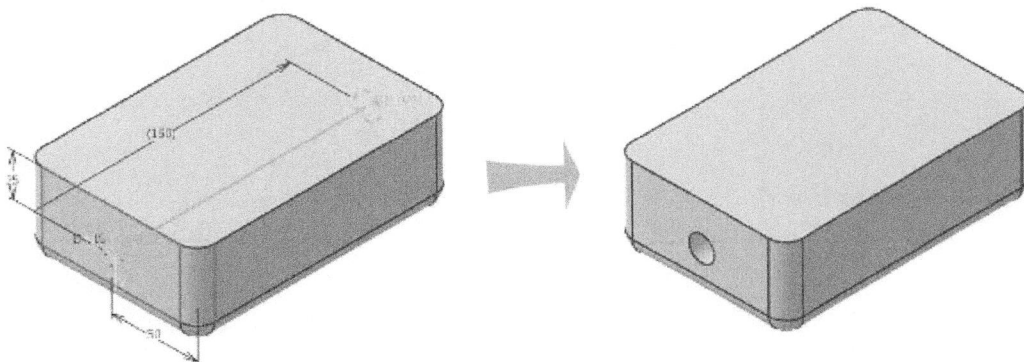

Fig 9-32 Creating a Hole

Right click on the Shell.1 feature in the Spec Tree and choose Define in Work Object in the pop-up menu. The model is updated as shown in Fig 9-33.

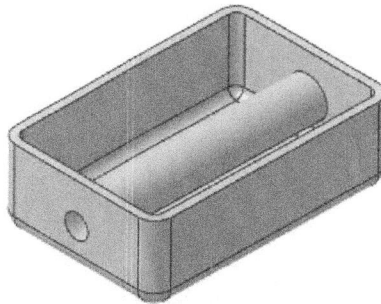

Fig 9-33 Completed Model

Exercise 71: Changing the Sketch Support (ch09_004.CATPart)

In this exercise, we will practice the following modeling techniques.

1. Delete a sketch curve and create a new one.
2. insert a reference plane after the desired feature and before the feature to use it.
3. Change the sketch support with the inserted reference plane.
    1. Open the given file ch09_004.CATPart and double click the Sketch.1 feature.
    2. Delete the curve (A) shown in Fig 9-34.
    3. Create the arc (B) shown in Fig 9-35.
    4. Exit the Sketcher.

The Update Diagnosis dialog box. Note that Sketch.2 is selected in the dialog box.

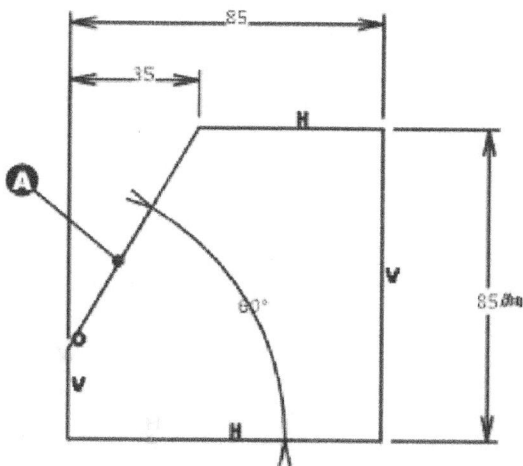

Fig 9-34 Given Sketch

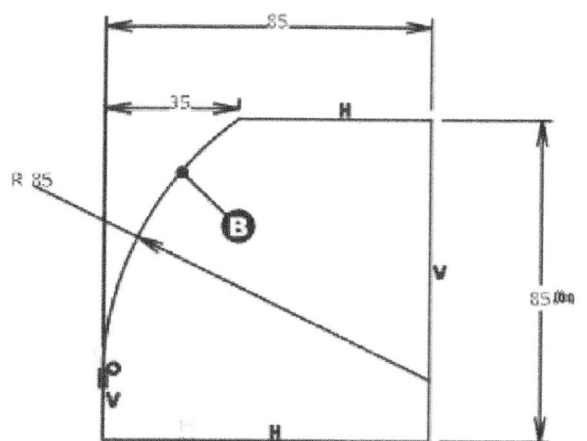

Fig 9-35 Modified Sketch

264

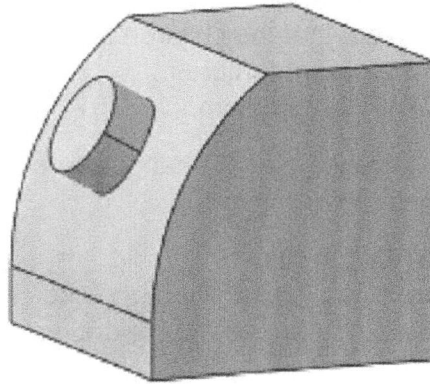

Fig 9-37 Updated Model

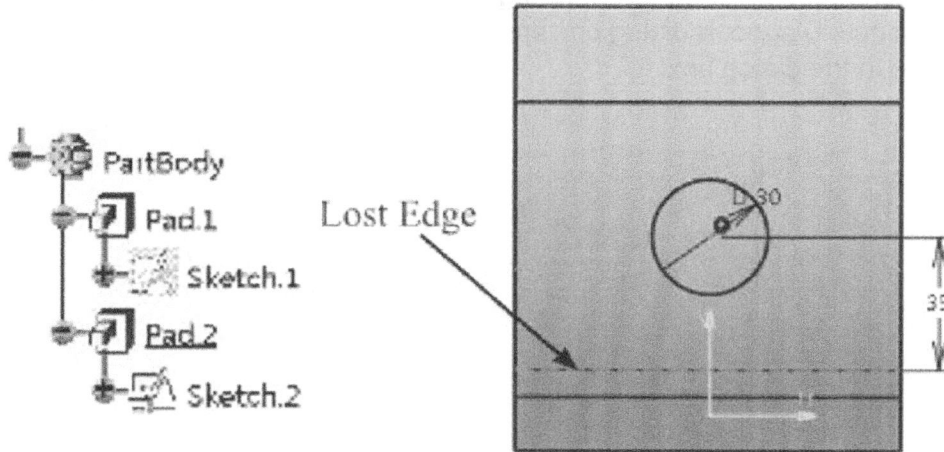

Fig 9-38 Sketch.2 Feature

5. Select Sketch.2 in the dialog box and press the Isolate button to break the link. Break the link of the Absolute Axis in the same way and close the dialog box. The 30 model is updated as shown in Fig 9-37.
6. Double click the Sketch.2 feature in the Spec Tree. Note that, if you isolate a sketch, the sketch feature is converted to a positioned sketch as shown in Fig 9-38. Note also that the dimension edge for the dimension 35 has been lost.
7. Exit the sketcher.
8. Close the file without saving.

(Note) Update Diagnosis

This dialog box appears when update problems occur. Read the Diagnosis column in the dialog box carefully. You can identify the causes of the update problem. The up- date problem in Exercise 04 occurred because the sketch support of the Pad.2 feature has been lost. TI1is kind of problem has to be resolved accurately. You can resolve the problem by using the buttons on the right of the dialog box.

1. Edit: Modification mode is invoked. In the case of Exercise 04, the Sketcher is invoked and you can modify the sketch.

2. Deactivate: Deactivates the feature with the problem. If you deactivate a feature, the feature disappears from the model. Note that the children features can also be affected.
3. Isolate: Break the link with the parent features.
4. Delete: Delete the feature ·with the problem.

Now, let's team how to create a reference plane, change the sketch support on it and modify the dimension 35 to reference the new edge.

1. Open the file ch09_004.CATPart again.
2. Modify the sketch as shown in Fig 9-35 and exit the sketcher.
3. Close the Update Diagnosis dialog box without taking any action.

We have to create a reference plane before the Pad.2 feature.

1. Right click on the Pad.1 feature and choose Define in Work Object in the pop-up menu.
2. Create a reference plane passing through the three vertices designated by arrows in Fig 9-39. The Update Diagnosis dialog box appears again as shown in Fig 9-40. Note that Sketch.2 is selected in the dialog box.

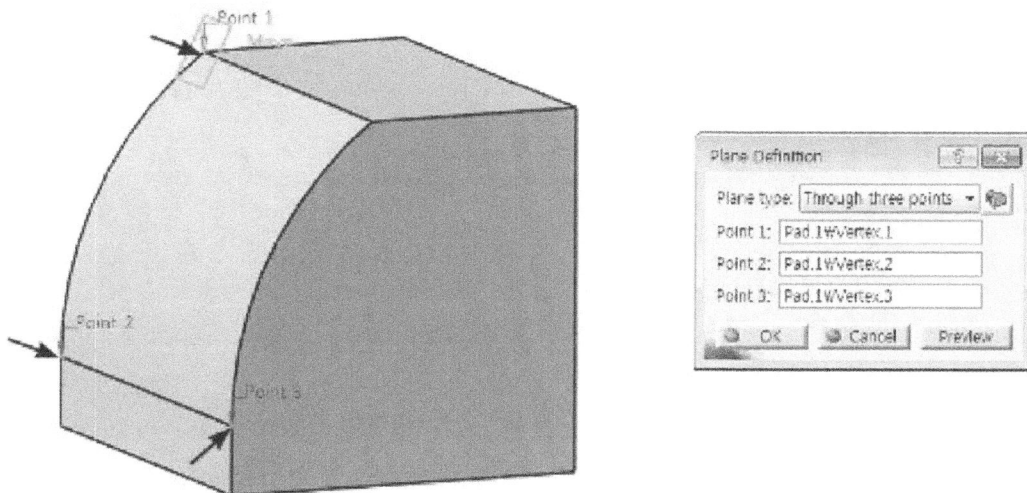

Fig 9-39 Reference Plane

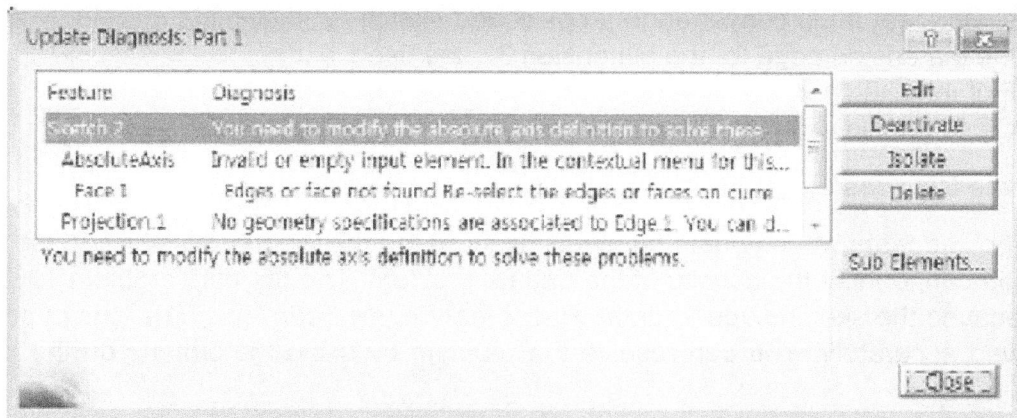

Fig 9-40 Update Diagnosis Dialog Box

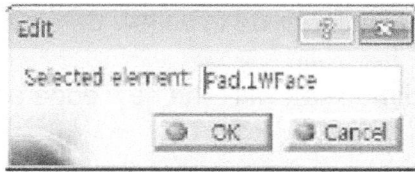

Fig 9-41 Edit Dialog Box

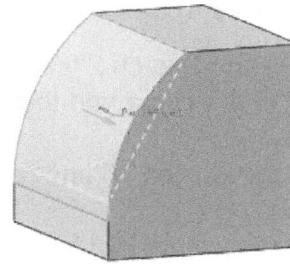

Fig 9-42 Resolving Error

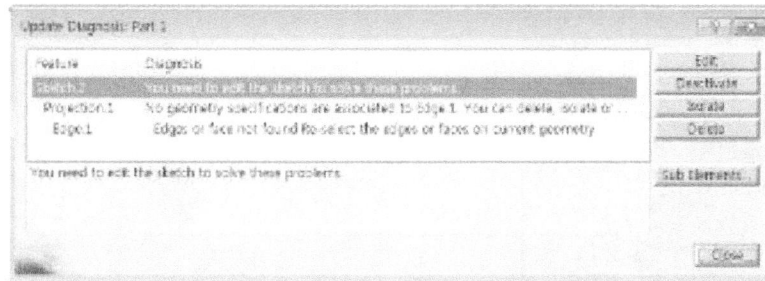

Fig 9-43 Update Diagnosis

3. Select Face.1 in the Update Diagnosis dialog box. Other buttons except for Edit become inactive.
4. Press the Edit button on the right of the Update Diagnosis dialog box. The Edit dialog box appears shown in Fig 9-41 and you are prompted to select an object. Note that the old lost sketch support is displayed by a yellow dotted line.
5. Select the reference plane that has been created in advance in the Spec Tree. The Plane. I feature is defined in work object.
6. Select the reference plane in the model. Make sure that Plane.1/Face is selected in the Edit dialog box.
7. Press the OK button in the Edit dialog box. The Update Diagnosis dialog box is shown like in Fig 9-43 which informs you that you need to edit the sketch to resolve the problem.
8. Close the Update Diagnosis dialog box.

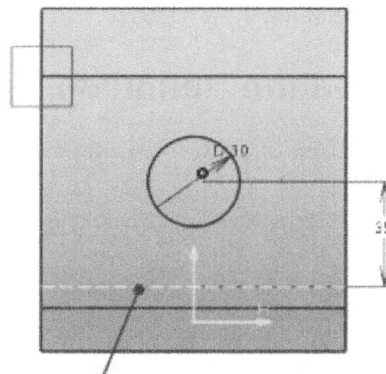

Yellow Dashed Line

Fig 9-44 Old Dimension

267

Now, let's modify the sketch.

1. Double click the Sketch.2 feature.   Note that the dimension 35 has been defined between the center of the circle and the old edge that is displayed in yellow dashed line as shown in Fig 9-44.
2. Delete the dimension 35 and create a new dimension witl1 the new edge as shown in Fig 9-45.
3. Delete the yellow dashed line.
4. Exit the sketcher.
5. Define the Pad.2 feature in a work object. Fig 9-46 shows the modified model.

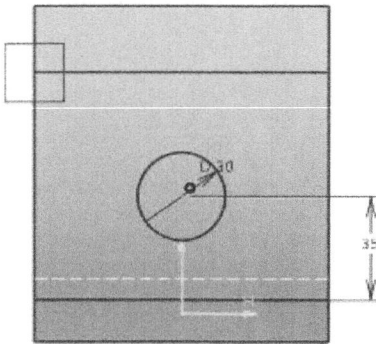

Fig 9-45 New Dimension

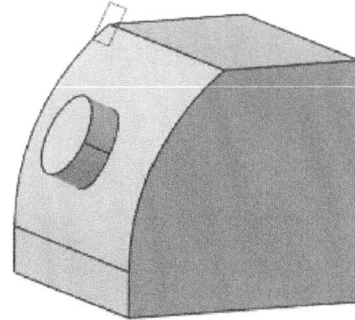

Fig 9-46 Comple ted Model

(Note) Purpose of Exercise 04

- Note that the purpose of this exercise is not to delete a feature but to modify the generated errors. Suppose that you have created a lot of features referencing the geometry of the Pad.2 feature. If you delete the Sketch.2 feature, all do instream features associated with the Pad.2 feature can be deleted or have update problems.

9.6 MODIFYING FEATURE DEFINITION

If you double click feature. such as Sketch-Based Features and Dress-Up Features, the feature definition dialog box appears. You can modify feature definition options in the dialog box. Types of modifying feature definitions can be classified as follows.

Approaches to Modifying Feature Definition Options

1. Reselecting target objects such as profiles and edges.
2. Modifying values
3. Modifying other options such as direction and thickness options.

9.6.1 Reselecting Target Objects

If you have created a feature on an existing geometry, you might have selected the geometry when you are applying a command. You can re-select geometry such as vertexes, edges and faces by invoking the feature definition dialog box. Examples of re-selecting objects for defining a feature arc as follows.

1. Limit element of Pad, Pocket and Hole feature
2. Edges of Fillet or Chamfer features
3. Axis of Shaft or Groove features
4. Faces, edges and points that have been selected while creating a reference element
5. A face that has been selected while creating a Draft or Shell feature

When you re-select a target object, you can click the selection field in the dialog box and select other objects in the model. You can create a target object such as a face, line or point by right clicking on the selection field. If you want to deselect objects, press the Shift key and select the object.

Exercise 72: Changing Limit Element of a Pad Feature (ch09_005.CATPart)

1. Open the given file ch09_005.CATPart.
2. Double click the Sketch.1 feature and create an R100 arc as specified by (A) in Fig 9-47 after deleting the corresponding line.
3. Exit the Sketcher. The Update Diagnosis dialog box appears as shown in Fig 9-48. Note that Face. I used as the limit element for the Pad.2 feature has been modified to a curved face. The software cannot substitute the limiting plane with the curved face. The user has Lo resolve the problem.

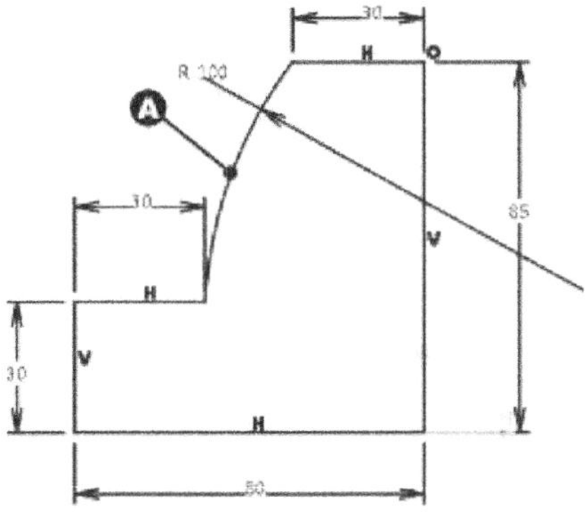

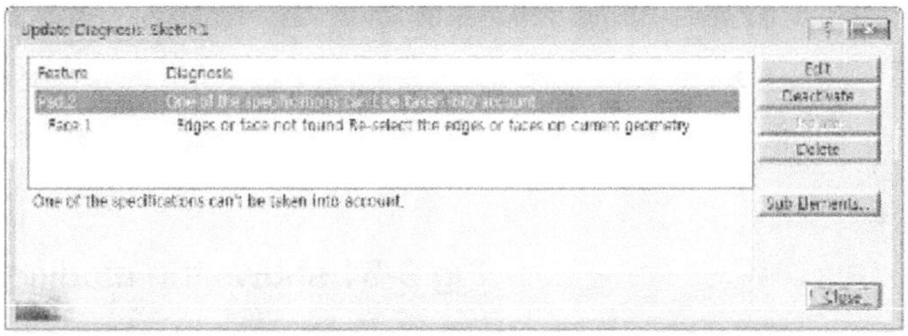

Fig 9-47 Modified Sketch

Fig 9-48 Update Diagnosis Dialog Box

4. Select Pad.2 in the dialog box and press the Edit button on the right The Pad Definition dialog box appears with the error message boxes shown in Fig 9-49.
5. Click OK in the error message boxes.

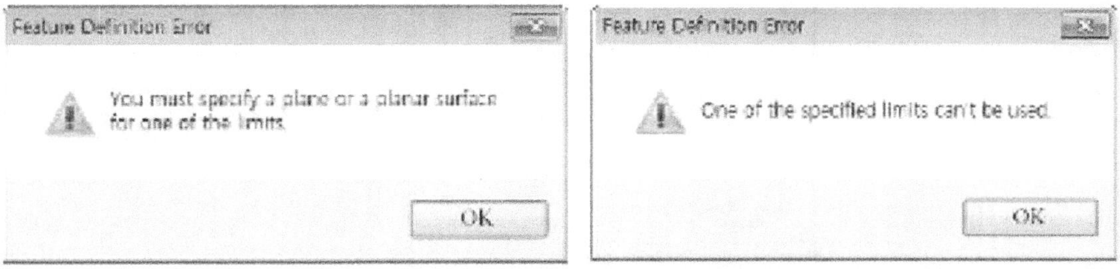

Fig 9-49 Error Messages

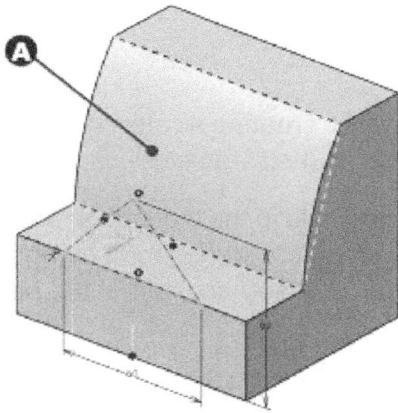

Fig 9-50 Selecting Limit Element   Fig 9-51 Updated Model

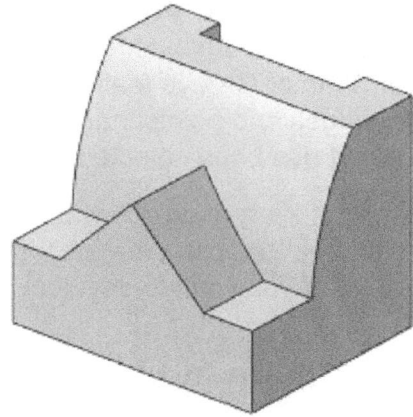

6. Modify the type of the First Limit to Up to surface. The Limit input box is activated.
7. Select the curved face O as shown in Fig 9 -50.
8. Press OK in the Pad Definition dialog box.

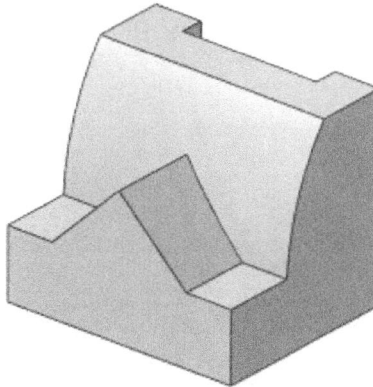

Fig 9-51 shows the modified part.

(Note) Spec Tree with Errors

- You can identify features with update er-rors in the Spec Tree.

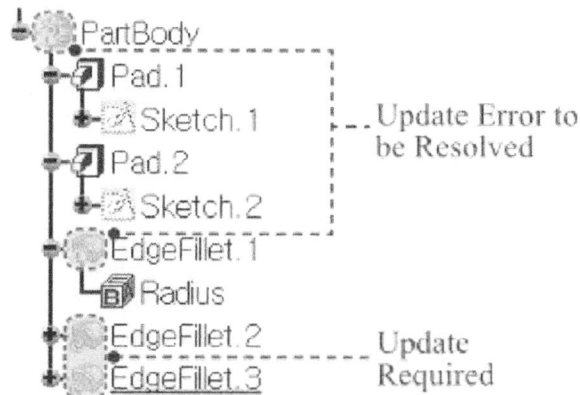

- Select Tools > Options in the menu bar. The Options dialog box is invoked after a while and you can set the option for managing update error in the General tab in Infrastructure > Part Infrastructure. If you check the Stop update on first error option, the update process will stop when it encounters the first error and the Update Diagnosis dialog box will appear.

Exercise 73: Selecting or Deselecting Fillet Edge

Let's modify the edges of fillets and resolve the errors encountered by deselecting and/or selecting new edges. We will not delete the fillet feature but modify the existing one.

Reviewing Modeling History

1. Open the given file ch09_006.CATPart
2. Right click on EdgeFillet.1 in the Spec Tree and select Define in Work Object from the pop-up menu.
3. Define the other fillet features in work object one by one to review the modeling history.
4. Define in the last feature in work object.

Set an option so that the sketch vie w is not set normal to the sketch plane (Hint: Fig 9-52 Reviewing the Modeling History Tools> Options> Mechanical Design> Sketcher).

Modifying a Sketch

1. Double click Sketch.2 of the Pad.2 feature.
2. Delete the line (A) shown in Fig 9-53 and create three lines specified by (B) in Fig 9-53 Deleting Sketch Curve

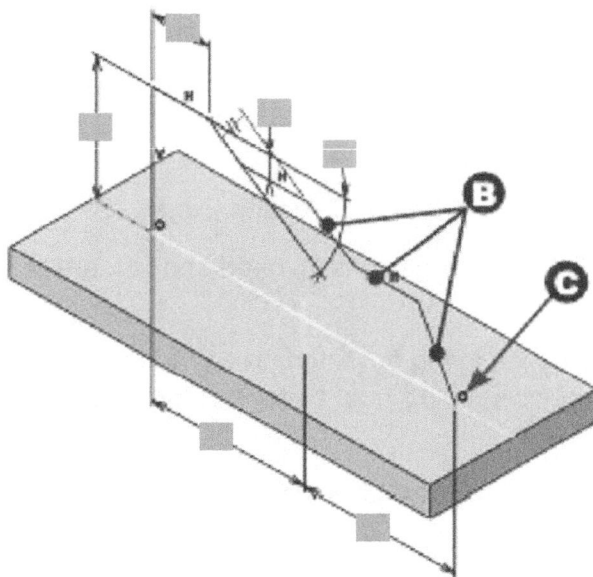

fig 9-54 Creating curves

Fig 9-54. The end point (C) of a line has to be coincident with the bottom line. Skip iso-constraint the sketch.

We can expect that an error will take place for the consecutive fillet feature because the edges will be missing. We will add new edges for the fillet feature.

Note that the purpose of this exercise is to modify the fillet, not delete it.

3. Exit the sketcher.

Resolving Errors

1. An Update Diagnosis dialog box. Read the message carefully.
2. Select EdgeFillet.1 and press the Edit button. Feature Definition Error message. One edge cannot be u ed and the edge is displayed as a dotted line.
3. Press the OK button in the error message box.

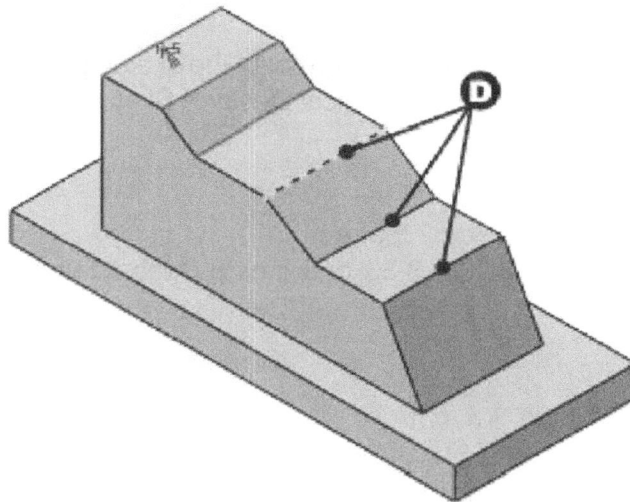

Fig 9-57 Selecting Edges

Note that the Edge Fillet Definition dialog box is invoked and you are prompted to select an edge or a face to edit the fillet

Select three edges specified by (D) in Fig 9-57 and press the OK button in the Edge Fillet Definition dialog box. The Update Diagnosis dialog box. Note that the error occurred in EdgcFillet.3 at this time.

Press the Edit button in the dialog box and click OK in the error message box.

Select the bottom edge specified by (E) in Fig 9-60 shows the final model after modification.

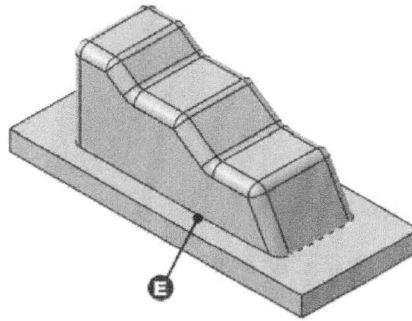

Fig 9-59 Selecting Edges

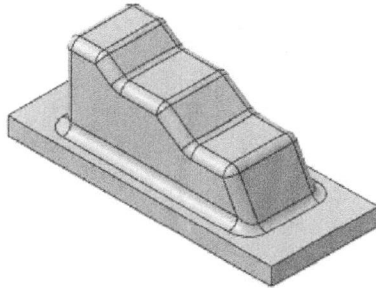

Fig 9-60 Comple ted Model

9.6.2 Modifying Profile

When you are studying several version s of design with various profiles, you have to be able to change the profile.

Types of Defining Profiles

1. Using the entire sketch
2. Using a Sub-element

Exercise 74: Re-Defining Profile (ch09_007.CATPart)

In this exercise, we will learn how to re-define a profile after adding a sketch curve.

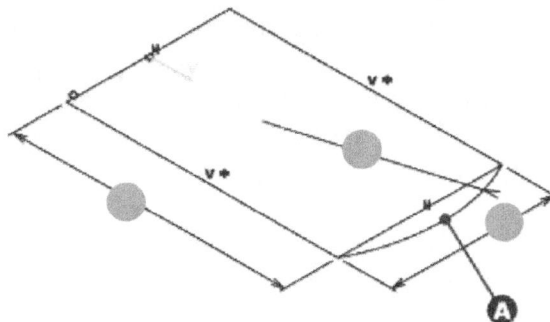

Fig 9-61 Adding a Sketch Curve

Reviewing Modeling History

1. Open the given file ch09_ 007.CATPart.
2. Review the modeling history of the part.

Modifying Sketch

1. Double click the Sketch.1 feature.
2. Add an R65 arc as specified by (A) in Fig 9-6 1.
3. Exit the sketcher.

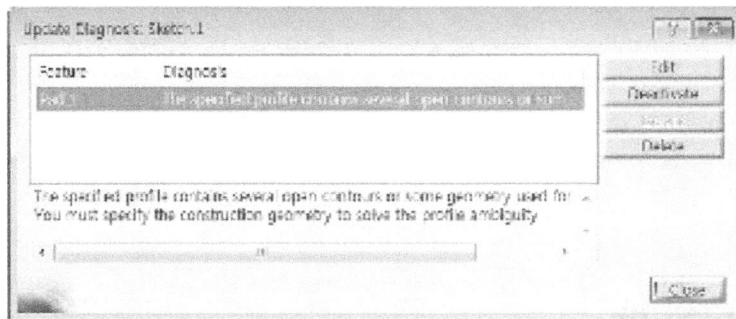

Fig 9-62 Update Diagnosis Dialog Box

The Update Diagnosis dialog box appears as shown in Fig 9-62. There is a problem in the profile of the Pad.1 feature.

Resolving the Error

Fig 9-63 Error Message

1. Select Pad.1 in the dialog box and press the Edit button on the right. The Pad Definition dialog box appears with the Feature Definition Error message box as shown in Fig 9- 63.
2. Read the message in the Feature Definition Error dialog box and press the OK button.
3. Right click on the Selection field of the Pad Definition dialog box and choose Go to profile definition ill the pop-up menu. The Profile Definition dialog box is invoked as shown in Fig 9-64.
4. Select Sketch.1 ill the list and press the Remove button.

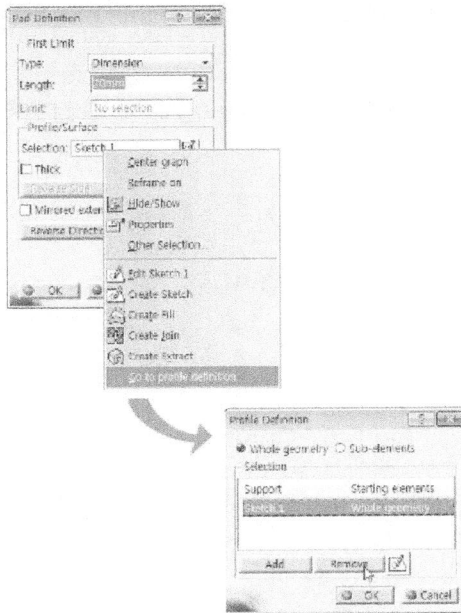

Fig 9-64 Deleting Profile

5. Select the Sub-elements option in the Profile Definition dialog box and select the curves including the arc as shown in Fig 9-65.

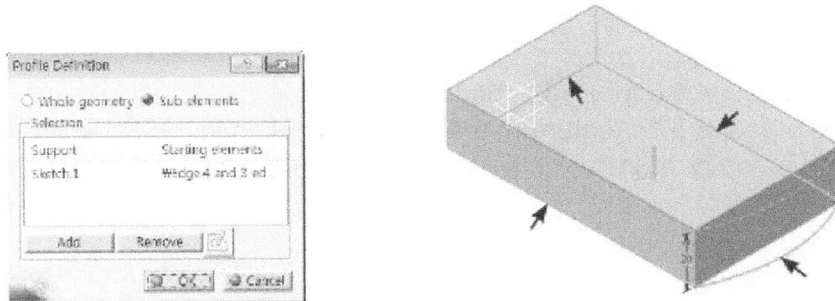

Fig 9-65 Defining a New Profile

6. Press OK in the Profile Definition dialog box.
7. Press OK in the Pad Definition dialog box.

An Update Diagnosis dialog box appears again as shown in Fig 9-66. The error is encountered because an edge has been projected on the second sketch and offset.

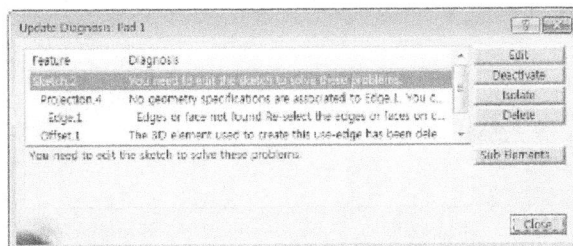

Fig 9-66 Update Diagnosis Dialog Box

We can re-select the edge to resolve the problem. But in this exercise, we will break the link between the sket.ch curves for simplicity.

1. Select Sketch.2 in the Update Diagnosis dialog box and press the Isolate button on the right.

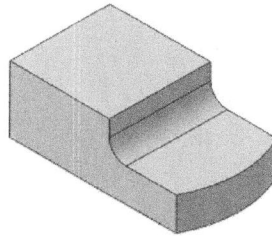

Fig 9-67 Completed Model

All errors have been resolved. Note that, as we did not delete the line in the first sketch, we can restore the previous model if it is required.

Exercise 75: Modifying a Section Profile and Adding a Feature (ch09_008.CATPart)

Modify the given part as shown in Fig 9-68 keeping to the requirements.

Requirements

1. Do not create a new sketch.
2. Modify the section profile for Pad.3 feature.
3. You can add a pad or hole feature at the desired location in the Spec Tree.
4. There should be no error in the completed mode l.

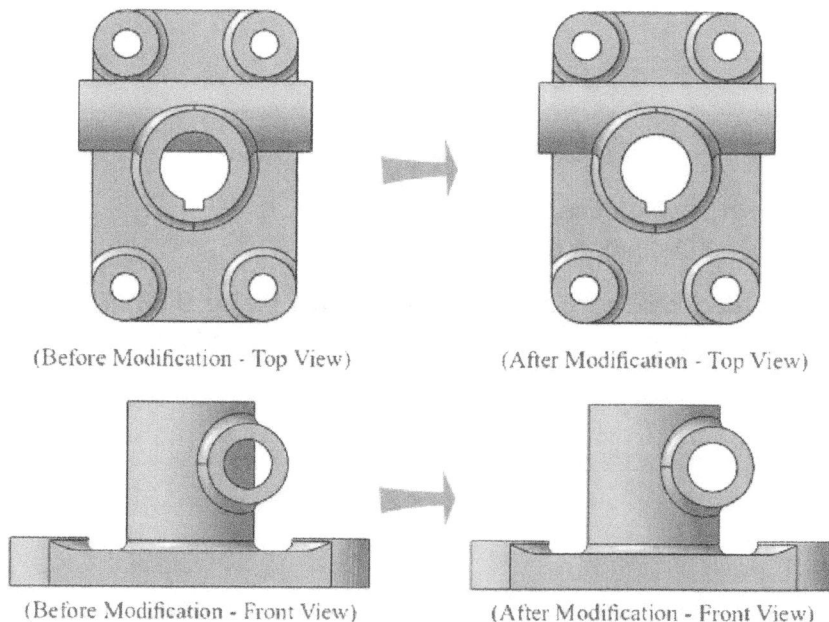

(Before Modification - Top View)   (After Modification - Top View)

(Before Modification - Front View)   (After Modification - Front View)

Fig 9-68 Before and After the Modification

276

(Note) Drag and Drop of a Feature

- You can drag a feature and drop it on the desi red location in the Spec Tree. The dragged feature is inserted after the feature. on which you drop.

Exercise 76: Inserting Features (ch09_009.CATPart)

Modify the given part according to the brief steps below. Rather than deleting features, either insert a new feature or modify the feature definition option.

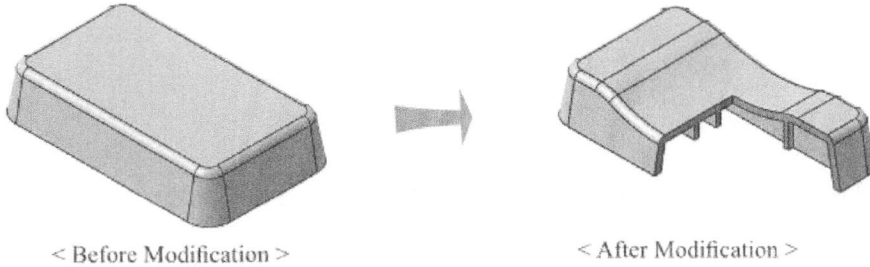

< Before Modification >   < After Modification >

Fig 9-69 Before and After the Modification

Step 1

1. Define the Oraft.1 feature in a work object and create a sketch as shown in Fig 9-70.
2. Create a pocket using the circle.

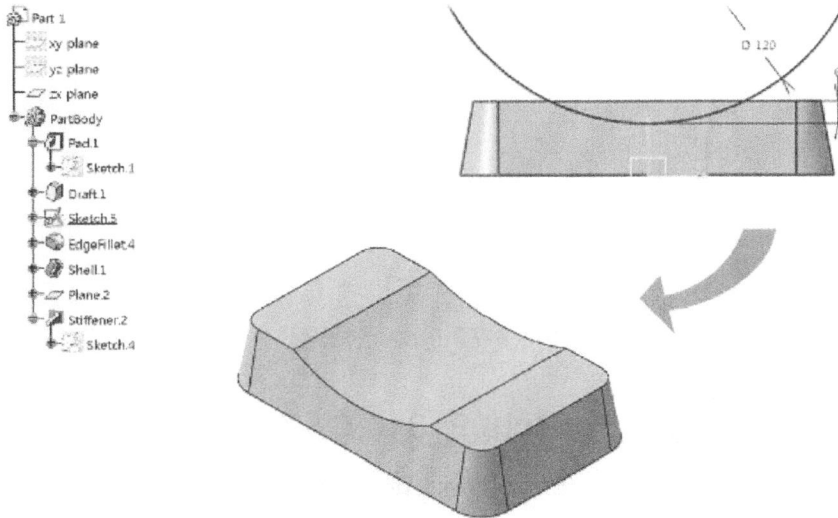

Fig 9-70 Modification Step 1

Step 2

Define the pocket feature created in Step 1 in a work object.

Apply an R20mm fillet on the edges specified by (A) in Fig 9-7 I before the EdgeFillet.4 feature.

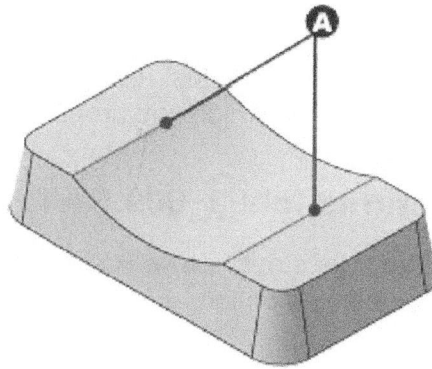

Fig 9- 71 Modification Step 2

Step 3

Define Stiffener.2 in a work object. Fig 9-72 shows the completed model.

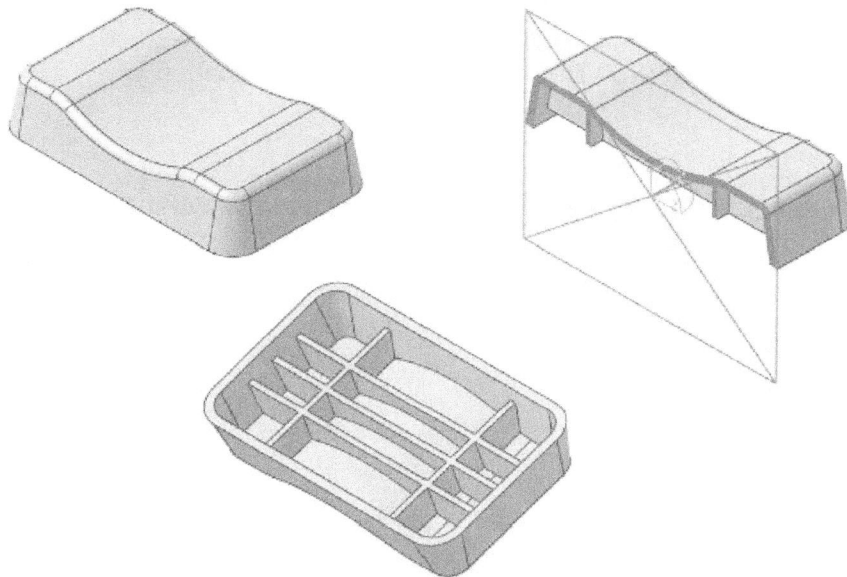

Fig 9-72 Final Model

Exercise 77: Resolving Error (ch09_010.CATPart)

Open the given file and resolve the error after modifying the profile according to the following procedure.

Procedure of Modification

1. Create a spline in the first sketch (Sketch.7) as shown in Pig 9-73. Skip iso-constraining the sketch.
2. Exit the Sketcher and resolve the error(s).

Fig 9-74 shows the pa11 before. and after the modification.

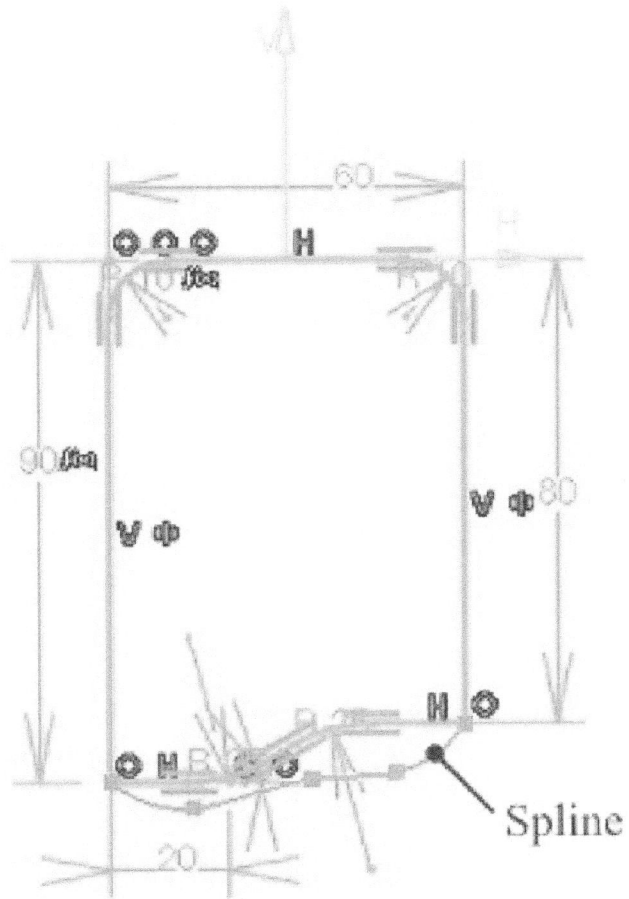

Fig 9-73 The Sketch

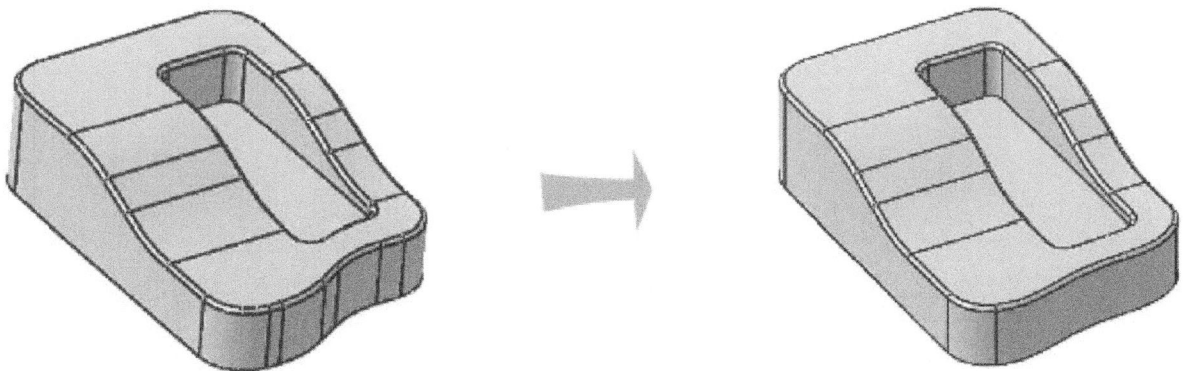

Fig 9-74 Before and After the Modification

Exercise 78: Joint Part (ch09_011.CATPart)

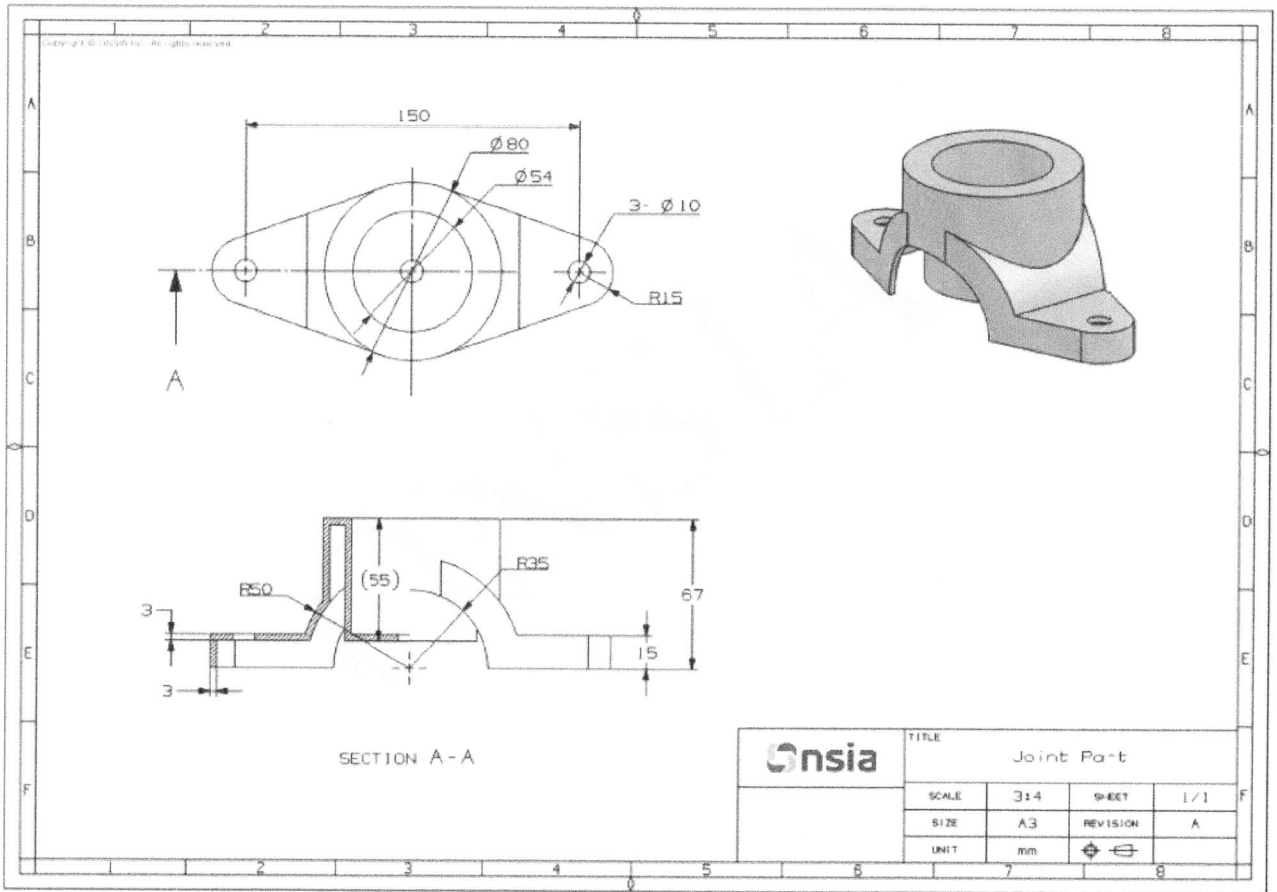

150

Ø80

Ø54

3- Ø10

R15

A

R50

(55)

R35

67

3

3

15

SECTION A-A

TITLE		Joint Part	
SCALE	3:4	SHEET	1/1
SIZE	A3	REVISION	A
UNIT	mm		

Fig 9-75 Drawing for Exercise 78

CHAPTER 10: ADVANCED MODELING: MULTI-BODY TECHNIQUES

10.1 MODELING WITH BODIES

In CATIA V5, you can create multiple bodies in a part file and perform Boolean operations between the bodi.es to construct a 3D model. There are several merits to creating models with multiple bodies.

- You can classify the geometry into several characteristic shapes.
- You can construct complex geometry efficiently.
- You can reuse each body as many times as you want.

As most final models are completed as a single body, when multiple bodies are created during the modeling process, they entail Boolean operations such as Add Remove and Intersect. Boolean operations are explained in the later section of this chapter.

10.1.1 Inserting Bodies

Two methods are available for inserting bodies.

1. Choose Insert > Body from the menu bar.
2. Choose Insert > Body in a Set from the menu bar.

If you insert a body with the first met hod, the name of the body is automatically allocated . You can modify the name by right clicking and choosing Properties on the name of body in the Spec Tree.

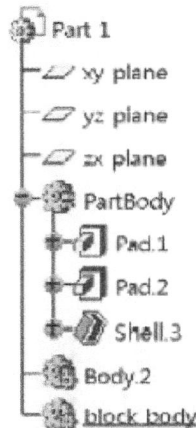

Part 1
xy plane
yz plane
zx plane
PartBody
  Pad.1
  Pad.2
  Shell.3
Body.2
block body

Fig 10-1 Inserted Bodies

If you insert a body using the second method , you can specify the name of the body and select the Father object in which to insert the body.

The newly created body is defined in a work object, and the features that are subsequently created are contained in the body. You can define another body in the work object by pressing MB3 > Define in Work Object on the desired body. You can also select the de- sired body in the Tools tool bar to define it in the work object.

Fig 10-2 Selecting Body in Tools Toolbar

Fig 10-3 shows a part with two bodies. A "block body" has been inserted, and the Pad.3 and Shell.2 features were created in the body.

Note that the PartBody is a basic body that is created automatically whenever you create a part file. The PartBody is located at the top level and becomes the base of the following modeling process. The inserted body can become the PartBody by using the Change Part Body option that is available by right clicking on the body object as shown in Fig 10-4.

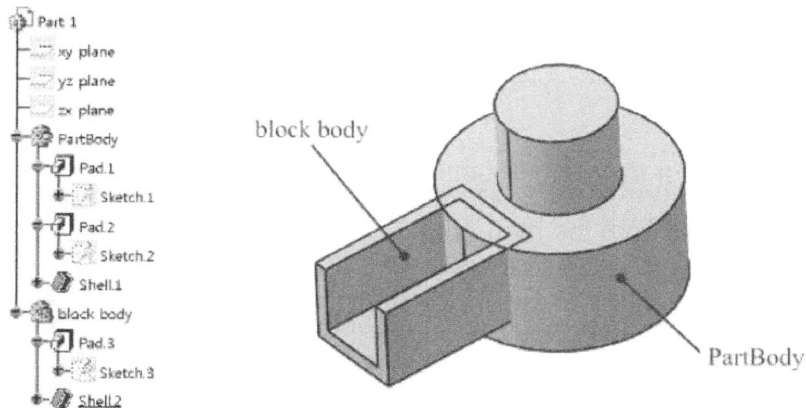

Fig 10-3 Part with Two Bodies

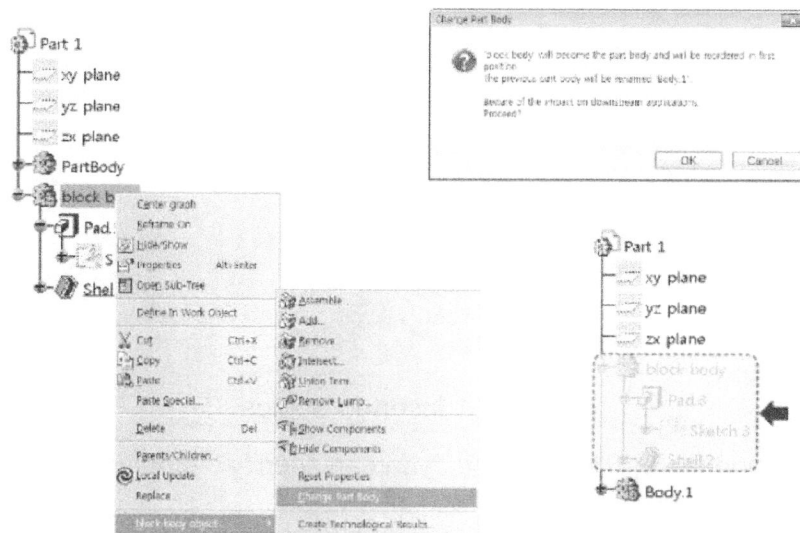

Fig 10-4 Changing the Pan Body

10.1.2 Geometrical Sets

You can group geometries into a type of folder which is called a Geometrical Set and Body. There are two kinds of geometrical sets: geometrical sets(GS) and ordered geometrical sets(OGS) . We should understand the characteristics and usages of geometrical sets and bodies to manage CATIA geometrics properly and to understand and efficiently modify modeling history.

Geometrical Set(GS)

- GS can contain objects such as sketches, reference elements and GSD (Generative Shape Design) elements which are not classified as bodies.
- GS can contain other GS but not the ordered geometrical set.
- GS can be created in a body that is created with the hybrid design option disabled.

Ordered Geometrical Set OGS

- OGS can contain sketches, reference elements and GSD elements such as sheet bodies.
- OGS can contain other OGS and bodies but not a GS.
- OGS can be created in a body that is created with the hybrid design option enabled.

Exercise 79: Inserting Bodies and Geometrical Sets (ch10_001.CATPart)

In this exercise, we will insert bodies and geometrical sets and create features in them.

Inserting Body and GS

1. Open the given file ch10_001.CATPart.
2. Take out the Insert toolbar.

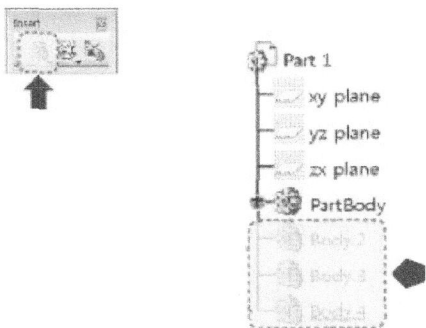

Fig 10-5 Inserting Bodies

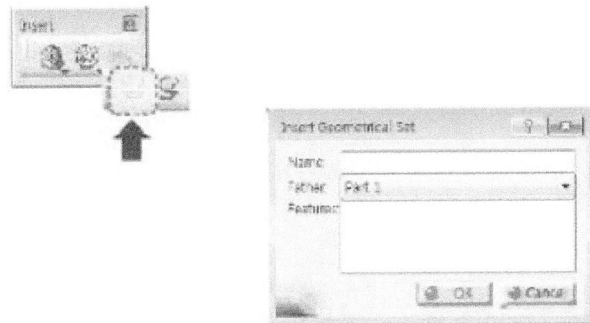

Fig 10-6 Inserting GS

3. Click the Body icon in the Insert toolbar three times to insert three bodies as shown in Fig I 0-5.
4. Click the Geometrical Set icon in the Insert toolbar and click OK in the dialog box to insert a GS with the de- fault name "Geometrical Set.1".
5. Right click on Body.2 in the Spec Tree and choose Properties.
6. Select the Feature Properties tab and enter "A" as the Feature Name.
7. Modify the name of Body.3 as "block body" and Body.4 as "C" in the same way.

283

8. Rename the GS as "sketch".

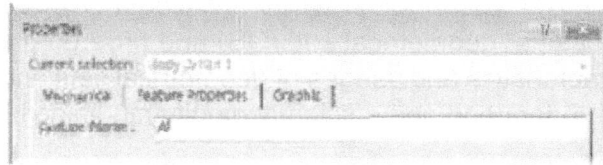

Fig 10-7 Renaming Feature

(Note) Alt + Enter

The Properties dialog box can be accessed by selecting a feature in the Spec Tree and pressing Alt + Enter on the keyboard.

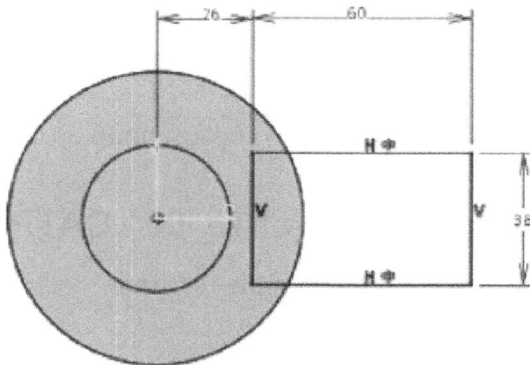

Fig 10-8 Sketch

Fig 10-9 Pad Feature

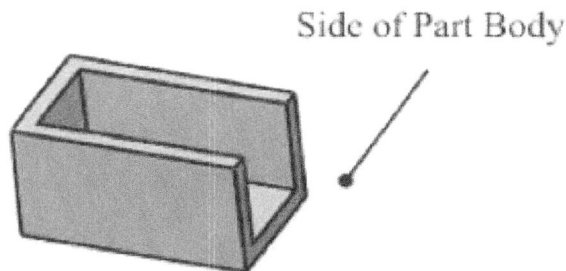

Fig 10-10 Applying Shell

Creating a Sketch

1. If you created the "sketch" GS at the end, it will have been defined in the work object. If not, define it in the work object by right cli c king on the "s ketch " GS and pressing "f on the keyboard.
2. Create a ketch on the middle circular plane as shown in Fig 10-8 and iso-constraint.
3. Exit the Sketcher.

The sketch is contained in the "sketch" GS.

284

Creating a Body

1. Define the "block body" in a work object.
2. Pad it by 30mm as shown in Fig 10-9.

Fig 10-11 Completed Model

Applying Shell

1. Hide the PartBody.
2. Apply a 5mm thick shell on the "block body" as shown in Fig 10-10.

10.2 BOOLEAN OPERATIONS

You can perform Boolean operations between bodies created in the same part file. Taking this approach in the modeling process, you can take advantage of the following benefits.

1. You can classify a part int o several characteristic shapes.
2. You can construct complex geometries efficiently.
3. You can reuse each body as many times as you want.

Although you may create several bodies during the mode ling process, in most cases they will construct a single body in the end. A single body can be constructed through a com- bination of Boolean operations. There are three types of Boolean operations.

1. Add
2. Remove
3. Intersect

Other operations that can be applied to the bodies are as follows.

1. Union Trim
2. Remove Lump
3. Assemble

10.2.1 Add

A body is added to another body. Add corresponds to the union in set theory.

If the two bodies are overlapped, the boundary will be merged . If the two bodies are separated, the two bodies possess their respective volumes, and they are recorded as a single body in the Spec Tree.

Exercise 80: Boolean Operation (Add) (ch10_002.CATPart)

Let's learn how to perform Boolean operations using the Add icon. We will add the two bodies created in Exercise 80.

1. Open the given file ch10_002.CATPart. You can use the result file of Exercise 80.

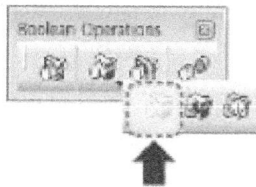

Fig 10-12 Add Icon

2. Take out the Boolean Operations toolbar and click the Add icon. The Add dialog box as shown in Fig 10-13 is invoked. Note that the Add selection field is activated.

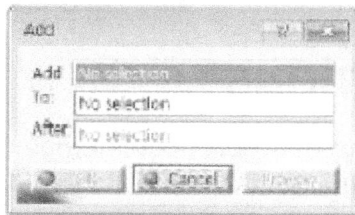

Fig 10-13 Add Dialog Box

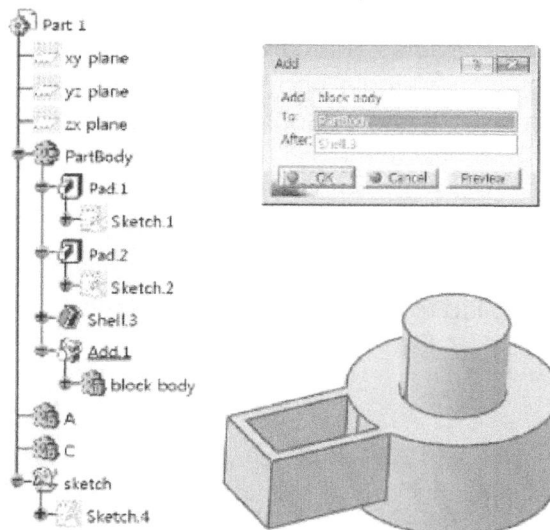

Fig 10-14 Completed Model

286

The Boolean operation is performed in such a way that the body selected in the Add field is added to the body selected in the to field. Properties of the to body are inherited.

3. Select the "block body" as the Add object. The to field is activated automatically.
4. Select the PartBody as the to object.
5. Press the OK button.

Fig 10-14 shows the completed model and the Spec Tree.

Exercise 81: Boolean Operation (Add) (ch10_003.CATPart)

Let's learn how to perfom1 Boolean operations using the Add pop-up menu. We will add the two bodies created in Exercise 81.

Fig 10-15 Add Option

Fig 10-16 Add Dialog Box

1. Open the given file ch10 _003.CATPart. Define the body "C" in a work object.
2. Place the mouse cursor on "block body" in the Spec Tree, right click and choose block body object > Add in the pop-up menu.

The Add dialog box as shown in Fig 10-16 appears. Note that C appears in the to field. This is because body C is a work object.

3. While the to field is activated, select PartBody in the graphic window or in the Spec Tree.

The PartBody is taken as the to object.

4. Press the OK button.

The result model and the Spec Tree are the same as that shown in Fig l0- 14.

Exercise 83: Deleting Boolean Operation (ch10_004.CATPart)

Let's learn how to delete the Boolean operation and the meaning of Aggregated option.

1. Open the given file ch10_004.CATPart. You can use the result file of Exercise 83.
2. Move the mouse cursor on the Adcl.1 operation, right click, and choose Delete. You can press the D key instead of selecting Delete in the pop-up menu.
3. Uncheck the (A) option marked in Fig 10-18.

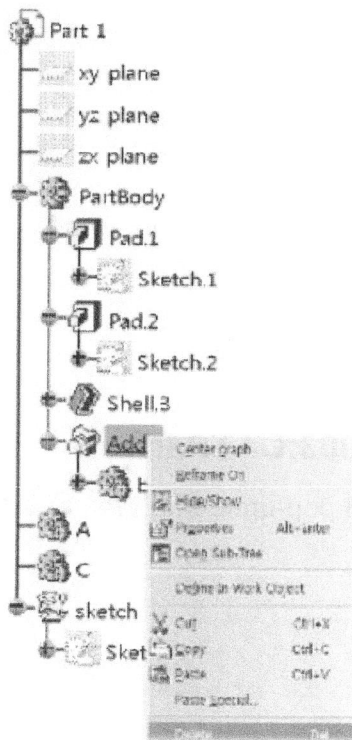

Fig 10-17 Delete Option

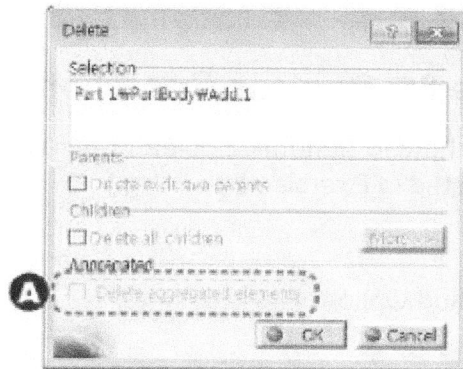

Fig 10-18   Delete Dialog Box

4.   Press the OK button.

The Spec Tree and the model are restored such that the contributing bodies are separated into two individual bodies.

If you have checked the option (A), the geometry in the "block body" might have been delete d together with the Add. I operation.

10.2.2 Union Trim

Using the Union Trim command the following two operations can be performed.

1.   Two bodies are Added (Union).
2.   A portion of a body is trimmed by using the surface of the other body (Trim). The surface that will be used as the trimming object has to enclose the section of the body to be trimmed.

Exercise 84: Union Trim (ch10_005.CATPart)

Let's learn the process of using Union Trim through an exercise.

1.   Open the given file ch10_005.CATPart.
2.   Click the Union Trim icon in the Boolean Operations toolbar. You are prompted to select the body to trim.
3.   Select Body.2 as the Trim object in the Spec Tree. Body.2 is designated in the Trim field of the Trim Definition dialog box.

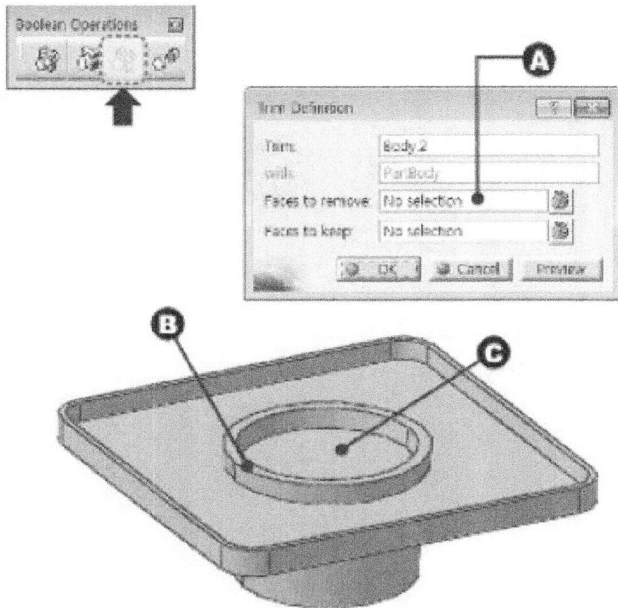

| Fig 10-19 Faces to Remove | Fig 10-20 Completed Model |

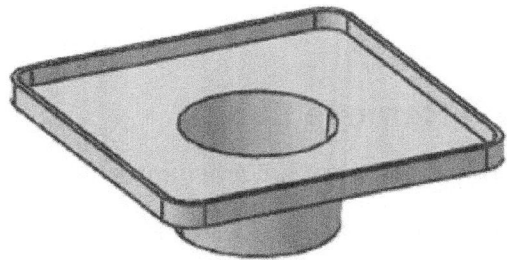

4. Click the Faces to remove field ((A) in Fig 10-19).
5. Select the face (B) in Body.2 and face (C) in the PartBody.
6. Press OK.

10.2.3 Remove

With the Remove operation, you can remove a body from another body. This operation corresponds to the difference set inset theory.

Exercise 84: Remove (ch10_006.CATPart)

Open the given file ch10_006.CATPart and perform the Remove operation according to the following alternative methods.

Method 1

1. Click the Remove icon in the Boolean Operations tool bar.
2. Select the Remove body and From body.
3. Check the result.

Method2

1. Right click on the "block" body and choose block object > Remove in the Spec Tree.
2. Check the result. Note that the PartBody is automatically designated as the From body.

The result part will be used for Exercise 84.

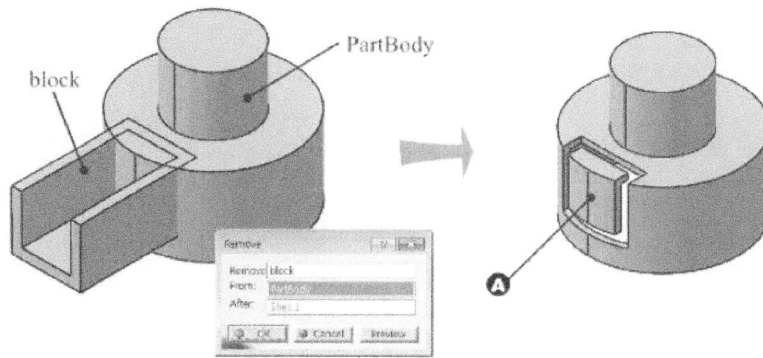

Fig 10-21 Remove Operation

10.2.4 Remove Lump

If a body consists of several lumps, you can remove them.

During the modeling process, lumps designated by (A) in Fig 10-21 can be generated unexpectedly. Unnecessary lumps can be removed using the Remove Lump command in the Boolean Operations toolbar.

Exercise 85: Remove Lump (ch10_007.CATPart)

Using the given file ch10_007.CATPart, perform the Remove Lump operation according to the following procedure.

1. Click the Remove Lump icon.
2. Select the body to trim.
3. Click the Face to remove selection field in the dialog box.
4. Select a face in the lump to be removed.
5. Press the OK button.

You can select the face to be kept in steps 3 and 4.

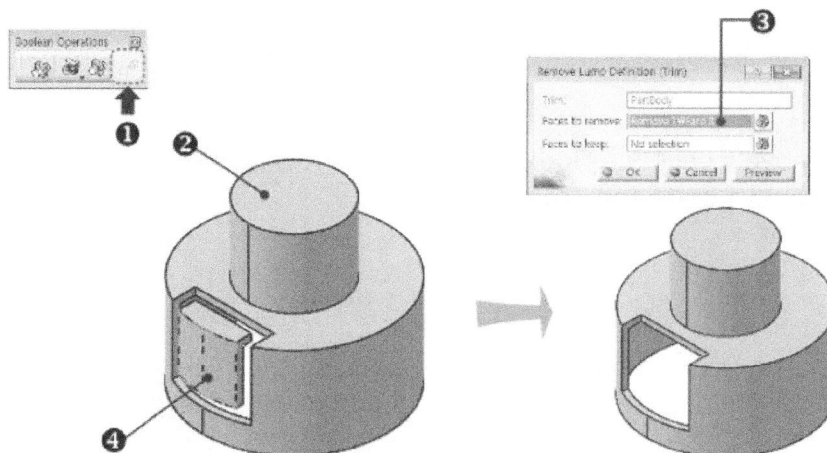

Fig 10-22 Remove Lump Operation

10.2.5 Intersect

The Intersect operation between two solid bodies leaves only the common portion of the vol ume and removes other po1tions from the two bodies.

Exercise 86: Intersect (ch10_008.CATPart)

Let's create the model shown in Fig 10-23 using the given sketches.

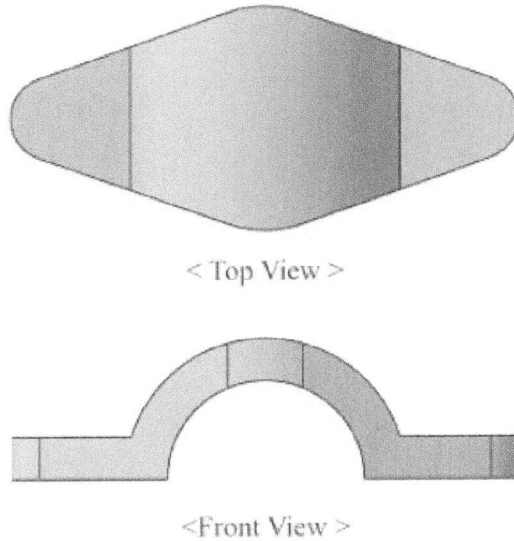

< Top View >

< Front View >

Fig 10-23 Model for Exercise

1. Open the given file ch10_008.CATPart
2. Click the Body icon in the Insert toolbar and rename it as "front".

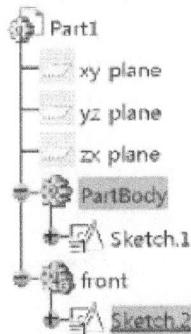

Fig 10-24 Creating the " front " Body

3. Drag the Sketch.2 feature and drop on the "front" body as shown in Fig 1 0-24.
4. Define the PartBody in a work object.
5. Pad the Sketch.1 feature by 60mm. The front view of the model is as shown in Fig 10-25.

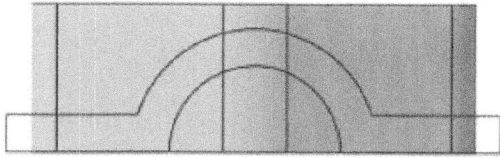

Fig 10-25 Front View

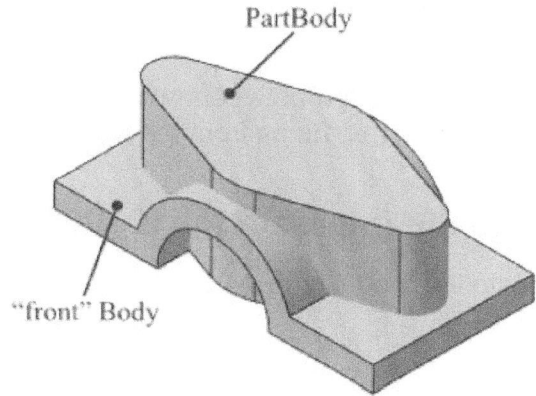

Fig 10-26 Two Bodies

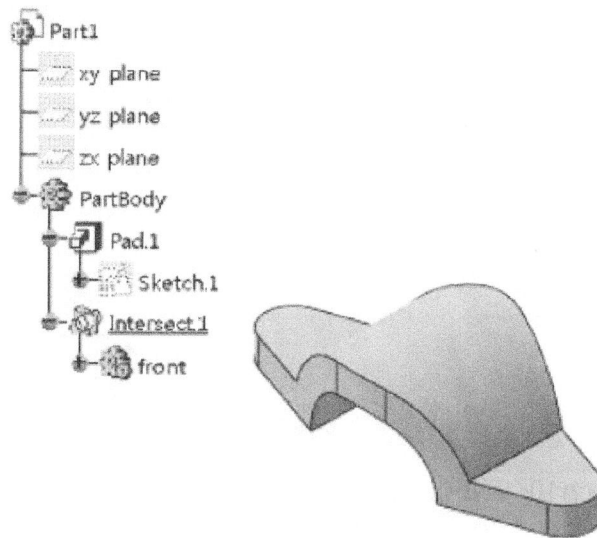

Fig 10-27 Completed Model

6. Define the "front" body in a work object and create a pad feature of 50mm length with the mirrored extent option using Sketch.2. Fig 10-26 shows the two bodies created in the PartBody and the "front" body.

7. Right click on the "front" body in the Spec Tree and choose front object > Intersection the pop-up menu.

Fig 10-27 shows the completed model and the Spec Tree.

Note that the PartBody cannot be used as an operand body. Therefore, Boolean operations are not available in the pop- up menu of the PartBody.

Exercise 87: Combination of Boolean Operations (ch10_009.CATPart)

Let's apply Boolean operations for the given bodies to obtain the resultant model as shown in Fig 10-28. Note that the edge specified by f3 in Fig 10-28 should not be dislocated.

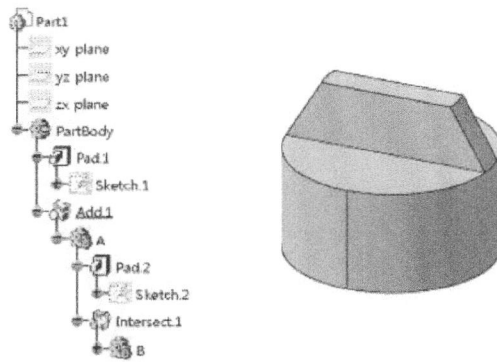

Fig 10-28 Completed Model

Procedure

1. Apply Intersect between the bodies "A" and "B" such that the resultant i s body "A".
2. Add the resultant body "A" to the PartBody.

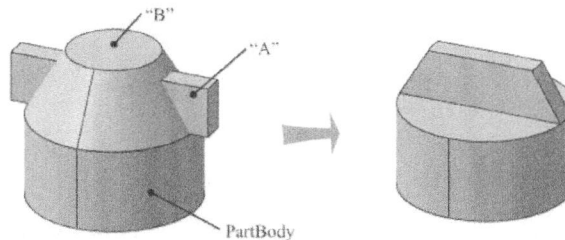

Fig 10-29 Applying Intersect

10.2.6 Assemble

Added bodies have a positive (+) or negative (-) polarity. If you assemble two bodies of the same polarities, they are added. If you assemble two bodies with different polarities, the body with - polarity is removed from the body with + polarity. Note that the PartBody always has + polarity.

The polarity of a body is determined by the first feature created in the body. If you create a feature that adds material such as pad or shaft, the body has + polarity and the plus sign is marked alongside with the gear symbol in the Spec Tree. If you create a feature that removes material such as pocket and groove, the body has - polarity and the minus sign is marked alongside with the gear symbol. Body.2 in Fig 10-30 has positive polarity and Body.3 has negative polarity. The PartBody doesn't have any sign.

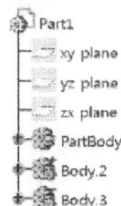

Fig 10-30 Polarity of Body

You can assemble two bodies with different polarity at the same time. If you assemble two bodies to the PartBody Body.2 is added to the PartBody and Body.3 is removed from the PartBody.

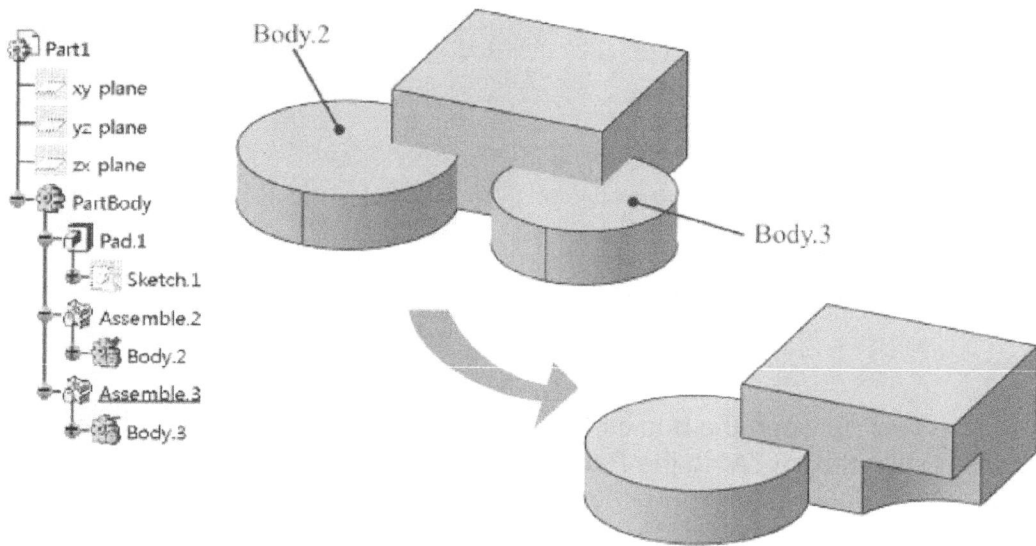

Fig 10-31 Result of Assemble

Exercise 88: Assemble (ch10_010.CATPart)

Given file is composed of three parts as shown in Fig 10 -32. Body.3 is contracted by 2mm than the PartBody. Complete the model according to the suggested procedure. Note that Body.2 has negative polarity an d Body.3 has positive polarity.

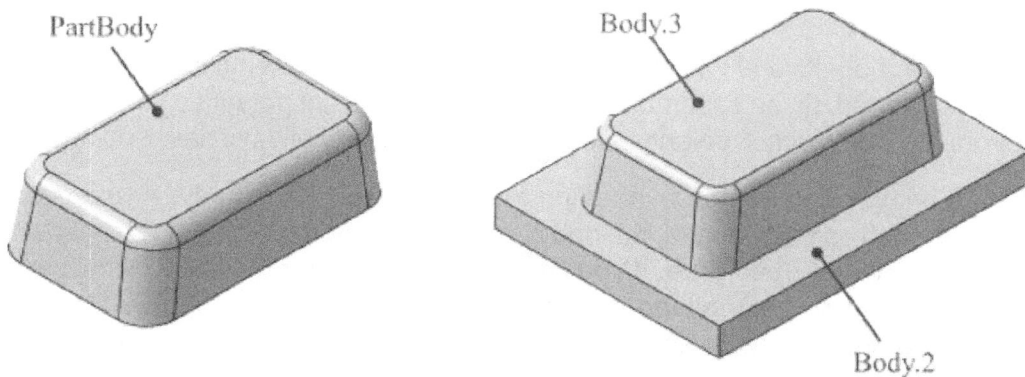

Fig 10-32 Given Part

Step 1

Add Body.3 to Body.2. The resultant body is Body.2 with negative polarity. Note that, if you want to add a body with the positive polarity to the body with the negative polarity , you have to use the Add Boolean operation.

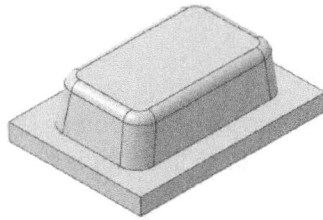

Fig 10-33 Body.2

Step 2

Create the sketch and pocket features as shown in Fig 10 -34. Note that you have to use the Pocket command because the polarity of Body.2 is negative.

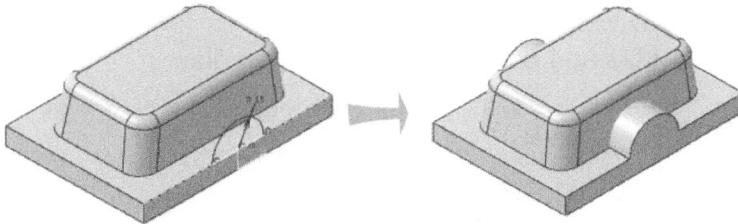

Fig 10-34 Added to Body.2

Step 3

Assemble Body.2 to the PartBody.

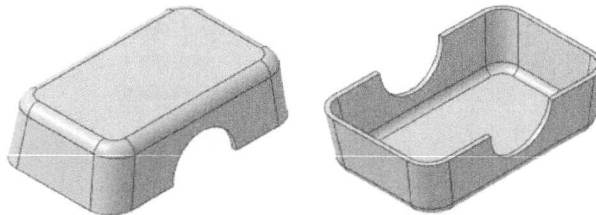

Fig 10-35 Completed Model

10.3.3 Reusing Bodies

Using the Paste Special command, you can copy and paste bodies in a part file and use them for the modeling process. You can also paste the body into another part file with or without links.

The Paste Special command is executed in two steps.

1. Copy the desired body in the Spec Tree or in the model by pressing Ctrl + C.
2. Choose Edit > Paste Special in the menu bar.

The following options are available in pasting the body.

1. As specified in Part document

Pastes the modeling history of the body. You can modify the history of the copied body afterwards.

 2. As Result With Link

Pastes the result geometry with links to the original body. The copied geometry is up-dated when you modify the original body. You can paste the copied body in a position where the Pattern commands are not applicable.

 3. As Result

Pastes the result geometry without links to the original body.

Exercise 89: Paste Special (ch10_011.CATPart)

In this exercise, we will learn two approaches for using the Paste Special command.

 1. Copy and paste a body with in a part file.
 2. Copy a body in a part file and paste it .in another part file.

Copy/Paste in a File

 1. Open the given file ch10_011.CATPart.
 2. Select the PartBody in the Spec Tree.
 3. Press Ctrl + C.
 4. Select the Product (Part 1) in the Spec Tree.
 5. Choose Edit> Paste Special in the menu bar.

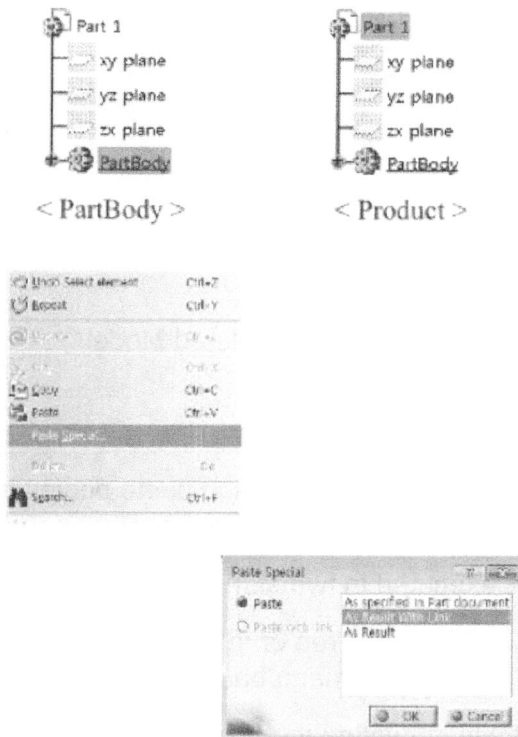

< PartBody >   < Product >

Fig 10-36 Procedure of Paste Special

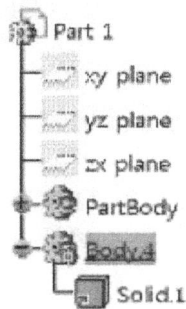

Fig 10-37 Pasted Body

6. Select the As Result With Link in the Paste Special dialog box as shown in Fig 10-36. Body.4 is inserted in the Spec Tree as shown in Fig 10 -3 7. The number of the feature may be different.

Note that a symbol is marked in front of the pasted feature Solid.1, which means that a link exists between the copied and original bodies.

Paste to Other File

1. Choose File > New in the menu bar.

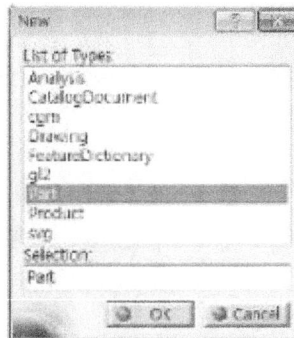

Fig 10-38 Types of File

2. Select Part as the type of the file in the New dialog box and press OK.

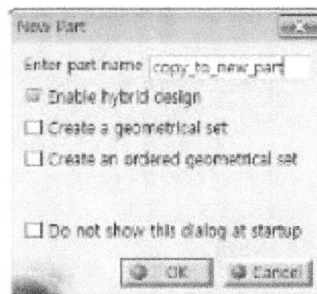

Fig 10- 39 Part Naming

3. Name the file as "copy_to_new_part" and press OK.

Now, we will display the two files horizontally.

4. Choose Window > Tile Horizontally in the menu bar. The display is changed as shown in Fig 10-40.
5. Select the PartBody in the file ch10_011 and press Ctrl + C.
6. Select the product "copy_to_new_part" designated by an arrow in Fig 10-40.

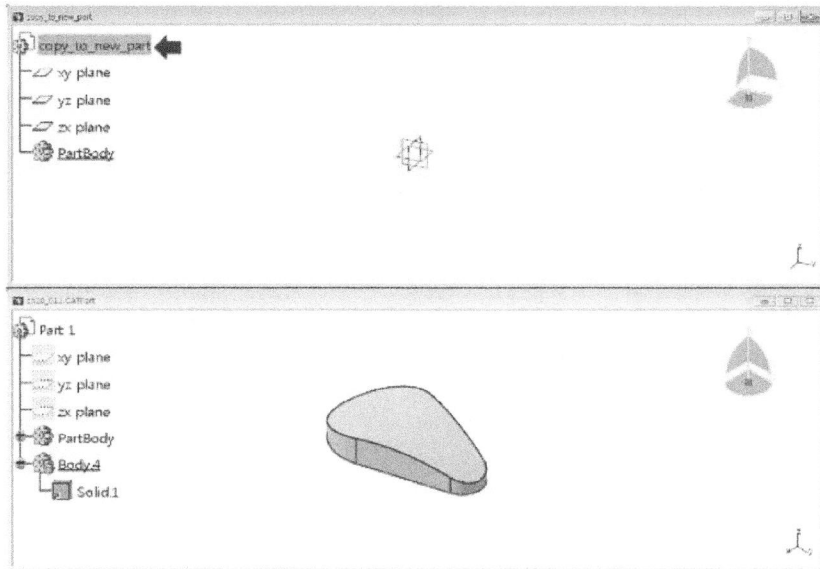

Fig 10-40 Two Files Displayed by Tile Horizontally

7. Choose Edit > Paste Special in the menu bar.

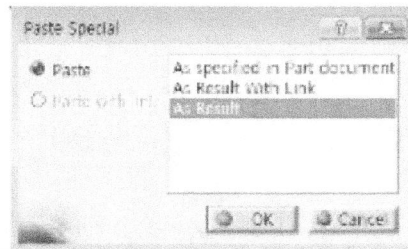

Fig 10-41 Paste Special Options

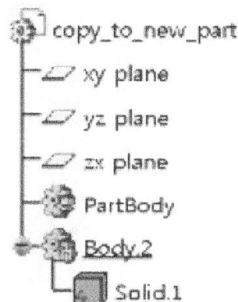

Fig 10-42 Pasted Body

Select the As Result option in the Paste Special dialog box. Body.2 is inserted in the Spec Tree of "copy_to_new_part" file.

Note that a symbol is marked in front of the pasted feature Solid.1, which means that the link between the copied and the original bodies has been broken. Therefore, the pasted body is not updated although you modified the original body in ch10_011.CATPart file.

10.4 GRAPHIC PROPERTIES

You can set different graphic properties such as color, opacity line types, etc. for each body. Various rendering styles can even be applied for each body in the same part file.

Exercise 90: Changing Graphic Properties (ch10_012.CATPart)

1. Open the given file ch10_012.CATPart.
2. Expand the PartBody in the Spec Tree.
3. Right click on Assemble.1 and choose Delete in the pop-up menu. Uncheck the Delete aggregated elements option in the Delete dialog box and press OK.

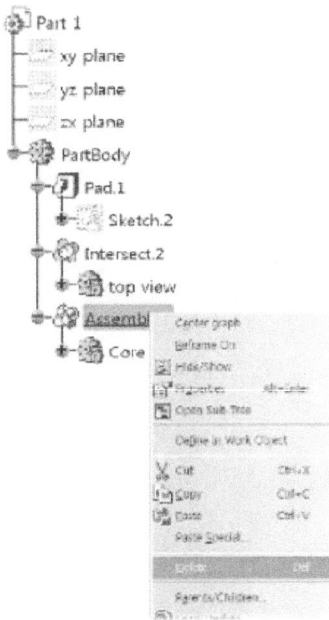

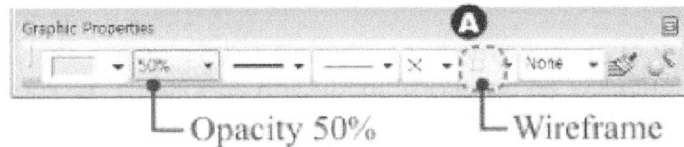

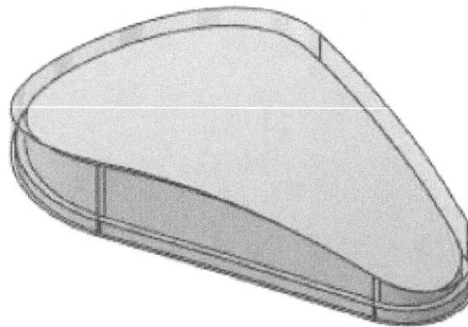

Fig 10-43 Deleting Boolean Operation   Fig 10-44 Changed Graphic Property

The "core" body is separated into an individual body.

4. Take out the Graphic Properties toolbar as shown in Fig 10-44.
5. Select the PartBody in the Spec Tree and change the Opacity to 50% as shown in Fig 10-44.
6. Select Wireframe for the option (A) designated in Fig 10-44.

You can identify the "core" body clearly.

(Note) view Mode

- Wireframe display option (A) is not yet applied. Note that the view mod e of the part is Shading with edges.
7. Select the "core" body and modify its color to Orange and its view mode to Shading with Edges ((A) in Fig 10-45).
8. Click the Customize View Parameters icon ((B) in Fig 10-46) in the View mode toolbar.
9. Select the Rendering style per object option ((C) in Fig 10-46) in the dialog box.

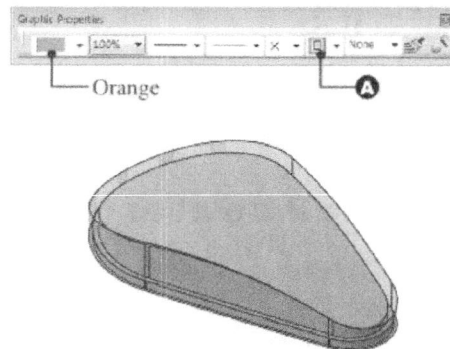

Fig 10-45 Graphic Property of Core Body

The Part Body is applied with Wire- frame mode and the "core" body is applied with Shading with Edges.

10. Select the view mode as Shaded with Edges.
11. Right click on the "core." body and choose Core object > Assemble.
12. Click OK in the Assemble dialog box.

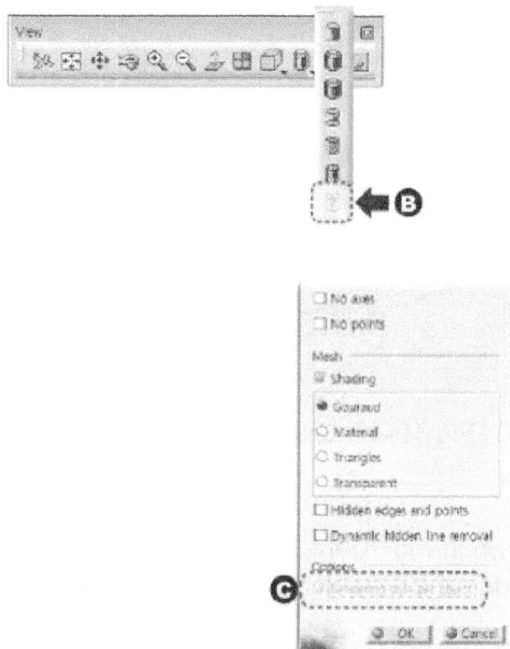

Fig 10-46 View Mode

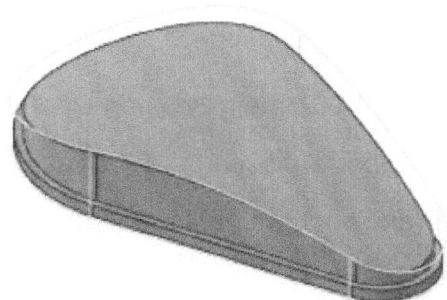

Fig 10-47 Result of Mixed View Mode

Fig 10-48 shows the result of the Assemble operation. The inner surface of the result body is colored orange.

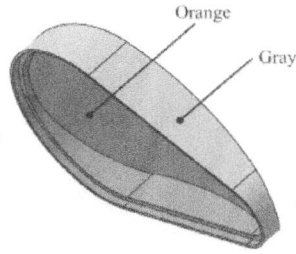

Orange
Gray

Fig 10-48 Result of Boolean Operation

Exercise 91: Modeling with Bodies (ch10_013.CATPart)

Using the given file ch10_013.CATPart, complete the part mode ling as shown in Fig 10-49.

1. Copy the given body and paste as a new body. Name it "core".
2. Add features to the "core" body.
3. Perform a Boolean operation to obtain the result body.

Refer to Fig 1 0-50 for eacl1 step and detail dimension in assembling the edge.

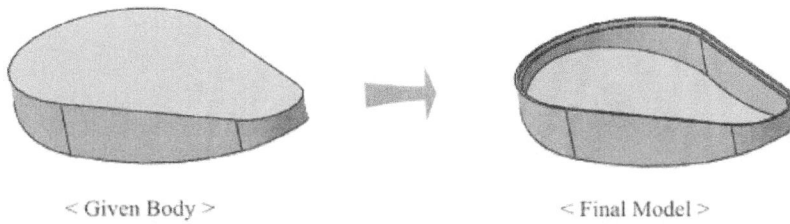

< Given Body >   < Final Model >

Fig 10-49 Mode I for Exercise

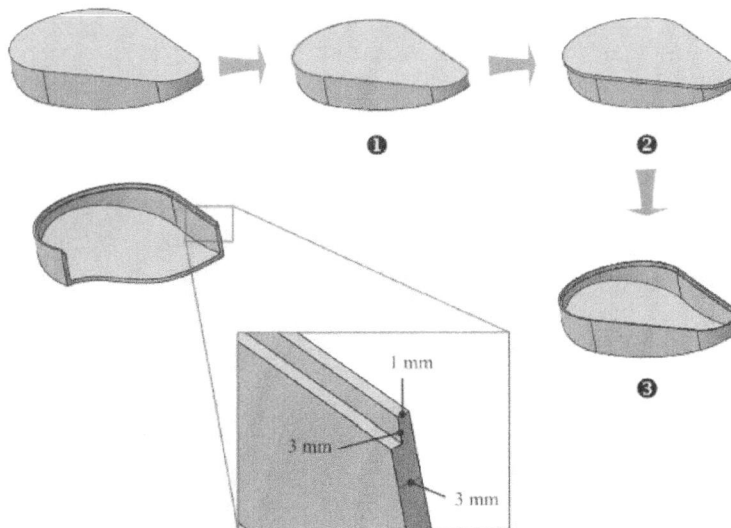

❶

❷

❸

1 mm

3 mm

3 mm

Fig 10-50 Modeling Procedure

Exercise 92: Stand Foot (Ch10_014.CATPart)

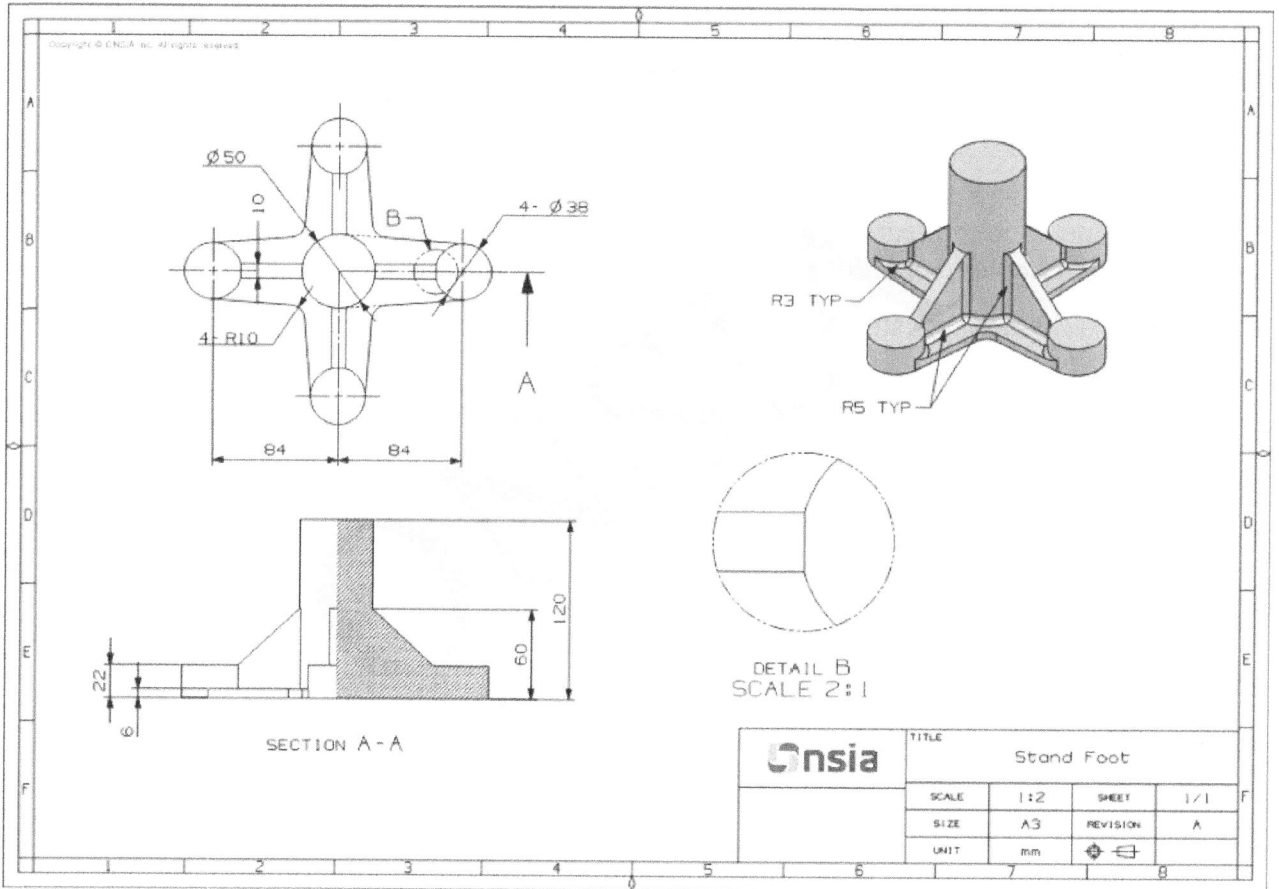

Fig 10-51 Drawing for Stand Foot

Exercise 93: Holder (Ch10_015.CATPart)

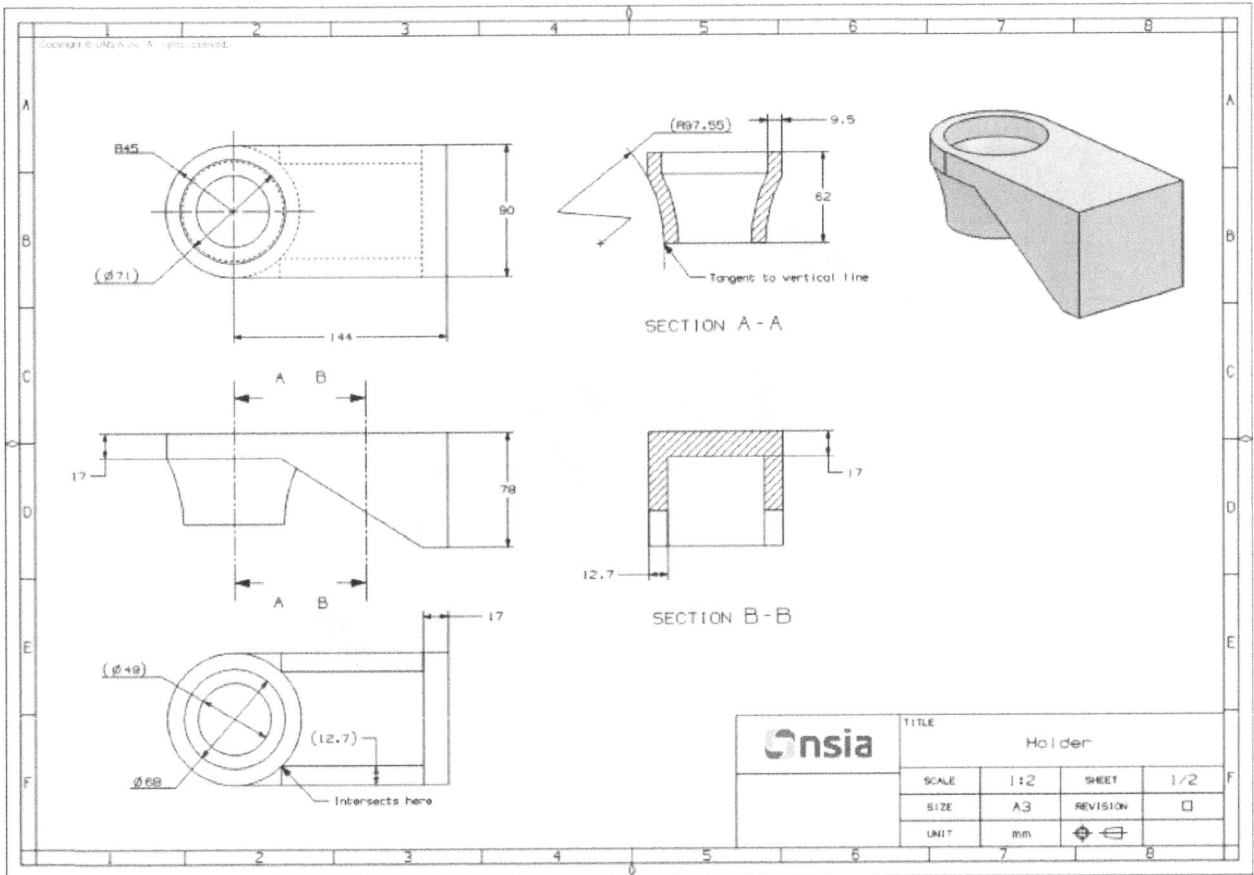

Fig 10-52 Drawing for Holder

Exercise 94: Lid of Electric Mixer (Ch10_016.CATPart)

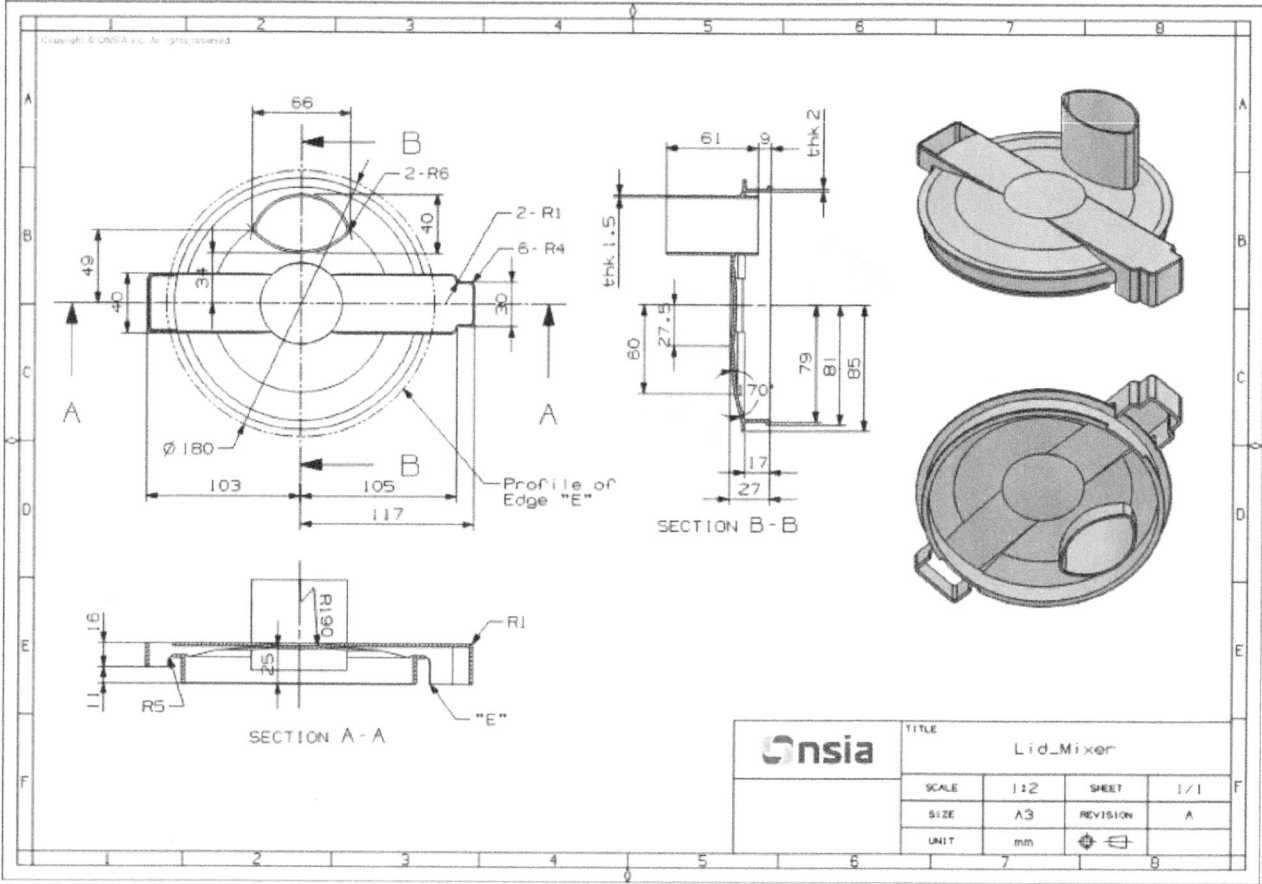

66

B

2-R6

2-R1

6-R4

49

40

3

30

Ø180

Profile of Edge "E"

103   105

117

SECTION A-A

61   9   thk 2

thk 1.5

60   27.5   79   81   85

170°

17

27

SECTION B-B

R190

25

R1

16

R5   "E"

SECTION A-A

TITLE	Lid_Mixer		
SCALE	1:2	SHEET	1/1
SIZE	A3	REVISION	A
UNIT	mm		

Onsia

Fig 10-53 Lid of Electric Mixer

CHAPTER 11: DUPLICATING SUCCESS: CLONING OBJECTS AND FEATURES

11.1 INTRODUCTION

Repeating the same modeling process several times is time consuming and tedious. Once a feature or object is created, you can escape from tiresome modeling repetition by applying commands that copy features or objects. Moreover, you can modify the result of the copy by changing the copy options. Fig 11-1 shows copying a hole to create four holes. The number of instances can be changed to eight as shown in Fig 11-2 by modifying the corresponding copy option. If the size of the instanced hole is changed, the sizes of all instances are updated.

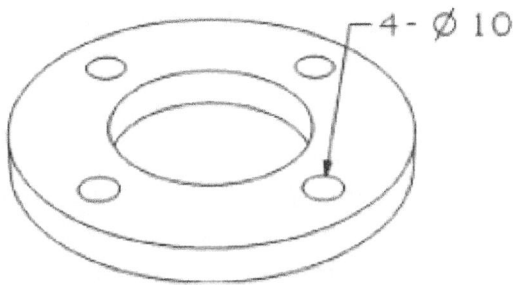

Fig 11-1 Four Holes

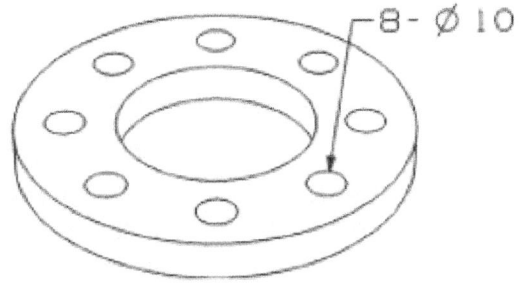

Fig 11-2 Eight Holes

11.2 TRANSFORMATION FEATURES

You can perform the following transformations using the commands in the Transformation Features toolbar.

1. Move or rotate features or bodies.
2. Mirror features.
3. Copy features or bodies as a pattern.
4. Scale a body uniformly or non-uniformly.

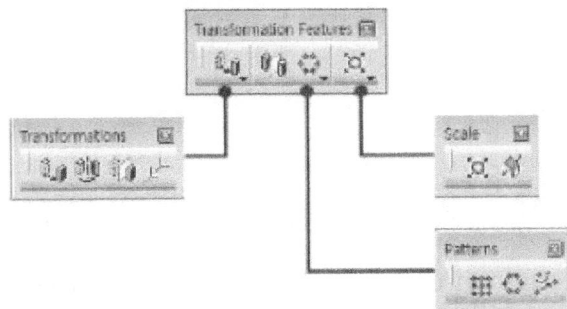

Fig 11-3 Transformation Features Toolbar

305

11.3 USER SELECTION FILTER

When you apply a command, you have to select objects by clicking the corresponding selection field in the dialog box. At that time, you can identify the type of available objects for selection in the User Selection Filter toolbar. Moreover, you can filter the types of objects for your selection by clicking icons in the User Selection Filter toolbar.

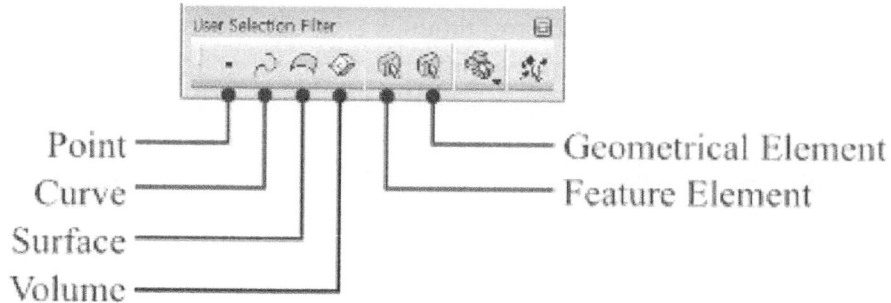

Fig 11-4 User Selection Filter

For example, if you click the Rectangular Pattern icon in the Transformation Features toolbar and click the Reference element selection field, the Curve Filter and Surface Filter are available in the category of both feature element and geometric al element. You can confine your selection to curves in the category of feature by clicking the Curve Filter and Feature Element Filter icon among the available filters.

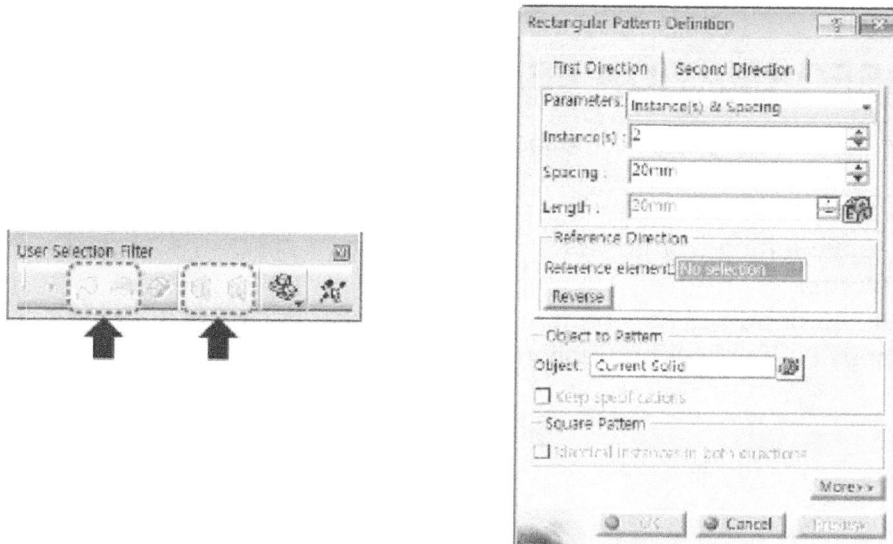

Fig 11-5 Selecting Reference Element

If you click the Circular Pattern icon in the Transformation Features toolbar and click the Object selection field, only the Volume Filter and Feature Element Filter arc available, which means that you can select only the volume type features.

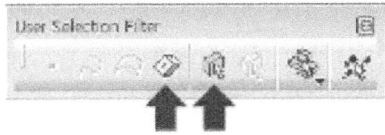

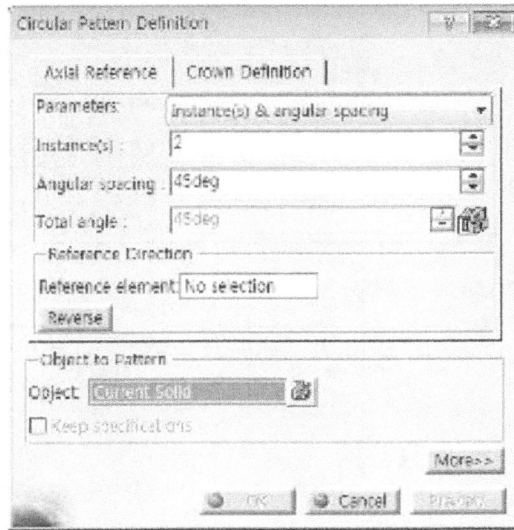

Fig 11-6 Selecting Object to Pattern

After using the user select ion filter, you are recommended to reset the filter. You can reset the selection filter by selecting the Reset Selection Filters option in the User Selection Filter toolbar. You can add the Reset Selection Filters option by dragging the command in the Customize dialog box and dropping on the User Selection Filter toolbar.

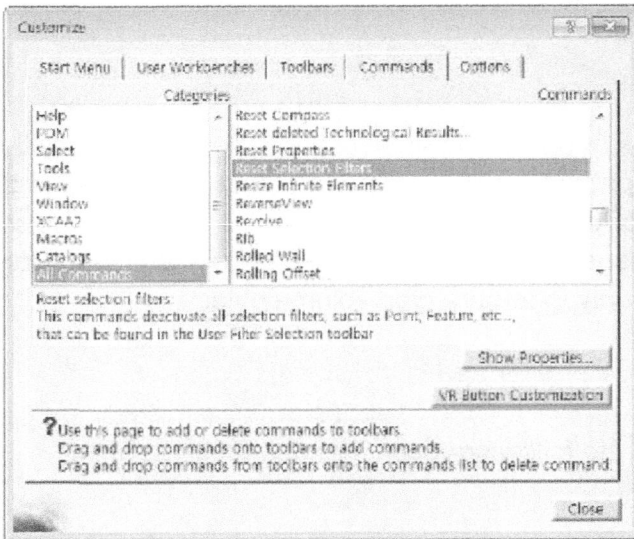

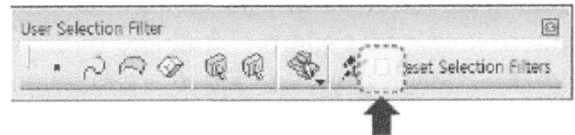

Fig 11-7 Reset Selection Filters Option

If the multiple select ion tool is available next to a selection field in a dialog box as shown in Fig 11-8, you can select multiple object for that option.

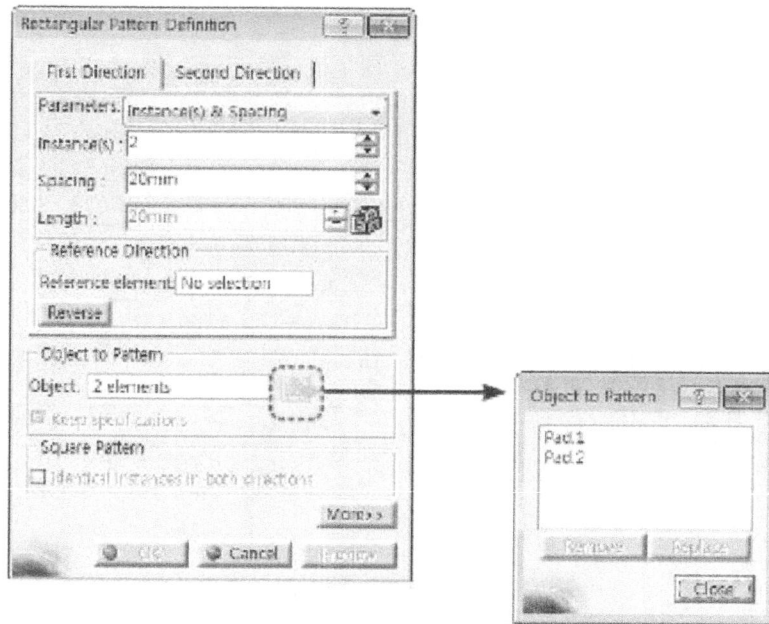

Fig 11-8 Multiple Selection Tool

11.4 PATTERN

You can create a pattern of features or bodies. Three types of patterns are available in CATIA V5.

1. Rectangular Pattern
2. Circular Pattern
3. User Pattern

A rectangular pattern create s a pattern of features or bodies in two directions. You can specify the number of instances ng each direction. A circular pattern creates a pattern of features or bodies by rotating about an axis. You can create a series of circular patterns along radial direction. A user pattern creates a pattern of features or bodies by specifying arbitrary locations   of instances. Note that the circular and user patterns can be applied only to feature type volume objects.

11.4.1 Rectangular Pattern

You can create a rectangular pattern according to the following recommended procedure.

Procedure

1. Click the Rectangular Pattern icon.
2. Specify the objects to copy. Note that Current Body is selected by default.
3. Select an element for the first direct ion and set the options for the pattern such as the number of instances, spacing, etc.
4. Select an element for the second direction and set the options for the pattern such as the number of instances, spacing, etc.
5. Click Preview and OK.

If you do not specify the object to pattern explicitly, the work body is patterned.

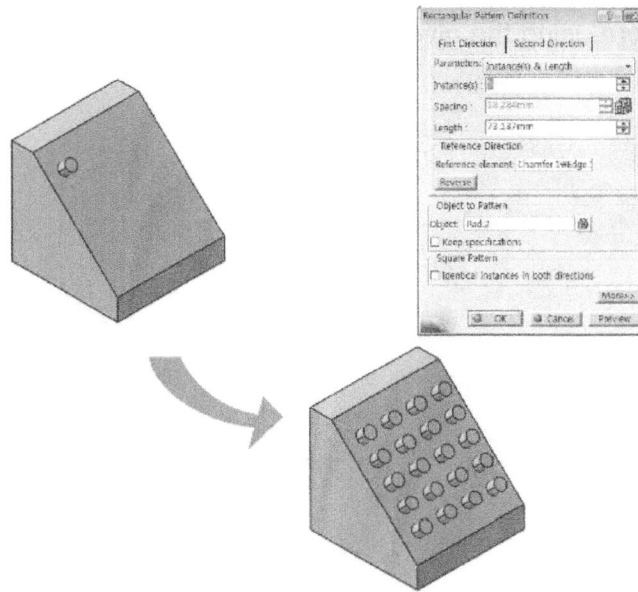

Fig 11-10 Creating a Rectangular Pattern

Parameters Option

The following types of Parameters options are available.

- **Instance(s) & Length:** Input the number of instances and total length. Spacing is calculated.
- **Instance(s) & Spacing:** Input the number of instances and spacing between instances. Total length is calculated.
- **Spacing & Length:** Input spacing between instances and total length. The number of instances are calculated.
- **Instance(s) & Unequal Spacing:** Input the number of instances and specify the spacing for each instance. You can modify the spacing by double clicking the values on the model.

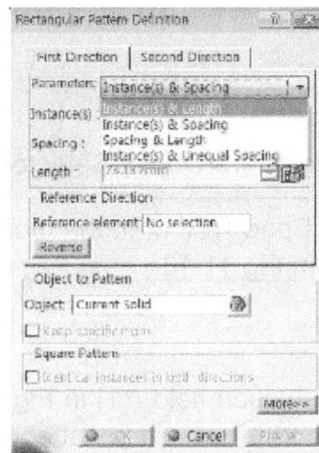

Fig 11-11 Parameters Option

309

Exercise 95: Create a rectangular pattern (ch11_001.CATPart)

Create a rectangular pattern using the given part. Note that the pattern should be centered on the chamfered surface.

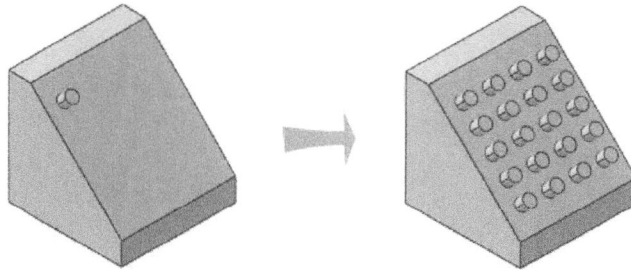

Fig 11-12 Rectangular Pattern

Executing Rec. Pattern

1. Open the given file ch11_001.CATPart.
2. Click the Rectangular Pattern icon in the Transformation Features toolbar.
3. Click the Object selection field in the Rectangular Pattern Definition dialog box.

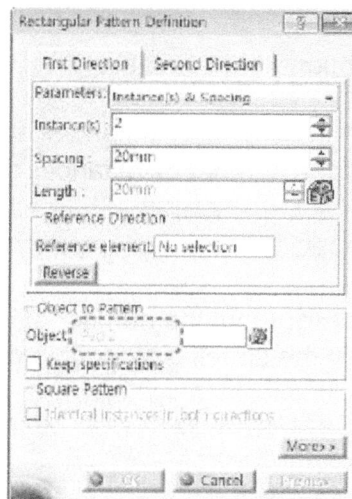

Fig 11-13 Object Selected

4. Select the Pad.2 feature in the Spec Tree or in the model. The selected object is designated in the selection field as shown in Fig 11-13.

Defining First Direction

1. Click the Reference element selection field ((1) in Fig 11-14) and select the-edge (2). Click the Reverse button if the direction of pattern is not correct.
2. Choose Instance(s) & Length in the Parameters dropdown list.
3. Enter 4 in the Instance(s) input box and 70mm in the Length input box.

310

4. Press the Tab key on the keyboard. The pattern for the first direction is previewed as shown in Fig 11-14.

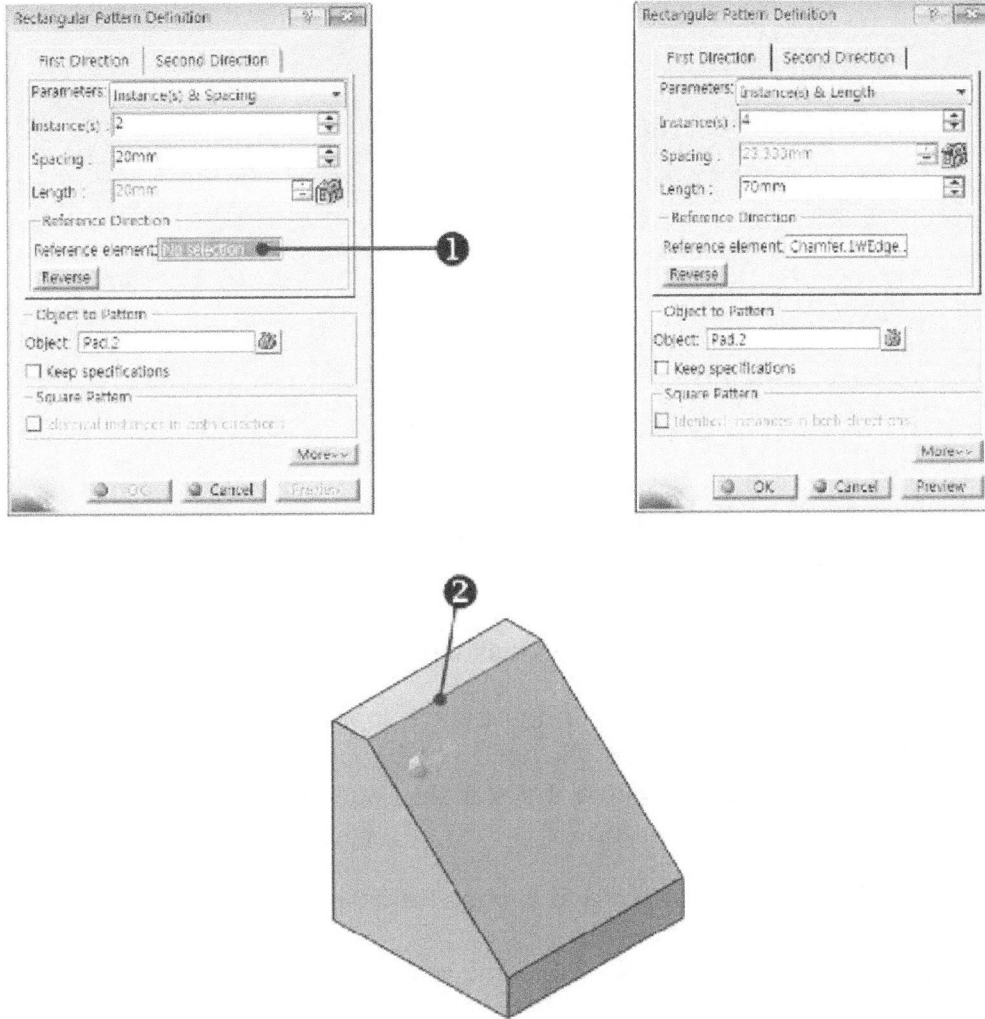

Fig 11-14 Defining First Direction

Defining Second Direction

To locate the pattern at the center along the second direction, we have to measure the length of the slanted edge and modify its value. You can do it according to the following procedure.

1. Press the Second Direction tab in the Rectangular Pattern Definition dialog box.
2. Click the Reference element field and select the edge (1) shown in Fig 11-5. Click the Reverse button if the direction of pattern is not connect.
3. Choose Instance(s) & Length .in the Parameters dropdown list.
4. Enter 5 in the Instance(s) input box.
5. Right click on the Length input box and choose Measure Item in the pop-up menu.
6. Select the edge (1), select the Keep measure option and click OK in the Measure Item dialog box.

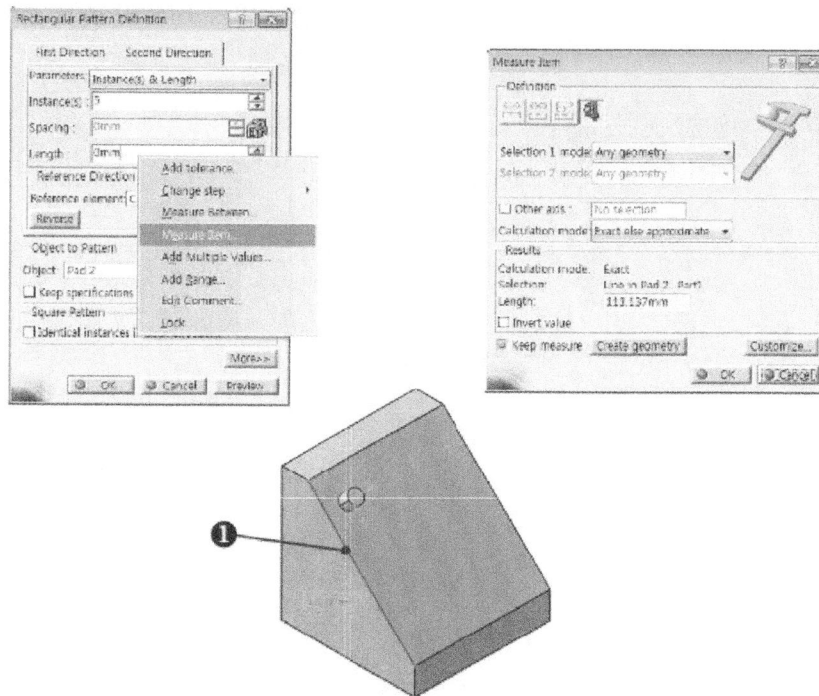

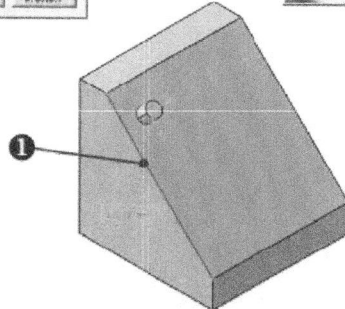

Fig 11-15 Measuring Hem

Note that the measured length is entered .in the Length input box. and the value is locked. The pattern is previewed as shown in Fig 11-16. We have to subtract 40mm from the length of the slanted edge so that the pattern is centered along the slanted edge. You can do this according to the following procedure.

1. Right click on the Length input box and choose Remove the link with measure in the pop-up me nu. Now, you can modify the value.
2. Add -40mm after the current length value and press the Tab key. The preview is updated as shown in Fig 11-18.
3. Click OK in the dialog box and hide the measured annotation in the Spec Tree.

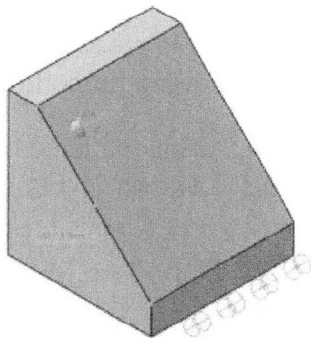

Fig 11-16 Preview

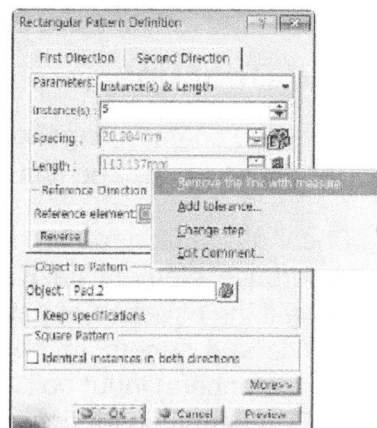

Fig 11-17 Removing Link

312

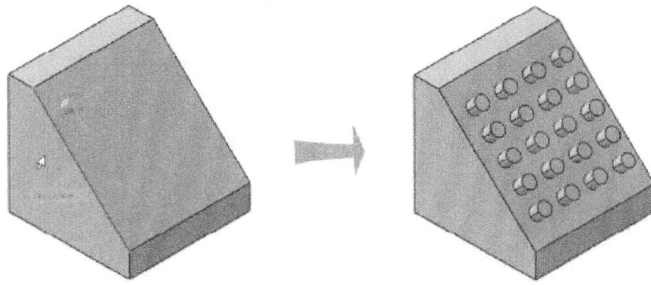

Fig 11-18 Result

Suppressing Instances

You can suppress some instances in the pattern feature by selecting the corresponding point location of the instances in the preview.

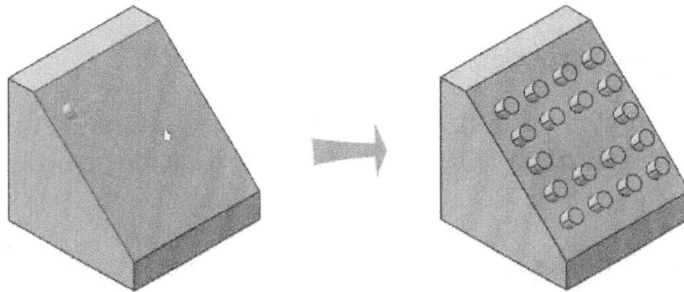

Fig 11-19 Suppressing instances

Keep Specifications

The feature creation option of the source object is applied to the instances. The pad feature shown in Fig 11-21 has been created with the Up to surface limit option and patterned.

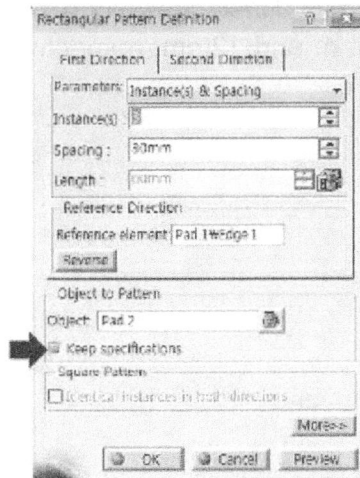

Fig 11- 20 Keep Specification Option

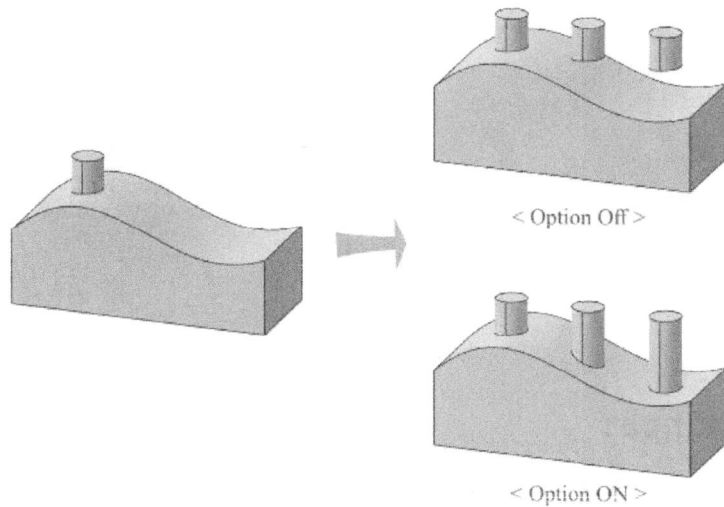

Fig 11-21 Using the Keep Specification Option

Patterning Several Features

To create a pattern of several feature(s), you can select the features in the Spec Tree in advance and click the Rectangular Pattern icon. Or, you can use the multiple selection too l beside the Object selection field.

The result of the pattern can be patterned in all but cannot be chosen together with other features.

Position of Object in Pattern Option

Press the More button in the Rectangular Pattern Definition dialog box. The dialog box is expanded, and the Position of Object in Pattern option is available. This option defines the location of the source feature among the instances of the pattern.

There is a pocket feature in Fig11-22 at the center of the base geometry. Suppose that you are creating a pattern for the pocket feature of 9 instances along the first direction and 4 instances along the second direction. Spacing is 20m m and 12mm, respectively. Fig 11-23 shows the preview of the pattern that has shifted to one side.

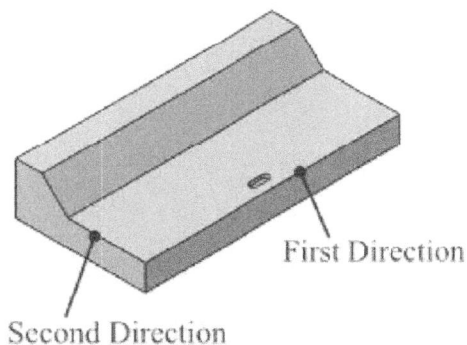

Fig 11-22 Source Feature

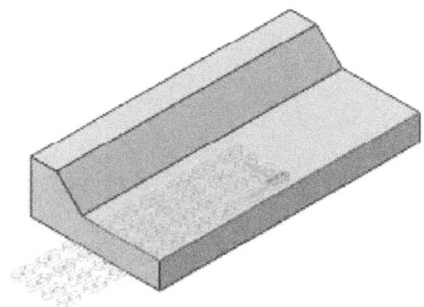

Fig 11-23 Preview of Partem

314

Press the More button in the Rectangular Pattern Definition dialog box and set the Position of Object in Pattern option as shown in Fig 11-24. A preview of the pattern is shown as in Fig 11-25. The source feature is located at a specified position among the instances of the pattern.

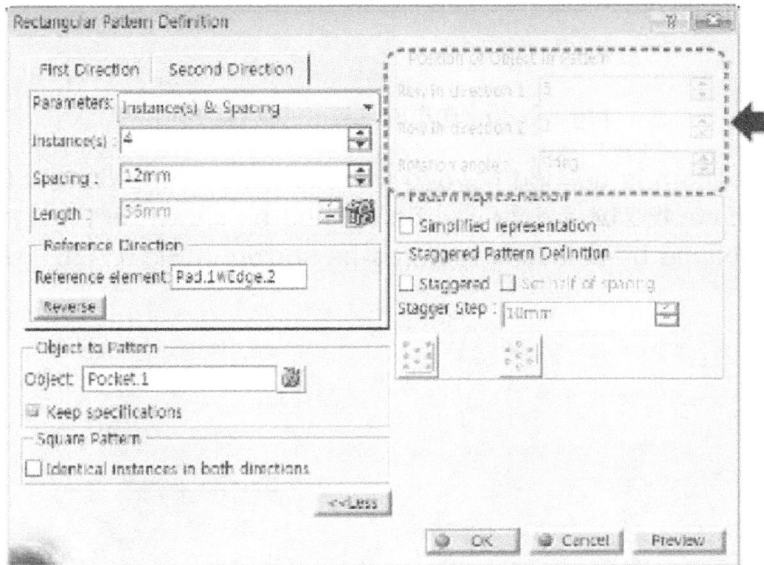

Fig 11-24 Position of Object in Pattern Option

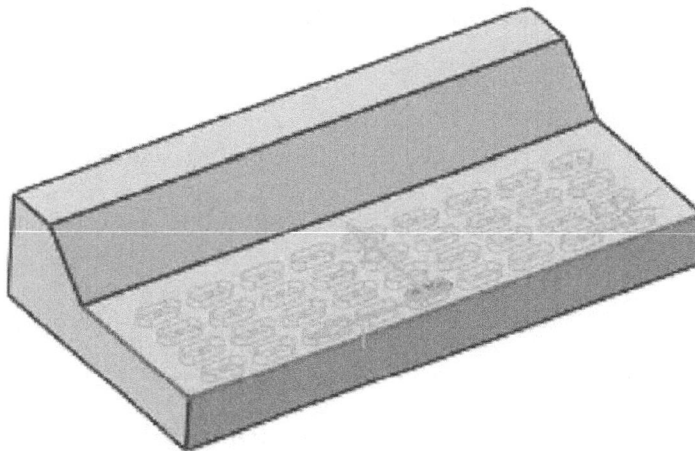

Fig 11-25 Preview of Pattern

Following cases have to be considered when you are copying features.

Dress-up features cannot be copied individually. You have to copy the parent features together that are required to define the dress-up features. If you select only a dress-up feature as the object to copy, the error message is displayed, and the current body is selected as the object.

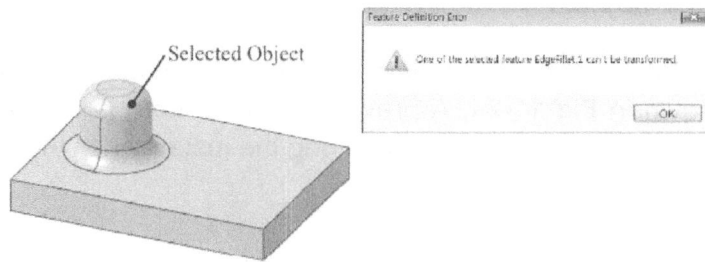

Fig 11-26 Feature Definition Error

When an instance of pattern is defined beyond the boundary of the current body the instance is created as a body in case the boundary can be defined as shown in Fig 11-27. However, if the boundary cannot be defined by selecting features as shown in Fig 11-28, you cannot create the pattern feature.

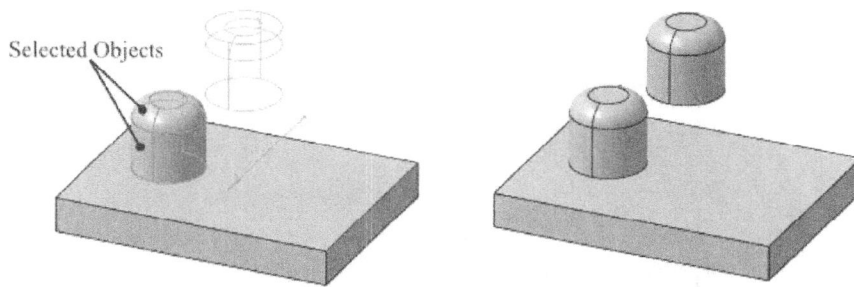

Fig 11-27 Instance out of the Boundary

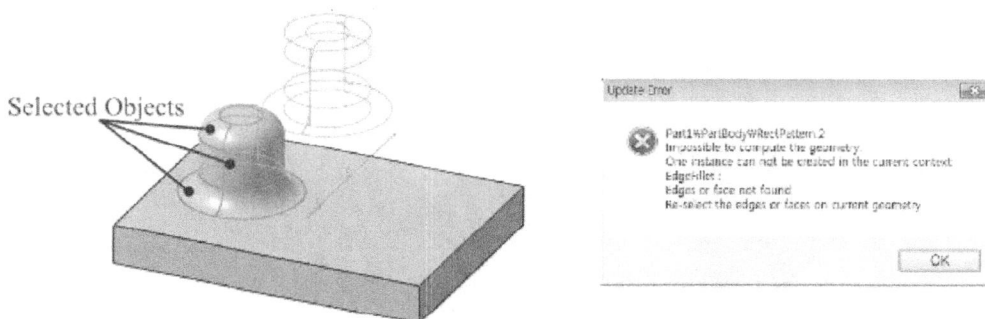

Fig 11-28 Update Error

11.4.2 Circular Pattern

You can create a pattern for features and a body by rotating about an axis.

Procedure

1. Click the Circular Pattern icon.
2. Specify the objects to copy. Note that Current Body is selected by default.
3. Select an element that will be used as the rotation axis.

4. Set other options for the pattern such as parameters, crown definition, etc.
5. Click Preview and OK

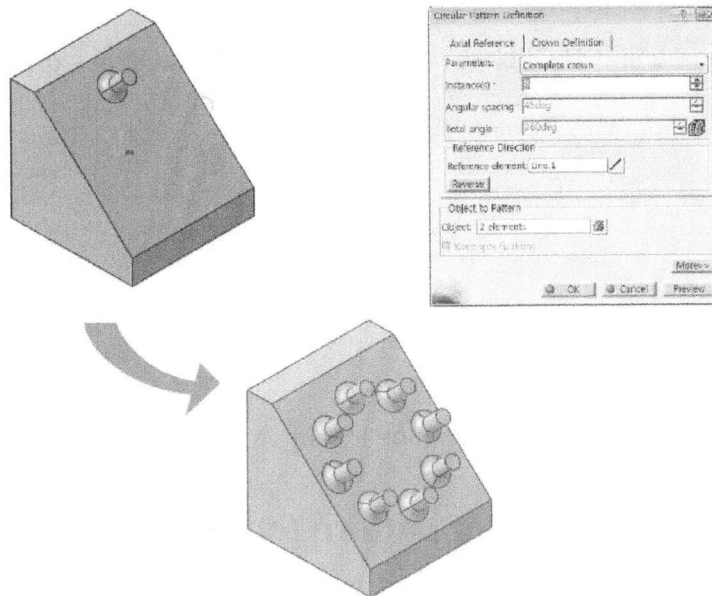

Fig 11-29 Creating a Circular Pattern

Parameters Option in the Axial Reference Tab

Instances of the circular pattern can be created along two directions. One is the circumferential direction and the other is the radial direction. A circumferential direct ion pattern can be defined in the Axial Reference tab. The following types of Parameters options are available.

- **Instance(s) & total angle:** Input the number of instances and total angle. The ang u- lar spacing is calculated.
- **Instance(s) & angular spacing:** Input the number of instances and angular spacing. The total angle is calculated.
- **Angular spacing & total angle**: Input the angular spacing and total angle. The number of instances is calculated.
- **Complete crown:** Create a specified number of instances in 360 degrees.
- **Instance(s) & Unequal angular spacing:** Input the number of instances and specify each angular spacing. You can modify the angular spacing by double clicking the values on the model.

Parameters Option in the Crown Definition Tab

A radial direction pattern can be defined in the Crown Definition tab. The following types of Parameters options are available.

- **Circle(s) & crown thickness:** Input the number of circles and thickness of the crown. The circle spacing is calculated.

317

- **Circle(s) & circle spacing:** Input the number of circles and circle spacing. The crown thickness is calculated.
- **Circle spacing & crown thickness:** Input the crown thickness and circle spacing. The number of circles is calculated.

Fig 11-30 explains the meaning of Circle Spacing and Crown Thickness graphically.

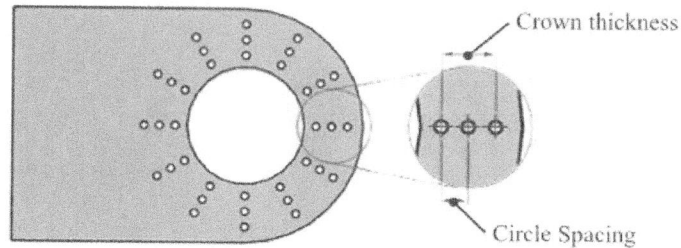

Fig 11-30 Options in Crown Definition

Exercise 95: Creating a circular pattern (ch11_002.CATPart)

Open the given file and create a circular pattern. We will define a reference line while creating the circular pattern.

Executing the Circular Pattern Command

1. Open the given file ch11_002.CATPart.
2. Select the Pad.2 and EdgcFillct.1 features in the Spec Tree.
3. Click the Circular Pattern icon in the Transformation Features toolbar.

Note that two elements are selected in the Object selection field.

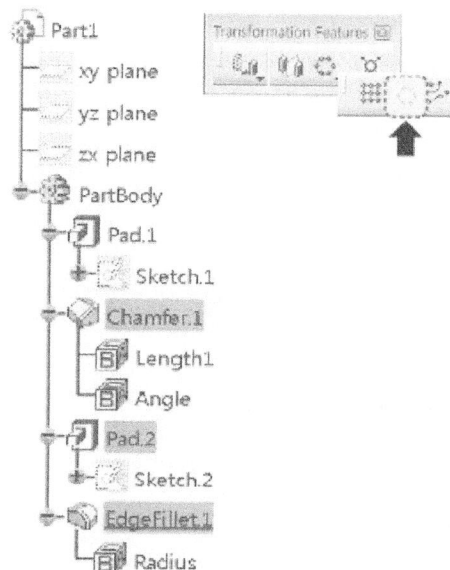

Fig 11-31 Selecting Features

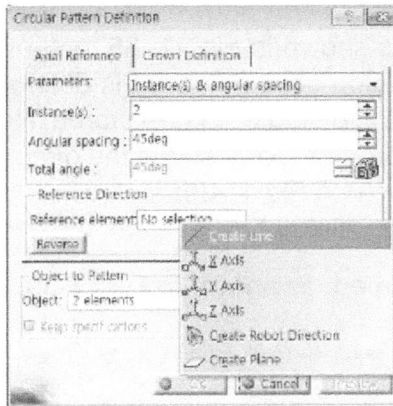

Fig 11-32 Create Line Menu

1. Right click on the Reference element selection field and choose Create Line in the pop-up menu. The Line Definition dialog box is invoked as shown in Fig 11-33.
2. Choose Point-Direction in the Line type dropdown list.
3. Right click on the Point select ion field and choose Create Point in the pop-up menu. The Point Definition dialog box is invoked as shown in Fig 11-34.

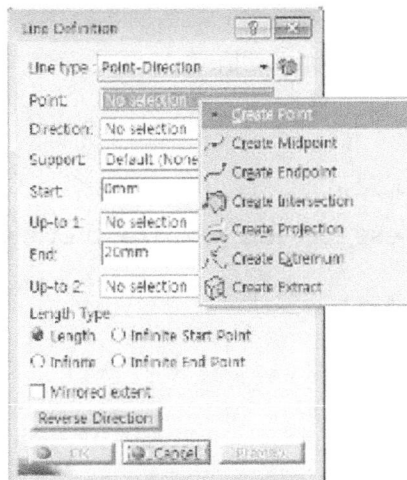

Fig 11-33 Line Definition Dialog Box

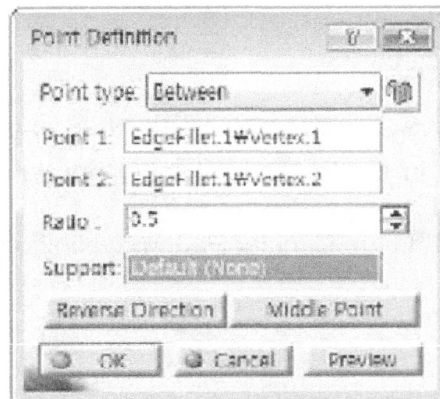

Fig 11-34 Point Definition Dialog Box

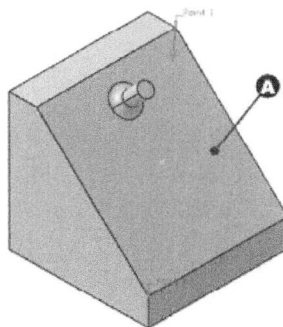

Fig 11-35 Selecting Points

319

4. Choose Between in the Point type dropdown List.
5. Select point 1 and point 2 as shown in Fig 11- 35, enter 0.5 in the Ratio input box and click OK in the Point Definition dialog box. The point is defined at the center of the two selected vertices and the Line Definition dialog box is re- stored. Note that the Direction selection field is highlighted, and you are prompt- ed to select the direction.
6. Select the face specified by (A) in Fig 11-35.
7. Click OK in the Line Definition dialog box.

Line is defined as the reference element as shown in Fig 11-36.

Fig 11-36 Reference Direction Defined

Other Options

1. Choose Complete crown in the Parameters dropdown list.
2. Enter 8 in the Instance(s) input box and press the Tab key. The preview of instances is updated.
3. Click OK in the Circular Pattern Definition dialog box.

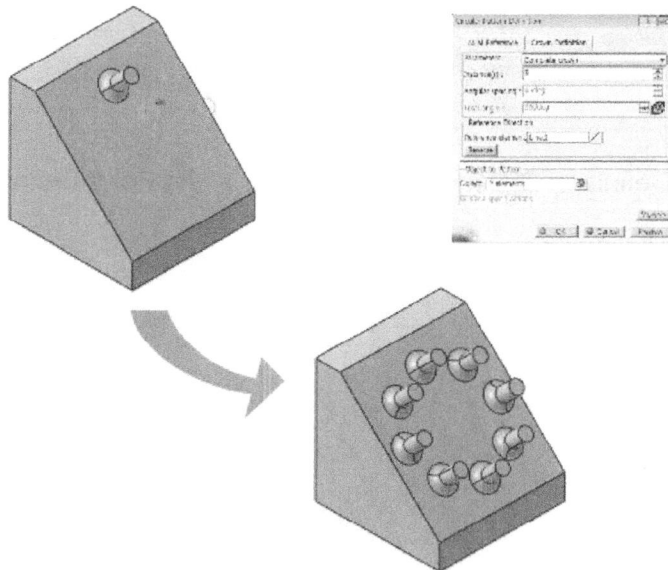

Fig 11-37 Completed Model

Exercise 96: Creating a circular pattern (ch11_003.CATPart)

Open the given part ch11_003.CATPatr and create a circular pattern as shown in Fig 11-38. Then double click the circular pattern feature and modify the Rotation of Instance(s) option so that the orientation of instances is maintained as shown in Fig 11-39.

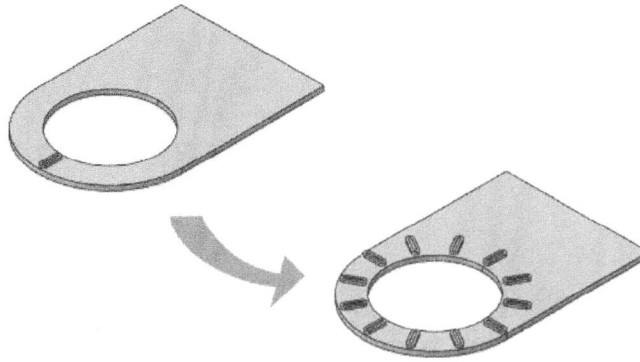

Fig 11-38 Circular Pattern

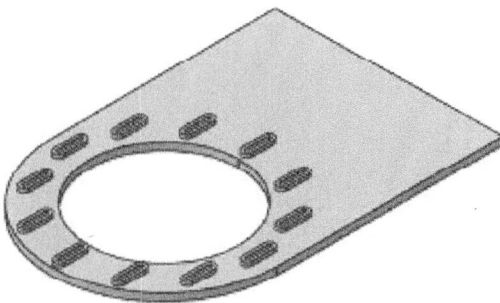

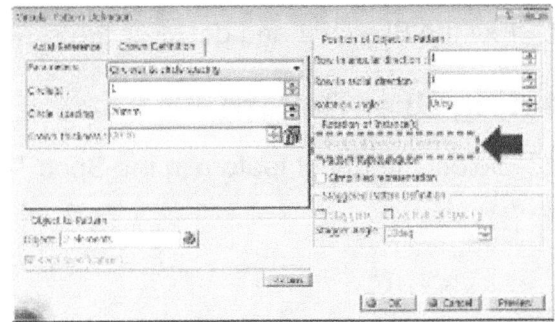

Fig 11- 39 Rotation of Instance (s) Option

11.4.3 User Pattern

The location of each instance of the pattern can be defined by a point. The po int is create d in Sketcher and constrained to a desired location.

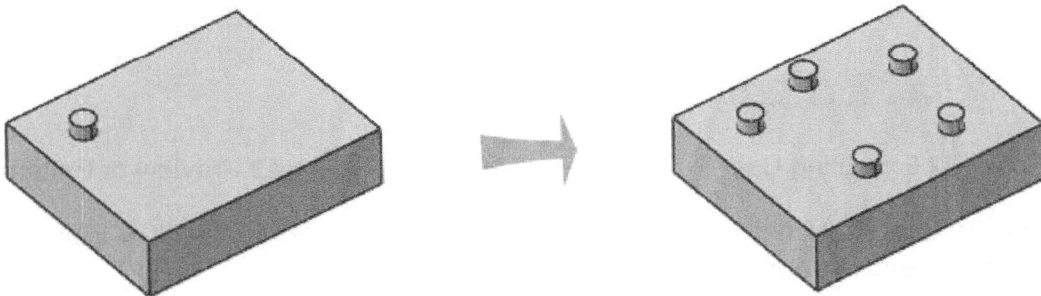

Fig 11-40 User Pattern

Exercise 97: Creating a User pattern (ch11_004.CATPart)

In this exercise, we will create a user pattern by defining the points in a sketch feature.

Creating a Sketch

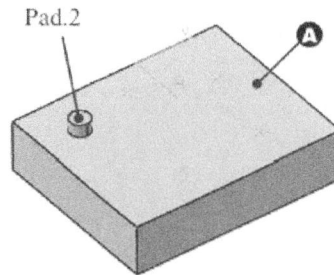

Fig 11-41 Creating a Sketch

1. Open the given file ch11_004.CATPart.
2. Define a sketch on the plane designated by (A) in Fig 11-41 and create points at an arbitrary location. Skip iso-constraining the points.
3. Exit the Sketcher and deselect the sketch.

Creating User Pattern

1. Select the Pad.2 feature in the Spec Tree.

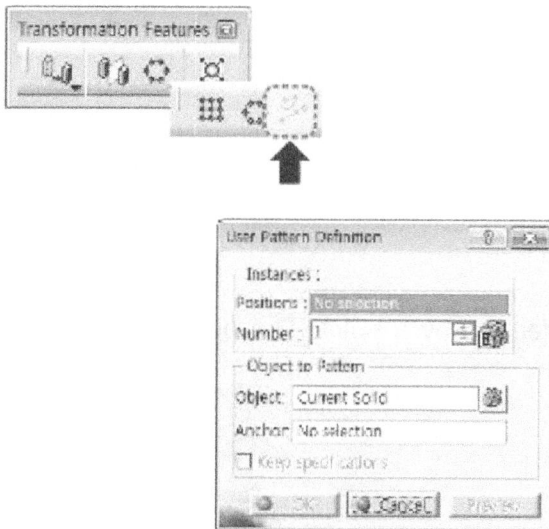

Fig 11-42 Executing User Pattern

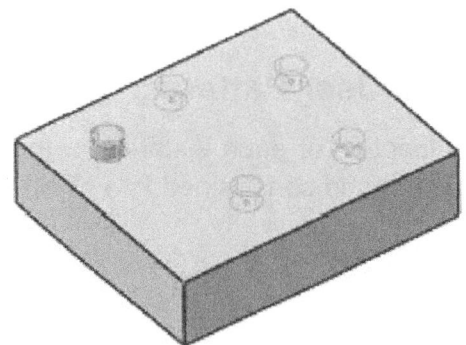

Fig 11-43 Preview of Pattern

2. Click the User Pattern icon. The Positions field is highlighted in the User Pattern Definition dialog box and you are prompted to select the sketch.
3. Select the sketch created in Fig 11-41. A preview is shown as in Fig 11-43.
4. Press the OK button.

11.5 MIRROR

You can copy features or a body reflectively against a plane. The reference plane or planar surface of the body can be used as the mirror plane.

To create a mirror for the feature(s) you have to select the features first and then press the Mirror button. Or you can click the Object field and select the feature in the Spec Tree or in the model. If you do not specify the object to pattern, the work body is mirrored.

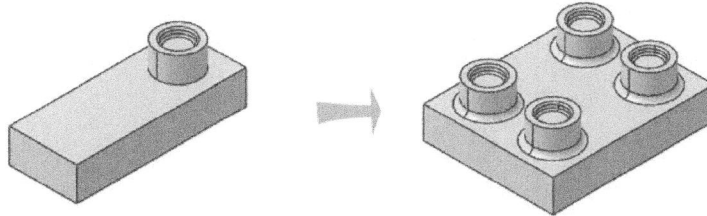

Fig 11-44 Mirror

Exercise 98: Mirroring Body and Feature (ch11_005.CATPart)

Let's create a mirror for the features and body.

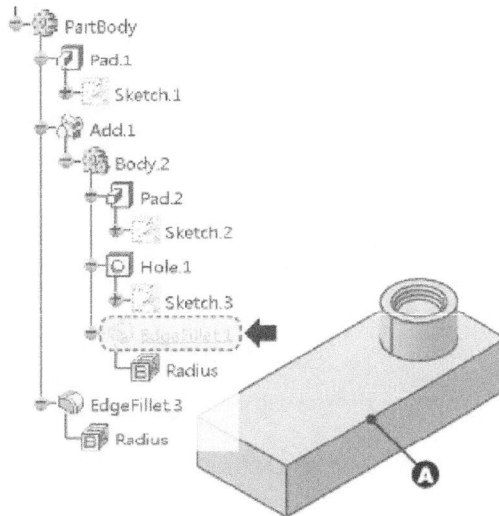

Fig 11-45 Defining in a Work Object

Mirroring Feature

1. Open the given file ch11_005.CATPart.
2. Expand the Spec Tree and define Edge Fillet. I in a work object.
3. Create a Normal to curve type reference plane at the center of the edge designated by (A) in Fig 11-45.
4. Press the Ctrl key and select the three feature in the Spec Tree as shown in Fig 11-46.
5. Click the Mirror icon.

Note that 3 elements are selected in the Object to mirror selection field in the Mirror Definition dialog box as shown in Fig 11-47. Th Mirroring element election field is highlighted and you are prompted to select a plane or a face.

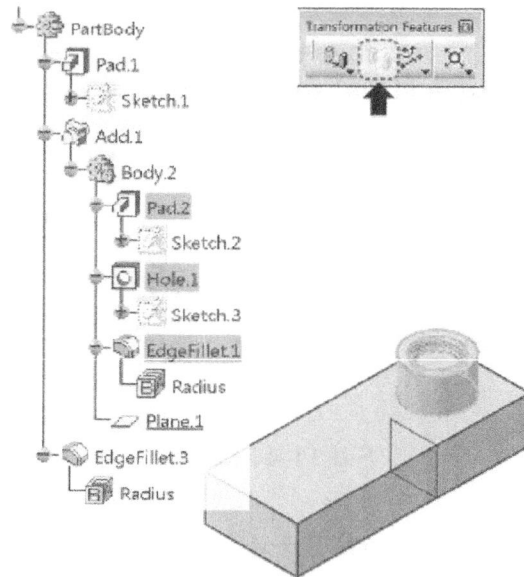

Fig 11-46 Executing Mirror

6. Select the reference plane (A) shown in Fig 11-48 as the Mirroring element.
7. Press the OK button.

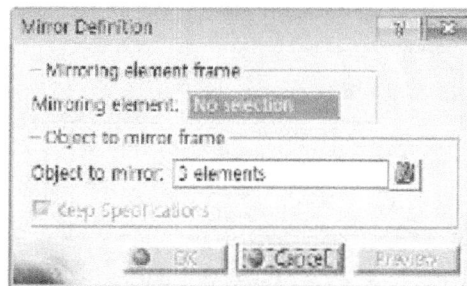

Fig 11-47 Mirror Definition Dialog Box

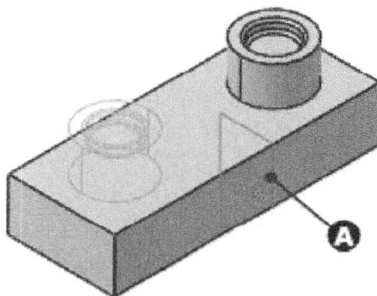

Fig 11-48 Preview

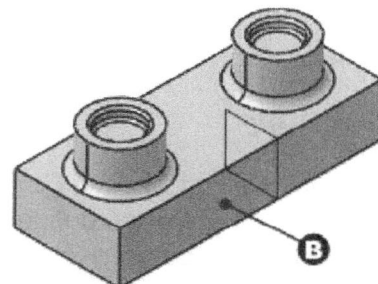

Fig 11-49 Fillet Added

Mirroring Body

1. Define the last feature in the Spec Tree in a work object.
2. Double click the EdgeFillet.3 feature and apply the fillet to the edge created by the mirror.
3. Click the Mirror icon.
4. Select the face (B) shown in Fig 11- 49.

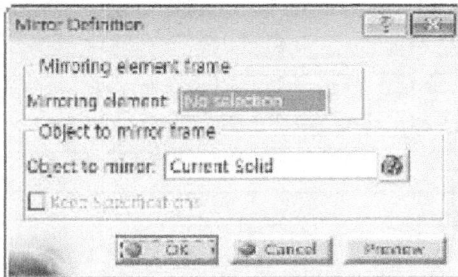

Fig 11-50 Mirror Definition Dialog Box

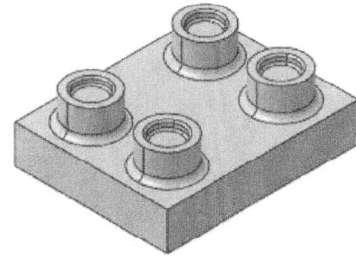

Fig 11- 51 Completed Model

Note that Current Solid is designated in the Object to mirror field in the Mirror Definition dialog box as shown in Fig 11-50. This means that a body has been selected as the source of the mirror.

5. Press the OK button.

Fig 11-51 shows the completed model.

11.6 SCALING A BODY

You can apply scale for the current body by using the Scale or Affinity command. Scaling is useful in modeling to take into account contract io n or expansion.

- **Scaling:** Uniform scaling is applied for each direction.
- **Affinity:** on-uniform scaling is applied for each direction.

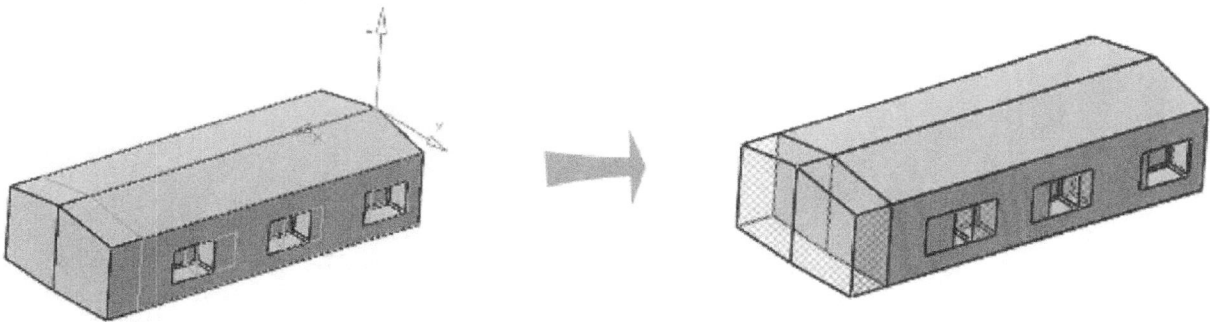

Fig 11-52 Scaling with Affinity Command (Ratio: X = 0.9, Y = 1, Z = 1)

Open the given file ch11_006.CATPart and create a rectangular pattern as shown in Fig 11- 54. The rectangular pattern has to be applied twice. One is for the feature designated by (A) and the other is for the feature (B).

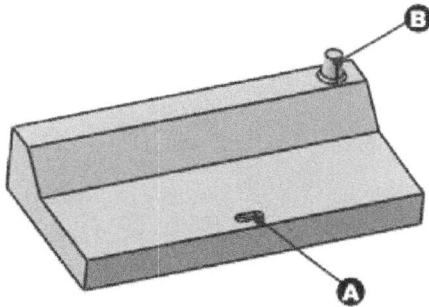

Fig 11-53 Model for Exercise

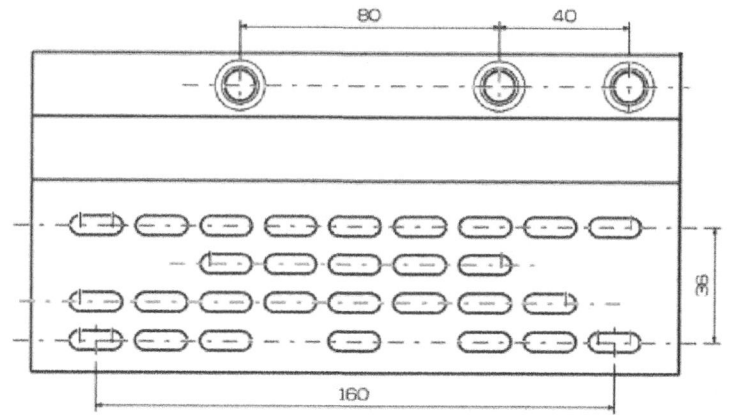

Fig 11-54 Pattern of the Features

Exercise 99: Rectangular Pattern (ch11_007.CATPart)

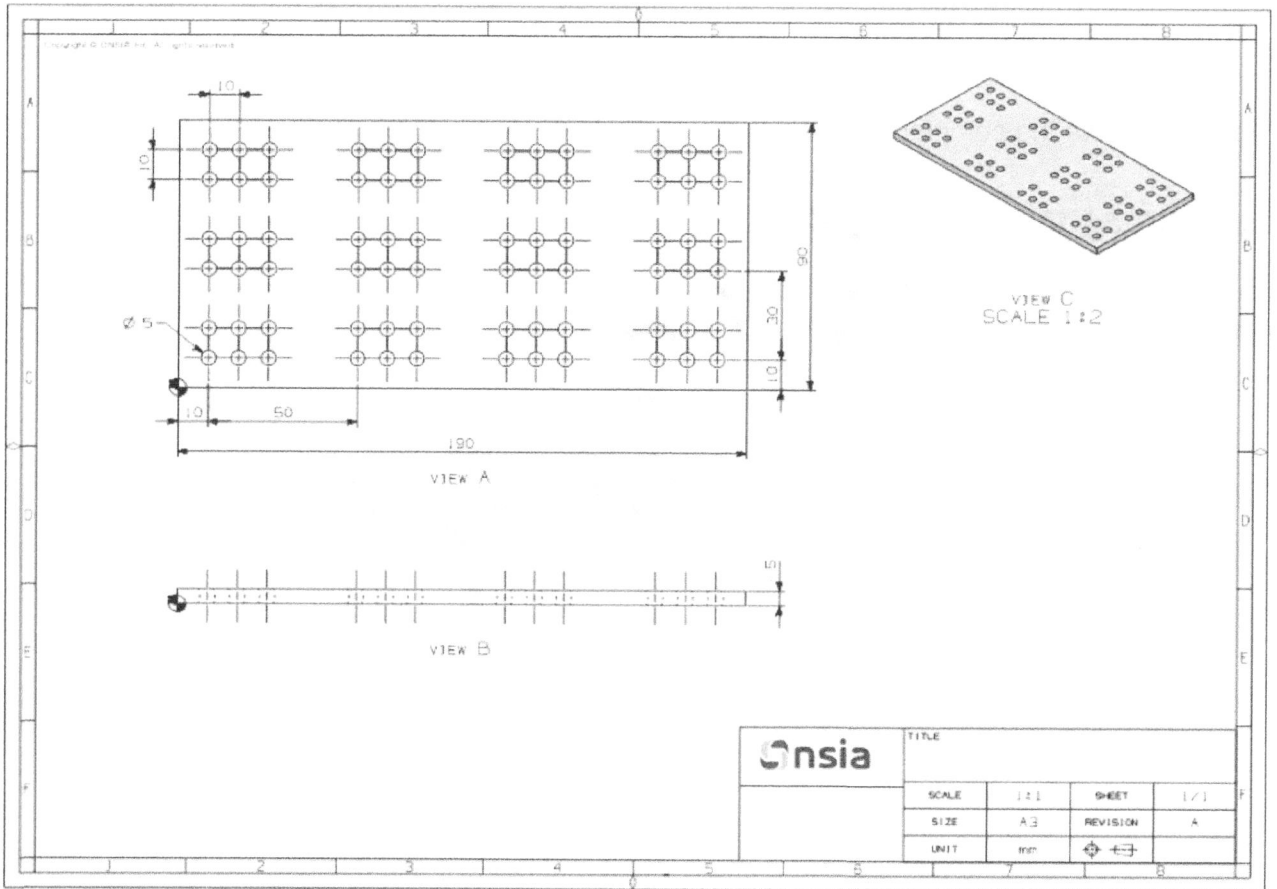

Fig 11-55 Drawing for Exercise 99

326

Exercise 100: Rectangular Pattern (ch11_008.CATPart)

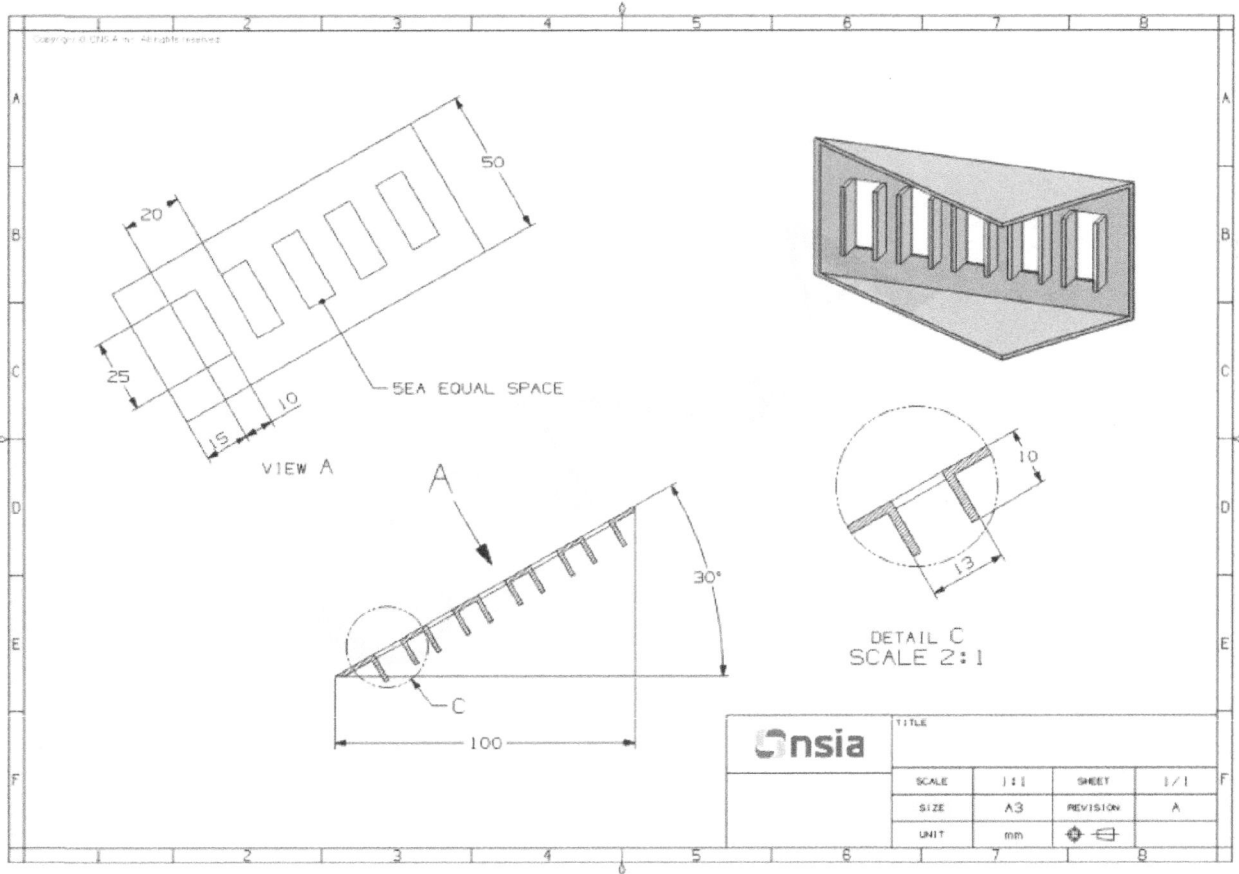

20

50

25

15   10

5EA EQUAL SPACE

VIEW A

A

30°

100

C

DETAIL C
SCALE 2:1

10

13

Onsia

TITLE				
SCALE	1:1	SHEET	1/1
SIZE	A3	REVISION	A
UNIT	mm		

Fig 11-56 Drawing for Exercise 100

327

Exercise 101: Rectangular Pattern (ch11_009.CATPart)

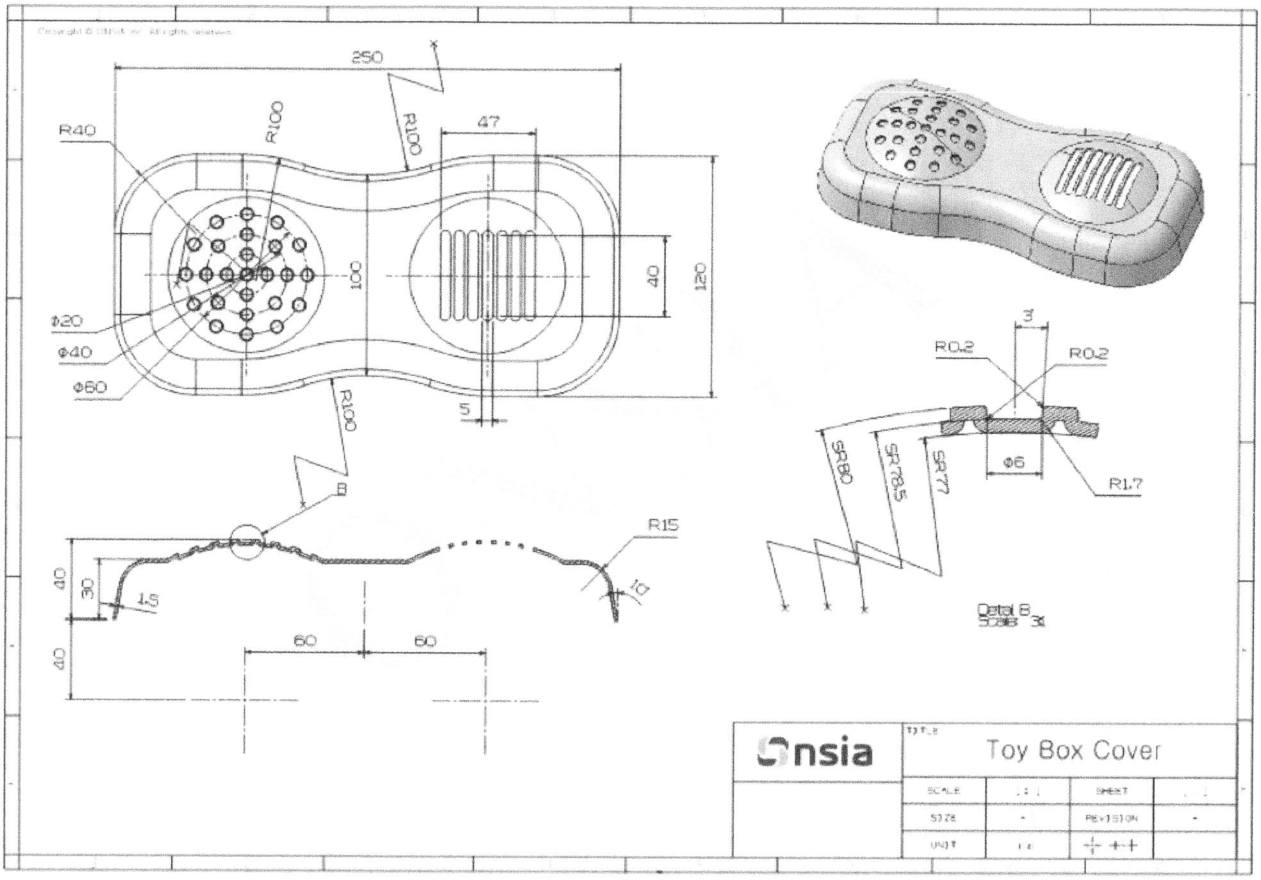

Fig 11-57 Toy Box Cover

Exercise 102: Fan Motor Cover (ch11_010.CATPart)

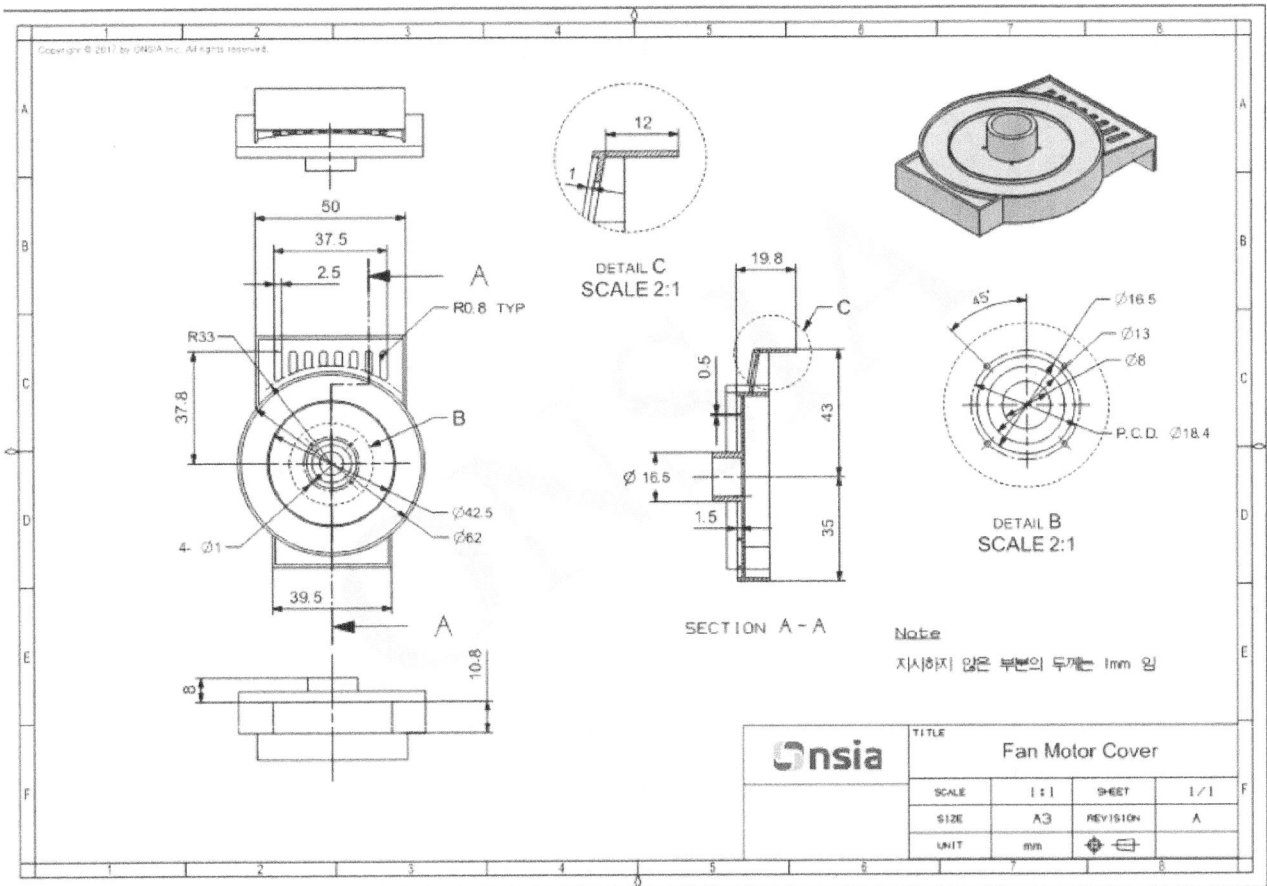

Fig 11-58 Fan Motor Cover

Exercise 103: Lampshade (ch11_011.CATPart)

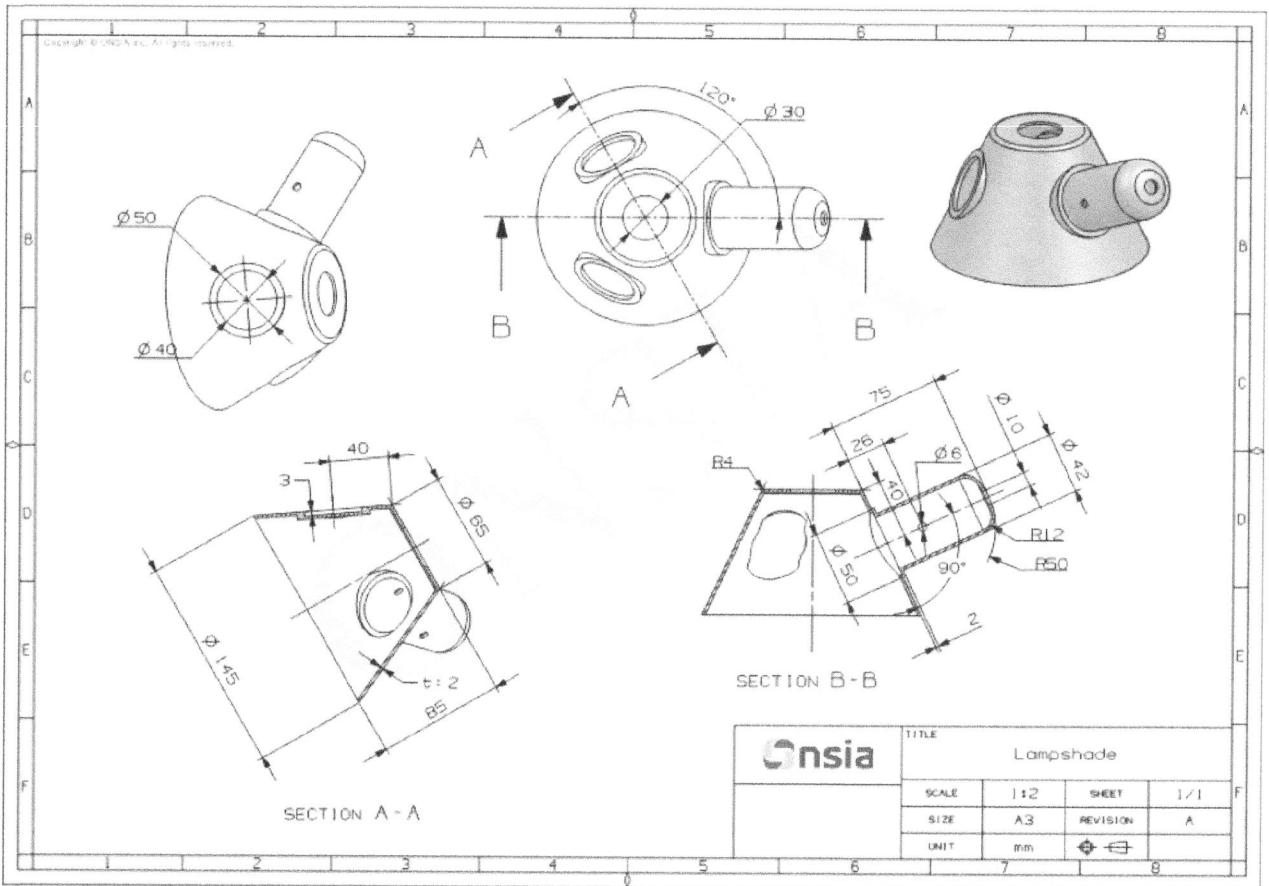

Fig 11-59 Lampshade

CHAPTER 12: COMPLEX SKETCH- BASED FEATURES: BEYOND THE BASICS

12.1 STIFFENER

A stiffener is created in a weak region of a part to resist against loading. In CATIA V5, you can create a stiffener conveniently using the Stiffener command in the Sketch- Based Features tool bar.

Create a sketch where you will create a stiffener and click the Stiffener icon in the Sketch- Based Features toolbar. You can use either the whole sketch curves or the sub-element of the sketch. Note that when you are using an open profile, the extension of the profile has to meet the part geometry.

Two modes are available for creating a stiffener feature.

> (1) From Side Mode.

> (2) From Top Mode.

12.1.1 From Side Mode

Apply thickness normal to the sketch plane and extrude the profile up to the existing geometry along a specified direction. If the extrusion of the profile does not meet the geometry, you cannot create the stiffener feature.

Procedure

1. Create a sketch on a plane normal to the thickness direction.
2. Click the Stiffener icon in the Sketch-Based Features toolbar.
3. Select the From Side mode in the Stiffener Definition dialog box.
4. Select the sketch and set the thickness and direction option.
5. Click OK in the dialog box.

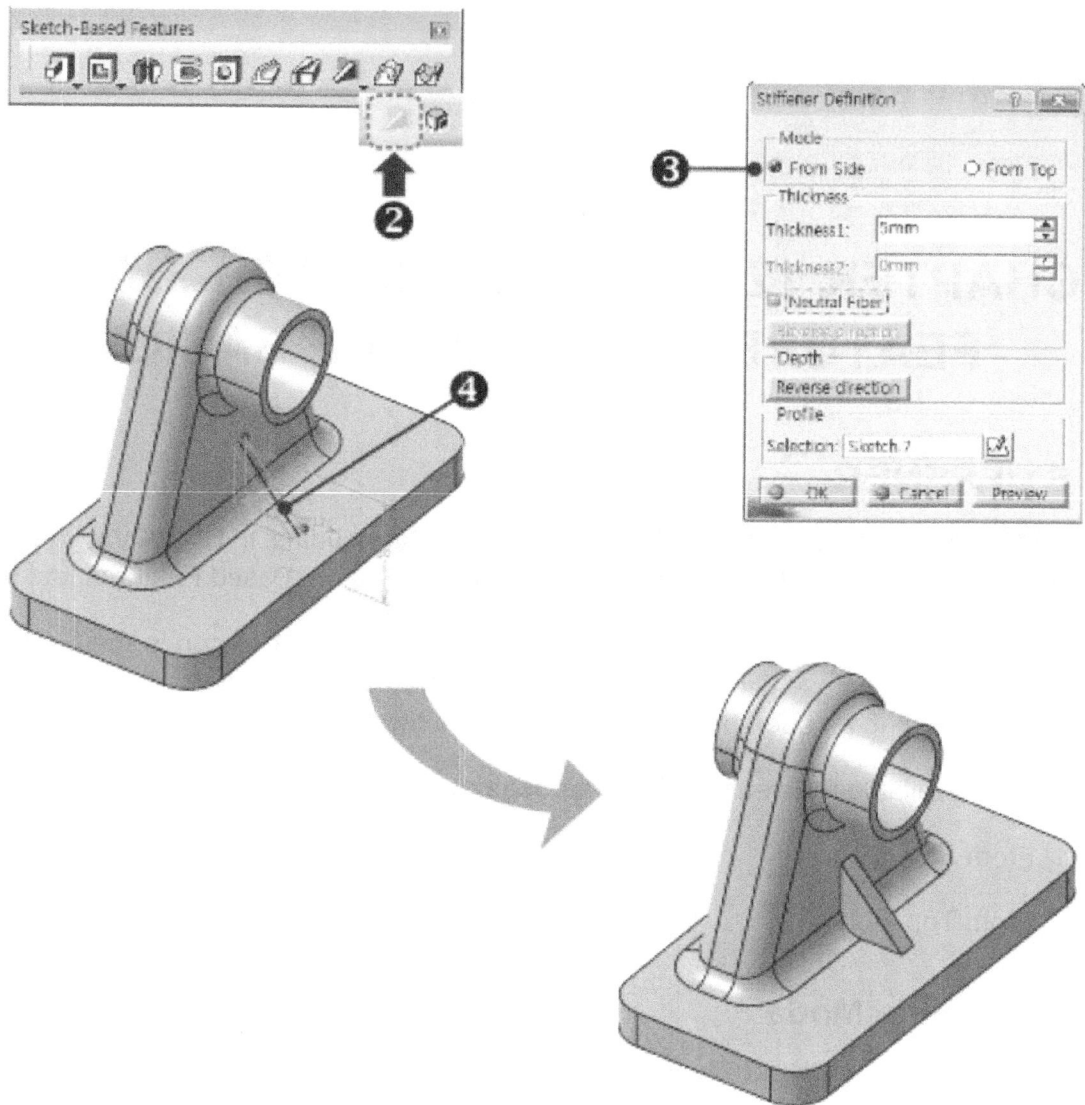

Fig 12-1 Creating Stiffener (From Side Mode)

12.1.2 From Top Mode

Apply thickness parallel to the sketch plane and extrude the profile up to the existing geometry along a specified direction. If the extrusion of the profile does not meet the geometry, you cannot create the stiffener feature.

Procedure

1. Create a sketch on a plane normal to the extrusion direction.
2. Click the Stiffener icon in the Sketch-Based Features toolbar.
3. Select the From Top mode in the Stiffener Definition dialog box.
4. Select the sketch and set the thickness and direction option.
5. Click OK in the dialog box.

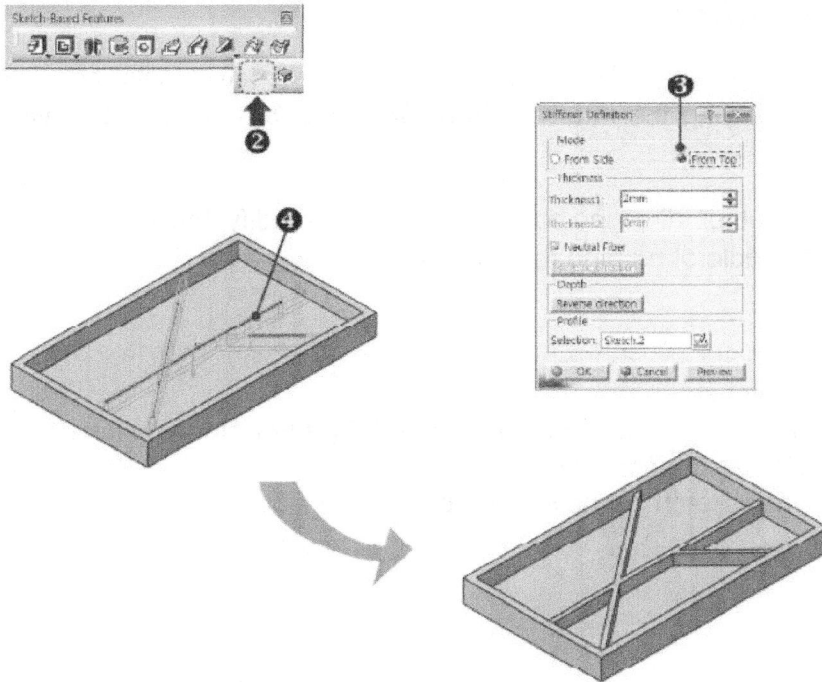

Fig 12-2 Creating Stiffener (From Top Mode)

Exercise 104: Creating Stiffener (ch12_001.CATPart)

Open the given file ch12_001.CATPart and create a stiffener as shown in Fig 12-3.

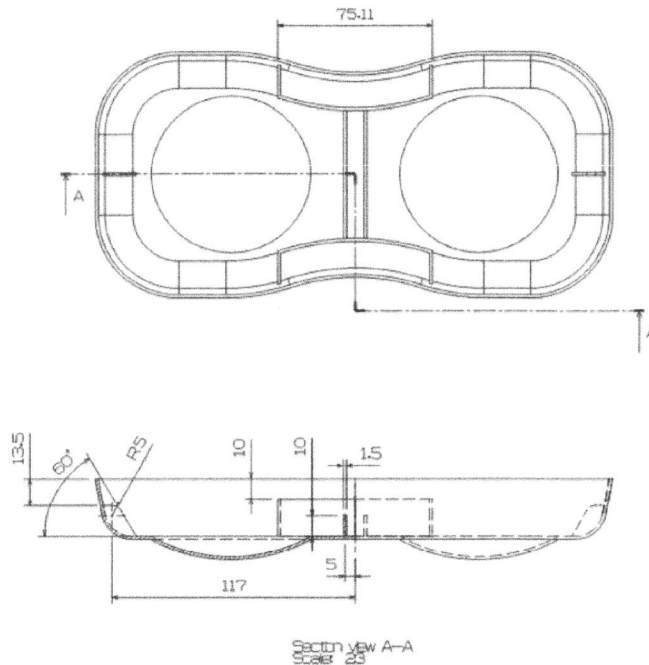

Section view A–A
Scale: 2:3

Fig 12-3 Creating Stiffener

12.2 SOLID COMBINE

This command extrudes two profiles and creates an intersection solid body. You can obtain the same geometry by applying the Intersect Boolean operation between the two bodies created by padding each profile.

You can specify the other direction for extrusion and modify the sketch dimensions by double clicking them in the middle of running the command.

Procedure

1. Create two sketches.
2. Click the Solid Combine icon in the Sketch-Based Features toolbar.
3. Select a sketch as the first profile.
4. Select the other sketch as the second profile.
5. Click OK.

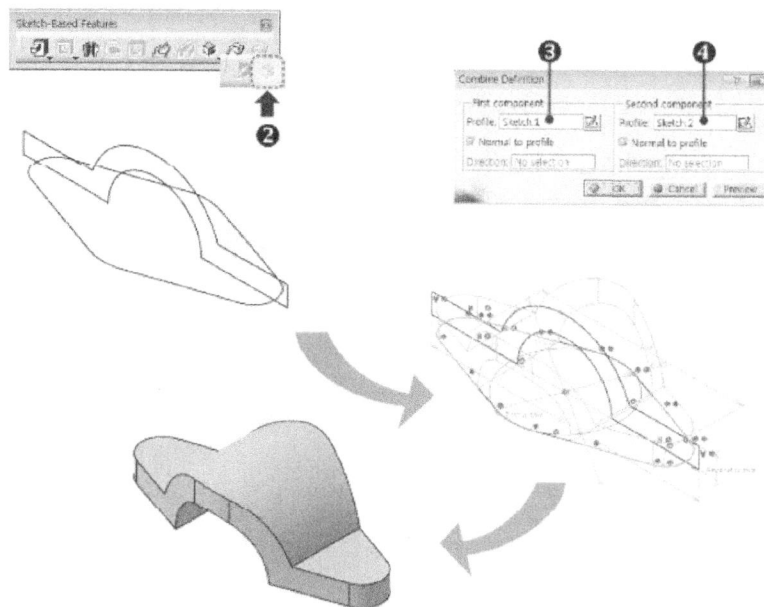

Fig 12-4 Creating a Combined Body

1.2.3 Rib

This command creates a solid body by sweeping a profile along a center curve.

Procedure

1. Create sketches that will be used for the center curve and for the profile.
2. Click the Rib icon in the Sketch-Based Features toolbar.
3. Select the profile.
4. Select the center curve.
5. Set the options and press OK.

Using the Sketch button next to the Profile and Center curve select ion field in the Rib Definition dialog box, you can create each sketch.

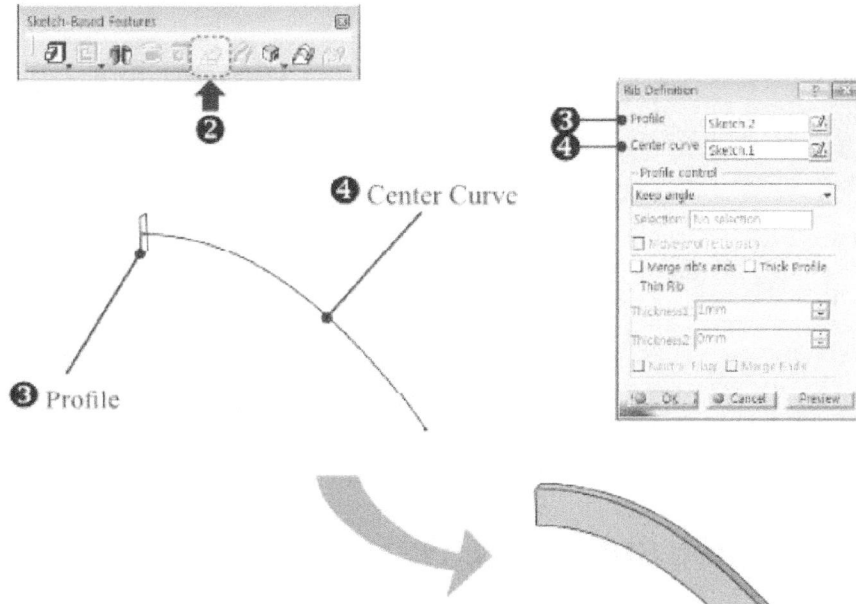

Fig 12-5 Creating a Rib Feature (Keep angle Option)

12.3.1 Keep Angle Option

Using the dropdown list in the Profile control option area, you can specify the direction of the profile. If you select Keep angle in the dropdown list, the profile is swept maintaining the angle between the profile and the tangent direction of the center curve.

When you create a sketch for a profile, it is recommended to define the Normal to curve type plane on the center curve and use the plane as the sketch support.

12.3.2 Pulling Direction Option

You can specify the pulling direction when you create a solid body sweeping a profile. As the angle between the pulling direction and the sketch support is maintained, the section area and shape is the same throughout the center curve.

A typical example of using this option is sweeping a sect ion along a spiral center curve. In this case, you have to set the pulling direction along the spiral center axis to maintain the action and orientation of the profile.

When you specify the pulling, you can select an edge, curve or plane. If you select a plane, the normal vector of the plane is designated as the pulling direction. Fig 12-6 shows an example of specifying the pulling direction as the xz plane. Note that the angle between the yz plane, which is nom1al to the xz plane, and the profile plane is the same at the be- ginning and at the end of the center curve.

335

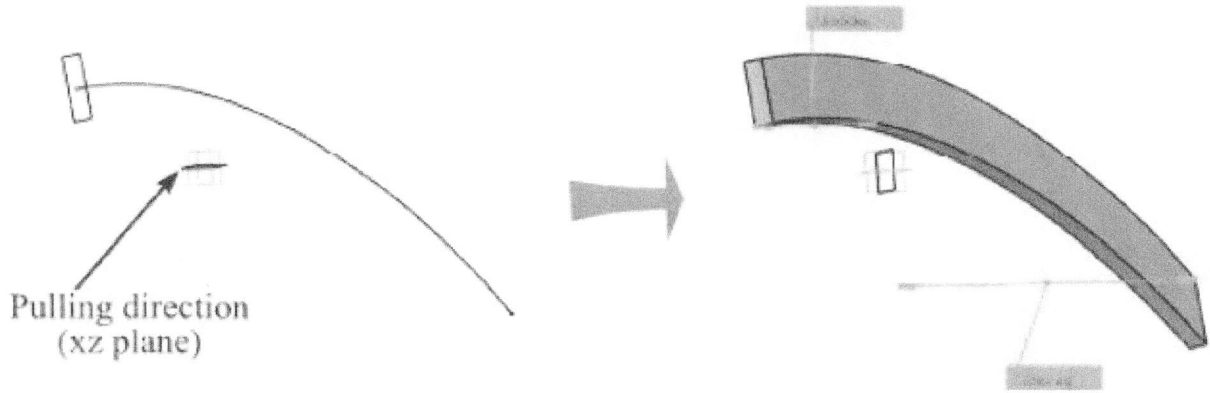

Fig 12-6 Specifying Pulling Direction

Exercise 105: Creating Stiffener (ch12_002.CATPart)

Open the given part ch12_002.CATPart and create a spring as shown in Fig 12-8. Choose an appropriate profile control option to obtain a desired result.

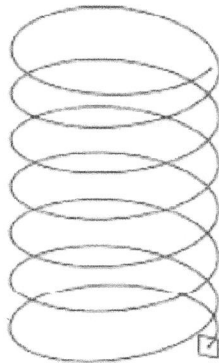

<Not Good>

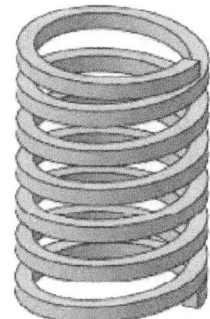

<Good>

Fig 12-7 Given Part

Fig 12-8 Spring

12.3.3 Reference Surface Option

If you select Reference surface as the Profile control option, the orientation of the sweep section can be controlled with reference to the designated surface. The angle be- tween the profile and the reference surface is maintained.

Note also that the Move profile to path option is activated when you are using the Reference Surface option.

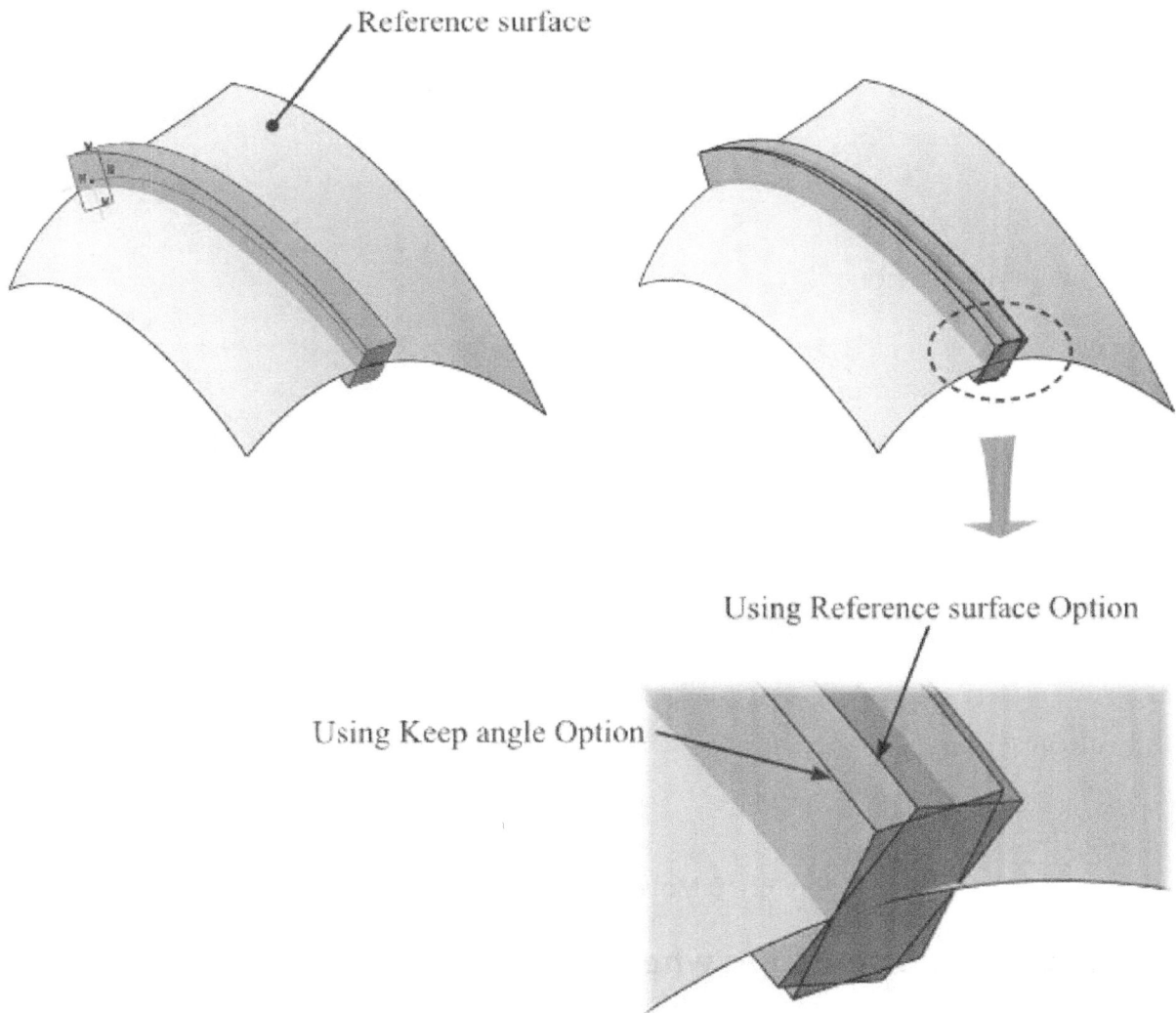

Reference surface

Using Reference surface Option

Using Keep angle Option

Fig 12-9 Reference Sur face Option

12.3.4 Move Profile to Path Option

When you have selected Reference surface or the Pulling direction option in the Profile control dropdown list, the Move profile to path option is activated.

Procedure

1. Click the Rib icon in the Sketch-Based Features toolbar.
2. Select a profile sketch.
3. Select a reference curve.
4. Click OK in the error message box.
5. Choose Reference surface as a profile control option and select a reference surface. Click OK if the error message box is encountered.
6. Check the Move profile to path option and click the blue arrow to reverse the direc tion.
7. Confirm the preview and press OK.

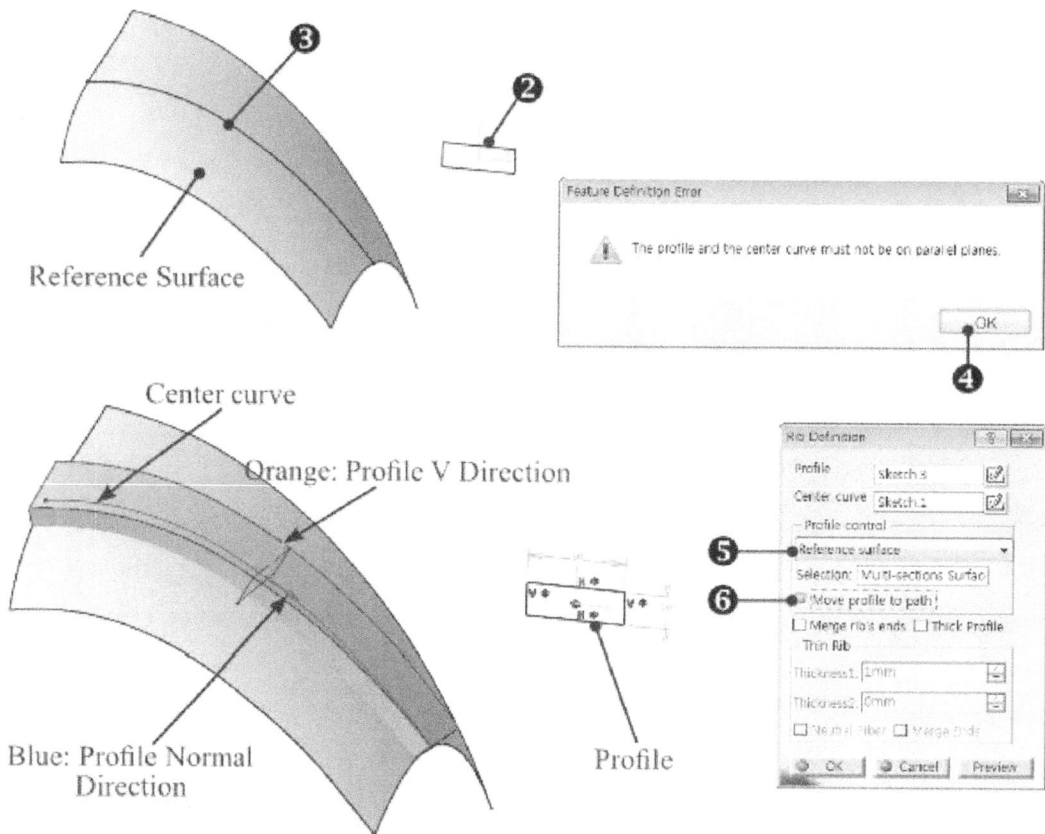

Reference Surface

Center curve

Orange: Profile V Direction

Blue: Profile Normal
Direction

Profile

Fig 12-10 Move Profile to Path Option

Rules of Section Orientation when the Profile is Moved

1. V direction of the profile is aligned to the orange arrow shown in the preview. The orange arrow can be either the normal direction of the reference surface or the pulling direction.
2. Local origin of the profile is swept along the center curve.
3. Normal direct ion of the profile is aligned to the blue arrow. The blue arrow is the tangent direction of the center curve.

12.3.5 Condition of Profile and Center Curve

The center curve can be closed or open, planar or non-planar. When you use a non-planar center curve, it has to be tangent continuous. Availability of the profile is determined by the condition of the center curve. The following table summarizes the usage of the Rib command according to the condition of the center curve and profile.

Closed Profile: Output geometry is always solid.

Open Profile:

- **Closed Center curve:** Thick Profile option has to be checked.
- **Open Center curve:**

338

- Thick Profile option is required for the first rib feature.
- Solid geometry can be created for the second or later features by specifying a proper Material side option.

(Note) Using Several Discontinuous Curve as the Center Curve

When you are using the Move profile to path option, you can create a rib feature along several discontinuous curves that are defined in a single sketch. Each rib feature is created as a respective solid geometry.

Exercise 106: Creating Flange Geometry (ch12_003.CATPart)

Using the given part ch12_003.CATPart, create a flange geometry as shown in Fig 12-11.

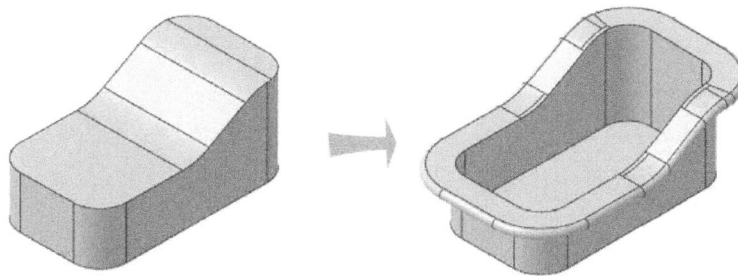

Fig 12-11 Container with Flange

1. Open the given file ch12_003.CATPart.
2. Define a sketch on the yz plane and create an inter sect ion point with the edge O as shown in Fig 12-12. Convert the point into a construction element.
3. Create a sketch as shown in Fig 12- 12 and exit the sketch.

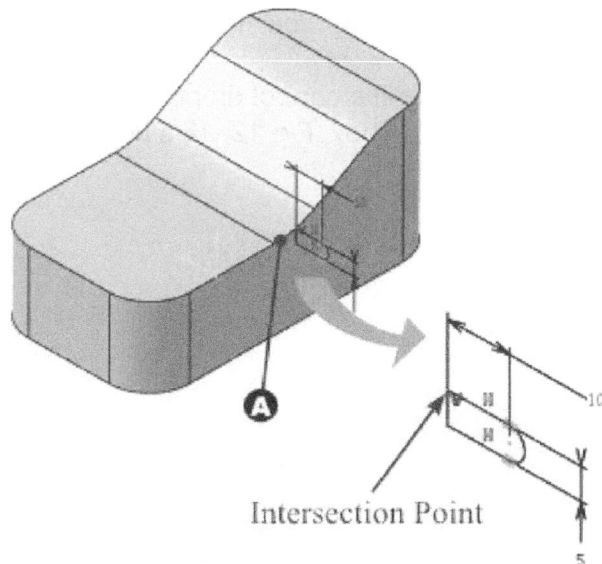

Intersection Point

Fig 12-12 Sketch for Profile

4. Click the Rib icon in the Sketch- Based Features toolbar and select the sketch as the profile.
5. Right click on the Center curve se- lection field and choose Create Extract in the pop-up menu ((A) in Fig 12-13).
6. Select the edge (B) shown in Fig 12 -14.   Note that the propagation type in the Extract Definition dialog box is Tangent continuity.

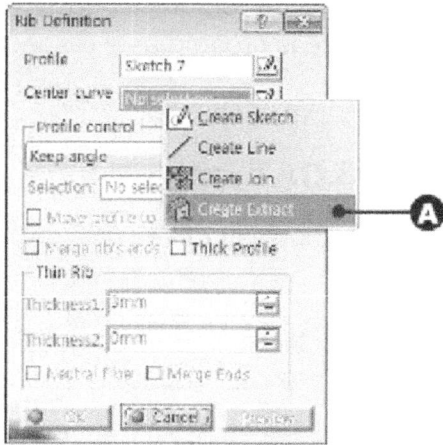

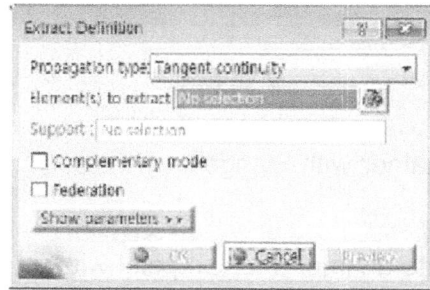

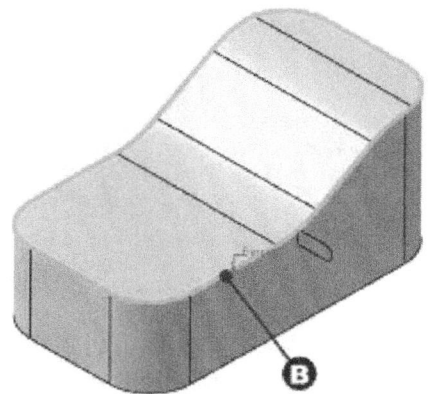

Fig 12-13 Extract Menu

Fig 12-14 Extracting Edge

7. Click OK in the Extract Definition dialog box. The rib feature is previewed as shown in Fig 12-15.
8. Choose Pulling direction in the Pro-file control dropdown list and select the xy plane.
9. Click OK in the Rib Definition dialog box. Fig 12- 16 s how s the mode l after creating the rib feature.

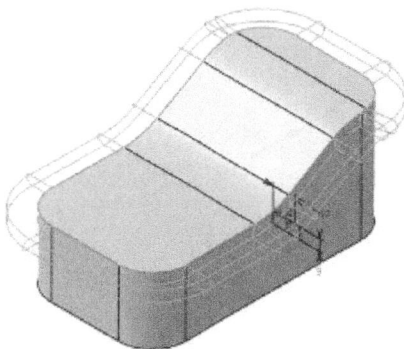

Fig 12-15 Preview

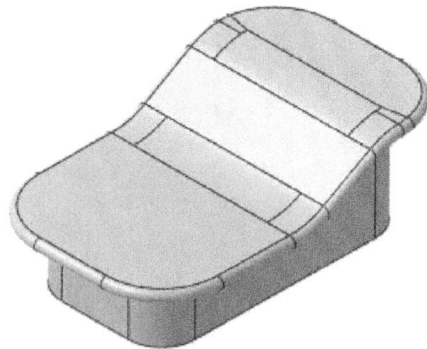

Fig 12-16 Result of Rib

10. Define a sketch on the bottom plane of the model.
11. Click the Project 3D Elements icon and create the projected curves as the construction elements by selecting the face (C) designated in Fig 12-17.

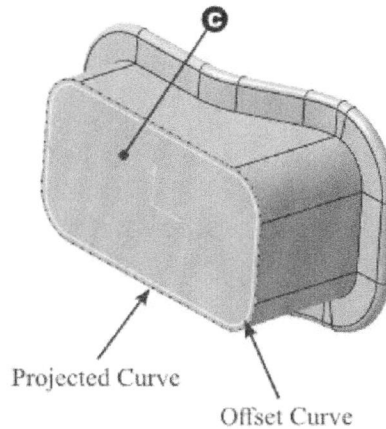

Fig 12-17 Creating a Sketch

12. Click the Offset icon and select the projected curves so that it is offset 3mm inward.
13. Convert the offset curves into the standard elements.
14. Exit the sketch and create a pocket feature as shown in Fig 12-18. Thickness for the bottom is 3mm.

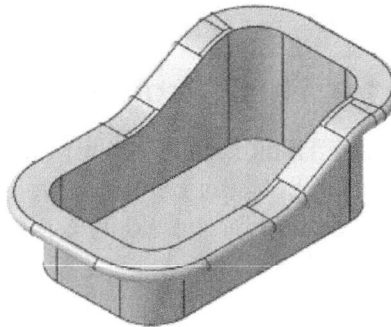

Fig 12- 18 Completed Model

(Note) Popup menu for Profile and Center Curve Selection Field

A pop-up menu is used for the following purposes.

- **Create Join:** Selects individual but connected curves or faces as a single object.
- **Extract:** Extracts faces from a solid or curves from a solid or surface and selects them as the profile or center curve.

12.3.6 Merge Ribs Ends Option

You can extend or trim the ends of a rib feature up to the existing geometry. Note that the ends of the feature have to be enclosed by the existing part geometry.

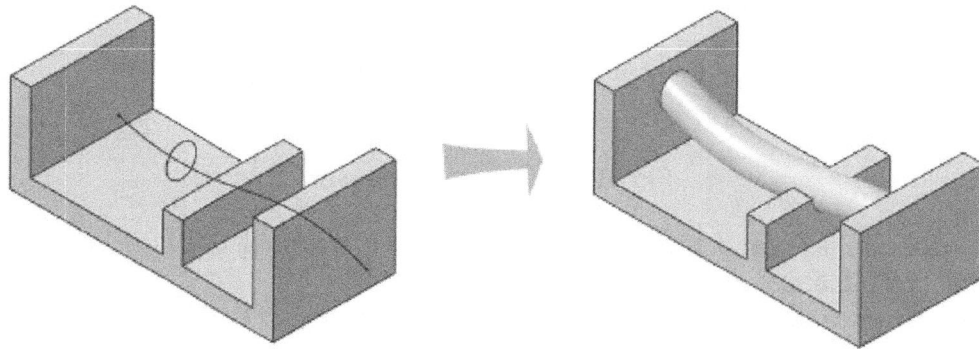

Fig 12-19 Merge Rib's Ends Option

12.3.7 Merge Ends Option for Thick Profile

When you create a rib feature with the Thick Profile option turned on, you can extend or trim the feature up to the existing geometry along both the center curve and profile. Note that the extension or trimming of the feature has to be enclosed by the existing part geometry.

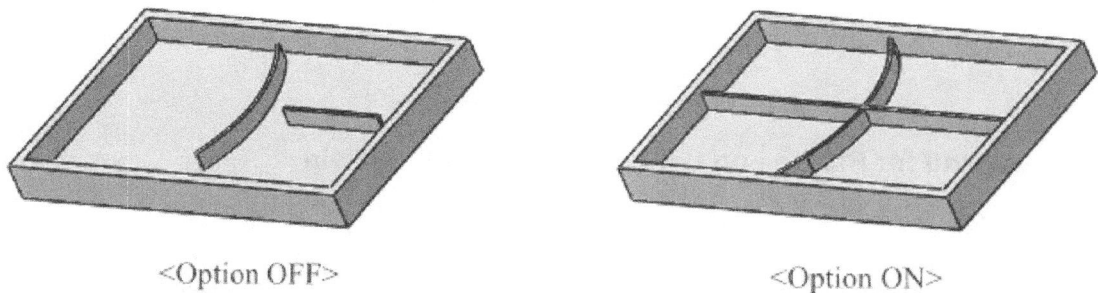

<Option OFF>   <Option ON>

Fig 12–20 Using Merge Ends Option

12.4 SLOT

You can remove material by sweeping a profile along a center curve. Options and usage of the Slot command is the same as those of the Rib command. Fig 12-21 shows a slot feature.

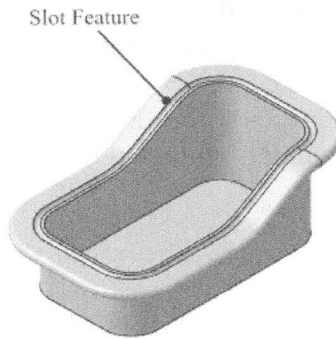

Fig 12-21 Slot Feature

12.5 MULTI SECTIONS SOLID

You can create a solid geometry by connecting several sections. The conditions and requirements for the major constituent are as follows.

1. **Section:** It has to be defined on a planar face and closed. Sections cannot intersect with each other. Each section has to be defined as an individual feature, i.e., individual sketch or curve.
2. **Guide:** It defines the connection method between sections. It has to pass through the intersect ion point with the sections.
3. **Spine:** It defines the orientation of the section. The spine has to be tangent and continuous. If you do not define a spine explicitly, it is computed automatically.

Exercise 107: Creating a Multi-Sections Solid (ch12 _004.CATPart)

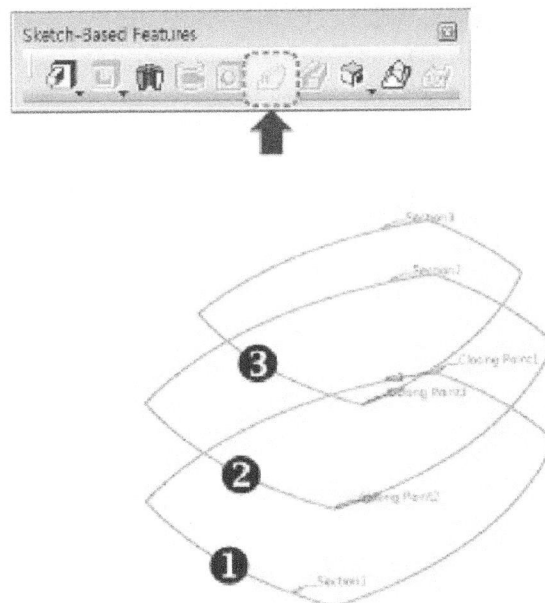

Fig 12- 22 Selecting Sections

343

1. Open the given file ch12_004.CATPart.
2. Click the Multi-sections Solid icon in the Sketch-Based Features toolbar. The status bar message prompts you to select a curve.
3. Select the section curve in order as shown in Fig 12-22. Check the closing points and the arrow direction. The closing point for the first section is located at a wrong point.

(Note) Connecting Sections

- Section is connected in order.
- Connects the closing points according to the section sequence and sweeps along the arrow direction.

4. Select the first section in the dialog box and click MB3 (right click).

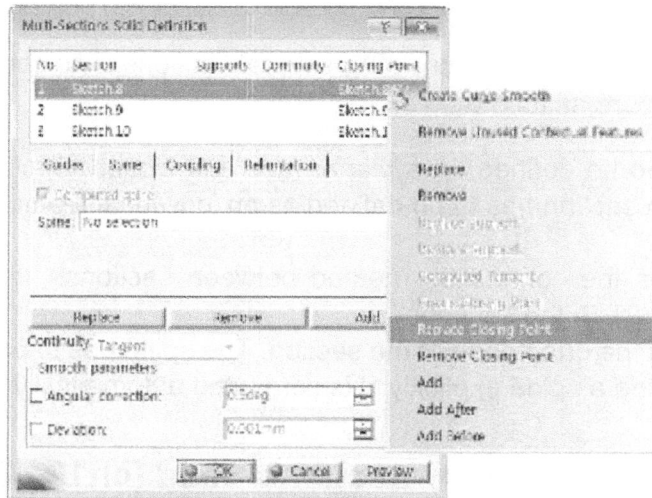

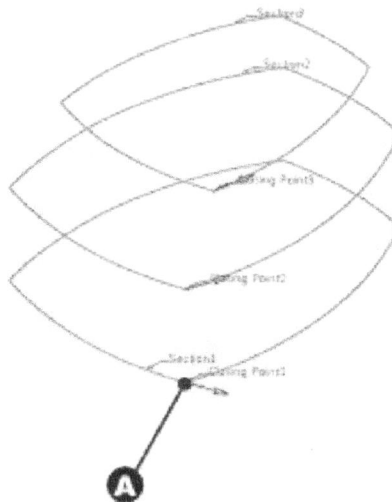

Fig 12-23 Modifying Closing Point

5. Select Replace closing point in the pop-up menu and select the point (A) designated in Fig 12-23. The arrow direction can be reversed by clicking its head.

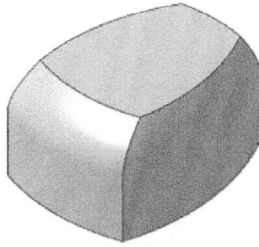

Fig 12-24 Comple ted Model

6. Click OK in the dialog box. Fig 12- 24 shows the result feature.

(Note) Impossible or Wrong!!

- If the location of the closing points is irregular or the direction is not the same, the multi-sections solid may not be created or be wrongly shaped.

12.5.1 Multi-Sections Solid with Guides

By defining guides to connect sections you can control the shape of the surface. Guides have to meet the following requirements.

Requirements of Guides

1. A guide has to intersect with all the sections.
2. When a face is used as a section, the guide has to be tangent to the adjacent surface at the section face.
3. Each guide has to be defined as an individual feature.

Exercise 108: Using Guides (ch12 _005.CATPart)

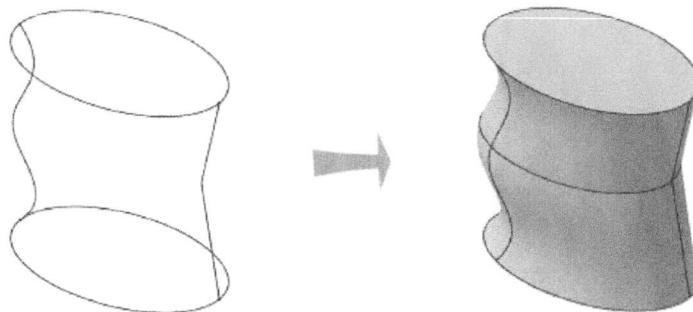

Fig 12- 25 Creating Multi-Sections Solid Using Guides

Creating a Guide Sketch

1. Open the given file ch12_005.CATPart.
2. Define the zx plane as the sketch sup- port. and create four intersection points with the ellipses as shown in Fig 12-26.

345

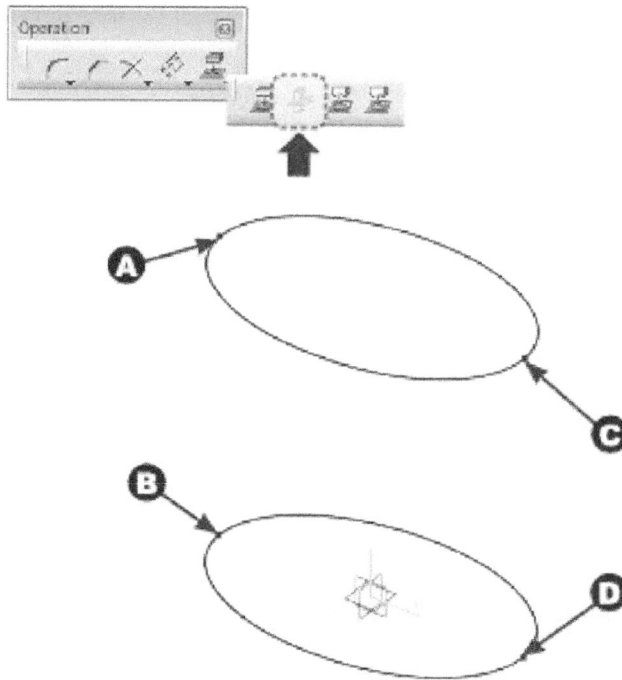

Fig 12-26 Intersection Point

3. Convert the two points (A) and (B) into the construct ion elements and delete the points (C) and (D).
4. Create a spine curve as shown in Fig 12-27. Points (A) and (B) have to be selected as the end points of the spline.
5. Exit the Sketcher workbench.
6. Create another sketch on the zx plane and create curves using the Profile command a shown in Fig 12-28.

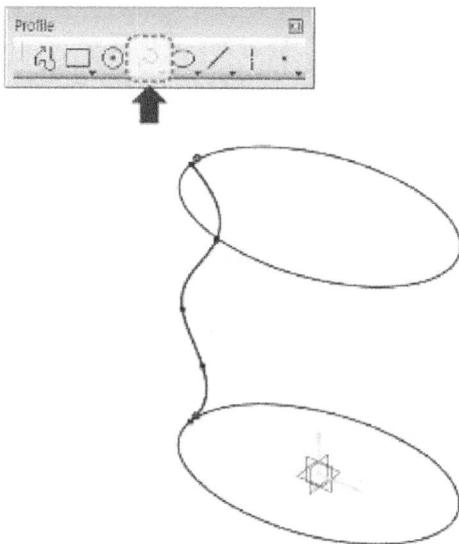

Fig 12-27 First Guide

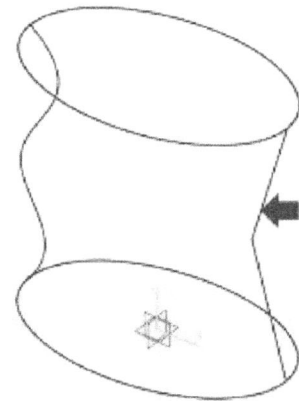

Fig 12-28 Second Guide

7. Exit the Sketcher workbench.

(Note) Condition of Guides

Each guide has to be defined as an individual feature. Therefore, the spline and the lines should not be created in the same sketch.

Creating Multi-Sections Solid

1. Click the Multi-sections Solid icon in the Sketch-Based Features toolbar.
2. Select the two sections ((1) and (2) in Fig 12-29).
3. Pick the region (3) in the dialog box.
4. Select the two guides ((4) and (5)).
5. Press the OK button in the dialog box. Fig 12-30 shows the result geometry.

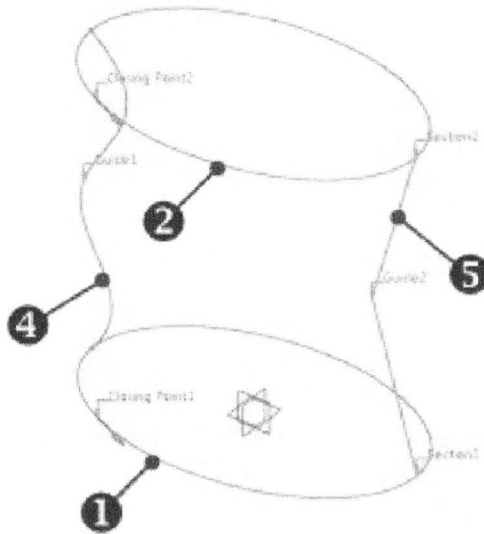

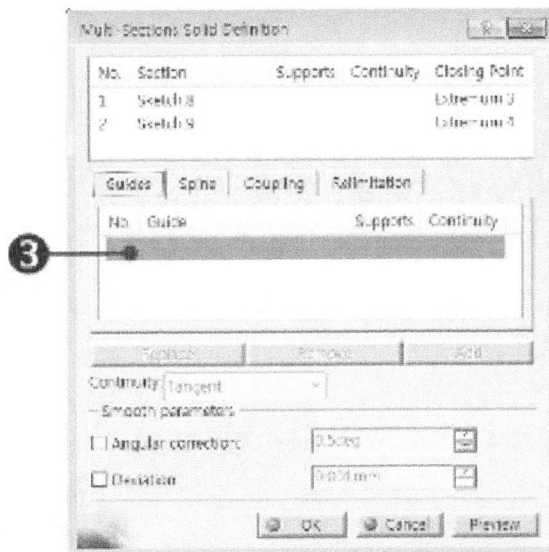

Fig 12-29 Selecting Sections and Guides

347

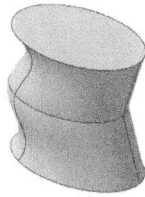

Fig 12-30 Comple ted Feature

12.5.2 Using a Spine for Multi-Sections Solid

A spine controls the surface composition so that the surface iso - parametric lines are aligned to the spine. You can specify the spine explicitly when you create a multi-sections solid. The spine has to meet the following requirements.

Requirements of Spine

1. Spine cannot be parallel to any of the sections.
2. Spine has to pass through the interior of all sections.
3. Spine has to be tangent and continuous.

Exercise 109: Using Guides (ch12 _006.CATPart)

1. Open the given file ch12_006.CATPart.
2. Create a multi-sections so lid by selecting sections (1) and (2) shown in Fig 12-31. Be careful about the direction of the arrow on the closing point.
3. Create a body by choosing Insert > Body in the menu bar and name it "spine' .
4. Click the Multi-sections Solid icon.
5. Hide the multi-sections solid feature which has already been create d and show the Sketch.2 and Sketch.3 features.

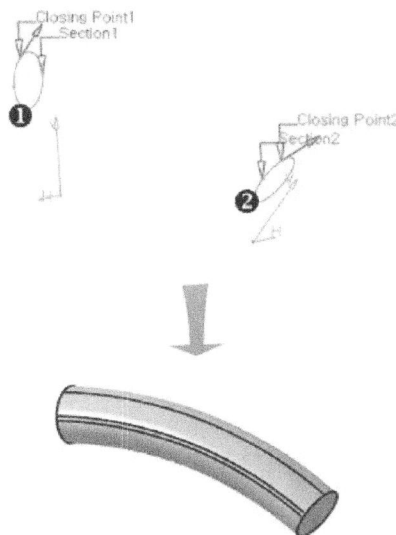

Fig 12-31 Creating a Multi-Sections Solid

6. Select the two sect ions (1) and (2) in the same way as in Fig 12-31.
7. Click the Spine tab in the dialog box and click the selection field O shown in Fig 12-32.
8. Select the Sketch. Spine feature as the spine ((2) in Fig 12-32).

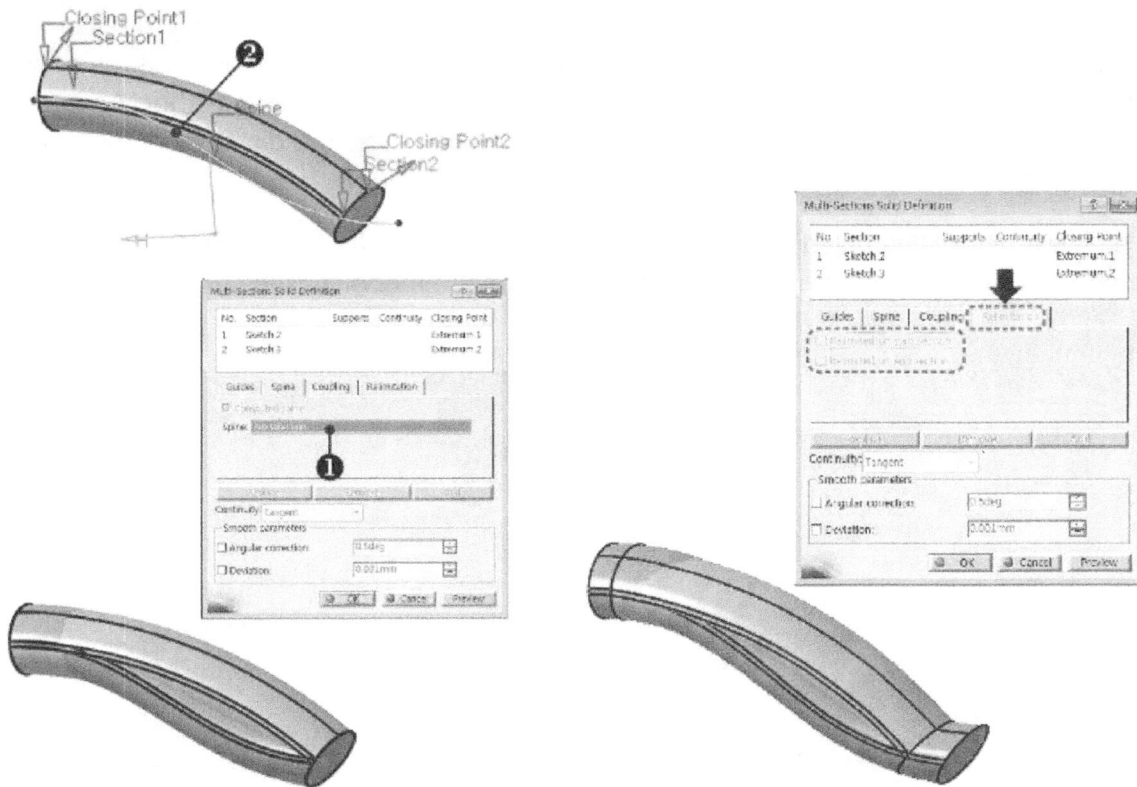

Fig 12- 32 Specifying a Spine Fig 12-33 Relimiting

9. Click OK in the dialog box. The result geometry is different to the former one.

(Note) Computed spin

- If you do not specify a spine explicitly, it is computed automatically. To remove the spine which is used for a multi-sections solid, turn on this option available in the Spine tab.

10. Double click the Multi-sections Solid feature in the "spine" body.
11. Click the Relimitation tab in the dialog box and uncheck the options shown in Fig 12-33.
12. Click OK in the dialog box. The part is created whole through the spine as shown in Fig 12-33.

(Note) Rules of Feature Limit

- **Relimit Option is ON:** Feature is created up to the section.
- **Relimit Option is OFF:**
    - No spine and no guides: Feature is created up to the sections.
    - No spine but with guides: Feature is created through the guides.
    - With spine and guides: Feature is created through the spine.
    - With spine but no guides: Feature is created through the spine.

349

o   With spine but docs not reach to the sections: Feature is created up to the sections.

12.5.3 Coupling and Closing Point

When CATIA V5 creates surfaces by connecting sections, it defines the and V direction grid first and then defines the surfaces. The U grid is based on sections and the V grid is based on coupling. A closing point defines the location of the first V grid and proceeds in defining other V grids following the arrow direction. Therefore, the lo cation of the closing point and the direction of the arrow play a very important role in creating multi-sections solids.

If you define a guide, it is taken as the V grid and is displayed as a line in the Shading with Edges view mode. Other grids may or may not be displayed on the model surface.

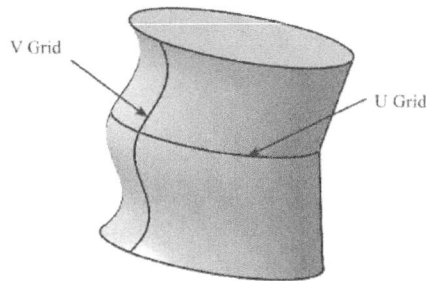

Fig 12-34 U and V Grids

Exercise 110: Modifying Coupling and Closing Point (ch12 _007.CATPart)

First Try

1. Open the given file ch12_007.CATPart.
2. Click the Multi-sections Solid icon and select the three sections in order as shown in Fig 12-35.

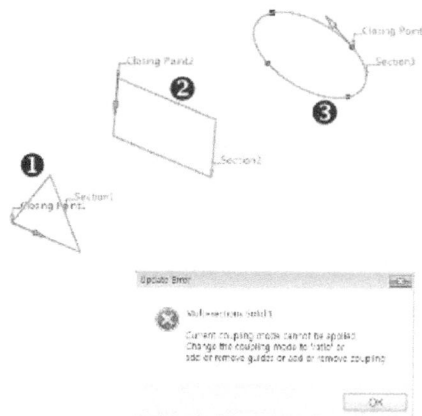

Fig 12-35 Update Error

3. Press the Preview button in the dialog box. An error message is encountered.
4. Press OK in the Update Error message box.
5. Press Cancel to close the dialog box.

Replacing Closing Point

1. Click the Multi-sections Solid icon and select the three sections in order as shown in Fig 12-35.
2. Select Closing Point 2 in the model preview. The corresponding section is highlighted in the dialog box.

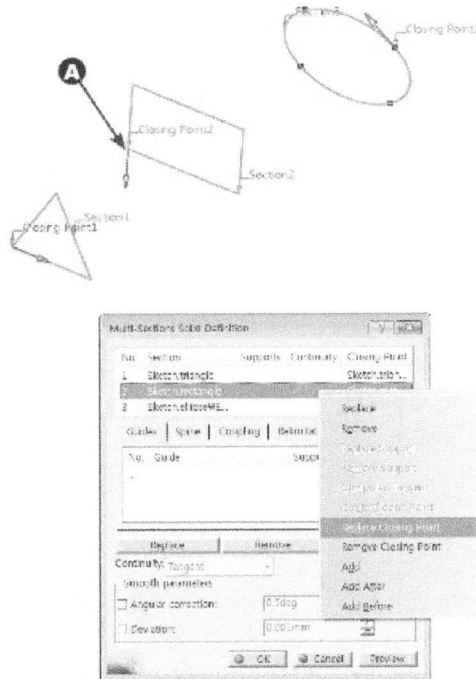

Fig 12- 36 Rep lacing Closing Point

3. Right click on the highlighted item and select Replace Closing Point as shown in Fig 12-36.
4. Select the point (A) designated in Fig 12-36.
5. Replace the Closing Point 3 for the ellipse with the point (A) as shown in Fig 12-37. Make sure that the arrow direction circulates for the same direction.

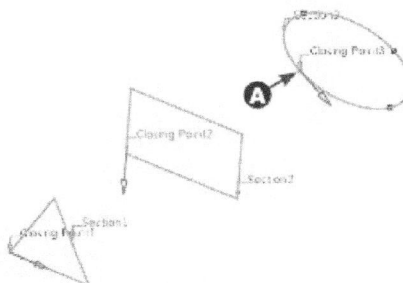

Fig 12-37 Replacing Closing Point 3

(Note) Tip!!!

- The point for Closing Point 3 has been defined in advance. If you want to select another point, you have to create the point in the sketch.

Defining Coupling

1. Click the Coupling tab in the dialog box.
2. Select Ratio in the Sections coupling dropdown list.

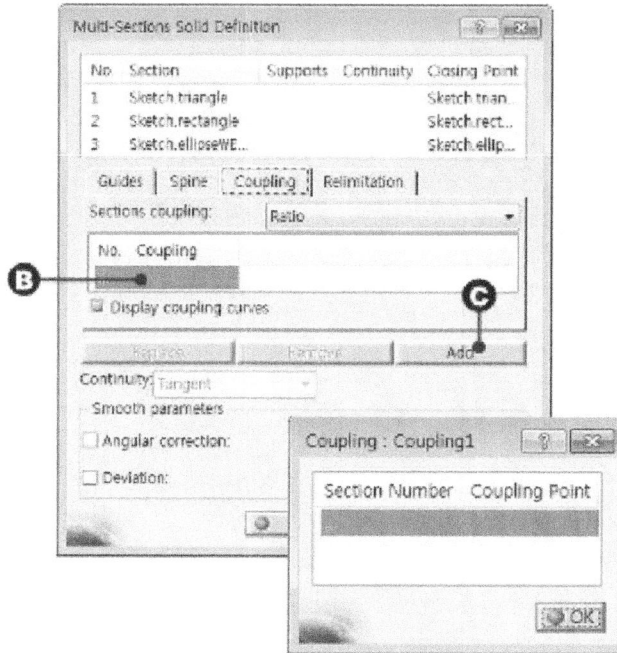

Fig 12-38 Defining Coupling

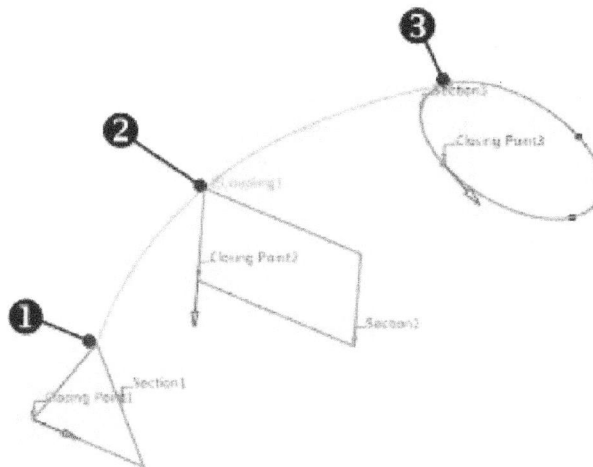

Fig 12-39 First Coupling

3. Click the option area (B) shown in Fig 12-38. Note the Add button (C) is available. Press the Add button.

The Coupling dialog box appears and the status bar message prompts you to select a coupling point.

4. Select three coupling points in order as shown in Fig 12-39. If all coupling points for the three sections are defined, the Coupling dialog box is closed.
5. Click the option area (A) shown in Fig 12-40 and press the Add button.
6. Select the three points in order as shown in Fig 12-40. Be careful not to select the coupling curve of the first coupling.
7. Define the third coupling as shown in Fig 1 2-40.
8. Press OK in the dialog box. Fig 12-41 shows the completed multi-sections solid feature.

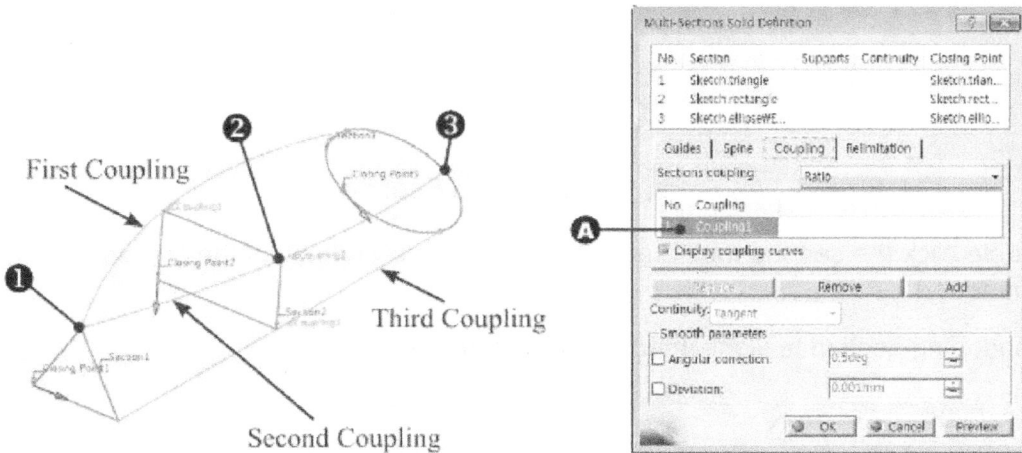

Fig 12-40 Second and Third Coupling

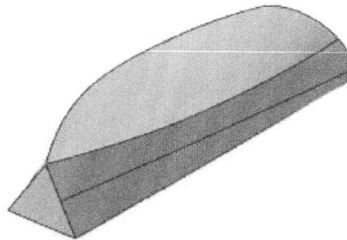

Fig 12- 41 Completed Model

Exercise 111: Tangent Surface (ch12 _008.CATPart)

If you create a multi-sections solid with more than three sections, the sections are connected smoothly. In this exercise, let's create a sharp bent feature by selecting the proper option.

1. Open the given file ch12_008.CATPart.
2. Create a multi-sections solid with the two sections as shown in Fig 12-42.

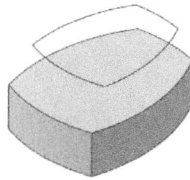

Fig 12-42 First Feature

3. Click the Multi-sections Solid icon and select the face (A) in Fig 12-43 as the first section and (B) as the second section. Then modify the closing point and arrow direction if required.
4. Click OK in the dialog box. A smooth connected feature is created as shown in Fig 12-43.

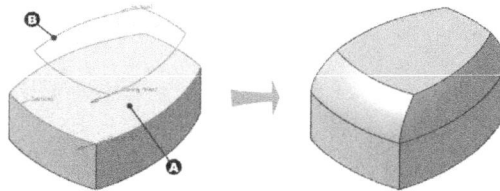

Fig 12-43 Second Feature

5. Double click the second multi-sections solid feature and select the first section in the model (Boundary).

The corresponding section is highlighted in the dialog box.

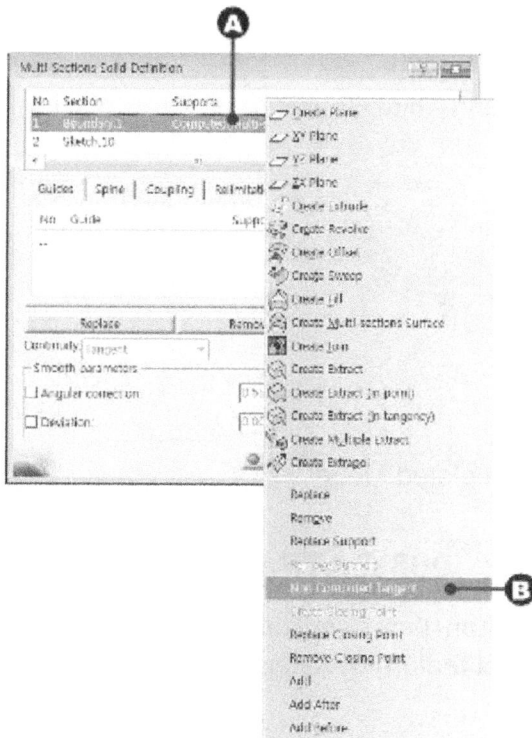

Fig 12-44 Removing Tangent

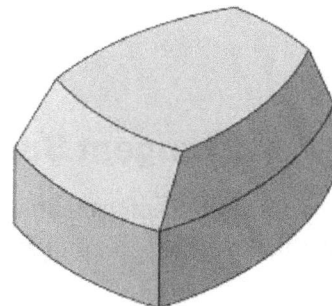

Fig 12-45 Sharp Bent Feature

6. Right click on the highlighted section ((A) in Fig 12-44).
7. Select Non Computed Tangent ((B) in Fig 12-44) in the pop-up menu.
8. Click OK in the dialog box. Fig 12-45 shows the feature with a sharp bent connection.

(Note) Tangent Connection

If you select a face as the first or last section, the multi-sections solid is created tangent with the adjacent surface.

12.6 REMOVED MULTI-SECTIONS SOLID

Using the Removed Multi-sections Solid icon in the Sketch-Based Features toolbar you can remove solid geometry by connecting sections. The options are the same as the Multi-sections Solid command. Fig 12-46 shows an example of removing solid geometry by creating multi-sections solid.

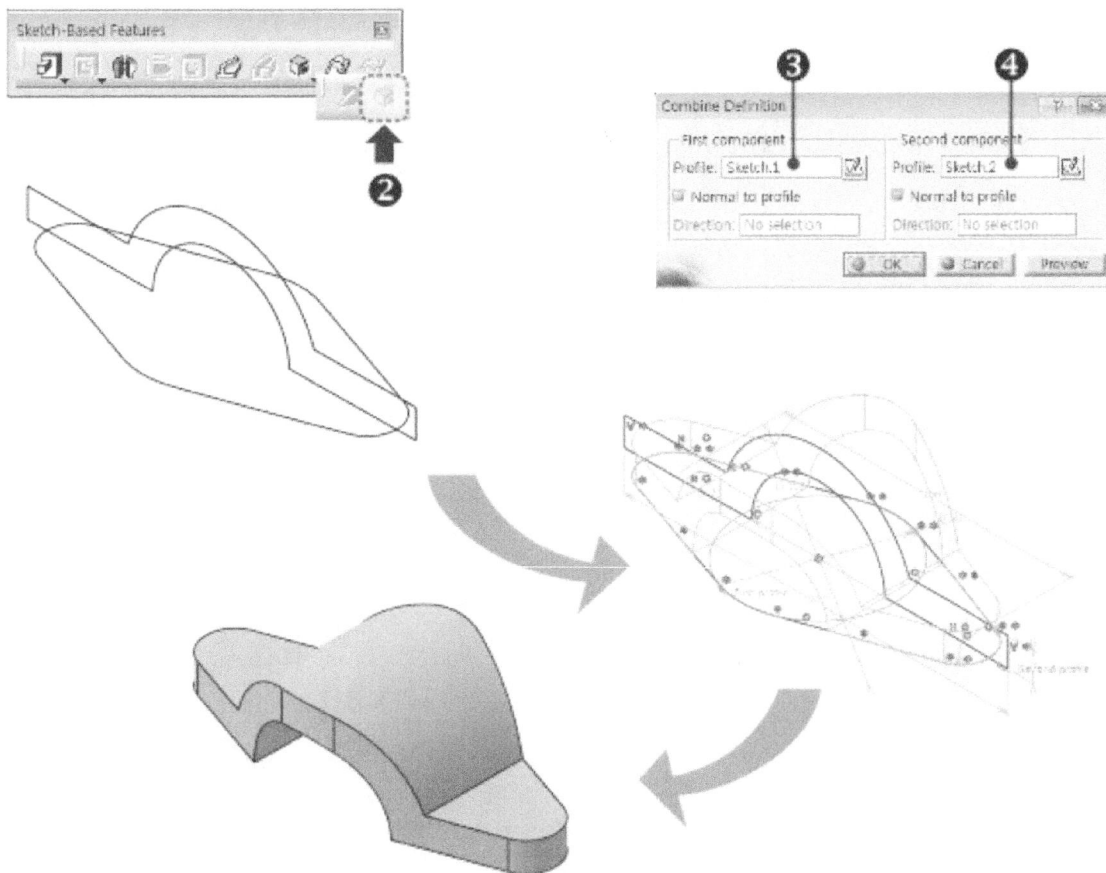

Fig 12-46 Removing with Multi-sections Solid

(Note) Angular correction and Deviation

- **Angular correction:** This option defines allowable tolerance for the tangent continuity of the spine. If here exists discontinuity smaller than the value in the Angular correction option, the surface is generated tangent.

355

- **Deviation:** This option defines allowable deviation from the guide. Note that in some cases, the multi-sect ions solid feature cannot ensure the guide curves.
- If you increase the two values, the possibility for creating the feature may increase. However, the result feature may deviate significantly from the desired shape.

Exercise 112: Tangent Surface (ch12 _009.CATPart)

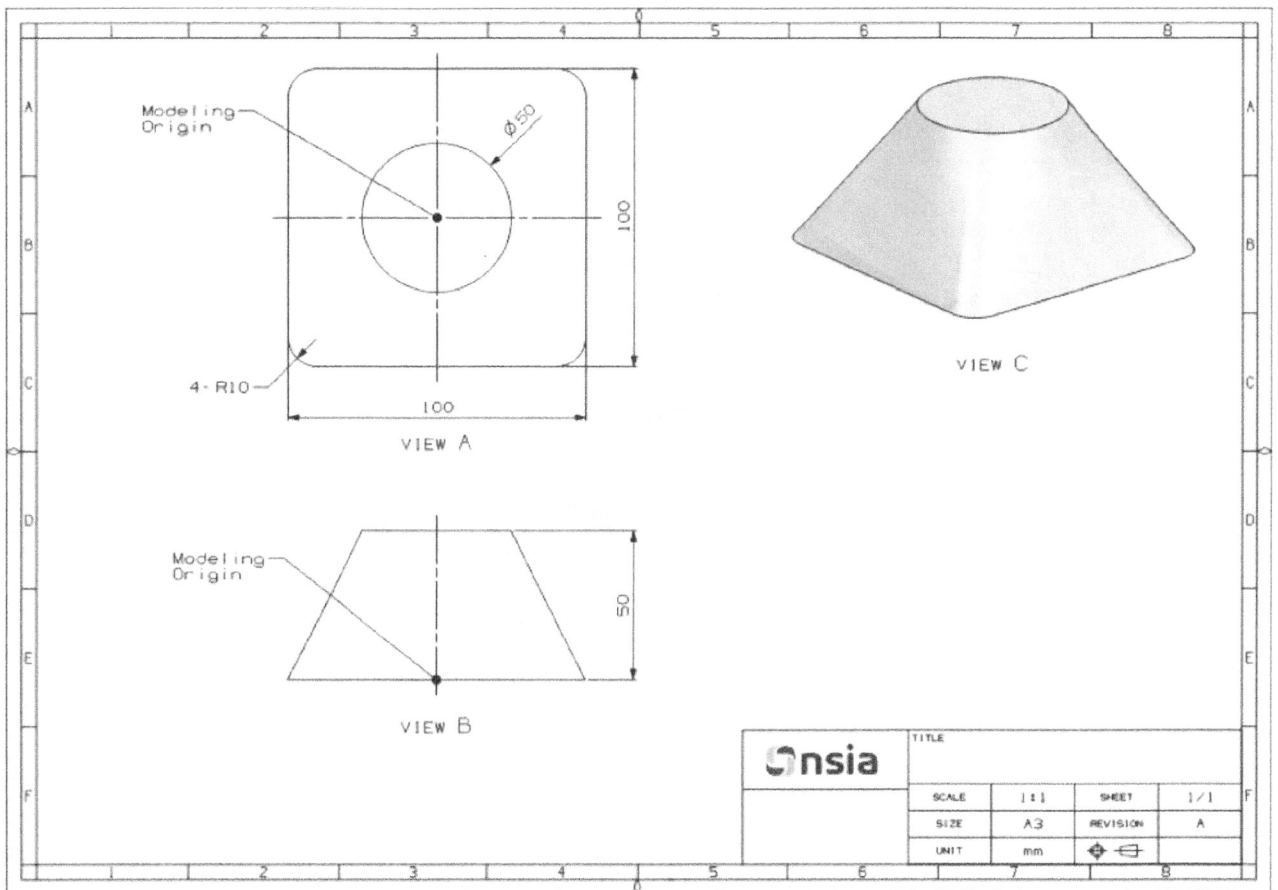

Fig 12-47 Drawing for Exercise 112

Exercise 113: Tangent Surface (ch12 _010.CATPart)

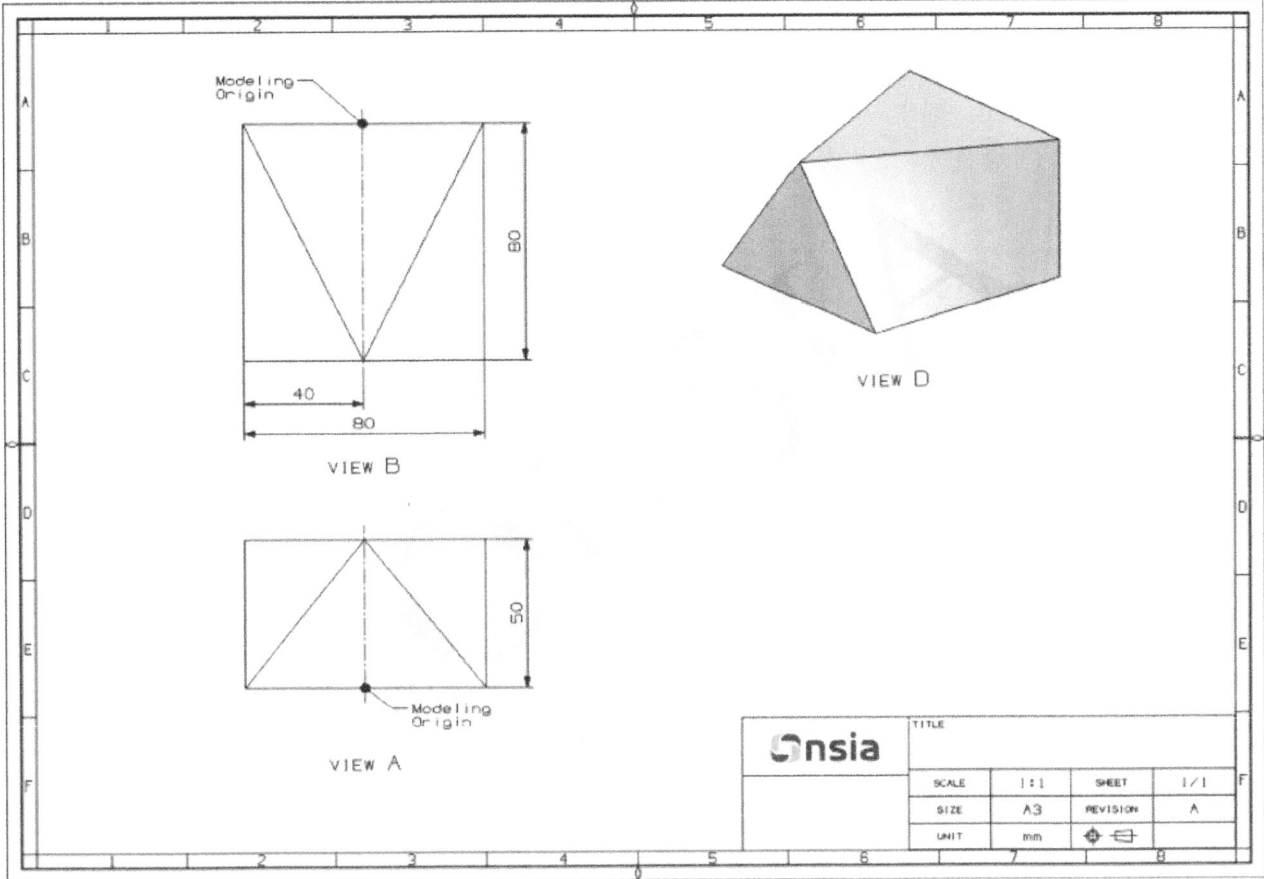

Fig 12-48 Drawing for Exercise 113

Exercise 114: Tangent Surface (ch12 _011.CATPart)

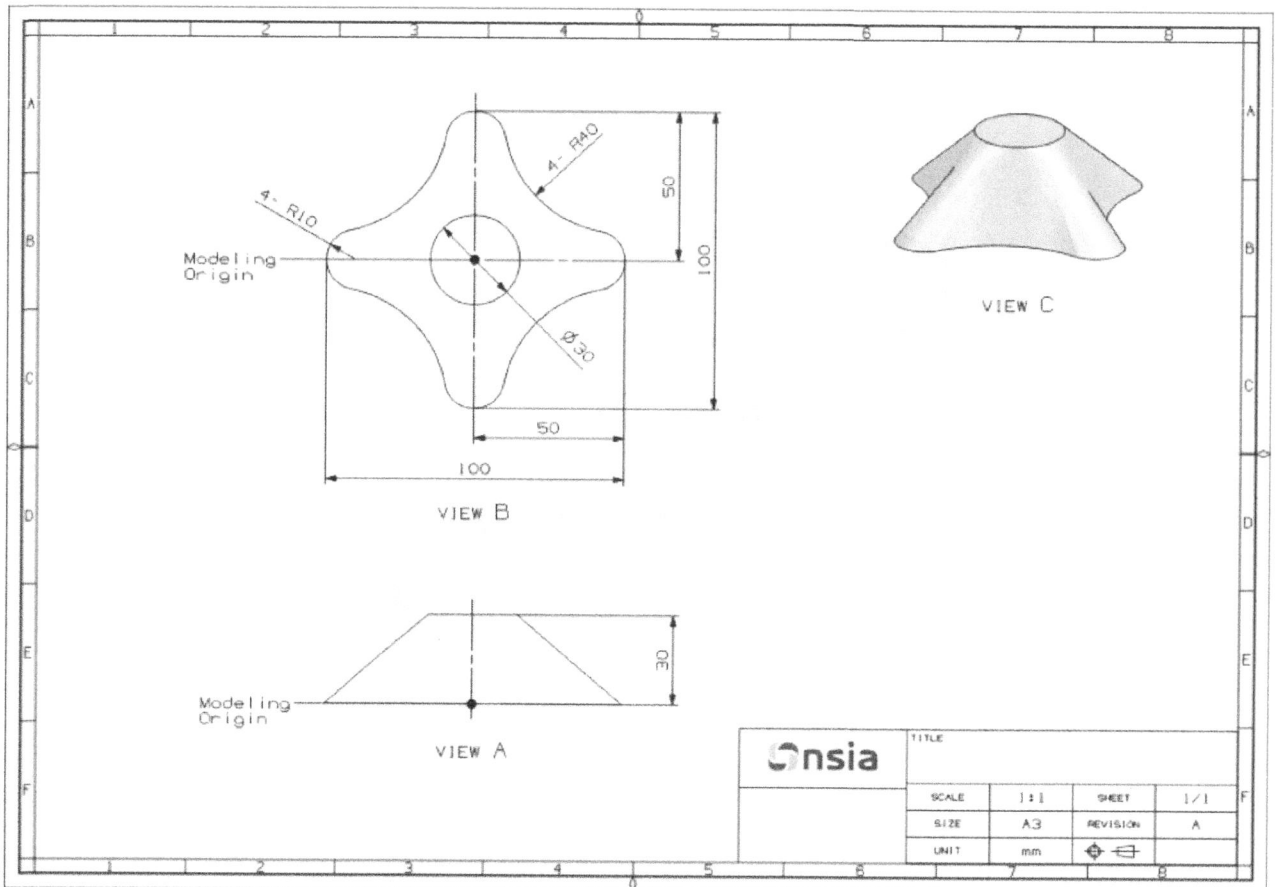

VIEW C

4 - R40

4 - R10

Modeling
Origin

Ø30

50

100

50

100

VIEW B

Modeling
Origin

30

VIEW A

Onsia

TITLE				
SCALE	1:1	SHEET	1/1
SIZE	A3	REVISION	A
UNIT	mm		

Fig 12-49 Drawing for Exercise 114

Exercise 115: Tangent Surface (ch12 _012.CATPart)

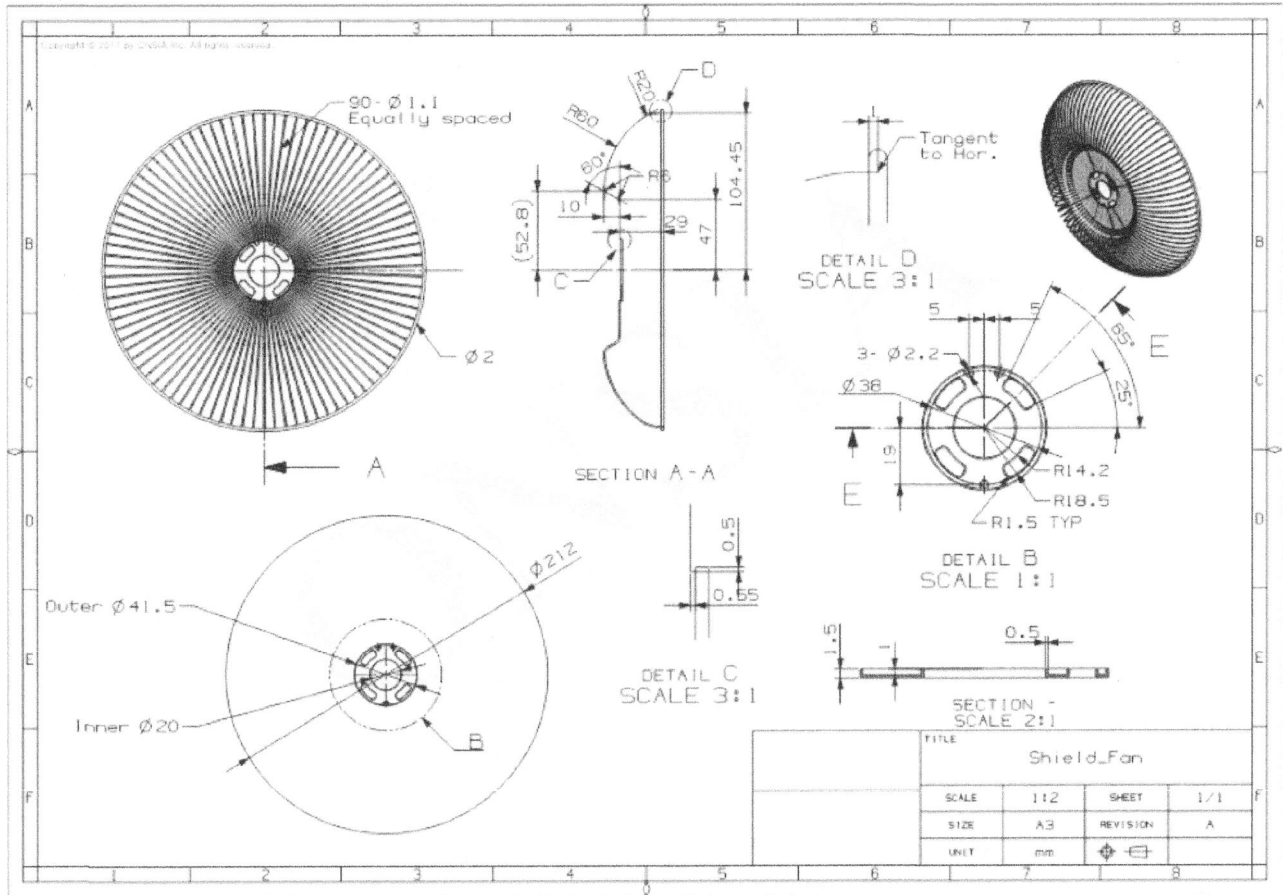

Fig 12- 50 Fan Shield

CHAPTER 13: DRIVING DESIGNS WITH FORMULAS

13.1 FORMULAS

Using the Formula command, you can apply your design intent in your model. You can create a dimension that is linked to another dimension, create parameters and use predefined functions to calculate a desired value.

13.2 Defining a Formula

You can define a formula for the value in a feature. creation dialog box where the Edit Formula menu is available by right clicking on the input box. Fig 13-2 shows the Formula Editor dialog box.

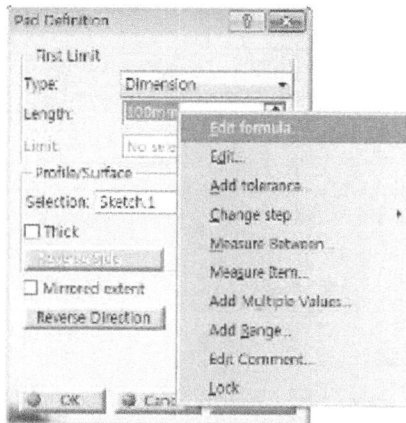

Fig 13-1 Edit Formula Menu

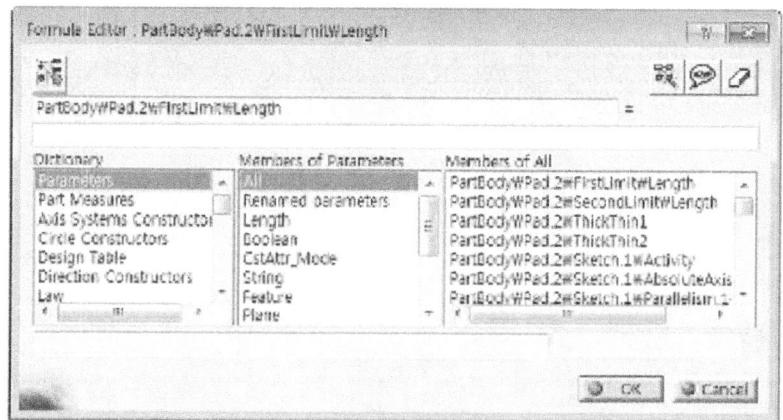

Fig 13-2 Formula Editor Dialog Box

Exercise 116: Linking Dimension (ch13 _001.CATPart)

Defining a Function

1. Open the given part ch13_001.CATPart.

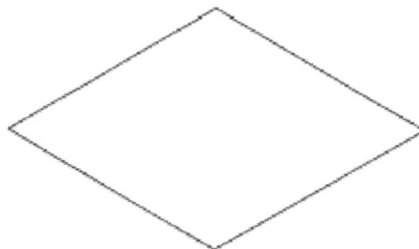

Fig 13-3 Given Part

2. Click the Pad icon in the Sketch-Based Features toolbar.

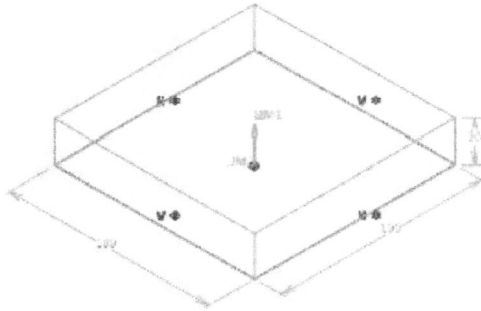

Fig 13-4 Preview

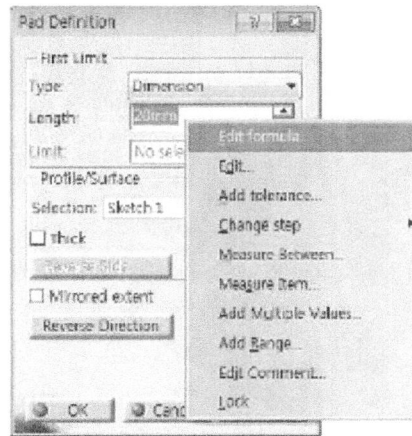

Fig 13-5 Edit Formula Pop-up Menu

3. Select the given sketch as a profile. The pad feature is preview ed as shown in Fig 13-4.
4. Right click on the Length input box and choose Edit formula in the pop-up menu. The Formula Editor dialog box is invoked.
5. Select the sketch feature. The dimensions in the sketch are displayed as shown in Fig 13-6.

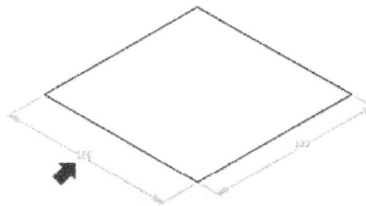

Fig 13-6 Dimensions

6. Select the dimension specified by the arrow in Fig 13-6. The corresponding parameter is entered in the function input field as designated by the arrow in Fig 13-7. The parameter First limit of the Pad.1 feature has been linked to the parameter Length.12 of the Sketch.1 feature. Note the equal symbol between two parameters.

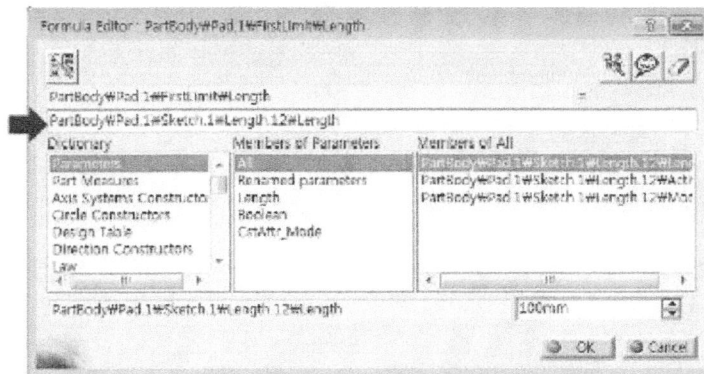

Fig 13-7 Formula Editor

Fig 13-8 Cube

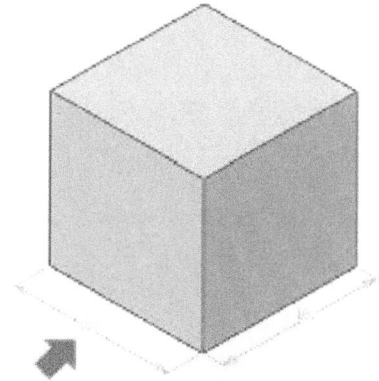

Fig 13-9 Selecting Dimension

7. Click OK in the Formula Editor dialog box.
8. Click OK in the Pad Definition dialog box. Fig 13-8 shows the cube.

Modifying the Source Dimension

1. Click the Formula icon in the Know- ledge toolbar.
2. Select the Sketch.1 feature in the Spec Tree. The dimensions for the selected feature are displayed as shown in Fig 13-9.
3. Select the dimension specified by the arrow in Fig 13-9. The parameter is highlighted in the Formulas dialog box as shown in Fig 13-10.
4. Enter 200mm in the value input box and press the Tab key, The color of the part turns to red.
5. Click OK in the Formulas dialog box. The model is updated as shown in Fig 13-11.

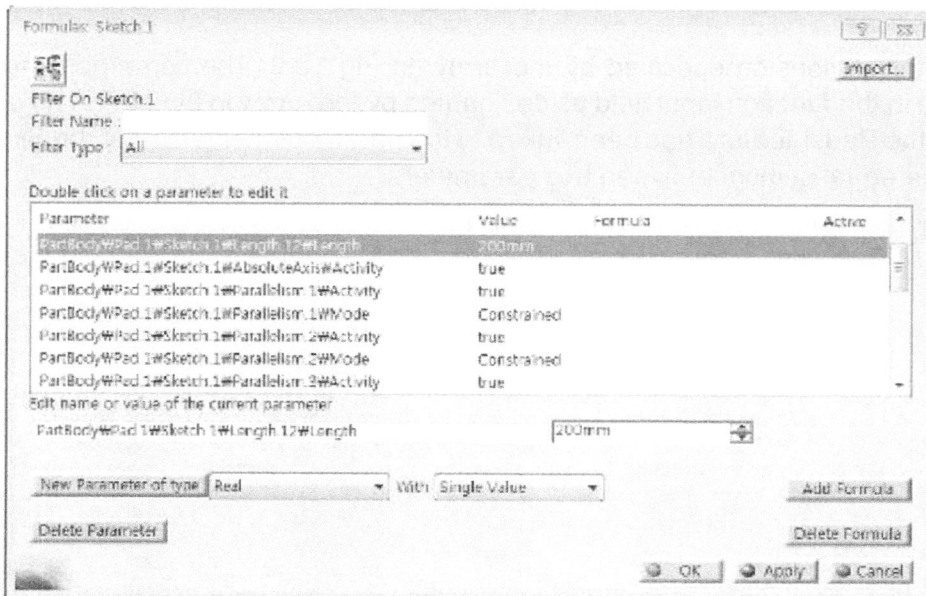

Fig 13-10 Modifying Value

362

Fig 13-11 Updated Model

1.3.3 Using Measured Parameter

If you measure distance, item or inertia with the Keep measure option, the result of the measurement is recorded in the Spec Tree. You can identify its name in the Formulas dialog box and use the parameter to define other parameters.

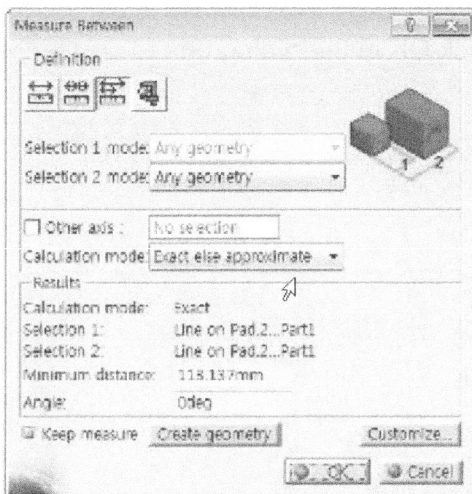

Fig 13-12 Keep Measure Option

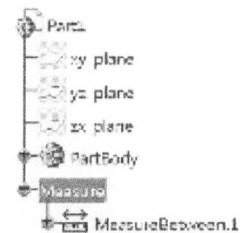

Fig 13-13 Spec Tree

Exercise 117: Linking Dimension (ch13 _002.CATPart)

The location of the boss of the given model is not defined exactly. Let's create four bosses symmetrically along the slanted edge using formula.

Measuring

Fig 13-14 feature Hem Dialog Box

1. Open the given part.
2. Click the Measure Item icon in the Measure toolbar.
3. Turn on the Keep measure option.
4. Turn on the Curve Filter and select the slanted edge.
5. Click OK in the dialog box. The length of the slanted edge is displayed in the model as designated by (A) in Fig 13-15.
6. Click the Measure Between icon in the Measure toolbar.
7. Select the edge and center of the boss and click OK in the dialog box to create the distance as designated by (B) in Fig 13-15.

Renaming the Parameters

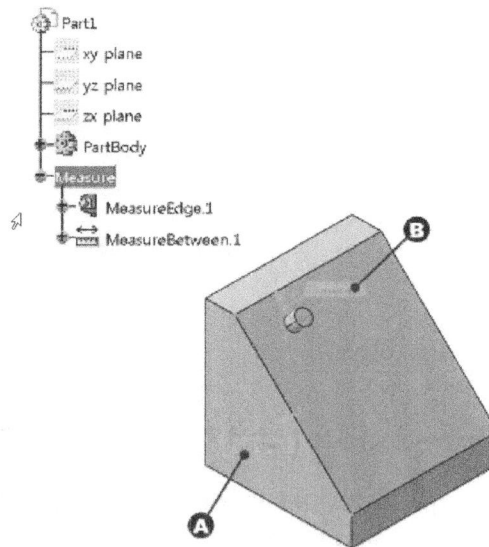

Fig 13-15 Measured Result

1. Click the Formula icon in the Know- ledge toolbar.
2. Select Measure Edge.1 in the Spec Tree. Note that the parameters related to the measurement are shown in the Formula dialog box and the parameter Length is highlighted.
3. Enter "diagonal" in the parameter edit box and press the Tab key. Press OK in the dialog box.

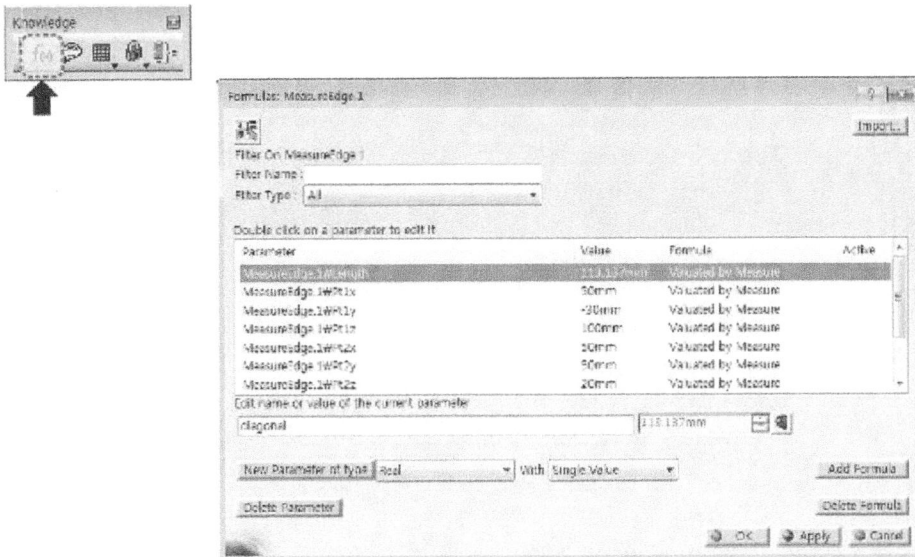

Fig 13-16 Renaming Parameter

You can also rename the parameter by double clicking a parameter in the Spec Tree.

4. Expand Measure Between.1 in the Spec Tree, double click Length and rename the parameter as "margin".

You can display only the renamed parameters as shown in fig 13-17 by applying the corresponding filter type in the Formulas dialog box.

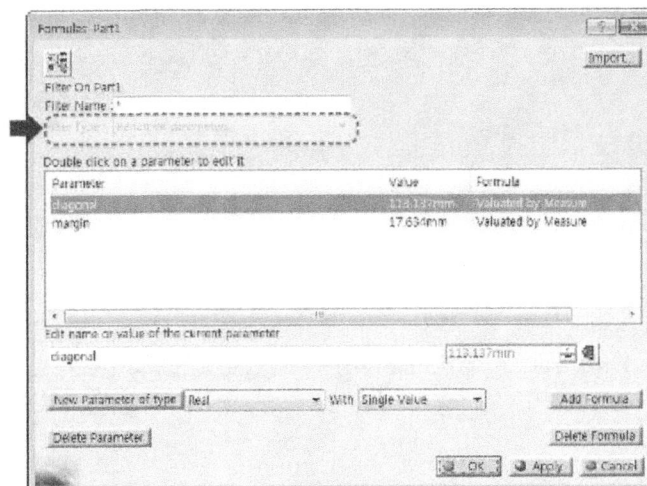

Fig 13-17 Filter Applied

Creating Pattern

1. Click the Rectangular Pattern icon in the Transformation Features toolbar.
2. Choose instance(s) & Length in the Parameters dropdown list.
3. Right click on the Length input box and note that the Edit Formula menu is not available in the pop-up menu.

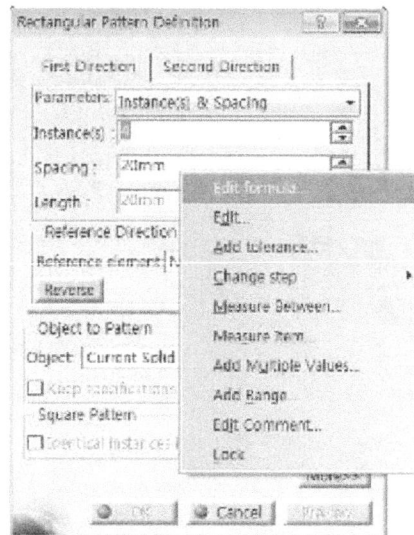

Fig 13-18 Edit Formula Menu

4. Choose instance(s) & Spacing in the Parameters dropdown list.
5. Enter 4 in the instance(s) input box.
6. Right click on the Spacing input box and choose Edit Formula in the pop-up menu.
7. Select the Measure item in the Spec Tree and double click "diagonal" in the Members of All list box. Note that the name of the parameter is entered in the edit box as shown in Fig 13-19.
8. Modify the edit box as designated by the arrow in Fig 13-20 and click OK in the dialog box.

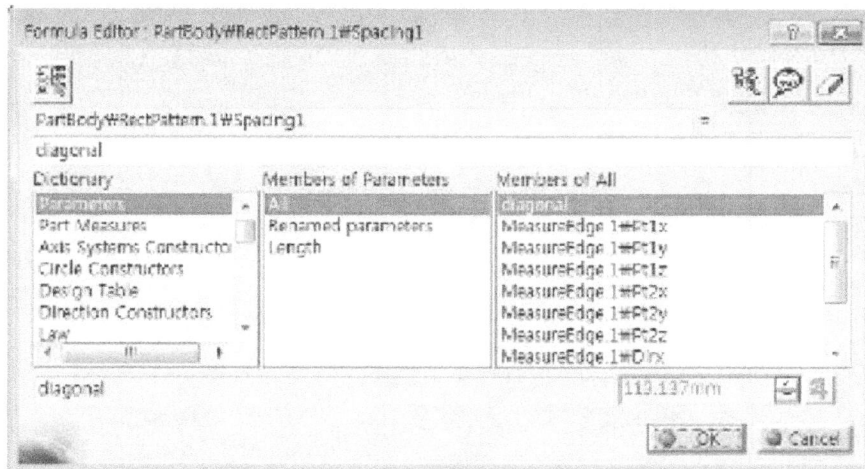

Fig 13-19 Entering Parameter

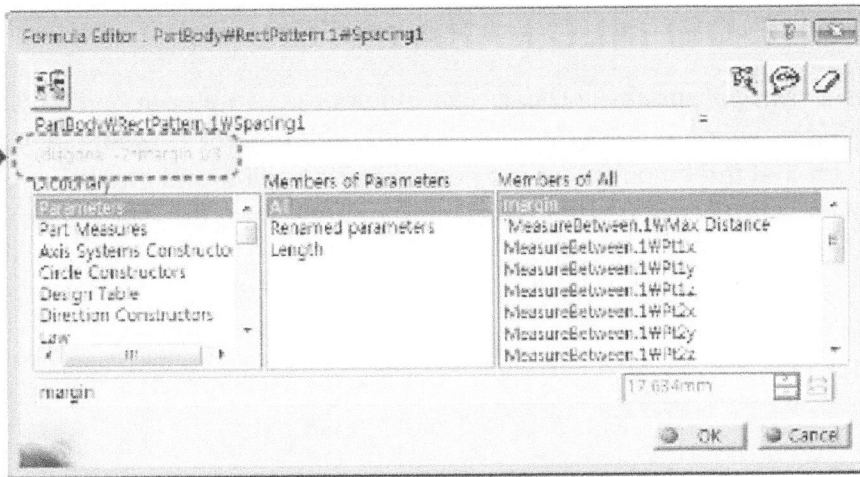

Fig 13-20 Modified Function

9. Define the reference direction and select the boss as the object to pattern. Preview of the rectangular pattern is available as shown in Fig 13-21. Note that you have to select the pad feature.

10. Click OK in the Rectangular Pattern Definition dialog box. Fig 13-22 shows the result.

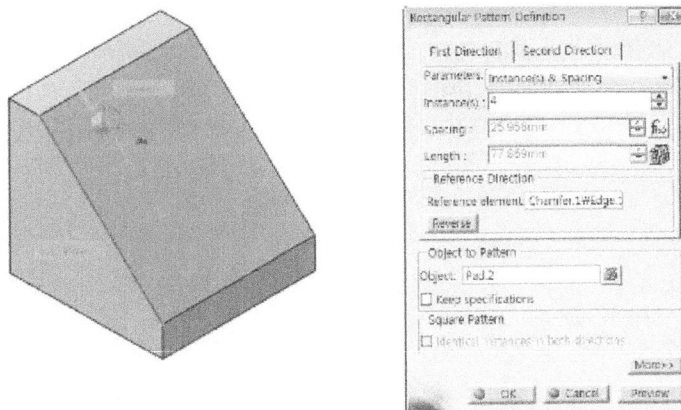

Fig 13-21 Preview of Pattern

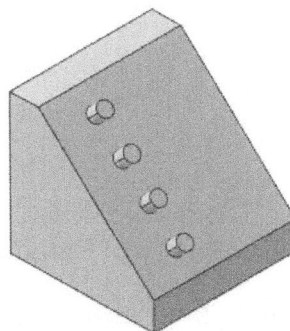

Fig 13-22 Completed Model

367

13.4 USING PRE-DEFINED PARAMETER

You can define your own parameter and calculate another parameter such that it satisfies desired condition by using your own parameter and pre-defined parameter. For example, you can define the radius of an arc such that the length of an arc has a specific value and that the center angle is pre-defined. If you define a desired arc length and center angle, then the radius of the arc is updated automatically.

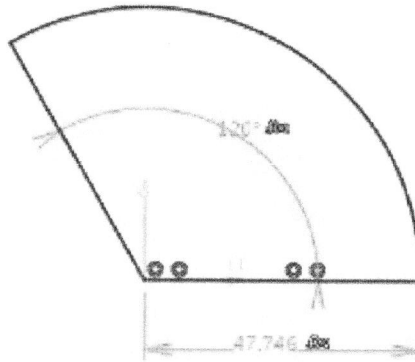

Fig 13-23 Calculating Radius

Note that you have to determine the type of new parameter when you are creating your own parameter. You can create a desired type of parameter by choosing the type in the area specified by the a1Tow in Fig 13-24 and pressing the New Parameter of type button.

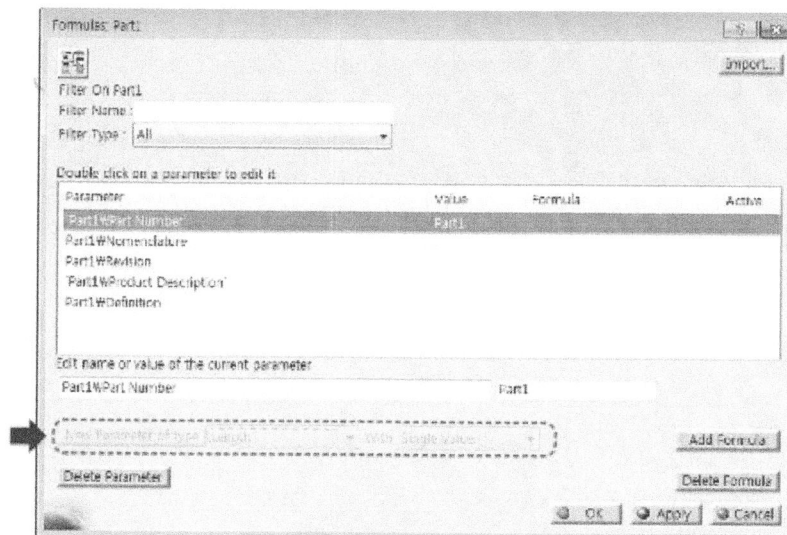

Fig 13-24 Type of Parameter

You can define a parameter using formula by pressing the Add Formula button in the Formulas dialog box. Fig 13-25 shows defining a new parameter with length type. Note that the units for each term have to be homogeneous. Therefore, when you add or subtract a constant, you have to append

368

correct unit behind the number. If you add or subtract a number without the unit, a syntax error will be invoked as shown in Fig 13-26 and CAT IA will use the international system unit, which may result in a wrong value as specified by the anow in Fig 13-27.

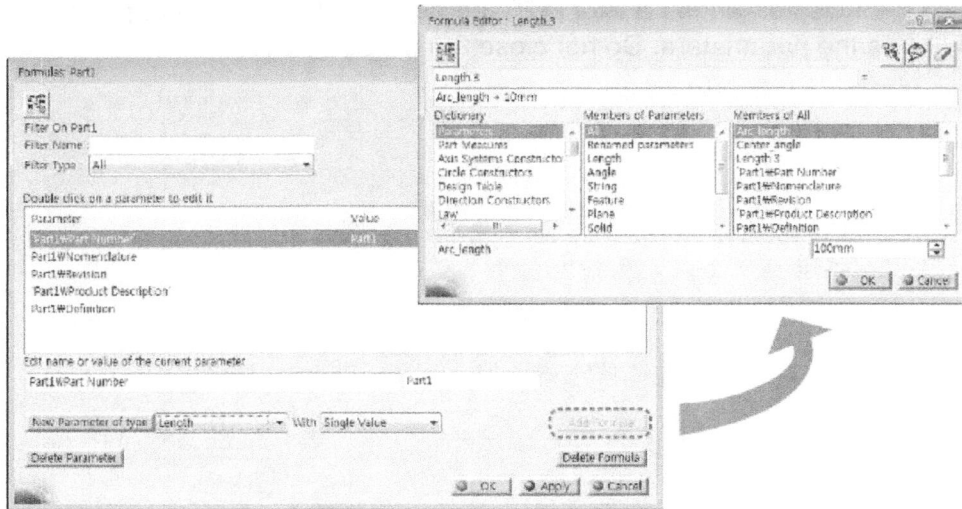

Fig 13-25 Adding Formula

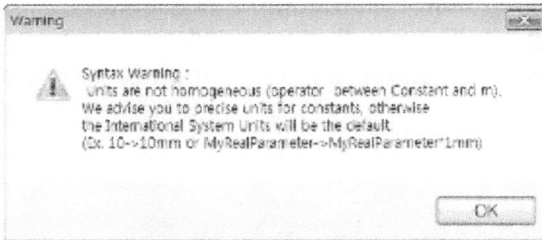

Fig 13-26 Syntax Error

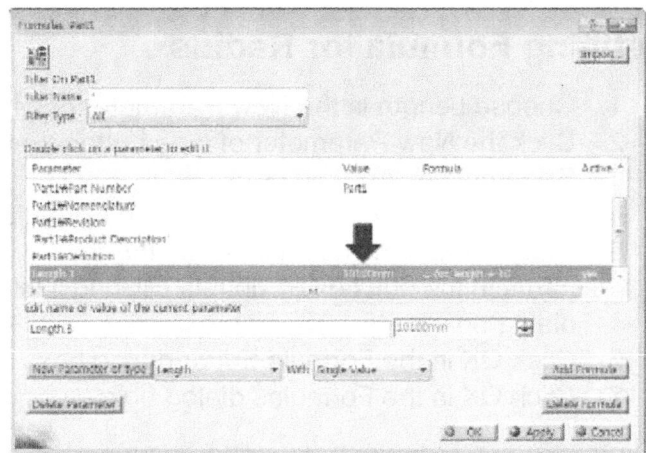

Fig 13-27 Wrong Value Assigned

Create an arc such that. you can choose the desi red length and center angle and the radius is determined automatically.

Exercise 118: Using Pre-defined Parameter (ch13 _003.CATPart)

Defining User Parameter

1. Create a new part file with the name of ch13 _003.CATPart.
2. Click the Formula icon in the Knowledge toolbar.
3. Choose Length in the New Parameter of type dropdown list.

4. Click the New Parameter of type button. Length.1 is created in the parameter list.
5. Rename it as Arc_length, assign 100 mm   as the initial value and press the Tab key.
6. Choose Angle in the New Parameter of type dropdown list.
7. Click the New Parameter of type button. Angle .1 is created in the parameter list.
8. Rename it as Center_angle, assign 120deg as the initial value and press the Tab key. Fig 13-28 shows the parameters. Do not close the dialog box yet.

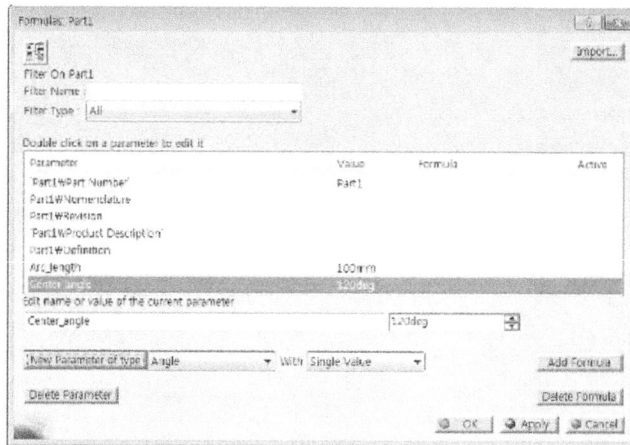

Fig 13-28 Parameters Created

Defining Formula for Radius

1. Choose Length in the New Parameter of type drop down list.
2. Click the New Parameter of type button. Length.2 is created in the parameter list.
3. Rename it as Arc_radius.
4. Click the Add Formula button in the Formulas dialog box while Length.2 is selected.
5. Enter formula as designated by the an ow in Fig 13-29. Note that you can enter parameter name in the edit box by double clicking it in the Members of All list box in the Formula Editor dialog box.
6. Click OK in the Formula Editor dialog box.
7. Click OK in the Formulas dialog box.

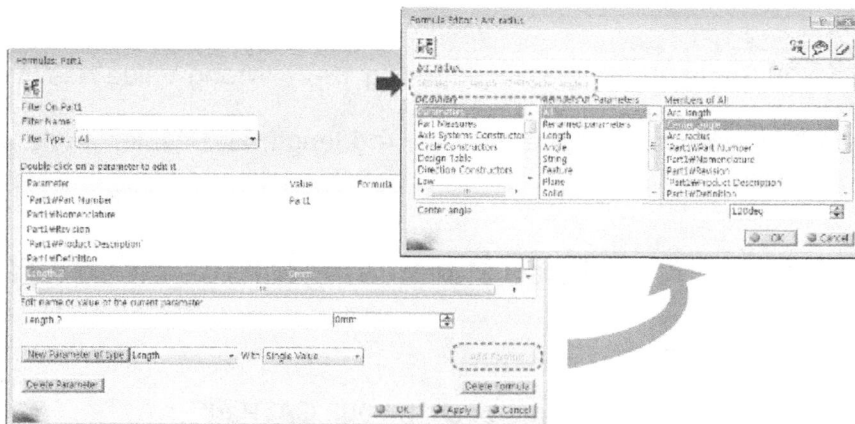

Fig 13-29 Formula Entered
370

Creating Sketch

1. Define a sketch on the xy plane.
2. Create an arc, apply the angular dimension and edit formula as shown in Fig 13 - 30.
3. Apply the radius dimension and edit formula as shown in Fig 13-31.
4. Exit the sketcher.

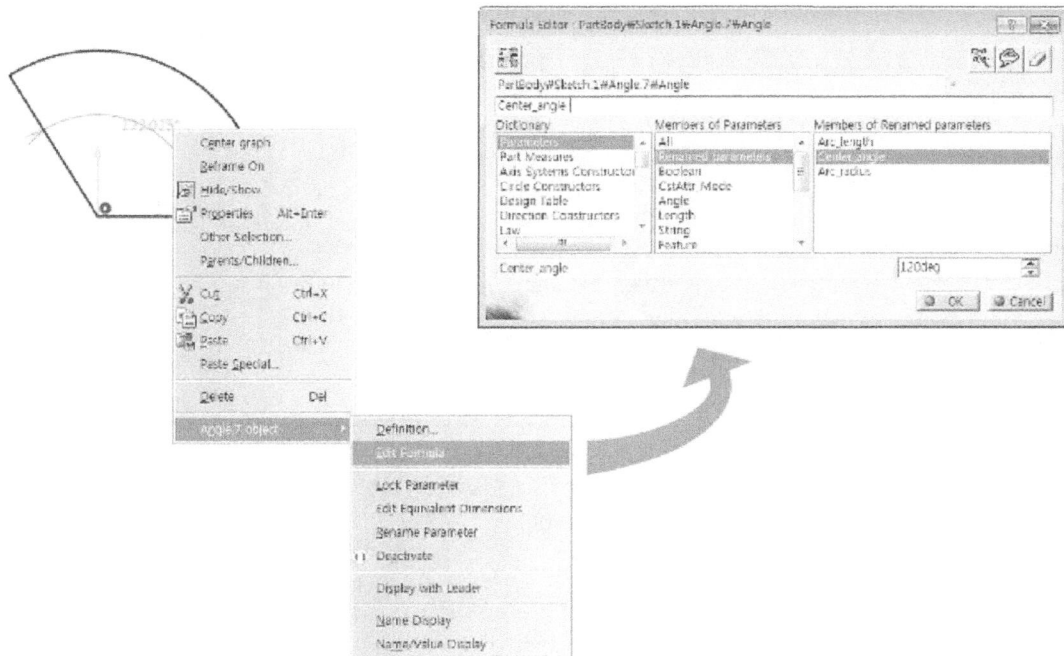

Fig 13-30 Editing Angular Dimension

Fig 13-31 Editing Radius Dimension

5. Create a 10 mm pad feature.
6. Measure the arc length as shown in Fig 13-32. Note that you can measure the arc length by clicking the Customize button in the Measure Item dialog box and choosing Length in the Measure Item Customization dialog box.

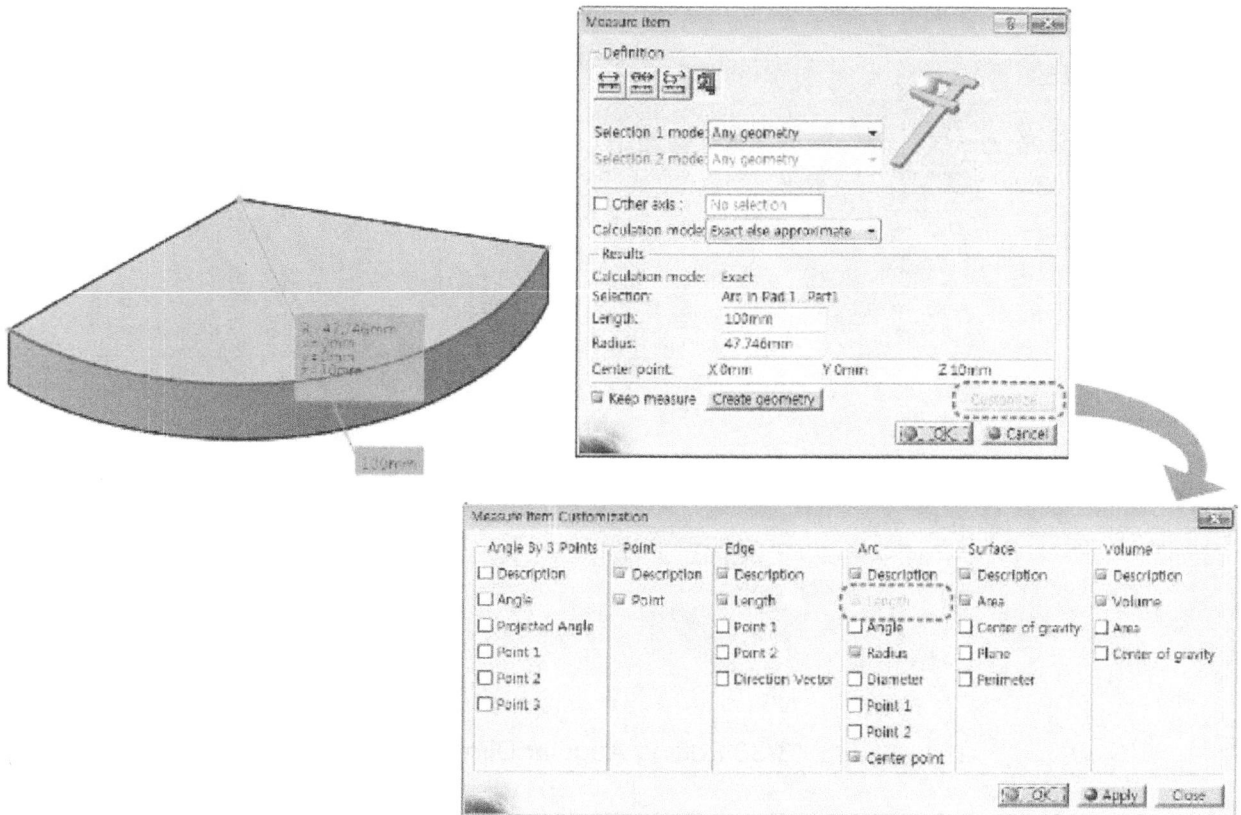

Fig 13-32 Measuring Arc Length

Modifying Desired Arc Length

1. Click the Formula icon in the Knowledge toolbar.
2. Choose Renamed Parameters in the Filter Type dropdown list.
3. Modify the value of Arc_length from 100mm to 200mm and press the Tab key.
4. Click OK in the Formulas dialog box.
5. Expand the Measure node in the Spec Tree, right click on the Measure Edge.1 and choose Local Update in the pop-up menu. The annotation of measurement is updated as shown in Fig 13-34. You can see that the radius is updated to cope with the modified arc length. You can also modify the center angle.

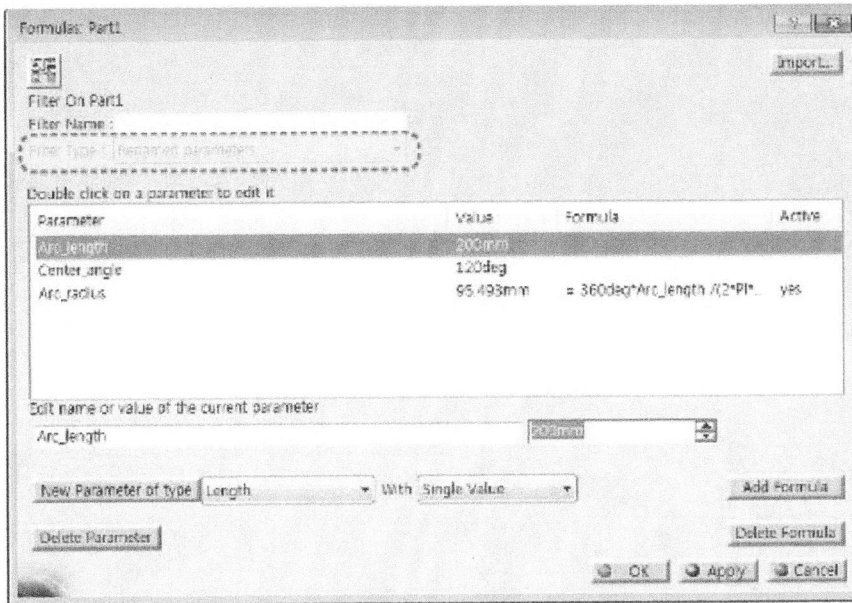

Fig 13-33 Modifying Arc_length

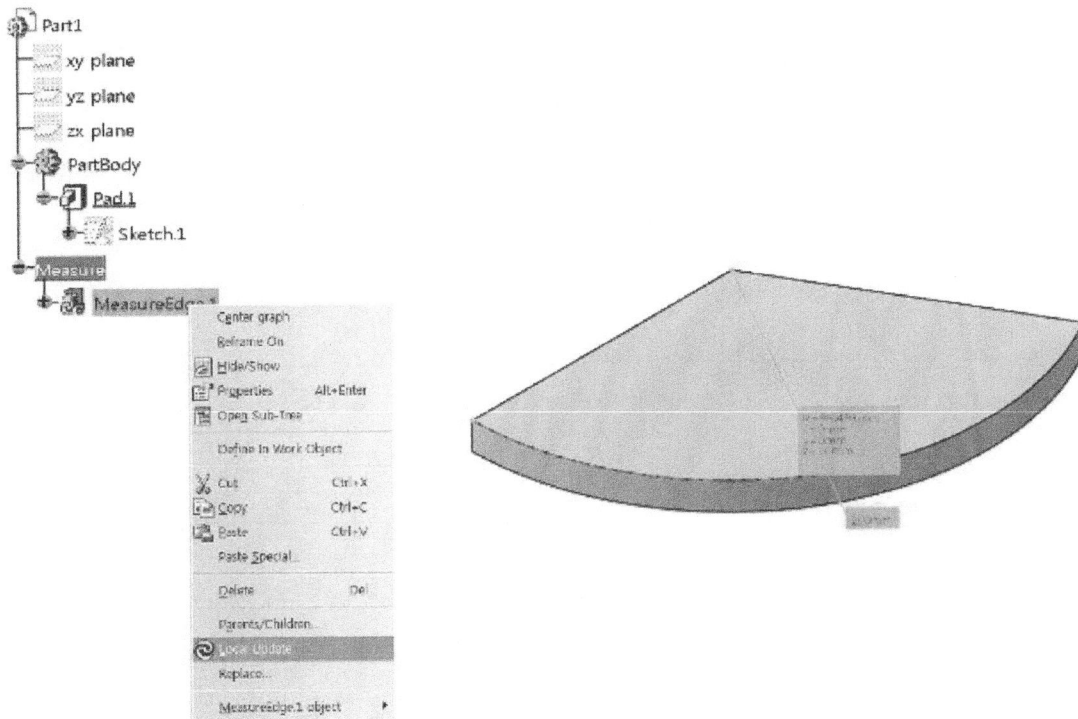

Fig 13-34 Updated Arc_length

Exercise 119: Using Measured Parameter (ch13 _004.CATPart)

Create the model shown in Fig 13-35 such that the dimension marked () should aways have the same value as the difference of the radius.

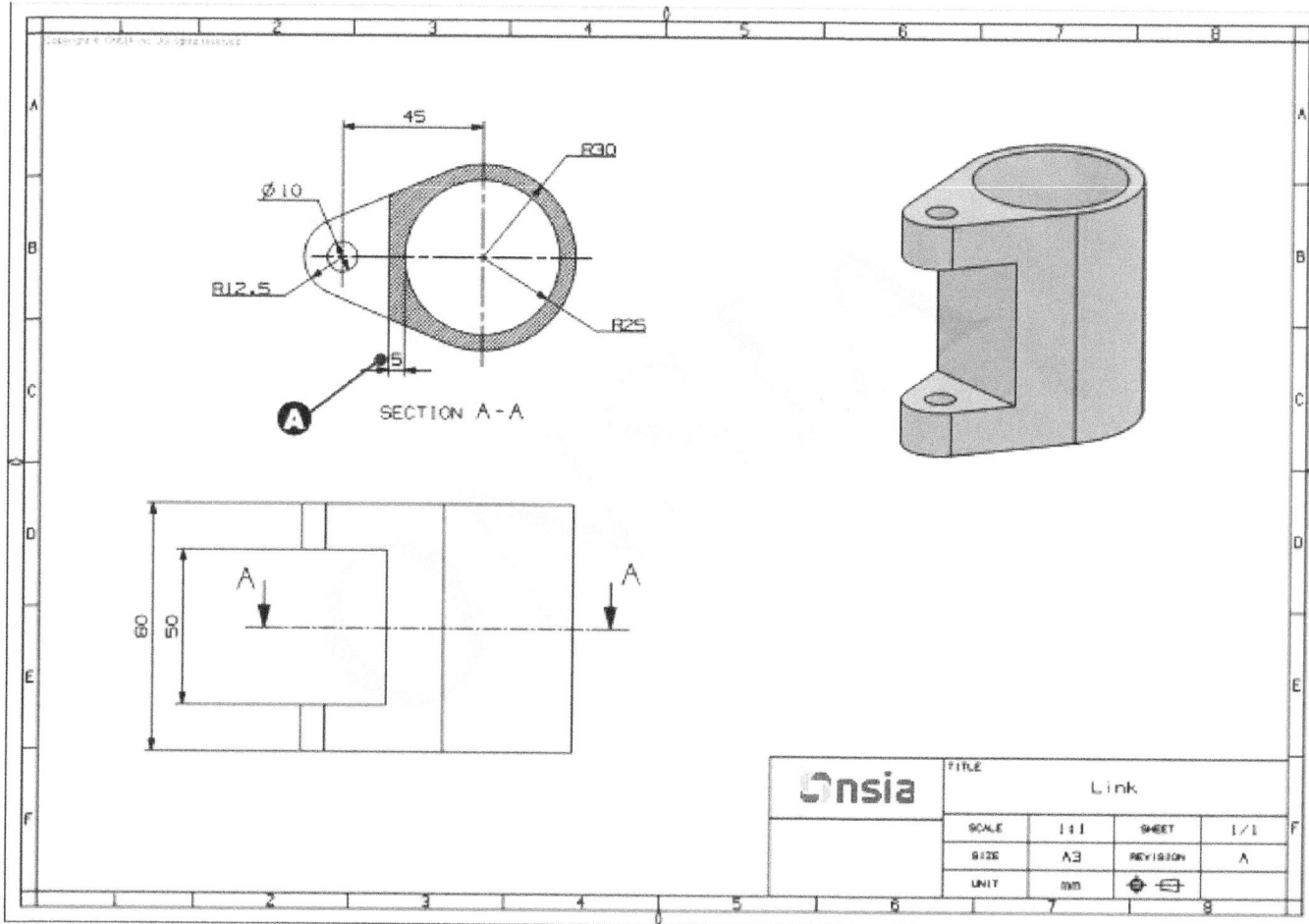

SECTION A-A

TITLE		Link	
SCALE	1:1	SHEET	1/1
SIZE	A3	REVISION	A
UNIT	mm		

Fig 13-35 Drawing of Link

374

CHAPTER 14: CONSTRUCTING ASSEMBLIES: STRATEGIES AND TECHNIQUES (BOTTOM-UP ASSEMBLY, TOP-DOWN ASSEMBLY)

14.1 INTRODUCTION

Products we use every day are in an assembled form. In the CATIA V5 Part Design workbench, we have been creating individual parts using a computer. After completing the part design, the parts will be manufactured in real life and then assembled so that they function as intended as a complete product. The products will undergo testing if required and then be sold to customers if they pass the tests.

Suppose that we are manufacturing individual parts just after completing the design. If there are problems in the actual assembly, it will take a lot of time, effort and money to correct the design mistakes.

On the other hand, We can replicate assembly on the computer for every part that constitutes the product. We can check interferences, the mechanism and basic physical characteristics such as weight, center of mass, etc. by using the Assembly Design workbench in CATIA V5. If design mis takes are found during the checking proc ess, we can modify the design within the assembly context by invoking the Part Design workbench.

14.2 TERMS AND DEFINITIONS

14.2.1 Part

A part in general refers to a single volume solid geometry that is created in the Part Design workbench. We have learned how to create parts in previous chapters. A part file with the extension CAT Part contains all the information required in constructing the part geometry. In general, a part file contains only one part, i.e. you will not create two or more individual parts within a part file as separate solid bodies.

14.2.2 Product

A product refers to an assembly constructed with many parts. Information on constructing the assembly is recorded in the product file with the extension CAT Product. A product file can contain other products and components.

14.2.3 Component

If parts are assembled in the CAT Product file to construct an assembly, they are called components.

Parts used as components do not contain information on defining the part geometry. Instead, the part components only show the resulting geometry and have their own independent appearance, position and orientation.

A component can be an assembly which contains other part components. This type of component is called an assembly component to distinguish it from a part component. An assembly component is like a product, but it is not saved as a separate CAT Product file whereas a product can be saved as a CAT Product file. Actually. assemblies such as engines and transmissions which can be manufactured and managed as intermediate products have to be assembled in a CAT Product file. On the other hand, conceptual assemblies such as pipes and harnesses which do not need to exist as CAT Product files, are assembled in components.

14.2.4 Sub-assembly

Sub-assembly is a general term to refer to an assembly that is used as a component. In CATIA V5. if a product is inserted into another product as a component, it can be called a sub-assembly. An assembly component can also be created in a product as a sub-assembly.

14.2.5 Master Part

The information data for constructing a 3D model geometry is contained in a part file. If a part is used as a component, it is called a master part to distinguish it from the component.

14.2.6 Instance

Products and components can be referred to as in stances which can have their own color, appearance, position and orientation. Suppose that an automobile is assembled with 100 bolts pointing to the same master part. Each bolt can have its respective color, appearance, position and orientation although they have the same geometry.

14.2.7 BOM (Bill of Material)

BOM refers to a parts list which contains basic information on the parts that constitute a product.

14.2.8 Bottom-Up Assembly Design

Bottom-Up assembly design refers to an assembly process starting from the bottom of the assembly structure to construct the top assembly. Looking at Fig 14 -1, parts A through F are designed in advance independently and assembled to construct sub-assemblies, and finally to construct the top assembly.

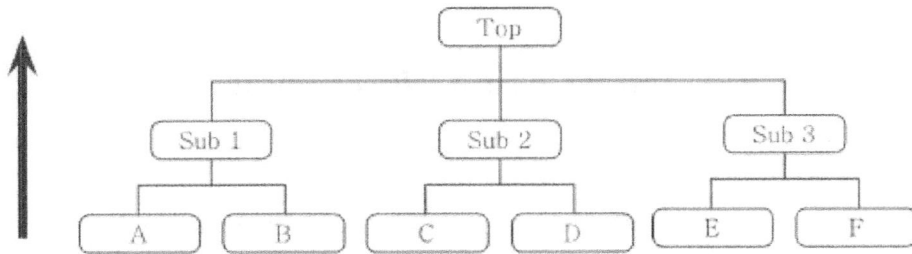

Fig 14-1 Concept Diagram of Bottom-Up Assembly Design

14.2.9 Top-Down Assembly Design

A process of creating certain parts in the context of assembly is called a Top-Down assembly design. Referring to the diagram shown in Fig 1 4-2, the top assembly is constructed with the parts A, B, C, E and F and then the missing part D is created in the Part Design workbench referencing the geometry and position of the other components. Yon can also modify a part in the context of assembly.

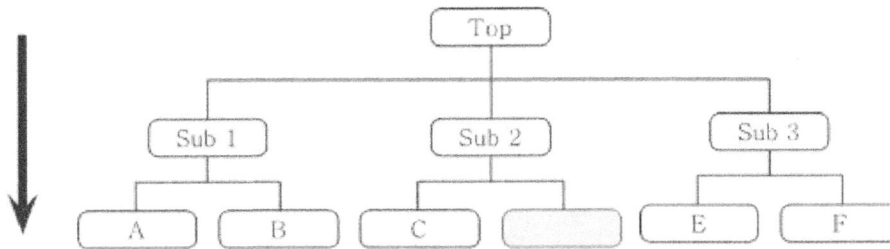

Fig 14-2 Concept Diagram of Top-Down Assembly Design

14.3 CONSTRUCTING AN ASSEMBLY

Constructing an assembly, in most cases entails assembling components in the Bottom up assembly design. We will move or constrain the components to define their position and orientation.

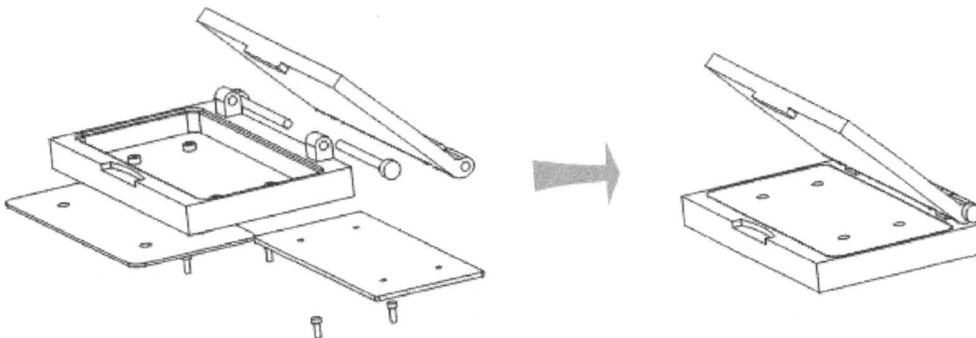

Fig 14-3 Constructing an Assembly

377

14.3.1 Invoking the Assembly Design Workbench

Using the Start Menu

To invoke the Assembly Design workbench, choose Mechanical Design > Assembly Design in the Start menu. You can invoke the Assembly Design workbench in this way while you have a file opened or with a new file.

If you have registered a Start Menu by customizing, the Assembly Design menu ap- pears in the start menu list as shown in Fig 14-4 (A).

When the Assembly Design workbench is invoked, a product named Product1 is created automatically and the toolbars to construct an assembly become available.

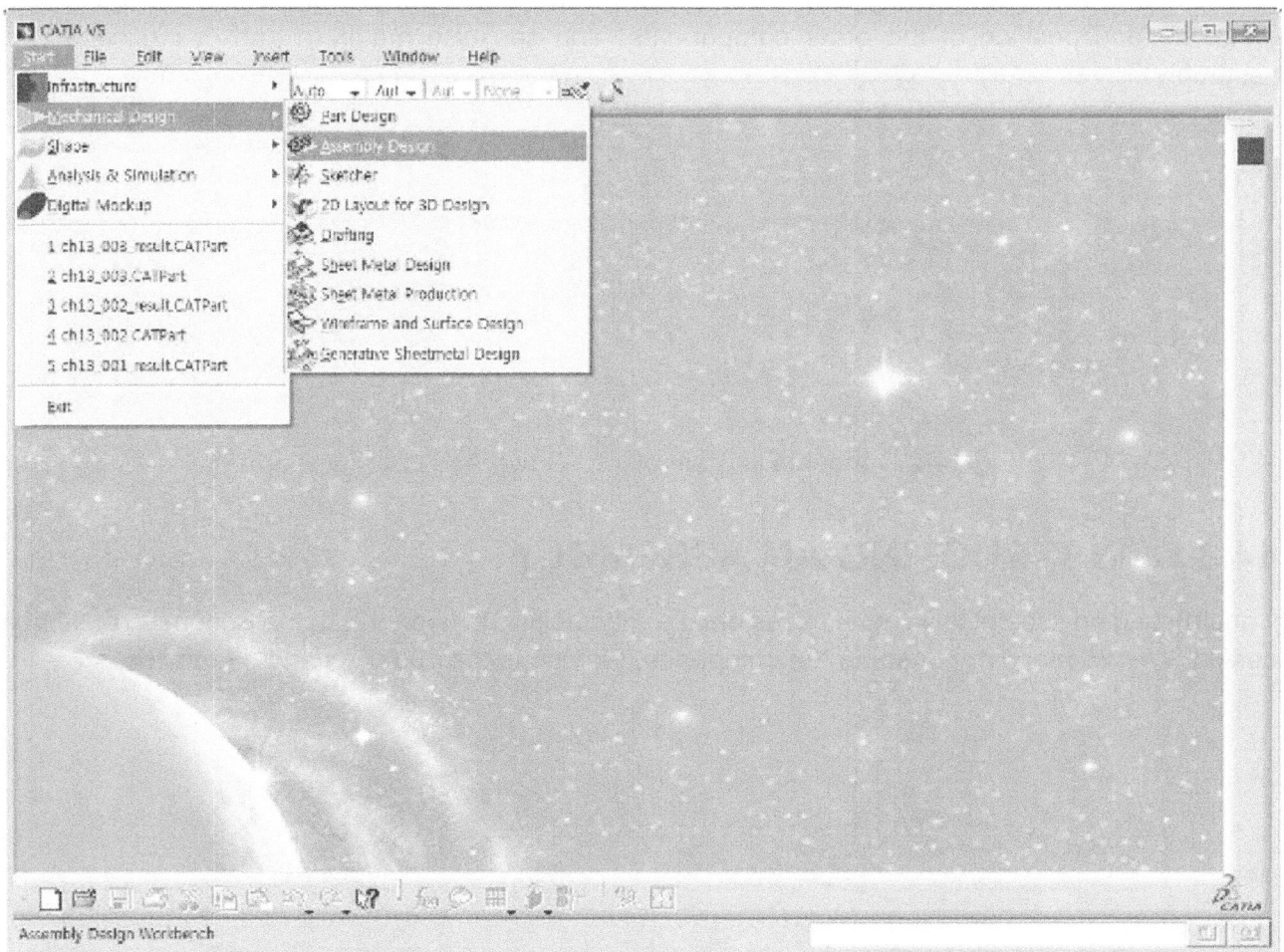

Fig 14-4 Invoking the Assembly Design Workbench

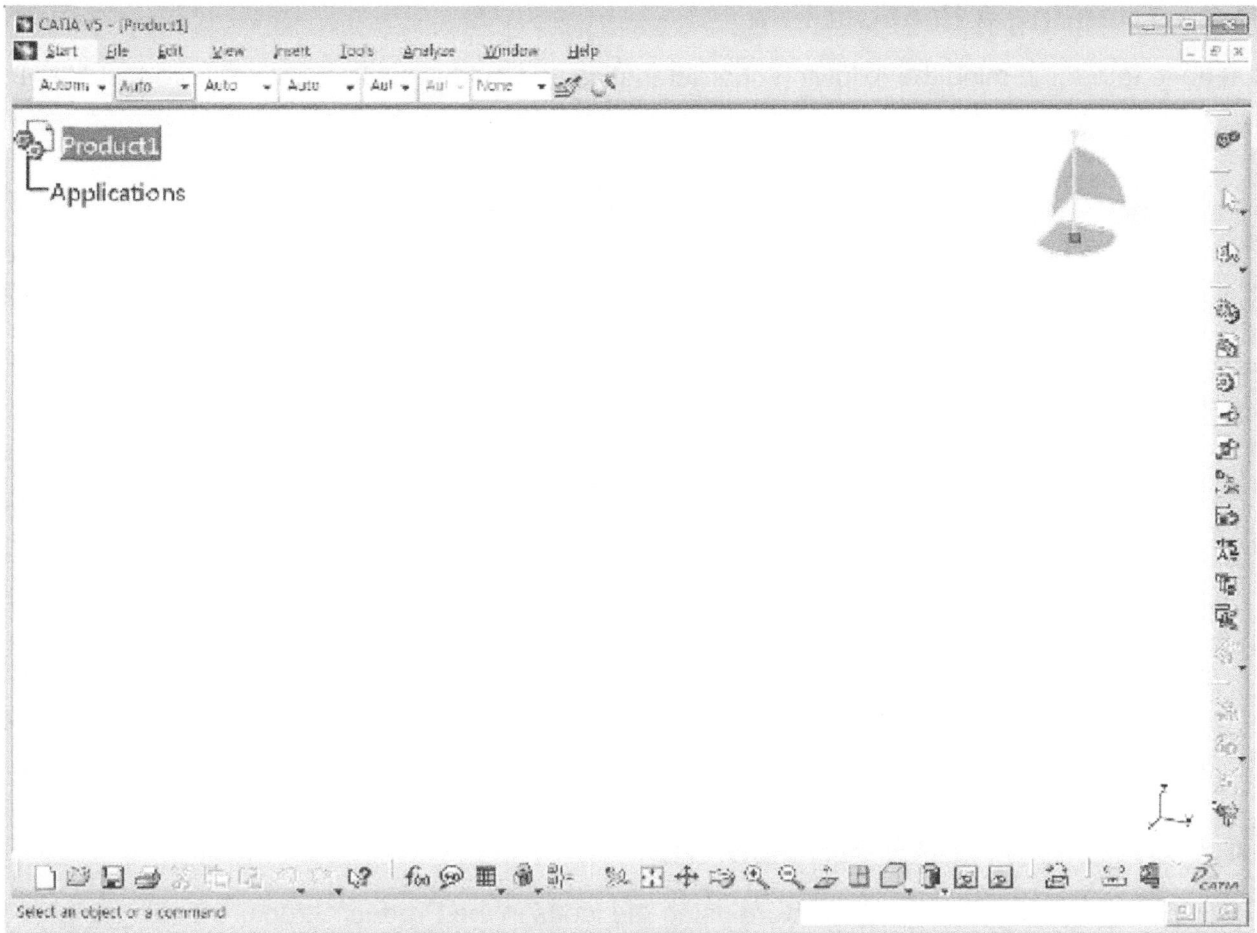

Fig 14-5 Screen of the Assembly Design Workbench

Using File > New Menu

Choose File > New in the menu bar. A New dialog box as shown in Fig 14-6 appears and you can specify the type of the file as a Product. Pressing the OK button, a product type new file is defined in the Assembly Design workbench as shown in Fig 14-5.

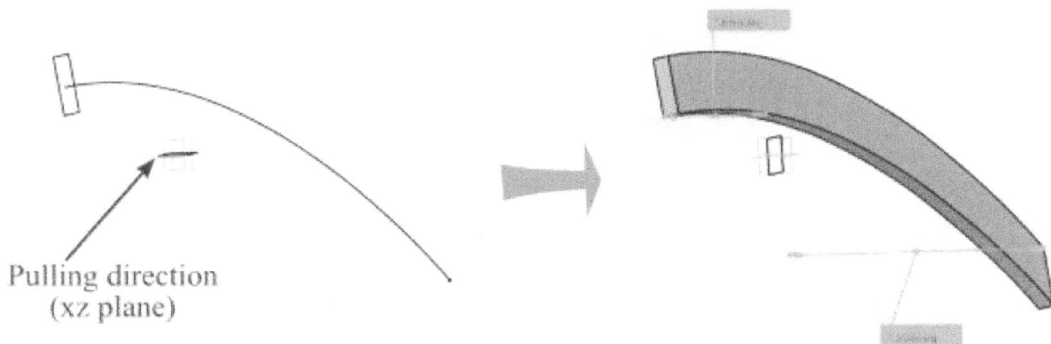

Pulling direction
(xz plane)

Fig 14-6 New Dialog Box

14.3.2 Creating a Product File

You have to bear in mind the following characteristics and guidelines in creating a product file.

1. File type is Product.
2. Extension of the product file is *.CATProduct
3. Save the product file in the same folder as the master part file.
4. Geometry of the component can be shown only when the master part file exists. Therefore, you have to have the product file and part files of the components at the same time to open and review the assembly status.

14.3.3 Key Functions of Assembly Design

The following are key functions that are available in the Assembly Design workbench.

1. **Creating an Assembly Structure:** You can create a product using part components and/or sub-assemblies.
2. **Constraining:** Define the position and orientation of each component.
3. **Checking interference:** Investigate if the volume of an instance intrudes other components.
4. **Part Modeling:** You can create a part referencing the geometry of other components.
5. **Creating a Disassembled Status:** You can disassemble the product to create an exploded assembly drawing.

14.4 CREATING AN ASSEMBLY

You can construct an assembly structure using the icons in the Product Structure Tools toolbar.

- **Component:** Inserts components in an assembly. I t is a sub-assembly that does not need to exist as a product file.
- **Product:** Inserts a sub-assembly. It is a sub-assembly that has to exist as a product file.
- **Part:** Inserts a new part component without any geometry. You can then create geometry in the part file.
- **Existing Component:** Inserts a part component that has already been created in the Part Design workbench.
- **Existing Component with Positioning:** Applies constraints while inserting a part component.

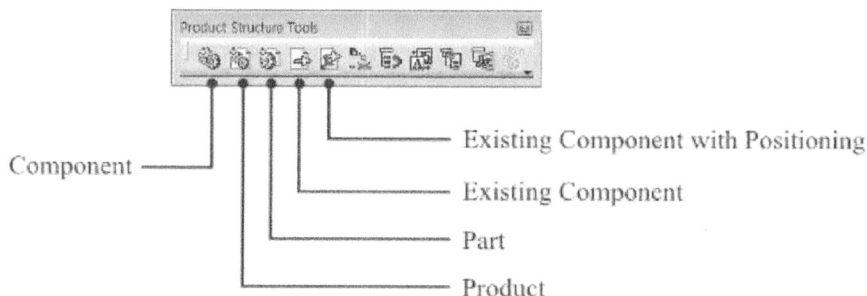

Fig 14-7 Product Structure Tools Toolbar

14.4.1 Inserting an Existing Part as a Component

A part can be inserted in a product in two steps.

- Step 1: Click the Existing Component icon in the Product Structure Tools toolbar.

Fig 14-8 Existing Component Icon

- Step 2: Select the product in the Spec Tree in which to insert the component.

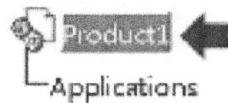

Fig 14-9 Selecting Product

Exercise 120: Creating a Product (Folder: ch14 _001)

Let's create a product using parts in the given folder ch14 _001.

Inserting a Component

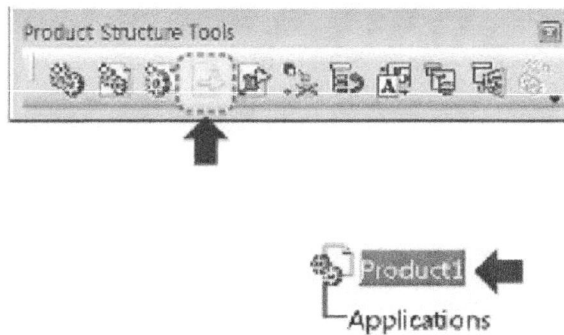

Fig 14-10 Inserting a Component

1. Execute CATIA V5 if it is not running already.
2. Close all files by choosing File > Close in the menu bar.
3. Choose File > New, et the file type as Product and press OK in the New dialog box.
4. Choose the Existing Component icon in the Product Structure Tools toolbar.

Read the status bar message.

Select a component into which the existing component will be inserted

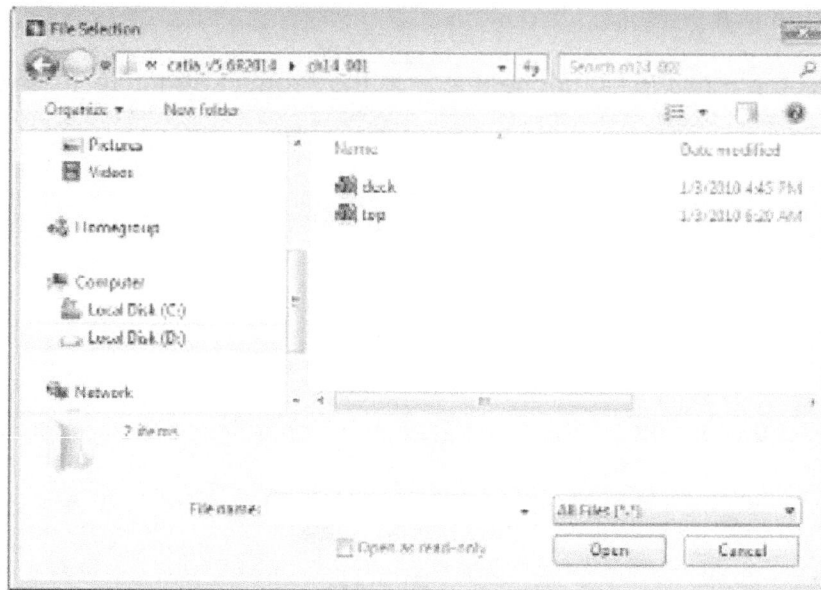

Fig 14-11 File Selection

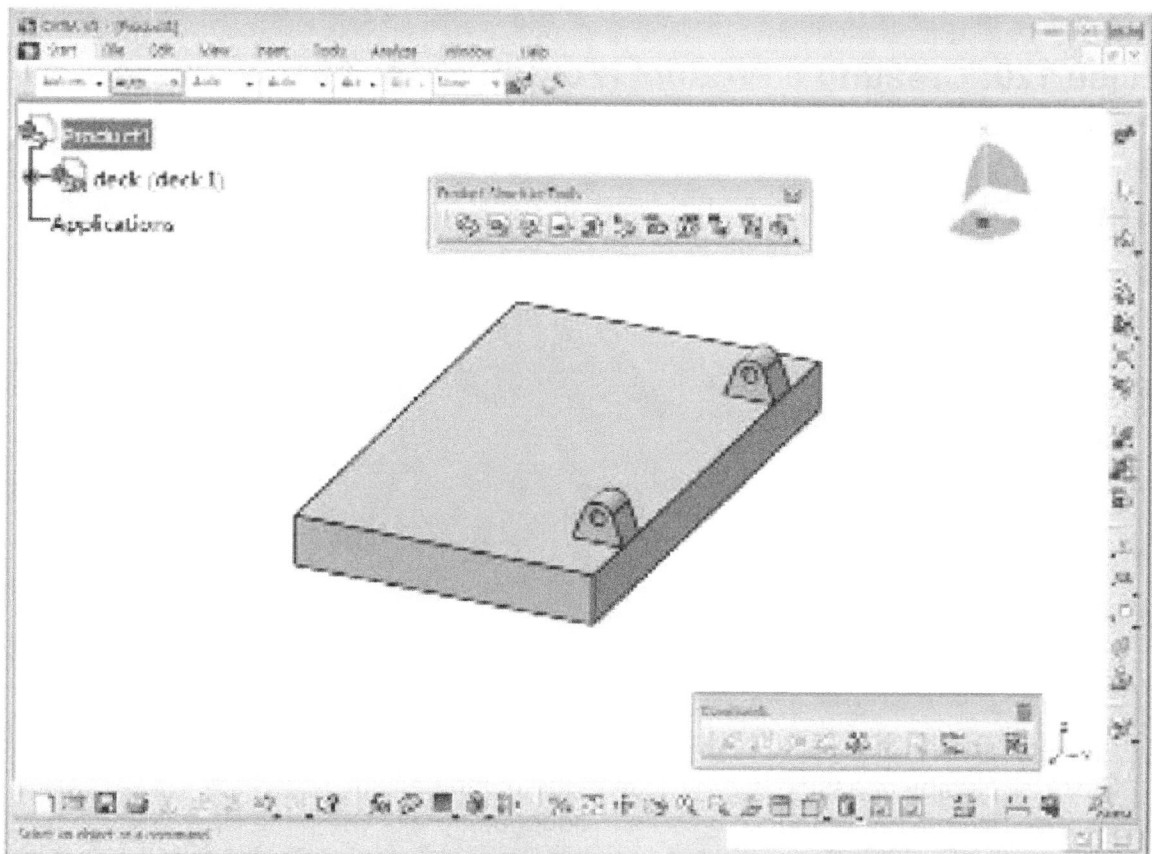

Fig 14-12 Inserted Component

5. Select Product1 in the Spec Tree. A dialog box as shown in Fig 14-11 ap- pear s.
6. Select deck.CATPart in the dialog box and press Enter or the Open button. The part is inserted as a component as shown in Fig 14-12.
7. Click the Existing Component icon again and select Product1 to insert top. CATPart.

Renaming

1. Right click on Product1 in the Spec Tree and select Properties.
2. Press the Product tab and input "notebook_assy" in the Part Number input box (refer to Fig 14-13).
3. Pres the OK button.

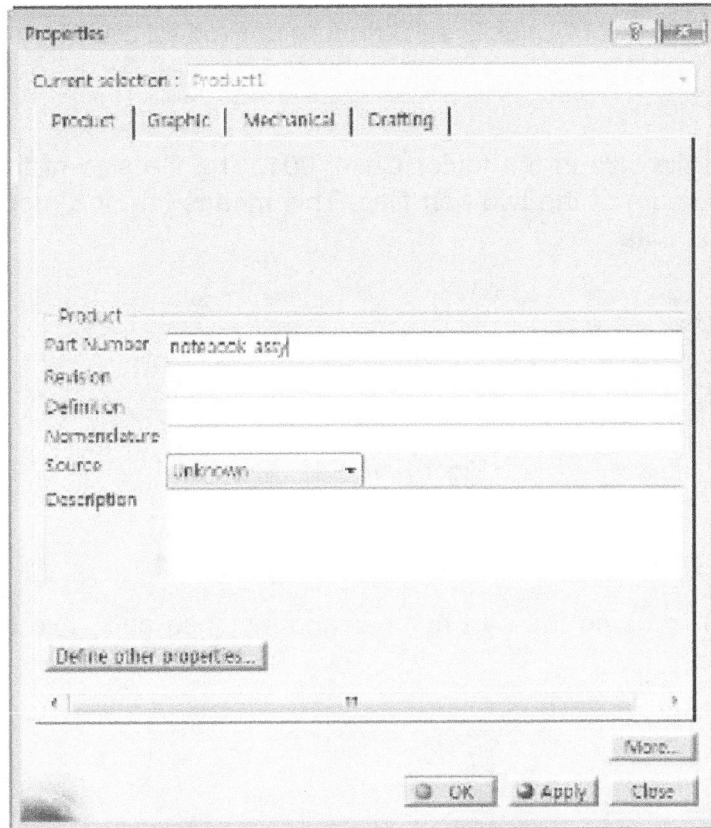

Fig 14-13 Setting Part number

4. Select File > Save in the menu bar. A Save As dialog box is invoked.
5. Save the product file in the same folder as the part file.

It is recommended that you do not close the product file before continuing wit h the next exercise.

14.4.2 Name of Product and Instance

Fig 14-14 shows the Spec Tree structure for the product file and the part file. The part number set in the part file is the component name in the product file. The name in the parent thesis (deck.1) is the instance name, which is required when you have to distinguish the name of each instance.

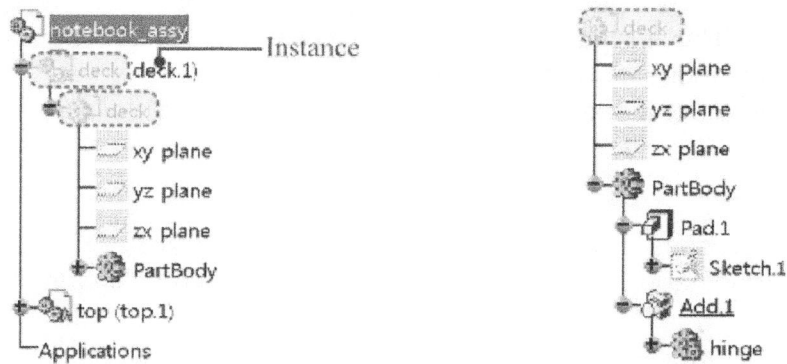

Fig 14-14 Spec Tree Structure of Product and Part

(Note) File Size

- Let's check the file size in the folder Ch14_001. The file size of the product file is much smaller than the sum of the two-part files. This means that the product file does not have part specification data.

Name ▲	Size	Type
deck.CATPart	137 KB	CATIA Part
notebook_assy.CATProduct	16 KB	CATIA Product
top.CATPart	120 KB	CATIA Part

Fig 14- 15 File Size

Exercise 121: Renaming and Save Management

In this exercise, we will rename the part number and instance and save the file using the Save Management command.

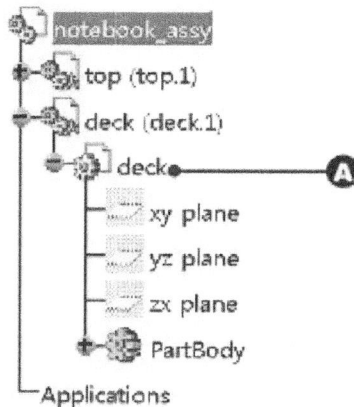

Fig 14-16 Spec Tree

1. Click the + symbol in front of the "deck" component and click the + symbol in front of the "deck" part The Spec Tree is expanded as shown in Fig 14-16.

2. Right click on (A) in Fig 14-16 and select Properties in the pop-up menu. A Properties dialog box is invoked as shown in Fig 14-17.
3. Press the Product tab and enter the Instance name ((B) in Fig 14-17) as bottom! and the Part Number ((C) in Fig 14- I7) as bottom.
4. Press the OK button in the dialog box.
5. Confirm that each name has been changed in the Spec Tree.
6. Choose File > Save Management in the menu bar. A Save Management dialog box is invoked as shm.vn in Fig 1 4-18. You can identify the modified file in the State column.
7. Select the Notebook_assy.CATProduct file and press the Save button on the right of the dialog box.
8. Select the deck.CATpart file and press the Save button.

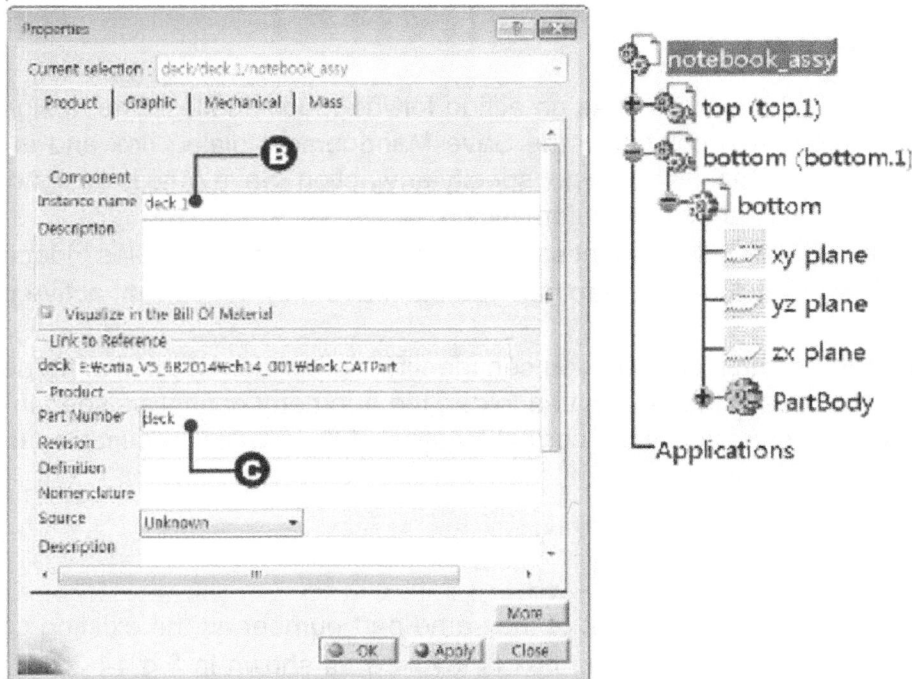

Fig 14-17 Renaming

9. Confirm that Save is assigned in the Action column in the dialog box as shown in Fig 14-19.
10. Press the OK button in the dialog box. The Save action is performed.

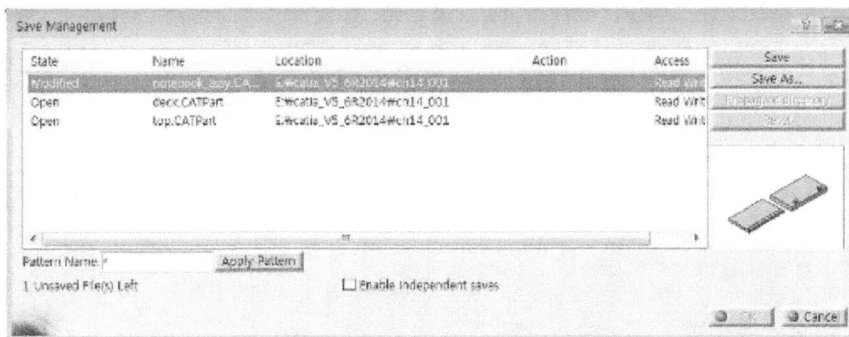

Fig 14-18 Save Management Dialog Box

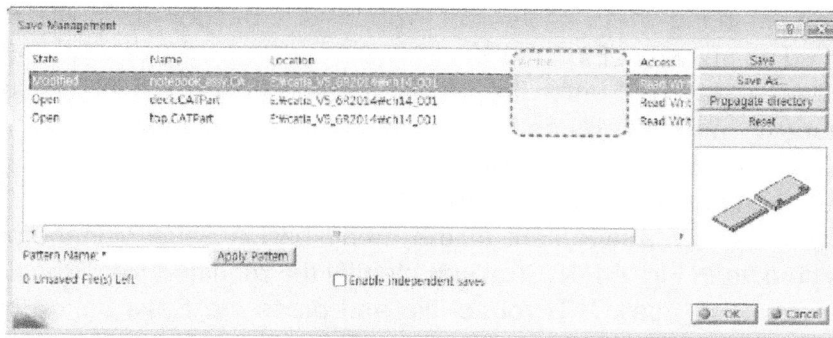

Fig 14-19 Action Column

(Note) Save Management

- You can specify Save or Save As an action for the modified files. The designated action is assigned in the Action column in the Save Management dialog box and is performed on pressing the OK button. If you do not specify any action, Save Auto is assigned in the Action column and the files are saved automatically.
- Checking the Enable independent saves option, you can save the files independently.
- Choosing File > Save in the menu bar, you can save only the current active product or part file.
- Looking at the Location column, you can identify the location of the file. If There arc no part files or product files in the designated folder, the geometry cannot be seen in the assembly. In this case, you can specify the correct location of the part or product files using the menu bar command Edit > Relink.

14.4.3 Part Number Conflicts

If you try to insert a different component of the same part number as the existing component in a product, the Part number conflicts dialog box is invoked as shown in Fig 14-20. If you press the Rename button in the dialog box, the Part Number dialog box appears and you can enter a different part number. If you press the Automatic rename button, an automatic part number is assigned.

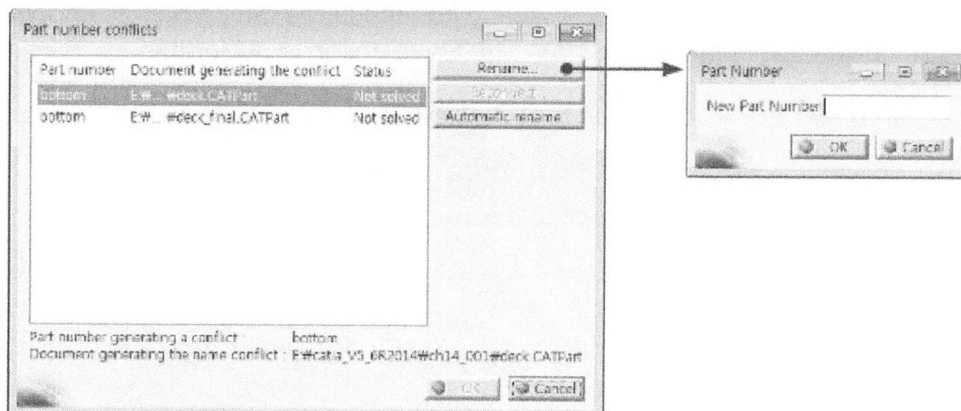

Fig 14-20 Part Number Conflicts Dialog Box

14.4.4 Closing Files

You can close a product file by choosing File > Close in the menu bar. Note that you cannot close each component or sub-product.

14.4.5 Opening a File

You can open a product file by choosing File > Open in the menu bar. You can choose Open as read-only option in the File Selection dialog box.

14.4.6 Activating Part File

You can activate a part £le by double clicking the pa1t number in the Spec Tree as shown in Fig 14-21. Note that the active file is highlighted in blue and that the workbench changes according to the type of the active file. For example, if you activate a part file, a workbench for modeling such as Part Design or Generative Shape Design is invoked.

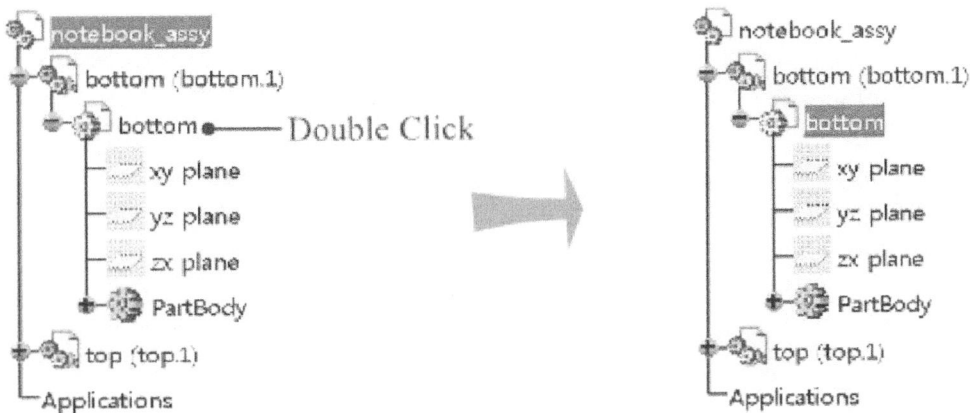

Fig 14-21 Activating a Part File

You can return to the Assembly workbench by double clicking the product name in the Spec Tree.

Activating a part file is a very important action when you are creating a model in the con- text of assembly, which will be explained in detail in Chapter 15. Note that the current active file is highlighted in blue and that you have to activate proper file to do your desired work That is to say, you have to activate a product file to do the assembly work and activate a part file to do the modeling work.

(Note) Low Light Mode

- You can identify current active file graphically by choosing the Low Light Mode option by accessing Options > Infrastructure > Product Structure and choosing the Low Light Mode option in the Product Structure tab.

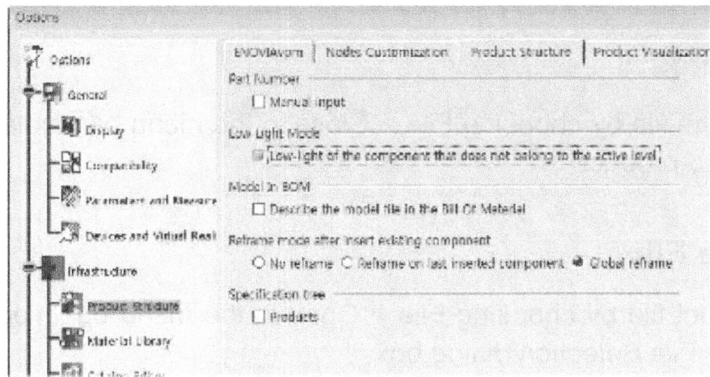

Fig 14-22 Low Light Mode Option

14.5 MOVE COMPONENT

When a component is inserted in the product, the Move toolbar is activated. You can move components either using the Manipulation icon in the toolbar or using the Compass on the top right in the graphic window.

Remember that we are moving or rotating components in the con text of assembly, which means that the manipulation operation does not have any impact on the part file.

Exercise 122: Move Component (Folder: ch14 _003)

1. Open the notebook_assy.CATProduct file.

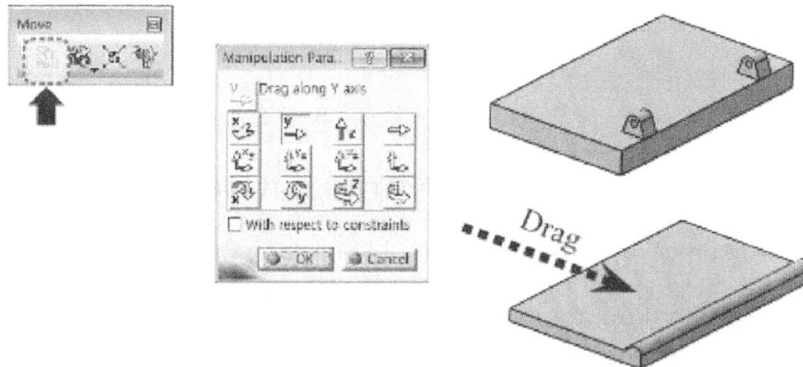

Fig 14-23 Moving Component

2. Click the Manipulation icon in the Move toolbar. The Manipulation Parameters dialog box is invoked. Note that the x (   ) button is activated.

3. Press the y (   ) button and read the status bar message.
4. Drag the " top" component along the Y direction.
5. Click OK in the Manipulation Parameters dialog box.

We will move the component along the Z direction using the Compass.

6. Right click on the Compass and choose Snap Automatically to Selected Object in the pop-up menu.

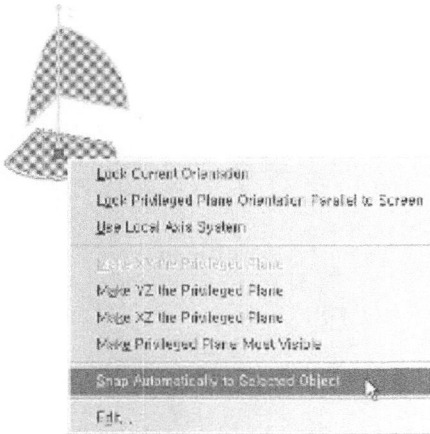

Fig 14-24 Compass Snap Option

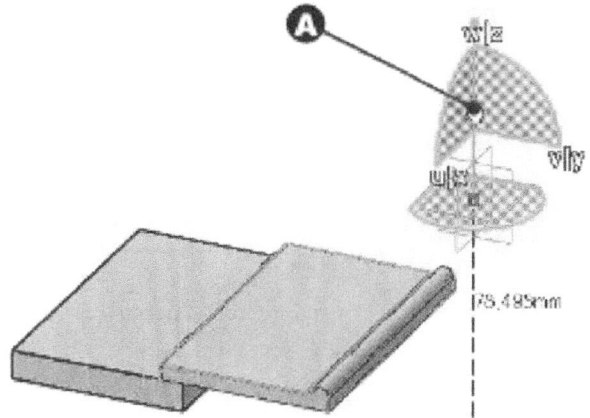

Fig 14-25 Dragging the Compass

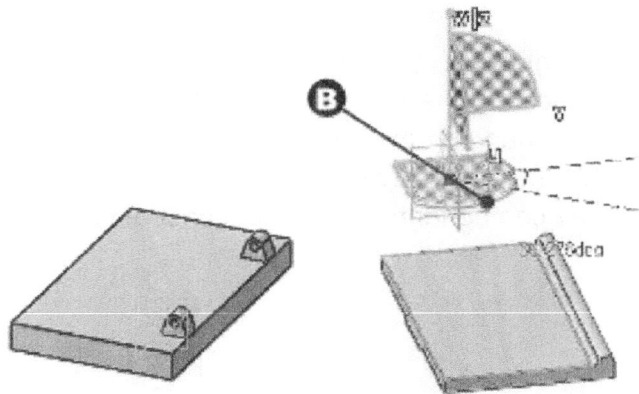

Fig 14-26 Rotating the Compass

7. Pick an arbitrary face of the " top" component. The Compass moves onto the " top" component and is colored yellow green.
8. Click the w/z axis line designated by (A) in Fig 14-25 and d rag it and drop to a proper location.
9. Click the arc on the bottom plane of the Compass as designated by (B) in Fig 14-26 and drag it to rotate the component.
10. Drag the red dot at the origin of the Compass and drop it on the coordinate shown in the bottom right corner of the graphic window.
11. Right click on the Compass and choose the Snap Automatically to Selected Object option in the pop-up menu to tum it off.

389

14.6 CONSTRAINING COMPONENTS

Using icons in the Constraints toolbar, you can constrain the movement or rotation of components within an assembly. Remember that the position and orientation of an object in the space can be defined completely with six degrees of freedom, i.e. three translational and three rotational degrees of freedom.

Fig 14-27 shows the Constraints toolbar.

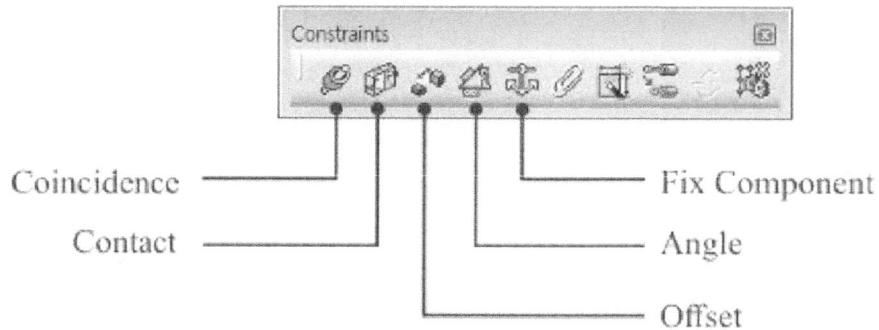

Fig 14- 27 Constraints Toolbar

14.6.1 Fix

When you are applying constraints to components, you have to determine a base component and fix it using the Fix Component icon in the Constraints toolbar. Other components are constrained with regard to the fixed component or the fully constrained components. A fully constrained component cannot move within the assembly with regard to the base component. Note that if there does not exist at least one fixed component, you cannot constrain the components fully.

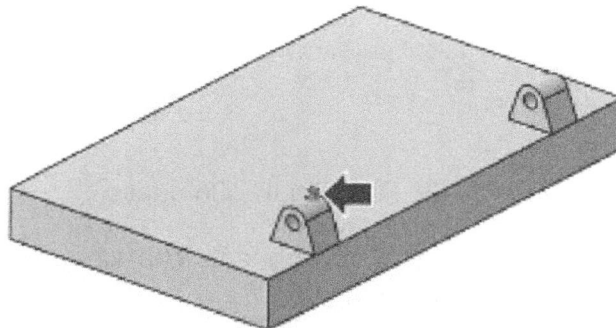

Fig 14-28 Fix Symbol

14.6.2 Coincidence

Using the Coincidence Constraint, you can align planar faces, points and lines with each other. In aligning two planar faces, the normal direction of the plane can be set using the Orientation option.

390

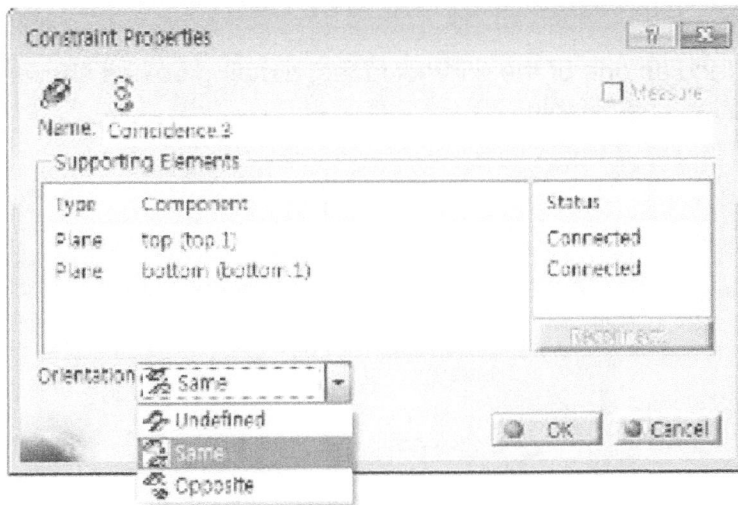

Fig 14-29 Constraint Properties Dialog Box or Coincidence

Fig 14-30 shows selecting the Same orientation option in aligning the two planes (A) and (B). The normal vectors of each plane are defined the same as each other.

Fig 14-31 shows selecting the Opposite orientation option. Note that the normal vector of plane (B) points in the opposite direction and is aligned to the normal vector of plane (A).

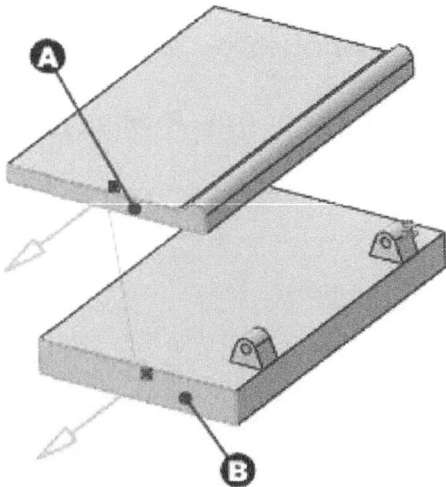

Fig 14-30 Same Orientation

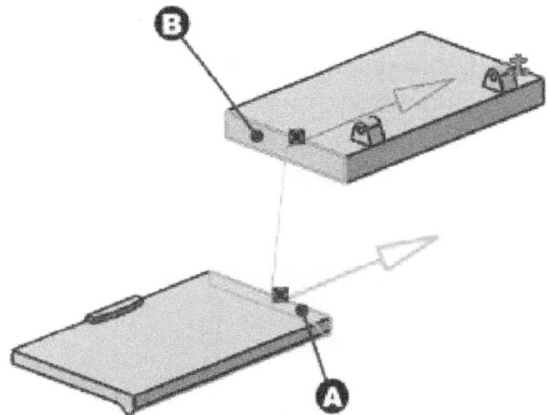

Fig 14-31 Opposite Orientation

14.6.3 Contact

Using the Contact Constraint icon in the Constraints toolbar, planar spherical and cylindrical face can be made to contact each other. If you have selected two planar faces, the result is the same as that of the Opposite orientation of the Coincidence constraint.

If you select a curved face as one of the contact faces, a dialog box as shown in Fig 14-32 appears and the Orientation option is available.

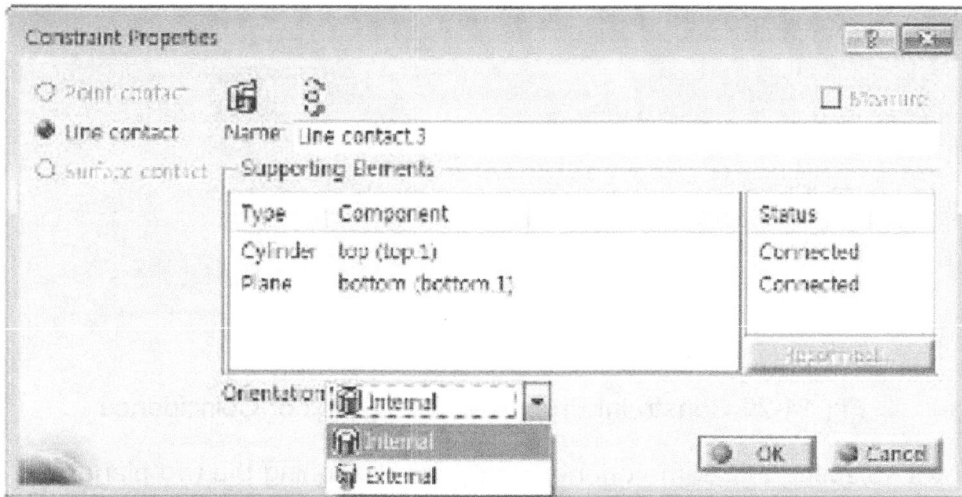

Fig 14-32 Constraint Properties Dialog Box of Contact

Exercise 123: Constraining a Component (Folder: ch14 _004)

Setting an Option

1. Open the file saved in Exercise 01. You can open the given file notebook_assy.CATProduct in the given folder ch14_004.
2. Choose Start > Mechanical Design > Assembly Design if you are not in the Assembly Design workbench.
3. Set the Update option to Automatic as shown in Fig 14-33.

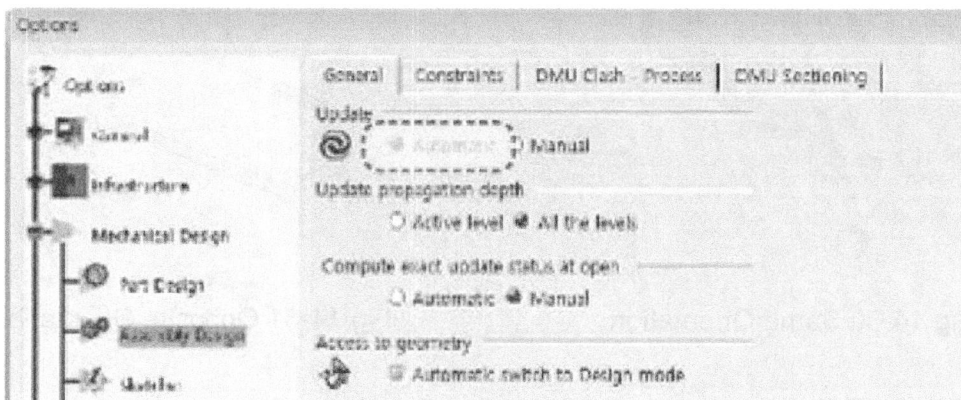

Fig 14-33 Update Option

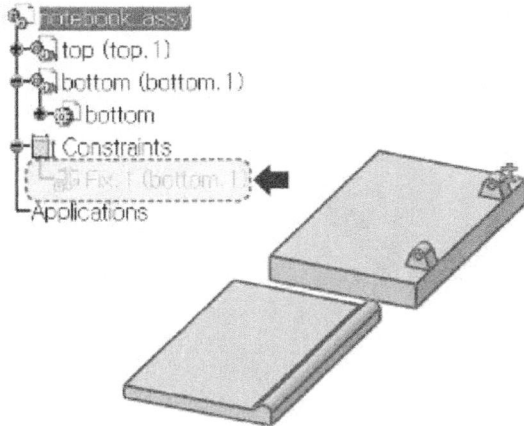

Fig 14-34 Applying Fix Component   Fig 14-35 Applying Coincidence

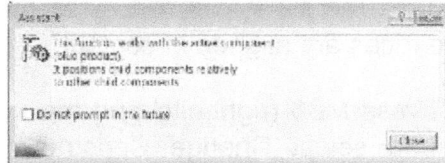

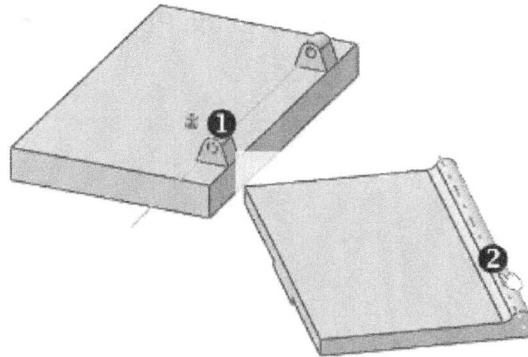

Fix

1. Choose Fix Component in the Constraints toolbar and read the status bar message.
2. Select the "bottom" component. A Fixed symbol appears on the component and in the Spec Tree.

Coincidence Constraint

1. Choose Coincidence Constraint in the Constraints toolbar.

Read the message in the Assistant dialog box. Check the Do not prompt in the future option and press Close.

The status bar message prompts you to select the first geometric element.

2. Select the centerline of the "bottom" component designated by (1) in Fig 14-35. Note that you have to click MB1 (left click) when the centerline is highlighted.

The status bar message prompts you to elect the second geometric element.

3. Select the centerline of the "top" component designated by (2) in Fig 14-35. Remember that you have to click MB1 (left click) when the centerline is highlighted.

The two centerlines are aligned as shown in Fig 14-36.

Contact Constraint and Change Constraint

Fig 14-36 Result of Coincidence

1. Choose Contact Constraint in the Constraints toolbar.
2. Select the two faces (3) and (4) as shown in Fig 14-36.

The two faces are aligned in contact.

3. Press MB3 (right click) on the symbol of the contact constraint that has just been applied and select Change Constraint from the pop-up menu. You can press MB3 on the corresponding constraint on the Spec Tree.
4. Select Coincidence in the Possible Constraints dialog box and press OK.

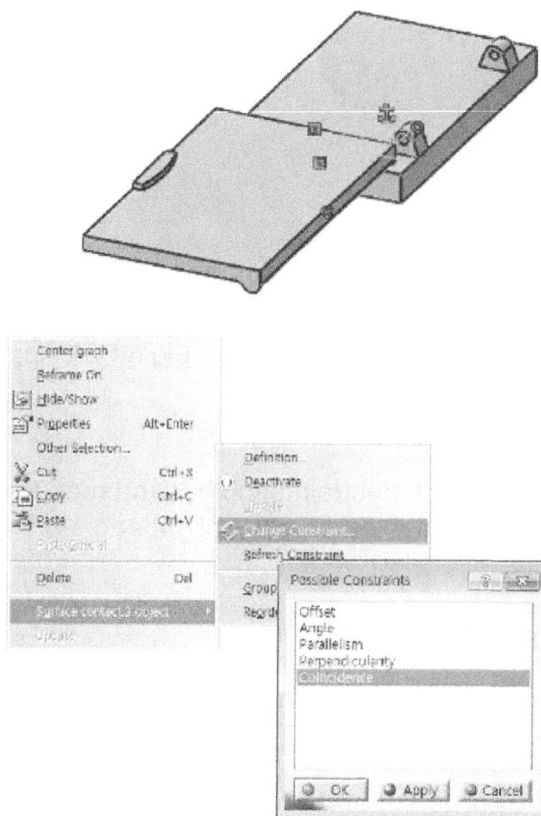

Fig 14-37 Changing Constraint

5. Double click the replaced Coincidence constraint.
6. Press the More button in the Constraint Definition dialog box.

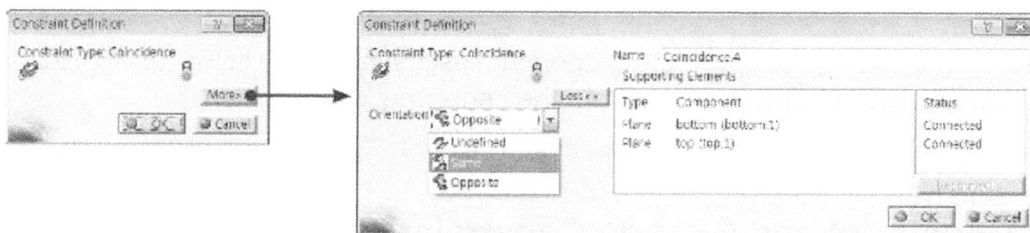

Fig 14-38 Orientation Option

7. Set the Orientation option to Same and press OK.

Fig 14-39 shows the result of the constraints.

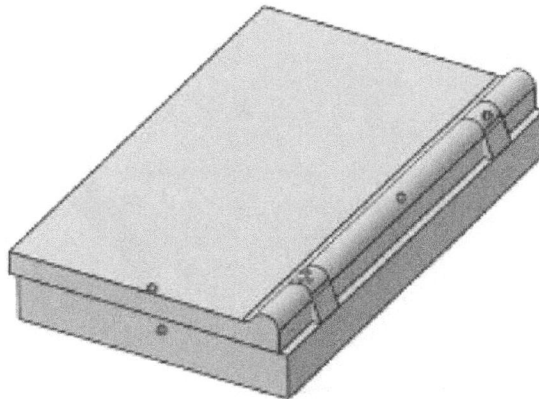

Fig 14- 39 Result of Constraints

8. Save the file.

(Note) Other Commands in the Constraints Toolbar

- **Offset:** Applied distance between objects.
- **Fix Together:** Binds several components into one. The bound components can be considered as a single component.
- **Quick Constraint:** Creates constraints automatically.
- **Flexible/Rigid Subassembly:** You can apply different constraints in the sub-assembly.
- **Change Constraint:** Substitutes a constraint for another.
- **Reuse Pattern:** Applies pattern for the components that are being assembled to a pattern feature.

14.6.4 Moving Components with the Snap Icon

In a similar method as applying constraints, we can move components with regard to the geometry of other components. Note that the constraint is not app lied, but the component moves as if the constraint has been applied.

Procedure

1. Click the Snap icon in the Move toolbar.
2. Select an element from the component to be moved.
3. Select an element from the base component.
4. Click the empty area in the screen to move the first selected component. You can click the green arrow to switch the alignment direction.

Note that the green arrow may or may not appear according to the type of element you selected.

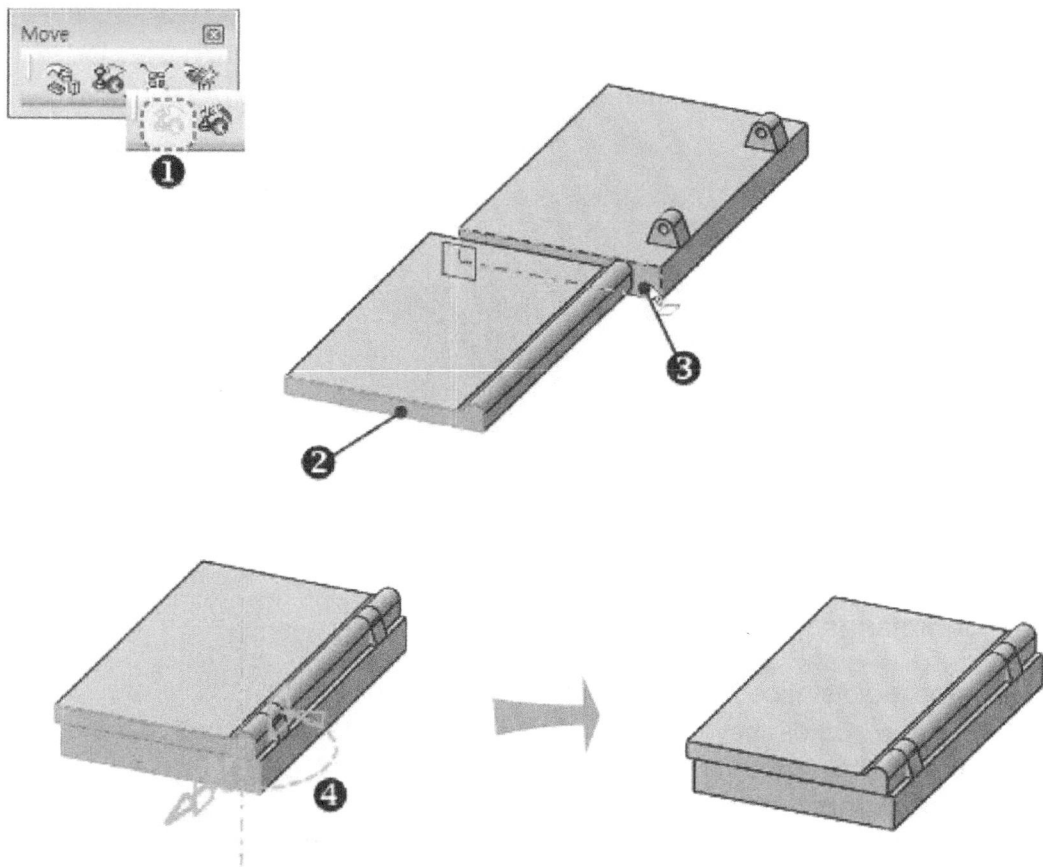

Fig 14-40 Moving Components with Snap Command

14.6.5 Moving Components with the Smart Move Icon

You can move a component in the same way as the Snap command. Note that you can apply constraints with the Automatic constraint creation option.

Procedure

1. Click the Smart Move icon in the Move toolbar.
2. Set the options in the Smart Move dialog box.
3. Select the first element in a component.
4. Select the second element in another component. The first component is snap ped to the second component and a yellow green arrow appears.
5. Click an empty area in the screen or press the OK button in the Smart Move dialog box.

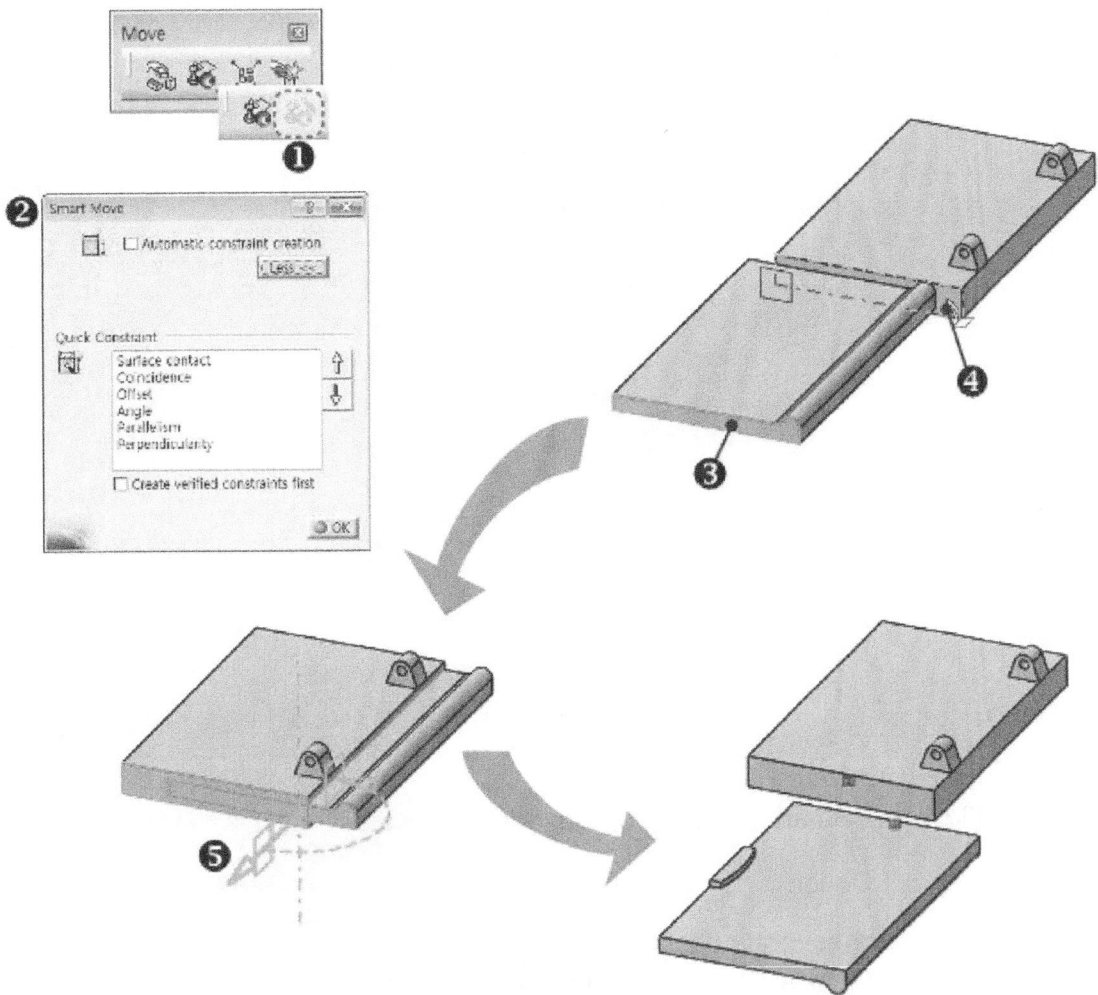

Fig 14-41 Applying Constraint with Smart Move Command

(Note) Component Preview and Quick Constraint Options

1. Component Preview

By selecting components in advance and then pressing the Smart Move button, the component is previewed in the Smart Move dialog box. The component is switched by pressing the Next component button. This method is useful when moving several components among many components or when you have to select components hidden by other components.

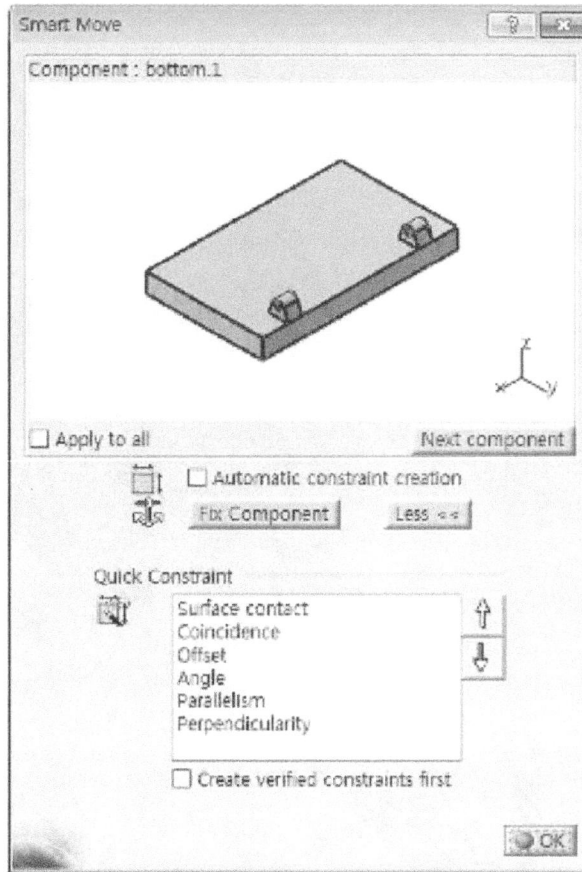

Fig 14-42 Smart Move Dialog Box after Pre-selecting Components

2. Quick Constraint Option

In cases where several constraints are available between the selected elements in the components, the upper type listed in the Quick Constraint option is applied with priority. For example, if you have selected two faces as shown in Fig 14-41, the Surface contact is applied instead   of Coincidence because the Surface contact is located at the top of the list.

14.6.6 Verifying Constraint Status

You can verify the status of constraints in two steps.

3. Verify the who le constraint status in the assembly.
4. Identify the degrees of freedom of each component.

To verify the status of constraint in an assembly, you have to activate the assembly by double clicking it in the Spec Tree. Then choose Analyze > Constraints in the men u bar. The assembly constraint status is displayed in the dialog box shown on the left of Fig 14-43. If you press the Degrees of Freedom tab the remaining degrees of freedom for the components can be identified.

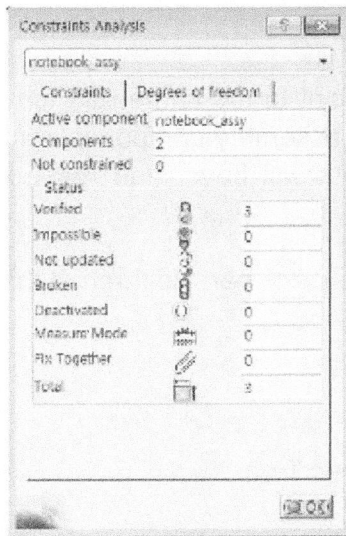

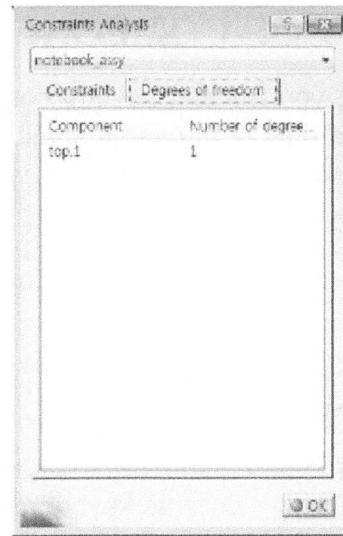

Fig 14-43 Verifying Stants of Assembly Constraint

To identify the remaining degrees of freedom of a component take one of the following procedures.

Using the Pop-up Menu

1. Activate the assembly in which the component is inserted.
2. Right click on the component and choose * object > Component Degrees of Free dom.

Using Analyze > Degree(s) of Free in the Menu Bar

1. Activate the assembly in which the component is inserted.
2. Choose Analyze > Degree(s) of Freedom in the menu bar.

The remaining degrees of freedom are displayed on the component by a corresponding symbol and detailed information is displayed in the Degree of Freedom Analysis dialog box as shown in Fig 14-44.

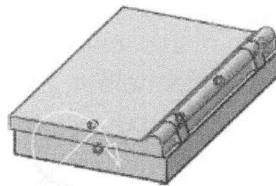

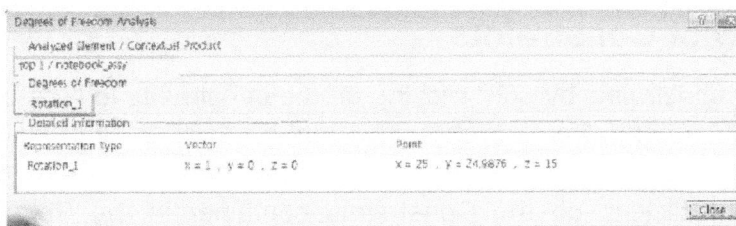

Fig 14-44 Identifying Component Degree of Freedom

14.7 COPY OF COMPONENTS

In most cases, you will add several component s which point to the same part file. For example, many bolts and nuts of the same standard will be used to assemble components in an assembly. The geometry of the bolts and nuts will be the same, but will have their respective positions, orientations and colors in the assembly.

You can add a component that points to the geometry of the same part file through the following two methods.

14.7.1 Copy/Paste

1. Select the part number of the components in the Spec Tree.
2. Press CTRL + C in the keyboard to copy the components.
3. Click the product where to paste the components.
4. Press CTRL + V in the keyboard to paste the components.

Note that the components will be overlapped in the graphic window. Therefore, you are recommended to move the pasted component.

14.7.2 Existing Component Icon

You can insert components as many times as required using the Existing Component command in the Product Structure Tools toolbar. Note that, if you choose a wrong file with the same geometry, file name or part number as the components that have already been inserted , you may be encountered with an error.

14.8 HIDE/SHOW

14.8.1 Hide/Show of Components

You can hide or show component by right clicking on the component in the Spec Tree and choosing Hide/Show in the pop-up menu. Note that this command is available while you are applying constraints by clicking an icon in the Constraints toolbar, and you can hide unnecessary components for applying constraints. Fig 14-45 shows the pop-up menu which is available with or without executing a command.

14.8.2 Hide/Show of Constraints

You can hide or show constraints by right clicking on the constraints to hide or show and choosing Hide/Show in the pop-up menu. You can select several constraints by pressing the CTRL or Shift key and hide or show the constraints at the same time as shown in Fig 14-46. You can hide or show all constraints by right clicking on the Constraints container in the Spec Tree and choosing Hide/Show in the pop-up menu.

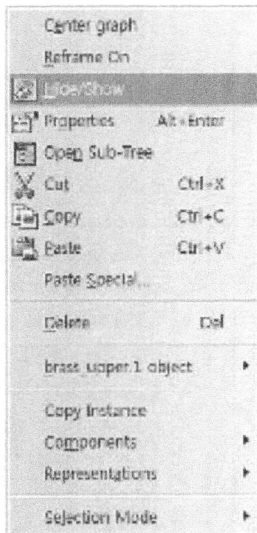

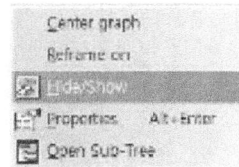

Fig 14-45 Hide/Show Menu of Components

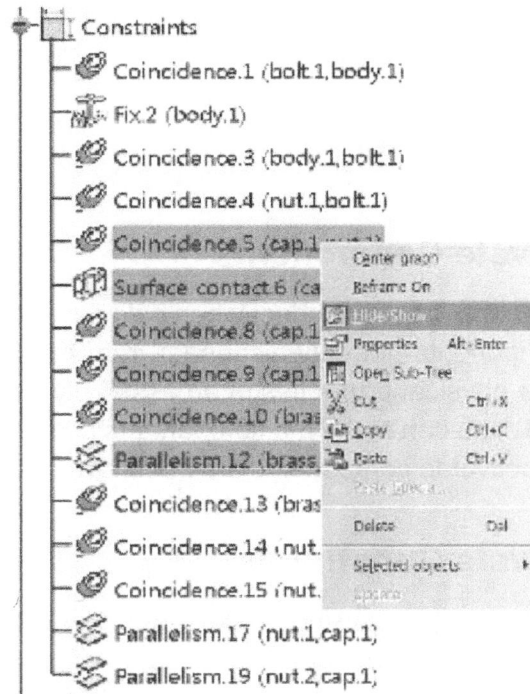

Fig 14-46 Hide/Show of Several Constraints

14.8.3 Identifying Component Constraint

Sometimes you need to identify constraints that have been applied for a certain component to modify or delete them. In this case, right click on the selected components and choose Selected objects > Component Constraints as shown in Fig 14-47. The constraints applied for the selected components are highlighted in the Constraints contain er in the Spec Tree as shown in Fig 14-48.

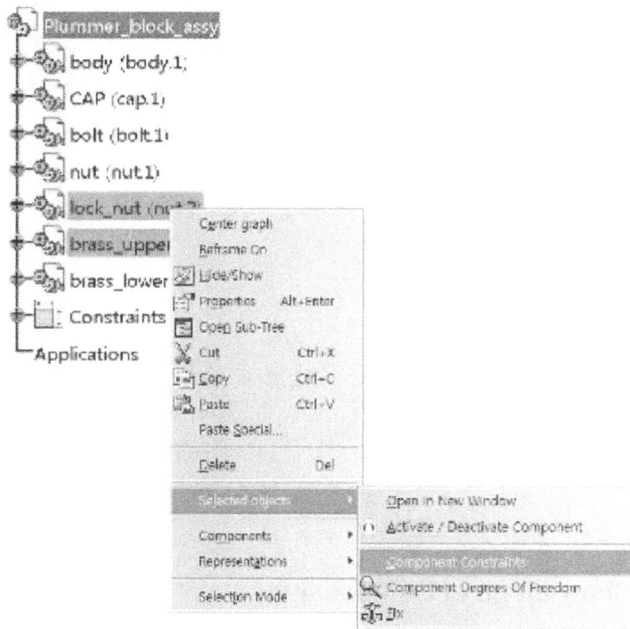

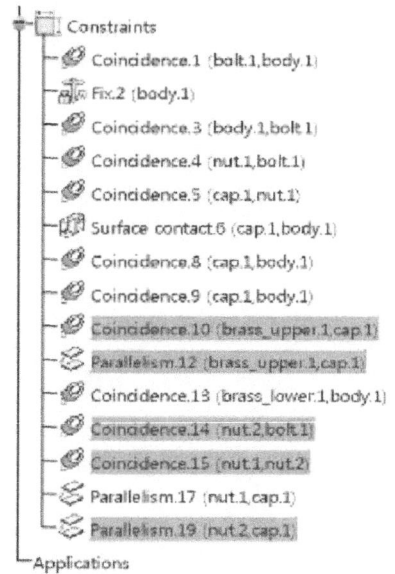

| Fig 14-47 Identifying Component Constraints | Fig 14-48 identified Constraints |

14.9 ACTIVATE/DEACTIVATE

14.9.1 Activate/Deactivate Components

You can exclude some components from a product when calculating the physical proper- ties of the product. The deactivated components not only disappear from the product but arc also not taken into account in calculating the physical properties of an assembly such as volume, mass, etc. with the Measure Inertia command. You can make the components active whenever required. Note that the hidden components or deactivated components are not shown in creating an assembly drawing.

14.9.2 Activate/Deactivate Constraints

You can deactivate constraints by right clicking on constraints and choosing Activate/De- activate in the pop-up me nu. The deactivated constraints do not take effect in constraining components as if the constraints are not applied. The difference between deactivating constraints and deleting them is that you can activate the deactivated constraints at any time you want. Deactivating constraints is useful when you make sure before you actually delete the constraints that you replace them with another constraint.

14.10 CONSTRUCTING SUB-ASSEMBLIES

You can construct sub-assemblies using the Product command or the Component command in the Product Structure Tools toolbar.

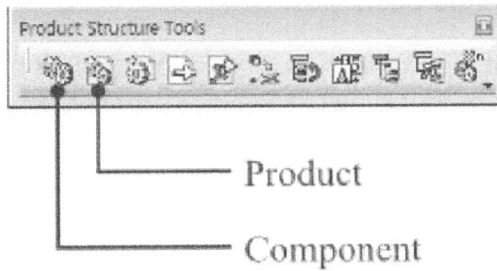

Fig 14-49 Product Structure Tools Toolbar

If you construct a sub-assembly using the Component icon in the Product Structure Tools toolbar, you cannot have a file for the sub-assembly. The component named Rings in Fig 14-50 has been created using the Component command. Note that the rings of piston assembly do not need to be managed as an actual sub-assembly in the real world, but you may need to manage the rings as a sub-assembly in the digital engine assembly.

The sub-assemblies such as Block_Assy, Head_Assy, Crank_Assy, Piston_Assy, etc. shown in Fig 14-50 have been constructed by using the Product icon in the Product Structure Tools toolbar because you need to manage them as sub-assemblies or assembled parts both in the digital engine assembly and in the real world engine assembly.

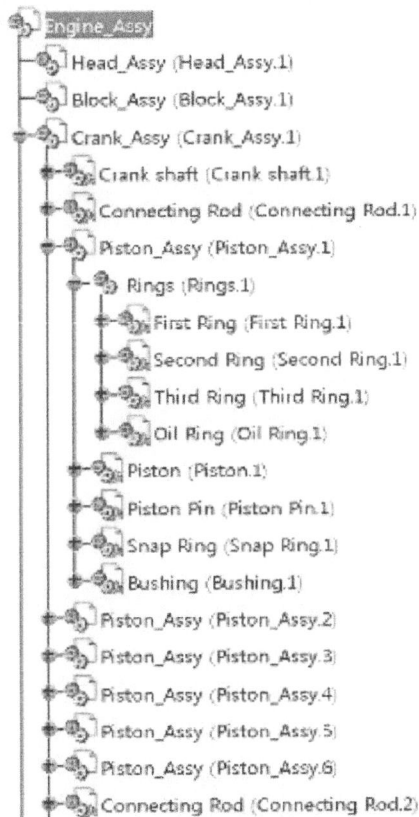

Fig 14-50 Product Structure of an Eugine Assembly

(Note) Manual Input of Part Number

- If you check the Manual Input option in the Options dialog box as shown in Fig 14-51, you can assign part number manually when you are creating a new product, component or part in an active product.

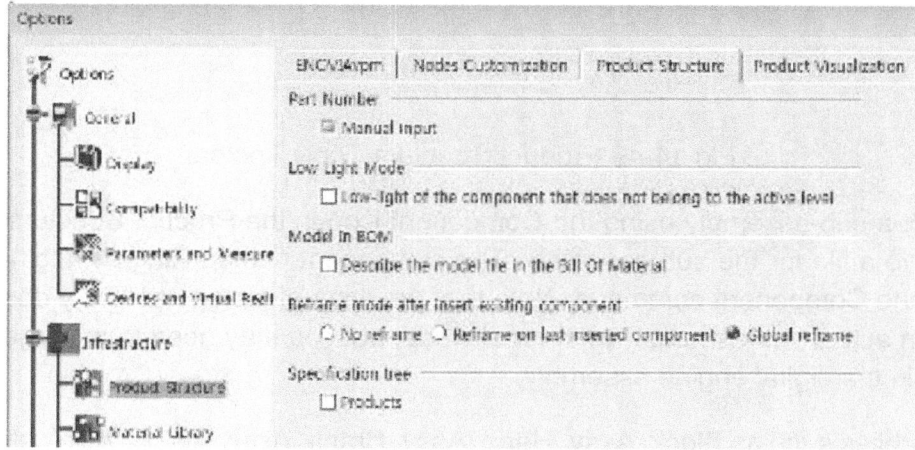

Fig 14-51 Manual Input Option

(Note) Filtered Selection

- Using the options in the Filtered Selection toolbar, you can select products or components conveniently.

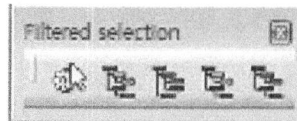

Fig 14-52 Filtered Selection Toolbar

(Note) Bounding Box

- If you display the manipulation bounding box, you can move a component by dragging the line of the bounding box.

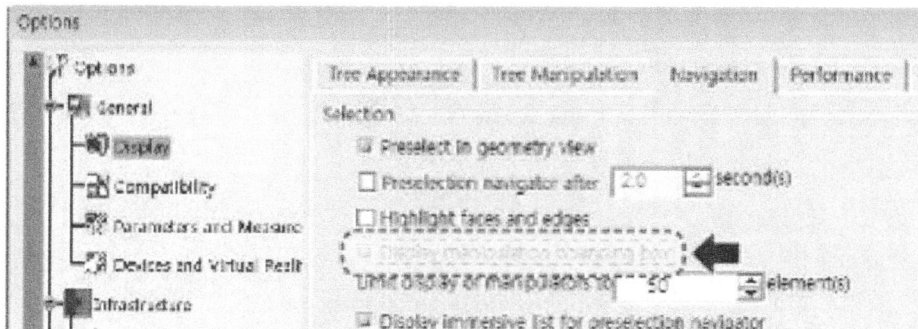

Fig 14-53 Displaying Bounding Box.

404

Exercise 124: Plummer Block (Folder: ch14 _005)

Construct the Plummer Block assembly using the given part file according to the suggested step.

Step 1

Create the Plummer Block assembly as shown in Fig 14-54. You are suggested to assemble it such that the faces of Cap and Body contact each other as designated by (A) in Fig 14-54 and that the two Brasses overlap as designated by (B).

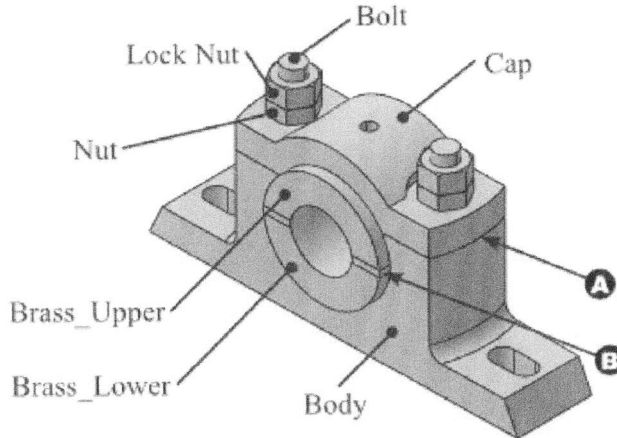

Fig 14-54 Wrong Assembly

Step 2

1. Identify the constraints that make the faces of Cap and Body contact by using the Component Constraint menu in the pop-up of the Cap component.
2. Deactivate the suspect constraint and make it sure by dragging the Cap component using the Compass.
3. Delete the suspect constraint and apply an appropriate one so that you can have the Plummer Block Assembly as shown in Fig 14 -55.
4. Correct other constraints if required.

Fig 14 - 55 Connect Assembly

Exercise 125: Laptop Assembly (Folder: ch14 _006)

Create a product using parts given in the folder ch14_006. The name of the product will be Laptop_assy.CATProduct.

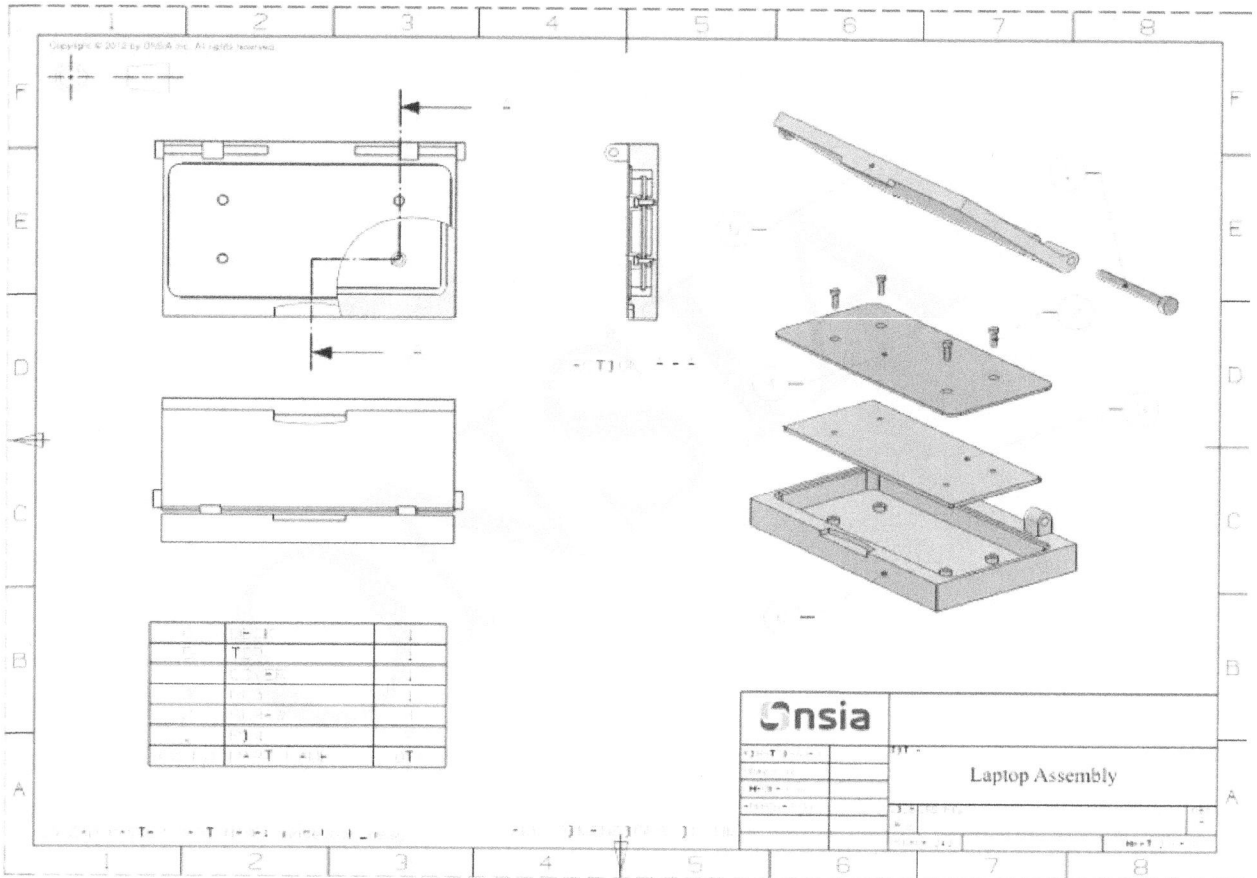

Fig 14-56 Laptop Assembly

ASSEMBLY DESIGN (TOP-DOWN ASSEMBLY)

15.1 CONTEXT CONTROL

The process of creating or modifying certain parts in the context of assembly is called Top-Down Assembly Design. When you are performing top-down assembly modeling, you need to understand exactly in which file you are doing which modeling process. The process of managing your work pa1t and the displayed part is called Context Control.

15.1.1 Load/Unload Components

You can unload or load the components in a product by right clicking on the product in the Spec Tree and choosing Load or Unload in the pop-up menu. If you unload components in a product all the components disappear in the graphics window, graphic and memory performances are improved and the Spec Tree is simplified as shown in Fig 15-2. You can load the unloaded components by choosing Load in the Components pop- up menu.

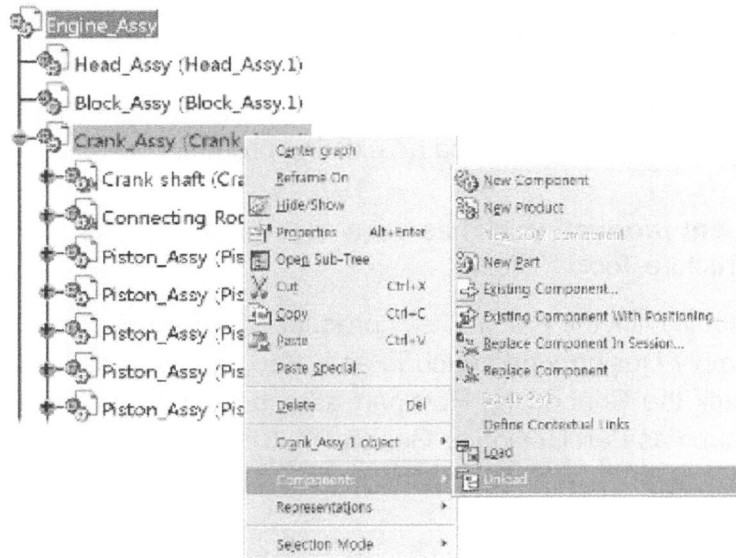

Fig 15-1 Unload Option

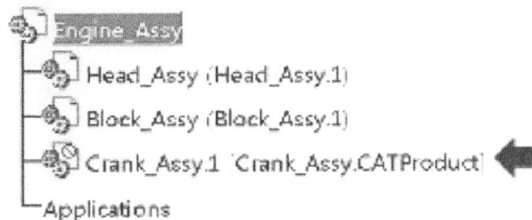

Fig 15-2 Unloaded Product

15.1.2 Edit Mode of Product or Part

You can enter the ed it mode of a product or a part by double clicking the part number in the Spec Tree. The product or part is activated and the corresponding workbench is activated. You can do the assembly or part design work according to the activated workbench. Note that the activated part or product is highlighted in blue in the Spec Tree.

You can identify the types of product or part by the symbol in the Spec Tree.

- : **Part product** which implies that the product is constructed by inserting an existing part file or by clicking the Part icon in the Product Structure Tools toolbar.

- : **Part** which can be defined in the part product.

- : **Product** which has been constructed by clicking the Product icon in the Product Structure Tools toolbar or by inserting an existing product file.

- : **Component product** which has been constructed by clicking the Component icon in the Product Structure Tools toolbar.

For example, if you double click the Piston_Assy product or the Rings product as designated by (A) in Fig 15-3, the Assembly Design workbench is activated, and you can do the assembly related work. If you double click the Connecting Rod part as specified by (B) in Fig 15 -3, the modeling related workbenches such as Part Design or Generative Shape Design is activated and you can do the modeling work.

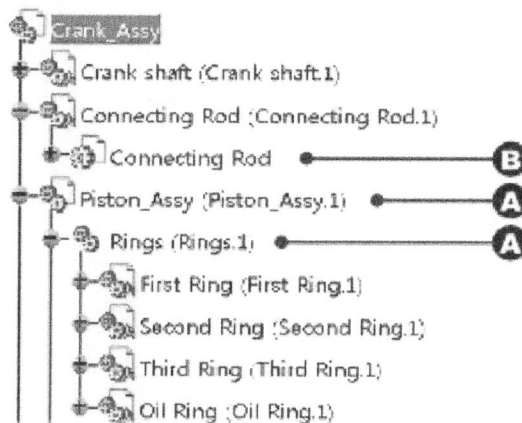

Fig 15-3 Structure of Crank Assembly

15.1.3 Open in New Window

If you double click a product or part in the context of an assembly, you can do the assembly or part design related work while investigating or referencing other parts in the open product. If you do not want to, you can open an individual product or sub-assembly or part in a new window by choosing Open in New Window in the product object pop-up me nu as shown in Fig 15-4. You can switch the files in the Window menu. Note that you cannot open the component product in a new window because the component product does not have an individual product file.

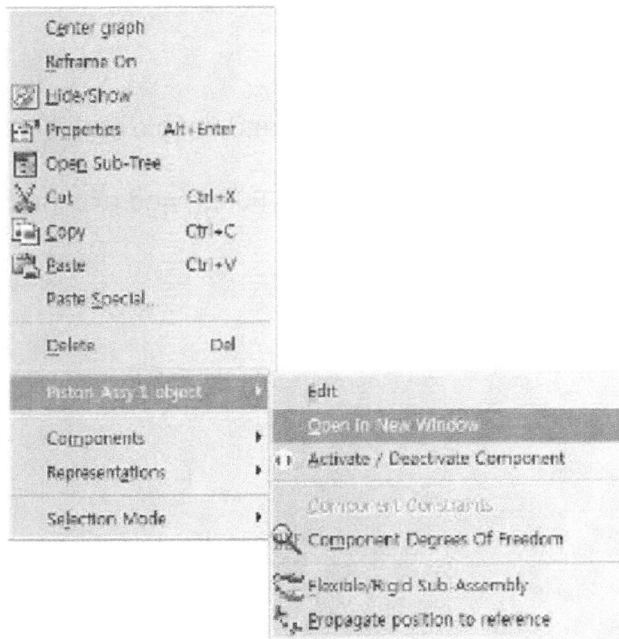

Fig 15-4 Open In new Window Menu

Exercise 126: Modifying Component and Applying Constraints (Folder: ch15 _001)

The two components in notebook_assy have the same size but are a different distance from the edge to the hinge centerline. Tn this exercise, we will modify the part to make the face (A) straight.

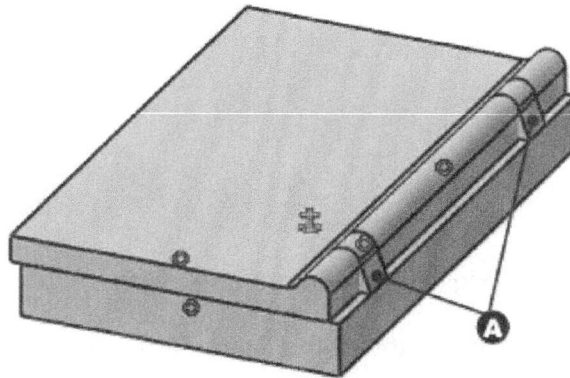

Fig 15-5 Geometry to be Modified

Modifying

1. Open the notebook_assy.CATProduct file given in the folder ch15_001.
2. Double click the 'bottom" part on the screen. Confirm that the Part Design workbench is invoked.
3. Press MB3 > Hide/Show on the "top" component to hide it.

4. Expand the Spec Tree as shown in Fig 15-6 and double click the Sketch.2 feature ((B) in Fig 15-6).
5. Modify the angular dimension from 70deg to 90deg and exit the Sketcher.
6. Show the "top " component.

Note that the assembly is not yet updated.

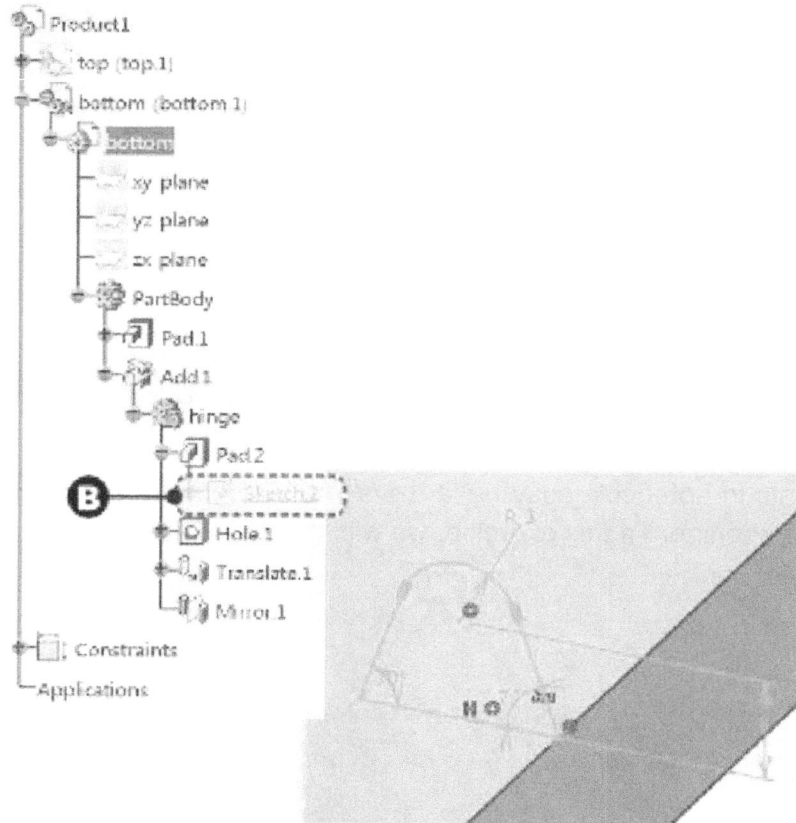

Fig 15-6 Sketch to be Modified

1. Double click the Product 1 at the top of the Spec Tree.

The assembly state is updated. If it is not updated automatically, press Ctrl + U

Applying Constraints

Collapse the Spec Tree.

410

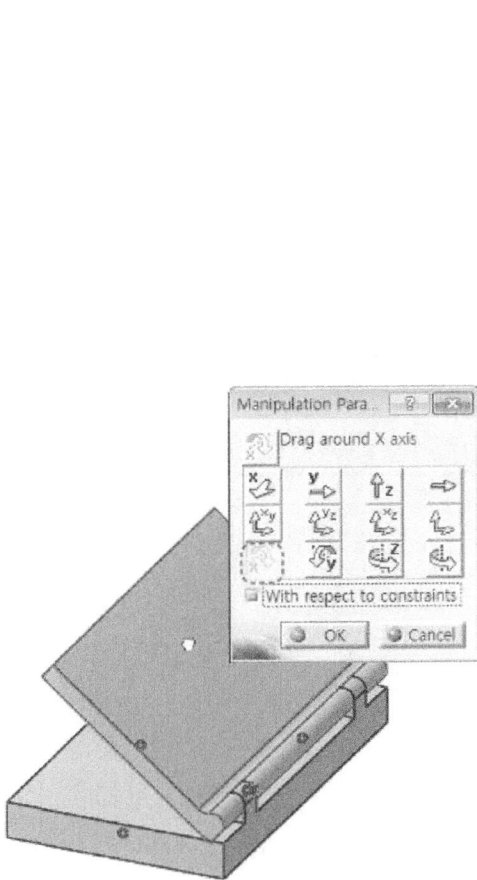

Fig 15-7 Rotating "top" Component

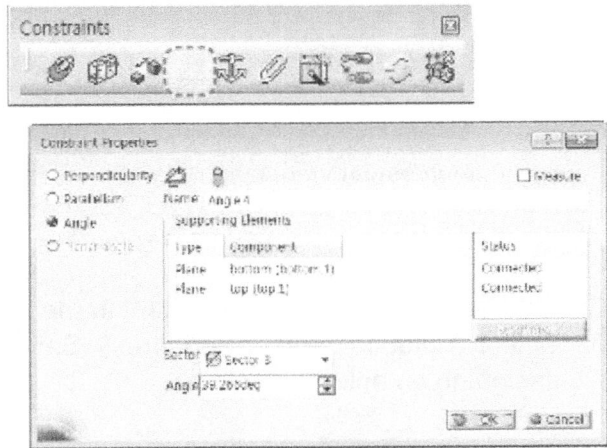

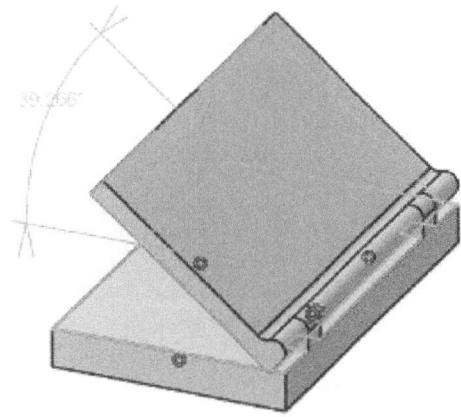

Fig 15-8 Applying Angular Dimension

2. Press the Manipulation icon in the Move toolbar, turn on the With respect to constraints option and rotate the "top" component about the x axis by dragging as shown in Fig 15-7.
3. Choose the Angled Constraint icon in the Constraints toolbar.
4. Select the upper face of the "bottom" component and the confronting face of the "top" face.

Note that you can select hidden elements by pressing the arrow key on the keyboard.

5. Select the pro per sector in the dialog box, enter 45deg and press OK.

Save

In this step, we will save the "deck" as a new version and the product file will not be changed.

411

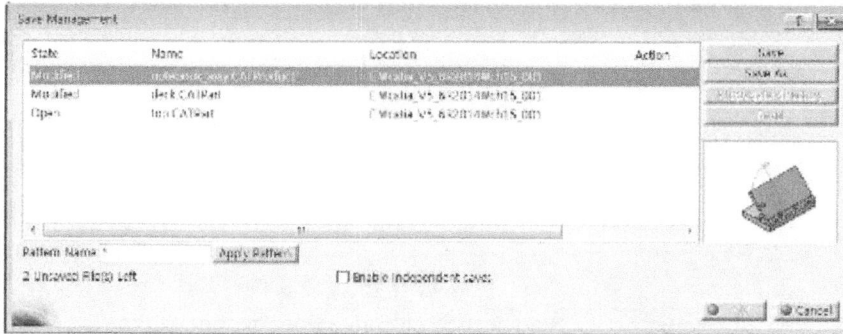

Fig 15-9 Save Management Dialog Box

1. Choose File > Save Management in the menu bar.
2. Select "notebook_assy" and press Save on the right. Remember that this step is only assigning an action.

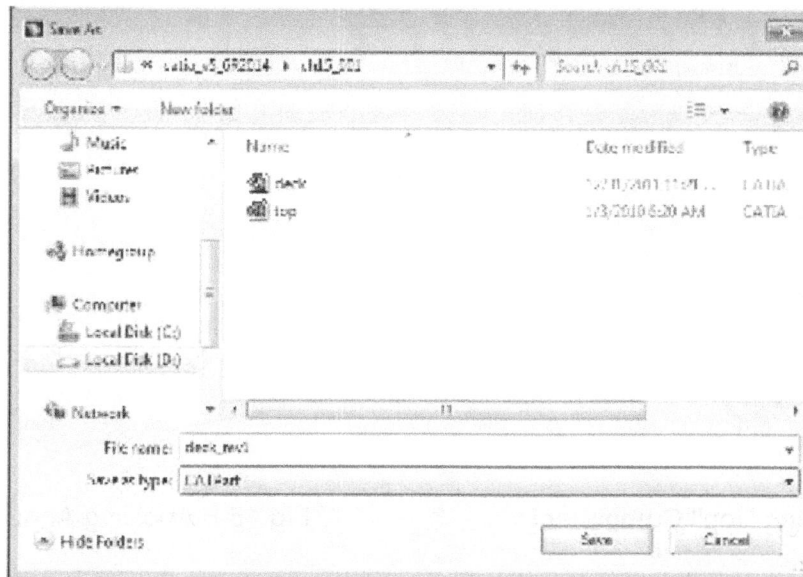

Fig 15-10 Save As Dialog Box

3. Select "deck" and press the Save As button. A Save As dialog box as shown in Fig 15-10 appears.
4. Enter the file name as "deck_rel1" and press the Save button in the Save As dialog box.

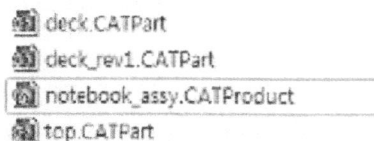

deck.CATPart
deck_rev1.CATPart
notebook_assy.CATProduct
top.CATPart

Fig 15-11 Files in Folder ch15_001

5. Confirm that the Name column has been updated in the Save Management dialog box.
6. Press the OK button in the dialog box. The assigned action is performed.

412

Files in the folder ch15_001 should be as shown in Fig 15-11.

1.5.2 Checking Interference

The purpose of assembling parts on a computer is to check for design errors before manufacturing the parts. The fundamental issue arising in checking an assembly is interference. We first assemble parts according to their design position and orientation and then check if the geometry of the part intrudes the volume of another part.

Component 1 in Fig 15-12 has a hole diameter φ30 which is smaller than the outer diameter φ 35 of Component 2. Therefore, we cannot assemble Component 2 into the hole of Component 1 using actual parts.

However, using 3D modeling software such as CATIA V5, we can assemble Component 1 and 2 irrespective of their sizes. Therefore, after assembling the components in their correct position, we need to check if they interfere with each other.

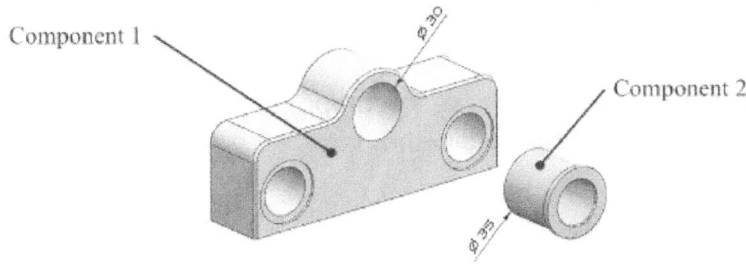

Fig 15-12 Assembly with Interference

15 .2.1 Types of interference

We can classify the status of interference into three types.

Clash

Fig 15-13 illustrates a clash state of interference. The volume of a component intrudes the volume of another component physically. In the case of a pressure fit, a very small amount of clash can happen by intention. However, if this happens in a general assembly condition, you have to modify the parts to avoid interference.

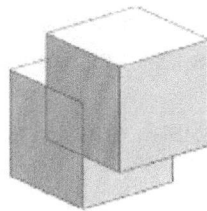

Fig 15-13 Clash State

Contact

Two parts contact each other along the face, edge or vertex. You may or may not need to modify the parts depending on your design intent.

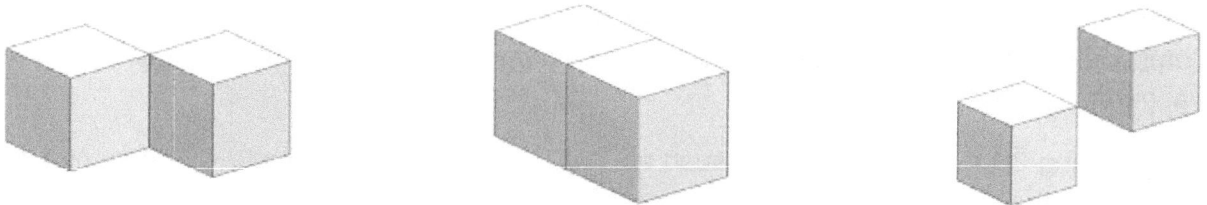

Fig 15-14 Contact State

Clearance

You can regulate minimum clearance between components. If the minimum clearance is smaller than the intended design, you have to modify the parts.

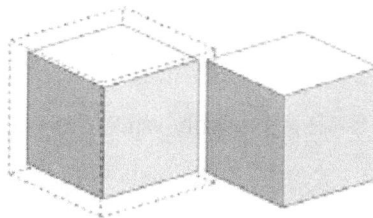

Fig 15-15 Clearance State

15.2.2 Checking Interference

You can check interference in CATIA V5 according to the following procedure.

Procedure

1. Click the Clash icon in the Space Analysis toolbar.
2. Set the options in the Check Clash dialog box and press Apply. The Check Clash dialog box is expanded, the preview window is invoked and interference is displayed on the assembly model.
3. Press the OK button in the Check Clash dialog box.

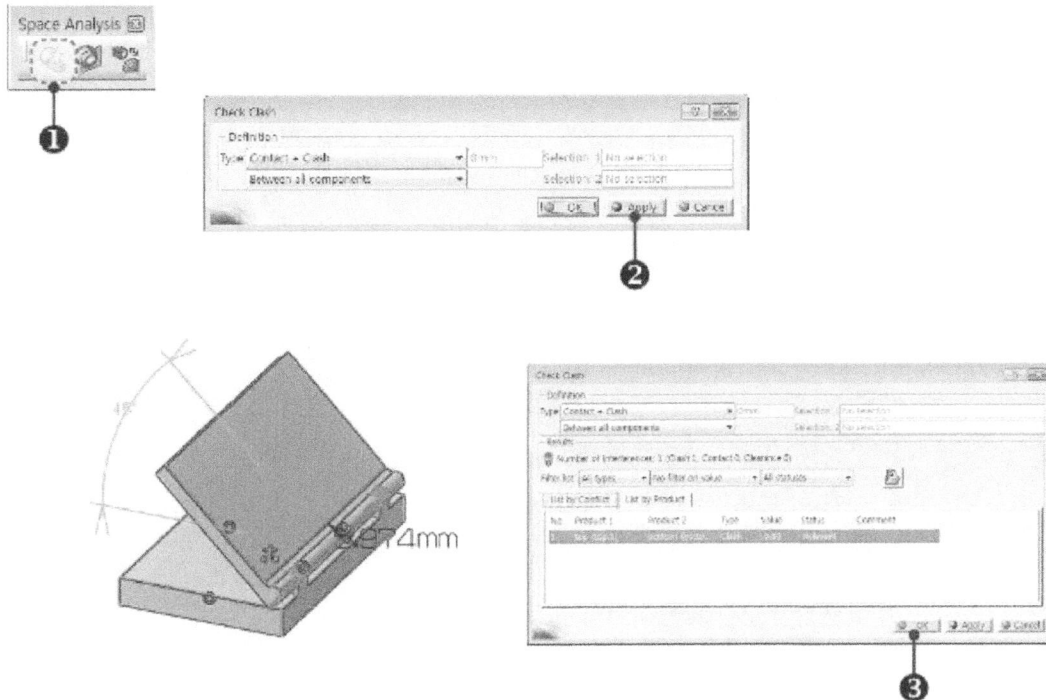

Fig 15-16 Checking Interference

In the first dropdown list of the Type option in the Check Clash dialog box, we set which type of interference to check for.

- **Contact+ Clash:** Checks the contact and clash state between components.
- **Clearance + Contact + Clash:** The clearance input area is activated. You can check for components that have clearance smaller than the specified value.

In the second dropdown list of the Type option in the Check Clash dialog box, we set the targe t objects for which to check for interference.

- **Inside one selection:** Selection 1 field is activated, and you can select several components to check for interference between them.
- **Selection against all:** Interference check is performed between the components that are selected in the Selection 1 field and the other components.
- **Between all components:** Interference check is performed between all components of the active product.
- **Between two selections:** Interference check is performed between the components selected in the Selection 1 field and the components selected in the Selection 2 field.

Exercise 127: Interference Check (Folder: ch15_002)

1. Open the notebook_a.ssy.CATProduct file given in folder ch15_002.
2. Choose the Clash button from the Space Analysis toolbar.
3. Leave the options as the default set-tings and press Apply.

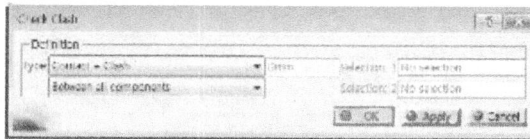

Fig 15-17 Executing Clash Check

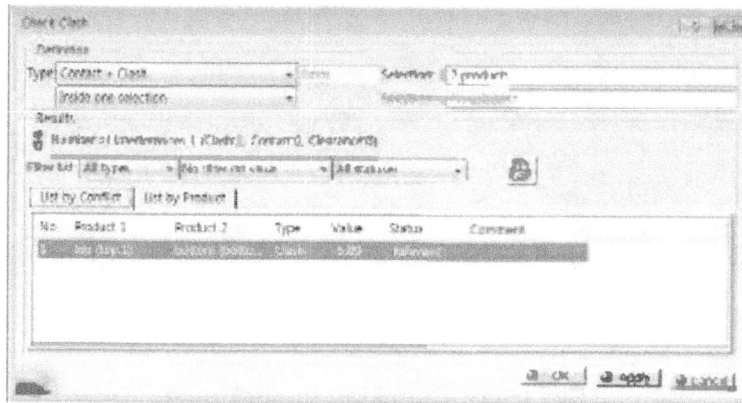

Fig 15-18 Check Clash Dialog box

The dialog box is expanded as shown in Fig 15-18 and the interference area is highlighted on the assembly model. The Preview window is invoked as shown in Fig 15-19 and you can investigate the interference region in detail.

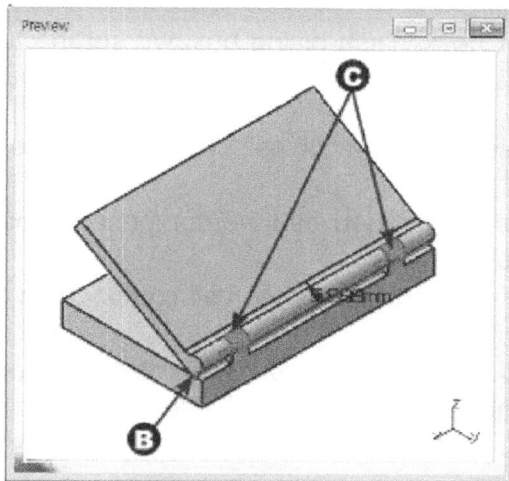

Fig 15-19 Result of interference Check

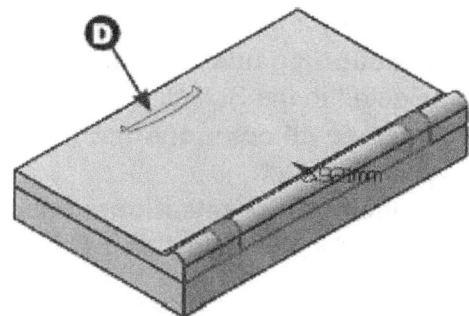

Fig 15-20 Result of interference Check ("top" component folded)

4. Close the Preview window and click OK in the Check Clash dialog box.

5. Modify the angular dimension between the two components to 0deg and check for interference as shown in Fig 15-20.

We will modify the parts to remove the interferences (B), (C) in Fig 15-19 and (D) in Fig 15-20 in the next exercise.

6. Press OK in the Clash Check dialog box and save the file.

15.3 MODIFYING PARTS IN THE CONTEXT OF ASSEMBLY

After checking for interference, we have to modify the parts if any undesired interference is detected between the components. When we modify the parts, it would be convenient if we could make reference to the geometry of the other components that will be assembled with the interested parts. This method of part modeling or modification is available if we activate the part component when the product file is opened.

Typical examples of modeling or modifying parts referencing the geometry of other components. include the following.

1. Create a sketch on the geometry of a component.
2. Use the face or surface of other components in defining a pad or pocket feature.
3. Create sketch elements by projecting or intersecting the geometry of other components.

If you have checked the Keep link with selected object option (refer to Fig 1-22), the geometry that has been created with reference to other components is updated according to the modification of the geometry or location of the component part. Therefore, you should not move the components after modeling in the context of assembly with the Keep link with selected object option turned on. On the other hand, if you have to move com-ponents after modifying parts that have links to other components, you should turn off the Keep link with selected object option.

Exercise 128: Modifying Parts (Folder: ch15_003)

In this exercise, we will modify the "top" and "bottom" component parts to remove the interferences (B), (C) in Fig 15-19 and (D) in Fig 15-20.

Setting an Option

1. Open the notebook_assy.CATProduct file given in folder ch15_002.

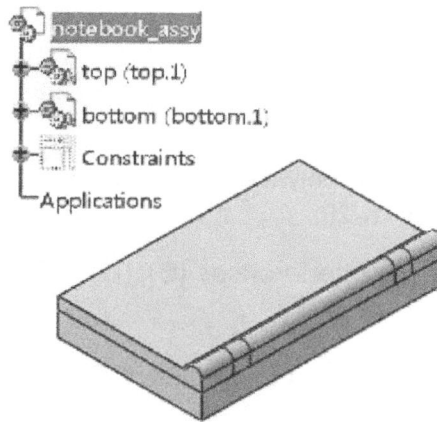

Fig 15-21 Hiding Unnecessary Specification

2. Select Tools > Options in the menu bar and tum off the Keep link with selected object option in the General tab of Infrastructure > Part Infrastructure.
3. Press MB3 (Right Click) > Hide / Show on Constraints in the Spec Tree to hide the constraint symbols as shown in Fig 15-21.

Modifying "top" Component

1. Double click the "top" component part in the Spec Tree as specified by the arrow in Fig 15-22.
2. Select Tools > Options in the menu bar and turn off the Position sketch plane parallel to screen option in Mechanical Design > Sketcher.
3. Press the Sketch button and select the face (A) of the "top" component shown in Fig 15-23 as the sketch support.

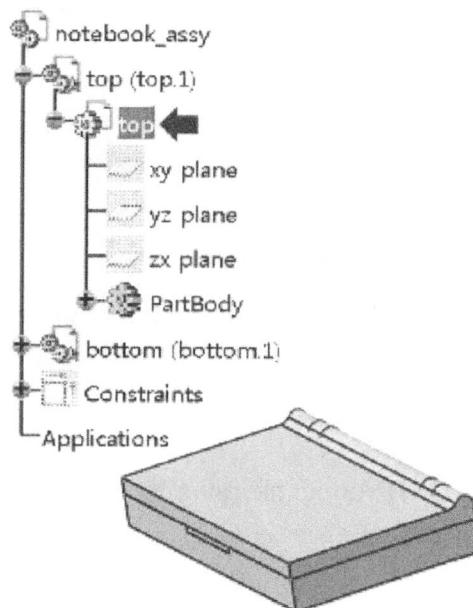

Fig 15-22 Activating "top" Component Part

4. Hide the "top" component.
5. Press the Project 30 Elements button.
6. Select the edges of the hinge support ((B) in Fig 15-24) to project onto the Sketch Support

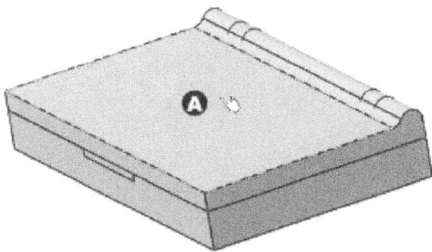

Fig 15-23 Sketch Support

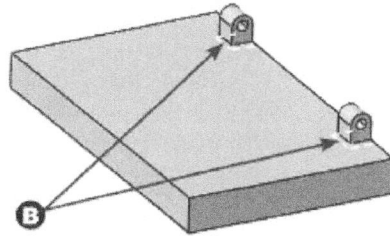

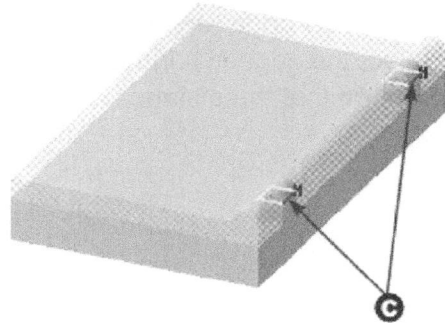

Fig 15-24 Creating Sketch

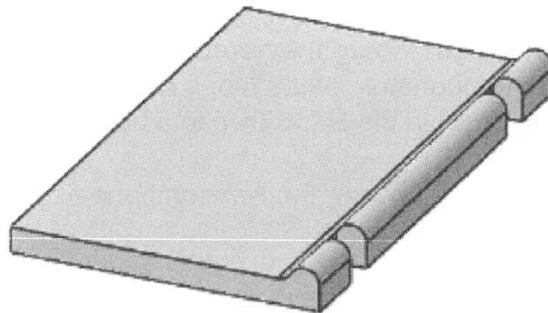

Fig 15-25 Modified "top" Component Part

7. Create lines (C) shown in Fig 15-24.
8. Exit the Sketcher.
9. Click the Pocket icon to remove the "top" component by extruding the sketch.
10. Ride the "bottom" component and show the "top" component. The "top" component is modified as shown in Fig 15-25.

The interference designated by (B) in Fig 15-24 is detected because the edge distance of the "top"' component is larger than the allowed hinge radius. We will apply a fillet to the edges.

11. Choose the Measure Between icon in the Measure toolbar.

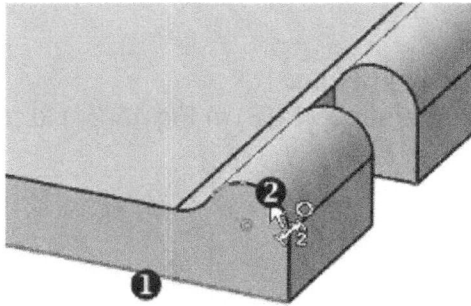

Fig 15-26 Measuring Distance

12. Select Any geometry as Section 1 mode and Arc center as Section 2 mode.
13. Select the edge (1) and arc (2) shown in Fig 15-26 in order.
14. Confirm that the distance is 5mm and press Cancel.

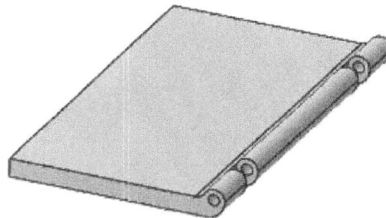

Fig 15-27 "top" Component Modified

15. Apply a 5mm fillet on the edges where interference is detected.
16. Create a 3mm diameter through hole at the hinge center. Fig 15-27 how the result model.
17. Double click "not ebook_assy" in the Spec Tree to activate it.
18. Show the bottom component.
19. Modify the angular dimension between the two components to 45°.
20. Perform the clash check.

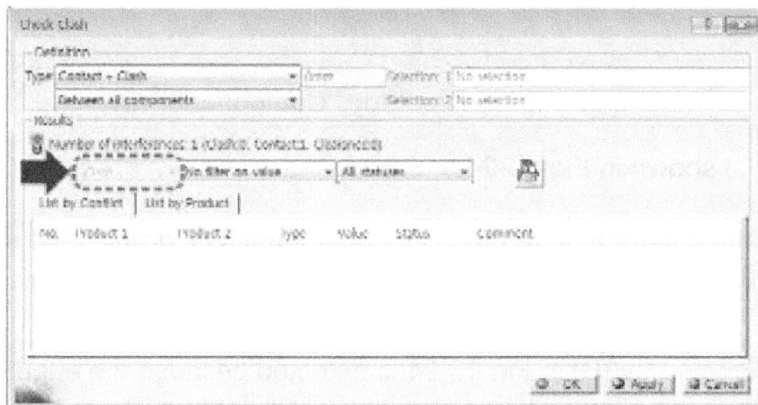

Fig 15-28 Interference Check

21. Set Filter list to Clash as shown in Fig 15-28.

22. Confirm that no interference is detected.

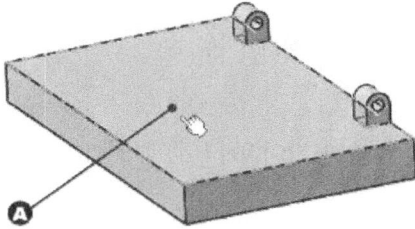

Fig 15-29 Sketch Support

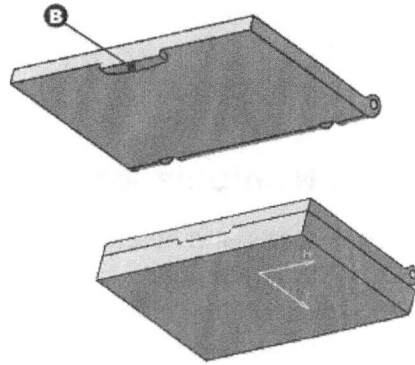

Fig 15-30 Projecting Edges

23. Close the Preview window, press OK in the Check Clash dialog box and choose File > Save All in the menu bar.

Modifying "bottom" Component

1. Modify the angle to 0deg.
2. Hide the "top" component.
3. Double click the "bottom" part in the Spec Tree.
4. Click the Sketch icon and select the face (A) shown in Fig 15-29.
5. Project the edges of face (B) shown in Fig 15-30.
6. Exit the Sketcher.
7. Click the Pocket icon and select the face (C) in Fig 15-31 as the first limit.

(Note) Tip!!

- You can hide or show component while you are running a command .

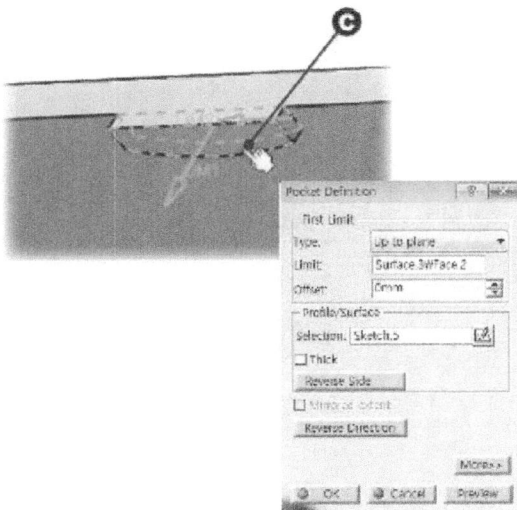

Fig 15-31 Creating a Pocket Feature

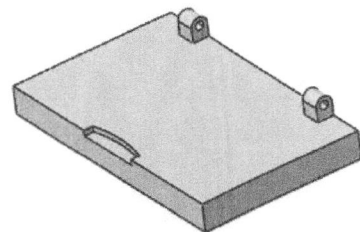

Fig 15-32 "bottom" Component Modified

Fig 15-32 shows the result of modifying the "Bottom" component.

8. Check for interference the same way as explained before and confirm that no interference is detected.
9. Save all fi!.es by choosing File > Save All in the menu bar.

Exercise 129: Manipulation Option

1. Show constraints and delete the angular dimension.
2. Press the Stop manipulate on clash button in the Move toolbar ((1) in Fig 15-33).
3. Click the Manipulation icon in the Move toolbar (2).
4. Press the Drag around any axis button (3).
5. Select the hinge centerline (4).
6. Drag the "top" component (5).

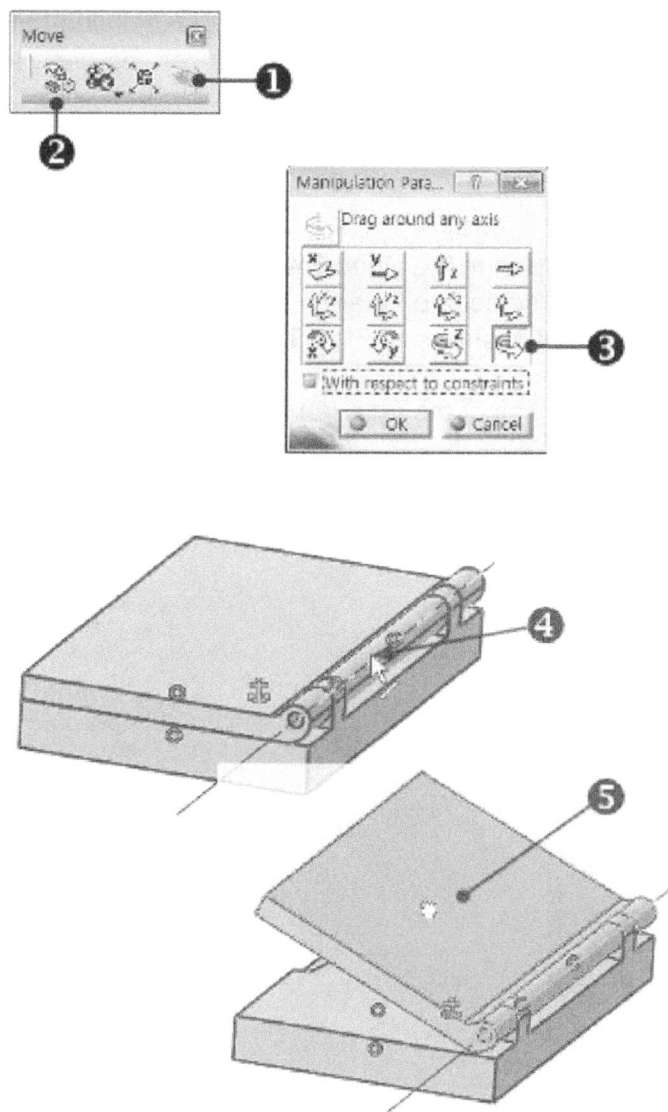

Fig 15-33 Stopping Manipulation on Clash

Manipulation stops when the "top" component clashes with the "bottom" component.

15.4 CREATING SUB-ASSEMBLIES AND NEW PART

15.4.1 Creating a New Product

You can create a new product in an existing product or component product and save it as a new product file. Click the Product icon in the Product Structure Tools toolbar and select a product or a component product in which you want to create a new product as a sub-assembly. Note that you cannot create a product in a part product. If you double click a product in the Spec Tree, an assembly related workbench is activated.

15.4.2 Creating a New Component Product

You can create a new component product in an existing product or another component product but you cannot save it as a new product file. Click the Component icon in the Product Structure Tools toolbar and select a product or a component product in which you want to create a new component product as a sub-assembly. Note that you cannot create a component product in a part product. If you double click a component product in the Spec Tree, an assembly related workbench is activated.

15.4.3 Creating a New Part Product

You can create a new part in an existing product or component product. Note that a part product, i.e., a part component, is created automatically to contain a part. Click the Part icon in the Product Structure Tools toolbar and select a product or a component product in which you want to create a new part product. The New Part: Origin Point dialog box is invoked as shown in Fig 15-34 and you can click the Yes or No button to define the origin point of the new part.

Note that you cannot create a part in a part product. If you double click a part product in the Spec Tree, an assembly related workbench is activated. If you double click a part in the Spec Tree, a modeling related workbench is activated.

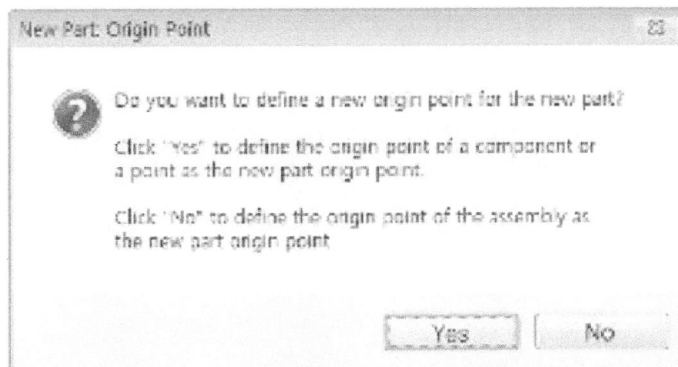

Fig 15-34 New Part: Origin Point Dialog Box

Exercise 130: Constructing Product Structure

Construct the product structure of an Engine product as shown in Fig 15-35 and save the files in a folder named ch15_005. Turn on the manual input option for part number as shown in Fig 14-51.

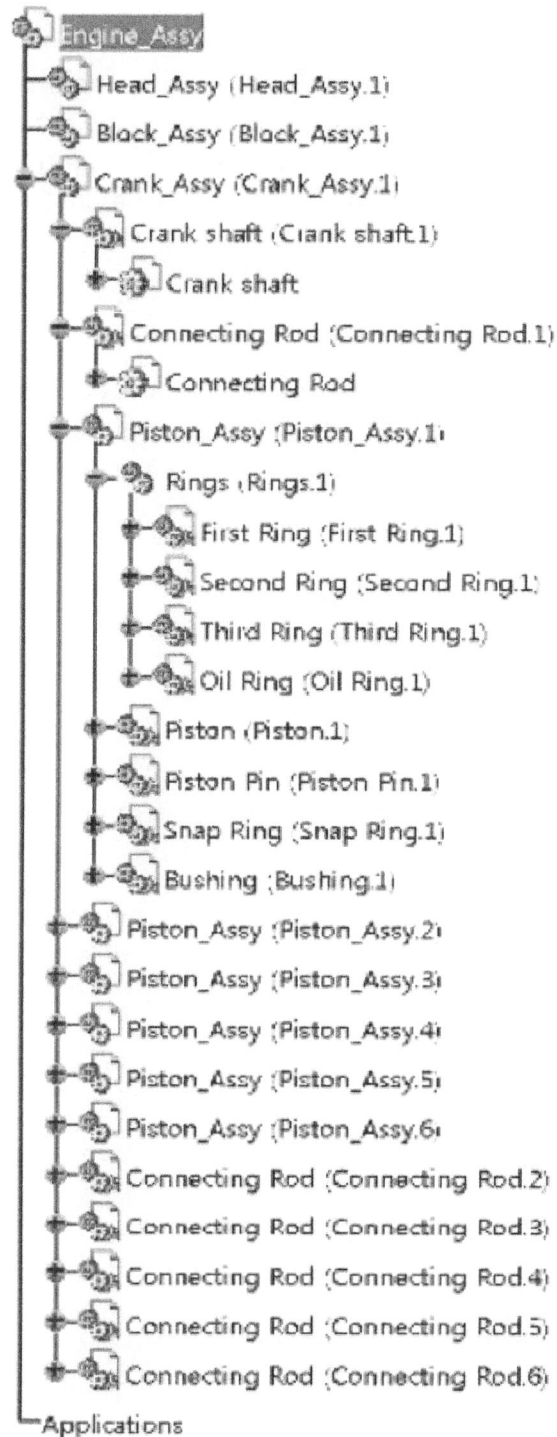

Fig 15-35 Product Structure of an engine Assembly

424

Exercise 131: Creating a Pin Part (Folder: ch15_006)

In this exercise, we will create a pin part to assemble the notebook_assy.

1. Open the notebook_assy.CATProduct file given in the ch15_006 folder.

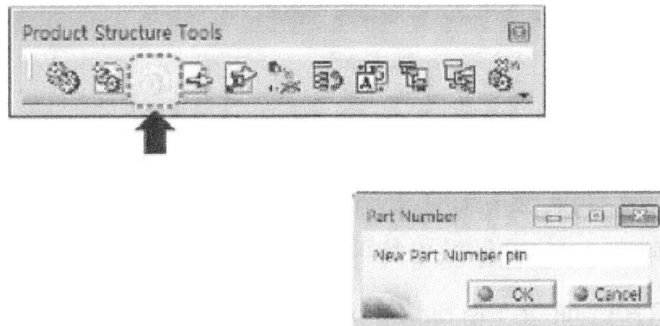

Fig 15-36 Naming Part

2. Turn on the manual input option for part number as shown in Fig 14-51.
3. Click the Part icon in the Product Structure Tools toolbar. The status bar message prompts you to select a component to insert a new part.
4. Select the "notebook_assy" in the Spec Tree.
5. Enter "pin" in the Part Number dialog box and press OK.
6. Press the Yes button in the New Part: Origin Point dialog box. You are prompted to define the new origin point.
7. Select the point (A) shown in Fig 15-37. Three planes are displayed at the origin of the new part as designated by (B) in Fig 15-37.

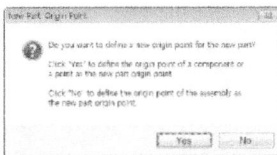

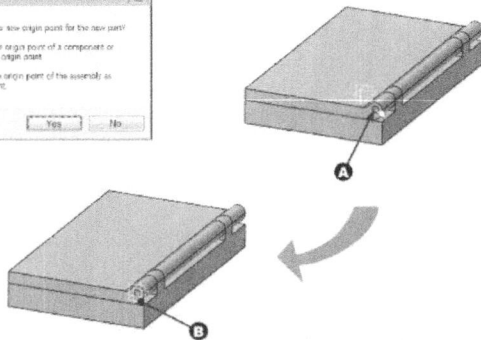

Fig 15-37 Defining the Part Origin

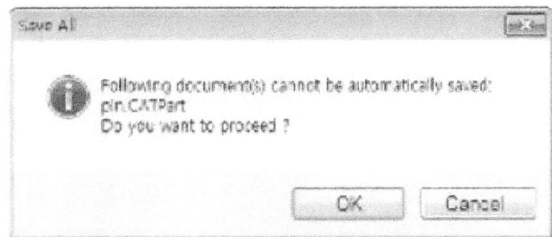

Fig 15-38 Save All Message

8. Choose File > Save All in the menu bar. Read the message as shown in Fig 15-38. Note that pin.CATPart cannot be saved automatically.
9. Press Cancel in the dialog box.
10. Choose File > Save Management in the menu bar.
11. Select the CATProduct file in the Save Management dialog box and press the Save button on the right.

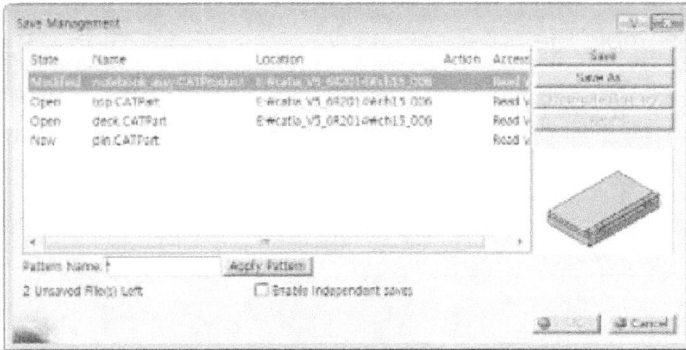

Fig 15-39 Save Management Dialog Box

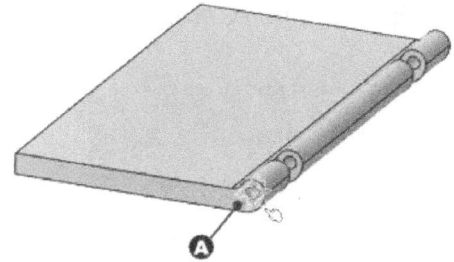

Fig 15-40 ketch Support

12. Select the pin.CATPart file in the dialog box and press the Save As button. Check the name of the file and press OK in the Save As dialog box.
13. Press OK in the Save Management dialog box.
14. Double click the "pin" component part in the Spec Tree.
15. Hide the "bottom" component.
16. Press the Sketch button and select the yz plane a designated by (A) in Fig 15-40.

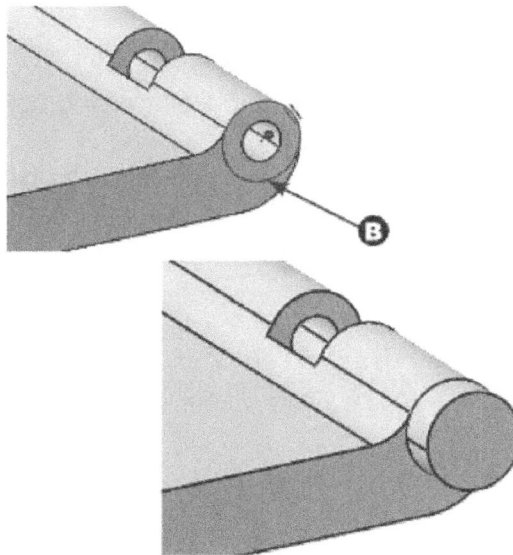

Fig 15-41 Creating Pin Head

17. Create circle (B) as shown in Fig 15-41 and exit the Sketcher.
18. Pad the circle by 3mm.
19. Create a 3mm diameter circle (C) on the inner plane of the pin head as shown in Fig 15-42.
20. Click the Pad icon and set the first limit to a 15mm offset plane of the plane (D) designated in Fig 15-42. Remember that you can select hidden elements by placing the mouse pointer on the hidden element and pressing the arrow key.
21. Save all modified files using the Save Management dialog box.

426

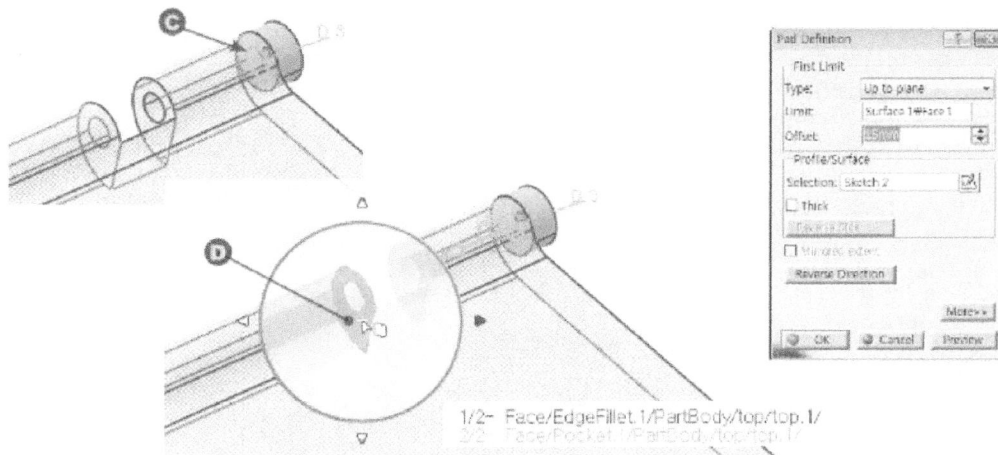

Fig 15-42 Creating Pin Body

15.5 USING FORMULAS

You can apply relations between parameters in different products or parts in the context of assembly in the same way as you have done in part design in Chapter 13. You can de- fine a parameter and assign a const ant value or measured value, etc. You can also define relation between parameters of different parts and make the relation maintained within the assembly. To do this, you have to turn on the Keep link with selected object option in the General tab of Infrastructure > Part Infrastructure.

Note that you can display the named parameters in the Spec Tree and select it to define a relation between parameters. To display the named parameters for a part in the Spec Tree, you have to check the Parameters option as designated by (A) in Fig 15-43. To Display relations between parameters in the Spec Tree, you have to check the Relations option as designated by (B) in Fig 15-43.

To display the named parameters and relations of product in the Spec Tree, you have to activate corresponding options in the Options dialog box as designated by (C) in Fig 15-44. Fig 15-45 shows the Spec Tree where the named parameters and relations are defined for part and product.

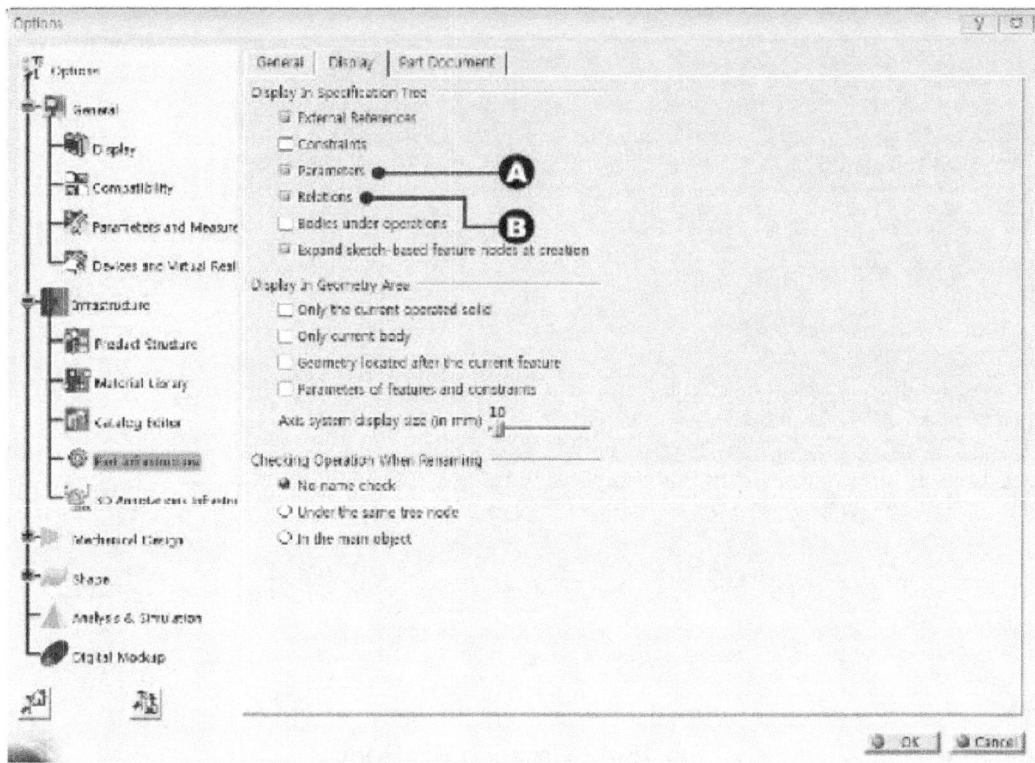

Fig 15-43 Display Options for Part Infrastructure

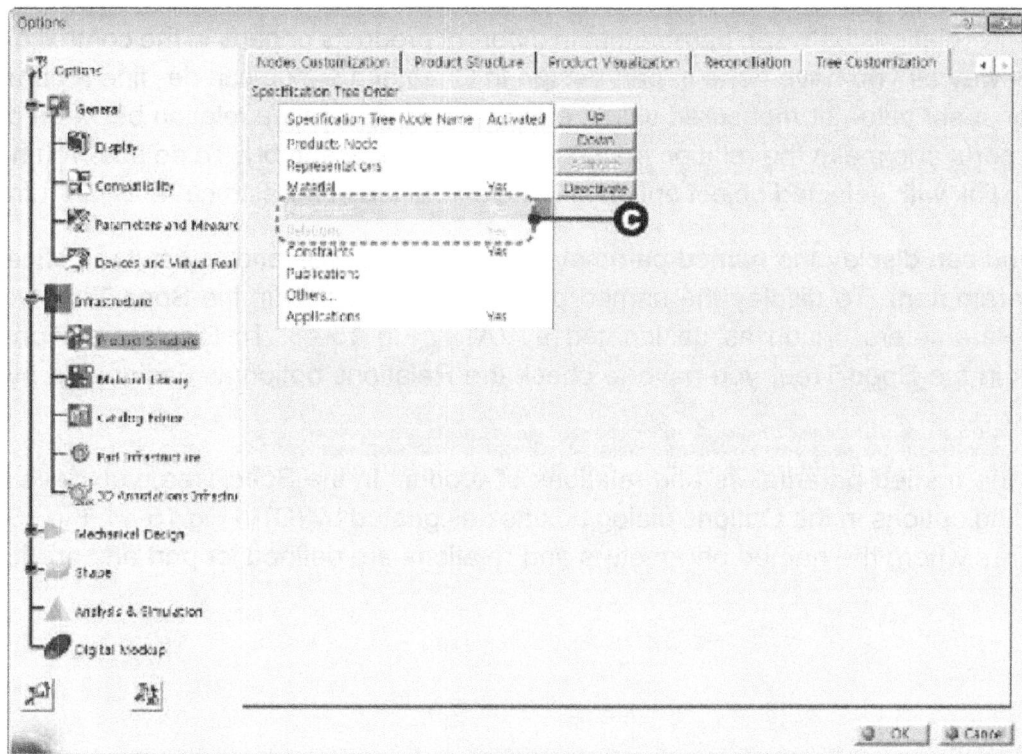

Fig 15-44 Display Options for Product Structure

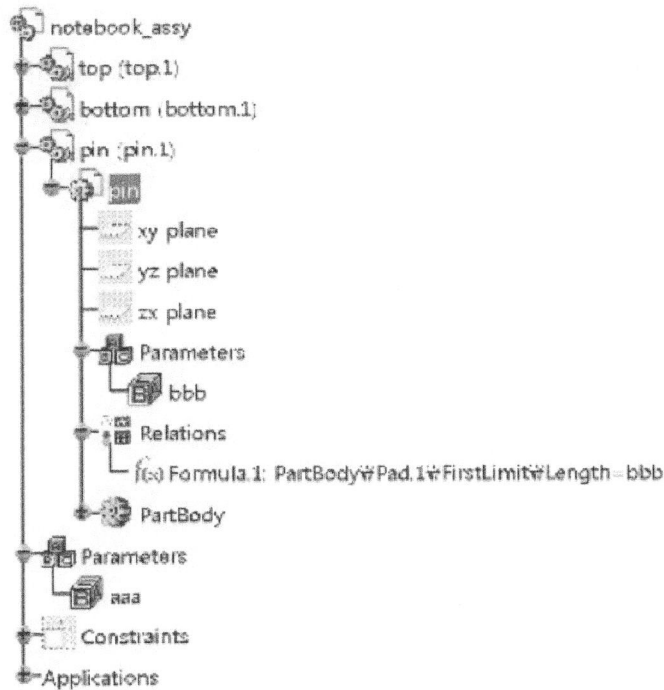

Fig 15-45 Parameters and Relations

Exercise 132: Defining Parameters and Relations (Folder: ch15_007)

In this exercise, we will define parameters in the "pin" part and in the "notebook_assy" product. Then, we will define inter-part relation between parameters in different files according to the following conditions.

1. Modify the parameter for hole diameter of the "top" component to " hole_dia".
2. Define a new parameter " head_height" in the "notebook_assy" product.
3. The height of pin head is the same as the parameter "head_heig bt".
4. The diameter of pin is 0.1 mm smaller than "hole_dia" of the "top" component.

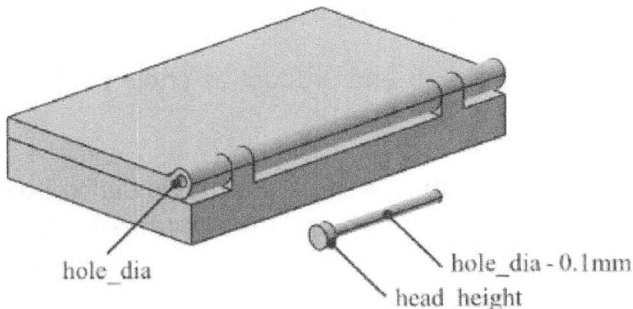

Fig 15-46 notebook_assy

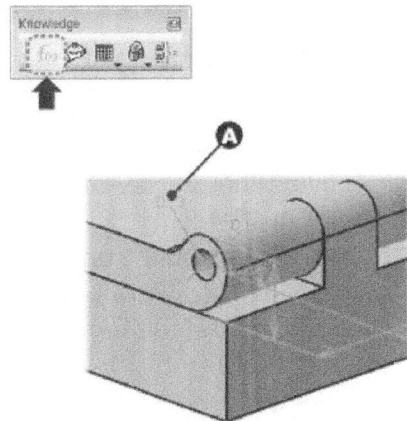

Fig 15-47 Diameter of Hole

Renaming "hole_dia"

1. Open the file notebook_assy.CATProduct in the given folder ch15_007.
2. Deactivate all assembly constraints and move the "pin" component as shown in Fig 15-46.
3. Click the Formula icon in the Knowledge toolbar.
4. Select the "top" part in the Spec Tree. The parameters in the "top' part are displayed.
5. Select the parameter relevant to the diameter of the hole in the "top" part as designated by (A) in Fig 15-47.
6. Erase the parameter that appear in the input area and enter "hole_dia" as designated by (B) in Fig 15-48 then press the Tab key.
7. Press OK in the Formulas dialog box.

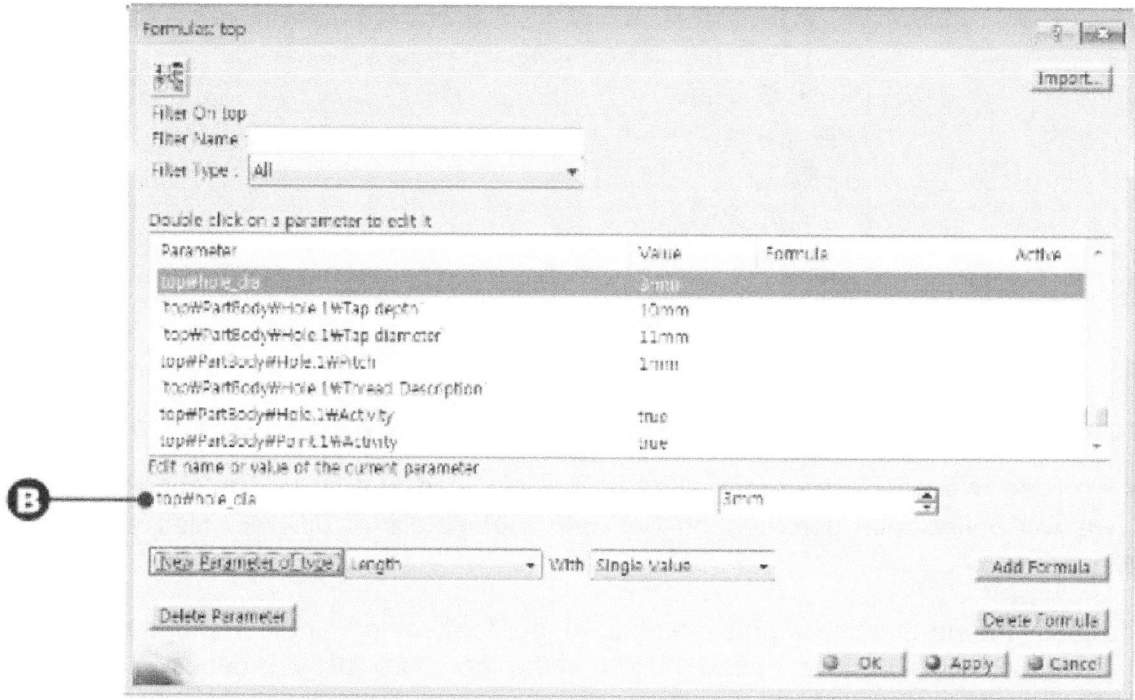

Fig 15-48 Parameter for Hole Diameter

Defining "head height"

We will define the parameter "head_height" in the "notebook_assy" product.

1. Activate the display of parameters and relations of part and product as shown in Fig 15-43 and Fig 15-44.
2. Click the Formula icon in the Knowledge toolbar.
3. Press the New Parameter of type button of the Length type in the Formulas dialog box.
4. Modify the default Length.1 as "head_height" and assign 3mm for the parameter as shown in Fig 15-49.
5. Press OK

The parameter is displayed in the Spec Tree.

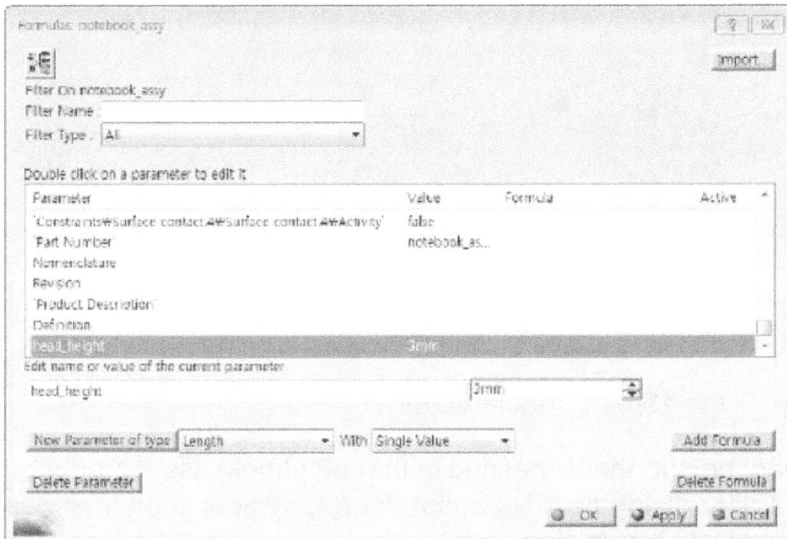

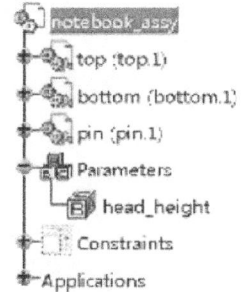

Fig 15-49 Defining "head_height"

Modifying Parameter in the "pin" component

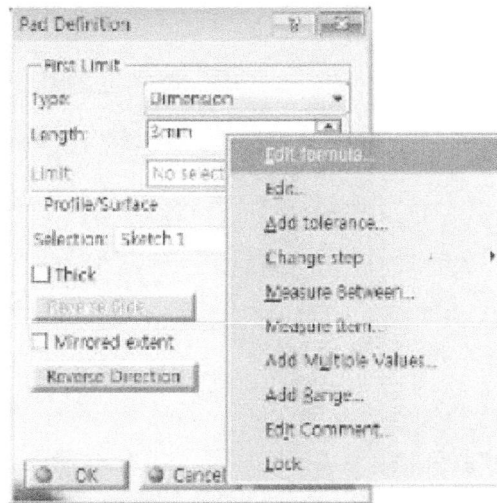

Fig 15-50 Edit Formula Menu

1. Select Tools > Options in the menu bar and turn off the Keep link with selected object option in the General tab of infrastructure > Part Infrastructure.
2. Double click the "pin" part to enter the edit mode. The Part Design workbench is executed.
3. Expand the Part Body node of "pin" and double click the Pad.1 feature.
4. Right click on the Length input box and choose Edit Formula in the pop-up menu The Formula Editor dialog box is invoked.

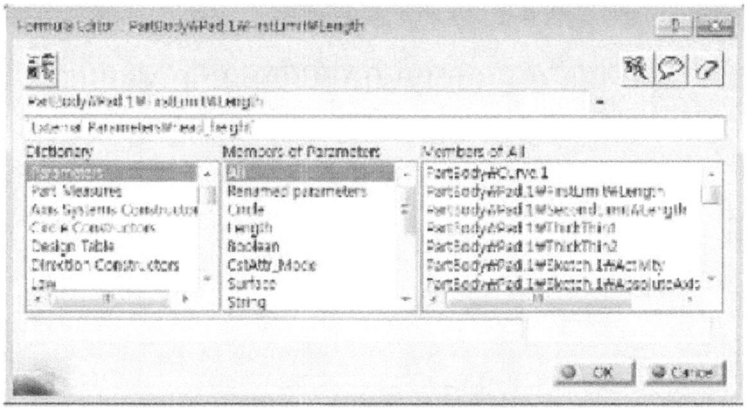

Fig 15-51 Formula Editor

5. Select the parameter "head_height" that is defined in the "notebook_assy" product.
6. Press OK in the formula Editor dialog box. Note that the f(x) symbol is marked beside the Length input box in the iPad Definition dialog box.
7. Press OK in the Pad Definition dialog box.

Relations are displayed in the Spec Tree as shown in Fig 15-52.

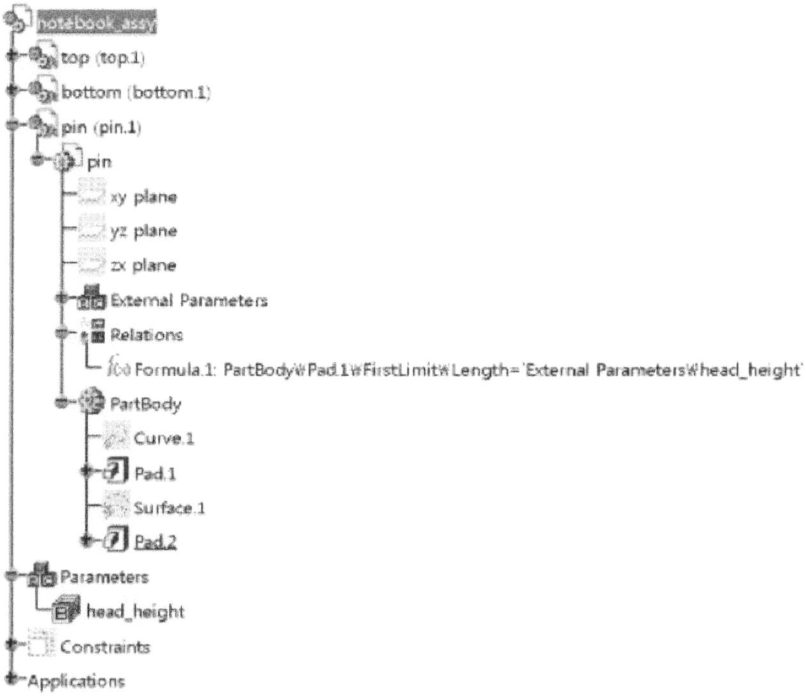

Fig 15-52 Relations Item in the Spec Tree

Modifying Parameter of Pin Diameter

We will modify the sketch parameter for pin diameter. Remember that we are in edit mode of the "pin" part.

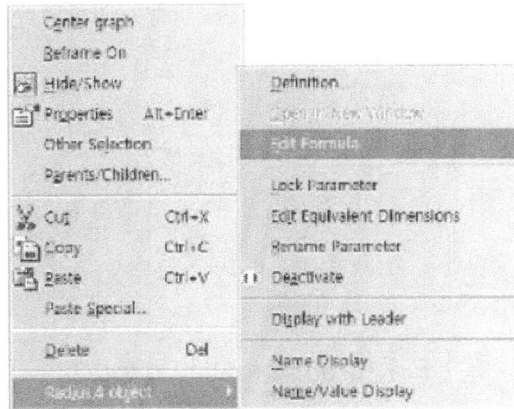

Fig 15-53 Edit Formula Menu

1. Double click Sketch.2 m the Spec Tree.
2. Right click on the radius dimension in the sketch and choose Radius.4 object > Edit Formula in the pop-up menu.

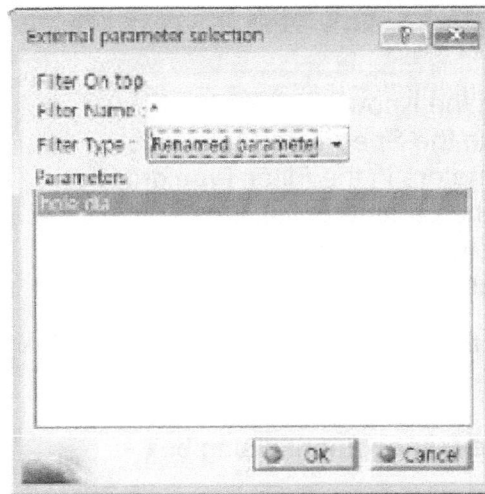

Fig 15-54 External Parameter Selection dialog box

3. Select the "top" part in the Spec Tree. The External parameter selection dialog box is invoked as shown in Fig 1 5-54.
4. Choose Renamed parameter in the Filter type dropdown list.
5. Select "hole_dia" and press OK.
6. Edit the parameter input box as shown in Fig 15-55. If the value 3mm appears in the input box, you should turn on the Keep link with selected object option. Note that you have to divide the diameter value by 2 because we are defining parameter for radius.
7. Press OK in the dialog box.
8. Exit the sketcher.

The second formula is registered in the Relations container in the "pin' part.

433

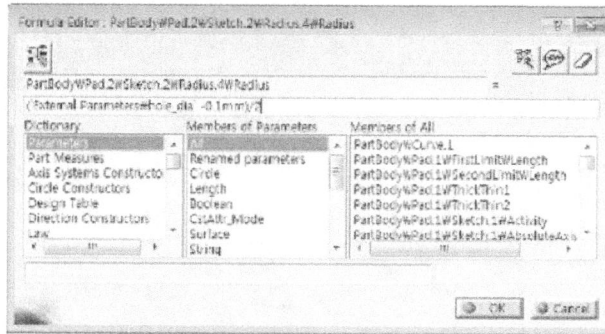

Fig 15-55 Formula Editor

Modifying "head height"

1. Double click the "notebook_assy" product.
2. Double click the parameter "head_height" in the Spec Tree.
3. Enter 5mm in the Edit Parameter input box.

Head height of the "pin" component is updated.

Modifying "hole_dia"

1. Click the Formula icon in the Knowledge toolbar.
2. Select the "top" product in the Spec Tree.
3. Choose Renamed Parameters in the Filter Type dropdown list in the Formulas dialog box.
4. Select "top\hole_dia" in the parameter list.
5. Enter 4 in the parameter input area and press the Tab key.
6. Press OK in the Formulas dialog box.

Note that the hole diameter of the "top" component is modified and that the diameter of "pin" is updated.

7. Save the files in the Save Management dialog box.

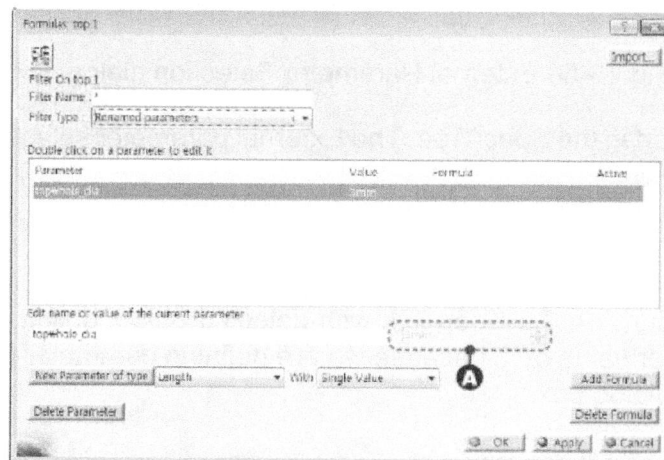

Fig 15-56 Formulas Dialog Box

Exercise 133: Assembling "pin" Component (Folder: ch15_008)

In this exercise, we will assemble two "pin" components and const rain them. Note that the rotational degree of freedom of the "pin" components will be constrained to the "top" component.

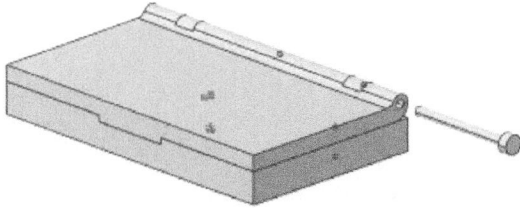

Fig 15-57 Moving Component

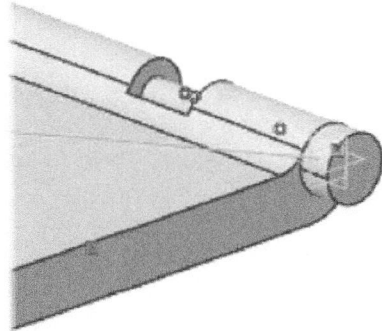

Fig 15- 58 Applying Constraint

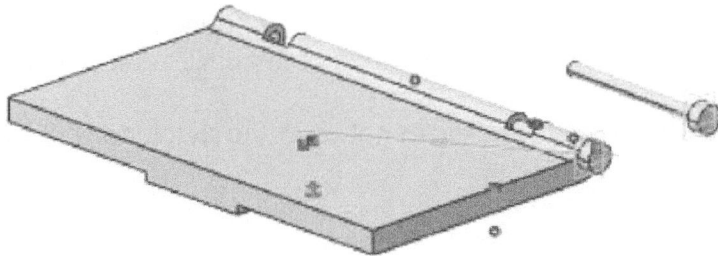

Fig 15-59 moving the Copied Component

1. Open the CATProduct file given in folder ch15_006.
2. Show all the assembly constraints and hide the "bottom" component.
3. Move the "pin" component as shown in Fig 15-57.
4. Apply a coincident constraint between the centerlines and a contact constraint between the faces of the pin he ad and the top component.
5. Show the planes in the pin part.
6. Apply the Angle Constraint/Parallelism between the xy plane of the "pin" component and the top face of the "top" component.
7. Select the "pin" component in the Spec Tree and press Ctrl + C.
8. Select the "notebook_assy" in the Spec Tree and press Ctrl + V.

(Note) Moving a Hidden Component

-   Turn on the snap option of the Compass and select the component to move in the Spec Tree. Then you can drag out the hidden component.
9. Move the copied component {pin.2) using the Compass as shown in Fig 15-59.
10. Apply a coincident constraint between the center line ((A) in Fig 15-60) of the pin.2 instance and the hinge centerline ((B) in Fig 15-60) in the "top" component.

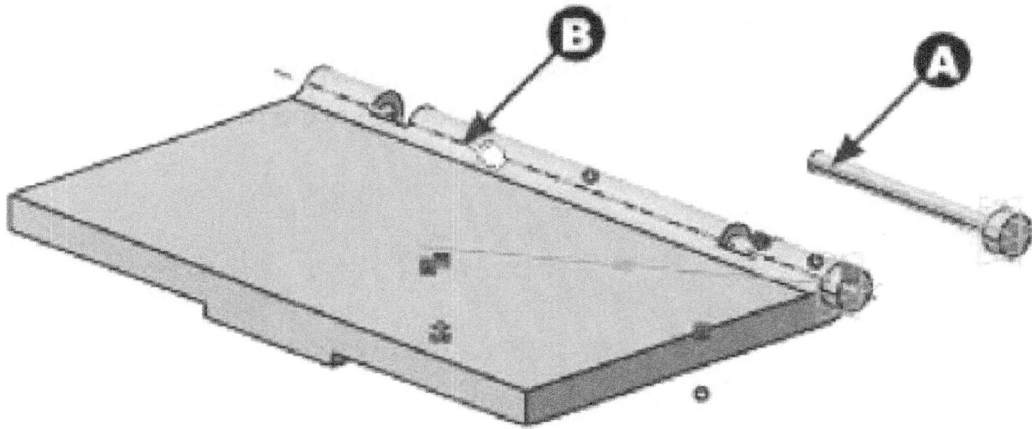

Fig 15-60 Applying Coincidence

If the pin.2 instance is absorbed in other component, press MB3 > Reframe On on the pin.2 product in the Spec Tree. You can identify the location of the pin.2 instance.

11. Drag out the pin.2 instance using the Compass or bounding box.
12. Apply a contact constraint between the face of the pin.2 head and the side face of the "top" component.
13. Apply the Angle Constraint/Parallelism between the xy plane and the top face of the "top" component.
14. Hide the planes in the "pin" part.
15. Hide all assembly constraints. Fig 15-6 I shows the final assembly.
16. Save all files.

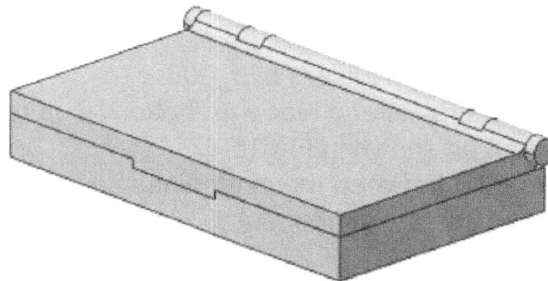

Fig 15-61 Final Assembly

15.6 PUBLICATION

You can publish geometrical elements and parameters and make them available for different users. This operation is useful when you are working with other designers in the context of assembly. You can publish elements and parameters for your part or assembly and then restrict other designers to be able to select only the published element by setting an option designated by the arrow in Fig 15-62. Note that the option does not take effect if you do not check the Keep link with selected object option.

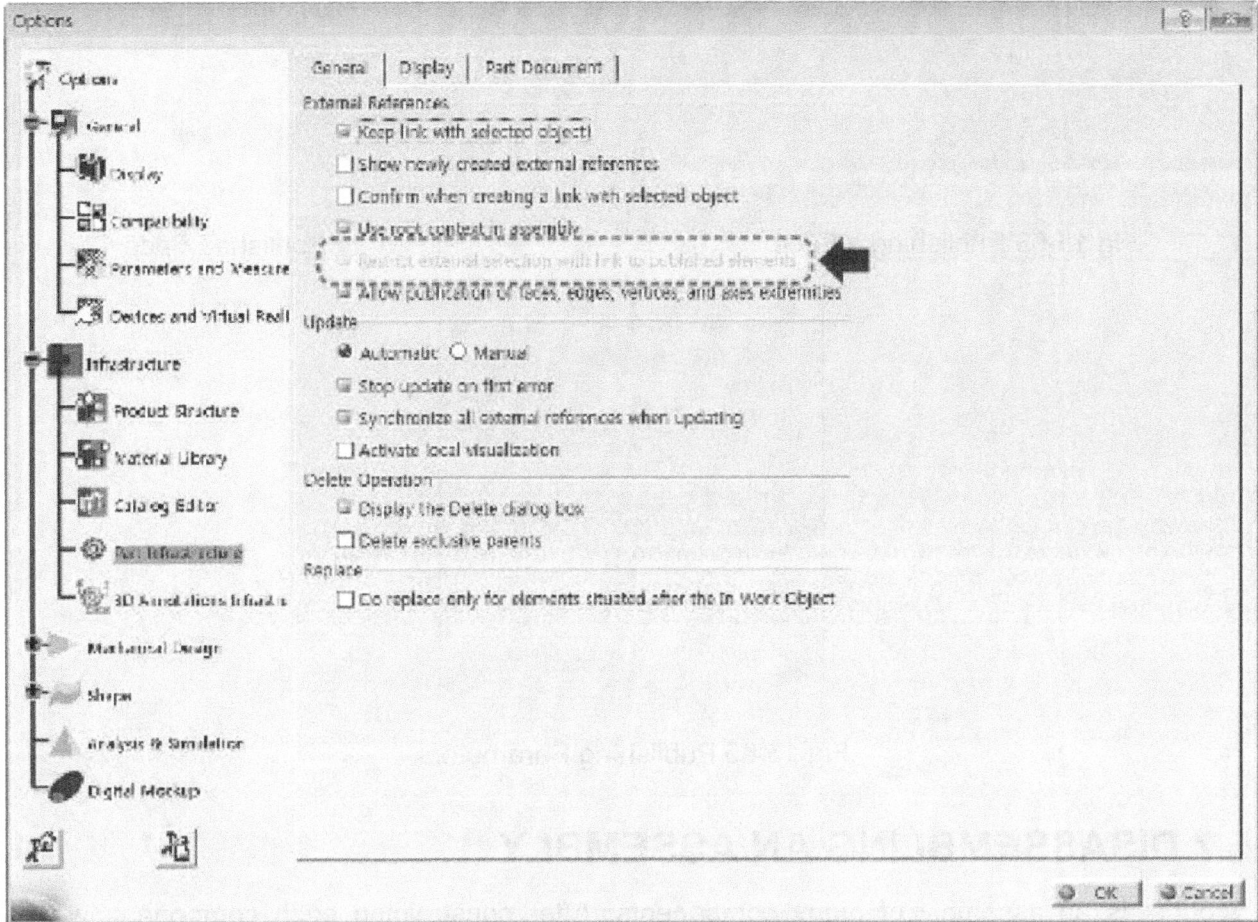

Fig 15-62 Option for Published Elements

You can publish geometrical elements or parameters by choosing Tools > Publication in the menu bar while you are editing a part or product. If you publish the face designate d in Fig 15-63 and set the opt io n designated in Fig 15-62, you can restrict the design of the "bottom" part to be able to select only the published face when the part is modified according to the process that we did in Exercise 03. The published element is registered in the Spec Tree as shown in Fig 15-64 and you can select it when you reference it.

You can publish parameters of component or part by pressing the Parameter button in the Publication dialog box. Note that para meters of a part can be published in the part editing mode.

Fig 15-63 Publishing a Face   Fig 15-64 Published Face

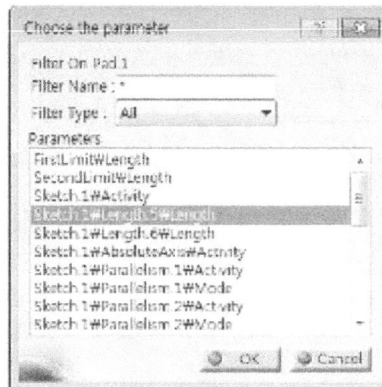

Fig 15-65 Publishing Parameters

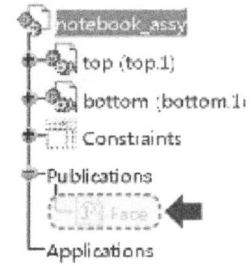

15.7 DISASSEMBLING AN ASSEMBLY

A product is an assembly of many components. After constraining each component, we can disassemble the components so that we can explain the assembly structure and create an assembly drawing. The assembled state can be restored by pressing the Update All button.

Procedure

1. Choose the Explode button from the Move toolbar.
2. Set the Explode option in the dialog box.
3. Press the OK button.

The depth option determines whether you will explode up to the sub-assembly level or only the components of the top assembly. In the Type dropdown list, you can set the method of exploding components: 3D, 2D or constrained. If you choose the Constrained type, a coincident constraint is maintained, and other constraints are neglected in order to disassemble the components. Fig 15-67 shows each exploded state of the notebook assembly.

If you want to exp lode the assembly with regard to a specific component, select the component as the fixed product.

438

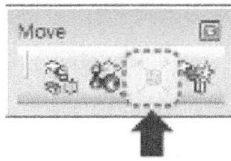

Fig 15-66 Explode Dialog Box

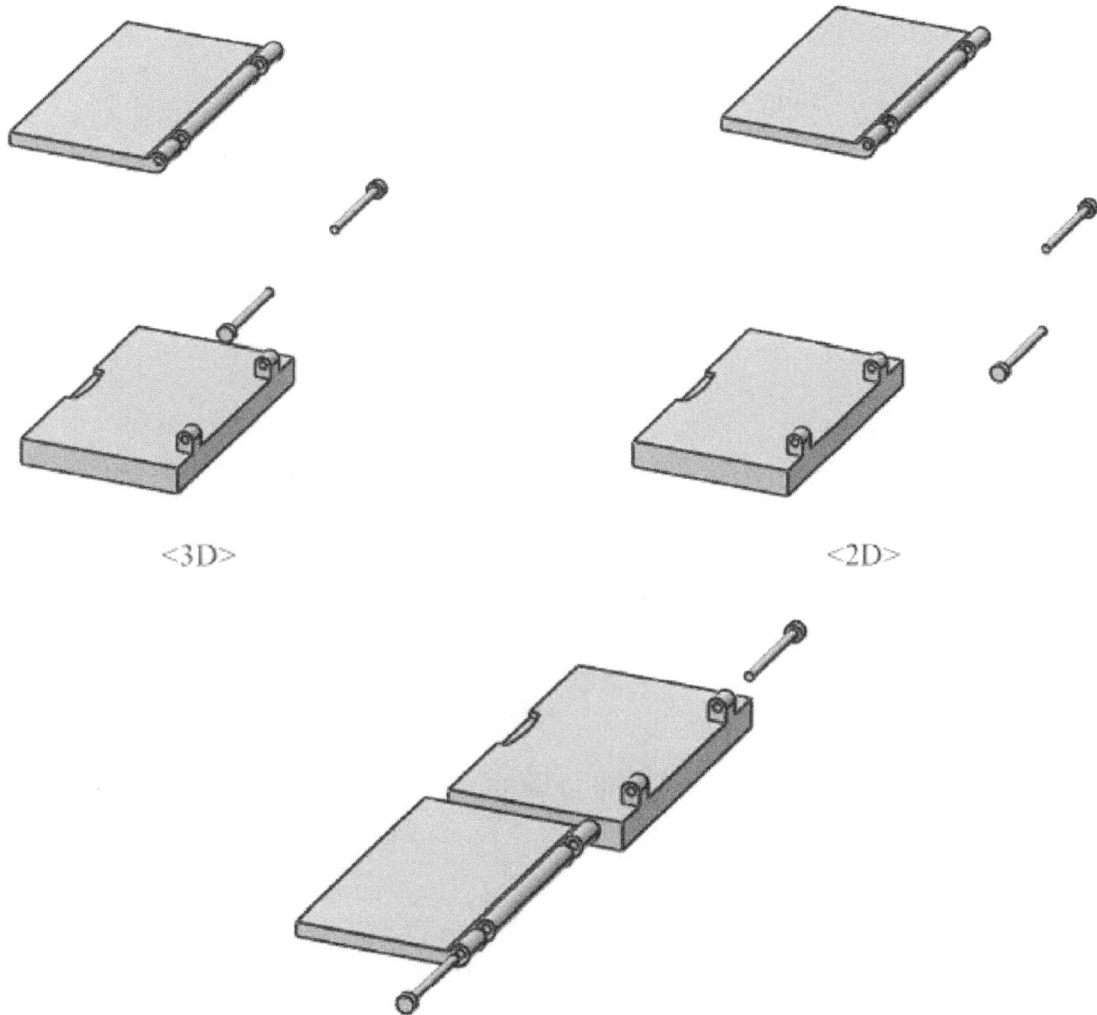

<3D>   <2D>

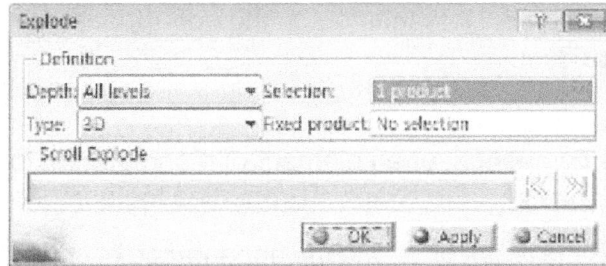

Fig 15-67 Types of Explosion

15.8 DISPLAY OF ASSEMBLY

15.8.1 Display of Components

Using the options in the Graphics Properties toolbar, you can modify the col or, opacity, line font, etc. of the components. Note that the change of appearance applies only to the components of the current active product.

1. Activate top assembly.
2. Select a component or an element of a component to modify its appearance.
3. Set the options in the Graphic Properties toolbar.

Fig 15-69 shows the result of setting the appearance of components in the "notebook_assy" product.

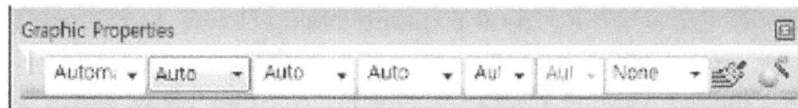

Fig 15-68 Graphic Properties Toolbar

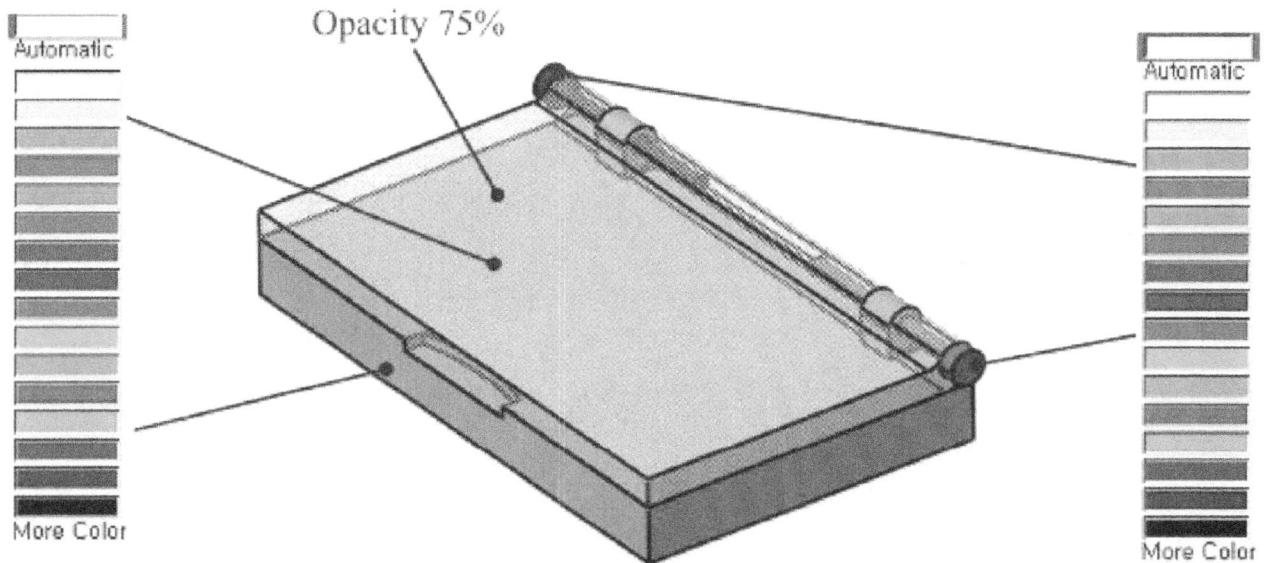

Fig 15-69 Setting Graphic Property

15.8.2 Sectioning

Using the Sectioning command in the Space Analysis too l bar, you can analyze a section of a product. You can investigate carefully the area where interference has been detected or the region of int e rest in a component or assembly. Each tab in the Section Definition dialog box provides the following functions.

- **Positioning:** Specifies the location of the section.

440

- **Result:** Sets the status of the section preview and process the section conditions.

If you press the Volume Cut button in the Result tab as specified by (A) in Fig 15-70, the section is displayed as shown in the figure. If you press the Result Window button as specified by (B) in Fig 15-70, the Section window is available, and you can rotate or flip the cut section by right clicking on the result window as specified by (C).

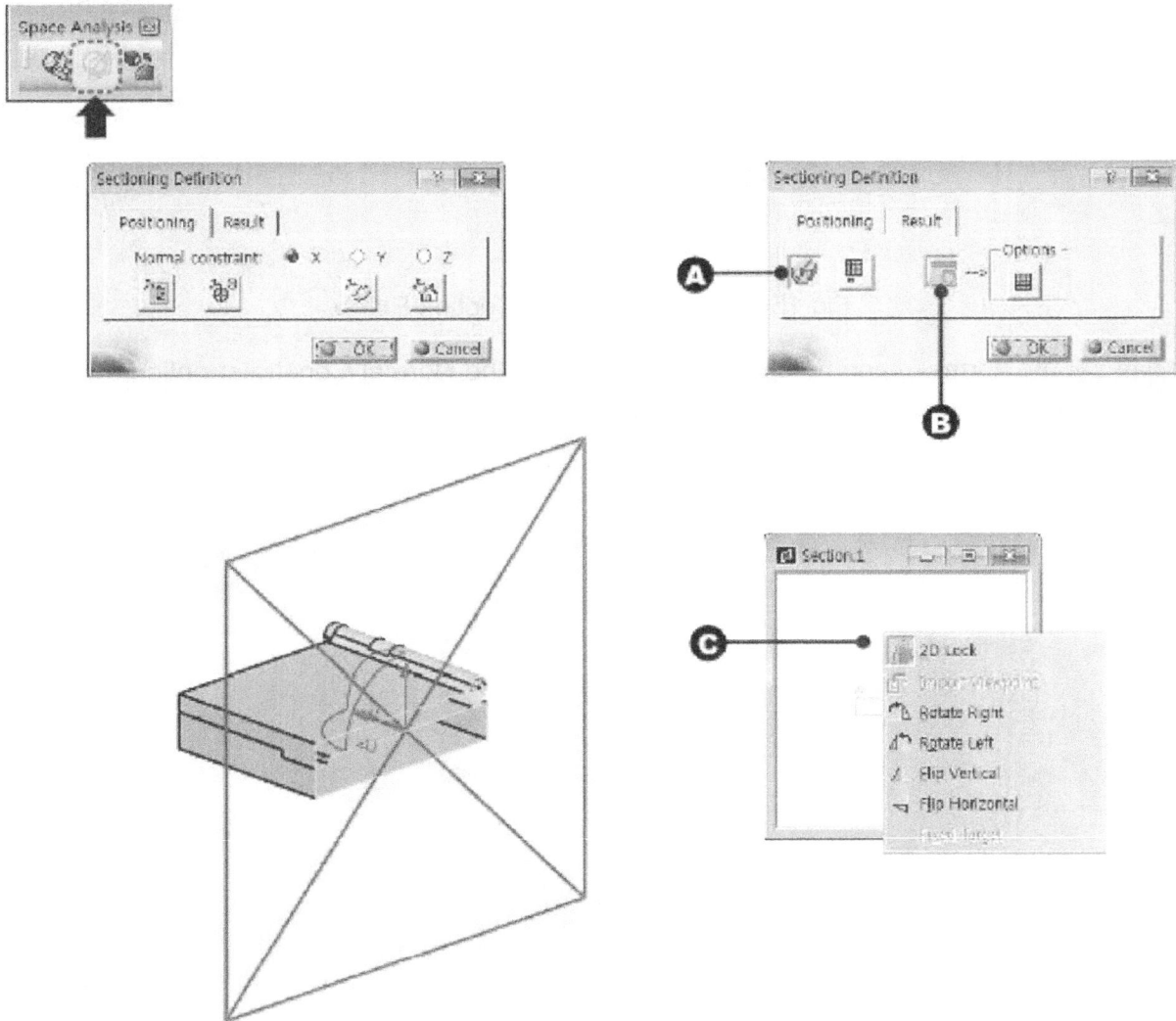

Fig 15-70 Sectioning an Assembly

You can manipulate the section plane by placing the mouse pointer on the section plane or coordinate system. You can move or rotate the section plane by dragging.

- **Move:** Place the mouse pointer on the section plane as shown in Fig 15-7 (A) and drag.
- **Resize:** Place the mouse pointer on the boundary edge of the plane as shown in Fig 15-71 (B) and drag.
- **Rotate:** Place the mouse pointer on the arc symbol designated by (C) in Fig 15-71 and drag.

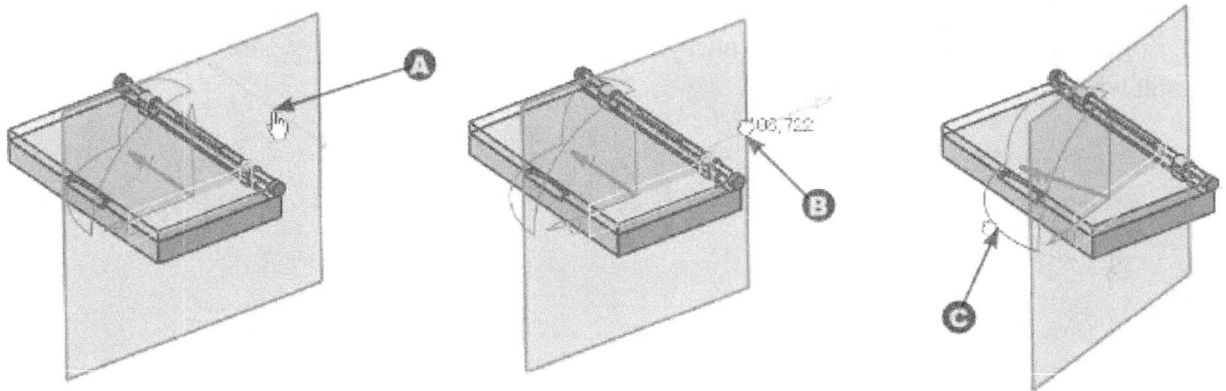

Fig 15-71 Manipulation of Section Plane

You can set the normal plane by choosing an option in the Normal Constraint option and you can reverse the view direction by pressing the Invert Normal button.

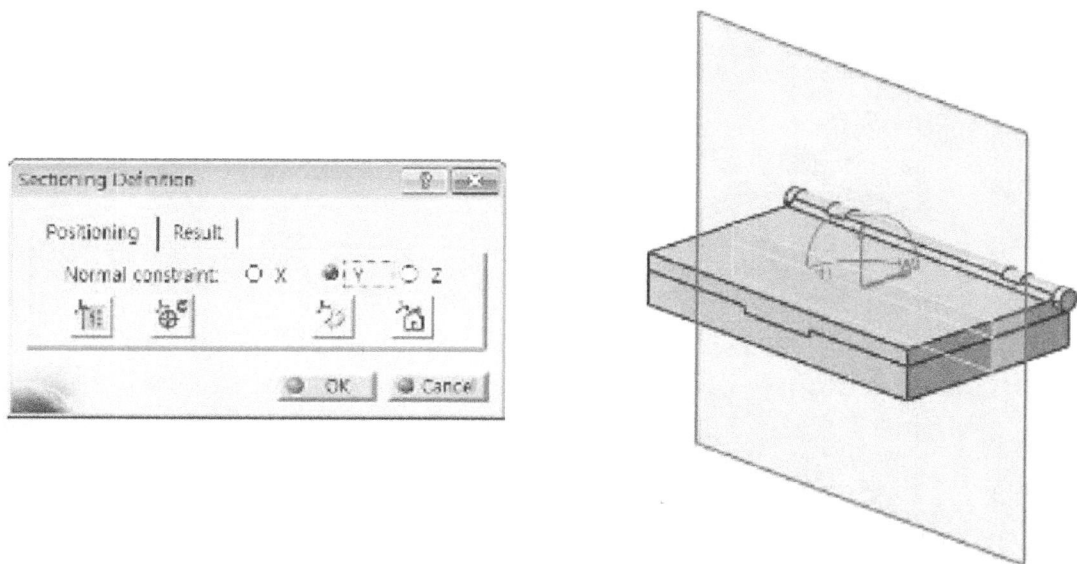

Fig 15-72 Changing Normal Direction

Exercise 134: Measuring Inertia (Folder: ch15_009)

1. Open the CATProduct file given in the folder ch15_009.
2. Click the Measure Inertia icon in the Measure toolbar.

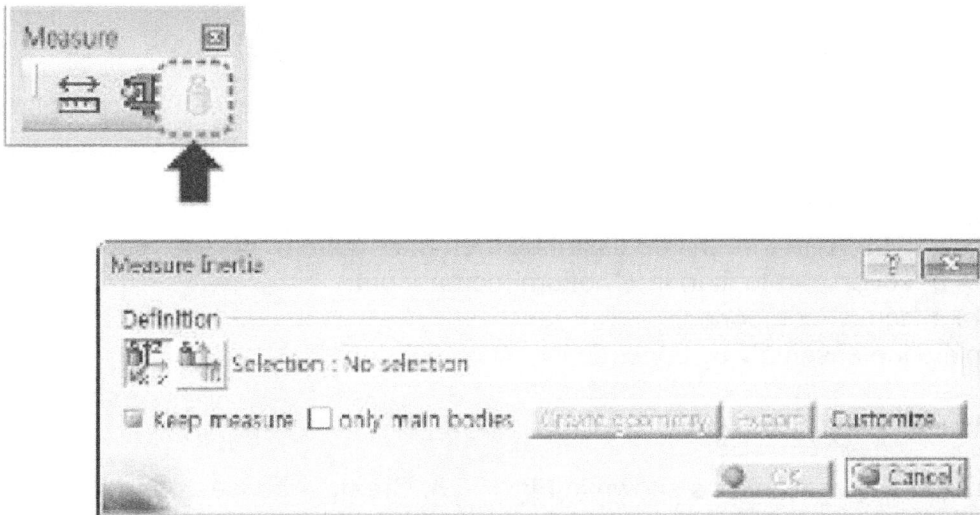

Fig 15-73 Measure Inertia Dialog Box

3. Check the Measure Inertia dialog box as shown in Fig 15-73. Note that the Measure 3D button is pressed.
4. Select the product to measure inertia in the Spec tree. ((A) in Fig 15-74)

The Measure Inertia dialog box is expanded and the result of measurement appears in region (B) designated in Fig 15-74.

5. Check the Keep measure option and press OK. The result of measurement is recorded in the Spec Tree.

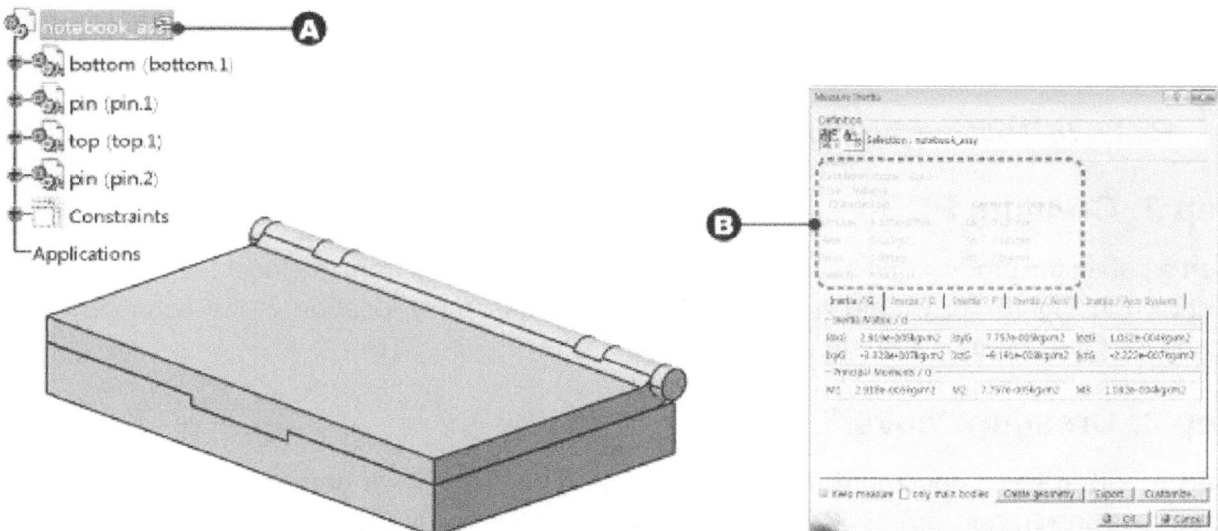

Fig 15-74 Measuring Inertia

443

Exercise 135: Measuring Inertia (Folder: ch15_010)

Open the CATProduct file given in the ch15_010 folder carry out the exercise according to the given procedure. Use your own dimensions and design intent for the unspecified dimension.

1. Modify the "bottom" component.
2. Create a "PCB" part that will be assembled on the " bottom" component.
3. Create a "cover' part to fit to the "bottom" component.
4. Create a "screw" component.
5. Complete the assembly by constraining all components.

Step 1: Modifying "bottom"

Modify the "bottom" component as shown in Fig 15-75. Create 4 bosses on which to assemble the "PCB" component by using the Rectangular Pattern command. Create a slot feature ((A) in Fig 15-75) of 1mm width and 1 mm depth on which to assemble the "cover" component.

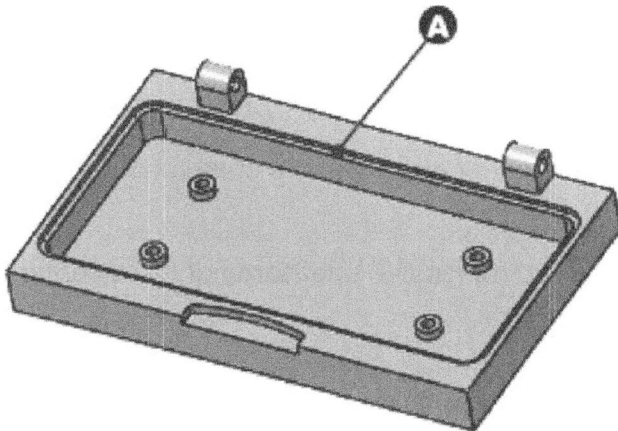

Fig 15-75 Modifying "bottom" Component

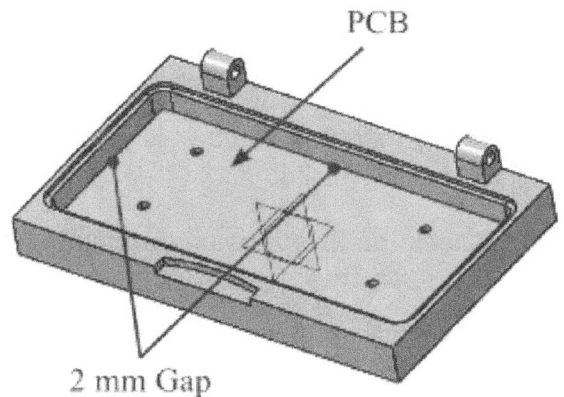

Fig 15-76 PCB Part

Step 2: Creating PCB

Insert a part in the product and save it as "PCB". Apply a 2mm gap from the inner face of the "bottom" as shown in Fig 15-76. Create a through hole at the assembly location of the boss center. The thickness of the "PCB" is 1.5mm.

Step 3: Creating "cover"

Insert a part in the product and save it as "cover". Apply a 0.1mm gap from the slot face of the "bottom" as shown in Fig 15-77. Create a boss downward up to the upper face. of "PCB" to assemble the "screw". The section of the assembly is shown in Fig 15-77.

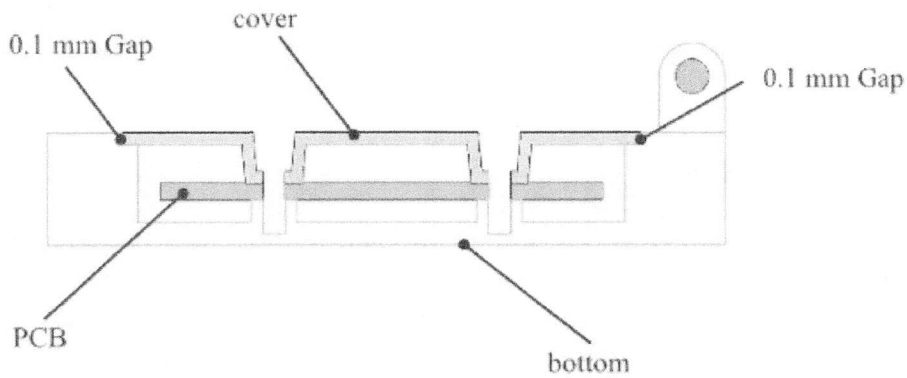

Fig 15-77 Section of the Assembly

Step 4: Creating "screw" and Completing

Create a proper sized screw and assemble it using the Reuse Pattern command. Constrain all components and save all files.

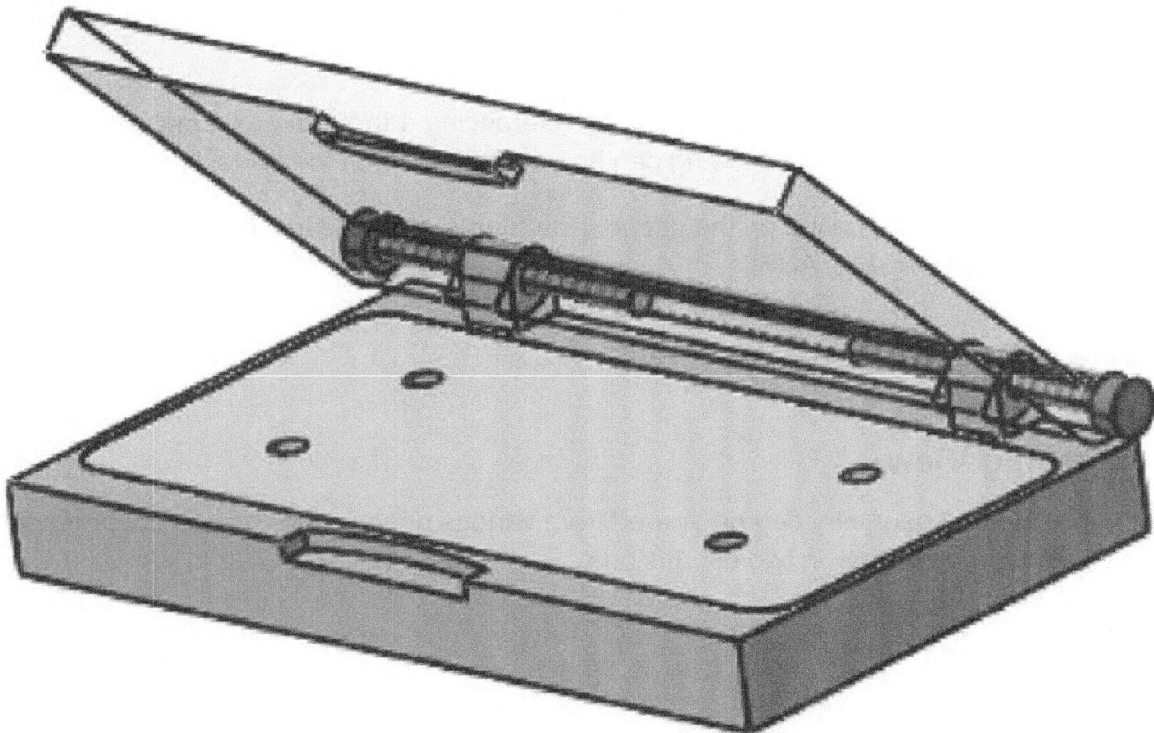

Fig 15-78 Completed Assembly

CHAPTER 15: BLUEPRINTING YOUR DESIGNS: DRAWING VIEW CREATION

16.1 INTRODUCTION

These days, three-dimensional design is widely adopted in designing products in manufacturing industries. If a product is designed using three-dimensional modeling programs such as CATIA V5 and manufactured on the basis of automation, there should be utilities available in the factory so that the manufacturing process can refer to the three-dimensional design data.

If the manufacturing process is based on a manual, such utilities to deal with the three-dimensional data are not required. In those cases, traditional drawings explaining the shapes and manufacturing methods of a part or product will be sufficient. Therefore, we have to be able to create drawings in three-dimensional modeling programs.

There are two types of drawings based on the objectives of drawings: a part drawing and an assembly drawing. A part drawing is created to manufacture individual part. An assembly drawing is created for assembly. The assembly sequence and path can be illustrated in a disassembled drawing view. Names, quantity, material, etc. of each component of an assembly can be included in the parts list.

In CATIA V5, we can create each drawing view by referencing a three-dimensional part geometry. If the part geometry is modified, the drawing can be updated to adapt to the design changes.

You can create your drawing based on the drawing standards available in CATIA V5; ISO, ISO_3D, JIS, JIS_3D, ASME_3D, ASME, ANSI.

16.2 TERMS AND DEFINITIONS

16.2.1 Drawing View

Three-dimensional part geometry can be viewed from various directions or can be cut or magnified to express its shape completely in two dimensions.

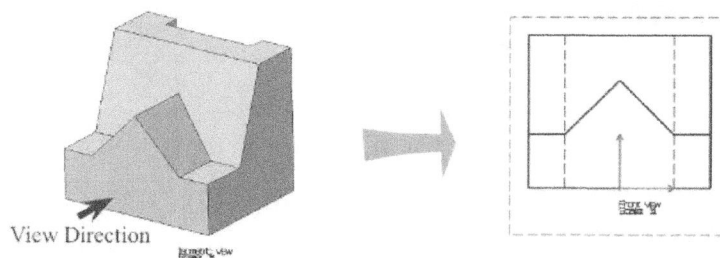

Fig 16-1 Drawing View

16.2.2 Title Block

Basic information for a drawing is recorded in the title block which is located in the bottom right of the drawing sheet. Fig 16-2 shows a typical title block that is available by default in CATIA V5.

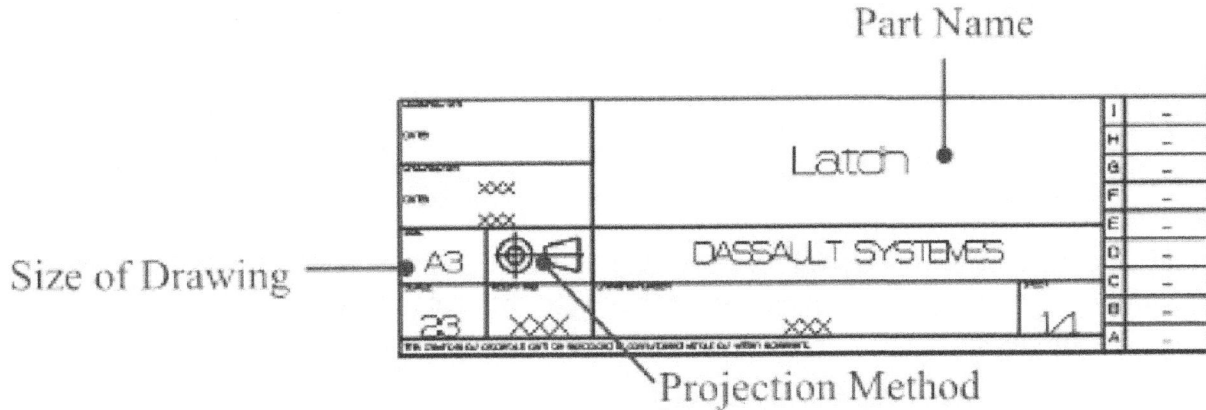

Fig 16-2 Title Block

16.2.3 Drawing Sheet

A manual drawing is created on a sheet. In a 2D drawing created with a CAD program, the size of the drawing, scale, drawing standard, projection method, etc. are defined in the drawing sheet.

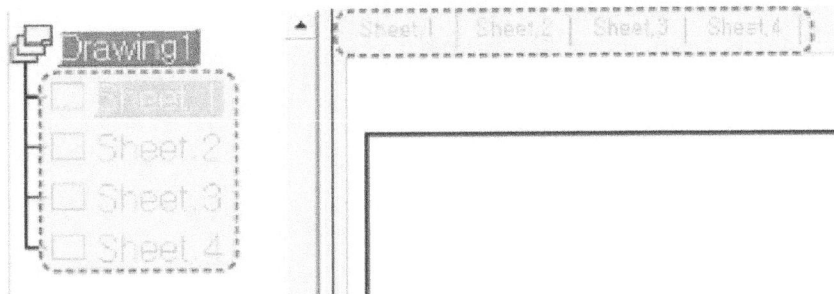

Fig 16-3 Drawing Sheets

16.3 CREATING A NEW DRAWING FILE

Choose File > New in the menu bar. A New dialog box as shown in Fig 16-4 appears. Select Drawing in the dialog box. You can enter "drawing" in the Selection input box. By pressing the OK button in the New dialog box a New Drawing dialog box appears as shown in Fig 16-5.

447

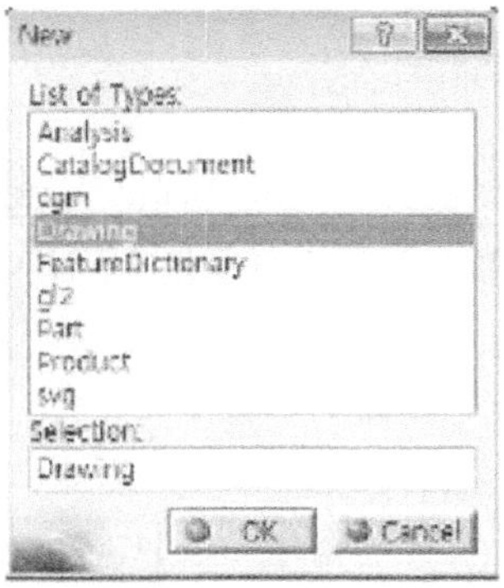

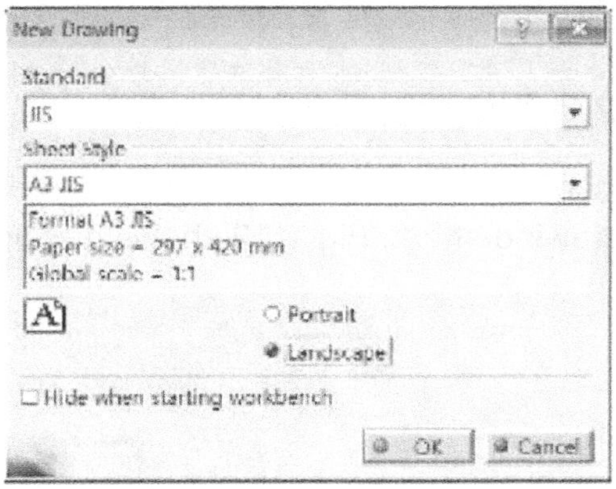

Fig 16-4 New Dialog Box

Fig 16-5 New Drawing Dialog Box

You can select the drawing standard and set the size and orientation of the drawing sheet in the New Drawing dialog box. By pressing the OK button in the dialog box, the Drafting workbench as shown in Fig 16-6 is invoked.

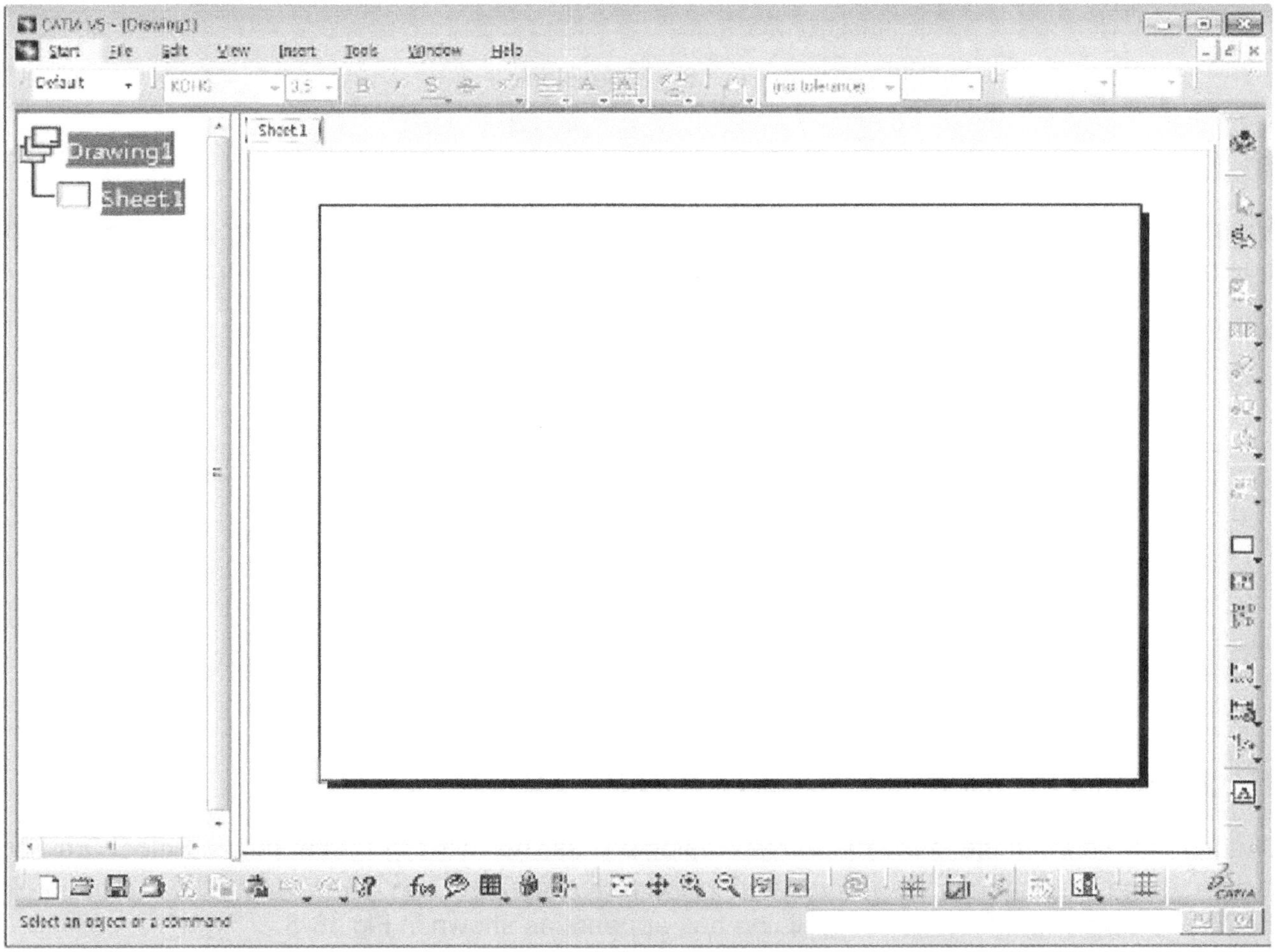

Fig 16-6 Drafting Workbench

16.4 DRAWING SHEET

The largest standard size of a sheet is A0 of which the dimension is 1189 mm x 841 mm. However, we cannot draw all necessary drawing views and annotations in a single sheet because we should not create texts and views too small. Bearing in mind that we have to print out the drawing at the end, the size of the texts and drawing views have to be easy and comfortable to read!. What, then, should we do in cases where we have to create a drawing for a part with great complexity in its geometry? All necessary drawing entities for those parts cannot be created in a single A0 sheet. We need to insert more drawing sheets and arrange the drawing views in several drawing sheets.

16.4.1 Creating a Drawing Sheet

In CATIA V5, we can insert additional drawing sheets if required by pressing the New Sheet icon in the Drawing toolbar as shown in Fig 16 -7. You can switch to each drawing view by double clicking the sheet in the Spec Tree ((A)in Fig 16-7) and selecting the tab. ((B) in Fig 16-7).

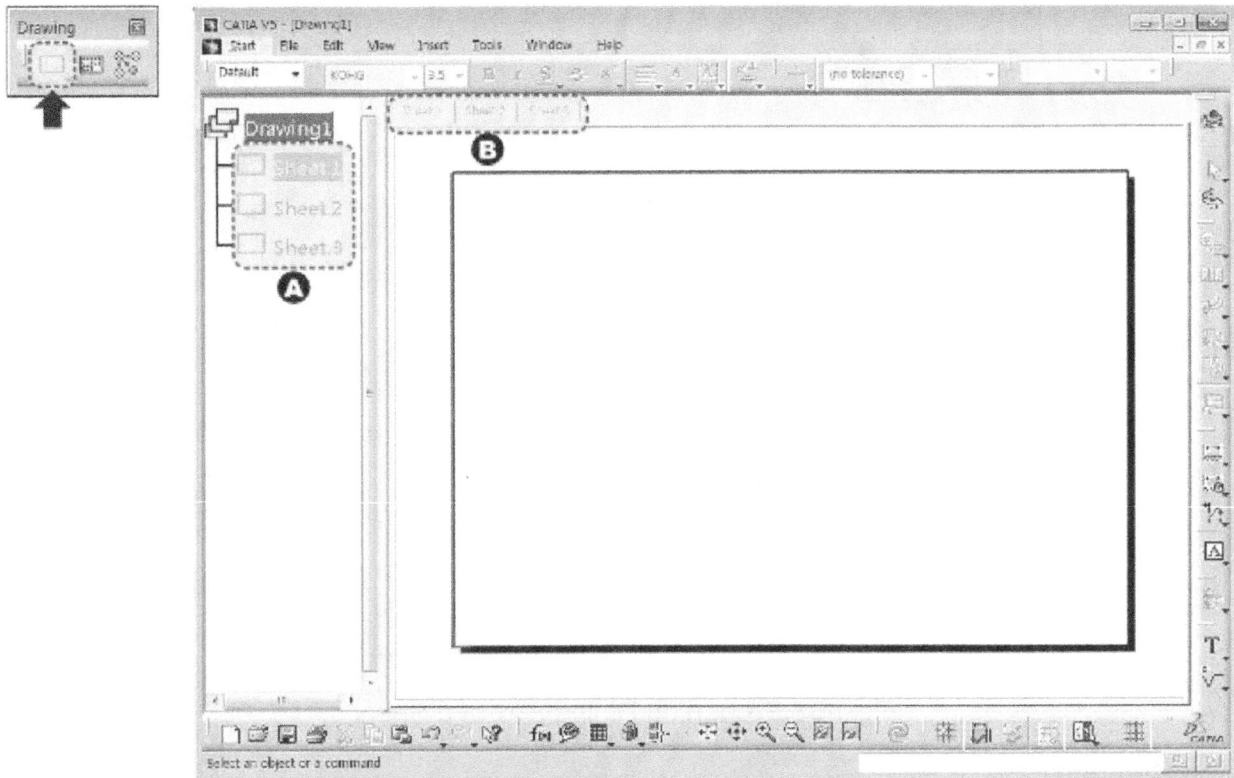

Fig 16-7 A Drawing File with Three Drawing Sheets

16.4.2 Setting a Drawing Sheet

Press MB3 (right click) > Properties on the sheet shown in Fig 16-70. The Properties dialog box as shown in Fig 16-8 appears and the basic settings for the sheet can be defined or modified. You can modify the name of the sheet, scale, drawing size and standard, projection method, etc. in the dialog box.

If you choose ISO as the drawing format, the Projection Method option is set as the First angle standard by default. If you choose JIS as the drawing format, the Projection Method option is set as the Third angle standard by default.

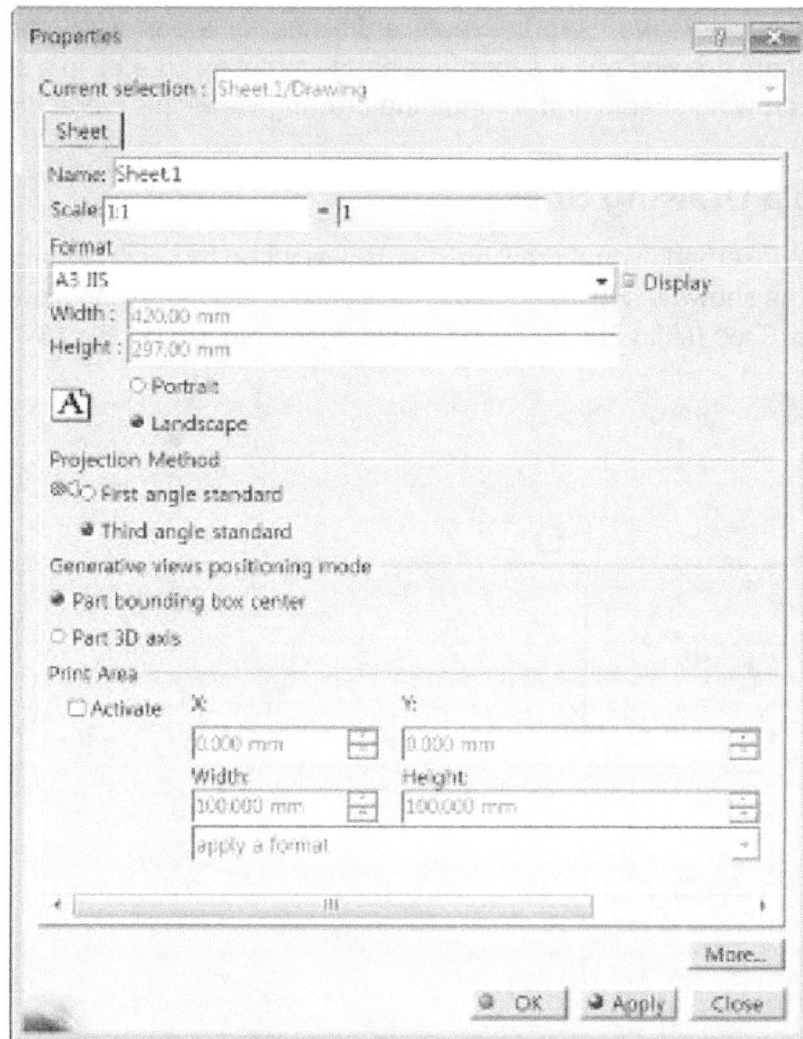

Fig 16-8 Properties Dialog Box of a Sheet

(Note) Hiding Grid

- Grid lines can be hidden by releasing the Sketcher Grid option in the Visualization.

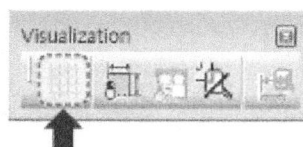

16.5 DRAWING VIEWS

To illustrate a three dimensional shape in a 2D sheet, we can create various types of drawing views to express the full shape without missing any aspect of it. ole that a smaller number of drawing views is preferable for the simplicity of the drawing. After creating all necessary drawing views, we create the dimensions and drawing symbols.

Various drawing views can be created with the icons in the sub-toolbars of the View toolbar.

- **Projections:** Drawing views arc created according to the view direction.
- **Sections:** A part is cut at a location or at an angle and is viewed.
- **Details:** A complex portion of another view is magnified.
- **Clippings:** A drawing view is clipped out leaving only the portion in the boundary.
- **Break View:** A part is cut out by a closed boundary or at a location.

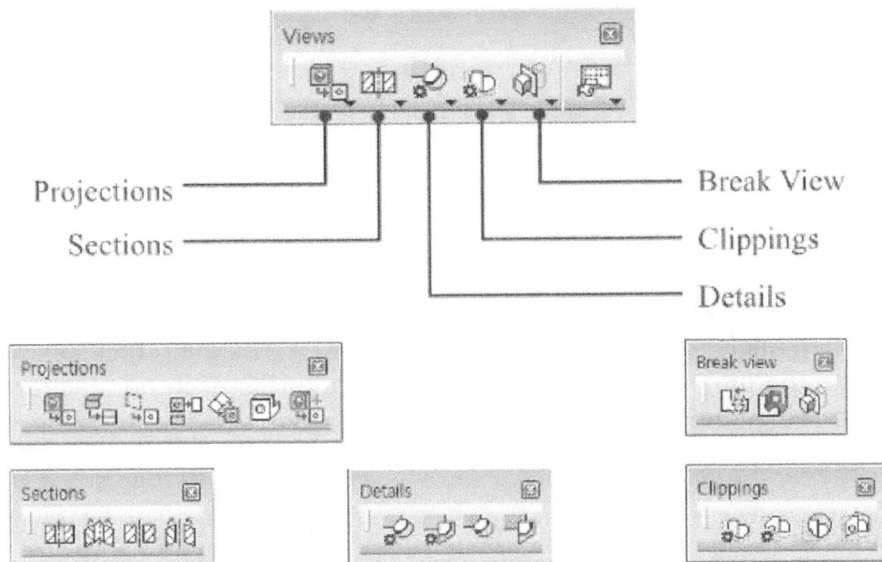

Fig 16-9 Views Toolbar

16.5.1 Projection View

You can create a view projected along a specified direction.

Exercise 136: Using Measured Parameter (ch16 _001.CATPart)

In this exercise, we will create project ion views for the given part ch16_001.CATPart according to the third angle projection standard.

1. Open the given part file ch16_001.CATPart.
2. Choose File > New in the menu bar.
3. Select Drawing in the New dialog box and press OK .
4. Set the options in the New Drawing dialog box as shown in Fig 16-10 and press OK.

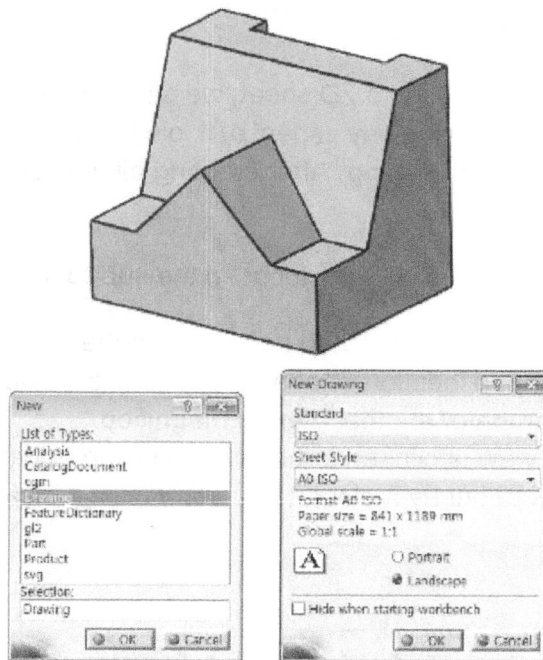

Fig 16-10 Invoking Drafting Workbench

Drafting workbench is invoked.

5. Press MB3 > Properties on Sheet.1 on the drawing Spec Tree.
6. Select the Third angle standard option ((A) in Fig 16 - 11) as the projection method and press OK. Note that the projection method is defined in the ISO drawing standard. If you choose JIS as the drawing standard, the Third angle standard is selected by default.

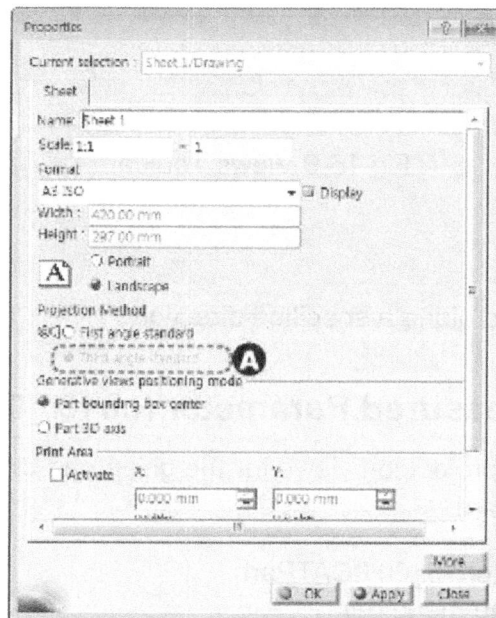

Fig 16-11 Projection Method Option

(Note) Projection Methods

- **1st Angle Projection**: A part is placed in the 1st quadrant in the space and is projected on each plane along the projection direction. The plane of projection is unfolded to arrange each projection view was shown in Fig 16-12.

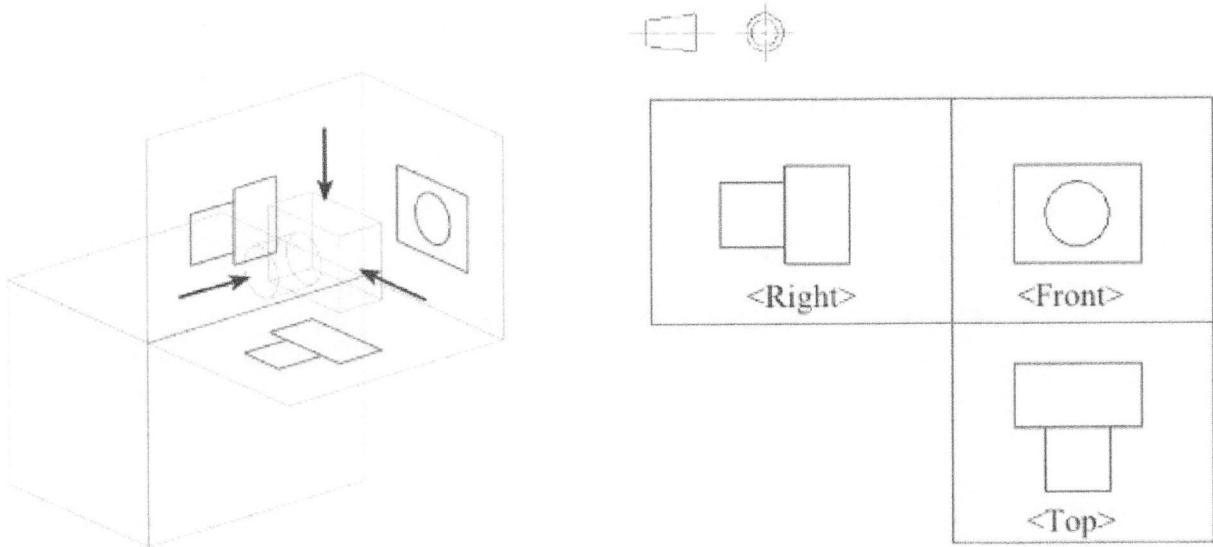

Fig 16-12 1st Angle Projection

- **3rd Angle Projection:** A part is placed in the 3rd quadrant in the space and is projected on each plane along the project ion direction. The plane of projection is unfolded to arrange each projection view as shown in Fig 16-13.

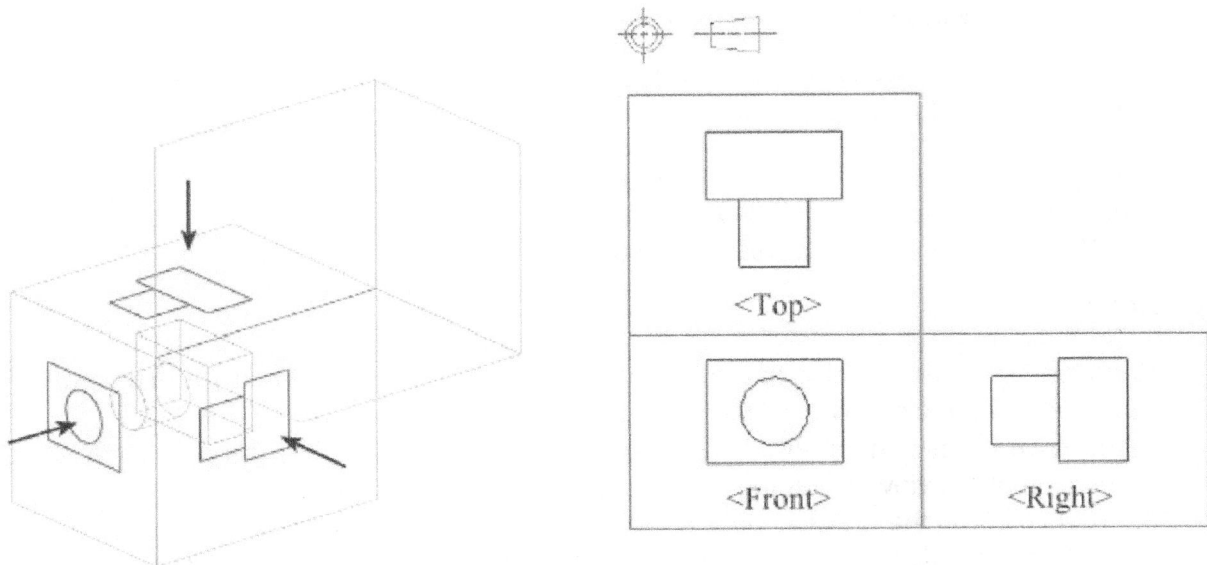

Fig 16-13 3rd Angle Projection

453

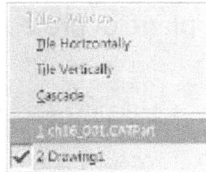

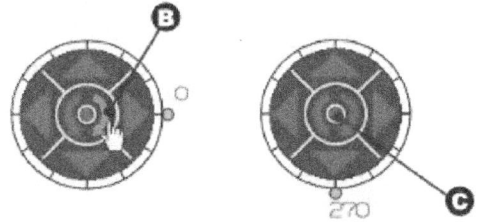

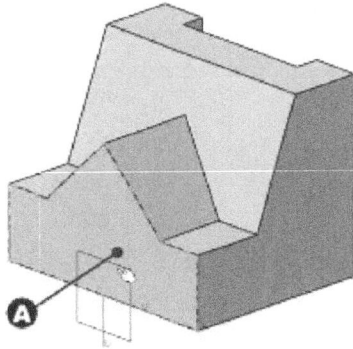

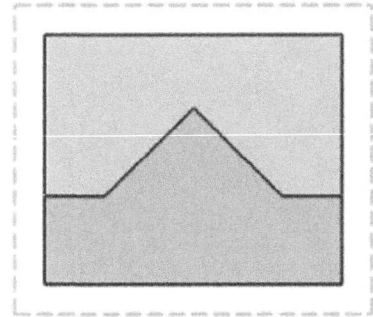

Fig 16-14 Selecting Front Plane

Fig 16-15 Rotation of the View

7. Click the Front View icon in the Views toolbar.

You are prompted to select a reference plane on the 3D geometry.

8. Select the part file in the Window menu. The part is shown in the main window.
9. Place the mouse cursor on plane (A) shown in Fig 16-14. A preview window appears. Click the plane with the mouse button 1. (Note that the user interface style is based on P2 configuration which can be set in Options > General > General in the menu bar.)

Th Drafting workbench is invoked and a blue knob appear on the top right of the screen. Be careful not to click MB1 (left click) on the screen.

10. Click (B) in fig 16-15 on the knob to rotate the drawing view.
11. When the view appears as shown in Fi g 1 6- 15, click the center of the knob (G in Fig 16-15). You can click an empty area in the screen.

(Note) Knob

- Knob functions are available in the P2 and P3 user interface style when you are creating the front and isometric drawing views.
- If you have made a m is take in placing the view, you can modify the reference plane or orientation of the view according to the following procedure.
  1. Right click on the drawing view in the Spec Tree or view boundary.
  2. Select Front view object > Modify Projection Plane from the pop-up menu.
  3. Select the reference plane in the 3D geometry.
  4. Define the orientation using the Knob and create a view.

12. Place the mouse cursor on the boundary of the view and drag around the bottom left of the sheet.

13. Take out the Projections sub-toolbar from the View tool bar and press the Projection View button.

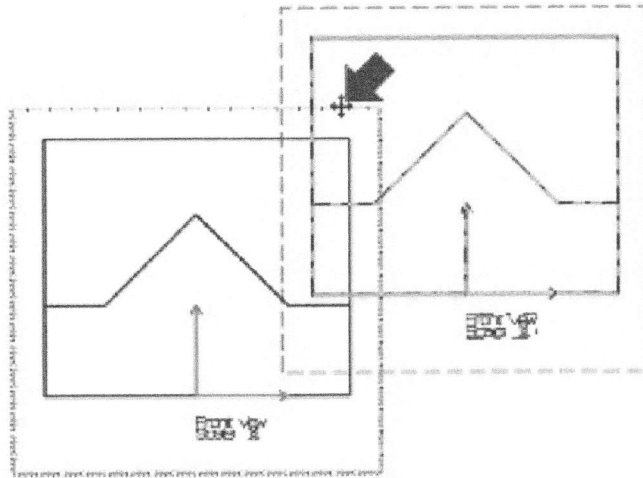

Fig 16-16 View Positioning

14. Place the mouse cursor on the right of the front view. Right view appears as shown in Fig 16-17. Click MB1 (left click) to generate the right view.

(Note) Active View

The view boundary of an active view is highlighted in red on the screen and in blue in the Spec Tree. You can double click a view to activate it.

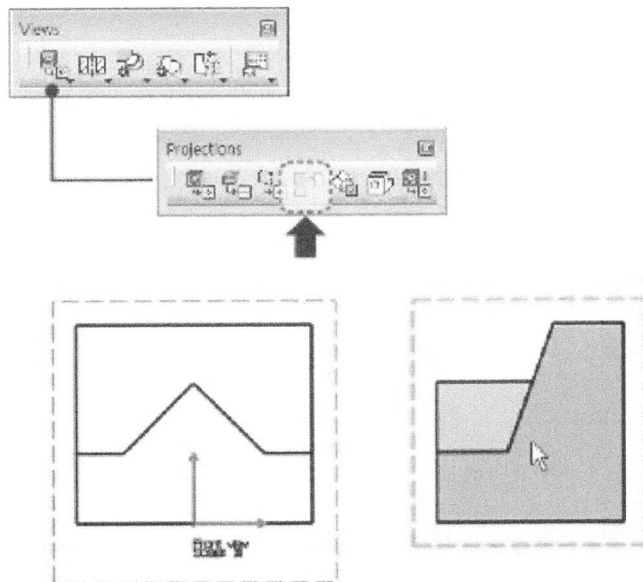

Fig 16-17 Creating a Right View

15. Create a top view using the Projection View command as shown in Fig 16-18.
16. Press the Fit All In button in the View toolbar.

The sheet size is too large. Note that we have chosen AO ISO in Fig 16-10. Let's down-size the sheet.

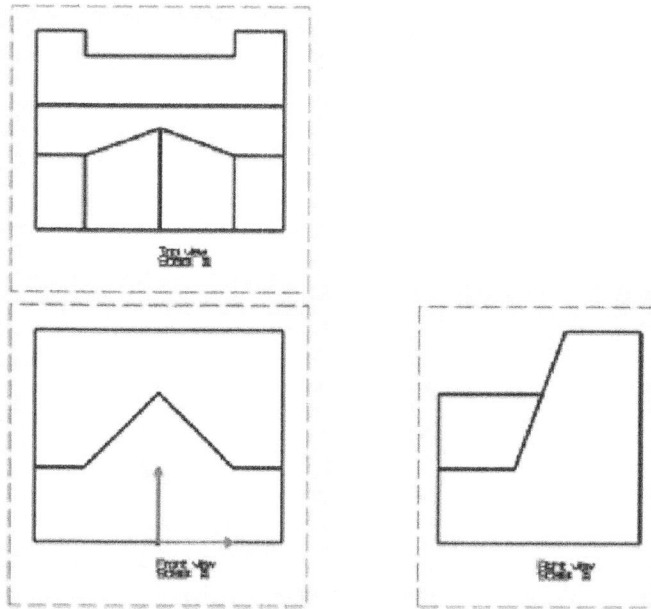

Fig 16-18 Top View

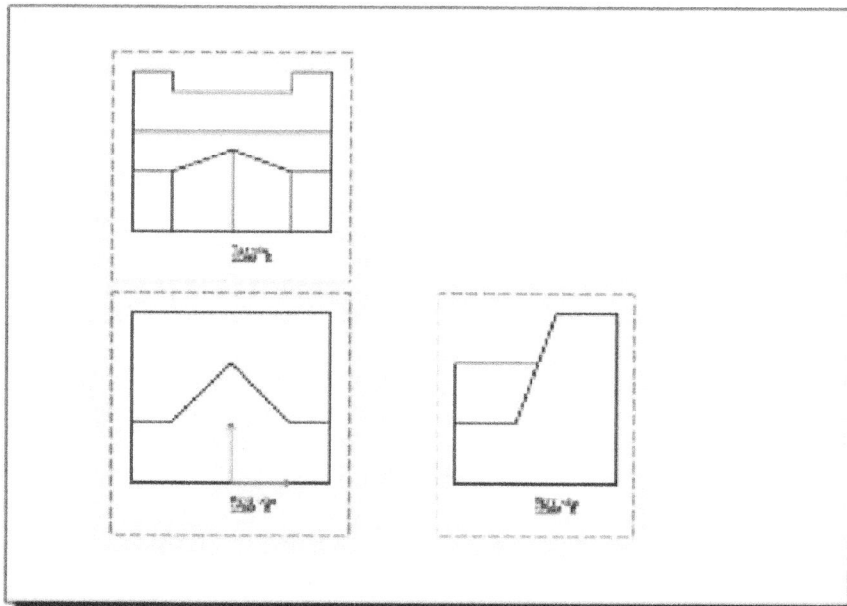

Fig 16-19 Arranged Views

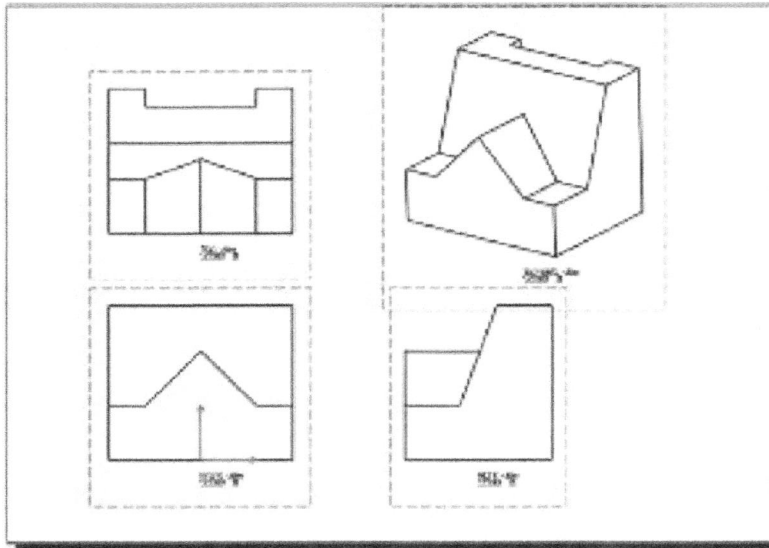

Fig 16-20 Isometric View

17. Press MB3 (right click) > Properties on Sheet.1 in the Spec Tree and select A3 ISO in the Format dropdown list.
18. Drag the active view and drop inside the sheet. Other views are moved together.
19. Pres the Fit All In once again.

Views are arranged as shown in Fig 16-19.

20. Choose Window > Tile Horizontally in the menu bar.
21. Click the drawing window and choose Isometric View in the Projections toolbar.
22. Select the front face in the part window.
23. Adjust the orientation and position of the view and generate the isometric view.
24. Choose File > Save in the menu bar.
25. Name the drawing file ch16_001.CATDrawing. It is recommended to use the same file name.

16.5.2 View Properties

Press MB3 (right click) > Properties on a view in the Spec Tree. The Properties dialog box as shown in Fig 16-21 appears and you can set the options for the drawing view. The dialog box is also invoked by right clicking on the view boundary and choosing Properties in the pop-up menu.

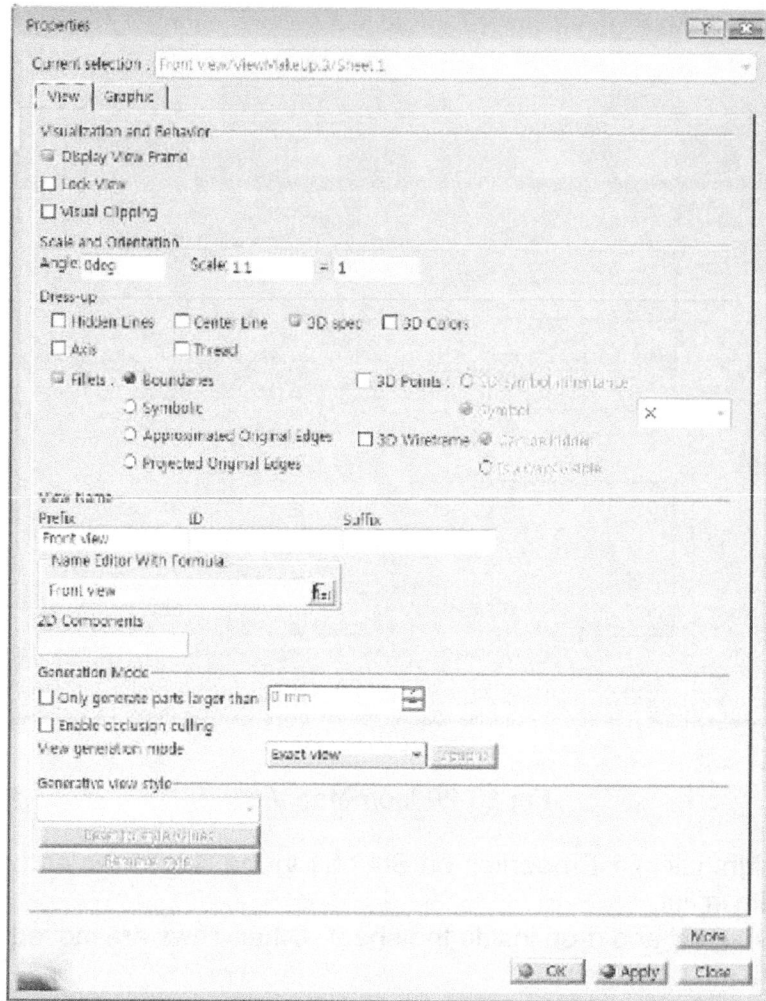

Fig 16-21 View Properties Dialog Box

Exercise 137: Setting the View Properties

1. Open the file created in Exercise 01.
2. Press MB3 > Properties on the front view and check the Hidden Lines option in the Dress-Up option area. Hidde n lines are displayed as shown in Fig 16-22.

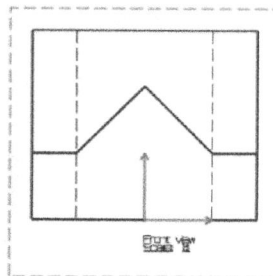

Fig 16-22 Hidden Lines

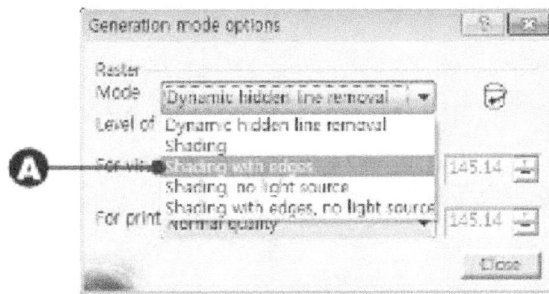

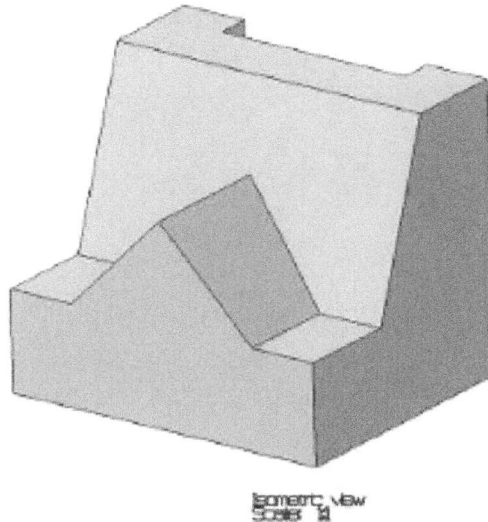

Fig 16-23 Shaded Raster Image

3. Set the Hidden Lines option for the right view.
4. Press MB3 > Properties on the iso-metric view.
5. Select Raster in the View generation mode option and press the Option button. Then select Shading with edges ((A) in Fig 16-23) in the Raster Mode dropdown list and close the dialog box.
6. Press the OK button in the Proper• ties dialog box. Isometric view is displayed in shaded raster mode as shown in Fig 16-23.
7. Modify the scale of each view to 4:5.
8. Save the drawing file and close.

Exercise 138: Creating an Auxiliary View (ch16 _003.CATPart)

Let's create an auxiliary view which is defined by projecting a view along a specified direction.

1. Open the given file ch16_003.CA Part.
2. Choose File > New in the menu bar.
3. Select Drawing in the New dialog box and press OK.
4. Choose the A3 ISO sheet style in the New Drawing dialog box and press OK. Drafting workbench is invoked.
5. Set the projection method a shown in Fig 16-11.

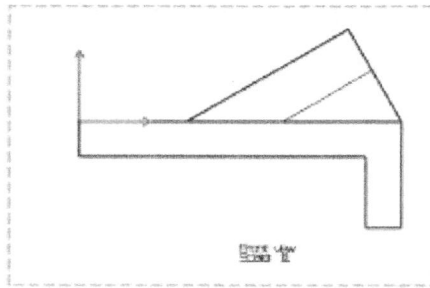

Fig 16-24 Front View

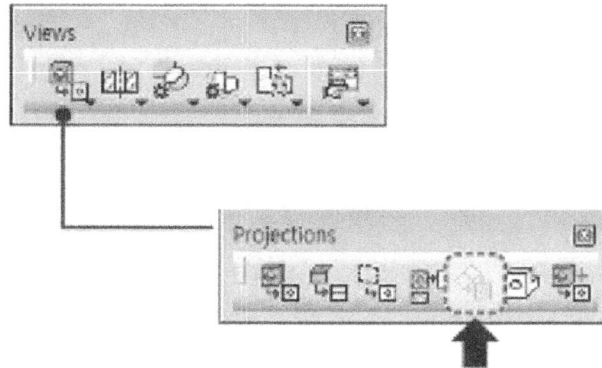

Fig 16-25 Auxiliary View Icon

6. Create a front view as shown in Fig 16-24.
7. Click the Auxiliary View icon in the Projections toolbar as shown in fig 16-25. You are prompted to select the starting point or a linear edge to define the orientation of the auxiliary view.
8. Select the edge (A) as shown in Fig 16-26. You are prompted to click to end.
9. Click MB1 (left click) at the location specified by (B) in Fig 16-26.

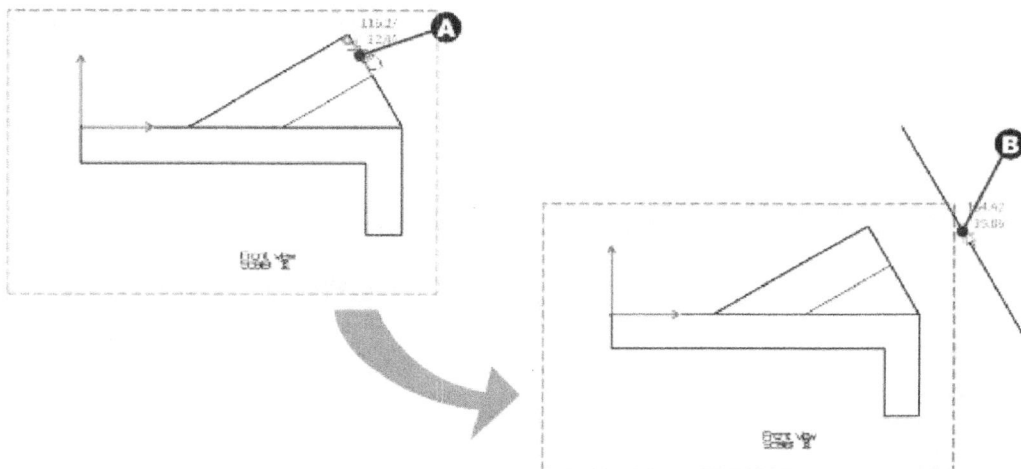

Fig 16- 26 Defining Orientation

460

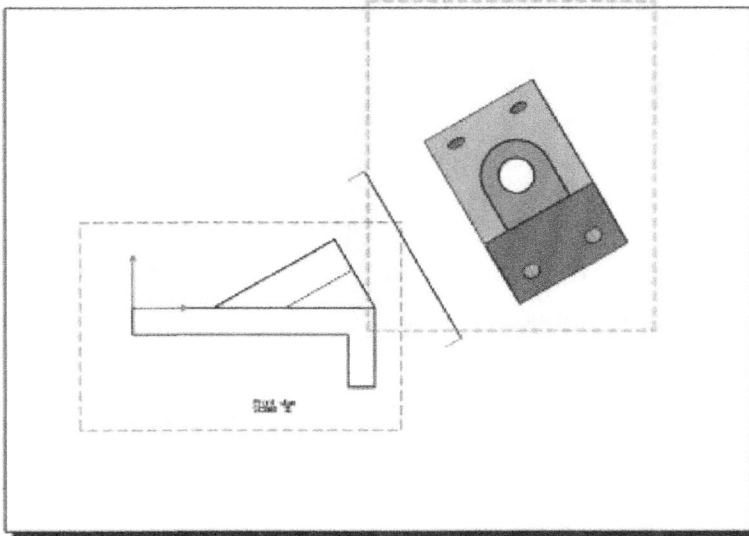

Fig 16-27 Preview of Auxiliary View

The preview of the auxiliary view is as shown in Fig 16-27

10. Click MB1 (left click) at desired location to create the auxiliary view as shown in Fig 16-28.

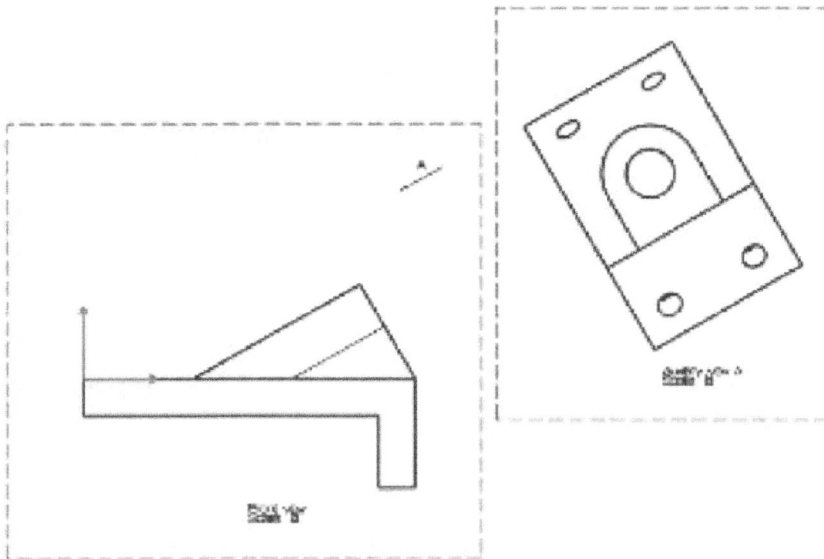

Fig 16-28 Auxiliary View Created

16.5.3 Section Views

By defining a cut line that passes through a specific location in the 3D geometry, you can express a complex shape exactly and effectively. In CATIA V5, four types of section views are available as shown in Fig 16-29.

461

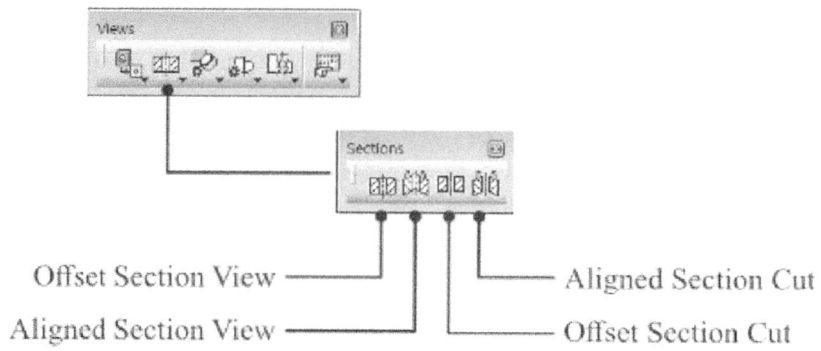

Fig 16-29 Sections Sub toolbar

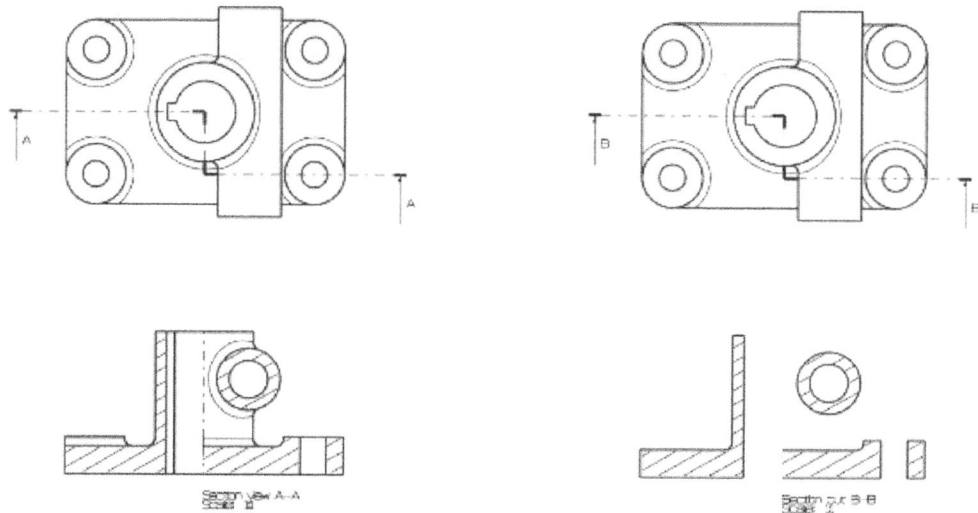

Fig 16-30 Offset Sections

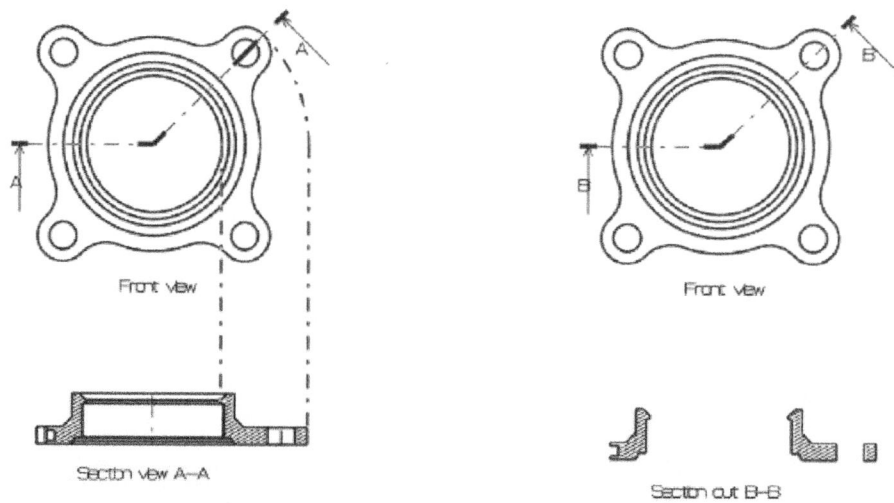

Fig 16-31 Aligned Sections

462

Exercise 139: Creating Section Views (ch16 _004.CATPart)

Let's create section views for the part given in ch16_004.CATPart.

Creating an Offset Section View

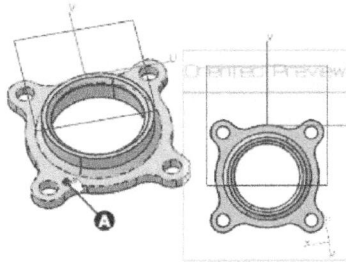

Fig 16-32 Front View

1. Open the given file ch16_004.CATPart.
2. Choose File > New in the menu bar and create a Drawing type file. Choose ISO for the drawing standard and A3 ISO for Sheet Style.
3. Select the third angle projection method.
4. Choose Window > Tile Horizontally in the menu bar.
5. Generate a front view by selecting the plane (A) designated in Fig 16-32.
6. Choose the Offset Section View from the Sections sub-toolbar.
7. Pick the points designated by (1), (2) in order and double click the point (3) as shown in Fig 16-33.
8. Place the mouse cursor around the point (4). The preview is shown attached at the mouse cursor.
9. Click MB1 (left click) at point (4) to generate the offset section view as shown in Fig 16-34.

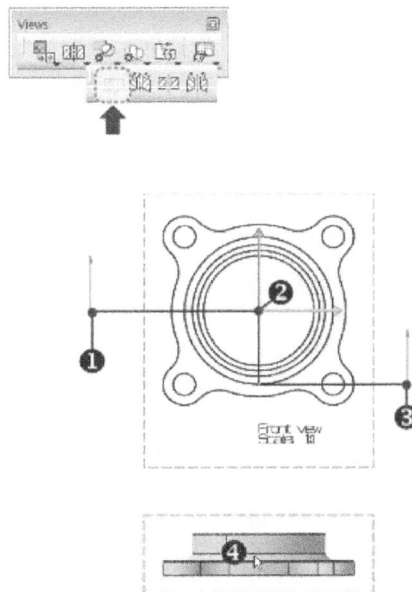

Fig 16-33 Creating Offset Section View

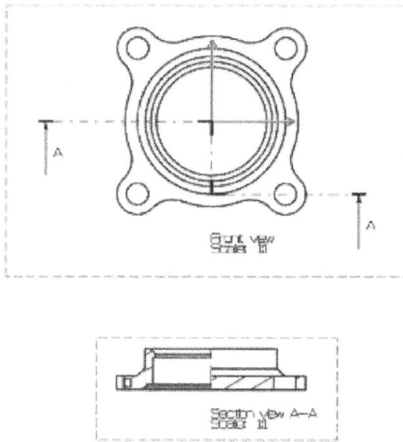

Fig 16-34 Offset Section View Created

(Note) Repositioning Section View

- You can reposition the view along the projection direction by dragging the boundary of the drawing view. Right click on the view boundary and select the View Positioning > Position In- dependently of Reference View option. You can move the view al an arbitrary location.

Creating an Aligned Section View

1. Choose the Aligned Section View button from the Views toolbar.
2. Select the circle center designated by (1) in Fig 16-35.
3. Select the point (2) and double click at the location (3) shown in Fig 16 - 35.

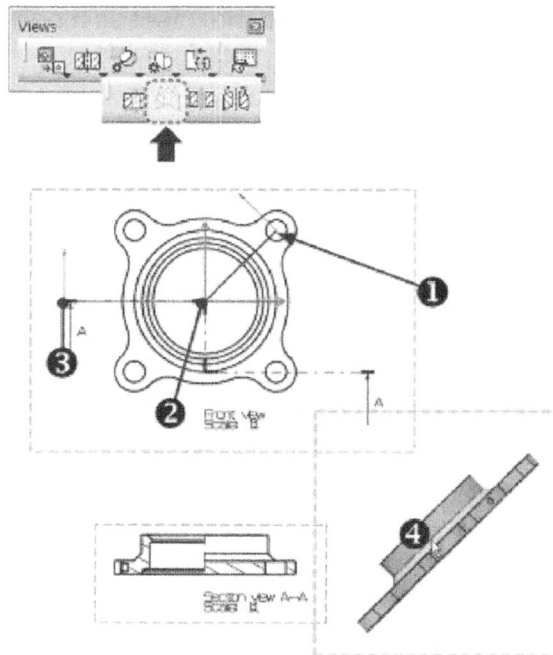

Fig 16-35 Creating Aligned Section View

464

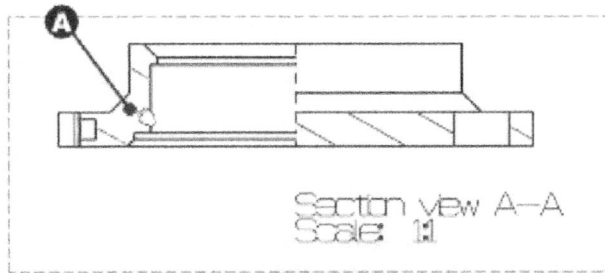

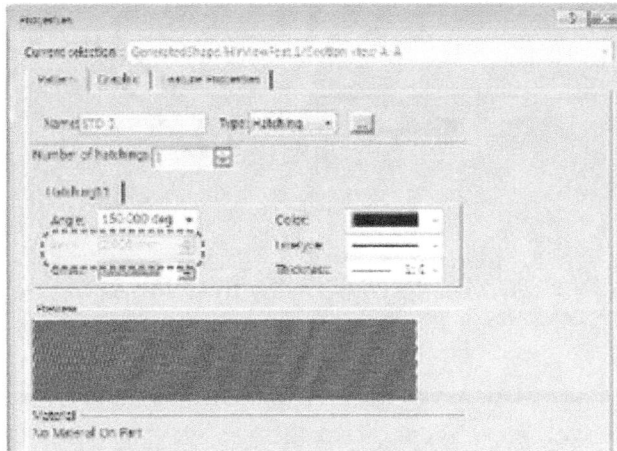

Fig 16-36 Properties of Hatching

1. Move the cursor to the location (4) and left click to generate the view. Note that aligned section view is located normal to the line defined by the first two point, i.e. the points (1) and (2) in Fig 16-35.
2. Double click the hatch line designated by (A) in Fig 16-36.
3. Enter 1 in the Pitch input area and press OK. The hatch line spacing is updated.
4. Close the file without saving.

(Note) Dragging Text

- You can move the view name text by dragging it. To turn off snapping, press the Shift key while dragging.

(Note) Redefining the Section Profile

- Double click on the section profile. The profile edition mode is invoked. The current section profile can be replaced by a new profile and the view direction can be inversed. After setting a new profile, press the End Profile Edition button.

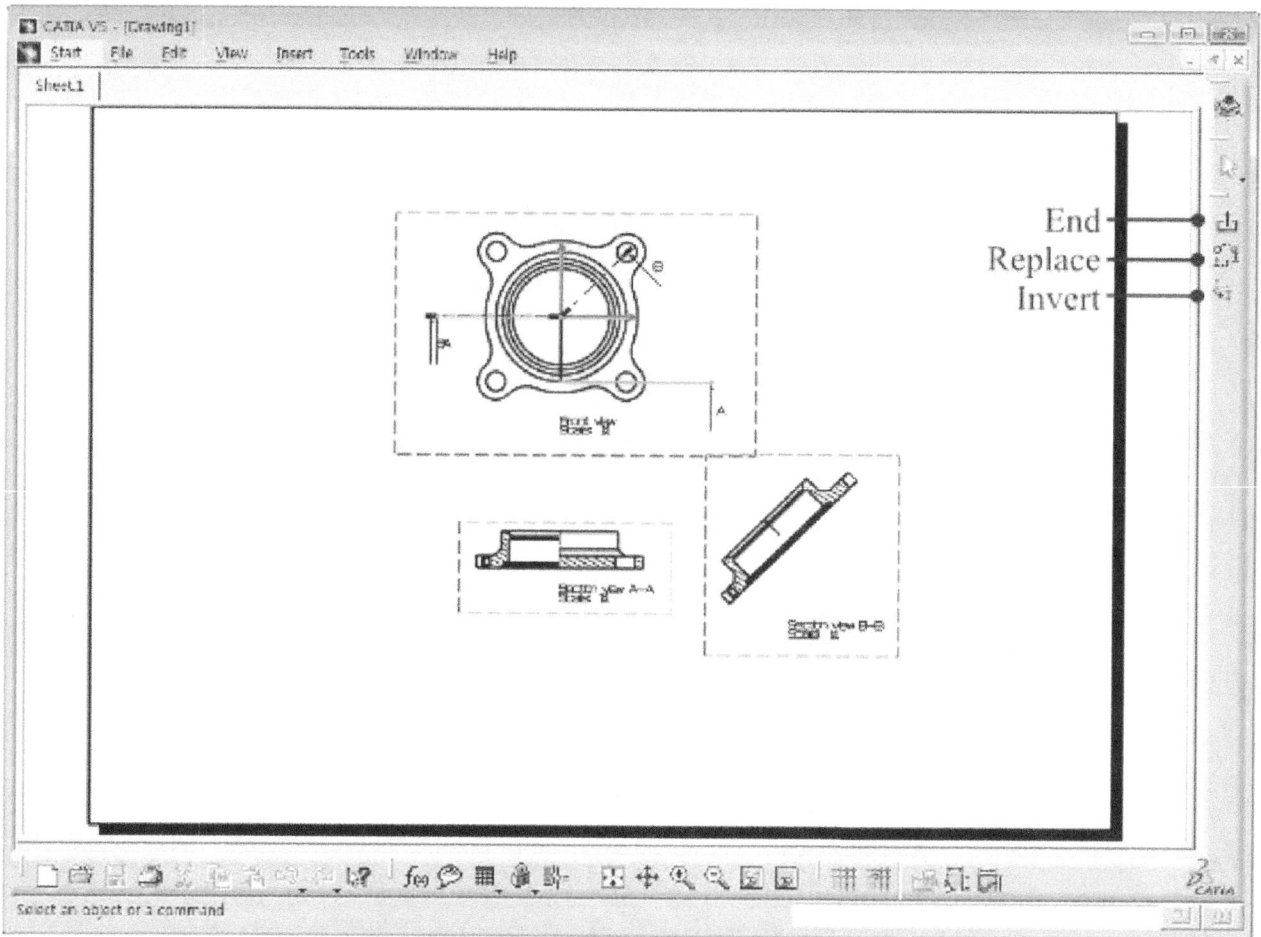

Fig 16-37 Redefining the Section Profile

When you select the first point in defining the section profile, the tools palette is invoked. Using the icons in this palette, you can set the angle of the profile with reference to an existing line. Keep to the following procedure.

1. Press a button in the Tools Palette toolbar.
2. Select a reference line.
3. Move the mouse cursor and click at the desired location.

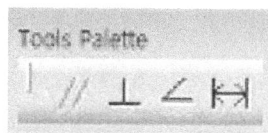

16.5.4 Detail Views

You can magnify a region of a drawing view to create a detail view by applying a higher calling ratio. You can even create another detail view for an existing detail view.

Procedure

1. Activate a view for which to create a detail view. (Press MB3 (right click) > Activate View on the view.)
2. Click an icon in the Details toolbar.
3. Define the region on the active view.
4. Specify the location of the detail view by clicking MB1 (left click).
5. Modify the scale by accessing the view properties option if required.

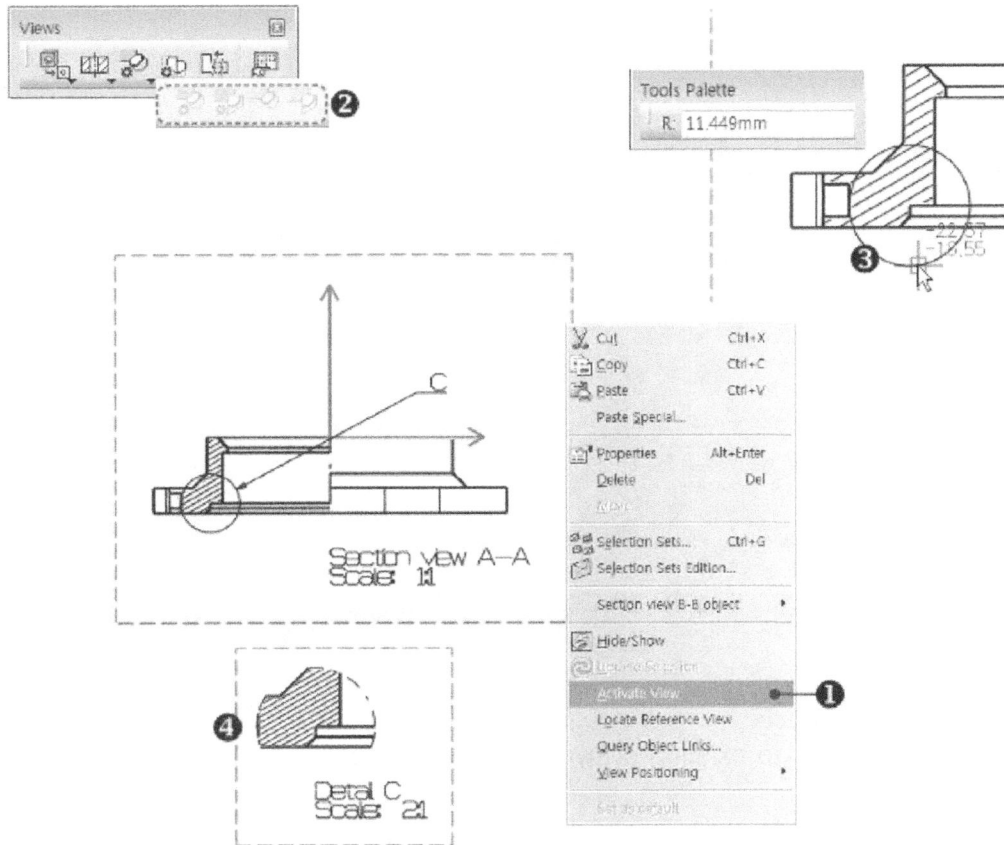

Fig 16-38 Creating a Detail View

16.5.5 Clipping Views

You can clip out an existing drawing view against a defined region. Note that you cannot create a clipping view for another clipping view or for a detail view. However, you can create a detail view for a clipping view.

Procedure

1. Activate a view for which to create a clipping view. (Press MB3 (right click) > Activate View on the view.)
2. Click an icon in the Clippings toolbar.

3. Define the region on the active view. If a closed clipping boundary is defined, the geometry outside of the region is clipped.

To restore the unclipped view, right click on the clipping view boundary and select view object > Unclip in the pop-up menu.

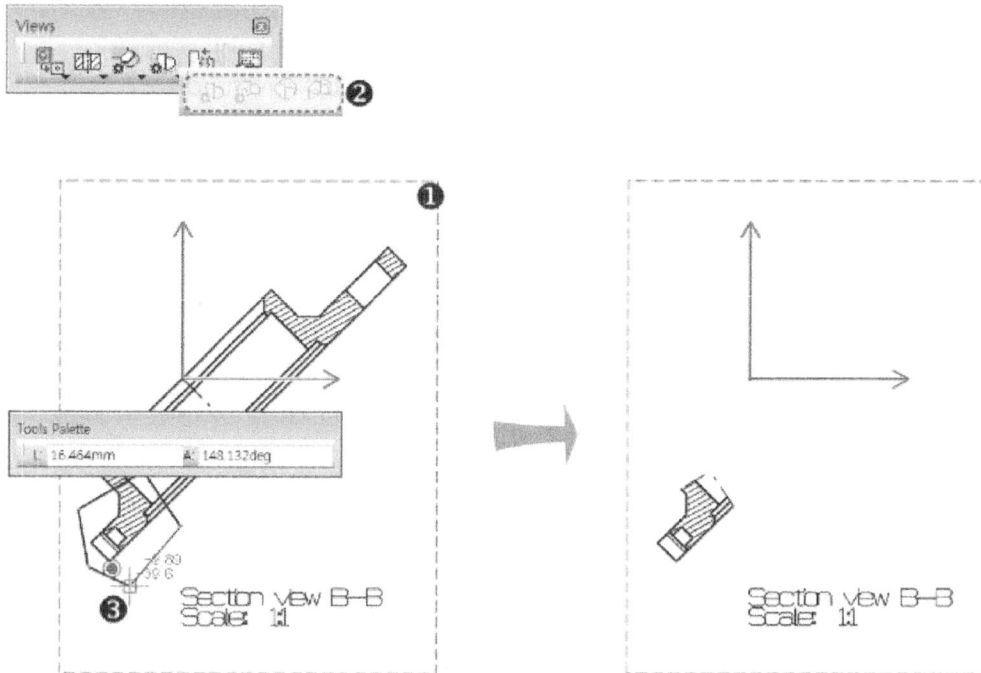

Fig 16-39 Creating a Clipping View

16.5.6 Break Views

You can break a portion of an existing drawing view. The following three types of break views are available in CATIA V5.

1. **Broken View**: Break out along uniform section of a part in the middle.
2. **Breakout View:** Break out a region at a specific depth.
3. **Add 3D Clipping:** Break out a 3D geometry using planes or clipping box.

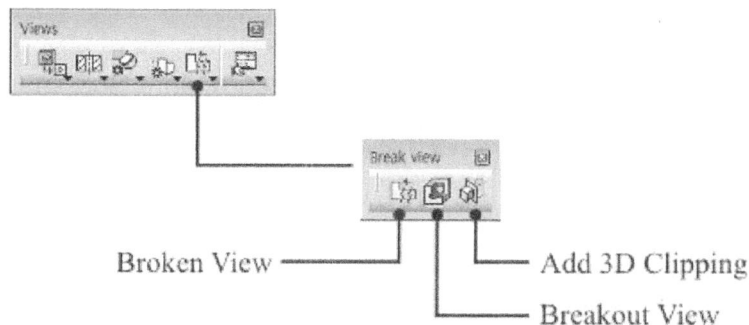

Fig 16-40 Break View Sub-toolbar

Exercise 140: Creating Broken Views and Breakout view (ch16 _005.CATPart)

Creating a Broken View

1. Open the given file ch16_005.CATPart.
2. Create a drawing file as the same name as the part file with the 3rd angle projection method.
3. Create a front view selecting the xy plane as the front.

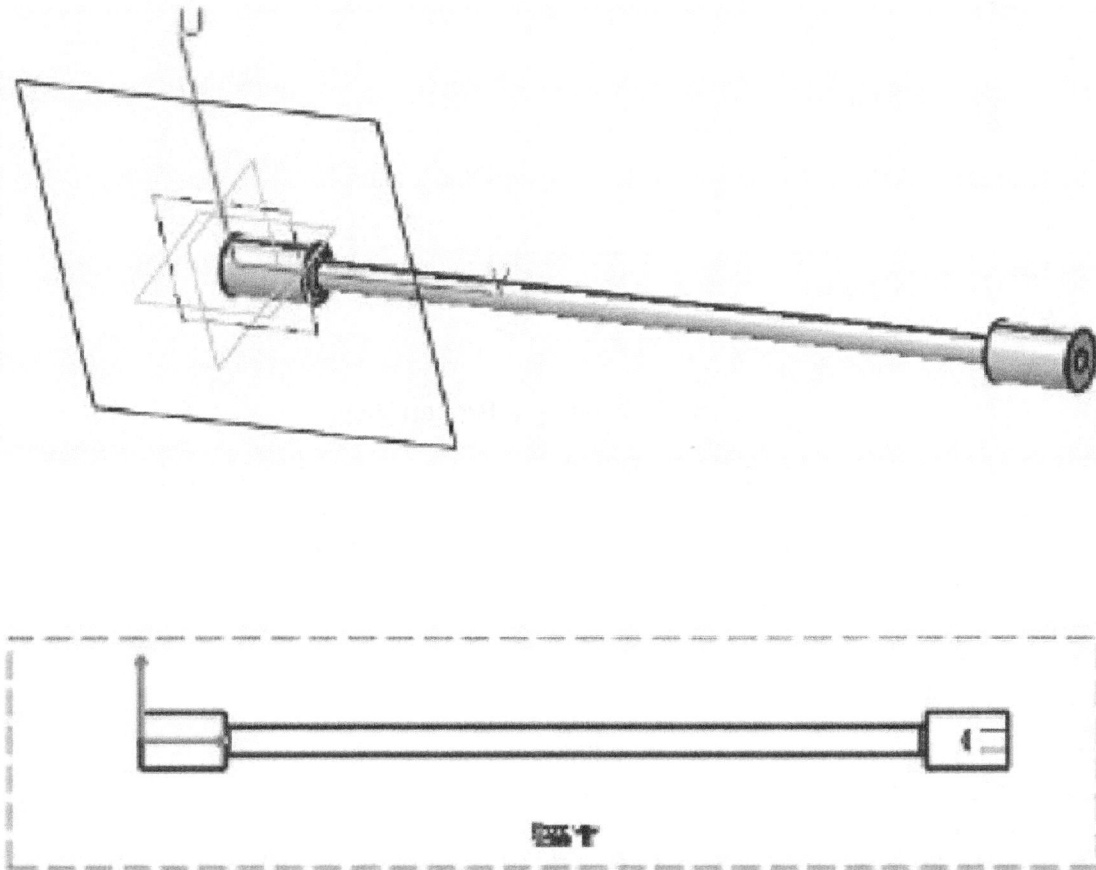

Fig 16-41 Creating a Front View

It is long compared with the section and the section is uniform.

4. Click the Broken View icon in the Break view toolbar.

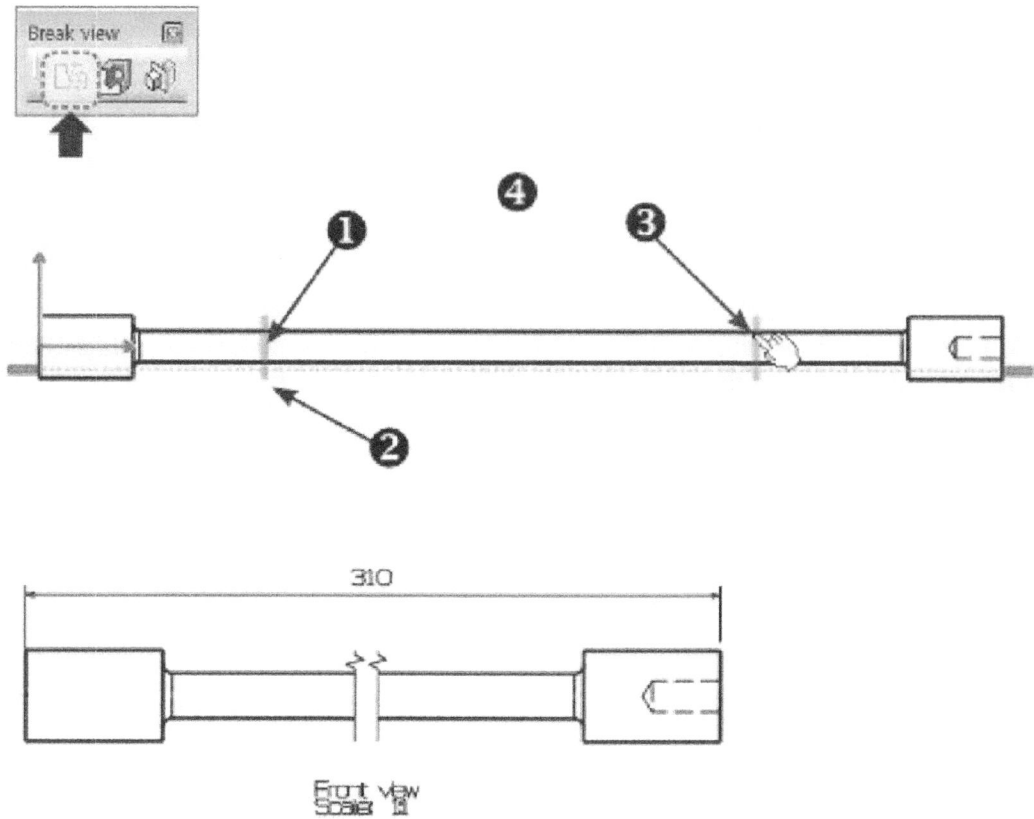

Fig 16-42 Creating a Broken View

5. Select the point (1) inside the geometry as shown i n Fig 16-42 as the first point.
6. Select the region (2) to specify a vertical break direction. A green vertical line is defined.
7. Select the point (3) inside the geometry as shown in Fig 16-42 as the third line.
8. Pick an arbitrary point i11 the sheet ((4) in Fig 16-42). The front view is converted to a broken view.

Creating a breakout view

1. Create another front view and a projection view on the right as shown in Fig 16- 43 to create a breakout view.
2. Activate the front view.

Fig 16-43 Front View and Projection View

3. Click the Breakout View icon in the Break View toolbar.

4. Define the region to break out ((A) in Fig 16-44). Note that the boundary has to be closed. The 3D View window is invoked.
5. Click the Reference element selection field ((B) in Fig 16-44). You are prompted to select a 2D element to define the depth origin.
6. Select the circular edge on the right view ((C) in Fig 16-44).
7. Rotate the 3D geometry to check the cut depth as shown in Fig 16-45.

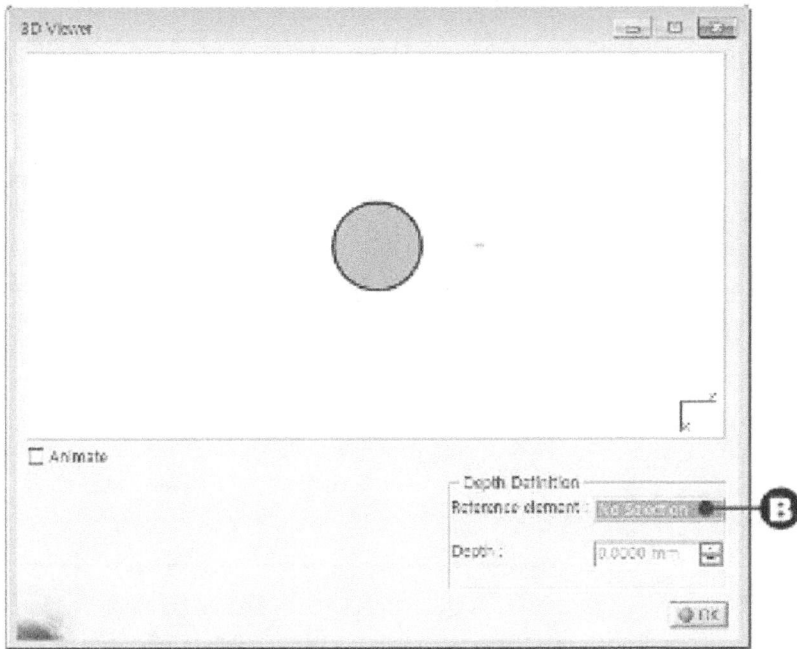

Fig 16-44 Defining Depth

8. Press OK in the 3D Viewer. A break out section is generated as shown in Fig 16-46.

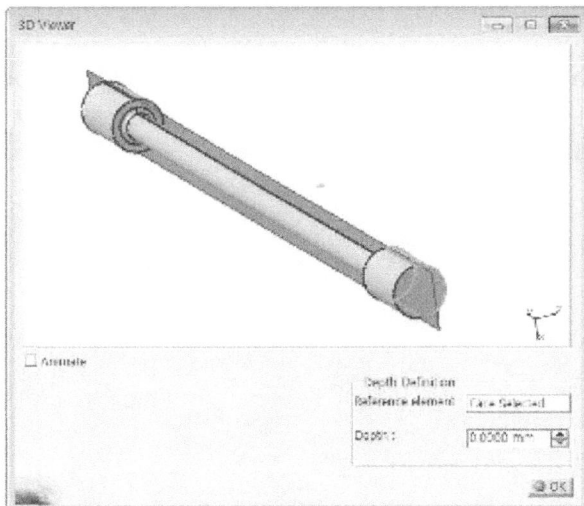

Fig 16-45 Face Selected

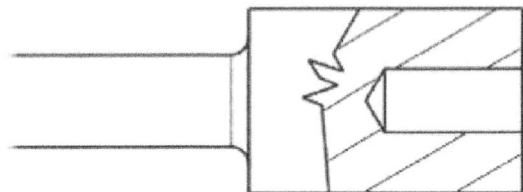

Fig 16- 46 Breakout View

(Note) Break Symbol

471

- You can select other types of break symbol by accessing the Properties dialog box of the break symbol.

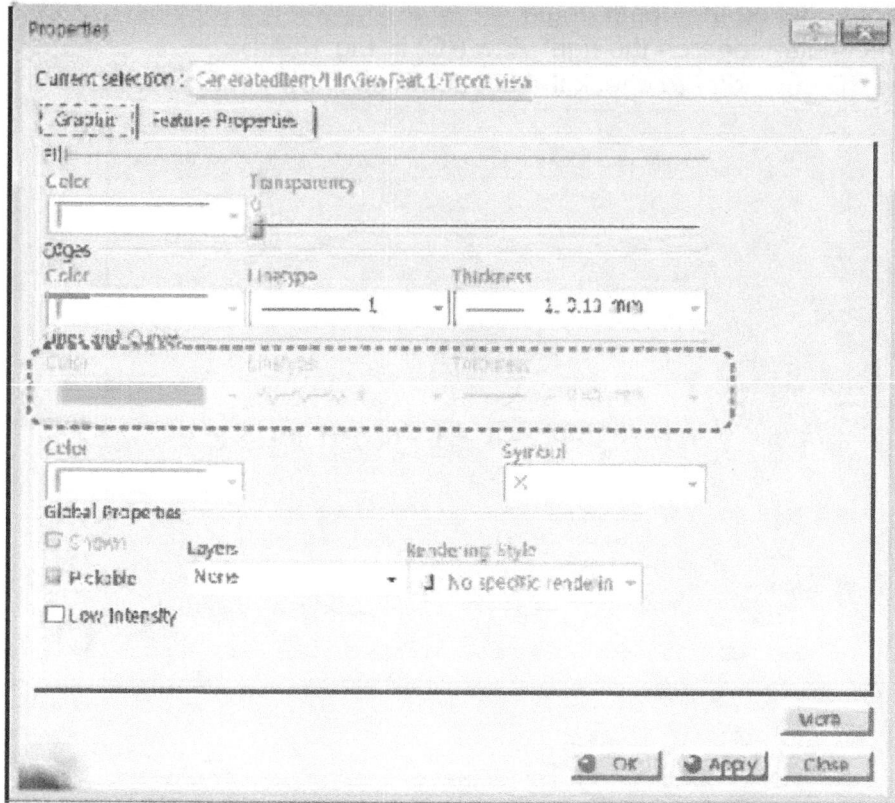

Fig 16-47 Break Line Types

16.6 VIEW POSITIONING

You can reposition a drawing view by dragging the view boundary. Note that you have to turn on the boundary option in the Visualization toolbar. Other view positioning option s are available by right clicking on the view boundary as shown in Fig 16-48.

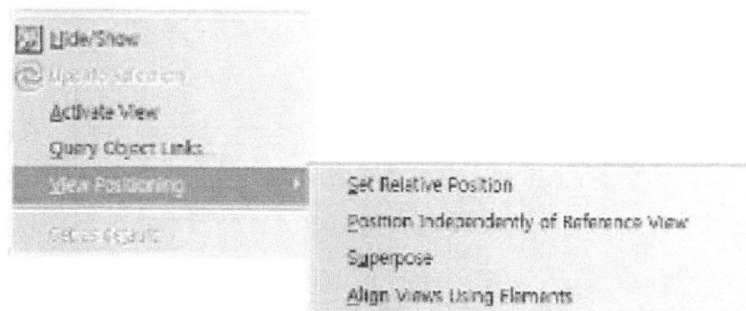

Fig 16-48 View Positioning Options

16.6.1 Set Relative Position

If you right click on the view boundary and choose View Positioning > Set Relative Position, you can set relative position of a drawing view as follows.

- **Drag (A):** View is repositioned along the relative line.
- **Drag (B):** Vie w is rotated by rotating the relative line with respect to the reference point. Fig 16-50 shows the rotated view.
- **Click (C):** Base point of the view is changed by selecting a point in the drawing view. Fig 16-51 shows the modified base point.

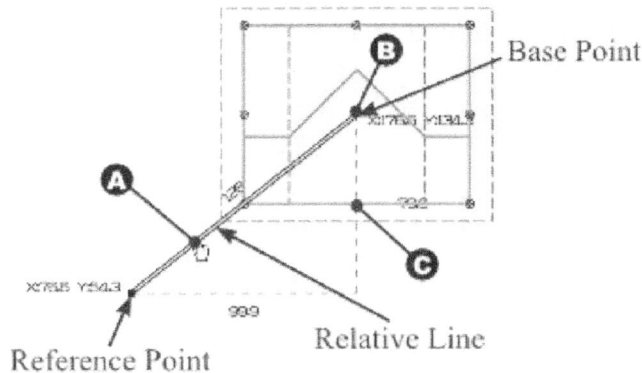

Fig 16-49 Setting Relative Position

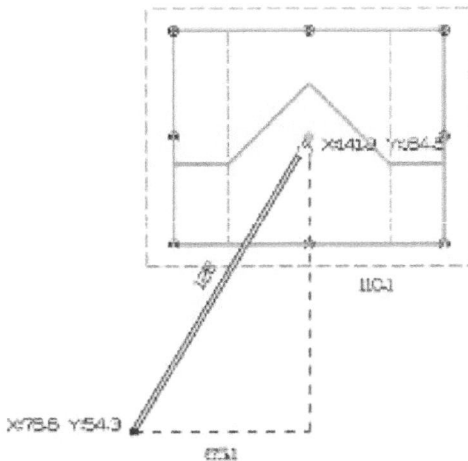

Fig 16-50 Rotated View   Fig 16-51 Modified Base Point

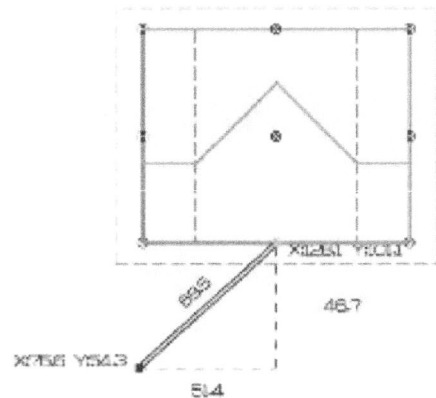

16.6.2 Position Independently of Reference View

Drawing views that reference other view are aligned to the reference view m1d you cannot drag the view free of the. reference view by default. If you choose the Position Independently of Reference View option in the pop-up menu by right clicking on the view boundary, you can drag the view at any location. You can choose the Position According to Reference View option later to align to the reference view.

16.6.3 Superpose

A view can be superimposed to another view as shown in Fig 16-52.

16.6.4 Align Views Using Elements

You can align drawing views by choosing elements in each view. To align bottom line of view (D) in Fig 16-53 right click on the boundary and choose View Positioning > Align View Using Elements in the pop-up menu. You are prompted to select the element to be aligned. Select the bottom line (1) in view (D) in Fig 16-53. You are prompted to select the reference element. Select the bottom line (2) in view (E).

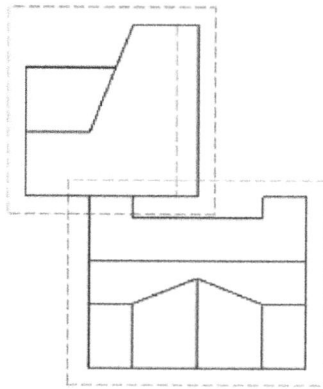

Fig 16-52 Superimposed Views

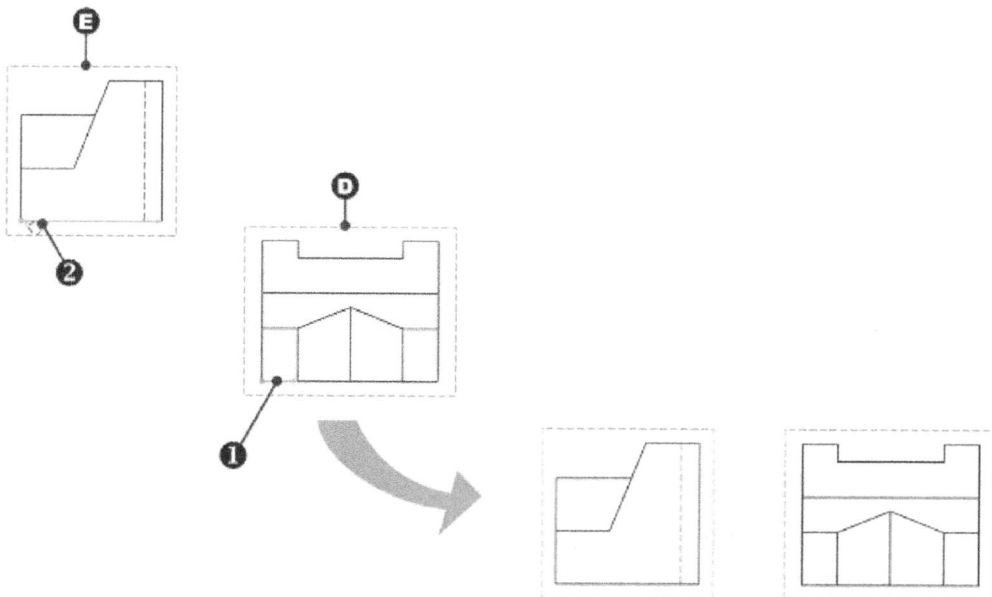

Fig 16-53 Aligning Views Using Elements

474

16.7 Modifying Part Geometry

While you are creating a drawing, you can modify the 3D part by opening the file with the menu Edit > Links. You can open the 3D part file while you have opened only an existing drawing file.

Select the Pointed documents tab in the Link of document dialog box. You can identify the path and the name of the part file and open or replace the part file. Note that you have to update the drawing file after modifying the geometry of the part.

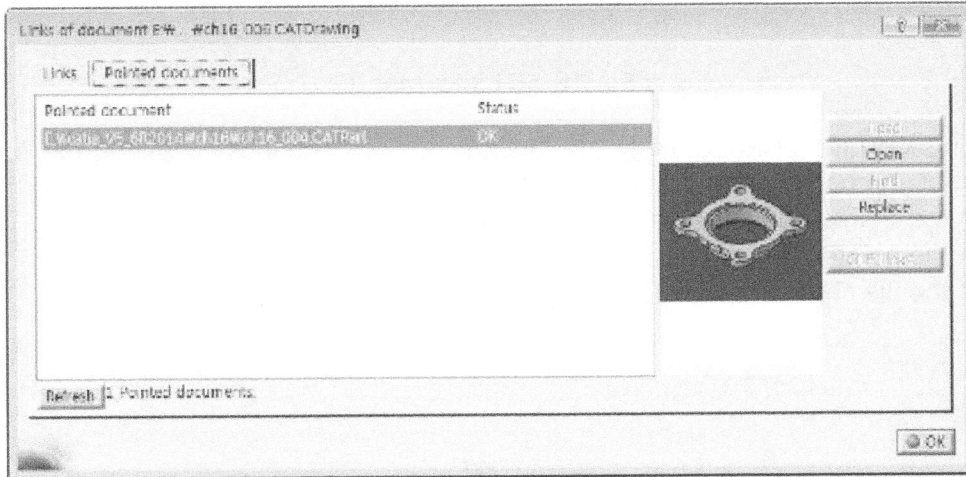

Fig 16-54 Opening a Linked 3D Part

Exercise 141: Modifying the Linked Part (ch16 _006.CATPart)

In this exercise, we will correct the linked part for a drawing file and modify the geometry of the linked part.

1. Open the given drawing file ch16_006.CATDrawing.
2. A message as shown in Fig 16-55 appears and prompts you to relocate the 3D part file.

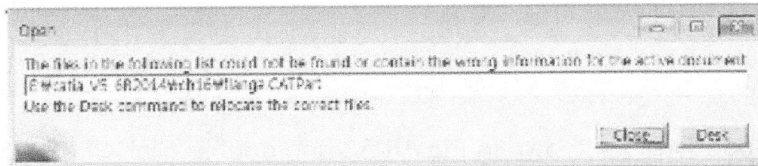

Fig 16-55 Open Information

3. Press the Desk button in the Open information box. The Desk workbench is invoked.

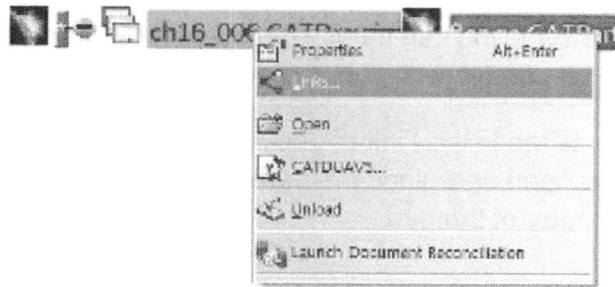

Fig 16-56 Links Menu

4. Right click on the drawing file in the Desk window and choose Links in the pop-up menu. Note that you can choose Edit > Links after closing the Open information box.
5. Select the Pointed documents tab in the Links of document dialog box.
6. Select the pointed document and press the Replace button on the right.
7. Select the file ch16_004.CATPart given in the same folder as the drawing file.

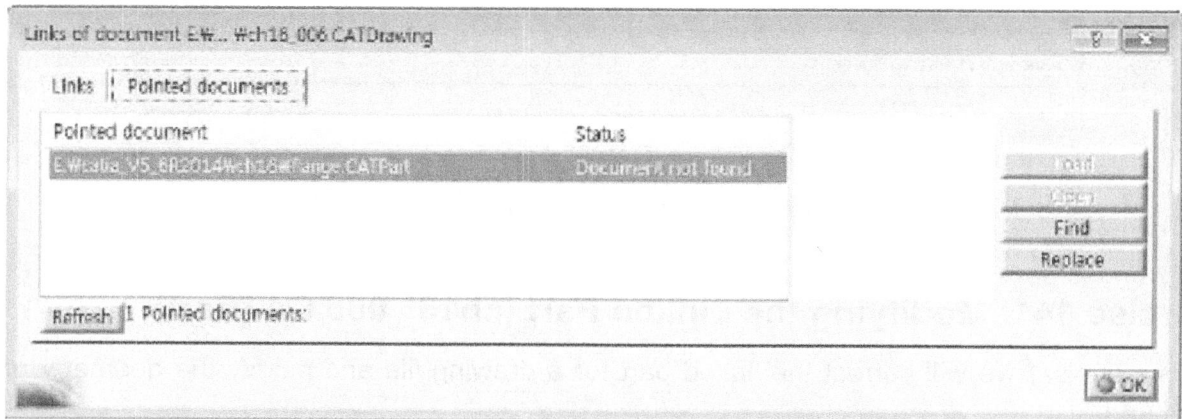

Fig 16-57 Links of document Dialog Box

8. Select the re-linked pointed document in the dialog box and press the Open button on the right.

Confirm that the part file ch16_004.CATPart has been opened in the Part Design workbench.

9. Expand the Spec Tree as shown in Fig 16-58 and double click Sketch.1.
10. Press the Normal View icon in the View tool bar once or twice to align the sketch plane. Modify the dimension (A) specified in Fig 16-58 to 8 and exit the Sketcher.
11. Select Window in the menu bar and display the drawing file.

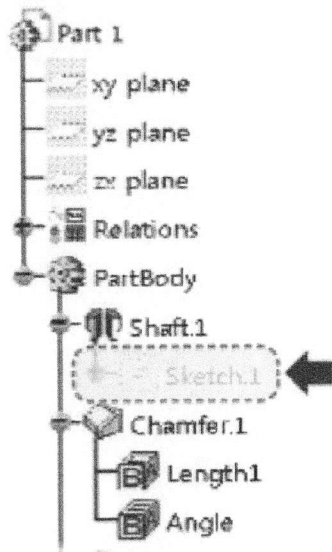

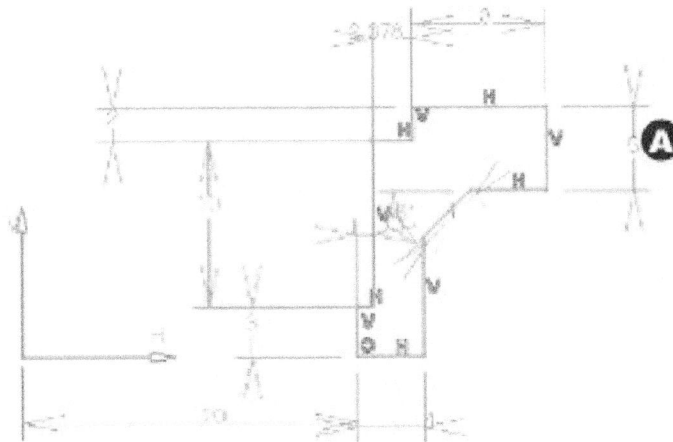

Fig 16-58 Modifying the Sketch Dimension

12. Press the Update (⊚) button in the Update toolbar . You can press MB3 > Update Selection on Sheet. I in the Spec Tree.

13. Choose File > Save Management in the menu bar and save the part file and the drawing file.

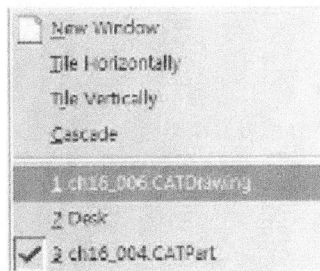

Fig 16-59 Displaying the Drawing

477

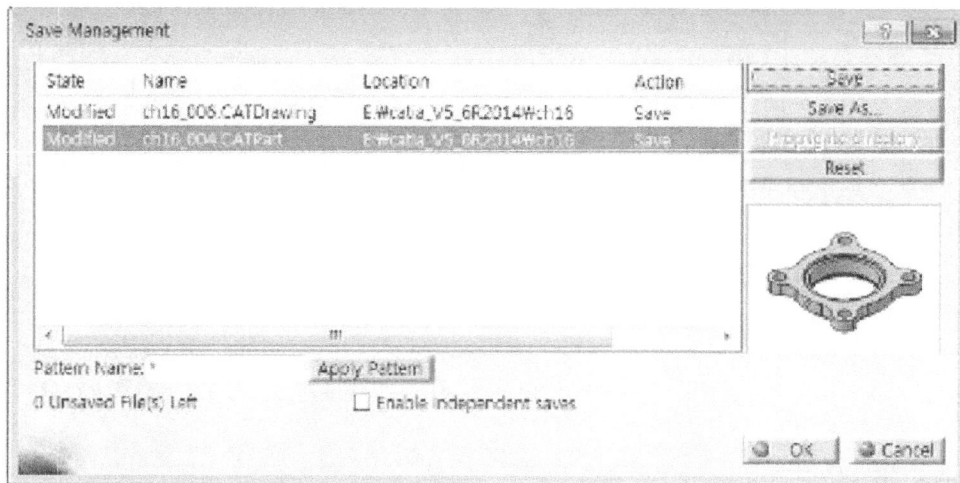

Fig 16-60 Save management Dialog Box

16.8 INSERTING FRAME AND TITLE BLOCK

You can insert a drawing frame and title block. Some frames and title blocks are supplied by default, or you can create your own frame and title block.

Procedure

1. Choose Edit > Sheet Background in the menu bar.
2. Choose Insert > Drawing > frame and Title Block in the menu bar.
3. Select the style of the title block, specify an action and press OK.
4. Choose Edit > Working Views in the menu bar.

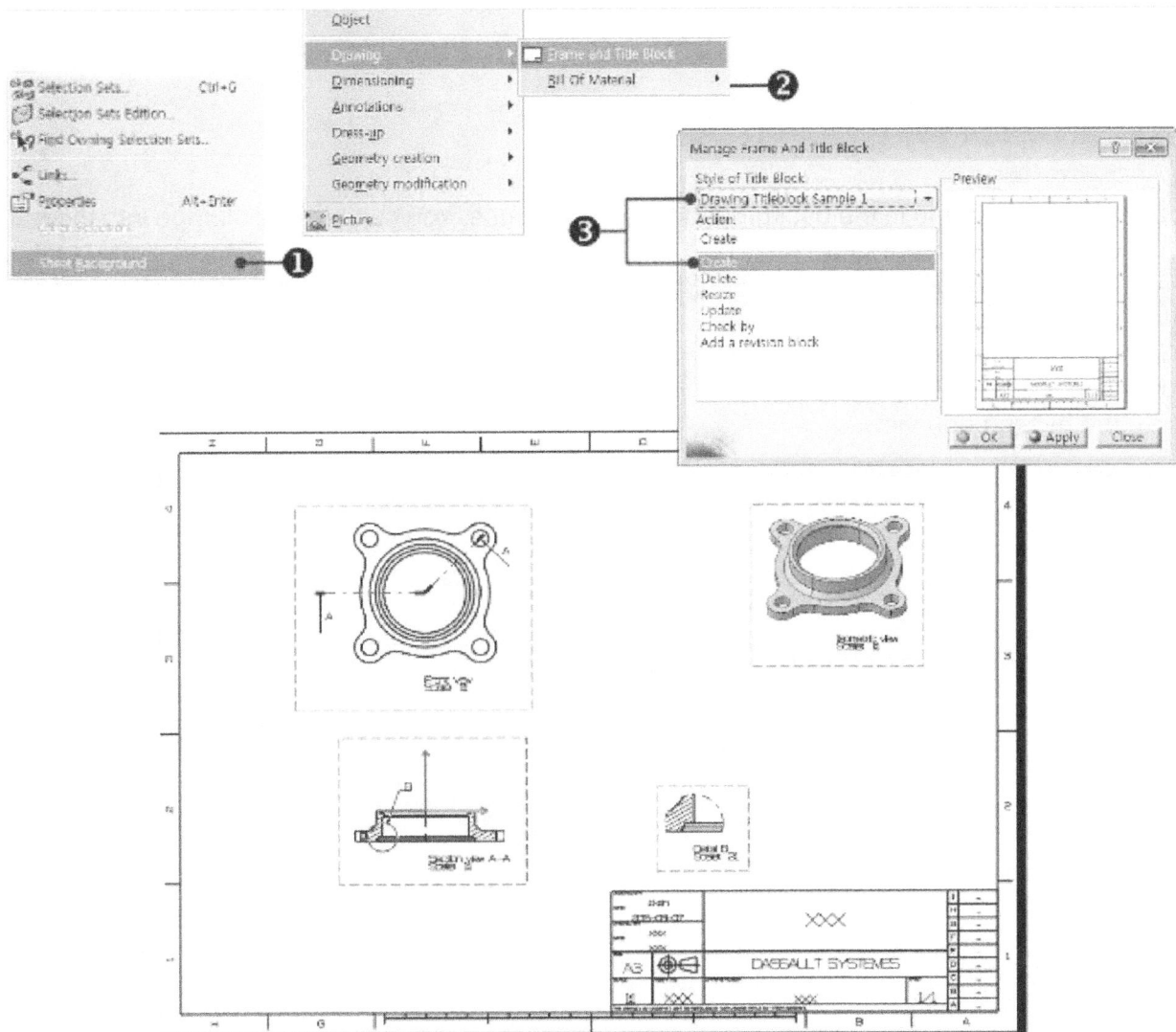

Fig 16-61 Inserting Frame and Title Block

16.8.1 Action

The frame and title block are applied for the current drawing sheet as a one-off. Therefore, if the size of the drawing has been changed after inserting the frame, you have to choose the Resize action and press OK to update the frame size.

To delete the frame and title block for the current drawing, select Delete as the action and press OK.

16.8.2 Creating a Frame for Company

You can create your own frame and title block in accordance with the following procedure.

1. Create an empty drawing file.
2. Insert a frame in the background.

3. Modify the frame in the background for your own use. You can insert an image into the frame using the Insert > Picture menu.
4. Exit to working view by selecting Edit > Working View in the menu bar and save and close the drawing file.
5. Create a drawing file for a part.
6. Choose File > Page Setup in the menu bar and insert the above created drawing file as the background view.

Fig 16-62 Page Setup Dialog Box

Exercise 142: Creating Drawing Views (ch16 _007.CATPart)

Create drawing views exactly as shown in Fig 16-63 for the given part ch16_007.CATPart.

Hints

1. Auxiliary view C can be created by activating the section view and by using the Auxiliary View icon in the Projections sub-toolbar.
2. View boundaries can be hidden by turning off the corresponding icon in the Visualization toolbar shown below.

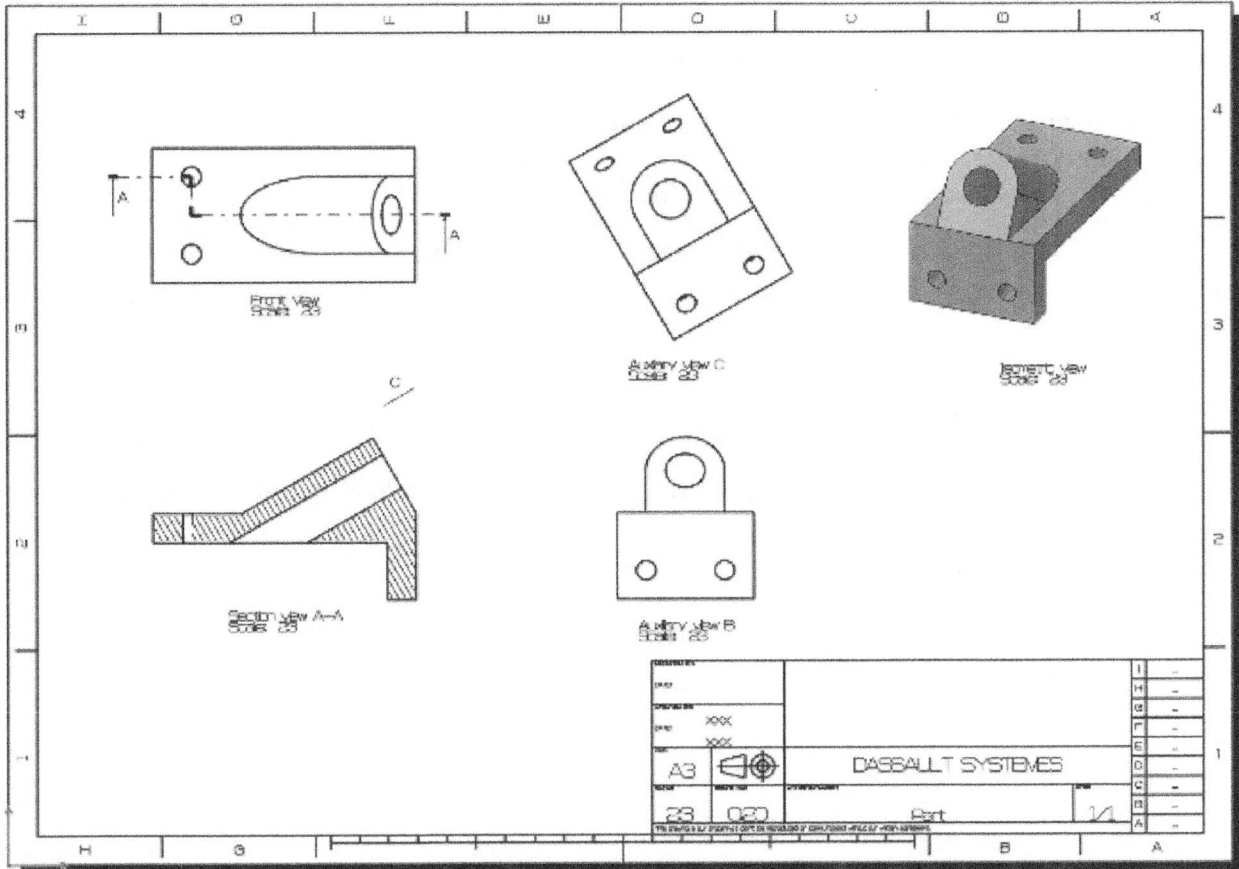

Fig 16-63 Drawing for Exercise

CHAPTER 16: FINALIZING DRAWINGS: DIMENSIONS, ANNOTATIONS, AND EXPLODED VIEWS

17.1 GENERAL PROCEDURE OF CREATING DRAWINGS

The major interest of Chapter 16 was explaining how to create various types of drawing views. The general procedure for creating drawings in CATIA V5 is as follows.

1. Open a part file for which to create a drawing.
2. Create a drawing file.
3. Set the sheet property and insert a frame and title block.
4. Create drawing views.
5. Create center lines, dimensions, annotations, etc.

In this chapter we will learn how to create center lines, axis, dimensions and annotations and how to set the options to improve their appearances. Basic topics in creating assembly drawings will also be explained in the chapter.

17.2 CREATING DIMENSIONS

Using the icons in the Dimensions sub-toolbar, you can create various types of dimensions in the drawing views.

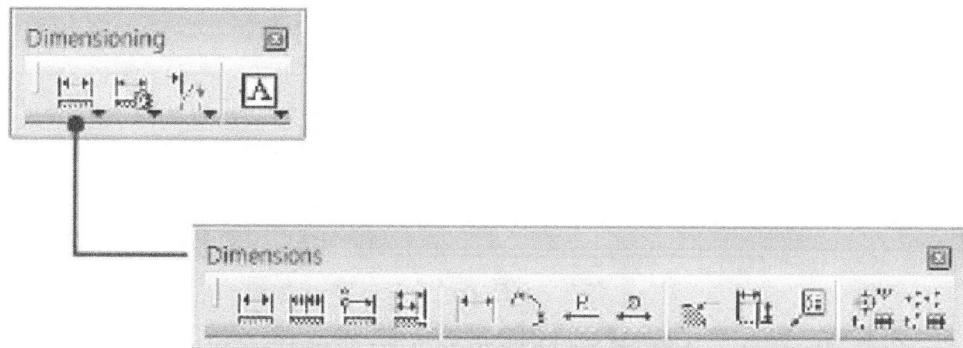

Fig 17-1 Dimensions Toolbar

17.2.1 Dimension Options

Dimensions can be created either with or without association to the geometry. If you create a dimension with association to the geometry, the dimension is updated when you modify the linked part parametrically. The di me ns ion associativity opt io n can be set in the Dimension tab in the Options dialog box as specified by (A) in Fig 17-2.

482

If you select Only create non-associative dimensions, the dimensions are not updated even if you modify the linked part parametrically. If you select Never create non-associative dimensions, all the dimensions are created with association to the part geometry. Note that this option is not available when the drawing views are isolated from the part geometry.

When you create geometry entities in the drawing view using the commands in the Geometry Creation toolbar and apply a dimension to them, check the Create driving dimension option ((B) in Fig 17-2). The lines and curves can be driven by modifying the dimension value.

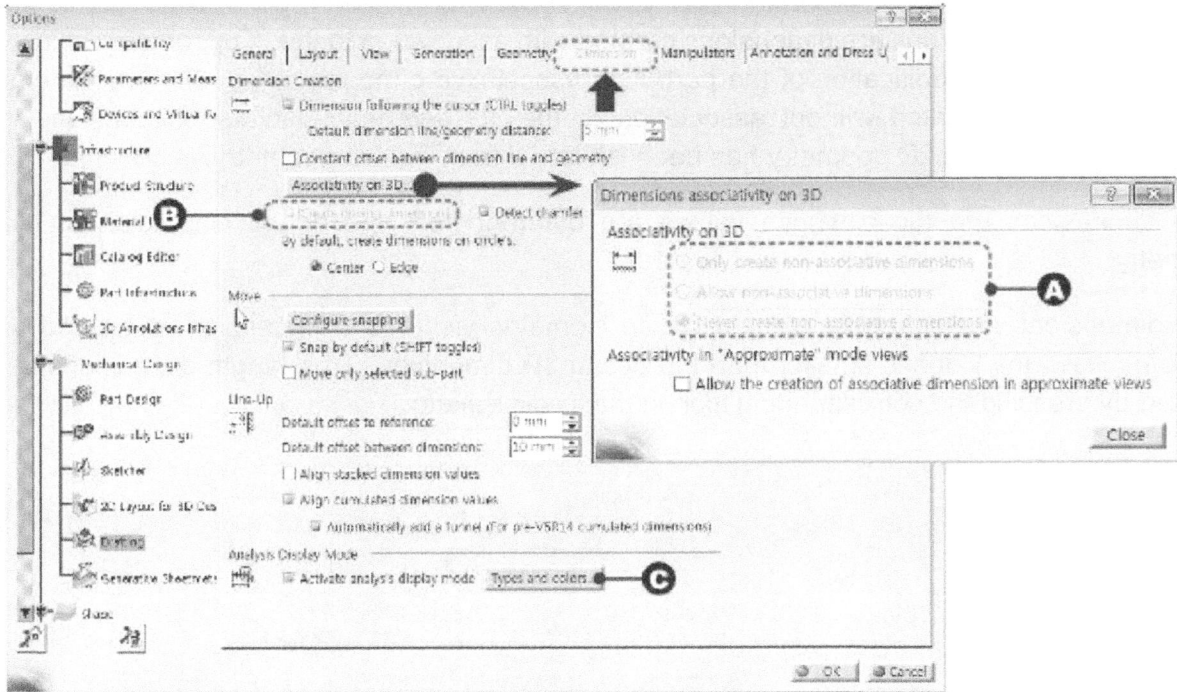

Fig 17-2 Dimensions Option

17.2.2 Display of Dimensions

Types of dimensions can be identified by the display color. The function app lies when the Analys is Display Mode button in the Visualization toolbar is pressed.

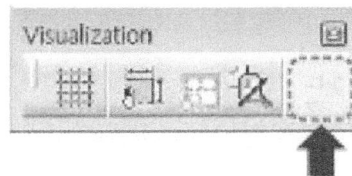

Fig 17-3 Visualization Toolbar

Pressing the Analysis Display Mode button is the same as checking the Activate analysis display mode option in the dimension option shown in Fig 17-2.

Press the Types and colors button in the Options dialog box as specified by (C) in Fig 17-2. You can set the display color for each type of dimension in the Types and colors dialog box shown in Fig 17-4.

Not-up-to-date dimensions are dimensions created with association to the 3D geometry which have to be updated after modification of the part. Non associative dimensions (on 3D) are dimensions which have been created without association to the 3D geometry. Isolated dimensions are dimension s where the 2D geometry has been iso late d from the 3D geometry.

Fake dimensions are those whose values are different from the actual dimension of the 2D geometry.

True dimensions are generally created on an isometric view. If a dimension is created on an isometric view, the value is smaller than the actual 3D dimension. True length dimensions can be created by pressing the corresponding icon in the Tools Palette.

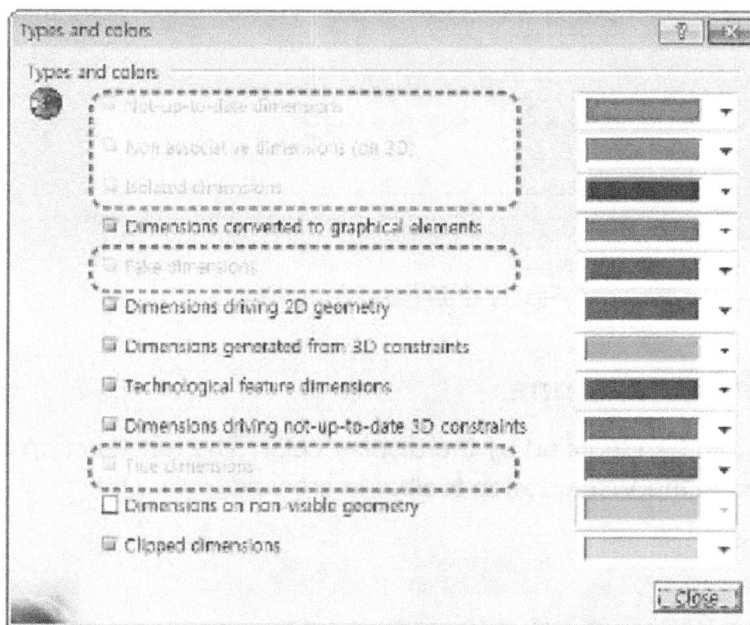

Fig 17-4 Types and colors Dialog Box

Exercise 143: Creating Dimensions (ch17 _001.CATPart)

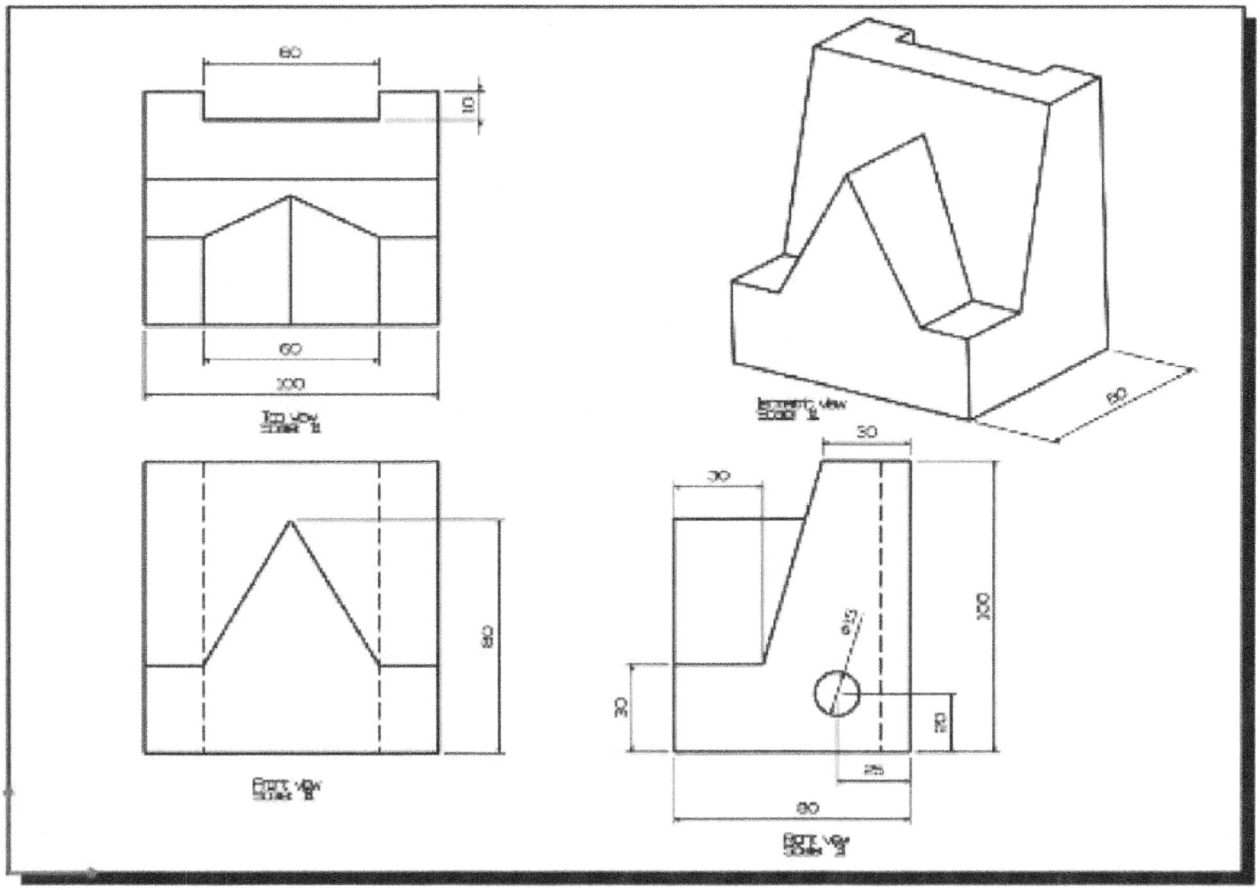

Fig 17-5 Drawing of Guide Block

Creating Dimensions

1. Open the given drawing file ch17_001.CATDrawing.

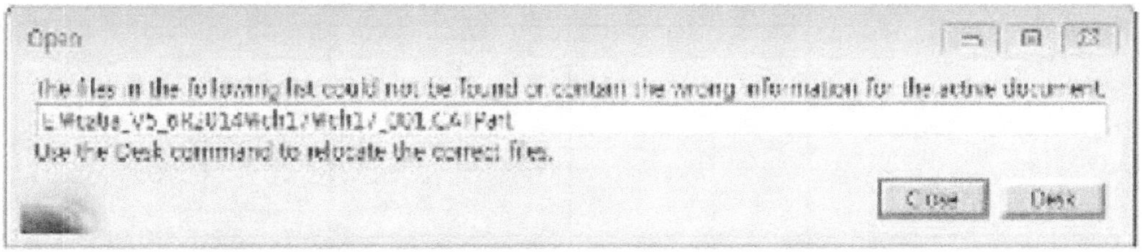

Fig 17-6 Open intonation

2. Close the Open information box.
3. Choose Tools > Options in the menu bar and set the dimension options as shown in Fig 17-2.

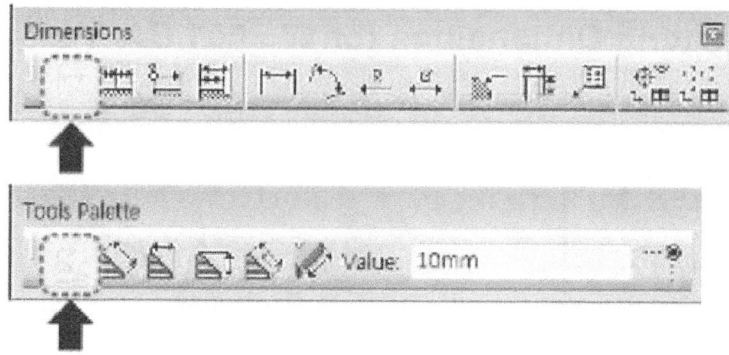

Fig 17-7 Dimension Icon

4. Click the Dimensions icon and select an element to create a dimension. The error message shown in Fig 17-8 appears.
5. Click OK in the message box.

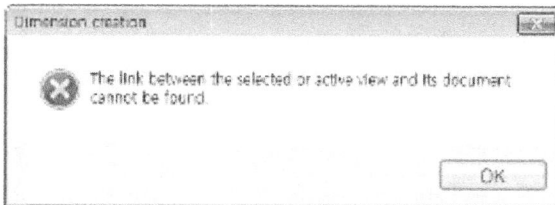

Fig 17-8 Dimensioning Error

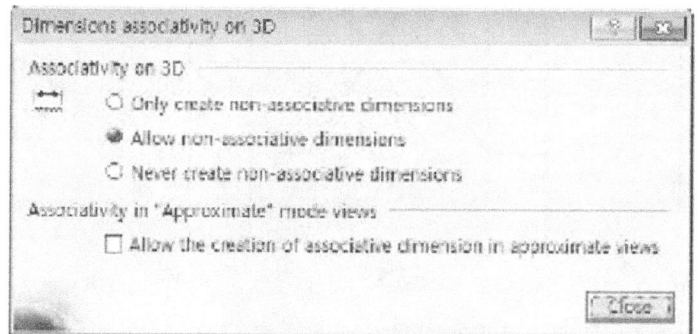

Fig 17-9 Dimensions Option

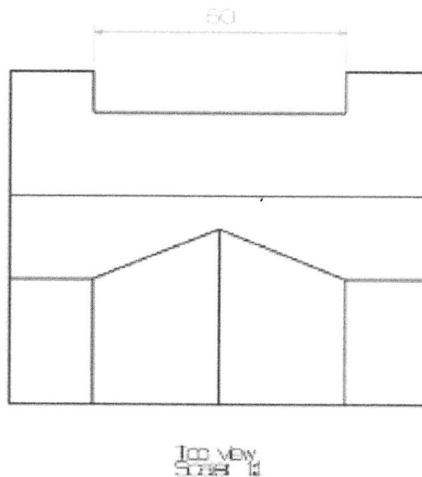

Fig 17-10 Non-associative Dimension

6. Choose Tools > Options in the menu bar and set the dimension options as shown in Fig 17-9.

486

7. Click the Dimensions icon in the Dimensions toolbar and create dimensions as shown in Fig 17-10. Note that a non-associative dimension is created in gray according to the color setting shown in Fig 17-4.
8. Choose Edit > Links in the menu bar.
9. Select the Pointed Document tab, press the Replace button on the right and select ch17_guide_block.CATPart.
10. Press OK in the Links of document dialog box. Note that the drawing file, sheet and drawing views are in a state that requires an update.
11. Press CTRL + U to update the drawing. The non-associative dimension turns to a not-up-to-date dimension because the dimension is still not associative to the linked part. Note that associativity is not established automatically.

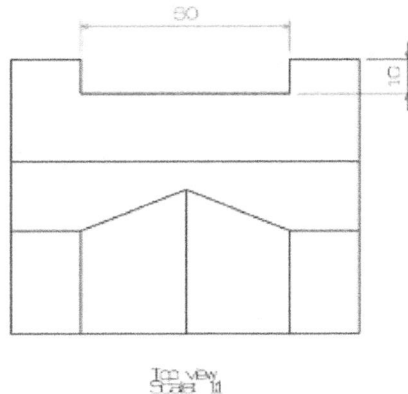

Fig 17-11 Updated Drawing View

12. Click the Dimensions icon and create dimension 10 as shown in Fig 17-11. An associative dimension is created.
13. Click Re-route Dimension icon in the Dimensioning toolbar.

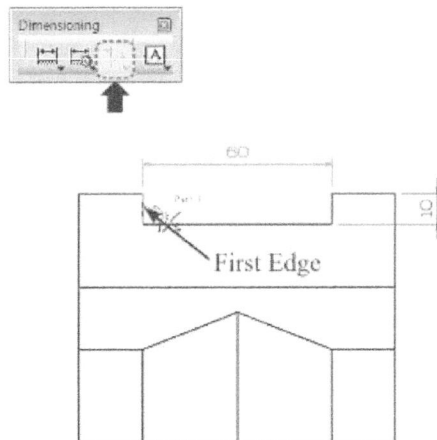

Fig 17-12 Re-route Dimension Icon

14. Select the not-up-to-date dimension 60. You are prompted to select the first element.
15. Select the first edge as shown in Fig 17-12. You are prompted to select the second element.

487

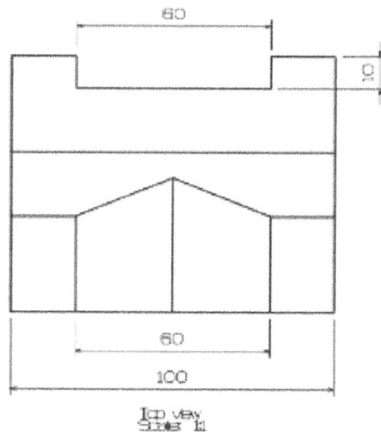

Fig 17-13 Dimensions

16. Select the other edge on the opposite side. The dimension now changes to the associative dimension.
17. Double click the Dimensions icon and create dimensions on the top view as shown in Fig 17-13.

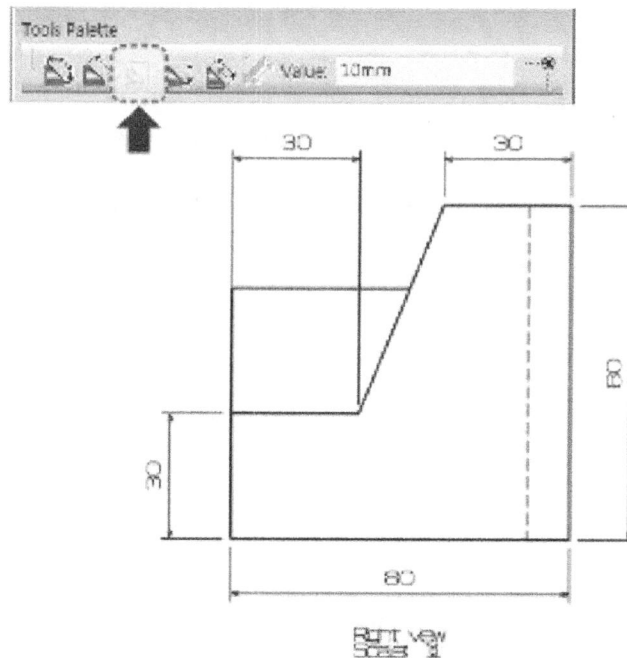

Fig 17-14 Dimensions on the Right View

Create dimensions on the right view a shown in Fig 17-14. You may need to use an appropriate option in the Tools Palette to create each dimension.

(Note) Dragging the View Label

- You can drag the view label without snapping by pressing the Shift key.

18. Choose Tools> Options in the menu bar and set the Associativity on 3D option as shown in Fig 17-15.

19. Create dimensions on the front view as shown in Fig 17-15. Note that the color of the dimension is displayed in a different color.

Modifying Part

1. Choose Edit > Links in the menu bar.

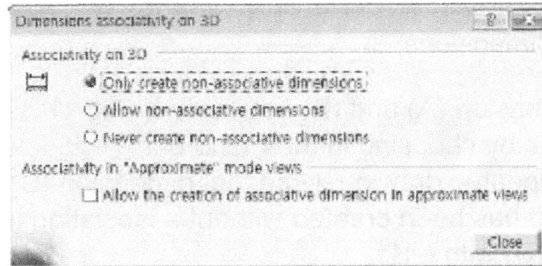

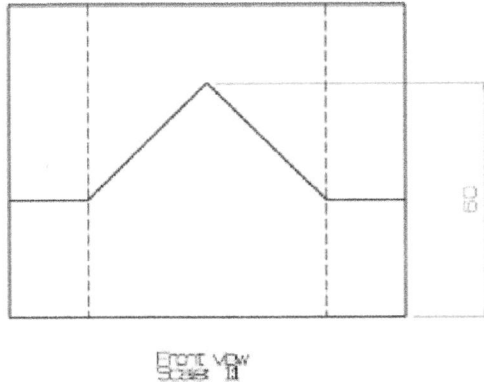

Fig 17-15 Dimensions on the Front View

Select the Pointed Document tab, check the path and name of the linked part and press the Open button.

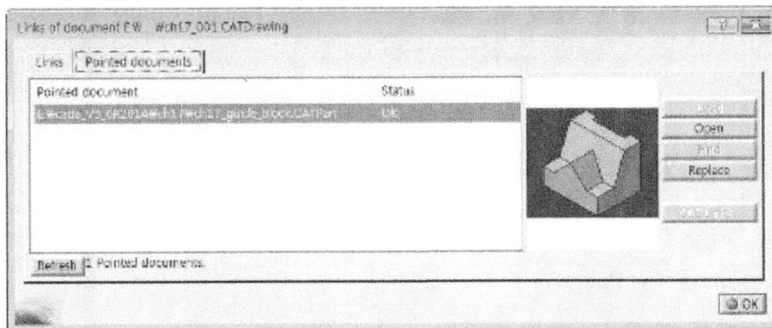

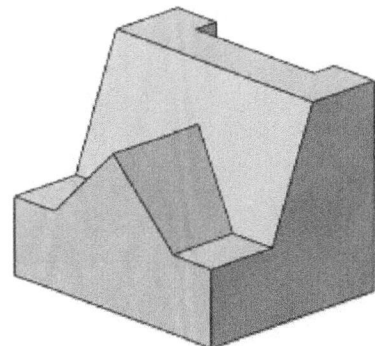

Fig 17-16 Linked Part

(Note) Links Menu

With the menu Edit > Links, you can verify the path and name of the linked part. If the link points to the wrong path or file, you can specify the correct one by pressing the Replace button.

In generative drafting where you create a drawing for a part, you should not move the part file to another folder after creating the drawing. If you have moved the pa11 file, you have to link the correct one. This mechanism applies to the links of component parts in an assembly.

Fig 17-17 Modifying Sketch Dimensions

2. Modify the sketch dimension (A) and (B) as shown in Fig 17-17.
3. Display the drawing file by choosing in the menu bar > Window and update the drawing.
4. Fig 17-18 shows the updated drawing. Note that dimension (C) is updated. Dimension (D) is not updated because it has been created without association to 3D geometry.
5. Select the dimension (D) with MB1.
6. Re-route the dimension as we have done in Fig 17-11 and Fig 17-12.

(Note) Re-route Dimension

If you re-route the dimensioning object with the Re-route Dimension button, associativity to the geometry is re-established.

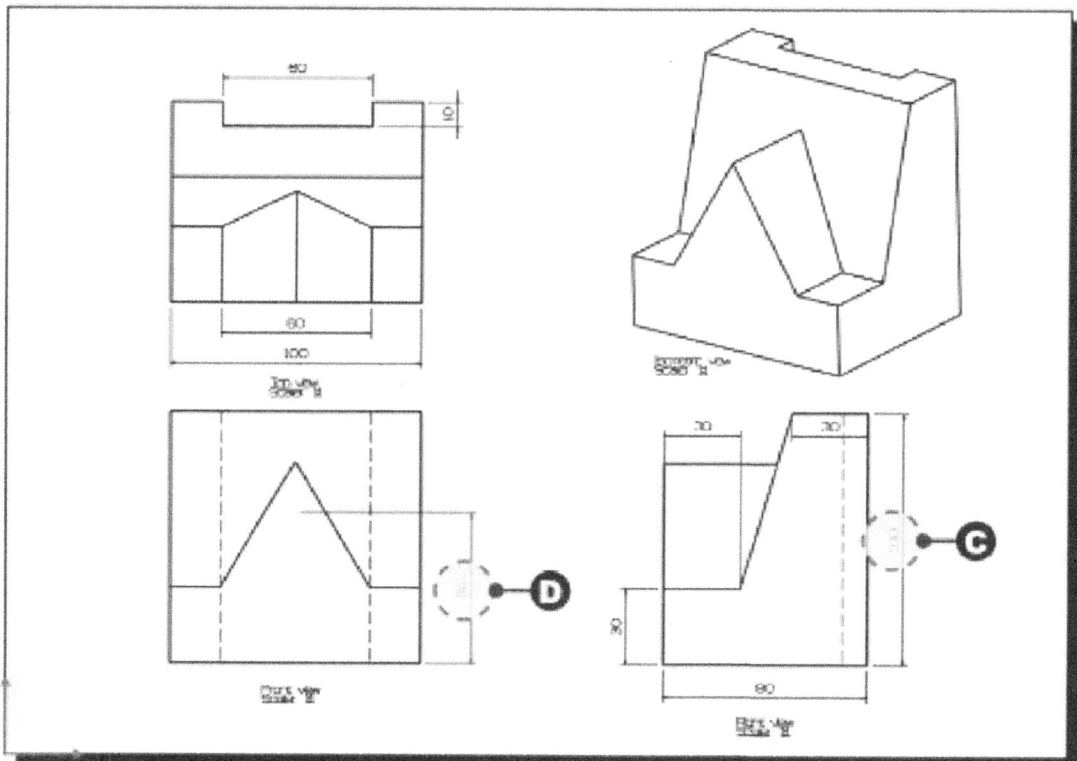

Fig 17-18 Updated Drawing

490

1. Activate the right view.
2. Click the Circle icon in the Geometry Creation toolbar and create a circle on the right view.
3. Set the Associative on 3D option as shown in Fig 17-19 and turn on the Create driving dimension option as specified by (B) in Fig 17-2.
4. Create dimensions for the circle as specified by (E) 's in Fig 17-1 9.

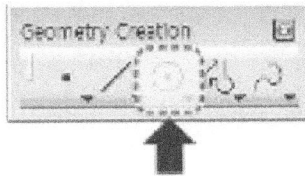

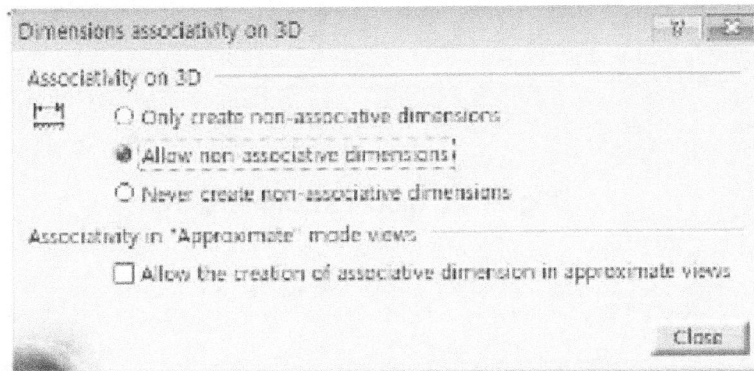

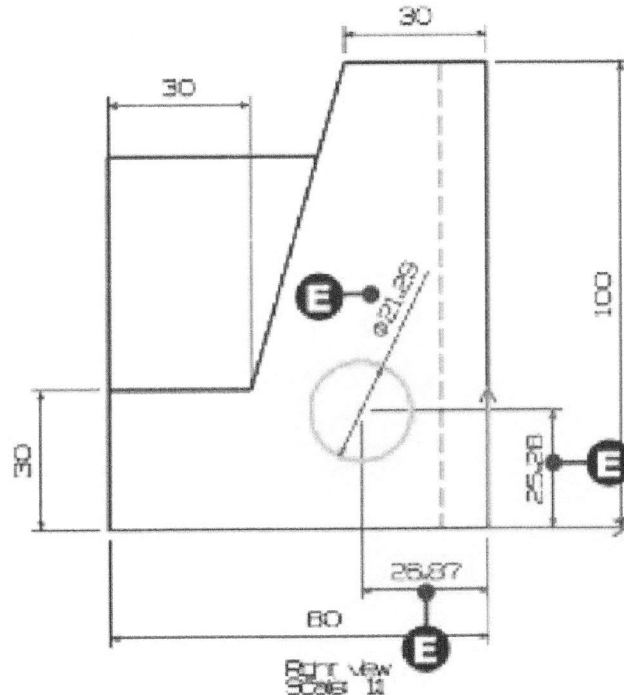

Fig 17-19 Adding 2D Geometry

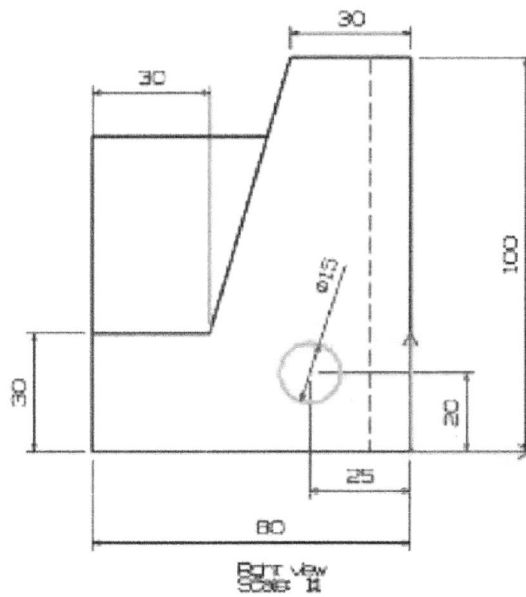

Fig 17-20 Modified Dimensions

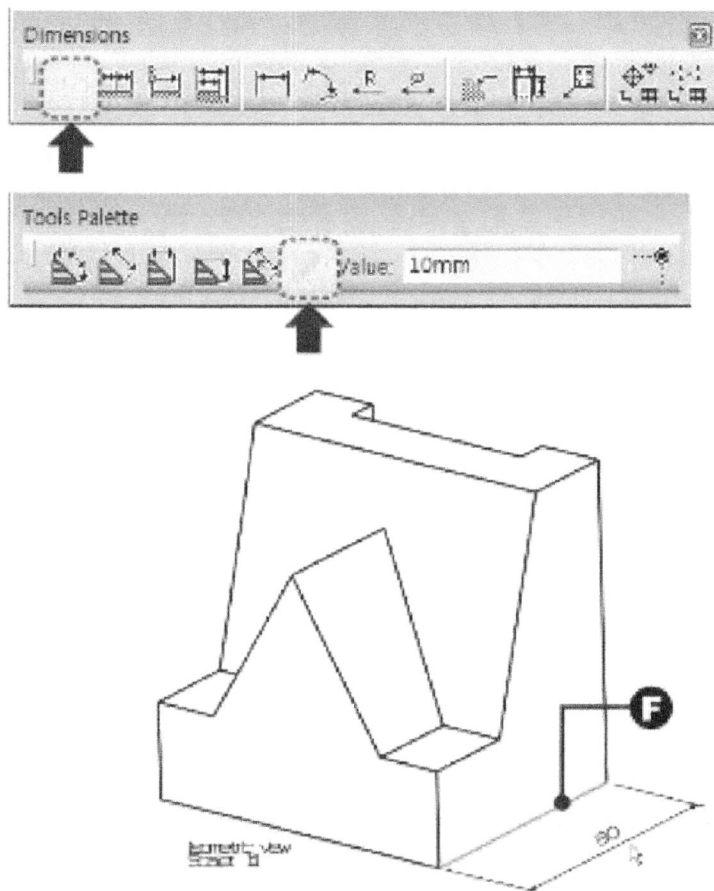

Fig 17-21 True Length Dimension

492

5. Modify the dimensions as s how n in Fig 17-20.

Confirm that the circle is updated when you modify the driving dimension.

Creating a True Length Dimension

Click the Dimension icon in the Dimensions toolbar and press the True length dimension button in the Tools Palette.

Select the bottom edge (F) in the iso-metric view as shown in Fig 17-21 and create the true length dimension.

Save the drawing file and 3D geometry file as *_modified as shown in Fig 17-22 and close all files.

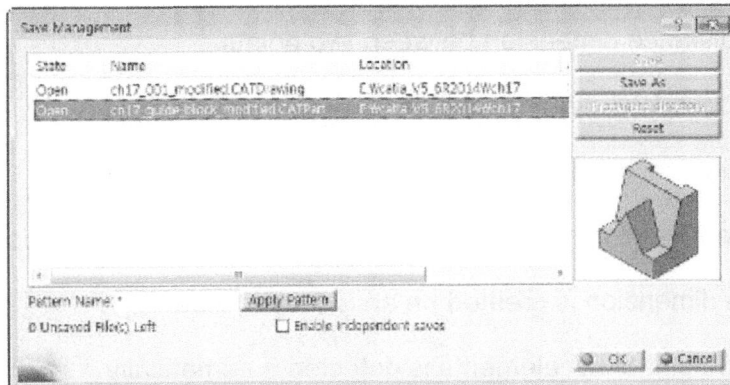

Fig 17-22 Save As

(Note) Visualization Too/bar

(A) Show or hide grids on tbc sheet.

(B) Show or hide constraints.

(C) Show or hide view boundaries.

(D) Turning on this icon, geo metrics that have been generated from a 3D part are dimmed.

(E) Turning on this icon, the dimension color setting is applied.

17.2.3 Tools Palette in Dimensioning

When you create dimensions with icons in the Dimensions tool bar, a Tools Palette shown in Fig 17-23 is invoked. You can set the direction option of the dimensions.

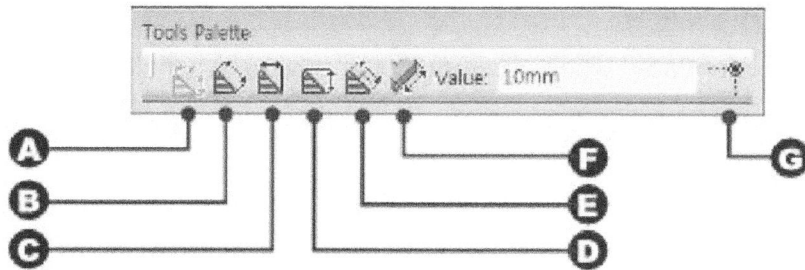

Fig 17-23 Tools Palette

(A) Dimension direction is inferred by the location of the mouse cursor. You can create a horizontal, vertical or distance dimension.

(B) Creates a distance dimension between two points.

(C) Creates a horizontal dimension.

(D) Creates a vertical dimension.

(E) You can create a dimension along or normal to a specified direction.

(F) True length dimension is created on an isometric view.

(G) Intersection point of 2D elements is detected automatically.

17.3 TYPES OF DIMENSIONS

With the Dimensions icon in the Dimensions toolbar, you can create Length/Distance Dimensions, Angle Dimensions, Radius Dimensions or Diameter Dimensions according to the selected 2D geometry. To create a specific type of dimension you have to choose the appropriate icon in the Dimensions toolbar as shown in Fig 17-24.

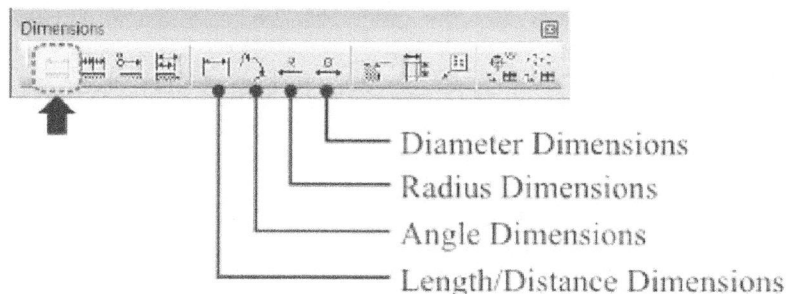

Fig 17-24 Dimensions Toolbar

With the Dimensions icon, you can create chained dimensions by selecting elements consecutively as shown in Fig 17-25. Chained dimensions, cumulated dimensions and stacked dimensions can he created using the respective icons in the Dimensions toolbar. Fig 1 7- 26 and Fig 17-27 show the cumulated dimension and stacked dimension, respectively.

494

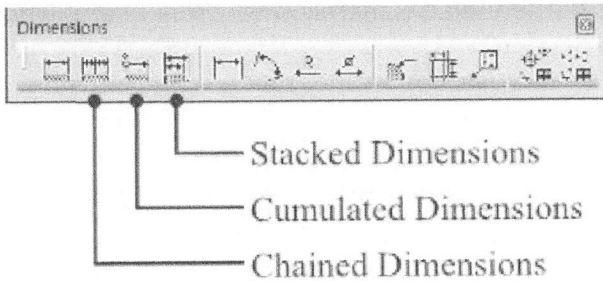

Stacked Dimensions
Cumulated Dimensions
Chained Dimensions

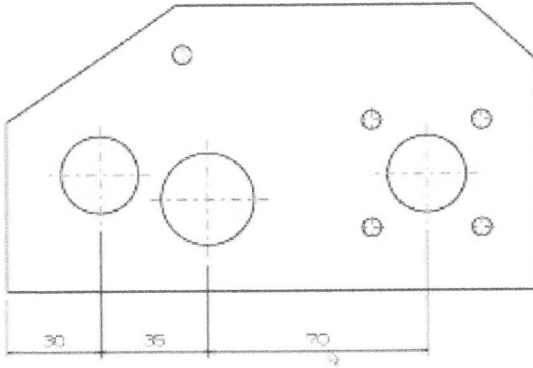

Fig 17-25 Chained Dimension

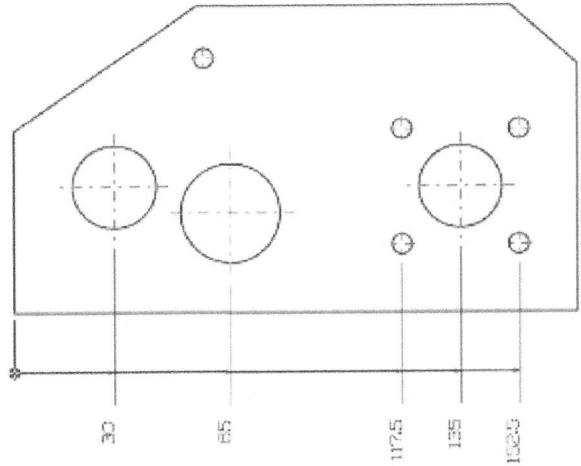

Fig 17-26 Cumulated Dimension

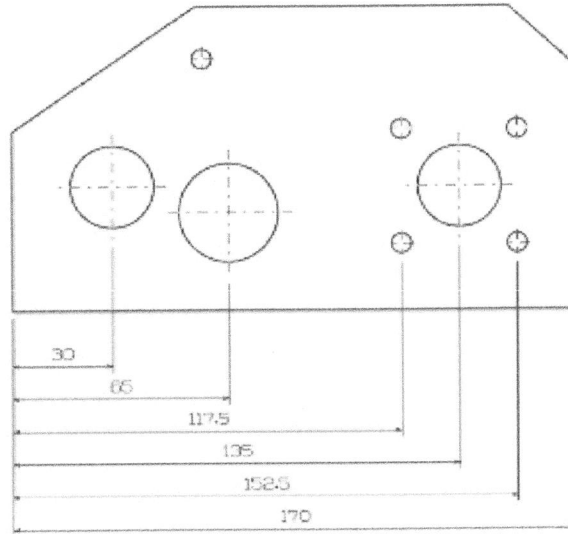

Fig 17-27 Stacked Dimension

17.4 DIMENSION POP-UP MENUS

While you are creating a type of dimension the pop-up menu is available by right clicking after selecting 2D geometries to dimension. The options that appear .in the pop-up vary according to the selected icons and 2D geometry. For example, if you click the Dimensions icon and select a curve or line, the pop-up men u shown in Fig 17-28 is available. You can add funnel and define value

495

orientation of the dimension text. Fig 1 7-29 shows the funneled dimension which is useful when dimensioning in narrow distance or length.

If you click the Dimensions icon and select two lines to create a distance dimension, the pop-up menu shown in Fig 17-30 is available. Note that you can apply half dimension in this case compared to the case of length dimension. If you click the Angular Dimensions icon and select two angled lines, the pop-up menu shown in Fig 17-31 is available. You can choose the sector of angular dimension by choosing one in the Angle Sector menu.

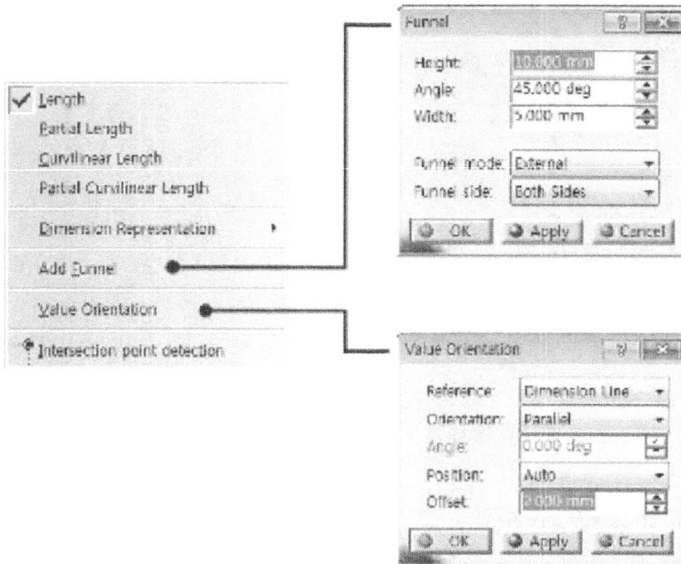

Fig 17-28 Pop-up Menu (Dimensions / Length of Curve)

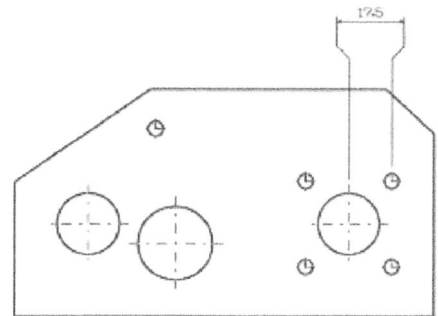

Fig 17-29 Funneled Dimension

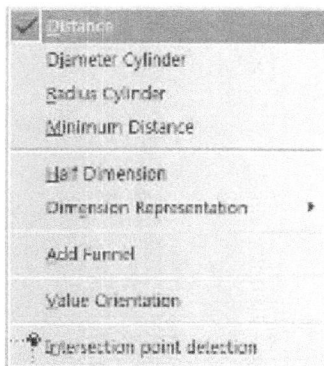

Fig 17-30 Pop-up Menu (Dimensions / Distance)

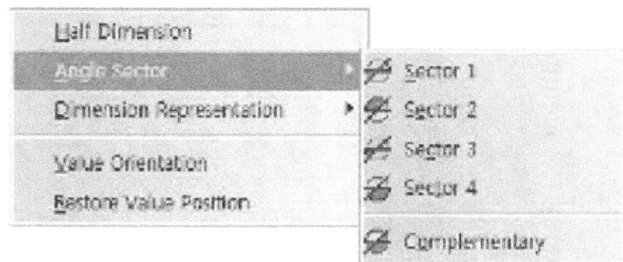

Fig 17-31 Pop-up Menu
(Angular Dimensions / Angled Lines)

If you click the Dimensions icon and choose a circle, the pop-up menu shown in Fig 17-32 is available. You can change the dimension type to a radius or diameter by choosing the Radius Center or the Diameter Center option or choose whether to extend the dimension line to center of circle or not.

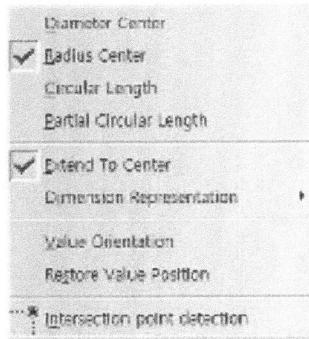

Fig 17-32 Pop-up menu (Dimensions / Circle)

If you click the Radius Dimensions icon and choose a circle, the pop-up menu show11in Fig 17-33 is available. If you click the Diameter Dimensions icon and choose a circle, the pop-up menu shown in Fig 17-34 is available.

You can select the Intersection point detection menu in the pop-up menu in all cases , which is the same as pressing the corresponding button in the Tools Palette.

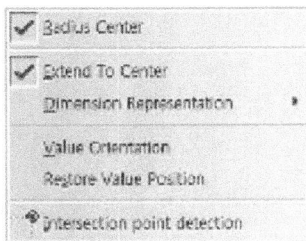

Fig 17-33 Pop-up Menu (Radius Dimensions / Circle)

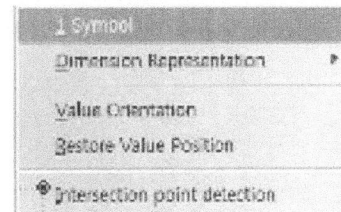

Fig 17-34 Pop-up Menu
(Diameter Dimensions / Circle)

If you click the Length/Distance Dimensions icon and select a circle and a line, the pop-up menu shown in Fig 17-35 is available. When the different anchor options are available for dimensioning distance, you can choose one in the Extension Lines Anchor option. Note that the result of anchor option varies according to the selected element and the location of selection. You can identify the location of ancho r points by pressing the CTRL key while you are creating a dimension. Note that you have to place the mouse cursor on the yellow mark.

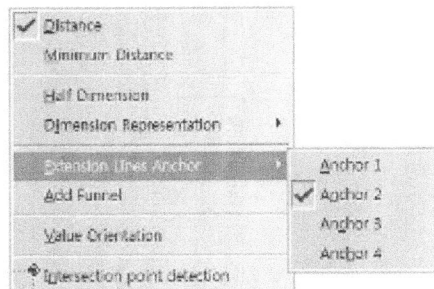

Fig 17-35 Pop-up Menu

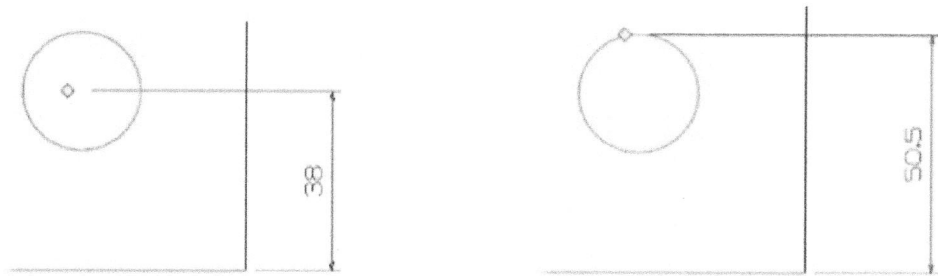

Fig 17-36 Distance Dimension with Different Anchor Option

17.5 ALIGNING DIMENSIONS

Using icons in the Positioning toolbar, you can align dimensions.

Procedure

1. Click the Line-Up icon in the Positioning toolbar.
2. Select a dimension to align.
3. Select a dimension or 2D element to align to.
4. Set the option in the Line-Up dialog box and press OK.

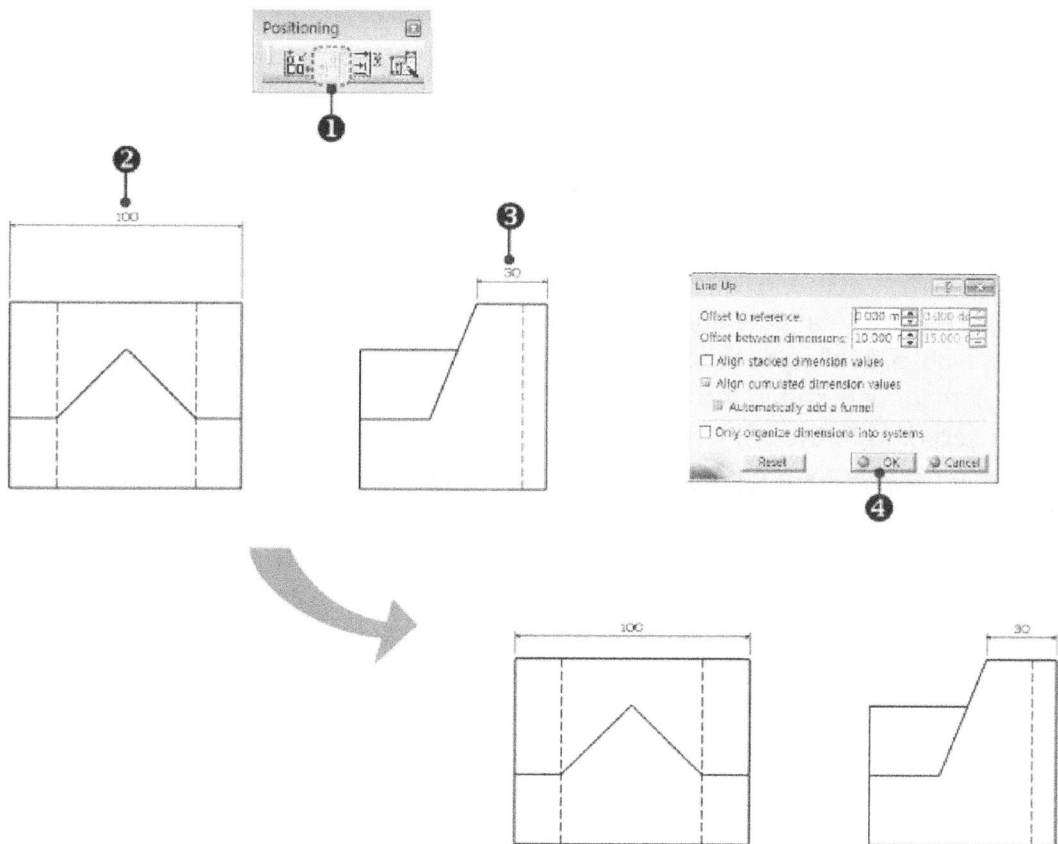

Fig 17-37 Aligning a Dimension

You can align several dimensions at the same time as shown in Fig 17-38. Note that you have to select the dimensions to align first and click the Line-Up icon, then select a dimension to align to.

Using the Offset to reference option, you can specify the distance from the reference object. Using the Offset between dimensions option, you can specify the spacing of several dimensions.

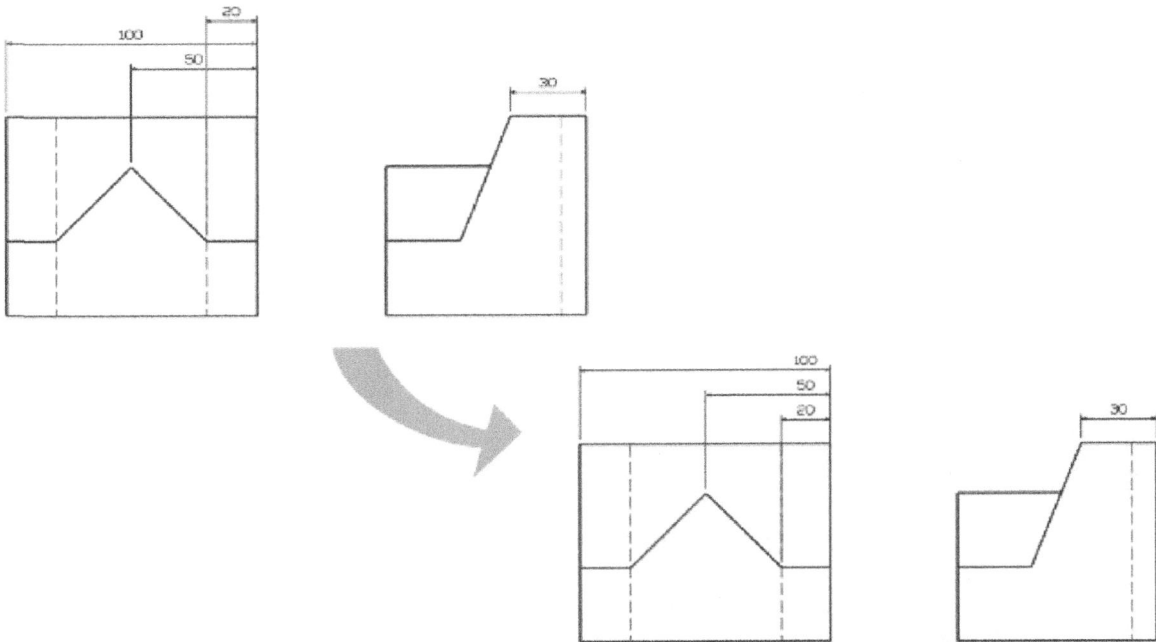

Fig 17-38 Aligning Several Dimensions

Using the Dimension Positioning icon in the Positioning too l bar, you can arrange dimensions in a drawing view automatically. Note that you have to activate the drawing view. Fig 17-39 shows the re-sult of automatic positioning of dimensions.

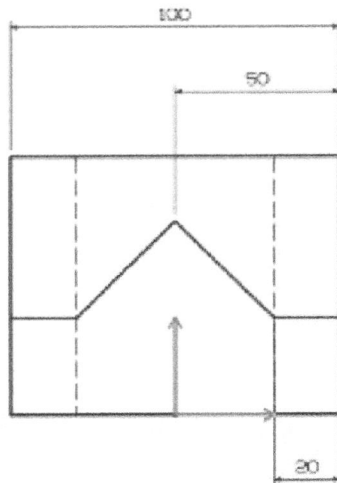

Fig 17-39 Automatic Positioning

499

17.6 Annotations

Drawing objects such as texts, tables, weld and roughness symbols, balloon and datum target symbols are called annotations. You can create text type annotations using the icons in the Text toolbar. Note that the annotations are created in an active drawing view.

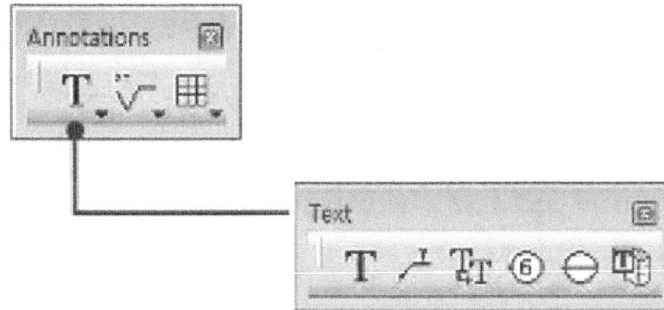

Fig 17-40 Text Toolbar

17.6.1 General Text

General text can be created according to the following procedure.

1. Activate a view for which to create text. (Press MB3 (right click) > Activate View on the view.)
2. Click the Text icon in the Text sub-toolbar.
3. Specify the location of the text. If you pick a location outside of the view, the boundary is extended.
4. Enter text in the Text Editor and press OK. If you want to insert a new line, you have to press Shift + Enter.

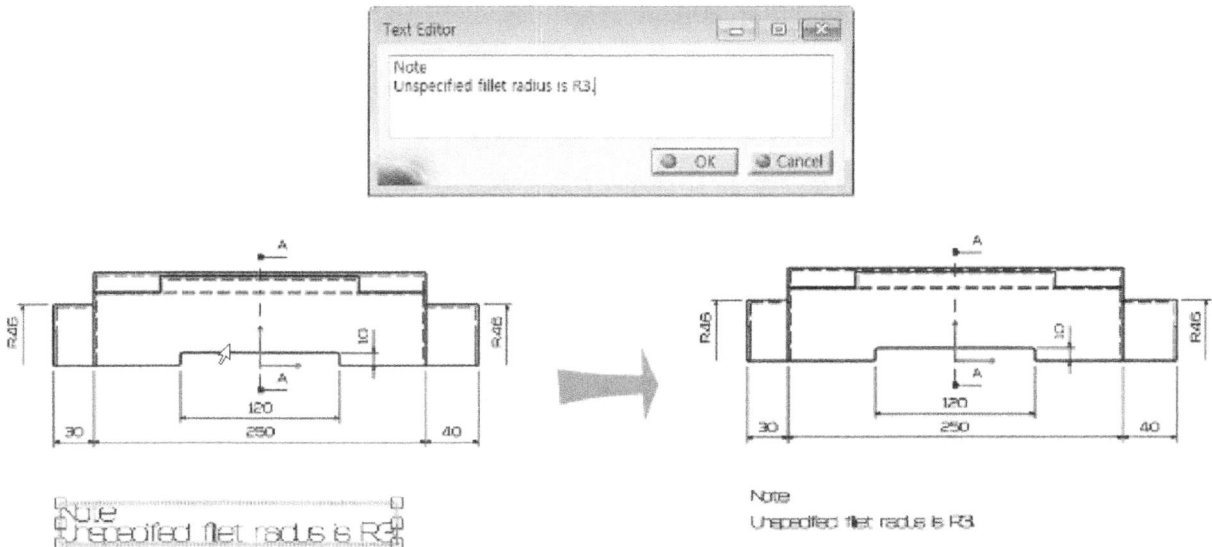

Fig 17-41 Adding Text

17.6.2 Leader Type Text

You can create the leader type text according to the following procedure. Each step number corresponds to that in Fig 17-42.

1. Activate a view for which to create text. (Press MB3 > Activate View on the view.)
2. Click Text with Leader icon in the Text toolbar.
3. Select the object to which attach the leader.
4. Specify the location of the text.
5. Enter text in the Text Editor and press OK.

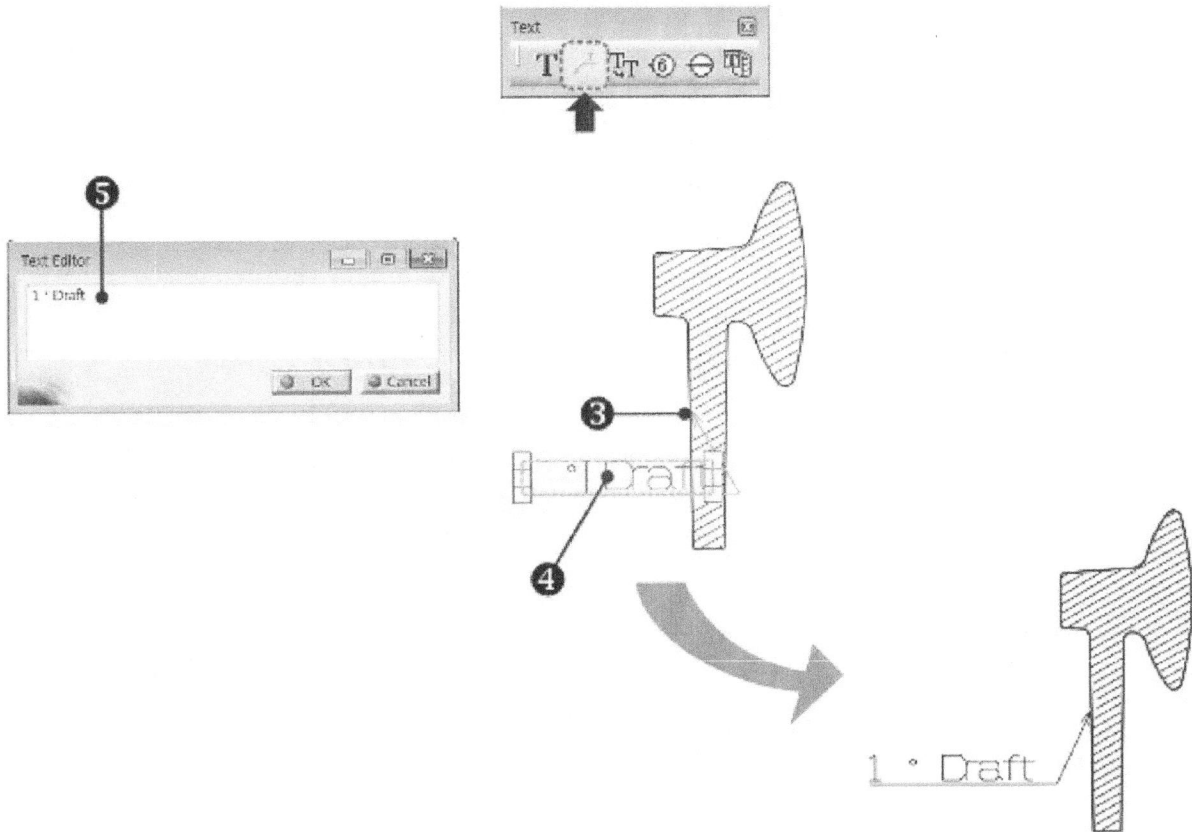

Fig 17-42 Creating a Text with Leader

17.6.3 Adding Leader

If you right click on a gen era l text or a leader type text, a pop-up menu shown in Fig 17-43 is available. Using the Add Leader option, you can specify as many objects as you want to designate by the text.

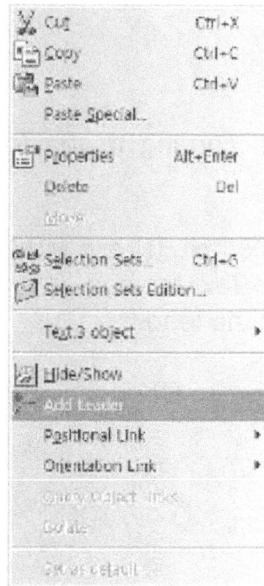

Fig 17-43 Pop-up Menu for Text

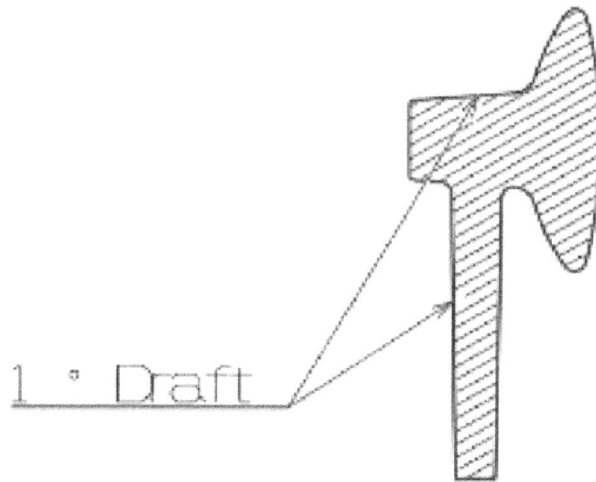

Fig 17-44 Text with Two Leaders

17.7 PROPERTIES OF DIMENSION AND ANNOTATION

17.7.1 Properties of Dimension

Right click on a dimension and select Properties. You can set the dimension properties in the dialog box shown in Fig 17-45. There are nine option tabs in the dialog box.

1. **Value**: Sets value orientation, dual dimension, format and fake dimenion.
2. **Tolerance**: Inserts tolerances.

3. **Dimension Line**: Sets the options for the dimension line.
4. **Extension Line**: Sets the options for extension lines.
5. **Dimension Texts**: Adds texts or symbols in front, back, above and below the main dimension text
6. **Font**: Sets the font of the dimension text.
7. **Text**: Sets appearances, position, orientation, etc. of the dimension text.
8. **Graphic**: Sets the color and type of the dimension line.
9. **Feature Properties**: Sets the name of the dimension.

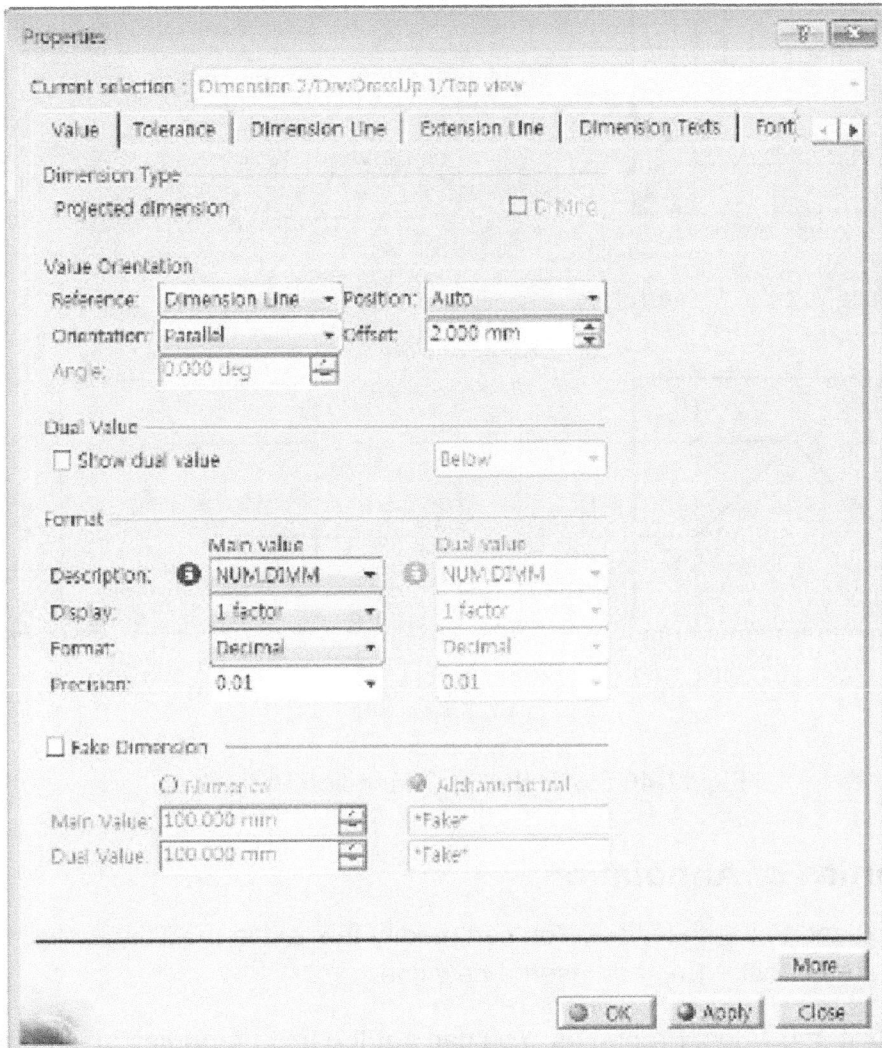

Fig 17-45   Dimension Properties Dialog Box

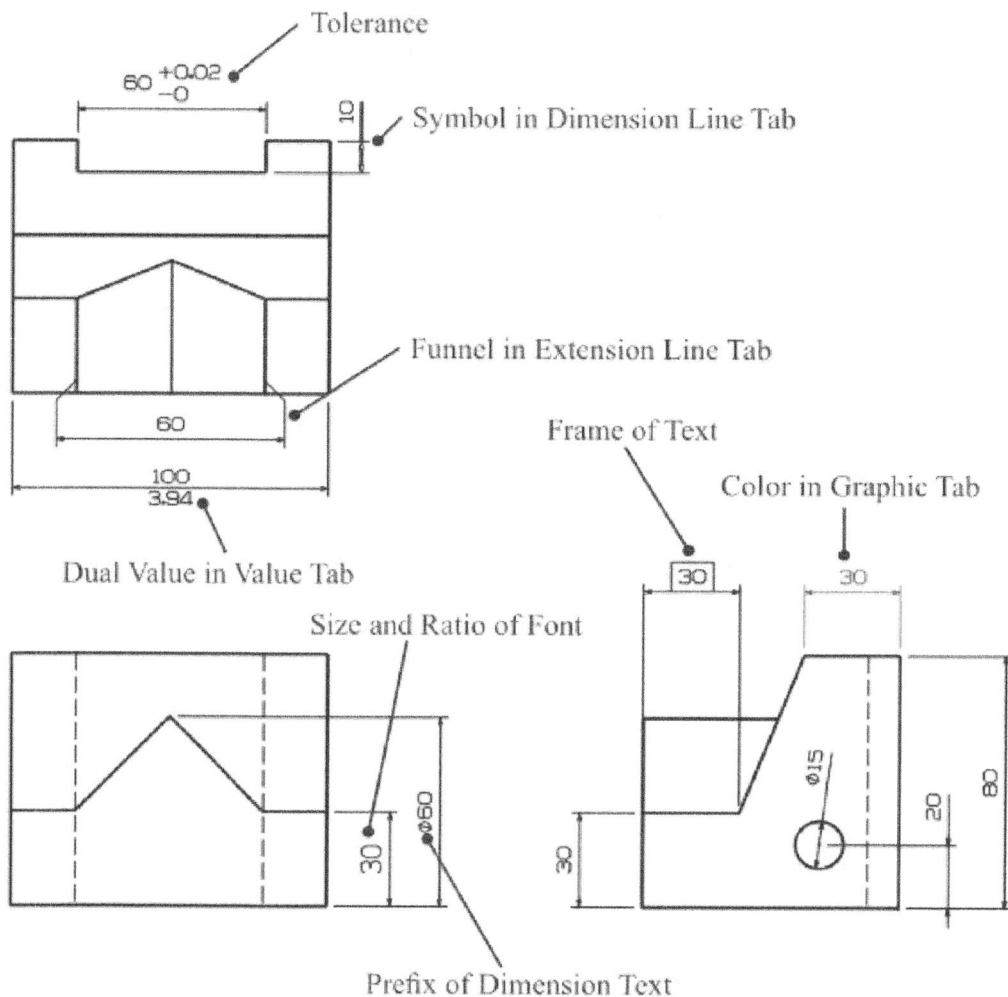

Fig 17-46 Examples of Dimension Properties

17.7.2 Properties of Annotation

Double click a text and text with leader. You can modify the text in the Text Editor dialog box. Note that you have to press Shift + Enter to insert a new line.

Right click on a text and select Properties. You can set the text properties in the dialog box shown in Fig 17-47. There arc four option tabs in the dialog box.

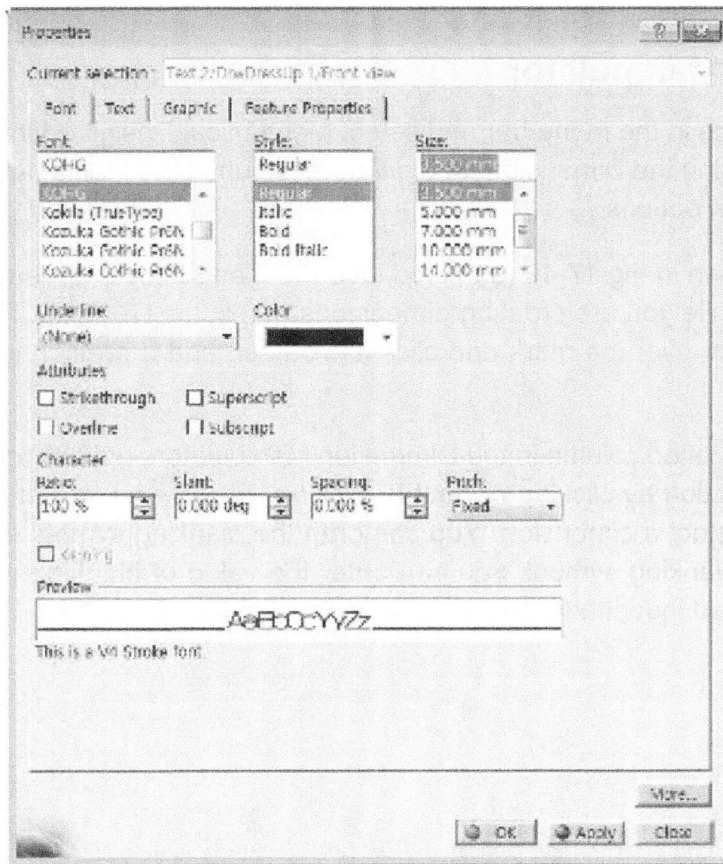

Fig 17-47 Text Properties Dialog Box

Place the mouse cursor on the text box. the cursor symbol changes to a hand and you can drag the text box. Clicking the text box, you can resize the text box by dragging the corner points.

If you click the text with leader, control point s are activated as shown in Fig 17-48 (a). You can drag the yellow point (A) in Fig 17-48 (a) to point to another object. You can drag the control point (B) to resize the stub as shown in Fig 17-48 (b).

Right click on the text with leader and select Add Leader. You can point to other objects with single text.

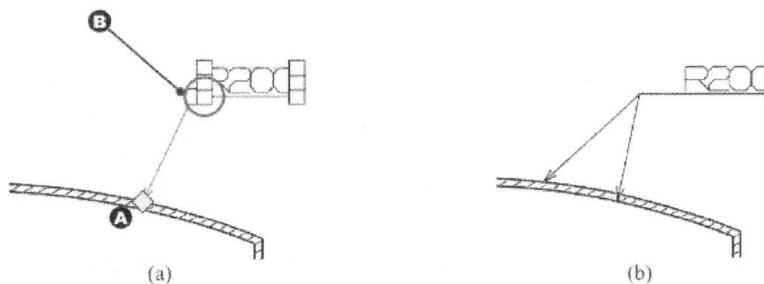

Fig 17-48 Modifying Text with Leader

505

17.7.3 Using the Manipulator

Choose Tools > Options in the menu bar and select Mechanical Design > Drafting on the left of the Options dialog box. Using the Dimension Manipulators option in the Manipulator tab, you can easily modify basic dimension options.

Set the options as shown in Fig 17-49 (a). A red inverted triangle mark appears in front and back of the main dimension while you are creating dimensions ((A) in fig 17-49(a)). Press the Ctrl key and move the mouse cursor over the mark and click it. You can add a prefix and/or suffix to the main text.

If you check the Modification column in the Dimension Manipulators option, you can take advantage of the manipulator function by clicking or double clicking the dimension. Set the options as shown in Fig 17-49 (h) and select a dimension. You can drag the blanking symbol ((B) in Fig 17-49(b)). If you double click the blanking symbol, you can enter the value of blanking in the input box. Each blanking can be dragged independently by pressing the Ctrl key.

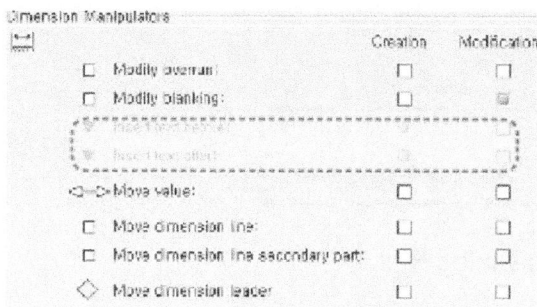
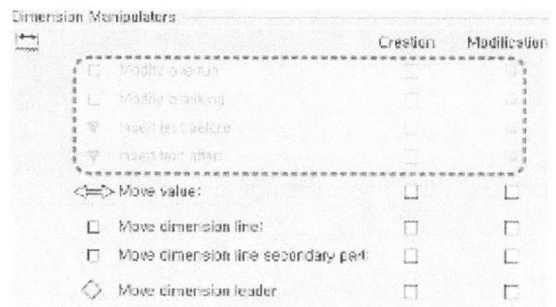

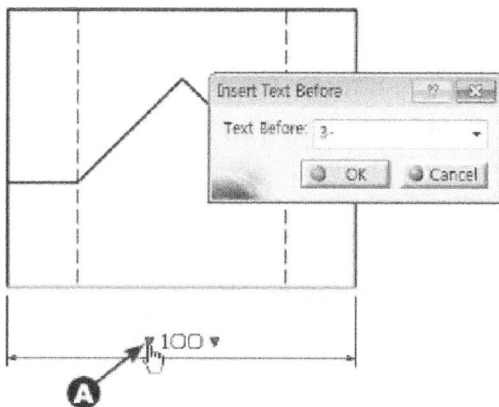
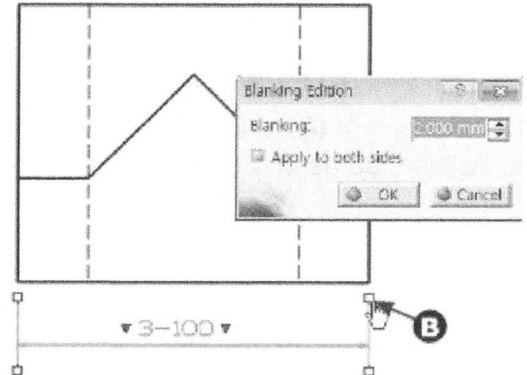

(a)   (b)

Fig 17-49 Creating and Modifying Dimension by Using Dimension Manipulator

By using the Copy Object Format button in the Graphic Properties toolbar, you can copy the proper ties of another objects. This function is useful in copying dimension properties.

Procedure

1. Select objects for which to modify their properties. You can select as many objects of the same type.
2. Press the Copy Object Format button in the Graphic Properties toolbar shown in Fig 17-50.
3. Select the object from which to copy the properties.

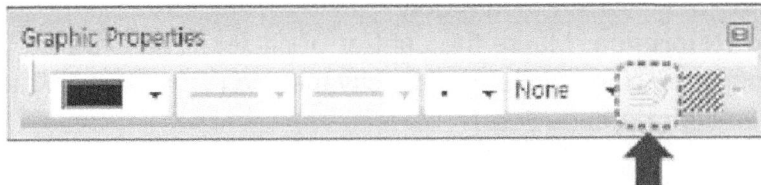

Fig 17-50 Copy Object Format Icon

17.8 CENTER LINES

If you check the Center Line option in the view properties dialog box, you can create center lines for the view at one time. Of course, you can delete certain center lines if necessary.

Using the icons in the Axis and Threads sub-toolbar of the Dress-up toolbar, you can create center lines for holes and the hole symbols one by one.

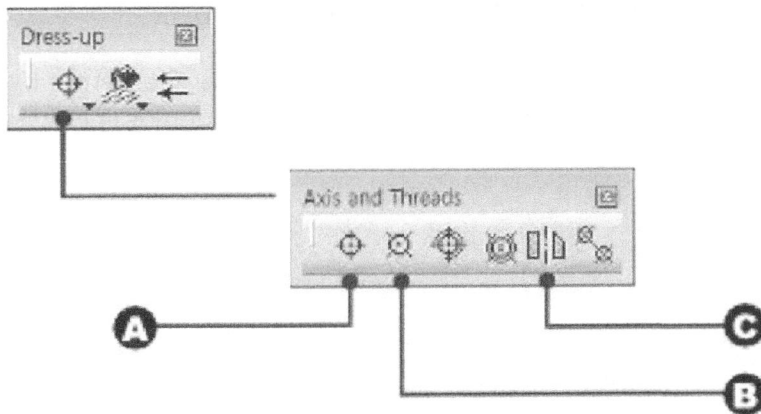

Fig 17-51 Axis and Threads Sub-toolbar

(A) Center Line: Marks the center of circles. The li ne s are aligned to horizonal and vertical all the time. You can resize the centerline by selecting it and dragging the end mark. If you press the Ctrl key, you can drag each line individually.

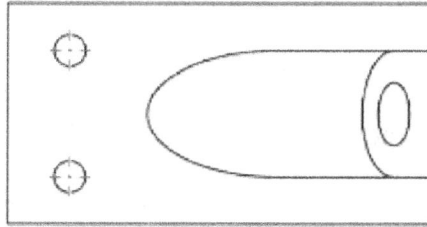

Fig 17-52 Center Line

(B) Center Line with Reference: Marks the cent er of circles. The lines are aligned to a specific direction. Press the icon, select the circle and specify the line (J) in Fig 17-53 as the reference. The center line is aligned to the reference line.

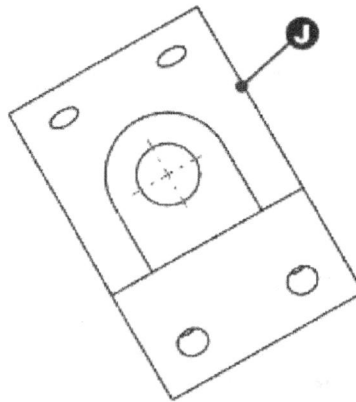

Fig 17-53 Center Line with Reference

(C) Axis Line: Creates a center line for a side view of a hole at the center by selecting two lines. The two lines do not need to be parallel. You can also create a center line by selecting two points.

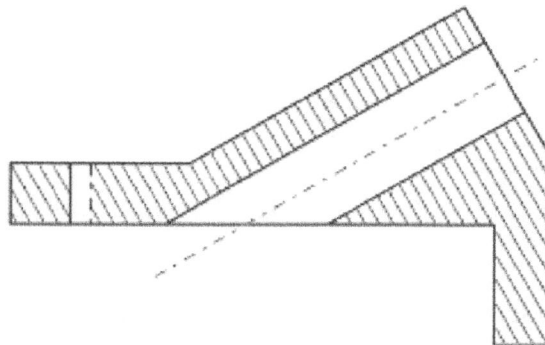

Fig 17-54 Axis Line

You can create the bolt circle centerline by using the Center Line with Reference icon according to the following procedure. Each step number corresponds to that in Fig 17-55.

1. Click the Center Line with Reference icon
2. Select the circle for bolt hole.
3. Select a circle that is concentric to the pitch circle as reference.
4. Select the centerline and drag the end mark by pressing the Ctrl key.

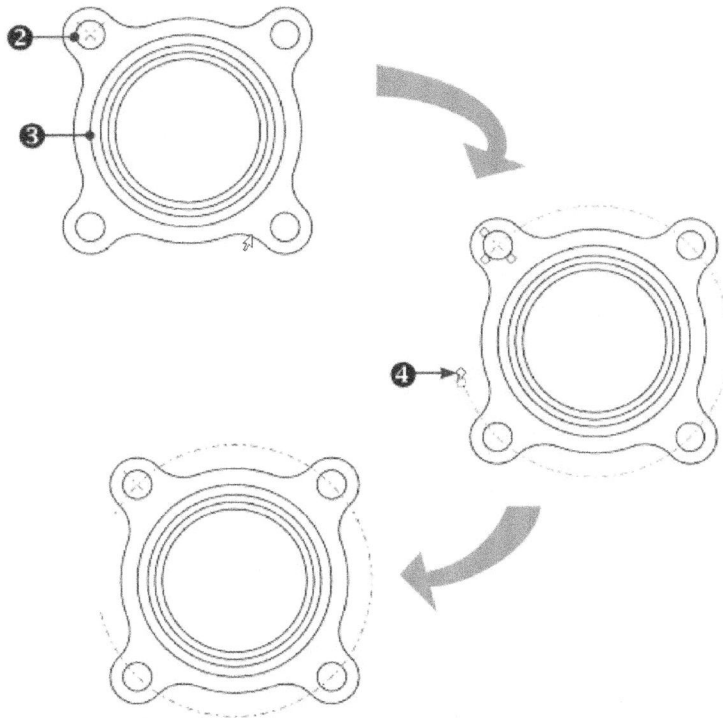

Fig 17-55 Creating Bolt Circle Center line

Exercise 144: Creating Linear Dimensions (ch17 _002.CATPart)

Create dimensions for the given part as shown in Fig 17-56. Note that one decimal place is applied for all dimension texts.

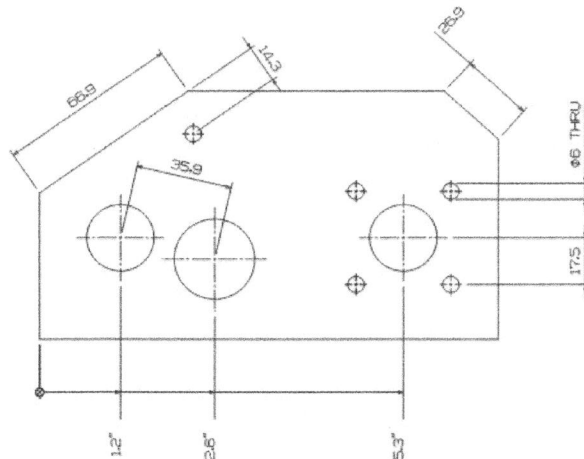

Fig 17-56 Drawing for Exercise 144

Exercise 145: Creating Linear Dimensions (ch17 _003.CATPart)

Create dimensions for the given part as shown in Fig 17-57.

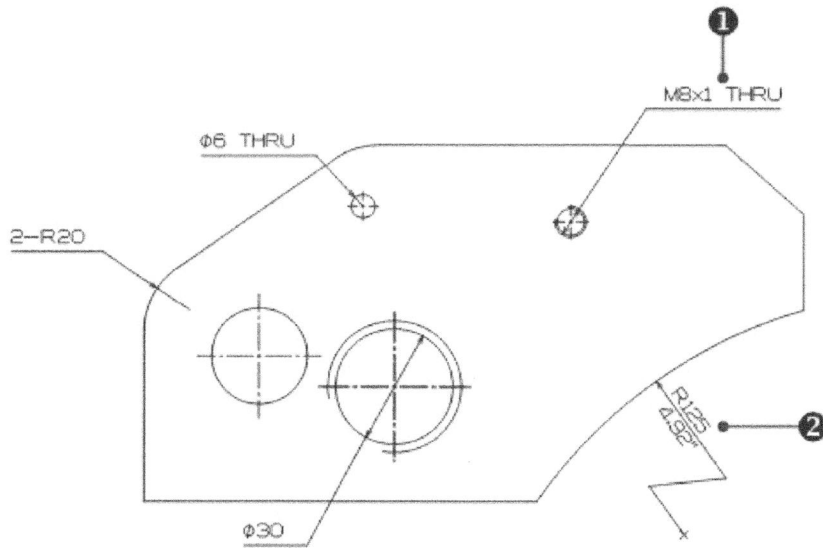

Fig 17-57 Drawing for Exercise 145

Hints!

The dimension (1) can be created by using the Thread Dimensions icon in the Dimensions toolbar.

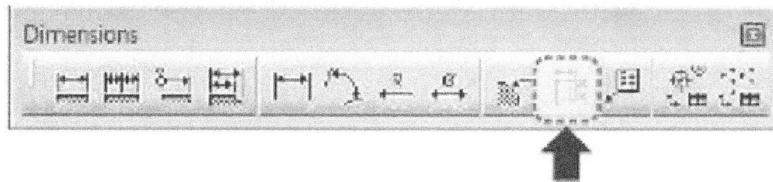

Fig 17-58 Thread Dimensions Icon

To apply this type of hole dimension, the hole has to be created by using the Threaded option and that the threaded type center line has to be created by using the icons shown in Fig 17-5 9. Note that the designated hole has been created with the M8xl spec as shown in Fig 17-60 in the given CATPart file.

Fig 17-59 Thread Type Centerline Icons

510

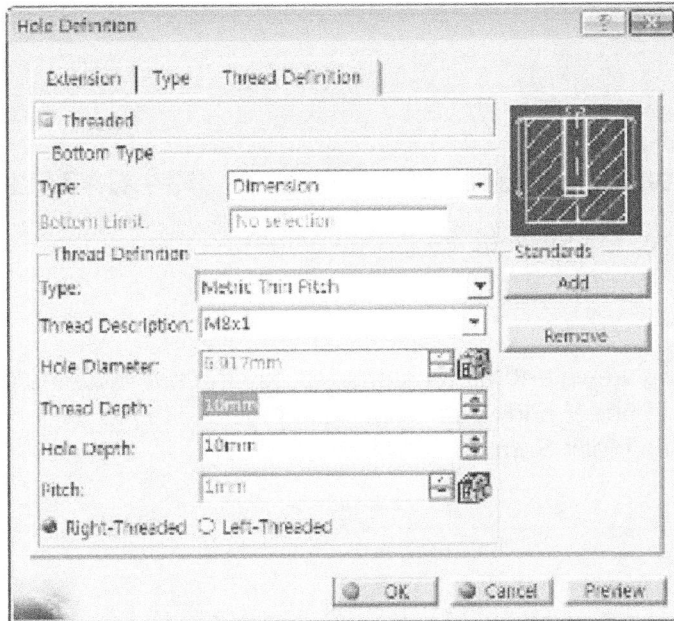

Fig 17-60 Thread Definition for Hole

The dimension (2) can be created by setting the Foreshortened option as shown in Fig 17-61 and the Dual Value option as shown in Fig 17-62.

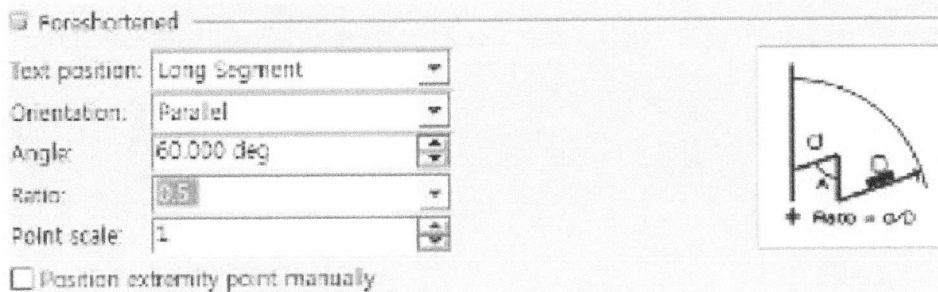

Fig 17- 61 Foreshortened Option

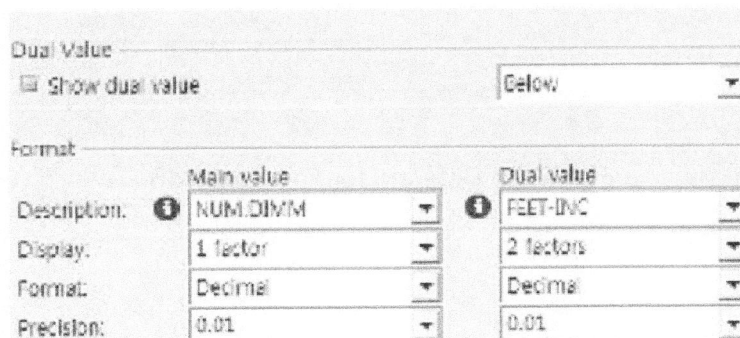

Fig 17-62 Dual Value Option

511

Exercise 146: Drawing for Bracket 2 (ch17 _004.CATPart)

Create a drawing as shown in Fig 17-63 for the given part.

Remarks

1. Create the drawing views and dimensions exactly the same as the given drawing.
2. Refer to the size of sheet and scale in the title block.
3. Apply Drawing Title block Sample 1 for frame.

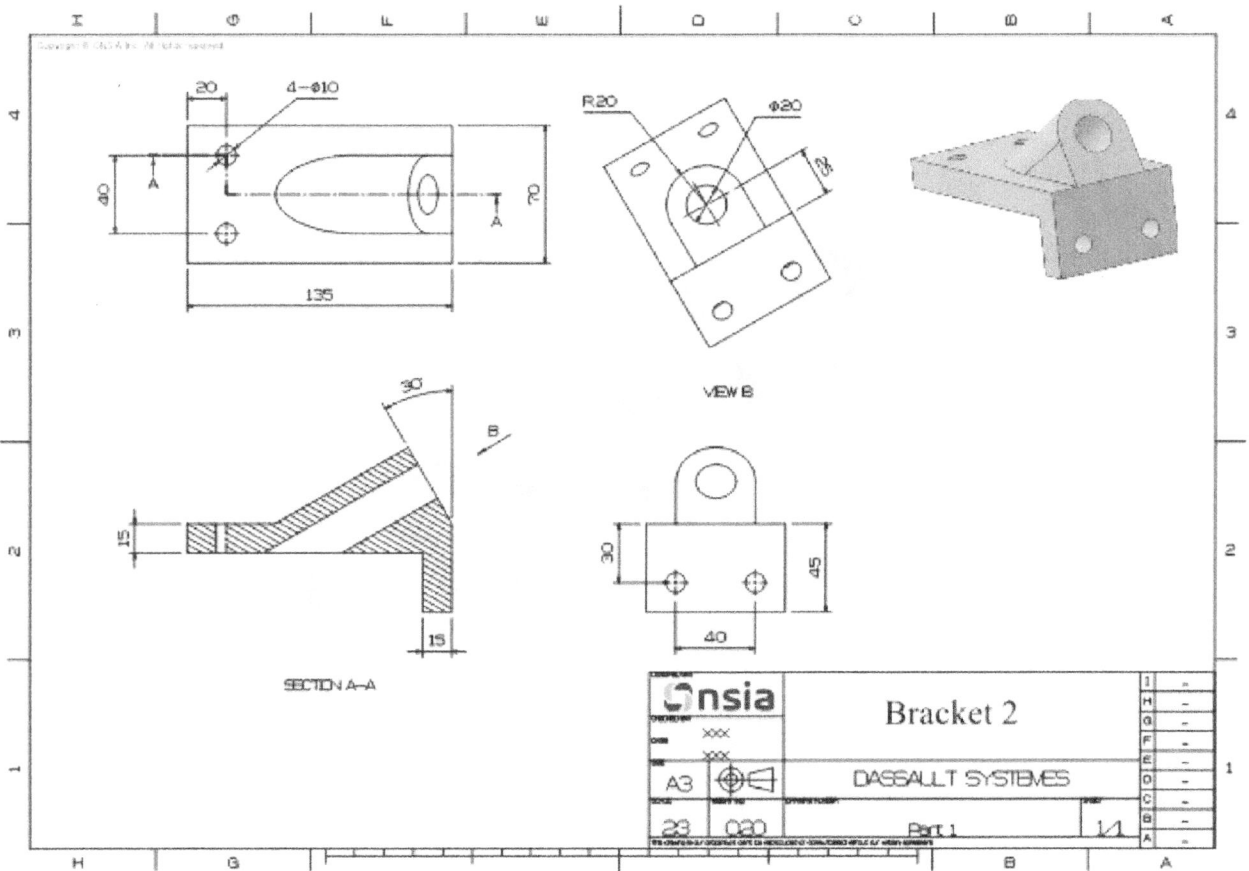

Fig 17-63 Drawing for Exercise 146

Exercise 147: Drawing for Plastic Cover (ch17 _005.CATPart)

Open the given part file ch17_005.CATPart and create a drawing as shown in Fig 17-64. For the isometric view use another given file ch17_005_drafted_filleted.CATPart.

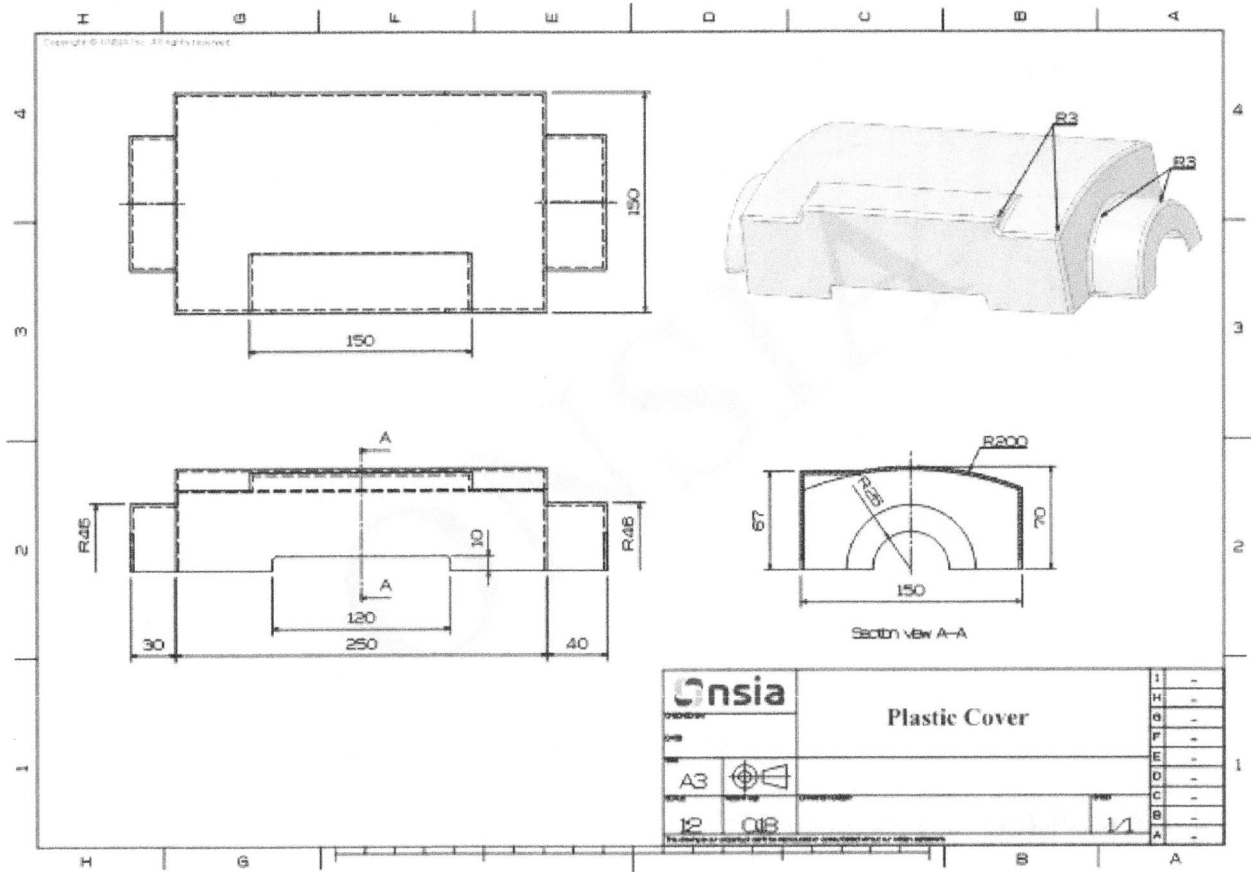

Fig 17-64 Drawing for Exercise 147

Exercise 148: Drawing for Toy Box Cover (ch17 _006.CATPart)

Open the given part file ch17_006.CATPa rt and create a drawing as shown in Fig 17-65.

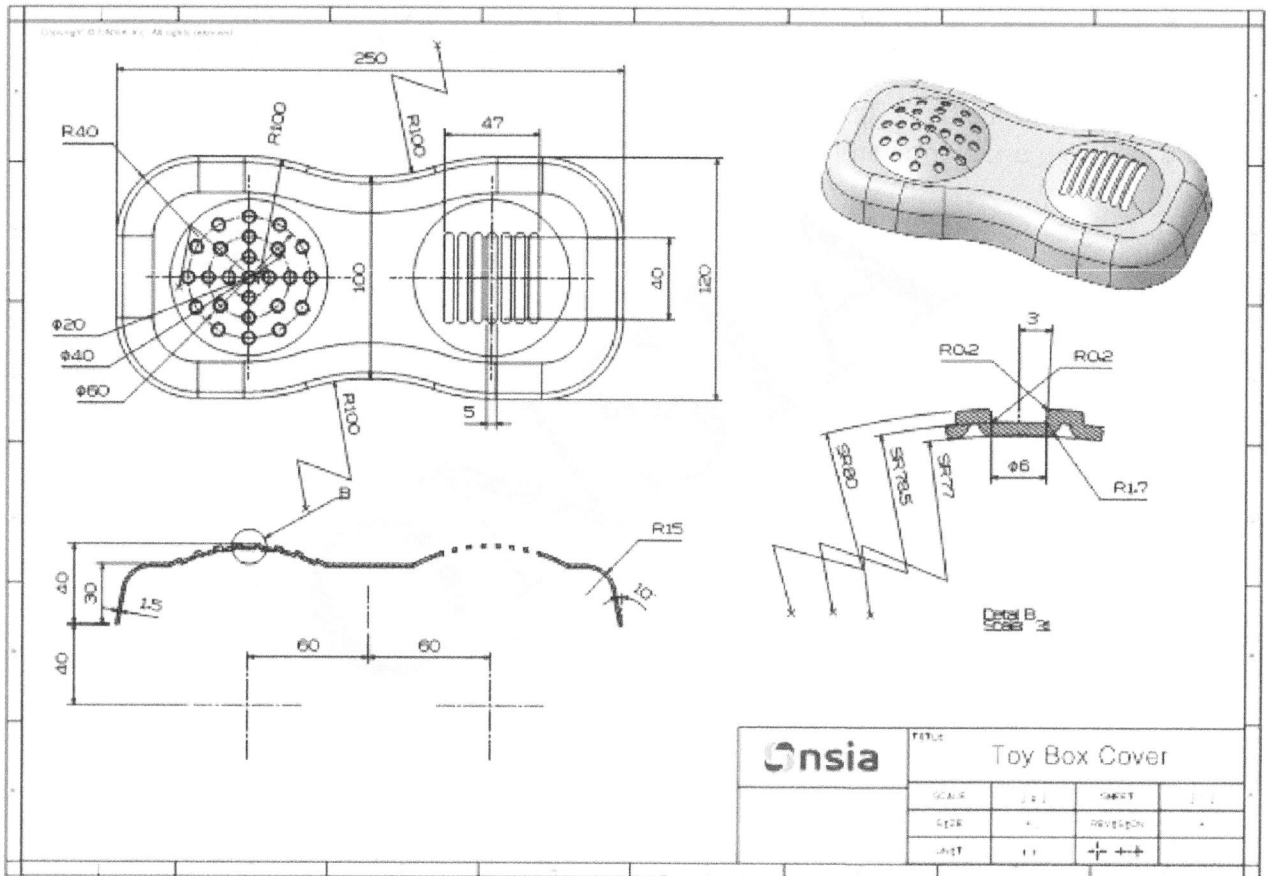

Fig 17-65 Drawing for Exercise 148

17.9 ASSEMBLY DRAWING

You can create a drawing for a product file. The purpose of creating an assembly drawing is to provide the information required for assembling a product. The assembly sequence and path can be illustrated in a disassembled drawing view. Names, quantity, material, etc. of each component of an assembly can be included in the parts list.

To create an assembly drawing, open the product file, create a drawing file and insert the drawing views as shown in fig 17-66 as you have done for part drawings. You can create a disassembled drawing view apply balloon annotations and include a BOM.

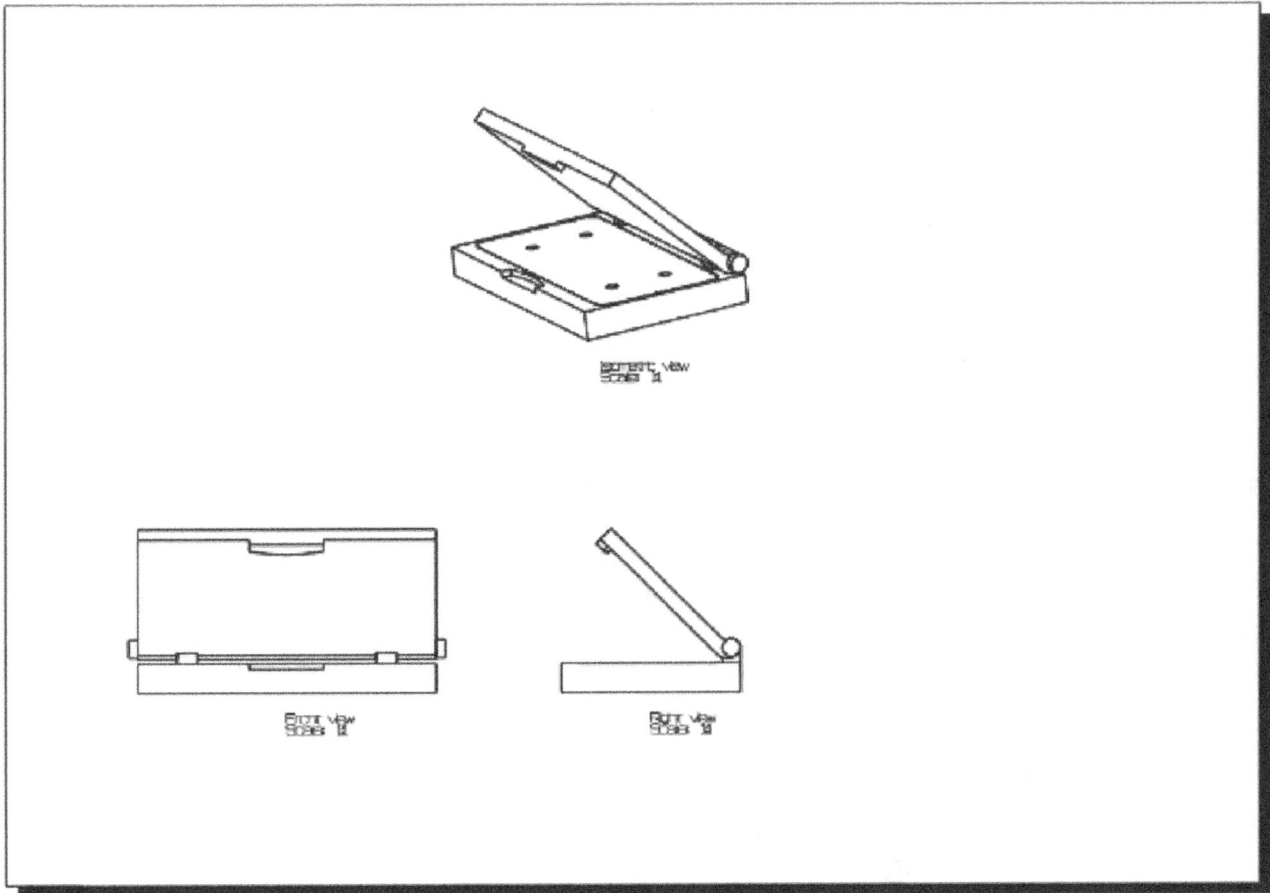

Fig 17-66 Assembly Drawing Views

17.9.1 Excluding Components in a View

You can deactivate certain components in the product file to refrain from appear in g in the drawing views. Right click on the component in the Spec Tree and select Activate/Deactivate Component in the pop-up menu as shown in Fig 17-67.

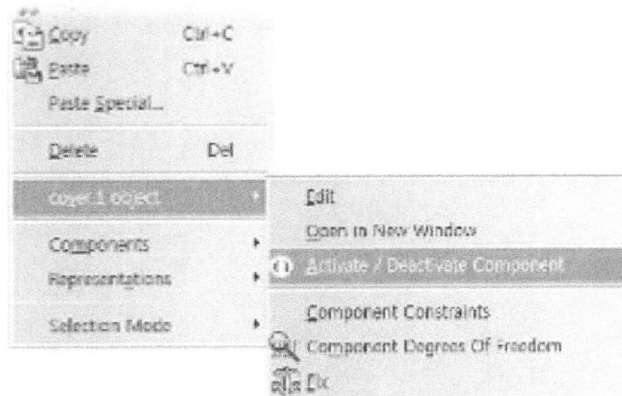

Fig 17-67 Activate / Deactivate Component Option

17.9.2 Excluding a Component from being Sectioned

When you create a section view for a product, you can exclude certain components from being cut. Note that this option has to be checked in the product file. Open the product file, select the component not to be cut in the section view and press MB3 (right click) > Properties. Select the Drafting tab in the Properties dialog box and check the Do not cut in section view option.

You can set components not to be used when projecting and be represented with hidden lines in the drawing views with the corresponding option in the Drafting tab.

Exercise 149: Creating Assembly Drawing View (Folder: ch17 _007)

Open the notebook_assy.CATProduct file in the given folder ch17_007 and create drawing views as shown in Fig 17-69.

Requirements

1. Exclude the "top" component from all drawing views.
2. The "screw" component should not be cut in Section View A-A.

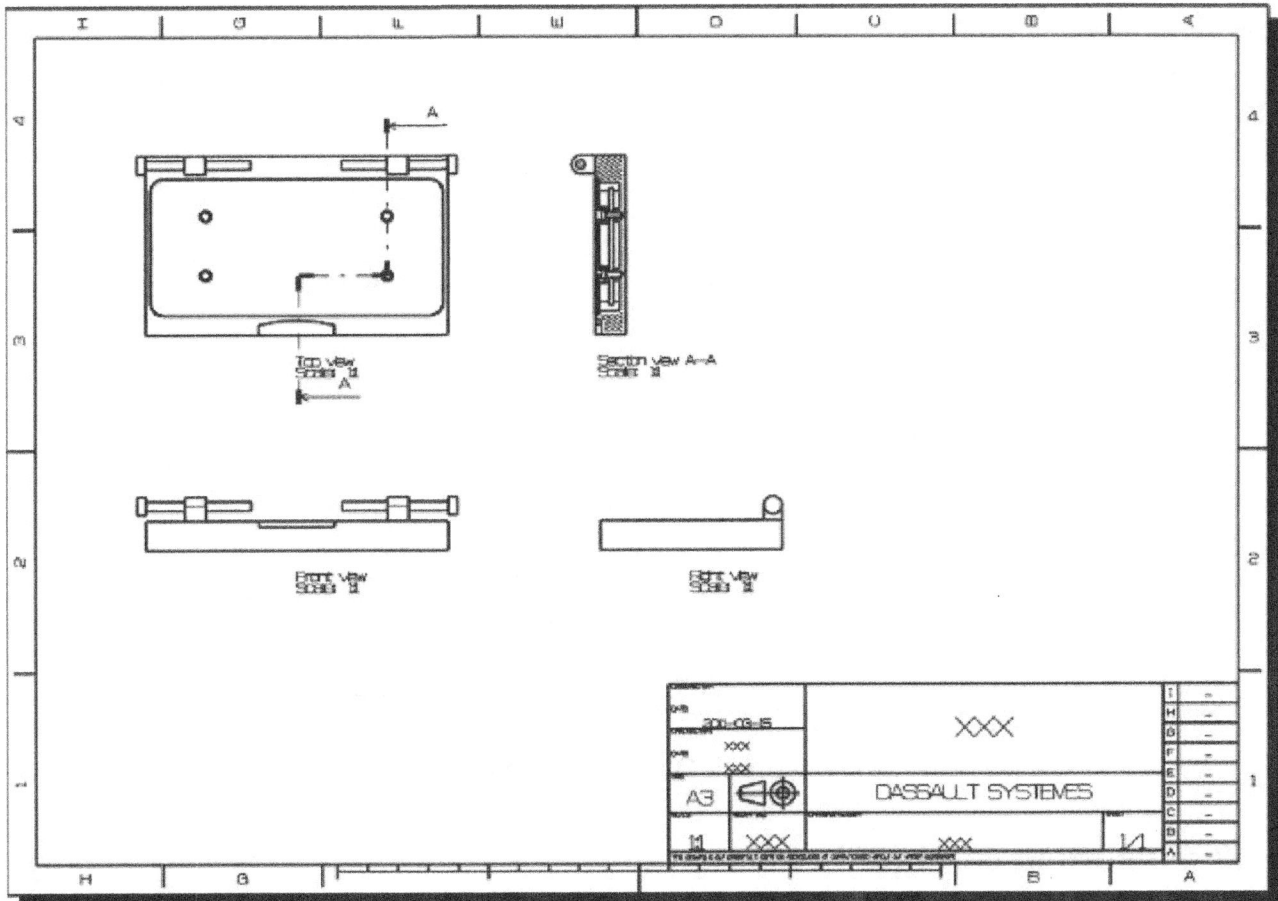

Fig 17-69 Assembly Drawing

17.9.3 Breakout View in an Assembly Drawing View

In the Assembly work bench, we assemble many components of a product. It is hard to describe the assembly state for interior components. In this case, the break out view can be helpful. The procedure is the same as that for the part drawing. Fig 17-70 shows the break out view of the notebook assembly.

The disassembled view, which will be explained later, shows the individual components in an arbitrary disassembled position. It does not show the components in the assembled position.

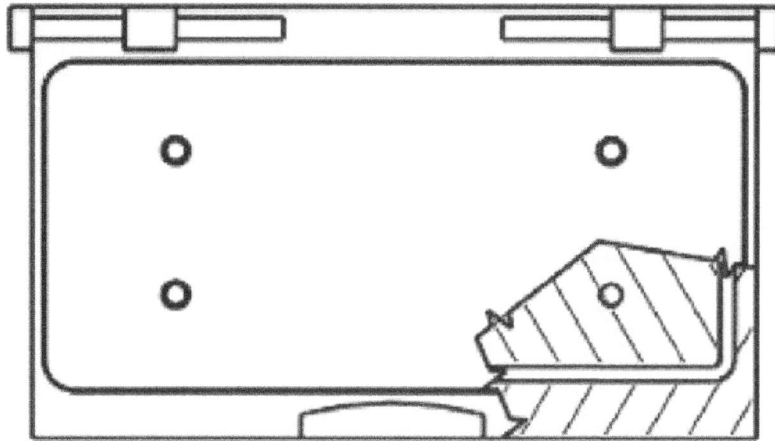

Fig 17-70 Break Out View of an Assembly

17.9.4 Inserting BOM (Bill of Material)

Most assembly drawings contain a BOM table, which is a kind of parts list that gives product information such as the number, name and material of components.

If you want the BOM table linked to the product file data contained in the numbering of balloon annotation, which will be explained later, you have to take the following procedure. Each step number corresponds to that in Fig 17-71.

1. Open a product file and create the drawing views.
2. Display the product file by choosing Window in the menu bar.
3. Click the Generate Numbering icon in the Product Structure Tools toolbar.
4. Select the top most product in the Spec Tree.
5. Set the options in the Generate Numbers dialog box and press OK.
6. Select Analyze > Bill of Material in the menu bar.
7. Press the Define formats button in the Bill of Material: xxx dialog box.
8. The items listed on the le ft of the Bill of Material: Define format dialog box are the items that will appear in the BOM table and the items on the right arc the ones that will not appear in the table. Select the items as shown in Fig 17-71 for example.
9. Close the two dialog boxes by pressing OK in each dialog box.

518

10. Save the product file.
11. Display the drawing file by choosing Window in the menu bar.
12. Activate one of the assembly drawing views, for example, the isometric view.
13. Choose Insert > Generation > Bill of Material > Bill of Material in the menu bar.
14. Pick the location to insert the BOM table, for example top left corner of the drawing sheet.

You can create the BOM table in the sheet not in a drawing view by double clicking the sheet. In this case a drawing view is not required. Choose Insert > Generation > Bill of Material > Bill of Material in the me n u bar, switch to the CATProduct file, select the product in the Spec Tree, return to the CATDrawing file and pick the location of the table on the sheet.

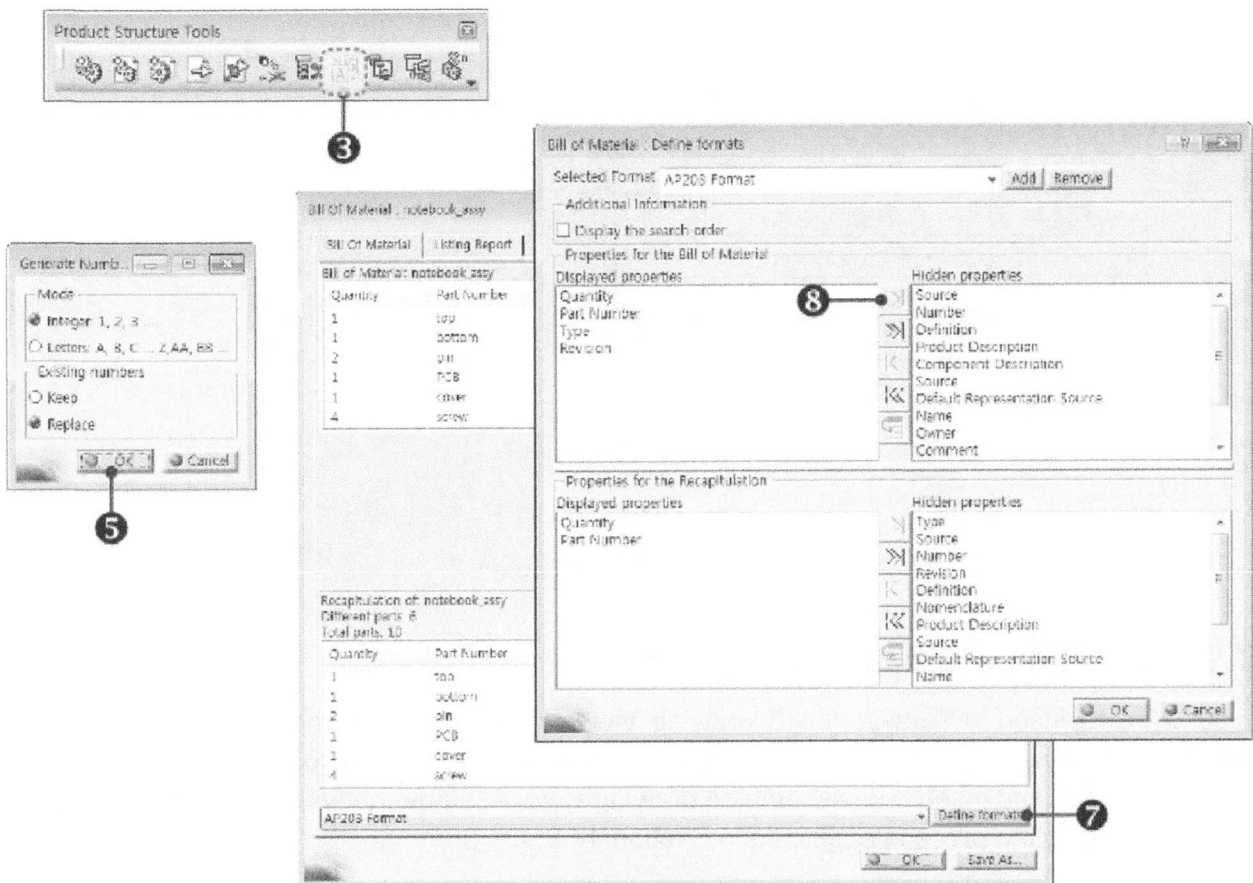

Fig 17-71 Procedure for Defining BOM Table

Bill of Material: Go Catia

Quantity	Part Number	Type	Nomenclature
1	Go Catia - 1	Part	
1	Go Catia - 2	Part	
1	Go Catia - 3	Part	
3	ISO Bolt	Part	
3	ISO Nut	Part	

Recapitulation of: Go Catia
Different parts: 5
Total parts: 9

Quantity	Part Number
1	Go Catia - 1
1	Go Catia - 2
1	Go Catia - 3
3	ISO Bolt
3	ISO Nut

Fig 17-72 BOM Table

17.9.5 Inserting a Disassembled View

If you want to insert a disassembled drawing view while other assembled drawing views are maintained in an assembly drawing, you have to create a scene first. Take the following procedure to create a scene and insert a disassembled drawing view. Assume that you have created the BOM table according to the process explained in Section 17.9.4.

1. Display the product file. Note that you are in the Assembly Design workbench.
2. Click the Enhanced Scene icon the Scenes toolbar.
3. Enter the name of the scene in the Enhanced Scene dialog box and press OK. Close the warning message that will appear. Note that the color of background changes to dark green.

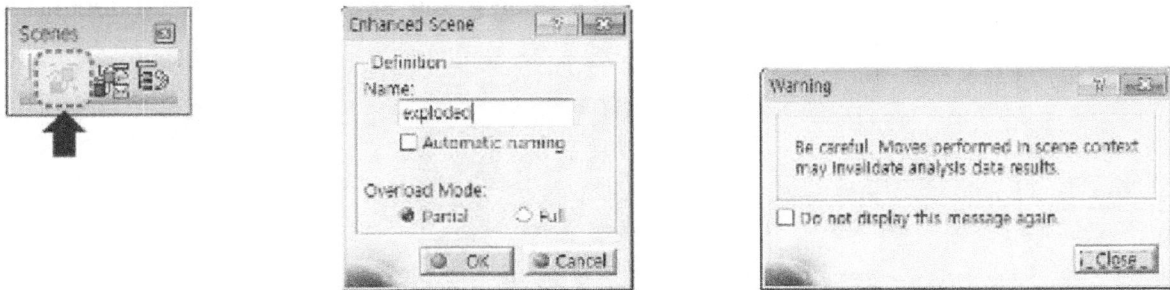

Fig 17-73 Defining a Scene

4. Click the Explode icon in the Enhanced Scenes toolbar. Components are exploded and you can modify the location of the exploded components using the Compass with the Snap Automatically to Selected Object option. You can use the Snap icon in the Move toolbar.

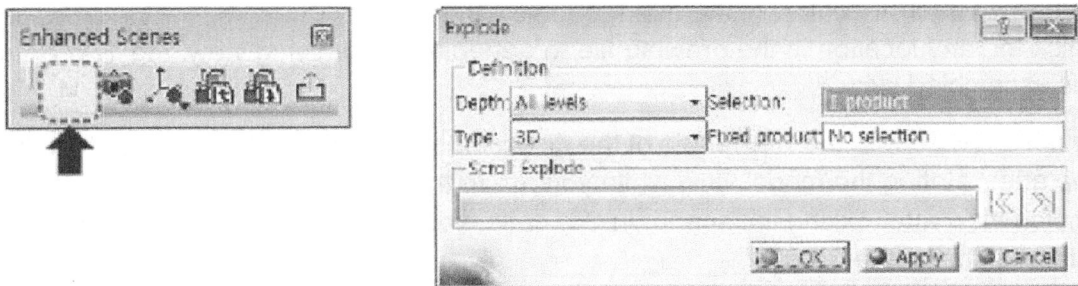

Fig 17-74 Creating Explosion

5. Display the drawing file.
6. Click the Isometric View icon in the Projections toolbar.

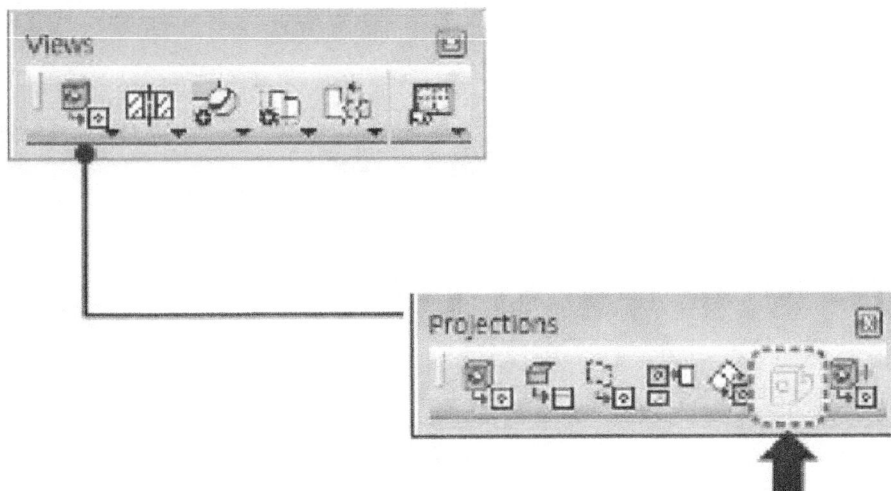

Fig 17-75 Isometric View Icon

7. Display the product file and rotate the model view according to your desire.

521

8. Select the name of the Scenes under Application in the Spec Tree of the product file. Note that you arc in the scene editing mode.

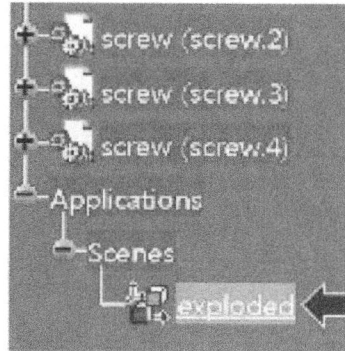

Fig 17-76 Selecting a Scene

9. Select an arbitrary object in the main graphic window.
10. Click the any location in the drawing file to generate the drawing view. Fig 17-77 shows the dis assembled view.

If you are not satisfied with the view angle of the disassembled view, you have to delete it and create a new one after rotating the model view while you are in the scene editing mode. You can create a disassembled view after exiting the scene. In this case, you can specify the view angle by choosing the front face of the isometric view.

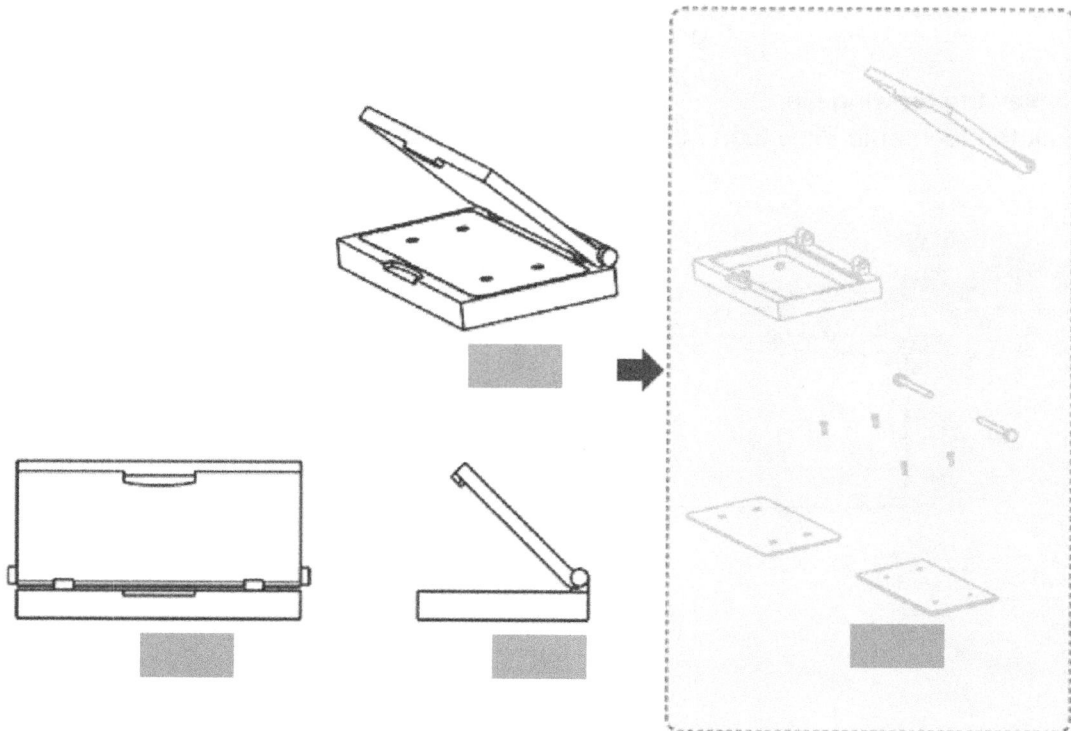

Fig 17-77 Disassembled View

17.9.6 Balloon Annotation

If you have generated component numbers as described in Section 17.9.4, you can insert balloon annotation automatically.

Activate the view to insert the balloon annotation, select Insert > Generation > Balloon generation in the menu bar. The annotation is generated for each component. You may have to adjust the location of the annotation if you are not satisfied with its distribution.

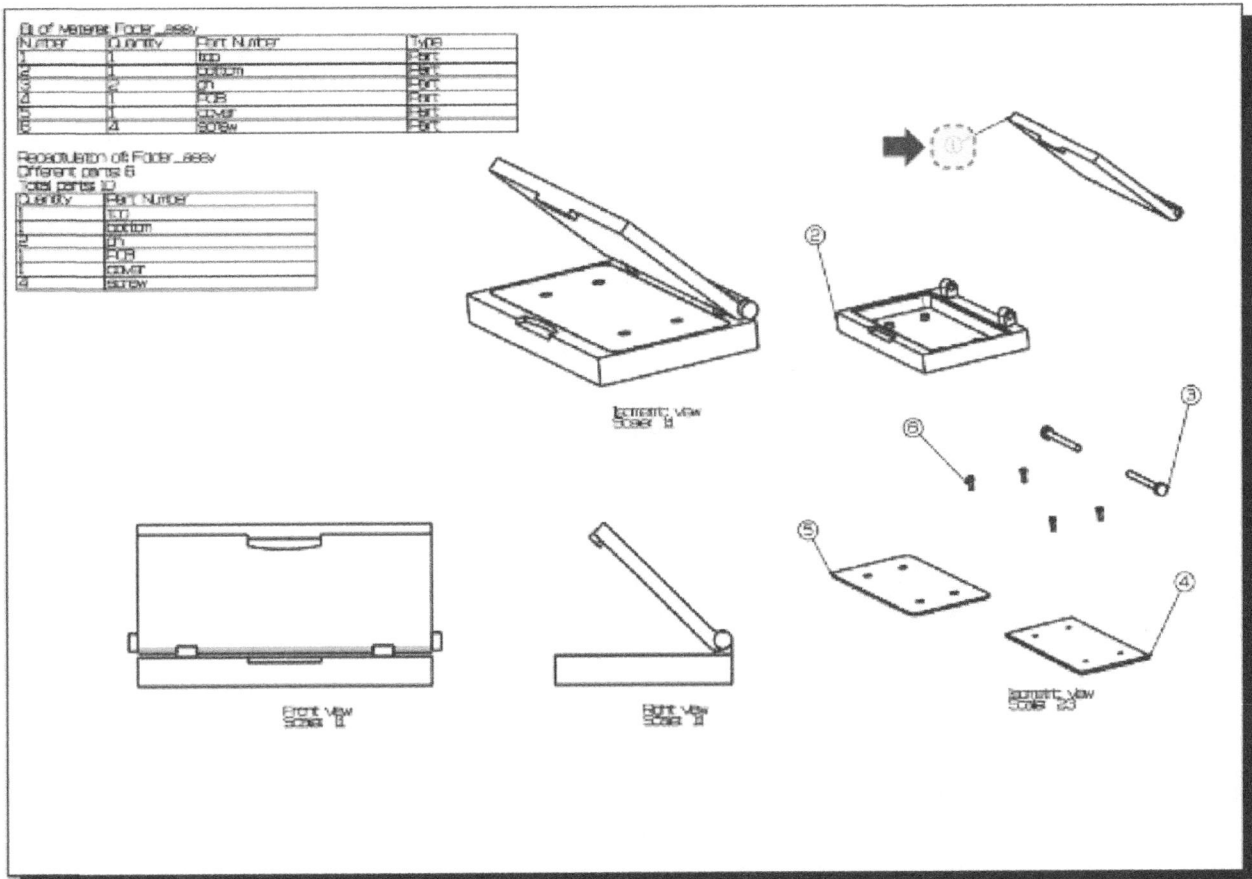

Fig 17-78 Inserting Balloon Annotation

17.10 CREATING A PDF FILE

Using File > Save As in the menu bar, you can create a PDF file for the drawing. Data translation to other formats is available with this menu.

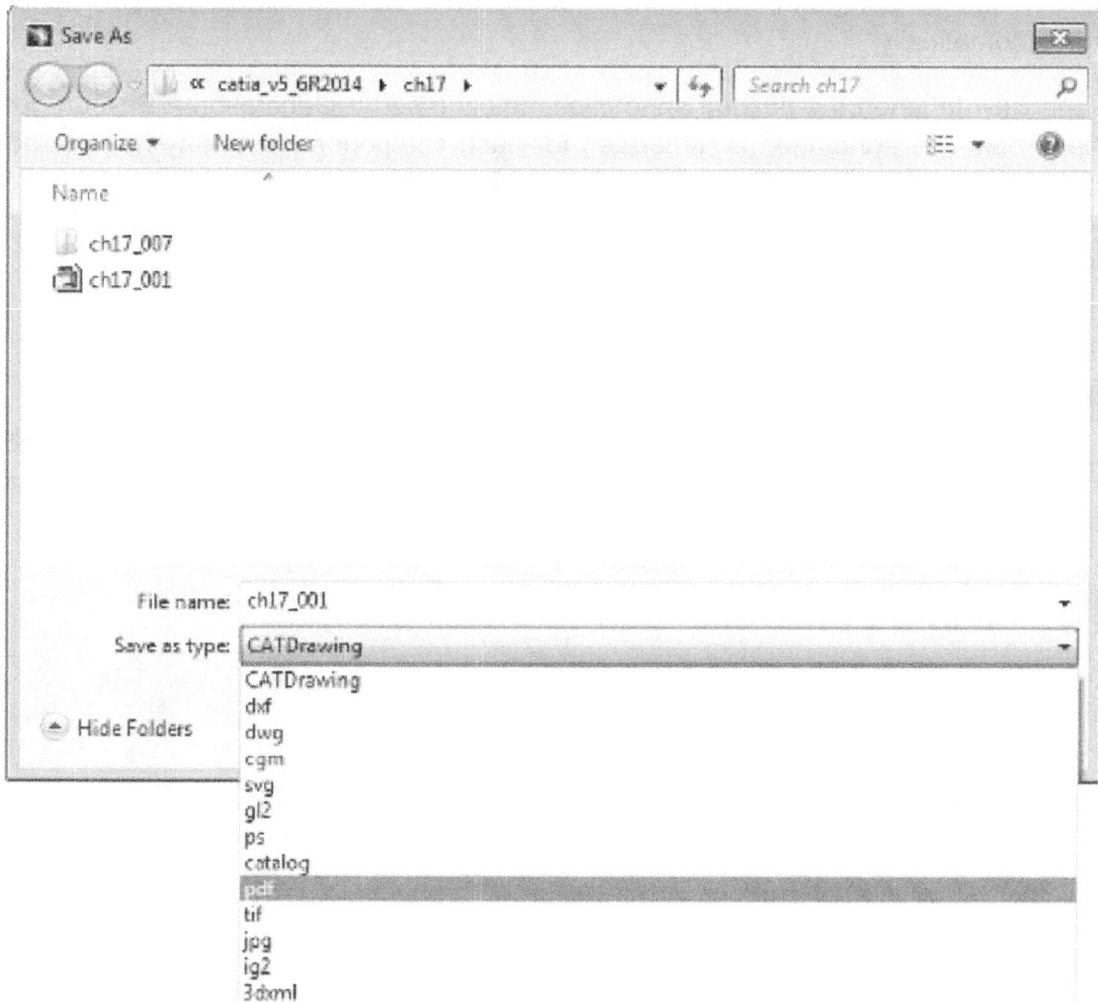

Fig 17-79 Save As Dialog Box

(Note) Translation Option

- By accessing Tools > Options in the menu bar, select General > Compatibility in the option item. You can set the translation graphics formats in the Graphics Formats tab.

CONCLUSION

As we reach the culmination of "Catia V5 2024 Guide for Beginners," it is time to reflect on the journey we have embarked upon together. From our initial foray into the basics of CATIA V5's interface to the complexities of assembly design and the intricacies of detailed drafting, this guide has aimed to equip you with the knowledge and skills to confidently use this powerful software tool.

Through the course of this book, you have been introduced to a broad spectrum of tools and techniques. You began by exploring the CATIA V5 workspace, learning to navigate and customize it to suit your needs. As you progressed into sketching and modeling, you tackled the essential building blocks of 3D design, learning how to translate a mental image into a digital reality. You have seen how sketch-based features form the backbone of your models and how dress-up features can refine them.

The detailed discussions on reference elements and parametric modification revealed the precision and control CATIA V5 offers, allowing you to create designs that are not only accurate but also flexible and responsive to change. The foray into advanced modeling techniques with multi-body design opened up new avenues for constructing complex models, and the replication of objects and features showed you ways to enhance efficiency in your work.

As your understanding deepened, you encountered the world of formulas and how they can be employed to create intelligent, dynamic designs. The chapters on assembly design introduced you to strategies for building coherent, functional assemblies that reflect the real-world complexities of mechanical systems.

In the later stages, you learned the crucial skills of generating drawing views, dimensioning, annotating, and presenting your designs. These skills bridge the gap between a virtual model and a physical product, ensuring your creations can be understood and manufactured according to your specifications.

Now, as you stand at the threshold of your next steps with CATIA V5, it is essential to recognize that this conclusion is not an end, but a milestone. The true test and application of your newfound knowledge begin with the projects you will undertake and the challenges you will resolve through design.

Remember that proficiency in CATIA V5, like any sophisticated tool, requires practice and persistence. The lessons and exercises in this guide serve as a solid foundation, but the expertise comes with time and continuous learning. Stay curious, explore the software further, and push the boundaries of your creativity and technical skill.

In the world of design and engineering, CATIA V5 is more than just a software application; it's a means of expression, a translator of innovation, and a facilitator of solutions. As you continue to develop your skills, you will contribute to the vast community of CATIA users worldwide, sharing ideas, pushing the envelope of what's possible, and shaping the future of design and manufacturing.

We encourage you to keep this guide at hand as you grow in your CATIA V5 journey. Revisit chapters, redo exercises, and always look for new ways to apply the principles you've learned. The field of CAD is dynamic, and so should be your learning. New features, updates, and methods are constantly emerging, and maintaining a student's mindset will keep you at the forefront of the industry.

As you move forward, consider joining forums, attending workshops, and collaborating with other CATIA V5 professionals. Each design challenge you encounter and each problem you solve enriches your understanding and fuels your growth.

In closing, let "Catia V5 2024 Guide for Beginners" be the springboard for your continued exploration into the vast, challenging, and ultimately rewarding world of computer-aided design with CATIA V5. The tools and techniques within these pages are your initial toolkit; your creativity and determination will define where you go from here.

Congratulations on completing this guide, and may your design journey be as fulfilling and exciting as the learning path that has led you here. Here's to the designs you will create, the problems you will solve, and the future you will help to shape with CATIA V5.

As we draw the curtain on our comprehensive guide, "Catia V5 2024 Guide for Beginners," we acknowledge the expansive landscape of knowledge we've traversed. From initiating your first sketch to perfecting complex assemblies, each chapter of this journey has been carefully designed to elevate your understanding and skill with CATIA V5.

Starting with the first principles of CATIA V5, you were introduced to a world where design meets technology. You learned to navigate the interface with agility, customizing your workspace to become an extension of your thought process. The foundational skills you have developed here will serve as the bedrock upon which your future projects will be built.

As you progressed to the sketching and modeling phases, you encountered the core of CATIA's design capabilities. You discovered how simple lines and curves can evolve into sophisticated 3D models that are precise and detailed. Each sketching exercise you completed was a step toward a fluent command of the digital language in which CATIA V5 speaks.

The chapters on sketch-based features brought you into a deeper dialogue with the software, teaching you to create solid, volumetric forms from two-dimensional outlines. Here, you've seen how a pad can extend into space, how a pocket can carve out material, and how every feature can be adjusted to fit the contours of your imagination.

As you engaged with reference elements and parametric modifications, you unlocked the secrets of precise and adaptable designs. This guide has demonstrated how the wise use of references can give you greater control over the most complex of geometries, and how parametric tools can make your models responsive to changes, reducing the need for time-consuming reworks.

By now, you've grasped the nuances of working with multiple bodies, understanding that each body can represent a distinct part of your assembly, a separate material, or even a different stage in the manufacturing process. This insight is key to mastering CATIA V5, as it allows for an organized approach to modeling that mirrors real-world construction and manufacturing sequences.

Your exploration of object and feature replication has opened up efficient avenues for manipulating and managing your designs. You've learned that the intelligent use of these tools can save time and ensure consistency, two vital aspects of professional design work.

The advanced sketch-based features and the use of formulas have propelled you into a new dimension of design capabilities. By now, you understand that with CATIA V5, you are not just creating static models but are capable of constructing intelligent designs that respond and adapt to varying parameters, akin to a living organism responding to its environment.

The penultimate chapters on assembly design invited you to think beyond individual components and consider the product as a whole. Whether you prefer a bottom-up or top-down approach, this guide has equipped you with the methodologies to construct assemblies that are logical, functional, and ready for real-world application.

In crafting drawing views and mastering dimensioning and annotation, you learned that a design's journey doesn't end with the model's completion. The creation of detailed, clear, and precise drawings is paramount, as it communicates your design intent and ensures the faithful realization of your project.

This book has aimed to be more than just an instructional manual; it has sought to be a companion on your journey from novice to confident CATIA V5 user. Remember, the examples and exercises within these pages are starting points—your unique challenges and projects will build upon them, further solidifying your expertise.

As you forge ahead, embracing continuous learning and development will be crucial. The landscape of CAD is ever-evolving, and CATIA V5 will continue to grow and change. Stay abreast of updates, connect with fellow designers, and participate in communities and forums. Every project you undertake enriches your experience and contributes to your personal and professional growth.

This conclusion, while signaling the end of the book, is truly an invitation to a beginning—the start of your independent journey with CATIA V5. It is a call to action to apply what you've learned, to explore, to create, and to innovate. In your hands lies the potential to design solutions to the challenges of tomorrow, to visualize the structures and mechanisms that will propel us into the future.

We hope that "Catia V5 2024 Guide for Beginners" has been an enlightening and empowering resource. May it continue to serve as a reference as you evolve in your career. As you close this book, remember that the real work, the most rewarding challenges, and the greatest achievements lie ahead. Keep learning, keep designing, and keep pushing the boundaries of what's possible with CATIA V5.

With every challenge comes an opportunity, and with every design, a chance to leave an indelible mark on the world. We wish you all the best as you embark on your new ventures. Let your creativity soar, your designs flourish, and your proficiency in CATIA V5 become second nature. Here's to a future shaped by your vision and crafted with your hands.

Made in the USA
Las Vegas, NV
20 May 2025